PETERSON'S
MASTER THE
SSAT & ISEE
2009

Jacqueline Robinson, M.S.
Dennis M. Robinson, Ed.M.

PETERSON'S
A **nelnet** COMPANY

PETERSON'S
A ⓝelnet COMPANY

About Peterson's, a Nelnet company
Peterson's (www.petersons.com) is a leading provider of education information and
advice, with books and online resources focusing on education search, test preparation, and financial aid. Its Web site offers searchable databases and interactive tools
for contacting educational institutions, online practice tests and instruction, and
planning tools for securing financial aid. Peterson's serves 110 million education
consumers annually.

For more information, contact Peterson's, 2000 Lenox Drive, Lawrenceville, NJ
08648; 800-338-3282; or find us on the World Wide Web at www.petersons.com/
about.

ISBN-13: 978-0-7689-2726-9
ISBN-10: 0-7689-2726-9

Printed in the United States of America

10 9 8 7 6 5 4 3 2   10 09 08

Seventh Edition

Petersons.com/publishing

Check out our Web site at www.petersons.com/publishing to see if there is any new information regarding the test and any revisions or corrections to the content of this book. We've made sure the information in this book is accurate and up-to-date; however, the test format or content may have changed since the time of publication.

Contents

Before You Begin

HOW TO USE THIS BOOK

Congratulations! You've just picked up the best high school entrance examination preparation guide you can buy. This book has all the answers to your questions about the SSAT and the ISEE. It contains up-to-date information, hundreds of practice questions, and solid test-taking advice. Here's how you can use it to get your best high school entrance exam score...and get into the secondary school of your choice.

- **Top 10 Strategies to Raise Your Score** gives you tried-and-true test-taking strategies.

- **Part I** contains answers to all your questions about the SSAT and the ISEE. You'll learn what kinds of questions to expect, how the tests are scored, what the questions look like, and how you can keep your cool on test day.

- **Part II** gives you your first chance to try your hand at sample questions from both exams. Practice Test 1: Diagnostic can show you where your skills are strong—and where they need some improvement.

- **Parts III, IV, V, and VI** lead you through the subjects of the exams. Here you will review word analysis and basic mathematics. Skim, scan, or study these reviews, depending on your *own* needs. You'll also learn about each question type you will see on your exam, and you'll find the detailed, step-by-step methods that take the guesswork out of answering those questions. These chapters let you in on the secrets smart test-takers know—secrets that can add valuable points to your test score.

- **Part VII** takes your hand as you face the part of the exam that some students find terrifying—the essay. You'll learn how to organize and express your ideas under time pressure.

- **Part VIII** contains four practice tests. Take at least one of your exams. Take both if time allows. Remember: practice makes perfect!

- The **Appendix** includes a chart of Private Schools at-a-Glance, which gives you valuable data on private secondary schools from *Peterson's Private Secondary Schools 2008*. These "snapshots" will help guide your search and also provide information about Advanced Placement (AP) subject areas and sports.

WHAT TO STUDY

Parts III through VII of this book provide content for you to review. Use the table below to determine which chapters to study for your test.

No.	Chapter	SSAT	ISEE
	Part III: Vocabulary Review		
5	Word Arithmetic	X	X
	Part IV: Verbal Ability Review		
6	Synonyms	X	X
7	Verbal Analogies	X	
8	Sentence Completions		X
	Part V: Reading Review		
9	Reading Comprehension	X	X
	Part VI: Mathematics Review		
10	Mathematics	X	X
11	Quantitative Ability	X	X
12	Quantitative Comparisons		X
	Part VII: Writing Sample Review		
13	Writing Mechanics	X	X
14	The Essay	X	X

SPECIAL STUDY FEATURES

Peterson's Master the SSAT & ISEE was designed to be as user-friendly as it is complete. It includes several features to make your preparation easier.

Overview

Each chapter begins with a bulleted overview listing the topics that will be covered in the chapter. You know immediately where to look for a topic that you need to work on.

Summing It Up

Each strategy chapter ends with a point-by-point summary that captures the most important points.

Test Yourself Quizzes and Exercises

Each chapter offers Test Yourself Quizzes and/or Exercises at the end of the chapter. Take as many quizzes and do as many exercises as you can. Use the results to determine where you still need work.

Bonus Information

In addition, be sure to look in the page margins of your book for the following test-prep tools:

NOTE

Notes highlight critical information about the format of the SSAT and the ISEE.

TIP

Tips draw your attention to valuable concepts, advice, and shortcuts for tackling the tests.

ALERT!

Whenever you need to be careful of a common pitfall or test-taker trap, you'll find an *Alert!* This information reveals and helps eliminate the wrong turns many people take on the exam.

AN IMPORTANT NOTE FOR EIGHTH AND NINTH GRADERS

You may find that some of the test questions that appear on the SSAT or ISEE are extremely difficult or cover material that you have not yet been exposed to. This is intentional. Keep in mind that the same upper-level exam is administered to students in grades 8, 9, 10, and 11. However, your final score will only be compared to the scores of other students in your grade. When the Secondary School Admission Test Board and the Educational Records Bureau send admission officers your scores, they'll include the average test scores of all students your age who have taken the test. No one expects you to compete against older students, so don't worry if you encounter vocabulary questions that seem too advanced or math concepts that you haven't mastered yet in school. It won't be held against you. Besides, because you're working with this book, you'll be better prepared to deal with those tough questions when you take the real test!

PARENTS' GUIDE TO PRIVATE SECONDARY SCHOOL

Parents—here's the information you need to navigate through the private secondary school choice and admission process. We've put together valuable advice from admission experts about choosing and applying to the school that's right for your child and your family. You'll be able to get answers to your questions about independent day schools, finding the perfect match, the admission application form, and how to pay for your child's private school education. Peterson's is here to help you and your family every step of the way, so be sure to also visit us online at www.petersons.com/privateschools for even more guidance and resources.

YOU'RE WELL ON YOUR WAY TO SUCCESS

Remember that knowledge is power. By using *Peterson's Master the SSAT & ISEE 2009,* you'll be studying with the most comprehensive preparation guide available and you'll become extremely knowledgeable about the test you're taking. We look forward to helping you raise your score. Good luck!

GIVE US YOUR FEEDBACK

Peterson's publishes a full line of resources to help you guide you through the admission process. Peterson's publications can be found at your local book store, library, and guidance office, and you can access us online at www.petersons.com.

We welcome any comments or suggestions you may have about this publication and invite you to complete our online survey at www.petersons.com/booksurvey. Or you can fill out the survey at the back of this book, tear it out, and mail it to us at:

Publishing Department
Peterson's, a Nelnet company
2000 Lenox Drive
Lawrenceville, NJ 08648

Your feedback will help us make your educational dreams possible.

TOP 10 STRATEGIES TO RAISE YOUR SCORE

1. **You don't really need to read the directions when you take your test.** By the time you actually sit down to take your exam, you've read this book, you've taken all of the practice tests you could find, and you've read enough test directions to fill a library. So when the exam clock starts ticking, don't waste time rereading directions you already know. Instead, go directly to Question 1. If, however, you don't feel as confident as we do about your abilities, then, read the directions.

2. **Question sets usually go from easiest to most difficult—you should, too!** Except for the reading comprehension questions, test questions follow this pattern. So, work your way through the earlier, easier questions as quickly as you can.

3. **The easy answer isn't always the best.** Remember, the hardest questions are usually at the end of a section and that also means the answers are more complex. Look carefully at the choices and really think about what the question is asking.

4. **An educated guess is always best.** The process of elimination is the best way to improve your guessing odds. Check out the answer choices and try to cross out any that you definitely know are wrong. If you're answering a question with five answer choices and you're able to knock out two choices, the odds go up to 33½ percent that you will be correct.

5. **It's smart to keep moving.** It's hard to let go, but sometimes you have to. Don't spend too much time on any one question before you've tried all of the questions in a section.

6. **For the ISEE, do not leave any blanks at the end of a test.** Keep track of your time and if you have questions remaining when time is almost up, try to answer the rest of the questions.

7. **You're going to need a watch.** If you're going to pace yourself, you need to keep track of the time—and what if there is no clock in the room or if the only clock is out of your line of vision? A word of warning: Don't use a watch alarm or your watch will end up on the proctor's desk!

8. **Keeping your place on the answer sheet saves time and test points.** Keep your place on the answer sheet by laying your test booklet on top of it so it acts as a line marker, moving the two as you mark an answer. This way you won't lose points by marking the right answer in the wrong row.

9. **Check and recheck if you have time.** If you finish a part before time is up, use the remaining time to check that each question is answered in the right space and that there is only one answer for each question.

10. **Relax, and good luck!**

PART I
HIGH SCHOOL ENTRANCE EXAM BASICS

All About the Tests

OVERVIEW

- **What are the high school entrance exams?**
- **How do I find out which exam I must take?**
- **If I have a choice of exams, how do I choose?**
- **What kinds of questions are asked on high school entrance exams?**
- **How are the exams structured?**
- **What do the answer sheets look like?**
- **How are the exams scored?**
- **Summing it up**

WHAT ARE THE HIGH SCHOOL ENTRANCE EXAMS?

The high school entrance exams are standardized tests. Independent, parochial, church-affiliated, and specialized public high schools use scores on these exams to help them make their admissions decisions.

There are a number of widely used standardized high school exams. The best known of these are the following:

- **SSAT,** the Secondary School Admission Test, which is administered eight times each year by the Secondary School Admission Test Board located in Princeton, New Jersey. Scores are accepted by more than 600 schools. Schools that accept SSAT scores include independent unaffiliated private day and boarding schools, non-diocesan Catholic schools or Catholic schools operated by religious orders, and non-Catholic religious-affiliated schools. The SSAT is offered at two levels—lower-level for students in grades 5, 6, and 7 and upper-level for students in grade 8 and above. The upper-level exam is administered to high school applicants, so this book concentrates on preparing you for the upper-level exam.
- **ISEE,** the Independent School Entrance Examination, which is administered by Educational Records Bureau of New York City. The ISEE is accepted by independent schools around the country, especially day schools.

chapter 1

The ISEE is accepted by all member schools of the Independent Schools Association of New York City and is the exam used by most of the independent schools in Philadelphia, San Diego, and Nashville. The ISEE is also the exam used by many non-Catholic religious-affiliated day schools. The ISEE is offered at three levels—lower-level for applicants for grades 5 and 6, middle-level for applicants for grades 7 and 8, and upper-level for high school applicants. This book is limited to preparation for the upper-level exam.

- **HSPT,** the High School Placement Test, which is administered by the Scholastic Testing Service of Bensenville, Illinois, and is used primarily by Catholic high schools. The HSPT is an examination specially designed for school systems with an 8/4 split. This means that the test measures aptitude and preparation for entrance to a four-year high school program. Because most Catholic high schools are organized in this manner, the HSPT is the exam of choice in more than 50 percent of Catholic schools nationwide. Some of the largest Catholic school systems in the country use the HSPT exclusively in selecting students for admission to their high schools. In Detroit, the HSPT is used for admission to public special academic high schools. Many independent Lutheran schools use the HSPT, as do a number of unaffiliated independent secondary schools. You will find full preparation for this test in *Peterson's Master the Catholic High School Entrance Exams.*

- **COOP,** the Cooperative Entrance Exam, published by CTB/McGraw-Hill of Monterey, California. The COOP is administered only to students planning to enter ninth grade. It is the exclusive entrance examination of the Archdiocese of New York; the Dioceses of Brooklyn, Rockland County, and Rockville Centre; and the Archdiocese of Newark, New Jersey. Use in other systems or in independent schools is scattered. Because the COOP is used almost exclusively by Catholic high schools, full preparation is offered in *Peterson's Master the Catholic High School Entrance Exams.*

- **SSHSAT,** the New York City Specialized Science High Schools Admissions Test administered by the New York City Board of Education. This exam is only for eighth and ninth graders who live in New York City and who wish to attend Bronx High School of Science, Brooklyn Technical High School, or Stuyvesant High School. Because the use of SSHSAT is so limited, this book offers no preparation for it. If you will be taking the SSHSAT, purchase *Peterson's New York City Specialized High Schools Admissions Test.*

- Lesser-known or individually constructed exams. Some schools construct their own exams or purchase standardized exams from small companies. The subjects and question styles of these exams cover a wide range of possibilities, but verbal, reading, and mathematics skills are sure to be included. You should find this book helpful for any exam.

HOW DO I FIND OUT WHICH EXAM I MUST TAKE?

Call the admissions offices of all schools to which you are applying and ask which exam each school requires or which exam results the school will accept. Ask also for the cutoff dates by which your scores must be received by the school. Find out if the school has made special arrangements for testing its applicants on a specific date at a convenient location.

IF I HAVE A CHOICE OF EXAMS, HOW DO I CHOOSE?

If all your schools will accept scores from either the SSAT or the ISEE, you can choose on the basis of convenience of testing date and location. Or, if you began your preparations early enough and have tried a sample of each exam in this book, you can choose the exam with which you feel more comfortable.

You can get lists of testing locations, dates, registration deadlines, and fees along with official test descriptions, official sample questions, and registration forms by writing or calling or by visiting the following Web sites:

> SSAT
> CN5339
> Princeton, NJ 08543
> 609-683-4440
> info@ssat.org
> www.ssat.org

> Educational Records Bureau
> 220 East 42nd Street, Suite 100
> New York, NY 10017
> 800-989-3721, Ext. 312 (toll-free)
> 212-672-9800
> 800-446-0320 (toll-free)
> isee@erbtest.org
> www.erbtest.org

WHAT KINDS OF QUESTIONS ARE ASKED ON HIGH SCHOOL ENTRANCE EXAMS?

The scope of questions is pretty limited for both the SSAT and ISEE. You will not find subject-specific questions—no grammar or spelling, no geography or science. But you will find questions testing your verbal, reading, and math skills—skills you've been working on since you were 6 years old.

Aside from the essay, which is not scored, all of the questions are multiple-choice—for each question, you have five choices on the SSAT and four choices on the ISEE. Multiple-choice questions make the test seem easier because you'll always have the correct answer in front of you—you just have to find it!

The Verbal Ability Sections

The verbal ability sections contain questions that test vocabulary and verbal reasoning. Both the SSAT and ISEE use synonym questions to test your vocabulary. The SSAT tests your verbal reasoning with analogy questions while the ISEE tests verbal reasoning with sentence completions.

Synonyms

Synonym questions present a single word and ask you to choose the word with the same or most similar meaning. This is a pure test of vocabulary, though word-building skills may help you figure out meanings of some unfamiliar words.

Analogies (SSAT only)

Analogies present a pair of words that have some logical relationship to one another. The correct answer consists of a pair of words with the same kind of relationship as the first pair.

Sentence Completions (ISEE only)

Sentence completion questions ask you to choose a word or words that fill in the blanks in a given sentence. They test how well you can use context clues and word meanings to complete a sentence.

Reading Comprehension

Reading comprehension questions relate to a passage that is provided for you to read. SSAT passages can be about almost anything. ISEE passages are based on social studies, humanities, or science readings, but they do not test your knowledge in these subjects. Regardless of the subject matter of the reading passage, the questions after it test how well you understood the passage and the information in it.

Mathematics Sections

The math sections on the SSAT and the ISEE are structured somewhat differently, but both exams seek to measure your understanding and application of quantitative concepts—that is, arithmetic, algebraic, and geometric concepts. It's important to know that these questions require either simple calculations or none at all. On the SSAT, you will see only standard multiple-choice questions, and the ISEE uses a combination of multiple-choice questions and quantitative comparisons.

Standard Multiple-Choice Questions

Standard multiple-choice questions give you a problem in arithmetic, algebra, or geometry. Then you choose the correct answer from the choices offered. Most of these problems involve number patterns, a small body of easily memorized information, and response choices that make it possible for you to estimate the correct answer. All but a few can be solved without pencil and paper.

Quantitative Comparisons (ISEE only)

Quantitative comparison questions test your skills in comparing information and in estimating. You'll see two quantities, one in Column A and one in Column B. Your job is to compare the two quantities and decide if one is greater than the other, if they are equal, or if no comparison is possible. These, too, can be determined without pencil and paper, particularly after you have reviewed the basic concepts in the math sections here.

HOW ARE THE EXAMS STRUCTURED?

SSAT

The SSAT is administered in six separately timed sections. The first section, Part I, is the writing sample. The other four sections, Part II, can appear in any order. Among the four sections you will always find two Quantitative sections, one Verbal (synonyms and analogies) section, and one Reading Comprehension section. *These may be arranged in any order the test-makers choose.* Every question on the multiple-choice part of the SSAT offers five answer choices lettered (A), (B), (C), (D), and (E).

Subject to the order of the sections, which may vary from booklet to booklet as a guard against cheating by looking at your neighbor's paper, here is a typical SSAT format and timetable:

FORMAT OF A TYPICAL SSAT

SECTION		NUMBER OF QUESTIONS	TIME ALLOWED
Part I:	Writing Sample		25 minutes
Part II:	Multiple-Choice		
Section 1:	Verbal	60 questions 30 Synonym questions 30 Analogy questions	30 minutes
Section 2:	Quantitative (Math)	25 questions	30 minutes
Section 3:	Reading Comprehension	40 questions based on approximately 7 reading passages	40 minutes
Section 3:	Quantitative (Math)	25 questions	30 minutes

ISEE

The ISEE is administered in five separately timed sections called "tests." The time limit for all tests is not identical, so all applicants at a given administration take the tests in the same order. However, your neighbor may get a booklet with different questions as a guard against cheating. The essay, which is the final "test" of the ISEE, is not scored and does not count. A photocopy of your essay is provided to each school as a writing sample.

Each multiple-choice question on the ISEE offers four answer choices. These are lettered (A), (B), (C), and (D).

Here is a typical ISEE format and timetable:

FORMAT OF A TYPICAL ISEE

SECTION		NUMBER OF QUESTIONS	TIME ALLOWED
Section 1:	Verbal Reasoning	40 questions	20 minutes
	Synonyms		
	Sentence Completions		
Section 2:	Quantitative Reasoning	35 questions	35 minutes
	Arithmetic/Algebra/		
	Geometry		
	Concepts/Understanding		
	Applications/Higher Order		
	Thinking		
	Quantitative Comparisons		
Section 3:	Reading Comprehension	40 questions based on approximately 9 reading passages	40 minutes
	Humanities Passages		
	Science Passages		
	Social Studies Passages		
Section 4:	Mathematics Achievement	45 questions	40 minutes
	Arithmetic Concepts		
	Algebraic Concepts		
	Geometric Concepts		
Section 5:	Essay		30 minutes

WHAT DO THE ANSWER SHEETS LOOK LIKE?

When you get the test booklet, you'll also get a separate sheet on which you'll mark your answers.

For each **multiple-choice** question, you'll see a corresponding set of answer ovals. The ovals are labeled from (A) to (D) on the ISEE and from (A) to (E) on the SSAT. Answer sheets are read by machines. Fill in your chosen answer ovals completely and boldly so there can be no mistake about which one you have chosen.

Take a look at the sample answer sheet below:

The only answers that will be registered correctly are 29 and 35. Question 30 isn't filled in completely, and Question 31 isn't dark enough, so the machine might miss them. Question 32 is a total mess—will the machine choose (A), (B), or (C)?

Since Question 33 has two ovals filled in, they cancel each other out, and this is registered as an omitted question. There's no penalty, but there's no credit either. The same will happen with Question 34; no answer, no credit.

HOW ARE THE EXAMS SCORED?

OK, you've answered all the questions, time is up (and not a moment too soon), and you turn in your answer sheet. What next? Off it goes to the machine at the central offices of the testing organization. The machine scans the sheet in seconds and calculates a score. How it calculates your score depends on which exam you were taking.

TIP

Keep your place on the answer sheet by laying your test booklet on top of it so it acts as a line marker, moving the two as you mark an answer. This way you won't lose points by marking the right answer in the wrong row.

ALERT!

When taking the SSAT, leave questions blank if you run out of time or have no idea what the answer is. Take a guess if you can rule out 2 of the 5 answer choices or if you have a pretty strong feeling about one choice. Never fill in the answer ovals randomly—it will cost you points!

TIP

Move quickly on the easy ones. The questions in a set usually go from easiest to hardest. Try to go through the easy ones quickly.

SSAT

The scoring of the SSAT is as follows: You get one point (+1 point) for each correct answer, and you lose one quarter of a point ($-\frac{1}{4}$ point) for each incorrect answer.

Omitted answers have no effect (0 points) on your score. Calculation of right answers minus one fourth of wrong answers yields your raw score. Do not worry that your standing on the exam may suffer in comparison to students in other grades taking the same upper-level exam. SSAT scores are scaled and reported in percentiles that compare only students within the same age and grade group.

ISEE

Scoring of the ISEE is uncomplicated. You receive one point for every question that you answer correctly. There is no penalty for a wrong answer. It receives no credit, but there is no deduction for the error. As with the SSAT, scoring and percentile ranking are done separately for members of each grade group taking the same exam. You will be compared only with your peers.

SUMMING IT UP

- The SSAT is a 3-hour test of verbal, quantitative, and reading ability.

- The ISEE is a 3-hour test of verbal and quantitative ability, reading comprehension, and mathematics achievement.

- The SSAT deducts one fourth of a point from your score for each incorrect answer. Random guessing will do no good. A calculated guess is always worthwhile.

- The ISEE gives you one point for each correct answer. Wrong answers do not affect your score. Leave no blanks.

- All SSAT quantitative questions are standard multiple-choice questions.

- Some ISEE mathematical questions are standard multiple-choice; some are quantitative comparisons.

- The essay is only a writing sample. It is not scored.

- On both exams all questions within each set, except reading comprehension, are arranged from easy to hard.

- Use a process of elimination to make educated guesses when you are not sure.

- Your percentile ranking is based on comparison of your score with students in your grade only.

- You *can* get a very good score even if you don't answer every question.

ALERT!

Don't spin your wheels. Don't spend too much time on any one question. Give it some thought, take your best shot, and move along.

NOTE

Guessing is always permissible, but is it always wise? That depends on whether or not you have a clue as to the possible answer, and it depends on which exam you are taking. If you're taking the SSAT, you will get penalized $\frac{1}{4}$ point for incorrect answers. Guess only if you can eliminate between 2 and 4 choices. You won't be penalized for guessing on the ISEE, so go ahead and take the chance. You have nothing to lose!

SSAT Questions

chapter 2

OVERVIEW

- **What can you expect on the test?**
- **How does the SSAT measure verbal ability?**
- **How does the SSAT measure quantitative ability?**
- **How does the SSAT measure reading ability?**
- **What is the writing sample?**
- **Summing it up**

WHAT CAN YOU EXPECT ON THE TEST?

The SSAT uses four question types to test your verbal and quantitative abilities and your reading comprehension. This chapter will describe each of them in turn and show you samples. Learning these question types in advance is the best way to prepare for the SSAT. They never change, so you'll know what to expect when you take the test. The SSAT also asks you to write a short essay on an assigned topic. This chapter will introduce you to the essay requirement.

HOW DOES THE SSAT MEASURE VERBAL ABILITY?

The SSAT measures your verbal ability with two question types:

1. Synonyms
2. Analogies

A verbal section consists of 60 questions; 30 of these questions are synonyms and 30 are analogies.

Synonym Questions

A synonym is a word with the same meaning or nearly the same meaning as another word. SSAT synonym questions ask you to choose the best synonym for a question word that is written in capital letters.

The directions for SSAT synonym questions look like this:

Directions: Choose the word or phrase whose meaning is most similar to the meaning of the word in CAPITAL letters.

Here are two sample SSAT synonym questions. Try each one on your own; then read the explanation that accompanies it.

1. NOVICE
   (A) competitive
   (B) clumsy
   (C) aged
   (D) beginner
   (E) impulsive

   The correct answer is (D). A NOVICE is a *beginner*, someone without experience. You may recognize the root of *novel*, meaning *new*, a clue to the definition.

2. CONVOY
   (A) hearse
   (B) thunderstorm
   (C) group
   (D) jeep
   (E) journey

   The correct answer is (C). A CONVOY is a *group* traveling together for protection or convenience. You have probably seen convoys of military vehicles traveling single file along the highway toward summer reserve camp.

Analogy Questions

Analogy questions ask you to match up pairs of words that are related in the same way. Each question starts with a word pair. Your job is to find or create another pair of words that is related in the same way as the first pair.

The directions for SSAT analogy questions look like this:

Directions: Find the relationship between the words. Read each question and then choose the answer that best completes the meaning of the sentence.

Here are two sample SSAT analogy questions. Try each one on your own before reading the explanation that accompanies it.

3. Lid is to box as cork is to
   (A) float
   (B) bottle
   (C) wine
   (D) blacken
   (E) stopper

   The correct answer is (B). The relationship is one of purpose. The purpose of a *lid* is to close a *box*; the purpose of a *cork* is to close a *bottle*. Cork is easily associated with all the choices, so you must recognize the purposeful relationship of the initial pair to choose the correct answer.

4. Poison is to death as
   (A) book is to pages
   (B) music is to violin
   (C) kindness is to cooperation
   (D) life is to famine
   (E) nothing is to something

   The correct answer is (C). This is a cause-and-effect relationship. *Poison* may lead to *death*; *kindness* may lead to *cooperation*. Neither outcome is a foregone conclusion, but both are equally likely, so the parallel is maintained. Choice (B) offers a reversed relationship.

HOW DOES THE SSAT MEASURE QUANTITATIVE ABILITY?

The SSAT tests your quantitative ability in two 25-question mathematics sections, that is, with 50 mathematics questions in all. The questions in each section measure your knowledge of algebra and quantitative concepts.

The directions are the same for both quantitative sections. Here's what they look like:

Directions: Calculate each problem in your head or in the scratch area of the test booklet and choose the best answer.

Here are four sample SSAT quantitative ability questions showing the range of mathematical questions. Try each of these on your own before you read the explanation that accompanies it.

5. $\frac{1}{4}$% of 1,500 =
   (A) 60
   (B) 15
   (C) 7.50
   (D) 3.75
   (E) 1.50

The correct answer is (D). $\frac{1}{4}$% written as a decimal is .0025. $(1,500)(.0025) = 3.75$. You could have done this problem in your head by thinking: 10% of 1,500 is 150; 1% of 1,500 is 15; $\frac{1}{4}$ of 1% = $15 \div 4 = 3.75$.

6. If psychological studies of juvenile delinquents show K percent to be emotionally unstable, the number of juvenile delinquents not emotionally unstable per 100 juvenile delinquents is
   (A) $100 - K$
   (B) $1 - K$
   (C) $K - 100$
   (D) $100 \div K$
   (E) $K \div 100$

The correct answer is (A). "Percent" means out of 100. If K percent are emotionally unstable, then K out of 100 are emotionally unstable. The remainder, $100 - K$, are not unstable.

7. A piece of wood 35 feet, 6 inches long was used to make 4 shelves of equal length. The length of each shelf was

(A) 9 feet, $1\frac{1}{2}$ inches.

(B) 8 feet, $10\frac{1}{2}$ inches.

(C) 8 feet, $1\frac{1}{2}$ inches.

(D) 7 feet, $10\frac{1}{2}$ inches.

(E) 7 feet, $1\frac{1}{2}$ inches.

The correct answer is (B). First convert the feet to inches. 35 feet, 6 inches = 420 inches + 6 inches = 426 inches. 426 ÷ 4 = 106.5 inches per shelf = 8 feet, $10\frac{1}{2}$ inches per shelf.

8. Angle *ABD* is a(n)

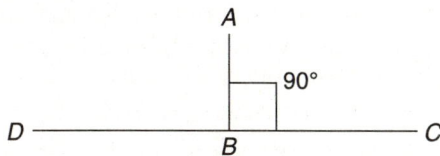

(A) straight angle and contains 180°.

(B) acute angle and contains 35°.

(C) obtuse angle and contains 360°.

(D) right angle and contains 45°.

(E) right angle and contains 90°.

The correct answer is (E). Angle *ABC* and angle *ABD* are supplementary angles. Since angle *ABC* = 90°, angle *ABD* must also equal 90° (180° − 90° = 90°). A right angle contains 90°.

You may have noted that only number 7 of the sample math questions required a pencil and paper calculation, because the numbers were a bit difficult to manipulate mentally. The others required application of a mathematical concept and very little calculation.

NOTE

Leave your calculator at home. You won't be able to use it on any of the tests. Instead, use the space provided in the test booklet for scratch work.

NOTE

The SSAT reading comprehension section is an open book test. The answers will always be directly stated or implied in the given passage.

HOW DOES THE SSAT MEASURE READING ABILITY?

The SSAT measures your ability to read quickly and to understand what you read by asking you questions about passages you must read. The 40 questions in a reading comprehension section are based on about seven reading passages.

The directions for SSAT reading comprehension questions look like this:

Directions: Carefully read each passage and the questions that follow it. Choose the best answer to each question on the basis of the information in the passage.

Here is a sample SSAT reading passage followed by four questions. Read the passage and try answering the questions on your own before reading the explanations.

> Cotton fabrics treated with the XYZ Process have features that make them far superior to any previously known flame-retardant-treated cotton fabrics. XYZ Process-treated fabrics are durable to repeated laundering and dry cleaning; are glow resistant as well as flame resistant; when exposed to flames or intense
> (5) heat form tough, pliable, and protective chars; are inert physiologically to people handling or exposed to the fabric; are only slightly heavier than untreated fabrics; and are susceptible to further wet and dry finishing treatments. In addition, the treated fabrics exhibit little or no adverse change in feel, texture, and appearance and are shrink-, rot-, and mildew-resistant. The treatment reduces strength only
> (10) slightly. Finished fabrics have "easy care" properties in that they are wrinkle-resistant and dry rapidly.

9. It is most accurate to state that the author in the preceding selection presents

    (A) facts but reaches no conclusion concerning the value of the process.

    (B) a conclusion concerning the value of the process and facts to support that conclusion.

    (C) a conclusion concerning the value of the process unsupported by facts.

    (D) neither facts nor conclusions, but merely describes the process.

    (E) the case for making all fabrics flame-retardant.

    The correct answer is (B). This is a combination main-idea and interpretation question. If you cannot answer this question readily, reread the selection. The author clearly thinks that the XYZ Process is terrific and says so in the first sentence. The rest of the selection presents a wealth of facts to support the initial claim.

10. For which one of the following articles would the XYZ Process be most suitable?
    (A) Nylon stockings
    (B) Woolen shirt
    (C) Silk tie
    (D) Cotton bed sheet
    (E) Polyester slacks

    The correct answer is (D). At first glance you might think that this is an inference question requiring you to make a judgment based upon the few drawbacks of the process. Closer reading, however, shows you that there is no contest for the correct answer here. This is a simple question of fact. The XYZ Process is a treatment for *cotton* fabrics.

11. The main reason for treating a fabric with the XYZ Process is to
    (A) prepare the fabric for other wet and dry finishing treatment.
    (B) render it shrink-, rot-, and mildew-resistant.
    (C) increase its weight and strength.
    (D) reduce the chance that it will catch fire.
    (E) justify a price increase.

    The correct answer is (D). This is a main-idea question. You must distinguish between the main idea and the supporting and incidental facts.

12. Which one of the following would be considered a minor drawback of the XYZ Process?
    (A) Forms chars when exposed to flame
    (B) Makes fabrics mildew-resistant
    (C) Adds to the weight of fabrics
    (D) Is compatible with other finishing treatments
    (E) Does not wash out of the fabric

    The correct answer is (C). Obviously a drawback is a negative feature. The selection mentions only two negative features. The treatment reduces strength slightly, and it makes fabrics slightly heavier than untreated fabrics. Only one of these negative features is offered among the answer choices.

WHAT IS THE WRITING SAMPLE?

At the beginning of each SSAT testing session, you must write a 25-minute essay on an assigned subject. This essay is not scored. It is duplicated and sent to each school as a sample of your ability to express yourself in writing under the same conditions as all other candidates for admission to the school.

The directions for the SSAT writing sample look like this:

Directions: Read the topic, choose your position, and organize your essay before writing. Write a convincing, legible essay on the paper provided.

Here is a sample SSAT essay topic. Try to organize and write an essay on this topic.

Topic: Bad things always happen in threes.

Assignment: Do you agree or disagree? Support your position with examples from your own experience, the experience of others, current events, or your reading.

SUMMING IT UP

- The SSAT measures verbal ability with two question types: synonyms and analogies.

- The SSAT measures quantitative ability in two sections of algebra and quantitative concepts.

- Calculators are not permitted. Instead, use the space provided in the test booklet for scratch work.

- The answers to the reading comprehension questions are based on information either directly stated or implied in the passages.

- At the beginning of each SSAT testing session, you must write a 25-minute essay on an assigned subject.

ISEE Questions

chapter 3

OVERVIEW

- **What can you expect on the test?**
- **How does the ISEE measure verbal ability?**
- **How does the ISEE measure quantitative ability?**
- **How does the ISEE measure reading comprehension?**
- **How does the ISEE measure mathematics achievement?**
- **What is the essay question?**
- **Summing it up**

WHAT CAN YOU EXPECT ON THE TEST?

The ISEE uses four question types to test your verbal and quantitative abilities and your achievement in mathematics and reading comprehension. This chapter will describe each of them in turn and show you samples. Learning these question types in advance is the best way to prepare for the ISEE. They never change, so you'll know what to expect and you won't have any unpleasant surprises when you show up to take the test. The ISEE also asks you to write a short essay on an assigned topic. This chapter will introduce you to the essay requirement.

HOW DOES THE ISEE MEASURE VERBAL ABILITY?

The ISEE measures your verbal ability with two question types:

1. Synonyms
2. Sentence completions

The verbal ability test consists of 40 questions. Twenty of these questions are synonyms and 20 are sentence completions.

Synonym Questions

A *synonym* is a word with the same meaning or nearly the same meaning as another word. ISEE synonym questions ask you to choose the best synonym for a capitalized word.

The directions for ISEE synonyms questions look like this:

Directions: Choose the word that is most nearly the same in meaning as the word in CAPITAL letters.

Here are two sample ISEE synonym questions. Try each one on your own; then read the explanation that accompanies it.

1. TENANT
   (A) occupant
   (B) landlord
   (C) owner
   (D) farmer

   The correct answer is (A). The most common sense of the word TENANT is *renter*. As such, the tenant is never the landlord. The owner may well be an occupant, but unless he or she occupies on a very temporary basis, he or she is not considered a tenant. A tenant farmer lives on and cultivates the land of another.

2. CALCULATED
   (A) multiplied
   (B) added
   (C) answered
   (D) figured out

   The correct answer is (D). CALCULATING may well include multiplying or adding in order to arrive at the answer, but not all calculations need be mathematical. It is the *figuring out* that is the *calculating*.

Sentence Completion Questions

Just as the name implies, sentence completions are "fill-in-the-blank" questions. ISEE sentence completion questions may have one or two blanks. Your job is to choose from among the answer choices the word or words that best fit each blank.

The directions for ISEE sentence completion questions look like this:

Directions: The blanks in the following sentences indicate that words are missing. If there is one blank, only a single word is missing. If there are two blanks, a pair of words is missing. Choose the one word or pair of words that will best complete the meaning of the sentence as a whole.

Here are two sample ISEE sentence completion questions, a one-blank question and a two-blank question. Try each one on your own before reading the explanation that accompanies it.

3. Utility is not _____, for the usefulness of an object changes with time and place.
   - **(A)** planned
   - **(B)** practical
   - **(C)** permanent
   - **(D)** understandable

   The correct answer is (C). If the usefulness of an object changes, then that usefulness is by definition not *permanent*.

4. A string of lies had landed her in such a hopeless _____ that she didn't know how to _____ herself.
   - **(A)** status .. clear
   - **(B)** pinnacle .. explain
   - **(C)** confusion .. help
   - **(D)** predicament .. extricate

   The correct answer is (D). "Hopeless predicament" is an idiomatic expression meaning "impossible situation." This is a reasonable position for one to be in after a string of lies. The second blank is correctly filled with a term that implies that she couldn't get out of the mess she had created.

HOW DOES THE ISEE MEASURE QUANTITATIVE ABILITY?

The ISEE tests your understanding of quantitative concepts and your ability to apply those concepts with two question types:

1   Standard multiple-choice questions

2   Quantitative comparisons

The quantitative reasoning test consists of 35 questions. About half of these are standard multiple-choice questions, and the remainder are quantitative comparisons.

Multiple-Choice

The directions for the standard multiple-choice questions look like this:

> **Directions:** Work each problem in your head or on the space available on the pages of the test booklet and choose the correct answer. All figures are accurately drawn unless otherwise noted. All letters stand for real numbers.

Here are two sample ISEE standard multiple-choice quantitative ability questions. Try each of these on your own before you read the explanation that accompanies it.

5. If $A^2 + B^2 = A^2 + X^2$, then B equals

    (A) $\pm X$

    (B) $X^2 - 2A^2$

    (C) $\pm A$

    (D) $A^2 + X^2$

    The correct answer is (A). Subtract A^2 from both sides of the equation: $B^2 = X^2$, therefore $B = \pm X$.

6. How much time is there between 8:30 a.m. today and 3:15 a.m. tomorrow?

    (A) $17\dfrac{3}{4}$ hrs.

    (B) $18\dfrac{1}{2}$ hrs.

    (C) $18\dfrac{2}{3}$ hrs.

    (D) $18\dfrac{3}{4}$ hrs.

The correct answer is (D). 12:00 = 11:60

From 8:30 a.m. until noon today: 11:60 − 8:30 = 3:30

3 hrs. 30 min.

From noon until midnight: 12 hrs.

From midnight until 3:15 a.m.: 3 hrs. 15 min.

Total: 3 hrs. 30 min. + 12 hrs. + 3 hrs. 15 min. = 18 hrs. 45 min. = $18\frac{3}{4}$ hrs.

Quantitative Comparisons

ISEE quantitative comparisons are probably not like any other math question you've ever seen. These questions present you with two quantities, one in Column A and one in Column B. Your job is to decide which quantity is greater, whether the two quantities are equal, or whether no comparison is possible. There are always four answer choices for this question type, and they are always the same. Here are what the directions look like:

Directions: For each of the following questions, two quantities are given—one in Column A, the other in Column B. Compare the two quantities and choose:

(A) if the quantity in Column A is greater

(B) if the quantity in Column B is greater

(C) if the quantities are equal

(D) if the relationship cannot be determined from the information given

Remember the following information as you tackle quantitative comparison questions:

• For some questions, information concerning one or both of the quantities to be compared is centered above the entries in the two columns.

• Symbols that appear in both columns represent the same thing in Column A as in Column B.

• Letters such as x, n, and k are symbols for real numbers.

• All figures are accurately drawn unless otherwise noted.

Here are two sample ISEE quantitative comparison questions. Try each of these on your own before you read the explanation that accompanies it.

Column A	Column B

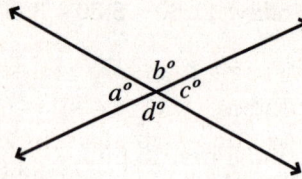

NOTE: Figure not drawn to scale.

7.

$$180 - a$$

$$d + c - b$$

The correct answer is (D).

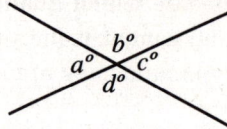

Since we do not know if $a > b$ or $a < b$, the relationship cannot be determined.

8.

$$\dfrac{\dfrac{2}{3}}{4}$$

$$\dfrac{2}{\dfrac{3}{4}}$$

The correct answer is (B).

$$\frac{\frac{2}{3}}{4} = \frac{2}{3} \cdot \frac{1}{4} = \frac{2}{12} \;\; vs. \;\; \frac{2}{\frac{3}{4}} = \frac{2}{1} \cdot \frac{4}{3} = \frac{8}{3}$$

Column A < Column B

HOW DOES THE ISEE MEASURE READING COMPREHENSION?

The ISEE measures your ability to read quickly and to understand what you read by asking you questions about passages that you must read. The 40 questions in the reading comprehension section are based on about nine reading passages. Because the ISEE is interested in both your level of reading and your ability to comprehend material from the sciences and from social studies, the content of the reading passages is based on social studies and science.

The directions for the ISEE test of reading comprehension look like this:

> **Directions:** Each passage is followed by questions based on its content. Answer the questions following each passage on the basis of what is stated or implied in the passage.

Here are samples of two ISEE reading passages, each followed by two questions. The first passage is a social studies passage and the second, a science-based passage. Read each passage and try to answer the questions on your own before you read the explanations.

> A large proportion of the people who are behind bars are not convicted criminals, but are people who have been arrested and are being held until their trial in court. Experts have often pointed out that this detention system does not operate fairly. For instance, a person who can afford to pay bail usually will not get locked up.
> (5) The theory of the bail system is that the person will make sure to show up in court when he is supposed to since he knows that otherwise he will forfeit his bail—he will lose the money he put up. Sometimes a person who can show that he is a stable citizen with a job and a family will be released on "personal recognizance" (without bail). The result is that the well-to-do, the employed, and those with families can
> (10) often avoid the detention system. The people who do wind up in detention tend to be the poor, the unemployed, the single, and the young.

9. According to the preceding passage, people who are put behind bars
   (A) are almost always dangerous criminals.
   (B) include many innocent people who have been arrested by mistake.
   (C) are often people who have been arrested but have not yet come to trial.
   (D) are all poor people who tend to be young and single.

The correct answer is (C). The answer to this question is directly stated in the first sentence. Choice (B) might be possible, but it is neither stated nor implied by the passage. The word *all* in choice (D) makes it an incorrect statement.

NOTE

In ISEE reading comprehension questions, the answers will always be directly stated or implied in the passage. You can think of it as an open book test!

10. Suppose that two men were booked on the same charge at the same time and that the same bail was set for both of them. One man was able to put up bail, and he was released. The second man was not able to put up bail, and he was held in detention. The writer of the passage would most likely feel that this result is

    (A) unfair, because it does not have any relation to guilt or innocence.

    (B) unfair, because the first man deserves severe punishment.

    (C) fair, because the first man is obviously innocent.

    (D) fair, because the law should be tougher on poor people than on the rich.

    The correct answer is (A). You should have no difficulty inferring this attitude from the tone of the passage.

      Fire often travels inside the partitions of a burning building. Many partitions contain wooden studs that support the partitions, and the studs leave a space for the fire to travel through. Flames may spread from the bottom to the upper floors through the partitions. Sparks from a fire in the upper part of a partition
    (5) may fall and start a fire at the bottom. Some signs that a fire is spreading inside a partition are: (1) blistering paint, (2) discolored paint or wallpaper, or (3) partitions that feel hot to the touch. If any of these signs is present, the partition must be opened up to look for the fire. Finding cobwebs inside the partition is one sign that fire has not spread through the partition.

11. Fires can spread inside partitions because

    (A) there are spaces between studs inside of partitions.

    (B) fires can burn anywhere.

    (C) partitions are made out of materials that burn easily.

    (D) partitions are usually painted or wallpapered.

    The correct answer is (A). This statement of fact is made in the second sentence.

12. If a firefighter sees the paint on a partition beginning to blister, he should first

    (A) wet down the partition.

    (B) check the partitions in other rooms.

    (C) chop a hole in the partition.

    (D) close windows and doors and leave the room.

    The correct answer is (C). Blistering paint (line 6) is a sign that fire is spreading inside a partition. If this sign is present, the firefighter must open the partition to look for the fire (lines 7–8). The way to open the partition is to chop a hole in it.

HOW DOES THE ISEE MEASURE MATHEMATICS ACHIEVEMENT?

The ISEE measures your mathematics achievement by asking you to answer math questions that relate to:

- Arithmetic concepts
- Algebraic concepts
- Geometric concepts

The mathematics achievement test consists of 45 questions, all of them of the standard multiple-choice type.

The directions for the mathematics achievement test look like this:

Directions: Read each question and choose the best answer based on calculations in your head or in the margins of the test booklet.

Here are four sample ISEE mathematics achievement questions. Try each of these on your own before you read the explanation that accompanies it.

13. If $\frac{3}{4}$ of a class is absent and $\frac{2}{3}$ of those present leave the room, what fraction of the original class remains in the room?

(A) $\frac{1}{4}$

(B) $\frac{1}{8}$

(C) $\frac{1}{12}$

(D) $\frac{1}{24}$

The correct answer is (C). If $\frac{3}{4}$ are absent, $\frac{1}{4}$ are present. If $\frac{2}{3}$ of the $\frac{1}{4}$ present leave, $\frac{1}{3}$ of the $\frac{1}{4}$ remain. $\frac{1}{3} \times \frac{1}{4} = \frac{1}{12}$ remain in the room.

NOTE

Leave your calculator and scratch paper at home. You can't use them on the test, but there will be space provided in the test booklet for scratch work.

14. A cog wheel having 8 cogs plays into another cog wheel having 24 cogs. When the small wheel has made 42 revolutions, how many has the larger wheel made?

(A) 10

(B) 14

(C) 16

(D) 20

The correct answer is (B). The larger wheel is 3 times the size of the smaller wheel, so it makes $\frac{1}{3}$ the revolutions: $42 \div 3 = 14$.

15. 75% of 4 is the same as what percent of 9?

(A) 25

(B) $33\frac{1}{3}$

(C) 36

(D) 40

The correct answer is (B). 75% of 4 = 3

$3 = 33\frac{1}{3}\%$ of 9

16. If $\frac{1}{2}$ cup of spinach contains 80 calories and the same amount of peas contains 300 calories, how many cups of spinach have the same caloric content as $\frac{2}{3}$ cup of peas?

(A) $\frac{2}{5}$

(B) $1\frac{1}{3}$

(C) 2

(D) $2\frac{1}{2}$

The correct answer is (D). $\frac{1}{2}$ cup spinach = 80 calories

$\frac{1}{2}$ cup peas = 300 calories

1 cup peas = 600 calories

$\frac{2}{3}$ cup peas = 400 calories

$400 \div 80 = 5$ half cups of spinach

$= 2\frac{1}{2}$ cups of spinach

WHAT IS THE ESSAY QUESTION?

At the end of each ISEE testing session, you must write a 30-minute essay on an assigned subject. This essay is not scored. It is duplicated and sent to each school as a sample of your ability to express yourself in writing under the same conditions as all other candidates for admission to the school.

The directions for the ISEE essay question look like this:

> **Directions:** Read the essay topic and decide what you want to say. Organize your thoughts carefully, then write a legible, coherent, and correct essay on the topic.

Here is a sample ISEE essay topic, also called a "prompt." Try to organize and write an essay on this topic.

Topic: An exchange student from China has just entered your school. What will you tell this student about student life at your school?

SUMMING IT UP

- The ISEE measures verbal ability with two question types: synonyms and sentence completions.

- The ISEE tests quantitative ability with two question types: standard multiple-choice and quantitative comparisons.

- The ISEE measures reading ability with reading comprehension questions based on information that is either directly stated or implied in the passages.

- The ISEE measure mathematics achievement with three question types: arithmetic, algebraic, and geometric concepts.

- Calculators are not permitted. Instead, use the space provided in the test booklet for scratch work.

- At the end of each ISEE test, you must write a 30-minute essay on an assigned subject.

PART II
DIAGNOSING STRENGTHS AND WEAKNESSES

CHAPTER 4   Practice Test 1: Diagnostic

Part II contains a Diagnostic Test to help you see where you stand. Take the Diagnostic Test first, to learn your strengths and weaknesses. Then use your results to develop a study plan.

Use the table below to determine which sections of the test to take.

No.	Section	SSAT	ISEE
1	Synonyms	X	X
2	Verbal Analogies	X	
3	Sentence Completions		X
4	Reading Comprehension	X	X
5	Quantitative Ability	X	X
6	Quantitative Comparisons		X

The Diagnostic Test does not contain an essay question. However, you will have chances to practice your writing skills in Part VII.

The sections on this Diagnostic may differ from your test in certain ways. For instance, all of the Diagnostic questions contain four answer choices, while the actual SSAT questions contain five answer choices. The Diagnostic sections may also be shorter than the sections on your test.

Though the Diagnostic will not be identical to the test you will take, it will still help you asses your *skill* levels. Once you know where you need work, you can better target your studying.

diagnostic test

ANSWER SHEET PRACTICE TEST 1: DIAGNOSTIC

Section 1: Synonyms (SSAT and ISEE)

1 Ⓐ Ⓑ Ⓒ Ⓓ	7 Ⓐ Ⓑ Ⓒ Ⓓ	13 Ⓐ Ⓑ Ⓒ Ⓓ	19 Ⓐ Ⓑ Ⓒ Ⓓ
2 Ⓐ Ⓑ Ⓒ Ⓓ	8 Ⓐ Ⓑ Ⓒ Ⓓ	14 Ⓐ Ⓑ Ⓒ Ⓓ	20 Ⓐ Ⓑ Ⓒ Ⓓ
3 Ⓐ Ⓑ Ⓒ Ⓓ	9 Ⓐ Ⓑ Ⓒ Ⓓ	15 Ⓐ Ⓑ Ⓒ Ⓓ	
4 Ⓐ Ⓑ Ⓒ Ⓓ	10 Ⓐ Ⓑ Ⓒ Ⓓ	16 Ⓐ Ⓑ Ⓒ Ⓓ	
5 Ⓐ Ⓑ Ⓒ Ⓓ	11 Ⓐ Ⓑ Ⓒ Ⓓ	17 Ⓐ Ⓑ Ⓒ Ⓓ	
6 Ⓐ Ⓑ Ⓒ Ⓓ	12 Ⓐ Ⓑ Ⓒ Ⓓ	18 Ⓐ Ⓑ Ⓒ Ⓓ	

Section 2: Verbal Analogies (SSAT Only)

1 Ⓐ Ⓑ Ⓒ Ⓓ	7 Ⓐ Ⓑ Ⓒ Ⓓ	13 Ⓐ Ⓑ Ⓒ Ⓓ	19 Ⓐ Ⓑ Ⓒ Ⓓ
2 Ⓐ Ⓑ Ⓒ Ⓓ	8 Ⓐ Ⓑ Ⓒ Ⓓ	14 Ⓐ Ⓑ Ⓒ Ⓓ	20 Ⓐ Ⓑ Ⓒ Ⓓ
3 Ⓐ Ⓑ Ⓒ Ⓓ	9 Ⓐ Ⓑ Ⓒ Ⓓ	15 Ⓐ Ⓑ Ⓒ Ⓓ	
4 Ⓐ Ⓑ Ⓒ Ⓓ	10 Ⓐ Ⓑ Ⓒ Ⓓ	16 Ⓐ Ⓑ Ⓒ Ⓓ	
5 Ⓐ Ⓑ Ⓒ Ⓓ	11 Ⓐ Ⓑ Ⓒ Ⓓ	17 Ⓐ Ⓑ Ⓒ Ⓓ	
6 Ⓐ Ⓑ Ⓒ Ⓓ	12 Ⓐ Ⓑ Ⓒ Ⓓ	18 Ⓐ Ⓑ Ⓒ Ⓓ	

Section 3: Sentence Completions (ISEE Only)

1 Ⓐ Ⓑ Ⓒ Ⓓ	7 Ⓐ Ⓑ Ⓒ Ⓓ	13 Ⓐ Ⓑ Ⓒ Ⓓ	19 Ⓐ Ⓑ Ⓒ Ⓓ
2 Ⓐ Ⓑ Ⓒ Ⓓ	8 Ⓐ Ⓑ Ⓒ Ⓓ	14 Ⓐ Ⓑ Ⓒ Ⓓ	20 Ⓐ Ⓑ Ⓒ Ⓓ
3 Ⓐ Ⓑ Ⓒ Ⓓ	9 Ⓐ Ⓑ Ⓒ Ⓓ	15 Ⓐ Ⓑ Ⓒ Ⓓ	
4 Ⓐ Ⓑ Ⓒ Ⓓ	10 Ⓐ Ⓑ Ⓒ Ⓓ	16 Ⓐ Ⓑ Ⓒ Ⓓ	
5 Ⓐ Ⓑ Ⓒ Ⓓ	11 Ⓐ Ⓑ Ⓒ Ⓓ	17 Ⓐ Ⓑ Ⓒ Ⓓ	
6 Ⓐ Ⓑ Ⓒ Ⓓ	12 Ⓐ Ⓑ Ⓒ Ⓓ	18 Ⓐ Ⓑ Ⓒ Ⓓ	

answer sheet

Section 4: Reading Comprehension (SSAT and ISEE)

1 (A) (B) (C) (D)   7 (A) (B) (C) (D)   13 (A) (B) (C) (D)   19 (A) (B) (C) (D)
2 (A) (B) (C) (D)   8 (A) (B) (C) (D)   14 (A) (B) (C) (D)   20 (A) (B) (C) (D)
3 (A) (B) (C) (D)   9 (A) (B) (C) (D)   15 (A) (B) (C) (D)   21 (A) (B) (C) (D)
4 (A) (B) (C) (D)   10 (A) (B) (C) (D)   16 (A) (B) (C) (D)   22 (A) (B) (C) (D)
5 (A) (B) (C) (D)   11 (A) (B) (C) (D)   17 (A) (B) (C) (D)
6 (A) (B) (C) (D)   12 (A) (B) (C) (D)   18 (A) (B) (C) (D)

Section 5: Quantitative Ability (SSAT and ISEE)

1 (A) (B) (C) (D)   9 (A) (B) (C) (D)   17 (A) (B) (C) (D)   25 (A) (B) (C) (D)
2 (A) (B) (C) (D)   10 (A) (B) (C) (D)   18 (A) (B) (C) (D)   26 (A) (B) (C) (D)
3 (A) (B) (C) (D)   11 (A) (B) (C) (D)   19 (A) (B) (C) (D)   27 (A) (B) (C) (D)
4 (A) (B) (C) (D)   12 (A) (B) (C) (D)   20 (A) (B) (C) (D)   28 (A) (B) (C) (D)
5 (A) (B) (C) (D)   13 (A) (B) (C) (D)   21 (A) (B) (C) (D)   29 (A) (B) (C) (D)
6 (A) (B) (C) (D)   14 (A) (B) (C) (D)   22 (A) (B) (C) (D)   30 (A) (B) (C) (D)
7 (A) (B) (C) (D)   15 (A) (B) (C) (D)   23 (A) (B) (C) (D)
8 (A) (B) (C) (D)   16 (A) (B) (C) (D)   24 (A) (B) (C) (D)

Section 6: Quantitative Comparisons (ISEE Only)

1 (A) (B) (C) (D)   7 (A) (B) (C) (D)   13 (A) (B) (C) (D)   19 (A) (B) (C) (D)
2 (A) (B) (C) (D)   8 (A) (B) (C) (D)   14 (A) (B) (C) (D)   20 (A) (B) (C) (D)
3 (A) (B) (C) (D)   9 (A) (B) (C) (D)   15 (A) (B) (C) (D)
4 (A) (B) (C) (D)   10 (A) (B) (C) (D)   16 (A) (B) (C) (D)
5 (A) (B) (C) (D)   11 (A) (B) (C) (D)   17 (A) (B) (C) (D)
6 (A) (B) (C) (D)   12 (A) (B) (C) (D)   18 (A) (B) (C) (D)

SECTION 1: SYNONYMS (SSAT AND ISEE)

20 Questions • 10 Minutes

Directions: Choose the word or phrase closest in meaning to the CAPITALIZED word. Mark the appropriate space on your answer sheet.

1. INTERMITTENTLY
   - (A) constantly
   - (B) annually
   - (C) using intermediaries
   - (D) at irregular intervals

2. DECEPTION
   - (A) secrets
   - (B) fraud
   - (C) mistrust
   - (D) hatred

3. ACCLAIM
   - (A) amazement
   - (B) laughter
   - (C) booing
   - (D) applause

4. ERECT
   - (A) paint
   - (B) design
   - (C) destroy
   - (D) construct

5. RELISH
   - (A) care
   - (B) speed
   - (C) amusement
   - (D) enjoy

6. FORTNIGHT
   - (A) two weeks
   - (B) one week
   - (C) two months
   - (D) one month

7. IMPOSE
   - (A) disguise
   - (B) escape
   - (C) require
   - (D) tax

8. ALIAS
   - (A) enemy
   - (B) sidekick
   - (C) hero
   - (D) other name

9. ITINERANT
   - (A) traveling
   - (B) shrewd
   - (C) insurance
   - (D) aggressive

10. AMPLE
    - (A) plentiful
    - (B) enthusiastic
    - (C) well-shaped
    - (D) overweight

11. STENCH
    - (A) puddle of slimy water
    - (B) pile of debris
    - (C) foul odor
    - (D) dead animal

12. SULLEN
    - (A) grayish yellow
    - (B) soaking wet
    - (C) very dirty
    - (D) angrily silent

13. TERSE
    (A) pointed
    (B) trivial
    (C) nervous
    (D) lengthy

14. INCREMENT
    (A) an improvisation
    (B) an increase
    (C) feces
    (D) specification

15. MISCONSTRUED
    (A) followed directions
    (B) led astray
    (C) acting to supervise
    (D) interpreted erroneously

16. VESTIGE
    (A) design
    (B) trace
    (C) strap
    (D) robe

17. CAPITULATE
    (A) surrender
    (B) execute
    (C) finance
    (D) retreat

18. EXTENUATING
    (A) mitigating
    (B) opposing
    (C) incriminating
    (D) distressing

19. SUBSERVIENT
    (A) underestimated
    (B) underhanded
    (C) subordinate
    (D) evasive

20. COLLUSION
    (A) decision
    (B) insinuation
    (C) connivance
    (D) conflict

SECTION 2: VERBAL ANALOGIES (SSAT ONLY)

20 Questions • 10 Minutes

Directions: Find the relationships among the words. Select the answer choice that best completes the meaning of the sentence. Mark the appropriate space on your answer sheet.

1. Red is to pink as black is to
   (A) beige
   (B) white
   (C) dark
   (D) gray

2. Youth is to young as maturity is to
   (A) people
   (B) parents
   (C) grandmother
   (D) old

3. One is to two as three is to
   (A) two
   (B) five
   (C) six
   (D) thirty

4. Light is to lamp as heat is to
   (A) furnace
   (B) light
   (C) sun
   (D) room

8/4/09

5. Week is to month as season is to
   - (A) year
   - (B) spring
   - (C) harvest
   - (D) planting

6. Square is to circle as rectangle is to
   - (A) round
   - (B) triangle
   - (C) oval
   - (D) cube

7. Choir is to director as team is to
   - (A) sport
   - (B) coach
   - (C) player
   - (D) athlete

8. Sand is to beach as black dirt is to
   - (A) earth
   - (B) plants
   - (C) water
   - (D) farm

9. Table is to leg as automobile is to
   - (A) wheel
   - (B) axle
   - (C) door
   - (D) fuel

10. Arouse is to pacify as agitate is to
    - (A) smooth
    - (B) ruffle
    - (C) understand
    - (D) ignore

11. Margarine is to butter as
    - (A) cream is to milk
    - (B) lace is to cotton
    - (C) nylon is to silk
    - (D) egg is to chicken

12. Woodsman is to axe as
    - (A) carpenter is to saw
    - (B) mechanic is to wrench
    - (C) soldier is to gun
    - (D) draftsman is to ruler

13. Worried is to hysterical as
    - (A) hot is to cold
    - (B) happy is to ecstatic
    - (C) lonely is to crowded
    - (D) happy is to serious

14. Control is to order as
    - (A) joke is to clown
    - (B) teacher is to pupil
    - (C) disorder is to climax
    - (D) anarchy is to chaos

15. Horse is to foal as
    - (A) donkey is to ass
    - (B) cow is to calf
    - (C) bull is to steer
    - (D) whinny is to moo

16. Sleep is to fatigue as
    - (A) water is to thirst
    - (B) rest is to weary
    - (C) pillow is to blanket
    - (D) fatigue is to run

17. Island is to ocean as
    - (A) hill is to stream
    - (B) forest is to valley
    - (C) oasis is to desert
    - (D) tree is to field

18. Drama is to director as
    - (A) class is to principal
    - (B) movie is to scenario
    - (C) actor is to playwright
    - (D) magazine is to editor

19. Request is to demand as
   (A) reply is to respond
   (B) inquire is to ask
   (C) wish is to crave
   (D) seek is to hide

20. Wood is to carve as
   (A) tree is to sway
   (B) paper is to burn
   (C) clay is to mold
   (D) pipe is to blow

SECTION 3: SENTENCE COMPLETIONS (ISEE ONLY)

20 Questions • 10 Minutes

Directions: Each question is made up of a sentence with one or two blanks. The sentences with one blank indicate that one word is missing. The sentences with two blanks indicate that two words are missing. Each sentence is followed by four choices. On the answer sheet, mark the letter of the choice that will best complete the meaning of the sentence as a whole.

1. Although fortune-tellers claim to _____ future happenings, there is no scientific evidence of their _____.
   (A) cloud .. ability
   (B) effect .. knowledge
   (C) foretell .. fees
   (D) predict .. accuracy

2. Great ideas have _____ youth: they are _____.
   (A) no .. petrified
   (B) eternal .. immortal
   (C) constant .. ephemeral
   (D) little .. frivolous

3. Each human relationship is unique, and the lovers who think there never was a love like theirs are _____.
   (A) foolish
   (B) blind
   (C) prejudiced
   (D) right

4. Rats give some _____ as scavengers, but this is over-balanced by their _____ activities.
   (A) help .. useful
   (B) service .. harmful
   (C) problems .. nocturnal
   (D) trouble .. breeding

5. Ancient societies gave authority to those who knew and preserved _____, for the idea of what was right lay in the past.
   (A) order
   (B) law
   (C) intelligence
   (D) tradition

6. The rare desert rains often come in _____, causing loss of life and property; thus, people living in an oasis think of rain with _____.
   (A) floods .. longing
   (B) torrents .. terror
   (C) sprinkles .. fear
   (D) winter .. snow

7. His admirers were not _____, for his essays were not widely known.
   (A) respected
   (B) numerous
   (C) ardent
   (D) interested

8. Archaeologists found ruins of temples and palaces, but no _____; it was as though these people never _____.
   (A) food .. lived
   (B) tombs .. died
   (C) plans .. built
   (D) monasteries .. worshipped

9. Safe driving prevents _____ and the endless _____ of knowing you have caused others pain.
   (A) disease .. reminder
   (B) tragedy .. remorse
   (C) accidents .. hope
   (D) lawsuits .. expense

10. A true amateur plays because he _____ the game and will not cheat because that would _____ the game.
    (A) studies .. lose
    (B) understands .. improve
    (C) knows .. forfeit
    (D) loves .. degrade

11. Companies have found it pays to have _____ handy when a meeting is likely to be _____.
    (A) food .. prolonged
    (B) secretaries .. enjoyable
    (C) telephones .. successful
    (D) money .. interesting

12. He _____ apart, for he prefers _____ to the company of others.
    (A) lives .. books
    (B) stays .. throngs
    (C) remains .. vivacity
    (D) dwells .. solitude

13. The Constitutional duty to "take care that the laws be faithfully executed" makes the president the head of law _____.
    (A) development
    (B) interpretation
    (C) education
    (D) enforcement

14. A reduction of the workweek to four days would certainly _____ the _____ industry.
    (A) destroy .. automobile
    (B) stimulate .. steel
    (C) improve .. electrical
    (D) benefit .. leisure

15. History tells us it took Athens less than a generation to change from a champion of _____ into a ruthless _____.
    (A) democracy .. republic
    (B) freedom .. tyrant
    (C) independence .. commonwealth
    (D) dictatorship .. liberator

16. The society was not _____ and required much outside aid.
    (A) philanthropic
    (B) destitute
    (C) democratic
    (D) self-sufficient

17. The _____ climate of the country _____ the delicate electronic equipment.
    (A) intolerable .. restored
    (B) dry .. vaporized
    (C) changeable .. demoralized
    (D) humid .. corroded

18. The value of _____ science to modern progress is _____.
    (A) research .. unimportant
    (B) physical .. unquestionable
    (C) medical .. unlikely
    (D) statistical .. unreliable

19. The final end of a nonadapting society is the same as for a nonadapting animal: _____.

(A) admiration

(B) resignation

(C) extinction

(D) immortality

20. Some temperamental actresses fail to understand that a director's criticism is aimed at their _____ and not at their _____.

(A) weaknesses .. conduct

(B) stupidity .. graciousness

(C) performance .. personality

(D) prosperity .. inability

SECTION 4: READING COMPREHENSION (SSAT AND ISEE)

22 Questions • 15 Minutes

Directions: Read each passage and answer the questions that follow it. Mark the appropriate space on your answer sheet.

If you are asked the color of the sky on a fair day in summer, your answer will most probably be "blue." This answer is only partially correct. Blue
(5) sky near the horizon is not the same kind of blue as it is straight overhead. Look at the sky some fine day and you will find that the blue sky near the horizon is slightly greenish. As your
(10) eye moves upward toward the zenith, you will find that the blue changes into pure blue, and finally shades into a violet-blue overhead.

Have you heard the story of a
(15) farmer who objected to the color of the distant hills in the artist's picture? He said to the artist, "Why do you make those hills blue? They are green, I've been over there and I know!"

(20) The artist asked him to do a little experiment. "Bend over and look at the hills between your legs." As the farmer did this, the artist asked, "Now what color are the hills?"

(25) The farmer looked again, then he stood up and looked. "By gosh, they turned blue!" he said.

It is quite possible that you have looked at many colors that you did not
(30) really recognize. Sky is not just blue; it is many kinds of blue. Grass is not plain green; it may be one of several

varieties of green. A red-brick wall frequently is not pure red. It may
(35) vary from yellow-orange to violet-red in color, but to the unseeing eye it is just red brick.

1. The title that best expresses the ideas of this passage is

(A) "The Summer Sky."

(B) "Artists vs. Farmers."

(C) "Recognizing Colors."

(D) "Blue Hills."

2. At the zenith, the sky is usually

(A) violet-blue.

(B) violet-red.

(C) greenish-blue.

(D) yellow-orange.

3. The author suggests that

(A) farmers are color-blind.

(B) perceived color varies.

(C) brick walls should be painted pure red.

(D) some artists use poor color combinations.

4. The word *zenith* in the first paragraph probably refers to
   (A) a color.
   (B) a point directly overhead.
   (C) a point on the horizon.
   (D) the hills.

While the Europeans were still creeping cautiously along their coasts, Polynesians were making trips between Hawaii and New
(5) Zealand, a distance of 3,800 miles, in frail canoes. These fearless sailors of the Pacific explored every island in their vast domain without even the simplest of navigational tools.

(10) In the daytime, the Polynesians guided their craft by the position of the sun, the trend of the waves and wind, and the flight of seabirds.

Stars were used during long
(15) trips between island groups. Youths studying navigation were taught to view the heavens as a cylinder on which the highways of navigation were marked. An invisible line
(20) bisected the sky from the North Star to the Southern Cross.

In addition to single canoes, the Polynesians often used twin canoes for transpacific voyages. The two
(25) boats were fastened together by canopied platforms that shielded passengers from sun and rain. Such crafts were remarkably seaworthy and could accommodate 60 to 80
(30) people, in addition to water, food, and domestic animals. Some of these vessels had as many as three masts.

These Pacific *mariners* used
(35) paddles to propel and steer their canoes. The steering paddle was so important that it was always given a personal name. Polynesian legends not only recite the names of the
(40) canoe and the hero who discovered a new island but also the name of the steering paddle he used.

5. The best title for this selection is
   (A) "European Sailors."
   (B) "The History of the Pacific Ocean."
   (C) "The Study of Navigation."
   (D) "Early Polynesian Navigation."

6. The Polynesians made trips to
   (A) New Zealand.
   (B) the Atlantic.
   (C) the Southern Cross.
   (D) Europe.

7. The word *mariner* means
   (A) propeller.
   (B) seaman.
   (C) paddle.
   (D) navigation.

8. This passage suggests that the Polynesians
   (A) trained seabirds to guide their canoes.
   (B) had seen a line in the sky that was invisible to others.
   (C) used a primitive telescope to view the heavens.
   (D) were astronomers as well as explorers.

The seasonal comings and goings of birds have excited the attention and wonder of all sorts of people in all ages and places. The oracles of
(5) Greece and the augurs of Rome wove them into ancient mythology. They are spoken of in the Books of Job and Jeremiah.

Nevertheless, it has been difficult
(10) for many to believe that small birds, especially, are capable of migratory journeys. Aristotle was convinced that the birds that wintered in Greece were not new arrivals, but merely
(15) Greece's summer birds in winter dress. According to a belief persisting in some parts of the world to this day, swallows and swifts do not migrate, but spend the winter in hibernation.
(20) (Swifts and swallows *do* migrate, just as most other Northern Hemisphere birds do.) Another old and charming, but untrue, legend enlists the aid of the stork in getting small birds to and
(25) from winter quarters: Small birds are said to hitch rides on the European stork's back.

It is clear why Northern Hemisphere birds fly south in the fall;
(30) they go to assure themselves of food and a more favorable climate for the winter months. It is also clear where most of the migrants come from and where they go. Years of bird-banding
(35) have disclosed the routes of the main migratory species.

But there are other aspects of migration that remain, for all our powers of scientific investigation, as
(40) puzzling and mysterious to modern man as to the ancients. Why do migrant birds come north each spring? Why don't they simply stay in the warm tropics the whole twelve
(45) months of the year? What determines the moment of departure for north or south? Above all, how do birds—especially species like the remarkable golden plover, which flies huge dis-
(50) tances directly across trackless ocean wastes—find their way?

9. The best title for this selection would be
   (A) "The Solution of an Ancient Problem."
   (B) "Mysterious Migrations."
   (C) "The Secret of the Plover."
   (D) "Aristotle's Theory."

10. Bird-banding has revealed
    (A) the kind of food birds eat.
    (B) why the birds prefer the tropics in the summer.
    (C) why birds leave at a certain time.
    (D) the routes taken by different types of birds.

11. Swallows and swifts
    (A) remain in Greece all year.
    (B) change their plumage in winter.
    (C) hibernate during the winter.
    (D) fly south for the winter.

12. The article proves that
    (A) nature still has secrets that man has not fathomed.
    (B) the solutions of Aristotle are accepted by modern science.
    (C) we live in an age that has lost all interest in bird lore.
    (D) man has no means of solving the problems of bird migration.

Using new tools and techniques, scientists, almost unnoticed, are remaking the world of plants. They have already remodeled sixty-five
(5) sorts of flowers, fruits, vegetables, and trees, giving us among other things tobacco that resists disease, cantaloupes that are immune to the blight, and lettuce with crisper
(10) leaves. The chief new tool they are using is colchicine, a poisonous drug, which has astounding effects upon growth and upon heredity. It creates new varieties with astonishing fre-
(15) quency, whereas such mutations occur but rarely in nature. Colchicine has thrown new light on the fascinating jobs of the plant hunters. The Department of Agriculture sends
(20) agents all over the world to find plants native to other lands that can be grown here and are superior to those already here. Scientists have crossed these foreign plants with
(25) those at home, thereby adding to our farm crops many desirable characteristics. The colchicine technique has enormously facilitated their work, because hybrids so often can
(30) be made fertile and because it takes so few generations of plants now to build a new variety with the qualities desired.

13. The title that best expresses the ideas of the paragraph is
(A) "Plant Growth and Heredity."
(B) "New Plants for Old."
(C) "Remodeling Plant Life."
(D) "A More Abundant World."

14. Mutation in plant life results in
(A) diseased plants.
(B) hybrids.
(C) new varieties.
(D) fertility.

15. Colchicine speeds the improvement of plant species because it
(A) makes possible the use of foreign plants.
(B) makes use of natural mutations.
(C) creates new varieties very quickly.
(D) can be used with sixty-five different vegetables, fruits, and flowers.

16. According to the passage, colchicine is a
(A) poisonous drug.
(B) blight.
(C) kind of plant hunter.
(D) hybrid plant.

Italy is a relatively small country. Its entire land area could be tucked into the borders of California, with plenty of room to spare, but Italy has *(5)* a population of more than 45,000,000 people. The country is 760 miles long and, at most points, only 100 to 150 miles wide.

Italy's southern, eastern, and *(10)* western borders are surrounded by water, making it a peninsula. To the north it is separated from France, Switzerland, Germany, and Yugoslavia by the towering mountain *(15)* chain known as the Alps.

About two thirds of the Italian peninsula is mountainous. In addition to the Alps, there are the Apennines, which run almost the entire length *(20)* of the country. This mountain chain is marked by the highly fertile river valleys that run across it.

Italy's climate is similar to that of Florida or California, except that *(25)* winters in the northern part of the country tend to be colder than in either of these states. The result is a long, productive growing season in much of the country.

(30) Tourists are often surprised at the full use to which the Italians put their soil. Because they are crowded in a small area, they cannot afford to let any land go to waste, and the *(35)* Italians are accomplished farmers. They have cultivated the fertile valleys and banks of the rivers as well as the northern plains regions. Mountainous areas have even been *(40)* utilized by cutting terraces into the steep slopes. Nearly half the population of Italy lives off the soil.

17. Which statement can be supported by the information in this passage?
    (A) Italy is separated from the rest of Europe by natural boundaries.
    (B) All of the Italian peninsula is a mountainous region.
    (C) Italy is a rather large country with a small population.
    (D) Few Italians cultivate the soil.

18. The winter climate of northern Italy is
    (A) similar to that of Texas.
    (B) comparable to that of Switzerland.
    (C) colder than winters in Florida.
    (D) similar to the winters in California.

19. The Italian peninsula
    (A) has a larger land area than California.
    (B) is 760 miles long and about 150 miles wide.
    (C) is longer than Florida.
    (D) has plenty of room to spare.

20. The Apennines are
    (A) river valleys.
    (B) plains.
    (C) mountains.
    (D) peninsulas.

21. Italy's northern border is formed by
    (A) rivers.
    (B) the Apennines.
    (C) water.
    (D) the Alps.

22. The northern plains and other flat areas of Italy make up how much of its land area?
    (A) About half
    (B) Two thirds
    (C) One third
    (D) Most of it

SECTION 5: QUANTITATIVE ABILITY (SSAT AND ISEE)

30 Questions • 30 Minutes

> **Directions:** Choose the correct answer to each question. Mark the appropriate space on your answer sheet.

1. Which square has half of its area shaded?

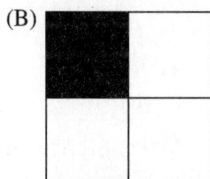

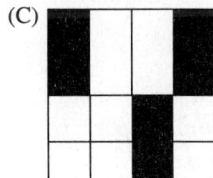

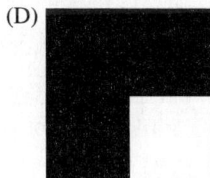

2. If 2 packages of cookies are enough for 10 children, how many will be needed for 15 children?
   - (A) 6
   - (B) 5
   - (C) 4
   - (D) 3

3. Which is equal to 9?
   - (A) 4×5
   - (B) 9×0
   - (C) 9×1
   - (D) 3×6

4. Jeff earns 12 dollars a week. Which of the following statements tells how many dollars he will earn in 5 weeks?
   - (A) $12 - 5$
   - (B) $12 \div 5$
   - (C) $12 + 5$
   - (D) 12×5

5. The distance from City X to San Francisco is 3 times the distance from City X to Chicago. How many miles away from City X is San Francisco? To solve this problem, what else do you need to know?
   - (A) The distance from Chicago to San Francisco
   - (B) The distance from City X to Chicago
   - (C) The city of origination
   - (D) Nothing else

6. If an odd number is subtracted from an odd number, which of the following could be the answer?
   - (A) 1
   - (B) 2
   - (C) 7
   - (D) 9

7. If $7 \times 6 = Y$, which is true?
   - (A) $Y \div 7 = 6$
   - (B) $Y \times 7 = 6$
   - (C) $7 \div Y = 6$
   - (D) $Y + 6 = 7$

8. $759 - 215 = \square$
   Which is closest to $\square$?
   - (A) 200
   - (B) 300
   - (C) 400
   - (D) 500

9. Edna bought 4 packages of balloons with 6 in each package, and 2 packages with 3 large balloons in each. How many balloons did Edna buy?

    (A) 10

    (B) 15

    (C) 26

    (D) 30

10. $a{\overline{\smash{\big)}\,4,028}}$ ^1

    What number is a?

    (A) 0

    (B) 1

    (C) 7

    (D) 4,028

11. $7 + \square = 15$

    Which number is equal to $\square$?

    (A) $15 \div 7$

    (B) $15 - 7$

    (C) 15×7

    (D) $15 + 7$

12. Colleen is 14 years old. She babysits for $4.50 an hour. Yesterday she baby-sat for $3\frac{1}{2}$ hours. Which shows how much she earned?

    (A) $14 \times \$4.50$

    (B) $2 \times 3\frac{1}{2}$

    (C) $3\frac{1}{2} \times \$4.50$

    (D) $(3\frac{1}{2} \times 2) \times \$4.50$

13.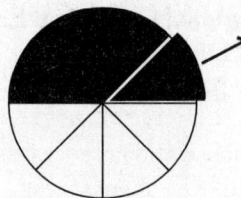

    Which of the following describes the chart above?

    (A) $\dfrac{4}{8} - \dfrac{1}{8}$

    (B) $\dfrac{4}{8} + \dfrac{1}{8}$

    (C) $\dfrac{4}{12} - \dfrac{1}{12}$

    (D) $\dfrac{4}{12} + \dfrac{1}{12}$

14. $8,862 < 8,\underline{}62$

    What number should be inserted to make the above statement correct?

    (A) 9

    (B) 8

    (C) 7

    (D) It cannot be determined by the information given.

15. A fence is being installed around the 156-meter perimeter of a swimming pool. How many posts will be used if they are spaced 12 meters apart?

    (A) 11

    (B) 12

    (C) 13

    (D) 14

16. What is 28,973 rounded to the nearest thousand?

    (A) 30,000

    (B) 29,000

    (C) 28,900

    (D) 28,000

17. The bakery received a shipment of 170 cupcakes that will be sold by the box. If each box holds 12 cupcakes, approximately how many boxes will be needed?

    (A) 8

    (B) 14

    (C) 20

    (D) 25

18.

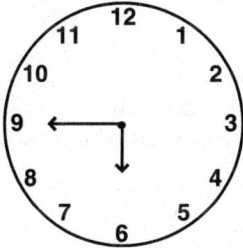

What time will it be in $3\frac{1}{2}$ hours?

    (A) 9

    (B) 9:15

    (C) 9:30

    (D) 9:45

19. Which of these number sentences is NOT true?

    (A) $\frac{3}{3} = \frac{5}{5}$

    (B) $\frac{5}{5} = \frac{6}{6}$

    (C) $\frac{8}{8} = 1$

    (D) $\frac{7}{8} = \frac{8}{7}$

20.

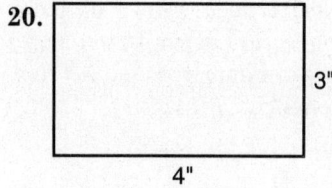

What is the area of this figure?

    (A) 1 sq. inch

    (B) 7 sq. inches

    (C) 12 sq. inches

    (D) 14 sq. inches

21. In order to make $\frac{7}{8}$ cup of salad dressing with our recipe, you add $\frac{1}{4}$ cup of vinegar to the oil. How much oil will you use?

    (A) $\frac{3}{8}$ cup

    (B) $\frac{5}{8}$ cup

    (C) $\frac{6}{8}$ cup

    (D) $\frac{3}{4}$ cup

22. Which digit is in the thousandths place?

    A   BC
    ↓   ↓↓
    5,000.072

    (A) Only A

    (B) Only B

    (C) Only C

    (D) B and C

23. Which is NOT true?

(A) $\dfrac{6}{8} = \dfrac{3}{4}$

(B) $\dfrac{2}{3} = \dfrac{6}{12}$

(C) $\dfrac{3}{4} = \dfrac{12}{16}$

(D) $\dfrac{3}{9} = \dfrac{6}{18}$

24. Which sequence of fractions is arranged in order of least to greatest?

(A) $\dfrac{1}{3}, \dfrac{1}{18}, \dfrac{1}{11}, \dfrac{1}{7}$

(B) $\dfrac{1}{18}, \dfrac{1}{11}, \dfrac{1}{7}, \dfrac{1}{3}$

(C) $\dfrac{1}{3}, \dfrac{1}{7}, \dfrac{1}{11}, \dfrac{1}{18}$

(D) $\dfrac{1}{8}, \dfrac{1}{7}, \dfrac{1}{11}, \dfrac{1}{3}$

25. In which of the following numbers does the digit 6 have a value 10 times greater than the value of the 6 in 603?

(A) 60

(B) 600

(C) 6,000

(D) 60,000

26. Which quotient would be approximately 5?

(A) $20\overline{)205}$

(B) $20\overline{)500}$

(C) $20\overline{)1000}$

(D) $200\overline{)1005}$

27.

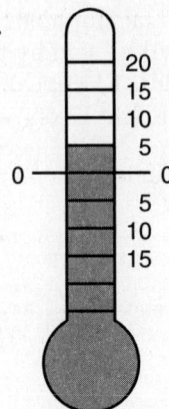

If the temperature decreases by 15 degrees below that shown on the thermometer, what will the new temperature be?

(A) 20°

(B) 10°

(C) −10°

(D) −20°

28. $5 \times (2 + x) = 15$

What number is x?

(A) 1

(B) 2

(C) 4

(D) 5

29. Which of the following has a quotient that is NOT smaller than the dividend?

(A) $0 \div 8$

(B) $1 \div 8$

(C) $2 \div 8$

(D) $8 \div 8$

30.

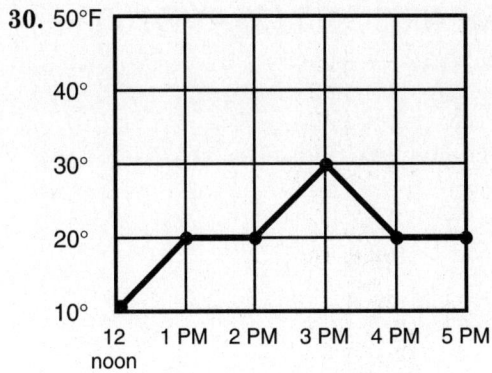

Which of the following is shown by the graph?

(A) There was no change in temperature between 1 and 2 p.m.

(B) There was no change in temperature between 3 and 4 p.m.

(C) The highest temperature occurred at 12 noon.

(D) The lowest temperature occurred at 5 p.m.

SECTION 6: QUANTITATIVE COMPARISONS (SSAT ONLY)

20 Questions • 20 Minutes

Directions: For each of the following questions, two quantities are given—one in Column A, the other in Column B. Compare the two quantities and mark your answer sheet as follows:

(A) if the quantity in Column A is greater

(B) if the quantity in Column B is greater

(C) if the quantities are equal

(D) if the relationship cannot be determined from the information given

Notes

- Information concerning one or both of the compared quantities will be centered above the two columns for some items.

- Symbols that appear in both columns represent the same thing in Column A as in Column B.

- Letters such as x, n, and k are symbols for real numbers.

- Figures are drawn to scale unless otherwise noted.

Column A	Column B		Column A	Column B

1.
$$2x + 3 = 5$$
$$3y + 7 = 10$$

| x | | y |

2.
$$\frac{x}{36} = \frac{1}{3}$$

| $\frac{4}{x}$ | | $\frac{1}{3}$ |

3. x is an integer

| x | | $\frac{x}{-1}$ |

4.

| Number of seconds in one day | | Number of minutes in April |

5.
$$9 < x < 10$$
$$9 < y < 11$$

| x | | y |

6.

| Area of a triangle with base 5 and height 7 | | Twice the area of a rectangle with base 5 and height 7 |

7.

$ABCD$ is a parallelogram

| AB | | DC |

Column A	Column B

8.

$$4 \cdot a \cdot 4 \cdot 4 = 3 \cdot 3 \cdot 3 \cdot 3$$

a	3

9.

A single discount of 10%	Two successive discounts of 5% and 5%

10.

$\sqrt{49} + \sqrt{16}$	$\sqrt{65}$

11. The average age of Alan, Bob, and Carl is 17.

The sum of Alan's age and Bob's age	The sum of Alan's age and Carl's age

12.

$$4 < a < 6$$
$$4 \le b \le 6$$

a	b

13.

$m<1+m<2+m<3$	$m<2+m<4$

14. Jack's salary is $\frac{3}{4}$ of Jim's salary and Joe's salary is $\frac{3}{2}$ of Jack's salary.

Jim's salary	Joe's salary

Column A	Column B

15.

$$AB = AC$$
$$m < A = 60°$$
NOTE: Figure not drawn to scale.

AB	BC

16.

$$a > b > c > 0$$

$\dfrac{a}{b}$	$\dfrac{a}{c}$

17.

The total surface area of a cube with edge 6	6 times the total surface area of a cube with edge 2

18.

5%	$\dfrac{1}{2}$

19.

$18 \cdot 563 \cdot 10$	$12 \cdot 563 \cdot 16$

20.

The number of posts needed for a fence 100 feet long if the posts are placed 10 feet apart	10 posts

ANSWER KEY AND EXPLANATIONS

Section 1: Synonyms (SSAT and ISEE)

1. D	5. D	9. A	13. A	17. A
2. B	6. A	10. A	14. B	18. A
3. D	7. C	11. C	15. D	19. C
4. D	8. D	12. D	16. B	20. C

1. **The correct answer is (D).** That which happens INTERMITTENTLY stops and starts again at intervals, or pauses from time to time. A pedestrian crossing light that is activated by a push button says "WALK" and "DON'T WALK" intermittently. You may see a relationship to *intermission*, which is a pause between parts of a performance.

2. **The correct answer is (B).** One who practices DECEPTION willfully tries to make another believe that which is not true to mislead or defraud. The verb on which this noun is based is *deceive*.

3. **The correct answer is (D).** To ACCLAIM is to greet with loud applause and approval. The winners of the World Series returned to the city to wild acclaim.

4. **The correct answer is (D).** To ERECT is to raise, construct, set up, or assemble. The adjective *erect* describes that which is vertical and straight up. You can see the relationship of verb and adjective.

5. **The correct answer is (D).** If you RELISH something, you enjoy it. You may be more familiar with the noun, with the relish that you put on your hot dog to make it more appetizing and to add to your enjoyment.

6. **The correct answer is (A).** A FORTNIGHT (fourteen nights) is a period of two weeks.

7. **The correct answer is (C).** To IMPOSE a tax is to place a tax upon the taxpayers and to require that it be paid. Be careful here. The *tax* (noun) is the object of *to impose* (verb), not the definition or a synonym.

8. **The correct answer is (D).** An ALIAS is an assumed name. The alias may be a pen name or a stage name, or may be a false name taken on for purposes of disguise.

9. **The correct answer is (A).** An ITINERANT peddler travels from place to place, selling his or her wares at each stop. The itinerant may follow an itinerary, a detailed outline of the proposed journey.

10. **The correct answer is (A).** That which is AMPLE is large, spacious, abundant, or plentiful. When referring to a figure, *ample* may imply *over-weight*, but the meaning of the word *ample* is simply *more than enough*.

11. **The correct answer is (C).** Stagnant water or a decaying dead animal may have a STENCH or foul odor. STENCH means *stink*.

12. **The correct answer is (D).** A SULLEN person is resentful, unsociable, and gloomy.

13. **The correct answer is (A).** TERSE means *concise* and *succinct*. It is the opposite of "lengthy" and has nothing at all to do with nerves or tension.

14. **The correct answer is (B).** An INCREMENT is a specified increase, usually a small one. Sometimes trying to figure out the meanings of words by looking at their roots just doesn't work. This word has nothing to do with "excrement" even though it looks like it.

15. **The correct answer is (D).** To MISCONSTRUE is to *misinterpret*. "Word arithmetic" works well with this synonym question. The prefix "mis" means *wrong*; the root is the same root as "construct," so to *misconstrue* is to *build up wrong* in one's mind.

16. **The correct answer is (B).** A VESTIGE is a *trace*. This is a difficult word, one that is picked up in the course of wide reading.

17. **The correct answer is (A).** To CAPITULATE is to *give in, give up,* or *surrender*. Capitulation is more a total act than a mere retreat.

18. **The correct answer is (A).** EXTENUATING is making light of something or lessening the real or apparent seriousness of something. In sentencing a guilty party, the judge may consider extenuating circumstances, details that make the guilt thinner or weaker. If there are extenuating or mitigating circumstances, the sentence may be lighter. If you missed this question, do not be upset. Both the word and its definition are very high-level words.

19. **The correct answer is (C).** SUBSERVIENT—serving under—means inferior, subordinate, or submissive.

20. **The correct answer is (C).** COLLUSION is a *conspiracy*, a *secret agreement*, or a *connivance*. Use of this word implies an illegal goal.

Section 2: Verbal Analogies (SSAT Only)

1. D	5. A	9. A	13. B	17. C
2. D	6. C	10. A	14. D	18. D
3. C	7. B	11. C	15. B	19. C
4. A	8. D	12. A	16. A	20. C

1. **The correct answer is (D).** The relationship is intensity or degree. PINK is a muted form of RED; GRAY is a muted form of BLACK. White is the opposite of *black*, while *dark* is one of *black's* characteristics.

2. **The correct answer is (D).** YOUTH is a noun form, YOUNG an adjective. Both refer to the early years. MATURITY is a noun form, OLD an adjective.

Maturity and *old* refer to the later years of existence.

3. **The correct answer is (C).** The relationship between the first two terms cannot be determined until you look at the third term and the choices. At first you might think, "Two follows one, so four should follow three." The problem is that "four" is not offered as an answer choice. Of the choices given,

SIX is most related to THREE, since SIX is *twice* THREE. Looking back at the first pair, you can see that TWO is *twice* ONE. Since the "times two" relationship applies to both sides of the proportion, choice (C) is the correct answer.

4. **The correct answer is (A).** The relationship is effect/cause. LIGHT is produced by a LAMP: HEAT is produced by a FURNACE. The sun also produces heat, but the *sun* is a natural source. *Lamp* in the original pair is an artificial source of light; *furnace*, the *best* answer, is an artificial source of *heat*.

5. **The correct answer is (A).** The relationship is part to whole. WEEK is part of MONTH; SEASON is part of YEAR.

6. **The correct answer is (C).** A SQUARE is angular, a CIRCLE rounded; a RECTANGLE is angular, an OVAL rounded. You might say "angular is to rounded as angular is to rounded."

7. **The correct answer is (B).** The relationship is that of object to actor. The DIRECTOR leads the CHOIR; the COACH leads the TEAM.

8. **The correct answer is (D).** The relationship is one of characteristic. SAND is the soil that is characteristic of the BEACH; BLACK DIRT is the soil that is characteristic of a productive FARM.

9. **The correct answer is (A).** This is a true functional relationship. The TABLE is supported by LEGS; the AUTOMOBILE is supported by WHEELS. It is important to narrow to the functional relationship in order to eliminate choices (B) and (C). Use of the part/whole relationship would yield too many correct answers.

10. **The correct answer is (A).** AROUSE and PACIFY are antonyms; AGITATE and SMOOTH are antonyms. If you know the meanings of the words, this is an easy analogy question. *Ruffle* is a synonym for *agitate*.

11. **The correct answer is (C).** The relationship is that of artificial to real or substitute to the real thing. MARGARINE is imitation BUTTER; NYLON is imitation SILK. *Lace* is often made from *cotton* but does not substitute for it.

12. **The correct answer is (A).** The relationship is a very specific functional one. The WOODSMAN uses an AXE to cut; the CARPENTER uses a SAW to cut. In all the other choices, we are offered a worker and a tool of his trade, but none of these tools is used specifically for cutting.

13. **The correct answer is (B).** The relationship is one of degree. One who is WORRIED may become HYSTERICAL (overwhelmed by fear); one who is HAPPY may become ECSTATIC (overwhelmed by joy).

14. **The correct answer is (D).** The relationship is one of cause and effect. CONTROL of a group results in ORDER; ANARCHY (lack of government or control) results in CHAOS (disorder).

15. **The correct answer is (B).** The relationship is one of degree (large/small) or, more specifically, that of parent to child. The HORSE is the parent of the FOAL; the COW is the parent of the CALF. *Donkey* and *ass* are synonyms. A *steer* is a *bull* raised for its meat.

16. **The correct answer is (A).** The best way to verbalize this relationship is to call it that of the cure to its ailment. SLEEP cures FATIGUE: WATER cures THIRST. Beware of the grammatical

inconsistency in choice (B). *Rest* cures "weariness," not *weary*. The relationship of choice (D) is effect to cause.

17. **The correct answer is (C).** This is a variation of the part-to-whole relationship. An ISLAND is a small body of land within and wholly surrounded by an OCEAN; an OASIS is a small, green, fertile spot within and wholly surrounded by a large arid expanse of DESERT.

18. **The correct answer is (D).** The relationship is that of actor to object. The DIRECTOR is responsible for the production of a DRAMA; the EDITOR is responsible for the production of a MAGAZINE. The *principal* is responsible for an entire school, not just a class. Responsibility for a single class rests with a teacher.

19. **The correct answer is (C).** The relationship is one of degree. To DEMAND is to REQUEST very strongly; to CRAVE is to WISH for very strongly. The terms in choice (A) are synonyms; in choice (D) antonyms; and in choice (B) cause and effect.

20. **The correct answer is (C).** At first glance, the relationship is object to action. However, this definition is not specific enough to allow for a single answer choice. A careful look at the possible answers helps lead to a refinement of the relationship to "creative manual action upon an object or medium that is changed by that action." The only answer with this relationship is choice (C), CLAY is to MOLD.

Section 3: Sentence Completions (ISEE Only)

1. D	5. D	9. B	13. D	17. D
2. B	6. B	10. D	14. D	18. B
3. D	7. B	11. A	15. B	19. C
4. B	8. B	12. D	16. D	20. C

1. **The correct answer is (D).** The first blank must be filled with what it is that fortune-tellers do. This narrows your answer to choices (C) or (D). There being no scientific evidence of their fees makes no sense, so the answer is choice (D).

2. **The correct answer is (B).** The sentence calls for synonyms, as the second clause merely expands upon the first. ETERNAL and IMMORTAL both mean everlasting.

3. **The correct answer is (D).** The second clause of the sentence is meant to corroborate the first. Since each human relationship is unique, the lovers who assume the uniqueness of their own relationship are RIGHT.

4. **The correct answer is (B).** The word "but" gives the clue that the blanks must be filled with contrasting terms. Choice (B) best meets this condition.

5. **The correct answer is (D).** If the idea of what was right lay in the past, then authority would have to be given to those who knew and preserved ancient lore and habits, e.g., TRADITION.

6. **The correct answer is (B).** Since the desert rains cause loss of life and property, people in an oasis must think of rain with TERROR, choice (B), or

fear, choice (C). The word that best fills the second blank will determine whether the correct answer is choice (B) or (C). Sprinkles, choice (C), would be unlikely to cause loss of life and property; TORRENTS, choice (B), is more appropriate.

7. **The correct answer is (B).** If the essayist's essays were not widely known, he would have few (not NUMEROUS) admirers.

8. **The correct answer is (B).** In light of the fact that archaeologists found temples and palaces, choices (A), (C), and (D) cannot be correct. The people clearly lived, thought, and built. Choice (B) presents a mystery, but it does create a logically correct sentence.

9. **The correct answer is (B).** Safe driving prevents TRAGEDY, choice (B), accidents, choice (C), and lawsuits, choice (D). The second part of the sentence, however, is reasonably completed only with choice (B).

10. **The correct answer is (D).** The purpose of amateur sports is recreation; the amateur participates for fun, for LOVE of the sport. (The word *amateur* is derived directly from Latin and means "lover.") Cheating is DEGRADING; it makes an activity less desirable.

11. **The correct answer is (A).** If there is to be a meeting, it might be well to have FOOD, choice (A), secretaries, choice (B), and telephones, choice (C), available. However, none of these is specifically needed at an enjoyable, choice (B), meeting or at a successful, choice (C), meeting. If the meeting is likely to be PROLONGED, choice (A), then it is worthwhile to provide FOOD.

12. **The correct answer is (D).** Choices (A) and (D) form excellent completions for this sentence. Choice (D) is the *best*

answer because SOLITUDE is in direct contrast to the company of others.

13. **The correct answer is (D).** Executing the laws requires law ENFORCEMENT.

14. **The correct answer is (D).** A four-day workweek would give workers much more LEISURE time, which would, in turn, greatly BENEFIT the LEISURE industry.

15. **The correct answer is (B).** The adjective *ruthless* (cruel) aptly describes a TYRANT. Since the sense of the sentence calls for contrast, a change from champion of FREEDOM to ruthless TYRANT fulfills the requirement.

16. **The correct answer is (D).** The reason that a society would need outside aid would be that the society was not SELF-SUFFICIENT.

17. **The correct answer is (D).** The sentence requires that there be a cause-and-effect relationship between the two words that fill the blanks. Only choice (D) meets this requirement.

18. **The correct answer is (B).** The meaning of any one of the choices would be equally appropriate for filling the first blank, although choice (A) would be grammatically incorrect. The words *value* and *progress* are positive words, suggesting the need for a positive completion for the second blank. The only positive second term is in choice (B).

19. **The correct answer is (C).** The final end is EXTINCTION.

20. **The correct answer is (C).** The role of a director is to perfect the PERFORMANCE through necessary criticism. A temperamental actress might misinterpret direction as PERSONAL criticism.

Section 4: Reading Comprehension (SSAT and ISEE)

1. C	6. A	11. D	15. C	19. B
2. A	7. B	12. A	16. A	20. C
3. B	8. D	13. C	17. A	21. D
4. B	9. B	14. C	18. C	22. C
5. D	10. D			

1. **The correct answer is (C).** The main idea, the topic of this passage, is looking closely at colors in order to truly recognize them. The farmer is the vehicle for making the point, and the sky and hills are used as illustrations.

2. **The correct answer is (A).** The last sentence of the first paragraph gives you this detail.

3. **The correct answer is (B).** You should be able to infer this answer from the passage. If not, you can choose the correct answer by eliminating all the other choices as being ridiculous.

4. **The correct answer is (B).** Reread the first paragraph carefully if you got this wrong. The phrase "moves up toward the zenith" should lead you to the correct answer.

5. **The correct answer is (D).** You should have no trouble finding the main idea of this passage.

6. **The correct answer is (A).** The first sentence tells us that the Polynesians made trips to New Zealand.

7. **The correct answer is (B).** The first sentence of the last paragraph makes clear that mariners are people.

8. **The correct answer is (D).** The third paragraph tells us how the Polynesians used the stars for navigation. People who study and understand movements of the stars are astronomers. Although the Polynesians used movements of seabirds as a guide during the daytime, they had not trained the birds. There is no mention of telescopes.

9. **The correct answer is (B).** The topic of the passage is bird migration and the mystery it has presented throughout the ages.

10. **The correct answer is (D).** The last sentence of the third paragraph makes this statement.

11. **The correct answer is (D).** You will find this information within the parentheses in the second paragraph.

12. **The correct answer is (A).** This is the point of the last paragraph.

13. **The correct answer is (C).** Choosing the title for this paragraph takes more than one reading of the paragraph. This is not an easy question. After a couple of readings, however, you should be able to conclude that the all-inclusive subject of the paragraph is the remodeling of plants. An equally correct title, not offered here, might be "Uses and Effects of Colchicine."

14. **The correct answer is (C).** Buried in the middle of the paragraph is the sentence: "It creates new varieties with astonishing frequency, whereas such mutations occur but rarely in nature."

15. **The correct answer is (C).** This question becomes easy to answer after you have dealt with the previous question.

16. **The correct answer is (A).** The third sentence states that colchicine is a poisonous drug.

17. **The correct answer is (A).** The second paragraph gives this information. All the other choices are actually contradicted in the passage.

18. **The correct answer is (C).** See the fourth paragraph.

19. **The correct answer is (B).** This is stated in the first paragraph. The first paragraph also states that Italy is smaller than California. The length of Florida is not stated in the paragraph. (When answering questions based upon a reading passage, you must base your answer only on what is stated or implied in the passage, not upon your personal information or opinion.)

20. **The correct answer is (C).** If you missed this, reread the third paragraph.

21. **The correct answer is (D).** See the second paragraph.

22. **The correct answer is (C).** If two thirds of the peninsula is mountainous (third paragraph), then one third must be made up of northern plains and other flat areas.

Section 5: Quantitative Ability (SSAT and ISEE)

1. A	7. A	13. A	19. D	25. C
2. D	8. D	14. A	20. C	26. D
3. C	9. D	15. C	21. B	27. C
4. D	10. D	16. B	22. C	28. A
5. B	11. B	17. B	23. B	29. A
6. B	12. C	18. B	24. B	30. A

1. **The correct answer is (A).** This square is divided into six sections, and three are shaded. Three is half of six.

2. **The correct answer is (D).** If 2 packages of cookies will serve 10 children, you may assume that 1 package will serve 5 children. Therefore, 3 packages will serve 15 children.

3. **The correct answer is (C).**
$4 \times 5 = 20$;
$9 \times 0 = 0$
$3 \times 6 = 18$;
$9 \times 1 = 9$

4. **The correct answer is (D).** $12.00 × 5 weeks = 12 × 5

5. **The correct answer is (B).** If C represents the distance from City X to Chicago, and S represents the distance from City X to San Francisco, then $3 \times C = S$. You must know the value of C in order to find S.

6. **The correct answer is (B).** An odd number subtracted from an odd number will always result in an even number. The only even number given is 2.

7. **The correct answer is (A).** Since $7 \times 6 = Y$, $Y = 42$. So $42 \div 7 = 6$.

8. **The correct answer is (D).** $759 - 215 = 544$, which, when rounded to the nearest hundred, is 500.

9. **The correct answer is (D).** $4 \times 6 = 24$ and $2 \times 3 = 6$; therefore, $24 + 6 = 30$.

10. **The correct answer is (D).** Any number divided by itself equals one.

11. **The correct answer is (B).** $15 - 7 = 8$; $7 + 8 = 15$

12. **The correct answer is (C).** Three numbers are given in this problem, but only two are necessary to solve the problem: the charge per hour and the number of hours Colleen baby-sat.

    $4.50 per hour $\times 3\frac{1}{2}$ hours =

    $4.50 $\times 3\frac{1}{2}$

13. **The correct answer is (A).** The pie has been divided into 8 pieces. One piece $= \frac{1}{8}$. Four pieces $= \frac{4}{8}$. Four pieces are left in this picture, and one is being taken away; therefore, $\frac{4}{8} - \frac{1}{8}$.

14. **The correct answer is (A).** The symbol < means "is less than." Using response A, the statement reads: 8,862 is less than 8,962.

15. **The correct answer is (C).** 156 meters $\div$ 12 meters = 13.

16. **The correct answer is (B).** In the number 28,973, the digit 8 is in the thousands place. The hundreds digit is greater than 5, so the next nearest thousand is 9; therefore, 29,000 is the answer.

17. **The correct answer is (B).** $170 \div 12 = 14$ with a remainder of 2. The closest number given is 14.

18. **The correct answer is (B).** The time is now 5:45. In 3 more hours it will be 8:45. Thirty minutes later the time will be 9:15.

19. **The correct answer is (D).**

    $\frac{3}{3} = \frac{5}{5} = 1$

    $\frac{5}{5} = \frac{6}{6} = 1$

    $\frac{8}{8} = 1$

    $\frac{7}{8} \neq \frac{8}{7}$

20. **The correct answer is (C).** The area of a rectangle is found by multiplying the length by the width. $4" \times 3" = 12$ square inches

21. **The correct answer is (B).** $\frac{1}{4} = \frac{2}{8}$, therefore, $\frac{7}{8} - \frac{2}{8} = \frac{5}{8}$.

22. **The correct answer is (C).** A is in the thousands place, and B is in the hundredths place.

23. **The correct answer is (B).** $\frac{2}{3} \neq \frac{6}{12}$; $\frac{2}{3} = \frac{8}{12}$; $\frac{6}{12} = \frac{1}{2}$

24. **The correct answer is (B).** The denominator of a fraction shows how many parts the whole has been divided into. Therefore, $\frac{1}{18}$ is less than $\frac{1}{11}$, etc.

25. **The correct answer is (C).** The 6 in 603 represents 600; $600 \times 10 = 6,000$.

26. **The correct answer is (D).** $1,005 \div 200 = 5$, with a remainder of 5. The answer is *approximately* 5.

27. **The correct answer is (C).** $5° - 15° = -10°$

28. **The correct answer is (A).** $5 \times (2 + 1) = 5 \times 3 = 15$

29. The correct answer is (A). $0 \div 8 = 0$. The other responses work out this way: Choice (B) $1 \div 8 = \frac{1}{8}$; Choice (C) $2 \div 8 = \frac{2}{8}$; Choice (D) $8 \div 8 = 1$. In $0 \div 8$, 0 is the dividend and 8 is the divisor. The quotient is the result obtained when the dividend is divided by the divisor.

30. The correct answer is (A). According to the graph, the temperature at 1 p.m. was 20°, and at 2 p.m. it was *still* 20°.

Section 6: Quantitative Comparisons (ISEE Only)

1. C	5. D	9. A	13. C	17. A
2. C	6. B	10. A	14. B	18. B
3. D	7. C	11. D	15. C	19. B
4. A	8. B	12. D	16. B	20. A

1. **The correct answer is (C).** Solving the equations, $x = 1$, $y = 1$.

2. **The correct answer is (C).** Solving for x, $x = 12$ or $\frac{4}{12} = \frac{1}{3}$.

3. **The correct answer is (D).** If $x > 0$, A is greater. If $x < 0$, B is greater. If $x = 0$, A and B are equal.

4. **The correct answer is (A).** 60 seconds = 1 minute; 60 minutes = 1 hour; 24 hours = 1 day; Seconds in 1 day $= 60 \cdot 60 \cdot 24$. There are 30 days in April; Number of minutes in April $= 60 \cdot 24 \cdot 30$. Without any computation, A has the greater factors.

5. **The correct answer is (D).** x and y can take on values so that A is greater, B is greater, or they are both equal.

6. **The correct answer is (B).**

   Area of triangle $= \frac{1}{2} \cdot 5 \cdot 7$

   Twice area of rectangle $= 2 \cdot 5 \cdot 7$

7. **The correct answer is (C).** Opposite sides of a parallelogram are congruent.

8. **The correct answer is (B).** If $64a = 81$, then $a =$ a little more than 1.

9. **The correct answer is (A).** Column A represents a greater discount since the full 10% is taken from the original price.

10. **The correct answer is (A).**

    $\sqrt{49} + \sqrt{16} = 7 + 4 = 11$

    $\sqrt{65}$ is a little more than 8.

11. **The correct answer is (D).** There is no information about the age of any of these.

12. **The correct answer is (D).** a and b can take on values to make either one greater or to make them equal.

13. **The correct answer is (C).** Each of these is 180°.

14. **The correct answer is (B).** If Jim's salary $= 8x$, then Jack's salary $= 6x$, and Joe's salary $= 9x$.

15. **The correct answer is (C).** There are 120° left between angle B and angle C. Since they must be congruent, they are each 60° and the triangle is equilateral.

16. **The correct answer is (B).** Since the numerators are the same, the fraction with the smaller denominator will be larger.

17. **The correct answer is (A).** Surface area of a cube is the sum of 6 equal squares.

    A $\qquad$ B

    $6 \cdot 6^2 \qquad 6 \cdot 6 \cdot 2^2$

    The factors are greater in A.

18. **The correct answer is (B).**

    $$\frac{1}{2} = .5$$

    $.5\% = .005$

19. **The correct answer is (B).**
    $18 \times 10 = 180; 12 \times 16 = 192$

20. **The correct answer is (A).** Since a post is needed at the very beginning as well as at the end, A requires 11 posts.

EVALUATING YOUR SCORE AND PLANNING YOUR STUDY TIME

Begin by entering on the score sheet the number of questions you got correct in each section and calculate your percentage score. Your scores on the actual exam will not be reported in percentages. You will receive percentile scores that compare your performance with that of other students your age and in your grade. Your percentile standing is very useful information for the school that must base its admission decision on your preparedness. For your purposes, however, the percent of questions you got right can help you compare your own performance on each question type. Your percent score can point out to you your own strengths and weaknesses and help you to plan your study time.

SCORE SHEET

SECTION	NO. CORRECT	÷	NO. OF QUESTIONS	=	× 100	= %
Synonyms (SSAT and ISEE)	____	÷	20	=	× 100	= %
Verbal Analogies (SSAT Only)	____	÷	20	=	× 100	= %
Sentence Completions (ISEE Only)	____	÷	20	=	× 100	= %
Reading Comprehension (SSAT and ISEE)	____	÷	22	=	× 100	= %
Quantitative Ability (SSAT and ISEE)	____	÷	30	=	× 100	= %
Quantitative Comparisons (ISEE Only)	____	÷	20	=	× 100	= %

As you look over your answer sheet, you may notice that you missed some of the earlier, "easier" questions and got some right near the end of a section. This should not surprise you. After all, you are an individual with your own interests, talents, and thought processes, and your current school may introduce some topics in a less usual order. If you were able to answer correctly many questions on the diagnostic exam, you are already ahead of the game. If you didn't get too far in the time limit or if you got many answers wrong, do not be discouraged. First consider your age and inexperience with some of the question styles. Then congratulate yourself that you had the foresight to plan a study program, and get to work.

Plot your standing on each section on the comparison chart for your test. Put a check mark into the boxes in which your scores fall. Now you can see at a glance exactly where you will have to concentrate your study. If you have lower percentage scores in certain areas, focus your preparation on those areas.

COMPARISON CHART—SSAT

	Percent Correct				
	0–30	31–45	46–60	61–75	76–100
Synonyms					
Verbal Analogies					
Reading Comprehension					
Quantitative Ability					

COMPARISON CHART—ISEE

	Percent Correct				
	0–30	31–45	46–60	61–75	76–100
Synonyms					
Sentence Completions					
Reading Comprehension					
Quantitative Ability					
Quantitative Comparisons					

PART III

VOCABULARY REVIEW

CHAPTER 5   Word Arithmetic
(SSAT and ISEE)

Word Arithmetic (SSAT and ISEE)

OVERVIEW

- Why do they test my vocabulary?
- How are words built?
- How do word parts work?
- List of common word parts
- Word list
- Summing it up

WHY DO THEY TEST MY VOCABULARY?

Your ability to understand and to use words is essential to all of your learning. If your test performance on verbal ability exams shows that you have a rich vocabulary, you are a good prospect for success at the schools to which you have applied.

HOW ARE WORDS BUILT?

The subject is not letters of the alphabet but rather the parts of words themselves. You can actually increase your vocabulary—and your test score—by learning about the structure of words. This will help you figure out the meanings of unfamiliar words you come across in the verbal ability section of your exam.

Knowing what the parts of words mean is the key to deciphering words you've never seen before. Let's take a look at the word *biography* and its parts. You know that a biography is something written about a person's life. How do the word parts tell you this? Well, the second part of the word, *graphy*, comes from a Greek word that means "writing." The first part of the word, *bio*, is also from Greek and means "life." Put them both together and you get . . . biography, the story of a person's life. If you add the Latin word for "self"—*auto*—you get . . . *autobiography*, a story you write about your own life. Think about some other words that use one or more of these parts, like *automobile*, *biochemistry*, and *autograph*. Can you see how the meaning fits the word parts?

TIP

**Practice word
arithmetic.** Words
are the sum of their
parts. If you come up
against an unfamiliar
word on your exam,
decipher its parts
and add them up to
get the meaning.

HOW DO WORD PARTS WORK?

Different kinds of word parts work together to make a fully functioning word. Think about it: If your car is going to do more than just sit there, it needs a collection of parts put together in the right way. Two steering wheels won't do you any good if you don't have a gas tank.

Each kind of word part has a specific purpose. There are three basic types of word parts:

1. *Prefixes* attach to the beginning of a root word to alter its meaning or to create a new word.

2. *Suffixes* attach to the end of a root word to change its meaning, help make it grammatically correct in context, or form a new word. Suffixes often indicate whether a word is a noun, verb, adjective, or adverb.

3. *Roots* or *stems* are the basic elements of a word that determine its meaning. Roots or stems are not words. They must be combined with prefixes, suffixes, or both. Groups of words from the same root word are called "word families."

A word can have a root, a prefix, and a suffix; it can have a root and two suffixes or a root and one prefix. The possibilities are endless (almost), but you must always have a root. Word analysis is a kind of arithmetic. Instead of adding numbers, we add the meanings contained in each part of an unfamiliar word. The sum of these parts is the definition of the whole word.

Use the word list that follows to expand your word horizons. Once you begin to learn the word parts on the list, you'll be able to take apart unfamiliar words like a master mechanic. As you make your way through the list, try to think of other words with the same parts. If you have time, check their meanings in a dictionary and take a look at the word origins in the entry.

LIST OF COMMON WORD PARTS

Prefix	Meaning	Example
a	not	amoral
ab	away from	absent
ad, ac, ag, at	to, against	aggressive, attract
an	without	anarchy
ante	before	antedate
anti, ant	against	antipathy, antonym

Prefix	Meaning	Example
bene	well	benefactor
bi	two	biannual
circum	around	circumvent
com, con, col	together	commit, collate
contra	against	contraband
de	from, down	descend
dis, di	apart, away	distract, divert
dom	home, rule	domicile, dominate
ex, e	out, from	exit, emit
extra	beyond, outside	extracurricular
in, im, ir, il, un	not	inept, irregular, illegal
in, im	in, into	interest, imbibe
inter	between	interscholastic
intra, intro	within	intramural
mal	bad	malcontent
mis	wrong	misspell
non	not	nonentity
ob	against	obstacle
omni	all	omnivorous
per	through	permeate
peri	around, about	periscope
poly	many	polytheism
post	after	postmortem
pre	before	premonition
pro	forward, for	propose
re	again, back	review, redeem
se	apart, away	seclude
semi	half	semicircle
sub	under	submarine
super	above	superimpose
sur	on, upon	surmount
syn, sym	together, with	sympathy
trans	across, beyond	transpose
un	not	unwelcome

Suffix	Meaning	Example
able, ible	capable of	applicable, reversible (*adj.*)
age	place, thing, idea	storage (*n.*)
al	pertaining to	instructional (*adj.*)
ance	relating to	reliance (*n.*)
ary	relating to	dictionary (*n.*)
ate	an action of	confiscate (*v.*)
cy	the quality of	democracy (*n.*)
ed	past action	subsided (*v.*)
ence	relating to	confidence (*n.*)
er, or	one who	adviser, actor (*n.*)
ic	pertaining to	democratic (*adj.*)
ing	present action	surmising (*v.*)
ion	the act or state of	radiation (*n.*)
ious	full of	rebellious (*adj.*)
ive	having the quality of	creative (*adj.*)
ize	to make	harmonize (*v.*)
ly	to do with the quality of	carefully (*adv.*)
ment	the result of	amusement (*n.*)
ness	the quality of being	selfishness (*n.*)
ty	condition of being	sanity (*n.*)

Stem	Meaning	Example
ag, ac	do	agenda, action
agri	farm	agriculture
aqua	water	aquatic
auto	self	automatic
biblio	book	bibliography
bio	life	biography
cad, cas	fall	cadence, casual
cap, cep, cept	take	captive, accept
capit	head	capital
ced, cede, ceed, cess	go	intercede
celer	speed	accelerate
chrom	color	monochromatic
chron	time	chronological

Stem	Meaning	Example
cide, cis	cut	incision
clude, clud, clus	close, close in	include, cluster
cog, cogn	knowledge of	recognize
cur, curs	run	incur, recur
ded	give	dedicate
dent, dont	tooth	dental
duce, duct	lead	induce, deduct
fact, feet, fict	make, do	perfect, fiction
fer, late	carry	refer, dilate
flect, flex	bend, turn	reflect
fring, fract	break	infringe, refract
graph, gram	picture, writing	graphic, telegram
greg	group, gather	gregarious
gress, grad	move	progress, degrade
hydr	water	hydrate
ject	throw	inject
jud	right	judicial
junct	join	conjunction
juris	law, justice	jurist
lect, leg	read, choose	collect
logue	speech, speaking	dialogue
logy	study of	psychology
loq, loc	speak	elocution
lude, lus	play, perform	elude
manu	by hand	manuscript
mand	order	remand
mar	sea	maritime
med	middle	intermediate
ment, mem	mind, memory	mention
meter	measure	thermometer
micro	small	microscope
min	lessen	miniature
mis, miss, mit	send	remit, dismiss
mot, mov	move	remote, remove
mute	change	commute

Stem	Meaning	Example
naut	sailor, sail	nautical
nounce, nunci	declare, state	announce, enunciate
ped, pod	foot	pedal
pel, pulse	drive, push	dispel, impulse
pend, pense	hang, way	depend, dispense
plac	please	placate
plic	fold	implicate
port	carry	portable
pose, pone	put, place	depose, component
reg, rect	rule	regulate, direct
rupt	break	disruption
scend, scent	move	ascent
scribe, script	write	describe
sec, sect	cut	bisect
sed	remain	sedentary
sert	state, place	insert
serve	keep, save	preserve
sist	stand, set	insist
spect	look	inspect
spire, spirat	breath, breathe	perspire
strict	tighten	restrict
tain	hold	detain
term	end	terminate
tort	twist	distort
tract	draw, drag	detract
vene, vent	come	intervene, invent
vict	overcome, conquer	evict
volve, volu	roll, turn	evolve, evolution

WORD LIST

The words in this list are grouped in "families," by their stems. The stems are arranged in alphabetical order. If you need help with words other than those listed here, check with your dictionary or thesaurus.

AQUA, AQUE: water

aquarium—a tank for fish and water plants

aquatic—having to do with water

aqueous—watery

subaqueous—under water

AUTO: self

autobiography—the story of one's life, written by oneself

autograph—a person's own signature

automatic—self-operating

automation—a system in which machinery does most of the work itself

BIBLIO: book

bibliography—a list of books used for reference

bibliolatry—worship of books

BIO: life

antibiotics—medicines that work against harmful life-forms in the body

biography—the story of a person's life

biology—the study of various life-forms

symbiosis—mutual interdependence of two different living organisms

CAP, CEP, CEPT: take

accept—to take in

capture—to take by force; to take prisoner

exception—something taken or left out

inception—the act of taking something in; a beginning

ED, CEDE, CEED, CESS: go, move

accede—to move toward; to grant

concede—to go with; admit

concession—an admission

exceed—to go over or outside of

excess—going over certain limits

intercede—to move between

precede—to go before or ahead of

proceed—to move forward

recede—to move back

secession—the act of moving apart; separation from the whole

CHRON: time

anachronism—something contrary to a particular era

chronometer—a tool that measures time

CIDE, CIS: cut

decide—to act; to cut off from further consideration

excise—to cut out or away

incision—a cut

CLUDE, CLUS: close, shut

exclude—to close or shut out

exclusive—having the quality of shutting out

include—to shut or close in

recluse—a person who shuts him- or herself away from others

seclude—to shut apart from

COG, COGN: knowledge of

cognizant—the quality of being knowledgeable

incognito—unknown; disguised

recognition—the act of knowing again; recalling

CUR, CURS: run

concurrent—running with; at the same time

cursory—the quality of running through quickly

precursor—a forerunner

recurrent—running again

DUCE, DUCT: lead

abduct—to lead away; to kidnap

conducive—having the quality of leading together; persuasive

deduce—to lead from; to conclude

introduce—to lead into

reduction—the act of leading backward; a loss

FACT, FECT, FICT: make, do

affectation—something made up; a pretense

defect—something made apart from the ordinary

effect—something done outwardly; a change

fictitious—made up; not true

FER: carry, bring

conference—the state of bringing together; a meeting

differ—to carry apart; to disagree

ferret—to force out of hiding; to search about

infer—to bring in; to conclude

offer—to carry out

preference—the act of bringing first or before

reference—the act of carrying back

transfer—to carry across

FLECT, FLEX: bend, turn

circumflex—an accent mark that is bent over a letter

flexible—able to be bent or changed

genuflect—to bend the knee to the floor

reflect—to bend or turn something back

reflex—a return movement; a response

FRING, FRACT: break

fracture—a break in something hard

infraction—the breaking of a rule

infringe—to break into

refract—to break up

GRAPH, GRAM: picture, writing

diagram—information in picture form

epigram—a brief piece of writing

graph—information in picture form

seismograph—a picture record of earth movements

telegram—communication using sound and writing

telegraph—communication with sounds that are translated into writing

GREG: group, gather

aggregation—a group

congregate—to gather together

gregarious—having the characteristic of getting along well in a group; social

segregate—to group apart; to keep groups separate

GRESS, GRAD: move

aggressive—the characteristic of moving toward something

degrade—to move down

graduate—to move from one level of prestige, proficiency, or experience to a higher one

ingredient—something that is moved into something else

progress—to move forward

regress—to move backward

upgrade—to move up

HYDR: water

dehydrate—to remove water from

hydrant—something that gives out water

hydraulic—relating to water power

hydrogen—water gas

hydrology—the study of water

hydrophobia—fear of water

hydrotherapy—cure by water

JECT: throw

conjecture—something thrown together; a guess

dejected—thrown down

eject—to throw out

inject—to throw in

projectile—an object to throw forward

subjected—thrown under

JUNCT: join

conjunction—a word that joins parts of sentences together

enjoin—to join into; to enforce

injunction—an enjoining action

junction—a joining of two parts of something

JURIS: law, justice

jurisdiction—sphere of legal authority

jurisprudence—legal science

jurist—an expert in law

LOGUE: speaking, speech

dialogue—speech between two people

epilogue—a short ending speech

eulogy—a speech of praise

monologue—one person's speech

prologue—a speech given as a foreword

LOQ, LOC: talk, speak

colloquy—talking together

elocution—clear speech

interlocutors—speakers

loquacious—the quality of being talkative

LUDE, LUS: play

allude—to refer to casually or indirectly

allusion—a reference to

delude—to deceive; to mislead

elude—to escape through cleverness

prelude—an introductory period before a main event

MAND: order, command

countermand—an order placed against another order

mandate—command

mandatory—ordered or required

remand—to order back

MANU: hand

manicure—care of the hands

manifest—as from an open hand; made obvious

manipulate—to handle

manual—a handbook; done by hand and not by machine

manuscript—a document written by hand

MEM, MENT: mind, memory

commemorate—to remember with

demented—out of one's mind

mention—a call to mind

reminisce—to call back memories

MIS, MISS, MIT: send

commit—to send together

dismiss—to send away

emit—to send out

remission—the state of being sent back

submit—to send under

transmit—to send across

PED, POD: foot

biped—an animal that walks on two feet

impede—to put a foot against; to obstruct

pedestrian—a person who is walking

podiatrist—a foot doctor

tripod—an object with three feet

PEL, PULSE: drive, push

dispel—to drive away

expel—to push out

impulse—to drive or push in

propel—to push forward

repel—to push back

PEND, PENSE: hang, weigh

appendix—part that hangs; a portion of a book usually found in the back

dispense—to apportion

expenditure—a sum paid out

impending—hanging over something

suspend—to hang from

PLAC: please

implacable—not able to be pleased or appeased

placate—to please

placebo—an inactive medicine designed to please or satisfy

placid—quiet, pleasing

PLI, PLIC: fold

implicate—to involve

pliable—easily folded or influenced

PONE, POSE, POSIT: place or put

components—units to be put together

depose—to put down

exponent—something or someone who puts something forth

oppose—to place against

proponent—a person who puts something forward; an advocate

PORT: carry, bring

deportation—the act of carrying out or away from

export—to carry trade out of a country

import—to carry trade into a country

report—to carry back

transport—to carry across

RECT, REG: to rule or lead, straight

erect—straightened upward

rectify—to straighten out; to correct

rectitude—moral uprightness

regulate—to rule

RUPT: break

disrupt—to break through or down

erupt—to break out

rupture—a break

SCEND, SCENT: climb

ascend—to climb up

condescend—to climb down with

descent—downward slope

transcend—to climb beyond

SCRIBE, SCRIPT: write

describe—to write about
inscription—something written in something else
prescription—written before receiving
proscribe—to write something out; to ban

SEC, SECT: cut

bisect—to cut in two
dissect—to cut apart
sector—a cutting or part of a whole

SERT: declare, state

assert—to state firmly
insert—to place within

SERVE: keep, save

conserve—to save (together)
preservation—the state of maintaining as before
reservation—something kept or saved aside

SIST: stand, set

desist—to stand away
inconsistent—not standing together; changing
insistent—having the quality of standing firmly

SPEC, SPECT: see, look

aspect—a way of looking at something
prospective—forward looking; future
spectrum—something seen broadly
speculate—to look at mentally

TAIN, TEN: hold

contain—to hold together
containment—the state of being held together
detain—to hold aside
retain—to hold back
tenacious—holding powerfully

TERM: end, limit

exterminate—to eliminate

interminable—not able to be ended; unending

terminate—to end

terminus—ending place

TORT: twist

contort—to twist together

distortion—something that twists away from the truth

extort—to twist away or out of

TRACT: draw, drag

attract—to draw toward

distraction—something that draws attention away from something else

extract—to draw out

intractable—not easily drawn or persuaded

protracted—drawn out

VENE, VENT: come

advent—a coming

circumvent—to avoid by going around

convene—to come together

intervene—to come between

VINCE, VICT: conquer, overcome

convince—to conquer

invincible—not able to be conquered

victor—conqueror

VOLVE, VOLU: roll, turn

convoluted—rolled or twisted together

evolution—the act of rolling forth; a gradual development

involve—to draw in

revolution—a rolling back; an overturning

EXERCISES: WORD ARITHMETIC

15 Questions

Directions: To get yourself started, take a look at these examples of word analysis and arithmetic.

Q PROCESSION

A *pro-* is a prefix that means "forward."

cess is a stem that means "go" or "move."

-ion is a noun suffix that means "the act of."

pro + cess + ion = *the act of going before*

Q RECEDING

A *re-* is a prefix that means "back."

cede is a stem that means "go."

-ing is an active word suffix.

re + ced + ing = *going back*

Q DISSECTED

A *dis-* is a prefix that means "apart."

sect is a stem meaning "cut."

-ed is a verb suffix showing past action.

dis + sect + ed = *cut apart or took apart*

Directions: Practice word arithmetic with these words. The List of Common Word Parts and the Word List will help you. Write a definition for each word in the space. The correct answers follow.

1. revision _____
2. audible _____
3. adhere _____
4. retract _____
5. projection _____
6. preclude _____
7. recline _____
8. erupt _____
9. regression _____
10. revolution _____
11. retain _____
12. inscription _____
13. divert _____
14. conduct _____
15. import _____

ANSWERS AND EXPLANATIONS

1. RE- *back, again;* VIS *look, see;* -ION *the act of*

   RE + VIS + ION = *the act of looking at or seeing again*

2. AUD *hear;* -IBLE *able*

   AUD + IBLE = *able to be heard*

3. AD- *to;* HERE *cling, stick*

   AD + HERE = *cling to*

4. RE- *back, again;* TRACT *draw, pull*

   RE + TRACT = *to draw back*

5. PRO- *forward;* JECT *throw;* -ION *the act of*

   PRO + JECT + ION = *the act of throwing forward*

6. PRE- *before;* CLUDE *close, close in*

   PRE + CLUDE = *to close in before*

7. RE- *back, again;* CLINE *lean*

   RE + CLINE = *to lean back*

8. E- *out;* RUPT *break*

   E + RUPT = *to break out*

9. RE- *back, again;* GRESS *move;* -ION *the act of*

   RE + GRESS + ION = *the act of moving backward*

10. RE- *back, again;* VOLU *roll;* -TION *the act of*

    RE + VOLU + TION = *the act of rolling again*

11. RE- *back, again;* TAIN *to hold;* -ED *indicates past action*

    RE + TAIN + ED = *held back*

12. IN- *in;* SCRIPT *write;* -ION *the act of*

    IN + SCRIPT + ION = *the act of writing in*

13. DI- *away, aside;* VERT *turn*

    DI + VERT = *to turn away*

14. CON- *together;* DUCT *lead*

    CON + DUCT = *to lead together*

15. IM- *in;* PORT *to carry*

    IM + PORT = *to carry in*

SUMMING IT UP

- Knowing what the parts of words mean is the key to deciphering words you've never seen before.

- Practice word arithmetic. Words are the sum of their parts.

- If you come up against an unfamiliar word on your test, decipher its parts and add them up to get the meaning.

PART IV
VERBAL ABILITY REVIEW

Synonyms (SSAT and ISEE)

OVERVIEW

- **How will synonym questions be presented?**
- **What do the synonym questions look like?**
- **How do you answer synonym questions?**
- **Summing it up**

HOW WILL SYNONYM QUESTIONS BE PRESENTED?

Synonyms are words with similar meanings, and synonym questions ask you to choose a word with a meaning similar to that of a given word or to complete a sentence.

Definition

This type of question presents a word in capital letters. You are asked to choose the word that is the closest to it in meaning.

> **Q** IMAGE
>
>   **(A)** newspaper
>
> → **(B)** picture
>
>   **(C)** fantasy
>
>   **(D)** oldest
>
> **A** **The correct answer is (B).** An *image* is a *picture*.

Sentence Context

This type of question presents a word printed in either italics or boldfaced type within a sentence. You are asked to choose a word that is closest in meaning to that word. The sentence context may give you clues to the meaning of the question word.

Q Miss Payne was a *garrulous* old gossip. *Garrulous* means

(A) complaining.

(B) overly friendly.

(C) careless.

→ (D) overly talkative.

A **The correct answer is (D).** *Garrulous* is an adjective describing the noun "gossip" in this sentence. Since adjectives answer the question "What kind?" *garrulous* must be telling what kind of gossip Miss Payne is. *Garrulous* is therefore a word that must have something to do with gossipy conversation.

WHAT DO THE SYNONYM QUESTIONS LOOK LIKE?

Both the SSAT and ISEE test you with straightforward synonym questions. They present a single word in capital letters and ask you to choose the word that is the best synonym for the question word.

Directions: Choose the word or phrase closest in meaning to the CAPITALIZED word.

Q PROFICIENT

(A) resentful

(B) amiable

(C) famous

→ (D) adept

A **The correct answer is (D).** Someone who is proficient is particularly good at doing a certain task or activity. *Adept* is a synonym for *proficient*.

HOW DO YOU ANSWER SYNONYM QUESTIONS?

To answer synonym questions, follow these four steps:

SYNONYMS: GETTING IT RIGHT

1 Read the question carefully. Consider *every* answer choice. One choice must always be the best response.

2 Eliminate obviously wrong responses immediately.

3 Use word-analysis techniques to help you with difficult words.

4 Try using the word in a sentence of your own; think about the meaning of the word as you have used it.

TEST YOURSELF QUIZZES

Use the following quizzes to help you determine what your weaknesses might be.

Mark every word you cannot define—capitalized word or answer choice. Look up these words in a dictionary and create your own personal vocabulary list for further study. See pages 110–111 for answers.

Test Yourself 1

Directions: Select the word that is closest in meaning to the CAPITALIZED word and circle the letter that appears before your answer.

1. CHASSIS
   - (A) frame
   - (B) body
   - (C) form
   - (D) lubrication

2. ENLIGHTEN
   - (A) reduce
   - (B) bleach
   - (C) educate
   - (D) absorb

3. AFFIRM
   - (A) prove
   - (B) validate
   - (C) sign
   - (D) stick

4. FROCK
   - (A) dress
   - (B) coat
   - (C) hermit
   - (D) veil

5. KEG
   - (A) beer
   - (B) nails
   - (C) barrel
   - (D) understanding

6. LOGO
   - (A) symbol
   - (B) copyright
   - (C) game plan
   - (D) magnet

7. MOUSY
   - (A) brown
   - (B) alcoholic
   - (C) gnawing
   - (D) timid

8. PARCH
   - (A) boil
   - (B) bum
   - (C) dry
   - (D) steam

9. REFUGE
   - (A) alibi
   - (B) shelter
   - (C) exile
   - (D) church

10. SKEPTIC
    - (A) doubter
    - (B) critic
    - (C) heretic
    - (D) opponent

11. TENUOUS
    - (A) boring
    - (B) impermanent
    - (C) nervous
    - (D) flimsy

12. VIE
    - (A) defeat
    - (B) hurry
    - (C) seek
    - (D) compete

13. ARMADA
    (A) fleet
    (B) battle
    (C) defeat
    (D) ship

14. DRIVEL
    (A) saliva
    (B) foam
    (C) tension
    (D) nonsense

15. BOOTY
    (A) piracy
    (B) riot
    (C) plunder
    (D) leather

16. PORTAL
    (A) dockside
    (B) carriage
    (C) peephole
    (D) gate

17. CAGEY
    (A) imprisoned
    (B) protected
    (C) shrewd
    (D) wild

18. JUMBO
    (A) egg
    (B) elephant
    (C) huge
    (D) mixture

19. MYTHICAL
    (A) ancient
    (B) religious
    (C) explanatory
    (D) imaginary

20. NUGGET
    (A) gold
    (B) candy
    (C) collision
    (D) lump

Test Yourself 2

Directions: Select the word that is closest in meaning to the CAPITALIZED word and circle the letter that appears before your answer.

1. ADULTERATE
    (A) cheat
    (B) age
    (C) shorten
    (D) idolize
    (E) dilute

2. BOARDER
    (A) carpenter
    (B) lumberman
    (C) edge
    (D) roomer
    (E) traveler

3. LEERY
    (A) obscene
    (B) uncontrolled
    (C) wicked
    (D) suspicious
    (E) sheltered

4. OVATION
    (A) speech
    (B) applause
    (C) egg dish
    (D) misjudgment
    (E) exaggeration

5. CORPULENT
   (A) ruddy
   (B) spiritual
   (C) bloody
   (D) overweight
   (E) gluttonous

6. DIVERT
   (A) behave
   (B) amuse
   (C) annoy
   (D) arrange
   (E) disclose

7. SUPERFICIAL
   (A) fantastic
   (B) family ties
   (C) real estate
   (D) well
   (E) without depth

8. COMBATIVE
   (A) honesty
   (B) posture
   (C) constructive
   (D) correction
   (E) argumentative

9. TRUCE
   (A) treaty
   (B) peace
   (C) pause
   (D) amnesty
   (E) silence

10. INTRIGUE
    (A) plot
    (B) jolly
    (C) dishonest
    (D) greedy
    (E) strict

11. SPECTRUM
    (A) rainbow
    (B) prism
    (C) range
    (D) magnifier
    (E) idea

12. PERILOUS
    (A) dangerous
    (B) waterproof
    (C) frightening
    (D) poor
    (E) perfect

13. INSENSITIVE
    (A) brief
    (B) lacy
    (C) uncaring
    (D) servile
    (E) sad

14. BENEFICIAL
    (A) bad luck
    (B) helpful
    (C) blessing
    (D) thanks
    (E) enlightenment

Test Yourself 3

Directions: Select the word that is closest in meaning to the CAPITALIZED word and circle the letter that appears before your answer.

1. HUMUS
   (A) nerve
   (B) topsoil
   (C) modesty
   (D) tonnage

2. INVALUABLE
   (A) useless
   (B) untrue
   (C) uniform
   (D) priceless

3. BELLIGERENT
   (A) warlike
   (B) windy
   (C) noisy
   (D) overweight

4. ACRID
   (A) burnt
   (B) smoky
   (C) bitter
   (D) artificial

5. RIFE
   (A) widespread
   (B) mature
   (C) quarrelsome
   (D) broken

6. TACIT
   (A) understood
   (B) sensitive
   (C) sticky
   (D) skillful

7. SHROUD
   (A) cummerbund
   (B) coffin
   (C) veil
   (D) wake

8. WRIT
   (A) law
   (B) order
   (C) deed
   (D) prohibition

9. DOWDY
   (A) young
   (B) fluffy
   (C) widowed
   (D) shabby

10. MAUDLIN
    (A) spotted
    (B) sentimental
    (C) silent
    (D) juicy

11. ULCER
    (A) pain
    (B) stomachache
    (C) sore
    (D) swelling

12. GREGARIOUS
    (A) haggling
    (B) sociable
    (C) quick
    (D) worm-like

13. SURLY
   (A) positively
   (B) confidently
   (C) unfriendly
   (D) overly

14. TOKEN
   (A) symbol
   (B) coin
   (C) omen
   (D) facsimile

15. ASYLUM
   (A) madness
   (B) illness
   (C) prison
   (D) sanctuary

16. PRUNE
   (A) raisin
   (B) fruit
   (C) trim
   (D) wrinkle

Test Yourself 4

Directions: Select the word that is closest in meaning to the CAPITALIZED word and circle the letter that appears before your answer.

1. AMORPHOUS
   (A) insomniac
   (B) drug-free
   (C) shapeless
   (D) headless
   (E) unloved

2. PALTRY
   (A) silo
   (B) larder
   (C) fowl
   (D) foul
   (E) meager

3. QUANDARY
   (A) swamp
   (B) prey
   (C) argument
   (D) nausea
   (E) puzzlement

4. STERLING
   (A) genuine
   (B) plated
   (C) excellent
   (D) shiny
   (E) heavy

5. TIC
   (A) click
   (B) twitch
   (C) check mark
   (D) insect
   (E) game

6. VALET
   (A) manservant
   (B) bootblack
   (C) chauffeur
   (D) doorman
   (E) rascal

7. BRUNT
   (A) wide end
   (B) heavy part
   (C) sore spot
   (D) harsh sound
   (E) weakest member

8. LIMPID
   (A) deep
   (B) clear
   (C) weak
   (D) blue
   (E) lame

9. NARRATE
   (A) write
   (B) dramatize
   (C) tell
   (D) summarize
   (E) explain

10. TRIATHLON
    (A) drunken brawl
    (B) dance
    (C) sporting event
    (D) wild party
    (E) long speech

11. MINCE
    (A) chop
    (B) meat
    (C) fruit
    (D) suet
    (E) pie

12. CORRUPT
    (A) dishonest
    (B) belittle
    (C) remove
    (D) portray
    (E) destroy

13. GARBLE
    (A) build
    (B) overeat
    (C) dazzle
    (D) drool
    (E) confuse

14. EBB
    (A) flow
    (B) wax
    (C) tide
    (D) wane
    (E) ocean

Test Yourself 5

Directions: Select the word that is closest in meaning to the CAPITALIZED word and circle the letter that appears before your answer.

1. GOAD
   (A) frog
   (B) tadpole
   (C) aspiration
   (D) prod
   (E) score

2. EQUABLE
   (A) hot
   (B) fair
   (C) measured
   (D) calm

3. GUILELESS
   (A) clumsy
   (B) clever
   (C) wistful
   (D) naïve

4. EXORBITANT
   (A) essential
   (B) lacking
   (C) literal
   (D) excessive

5. DESPERADO
   (A) cowboy
   (B) hunter
   (C) settler
   — (D) criminal

6. FATIGUE
   (A) femininity
   (B) length
   — (C) weariness
   (D) perseverance

7. DISPENSARY
   (A) military store
   — (B) infirmary
   (C) confessional
   (D) bus station
   (E) courtroom

8. JOGGLE
   (A) tinkle
   — (B) shake
   (C) shove
   (D) race
   (E) surprise

9. KEEPER
   (A) miser
   — (B) caretaker
   (C) box
   (D) jeweler

10. VOUCH
    (A) pay
    (B) repeat
    (C) agree
    (D) comfort
    — (E) guarantee

11. ACCRUE
    (A) blame
    — (B) accumulate
    (C) authorize
    (D) praise

12. ROUSE
    (A) complain
    — (B) awake
    (C) dig
    (D) annoy

13. PROLETARIAT
    —(A) workers
    (B) voters
    (C) royalty
    (D) judiciary

14. LIMBER
    (A) nowhere
    (B) tied
    — (C) loose
    (D) happy

15. HIATUS
    (A) mountain
    (B) cymbals
    (C) rumpus
    —(D) gap

16. UNBLUSHING
    (A) pale
    —(B) shameless
    (C) stoic
    (D) bold

Test Yourself 6

Directions: Select the word that is closest in meaning to the CAPITALIZED word and circle the letter that appears before your answer.

1. DELECTABLE
   (A) hindrance
   (B) enjoyable
   (C) explanation
   (D) debate

2. GAINSAY
   (A) repeat
   (B) somersault
   (C) deny
   (D) enjoy

3. FOREGONE
   (A) previous
   (B) later
   (C) ended
   (D) preordained

4. OTTOMAN
   (A) footstool
   (B) rug
   (C) sofa
   (D) blanket

5. GRATUITOUS
   (A) thankful
   (B) polite
   (C) unnecessary
   (D) annoying

6. OPULENT
   (A) busy
   (B) showy
   (C) abundant
   (D) enchanted

7. INTERMENT
   (A) apprenticeship
   (B) questioning
   (C) referral
   (D) burial

8. SUNDER
   (A) separate
   (B) vary
   (C) darken
   (D) depress

9. QUADRANT
   (A) perpendicular
   (B) right angle
   (C) quarter
   (D) corner

10. PORTENTOUS
    (A) overweight
    (B) ominous
    (C) overbearing
    (D) ostentatious

11. VAULT
    (A) boast
    (B) display
    (C) jump
    (D) defy

12. PONDER
    (A) brag
    (B) consider
    (C) beat
    (D) mimic

13. ETIQUETTE
   - (A) manners
   - (B) dress code
   - (C) wedding
   - (D) aristocracy

14. GOUGE
   - (A) measure
   - (B) scoop
   - (C) stuff
   - (D) stab

15. CUPIDITY
   - (A) greed
   - (B) love
   - (C) archery
   - (D) boldness

16. APOLOGIST
   - (A) defender
   - (B) petitioner
   - (C) prisoner
   - (D) repenter

Test Yourself 7

Directions: Select the word that is closest in meaning to the CAPITALIZED word and circle the letter that appears before your answer.

1. WHEEDLE
   - (A) breathe loudly
   - (B) give birth
   - (C) coax
   - (D) insinuate
   - (E) squirm

2. UNLETTERED
   - (A) pantomimed
   - (B) illustrated
   - (C) manuscript
   - (D) numbered
   - (E) illiterate

3. SOJOURN
   - (A) trip
   - (B) convent
   - (C) pilgrimage
   - (D) worry
   - (E) visit

4. PENSIVE
   - (A) sorrowful
   - (B) hanging
   - (C) thoughtful
   - (D) poor
   - (E) stingy

5. RADIATE
   - (A) heat
   - (B) expand
   - (C) illumine
   - (D) shine
   - (E) energize

6. TRACERY
   - (A) searching
   - (B) design
   - (C) copy
   - (D) track
   - (E) recording

7. AGOG
   (A) frightened
   (B) surprised
   (C) open
   (D) angry
   (E) upset

8. HIGHWAYMAN
   (A) truck driver
   (B) state trooper
   (C) mountain dweller
   (D) hermit
   (E) robber

9. BIBLIOGRAPHY
   (A) story of one's own life
   (B) story of another's life
   (C) list of books
   (D) footnote
   (E) card catalog

10. JOLLITY
    (A) piracy
    (B) peace
    (C) dessert
    (D) merriment
    (E) teasing

11. IGNOBLE
    (A) stupid
    (B) base
    (C) drunken
    (D) regal
    (E) erect

12. MUNIFICENT
    (A) lavish
    (B) urban
    (C) splendid
    (D) enormous
    (E) important

13. ODIOUS
    (A) impossible
    (B) perfumed
    (C) bad smelling
    (D) unpleasant
    (E) strange

14. CRONE
    (A) complainer
    (B) bee
    (C) hag
    (D) singer
    (E) friend

Test Yourself 8

Directions: Select the word that is closest in meaning to the CAPITALIZED word and circle the letter that appears before your answer.

1. CITADEL
   (A) castle
   (B) barricade
   (C) mansion
   (D) fort
   (E) church

2. INCORRIGIBLE
   (A) incredible
   (B) immaterial
   (C) unruly
   (D) selective
   (E) immovable

3. FURL
   (A) wave
   (B) flap
   (C) roll up
   (D) sail
   (E) billow

4. MORTIFY
   (A) change
   (B) embed
   (C) fasten
   (D) embarrass
   (E) piece together

5. FACILE
   (A) lithe
   (B) hairy
   (C) copy
   (D) partisan
   (E) easy

6. NOSEGAY
   (A) lunchbag
   (B) gold ring
   (C) bouquet
   (D) wreath
   (E) ribbon

7. GURNEY
   (A) cow
   (B) bubble
   (C) body bag
   (D) waterspout
   (E) stretcher

8. ETCH
   (A) print
   (B) engrave
   (C) paint
   (D) capture
   (E) frame

9. HAMLET
   (A) small pig
   (B) glove
   (C) basket
   (D) village
   (E) cabin

10. INSOLVENT
    (A) solid
    (B) liquid
    (C) bankrupt
    (D) suspended
    (E) mixture

11. KNACK
    (A) junk
    (B) ability
    (C) knowledge
    (D) sausage
    (E) noise

12. AVARICE
    (A) gluttony
    (B) starvation
    (C) intelligence
    (D) greed
    (E) wealth

13. SUCCUMB
    (A) yield
    (B) irritate
    (C) echo
    (D) succeed
    (E) refuse

14. PEER
    (A) equal
    (B) juror
    (C) legislator
    (D) judge
    (E) neighbor

Test Yourself 9

Directions: Select the word that is closest in meaning to the CAPITALIZED word and circle the letter that appears before your answer.

1. CISTERN
   - (A) water tank
   - (B) sewage system
   - (C) stew pot
   - (D) drainage pipe

2. FORSWEAR
   - (A) curse
   - (B) repent
   - (C) empty
   - (D) give up

3. DOUSE
   - (A) soak
   - (B) divine
   - (C) conjure
   - (D) depress

4. LITIGANT
   - (A) reader
   - (B) cleric
   - (C) wrapper
   - (D) suer

5. ORDINANCE
   - (A) ammunition
   - (B) rule
   - (C) simplification
   - (D) suffering

6. MARQUEE
   - (A) nobleman
   - (B) billboard
   - (C) canopy
   - (D) gemstone

7. IMPASSIVE
   - (A) active
   - (B) obstructive
   - (C) unfeeling
   - (D) fair

8. NEOPHYTE
   - (A) novice
   - (B) complainer
   - (C) baby
   - (D) wood nymph

9. HENCHMAN
   - (A) bartender
   - (B) gardener
   - (C) criminal
   - (D) follower

10. JUBILEE
    - (A) meeting
    - (B) year
    - (C) anniversary
    - (D) service

11. BAILIFF
    - (A) sailor
    - (B) moneylender
    - (C) dog
    - (D) court officer

12. TREMENDOUS
    - (A) frightening
    - (B) enormous
    - (C) shaking
    - (D) noisy

13. ROOT
(A) hurry
(B) hibernate
(C) dig
(D) perch

14. RAZE
(A) bum
(B) destroy
(C) loot
(D) obscure

15. REVULSION
(A) disgust
(B) insurgency
(C) twisting
(D) correction

16. GYRATE
(A) barbecue
(B) twist
(C) wobble
(D) spin

Test Yourself 10

Directions: Select the word that is closest in meaning to the CAPITALIZED word and circle the letter that appears before your answer.

1. WREAK
(A) smash
(B) rage
(C) poke
(D) emanate
(E) inflict

2. PHOBIA
(A) attraction
(B) love
(C) fear
(D) hatred
(E) illness

3. STATIC
(A) lively
(B) electrical
(C) unpleasant
(D) shocking
(E) inactive

4. AMULET
(A) omen
(B) necklace
(C) charm
(D) armband
(E) flask

5. HAZY
(A) polluted
(B) indistinct
(C) brown
(D) annoyed
(E) insane

6. KILN
(A) skirt
(B) plaid
(C) oven
(D) relative
(E) weight

7. MIGRATE
(A) go south
(B) sleep
(C) headache
(D) travel
(E) return

8. OFFICIOUS
(A) insulting
(B) formal
(C) meddling
(D) distant
(E) ceremonial

9. NIB
   (A) irritation
   (B) bite
   (C) bump
   (D) chill
   (E) point

10. GAINFUL
    (A) profitable
    (B) overflowing
    (C) enthusiastic
    (D) injurious
    (E) busy

11. FILAMENT
    (A) steak
    (B) thread
    (C) flavoring
    (D) decoration
    (E) failure

12. DELL
    (A) farm
    (B) barnyard
    (C) valley
    (D) bell
    (E) ring

13. COBBLE
    (A) limp
    (B) weave
    (C) eat greedily
    (D) repair shoes
    (E) shoe horses

14. UNNUMBERED
    (A) unclassified
    (B) countless
    (C) few
    (D) lettered
    (E) listed

15. IMPISH
    (A) disrespectful
    (B) mischievous
    (C) rash
    (D) unsaid
    (E) relentless

16. BICEPS
    (A) muscle
    (B) tweezers
    (C) dinosaur
    (D) rowboat
    (E) crossroads

17. THERAPEUTIC
    (A) manipulative
    (B) active
    (C) athletic
    (D) rigorous
    (E) curative

18. STAID
    (A) leftover
    (B) guest
    (C) sedate
    (D) dirty
    (E) immobile

19. PURIST
    (A) perfectionist
    (B) sanitarian
    (C) laundress
    (D) exorcist
    (E) steward

20. FETISH
    (A) charm
    (B) foot
    (C) dust ball
    (D) gremlin
    (E) hairdo

ANSWER KEY

Test Yourself 1

1. A	5. C	9. B	13. A	17. C
2. C	6. A	10. A	14. D	18. C
3. B	7. D	11. D	15. C	19. D
4. A	8. C	12. D	16. D	20. D

Test Yourself 2

1. E	4. B	7. E	10. A	13. C
2. D	5. D	8. E	11. C	14. B
3. D	6. B	9. C	12. A	

Test Yourself 3

1. B	5. A	8. B	11. C	14. A
2. D	6. A	9. D	12. B	15. D
3. A	7. C	10. B	13. C	16. C
4. C				

Test Yourself 4

1. C	4. C	7. B	10. C	13. E
2. E	5. B	8. B	11. A	14. D
3. E	6. A	9. C	12. A	

Test Yourself 5

1. D	5. D	8. B	11. B	14. C
2. B	6. C	9. B	12. B	15. D
3. D	7. B	10. E	13. A	16. B
4. D				

Test Yourself 6

1. B	5. C	8. A	11. C	14. B
2. C	6. C	9. C	12. B	15. A
3. D	7. D	10. B	13. A	16. A
4. A				

Test Yourself 7

1. C	4. C	7. B	10. D	13. D
2. E	5. D	8. E	11. B	14. C
3. E	6. B	9. C	12. A	

Test Yourself 8

1. D	4. D	7. E	10. C	13. A
2. C	5. E	8. B	11. B	14. A
3. C	6. C	9. D	12. D	

Test Yourself 9

1. A	5. B	8. A	11. D	14. B
2. D	6. C	9. D	12. B	15. A
3. A	7. C	10. C	13. C	16. D
4. D				

Test Yourself 10

1. E	5. B	9. E	13. D	17. E
2. C	6. C	10. A	14. B	18. C
3. E	7. D	11. B	15. B	19. A
4. C	8. C	12. C	16. A	20. A

EXERCISES: MEANING IN CONTEXT

Directions: Circle your answer to each question.

1. The change in procedure *stimulated* the men. *Stimulated* means
   (A) rewarded.
   (B) gave an incentive to.
   (C) antagonized.
   (D) lowered the efficiency of.

2. Courage is difficult to *instill* in a person. *Instill* means
   (A) measure exactly.
   (B) predict accurately.
   (C) impart gradually.
   (D) restrain effectively.

3. His report contained many *irrelevant* statements. *Irrelevant* means
   (A) unproven.
   (B) hard to understand.
   (C) not pertinent.
   (D) insincere.

4. He had a *prior* appointment with the manager. *Prior* means
   (A) private.
   (B) definite.
   (C) later.
   (D) previous.

5. The supply of pamphlets has been *depleted*. *Depleted* means
   (A) exhausted.
   (B) included.
   (C) delivered.
   (D) rejected.

6. Mr. Dorman asked for a *candid* opinion. *Candid* means
   (A) biased.
   (B) written.
   (C) frank.
   (D) confidential.

7. The patient had a serious *ailment*. *Ailment* means
   (A) illness.
   (B) food allergy.
   (C) operation.
   (D) problem.

8. His *nonchalance* was disturbing to the courtroom observers. *Nonchalance* means
   (A) interest.
   (B) poverty.
   (C) care.
   (D) indifference.

9. Our argument was based on *fundamental* economic principles. *Fundamental* means
   (A) adequate.
   (B) essential.
   (C) basic.
   (D) truthful.

10. He wishes to *terminate* the conversation. *Terminate* means
    (A) end.
    (B) ignore.
    (C) postpone.
    (D) continue.

11. Miss Fulton showed her *reluctance* to serve as a relief operator. *Reluctance* means
    (A) eagerness.
    (B) ability.
    (C) unreliability.
    (D) unwillingness.

12. His secretary was a *diligent* worker. *Diligent* means
    (A) incompetent.
    (B) careless.
    (C) cheerful.
    (D) industrious.

13. There is considerable *diversity* in the submitted suggestions. *Diversity* means
    (A) similarity.
    (B) triviality.
    (C) value.
    (D) variety.

14. The vehicle was left *intact* after the accident. *Intact* means
    (A) undamaged.
    (B) unattended.
    (C) a total loss.
    (D) repaired.

15. He *resolved* to act at once. *Resolved* means
    (A) offered.
    (B) refused.
    (C) hesitated.
    (D) determined.

16. The departmental rules were *rigorously* enforced. *Rigorously* means
    (A) usually.
    (B) never.
    (C) strictly.
    (D) leniently.

17. Relations between England and the United States are *amicable*. *Amicable* means
    (A) friendly.
    (B) tender.
    (C) accessible.
    (D) inimical.

18. I could plainly hear the *clamor* of the crowd. *Clamor* means
    (A) murmur.
    (B) noise.
    (C) questions.
    (D) singing.

19. He *declined* our offers to help him. *Declined* means
    (A) suspected.
    (B) misunderstood.
    (C) consented to accept.
    (D) refused.

20. It was reported that *noxious* fumes were escaping from the tanks. *Noxious* means
    (A) concentrated.
    (B) harmful.
    (C) gaseous.
    (D) heavy.

21. They are discussing *trivial* matters. *Trivial* means
    (A) of a personal nature.
    (B) very significant.
    (C) interesting and educational.
    (D) of little importance.

22. This equipment is *obsolete*. *Obsolete* means
    (A) complicated.
    (B) out of date.
    (C) highly suitable.
    (D) reliable.

23. The operator was commended for her *dexterity*. *Dexterity* means
    (A) skill.
    (B) punctuality.
    (C) courtesy.
    (D) cooperation.

exercises

24. The witness was *recalcitrant. Recalcitrant* means
(A) cooperative.
(B) highly excited.
(C) accustomed to hard work.
(D) stubbornly resistant.

25. He was asked to *placate* the visitor. *Placate* means
(A) escort.
(B) appease.
(C) interview.
(D) detain.

26. He was given considerable *latitude* in designing the program. *Latitude* means
(A) advice and encouragement.
(B) assistance.
(C) cause for annoyance.
(D) freedom from restriction.

27. This is the most *expedient* method for achieving the desired results. *Expedient* means
(A) inconvenient.
(B) expensive.
(C) efficient.
(D) time-consuming.

28. The men refused to give up their *prerogatives* without a struggle. *Prerogatives* means
(A) ideals.
(B) privileges.
(C) demands.
(D) weapons.

ANSWER KEY AND EXPLANATIONS

1. B	7. A	13. D	19. D	24. D
2. C	8. D	14. A	20. B	25. B
3. C	9. C	15. D	21. D	26. D
4. D	10. A	16. C	22. B	27. C
5. A	11. D	17. A	23. A	28. B
6. C	12. D	18. B		

1. **The correct answer is (B).** *Stimulate* comes from the word "stimulus." A stimulus is an incentive.

2. **The correct answer is (C).** "Impart gradually" is a synonym for the word *instill*.

3. **The correct answer is (C).** *Relevant* means "pertinent." The prefix *ir-* means "not." Therefore, the word *irrelevant* means "not pertinent."

4. **The correct answer is (D).** A *prior* appointment is one that was made previously.

5. **The correct answer is (A).** "Used up," "consumed," and "exhausted" are all synonyms for the word *depleted*.

6. **The correct answer is (C).** A candid opinion is expressed freely and honestly. "Frank" is a synonym for candid.

7. **The correct answer is (A).** "Sickness," "disease," and "illness" are all synonyms for the word *ailment*.

8. **The correct answer is (D).** "Apathy," "disinterest," and "indifference" are all synonyms for the word *nonchalance*.

9. **The correct answer is (C).** "Essential" and "basic" are both synonyms for the word *fundamental*. "Basic" is the best choice in this sentence.

10. **The correct answer is (A).** The stem *term* means "end." *Terminate* is a word that means to "bring to an end."

11. **The correct answer is (D).** *Reluctance* is a noun meaning "hesitation" or "unwillingness."

12. **The correct answer is (D).** A *diligent* worker is one who works very hard. "Industrious" is a synonym for *diligent*.

13. **The correct answer is (D).** The word *diversity* in this context means "differences that cover a broad range of possibilities."

14. **The correct answer is (A).** Try substituting each of the four choices in the sentence. *Intact*, which means "together" or "in one piece," is the best choice.

15. **The correct answer is (D).** In this context, the word *resolve* means to "make up one's mind firmly." "Determined" is a synonym of resolved.

16. **The correct answer is (C).** *Rigorously* or strictly enforced rules are kept without any exceptions.

17. **The correct answer is (A).** The stem *ami* means "friend." "Friendly" is a synonym of *amicable*.

18. **The correct answer is (B).** The words "plainly" and "crowd" are context clue words in this sentence. A *clamor* is an "uproar," a "great noise."

19. **The correct answer is (D).** To *decline* or refuse an offer is to "turn it down or away." The prefix *de-* means "down."

20. **The correct answer is (B).** *Noxious* means "injurious" and "harmful to health."

21. **The correct answer is (D).** *Trivial* means "insignificant."

22. **The correct answer is (B).** *Obsolete*, literally "grown out of use," means "out of date."

23. **The correct answer is (A).** *Dexterity* is "skill with the hands." The root is *dexter*, which refers to the right hand.

24. **The correct answer is (D).** *Recalcitrant*, literally "kicking back," means "disobedient" and "hard to handle."

25. **The correct answer is (B).** To *placate* is to "appease" or to "soothe."

26. **The correct answer is (D).** *Latitude*, literally "breadth," can then be interpreted as "freedom from narrowness."

27. **The correct answer is (C).** *Expedient*, related to *expedite*, refers to speed, efficiency, and practicality.

28. **The correct answer is (B).** *Prerogatives* are rights and privileges related to rank or position. The prefix *pre-* gives a clue.

EXERCISES: DEFINITIONS

Directions: Circle your answer to each question.

1. The word *cognizant* means
   (A) rare.
   (B) aware.
   (C) reluctant.
   (D) haphazard.

2. The word *denote* means
   (A) encumber.
   (B) furnish.
   (C) evade.
   (D) indicate.

3. To say that the information obtained was *meager* means it was
   (A) well received.
   (B) long overdue.
   (C) valuable.
   (D) scanty.

4. To *impair* means to
   (A) weaken.
   (B) improve.
   (C) conceal.
   (D) expose.

5. To say that a man's knowledge of the law is *extensive* means it is
   (A) factual.
   (B) broad.
   (C) sufficient.
   (D) hypothetical.

6. A regulation that is *rigid* is
   (A) precise.
   (B) clearly expressed.
   (C) strict.
   (D) rarely applied.

7. A *commendable* action is one that is
   (A) premeditated.
   (B) broad.
   (C) praiseworthy.
   (D) hypothetical.

8. A pamphlet that is *replete* with charts and graphs
   (A) is full of charts and graphs.
   (B) substitutes illustrations for information.
   (C) deals with the construction of charts and graphs.
   (D) is in need of charts and graphs.

9. To say that a document is *authentic* means it is
   (A) fictitious.
   (B) priceless.
   (C) well written.
   (D) genuine.

10. An *exacting* task is one that is
    (A) brief.
    (B) severe in its demands.
    (C) arithmetical in nature.
    (D) responsible.

11. A person who is *slovenly* is
    (A) neat and well dressed.
    (B) eager and ambitious.
    (C) lazy and slipshod.
    (D) aggressive and resentful.

12. A *vivacious* person is one who is
    (A) kind.
    (B) lively.
    (C) talkative.
    (D) well dressed.

13. *Peremptory* commands are those that are
    (A) unexpected.
    (B) military.
    (C) incomplete.
    (D) dictatorial.

14. To say that the order was *rescinded* means it was
    (A) revised.
    (B) misinterpreted.
    (C) canceled.
    (D) summarized.

15. To *extol* is to
    (A) summon.
    (B) praise.
    (C) reject.
    (D) withdraw.

16. The word *appraise* means
    (A) consult.
    (B) manage.
    (C) judge.
    (D) attribute.

17. A *diplomatic* person is
    (A) domineering.
    (B) verbose.
    (C) tactful.
    (D) deceitful.

18. A *potent* incentive is one that is
    (A) impossible.
    (B) not practical.
    (C) highly effective.
    (D) a possibility.

19. The word *monomial* refers to
    (A) one term.
    (C) soliloquy.
    (B) eyeglass.
    (D) one tone.

20. *Antitoxin* is used in cases of
    (A) corruption.
    (B) sanitary inspections.
    (C) disease.
    (D) construction.

21. A *fulcrum* is part of a
    (A) typewriter.
    (B) lever.
    (C) radio.
    (D) lamp.

22. A person who is *meticulous* in his or her work is
    (A) alert to new techniques.
    (B) likely to be erratic.
    (C) excessively careful of small details.
    (D) slovenly and inaccurate.

23. A *prolific* writer is one who is
    (A) productive.
    (B) talented.
    (C) popular.
    (D) forward looking.

24. To *oscillate* means to
    (A) lubricate.
    (B) decide.
    (C) waver.
    (D) investigate.

25. A *homogeneous* group of persons is
    (A) similar.
    (B) discontented.
    (C) teamwork.
    (D) different.

26. A *vindictive* person is one who is
    (A) prejudiced.
    (B) petty.
    (C) unpopular.
    (D) vengeful.

27. A *futile* effort is one that is
    (A) strong.
    (B) useless.
    (C) clumsy.
    (D) sincere.

28. To say that the speaker *amplified* his remarks means the remarks were
    (A) shouted.
    (B) analyzed.
    (C) expanded.
    (D) summarized.

29. An *innocuous* statement is one that is
    (A) forceful.
    (B) offensive.
    (C) harmless.
    (D) brief.

30. The word *cogent* means
    (A) confused.
    (B) opposite.
    (C) convincing.
    (D) unintentional.

exercises

ANSWER KEY AND EXPLANATIONS

1. B	7. C	13. D	19. A	25. A
2. D	8. A	14. C	20. C	26. D
3. D	9. D	15. B	21. B	27. B
4. A	10. B	16. C	22. C	28. C
5. B	11. C	17. C	23. A	29. C
6. C	12. B	18. C	24. C	30. C

1. **The correct answer is (B).** The stem *cogn* means "knowledge of."

2. **The correct answer is (D).** The prefix *de-* means "down." The word *denote* means to "note down."

3. **The correct answer is (D).** *Meager* means "scanty" or "very little."

4. **The correct answer is (A).** *Impair* means to damage or weaken, as in the sentence "The infection had *impaired* his hearing."

5. **The correct answer is (B).** *Extensive* means "wide-ranging" or "broad."

6. **The correct answer is (C).** *Rigid* is synonymous with "stiff" and "inflexible." A *rigid* regulation is one that has no exceptions.

7. **The correct answer is (C).** To *commend* is to praise, as in the sentence "The principal *commended* those students who had made the honor roll."

8. **The correct answer is (A).** "Filled," "stuffed," and "packed" are synonyms for the word *replete*.

9. **The correct answer is (D).** *Authentic*, literally "itself," means "reliable" or "legitimate."

10. **The correct answer is (B).** An *exacting* task must be done according to strict regulations and is therefore "strict in its demands."

11. **The correct answer is (C).** Synonyms include "sloppy" and "untidy," which are similar in meaning to the correct answer.

12. **The correct answer is (B).** *Vivacious* means "full of life."

13. **The correct answer is (D).** *Peremptory* commands tend to be absolute, which is similar to "dictatorial."

14. **The correct answer is (C).** The prefix *re-* means "back." A *rescinded* order is one that has been taken back.

15. **The correct answer is (B).** Even beyond "praise," to *extol* is to "praise highly."

16. **The correct answer is (C).** To *appraise*, literally "to set a price," means "to judge value."

17. **The correct answer is (C).** A *diplomat* is a person who is skillful in dealing with people.

18. **The correct answer is (C).** Something that is *potent* is powerful, or highly effective.

19. **The correct answer is (A).** The word *monomial* is used in algebra to indicate a single term.

20. **The correct answer is (C).** *Toxin* means "poison." The prefix *anti-* means "against." An *antitoxin* is a substance used against a poison or disease in the body.

21. **The correct answer is (B).** A *fulcrum* is the support for a lever when it is in operation.

22. **The correct answer is (C).** The *meticulous* person is extremely careful.

23. **The correct answer is (A).** *Prolific* means productive, as in the sentence "A *prolific* tree bears much fruit."

24. **The correct answer is (C).** *Oscillate* literally means "swing back and forth."

25. **The correct answer is (A).** The prefix *homo-* means "same."

26. **The correct answer is (D).** A *vindictive* or vengeful person bears a grudge or seeks revenge.

27. **The correct answer is (B).** A *futile* effort is bound to fail, or useless.

28. **The correct answer is (C).** Remarks might be *amplified*, or expanded, through the addition of more detail.

29. **The correct answer is (C).** *Innocuous* also means "noncontroversial" or "dull."

30. **The correct answer is (C).** *Cogent* means "pulled together" or "convincing."

answers exercises

EXERCISES: SYNONYMS

Directions: Circle your answer to each question.

1. ANTICIPATE
   (A) foresee
   (B) annul
   (C) approve
   (D) conceal

2. RELUCTANT
   (A) relaxed
   (B) drastic
   (C) constant
   (D) hesitant

3. FRUGAL
   (A) friendly
   (B) hostile
   (C) thoughtful
   (D) economical

4. IMPERATIVE
   (A) impending
   (B) impossible
   (C) compulsory
   (D) flawless

5. ACCESS
   (A) too much
   (B) admittance
   (C) extra
   (D) arrival

6. SUBSEQUENT
   (A) preceding
   (B) early
   (C) following
   (D) winning

7. HERITAGE
   (A) will
   (B) believer
   (C) legend
   (D) inheritance

8. CULTURED
   (A) malformed
   (B) decomposed
   (C) exiled
   (D) cultivated

9. ATONE
   (A) repent
   (B) rebel
   (C) sound
   (D) impotent

10. PREDATORY
    (A) introductory
    (B) intellectual
    (C) preaching
    (D) carnivorous

11. MAIL
    (A) armor
    (B) seaside
    (C) rapid travel
    (D) wool

12. FLORID
    (A) seedy
    (B) ruddy
    (C) hot
    (D) overflowing

13. FEASIBLE
    (A) simple
    (B) practical
    (C) visible
    (D) lenient

14. SUPPLANT
    (A) approve
    (B) displace
    (C) widespread
    (D) appease

15. PREVALENT
    (A) current
    (B) permanent
    (C) widespread
    (D) temporary

16. CONTEND
    (A) assert
    (B) agree
    (C) temper
    (D) appease

17. FLAGRANT
    (A) glaring
    (B) hopeless
    (C) engrossing
    (D) motioning

18. ENTHRALL
    (A) throw in
    (B) captivate
    (C) support
    (D) deceive

19. DESECRATE
    (A) improve upon
    (B) occupy
    (C) profane
    (D) hide

20. OSTRACIZE
    (A) delight
    (B) exclude
    (C) include
    (D) hide

21. EXORBITANT
    (A) priceless
    (B) worthless
    (C) extensive
    (D) excessive

22. OBLITERATE
    (A) annihilate
    (B) review
    (C) demonstrate
    (D) detect

23. AUSTERITY
    (A) priority
    (B) anxiety
    (C) self-discipline
    (D) solitude

24. CORROBORATION
    (A) expenditure
    (B) compilation
    (C) confirmation
    (D) reduction

25. SALUTARY
    (A) popular
    (B) beneficial
    (C) urgent
    (D) forceful

26. ACQUIESCE
    (A) endeavor
    (B) discharge
    (C) agree
    (D) inquire

27. DIFFIDENCE
- **(A)** shyness
- **(B)** distinction
- **(C)** interval
- **(D)** discordance

28. REPRISAL
- **(A)** retaliation
- **(B)** advantage
- **(C)** warning
- **(D)** denial

29. CAPITULATE
- **(A)** repeat
- **(B)** surrender
- **(C)** finance
- **(D)** retreat

30. REPUTABLE
- **(A)** star
- **(B)** capable
- **(C)** significant
- **(D)** honest

ANSWER KEY AND EXPLANATIONS

1. A	7. D	13. B	19. C	25. B
2. D	8. D	14. B	20. B	26. C
3. D	9. A	15. C	21. D	27. A
4. C	10. D	16. A	22. A	28. A
5. B	11. A	17. A	23. C	29. B
6. C	12. B	18. B	24. C	30. D

1. **The correct answer is (A).** *Anticipate* your opponent's arguments and prepare your responses.

2. **The correct answer is (D).** The frightened witness was a *reluctant* trial participant.

3. **The correct answer is (D).** She has saved a great deal of money because she lives *frugally*.

4. **The correct answer is (C).** It is *imperative* that you see a doctor before the rash spreads.

5. **The correct answer is (B).** Jim is the only person who has *access* to the safe.

6. **The correct answer is (C).** In *subsequent* meetings we will be discussing the progress of this project.

7. **The correct answer is (D).** Americans were left a wonderful *heritage* by their ancestors.

8. **The correct answer is (D).** *Cultured* pearls are less expensive than natural ones.

9. **The correct answer is (A).** The prisoner wanted to *atone* for his past crimes.

10. **The correct answer is (D).** Lions are *predatory* animals.

11. **The correct answer is (A).** Swords could not pierce a knight's suit of *mail*.

12. **The correct answer is (B).** *Florid* means ruddy, or reddish, as in "The salesman had a *florid* complexion."

13. **The correct answer is (B).** The engineers thought the bridge would be economically *feasible*.

14. **The correct answer is (B).** In industry today, new ideas are constantly being *supplanted* by even newer ones.

15. **The correct answer is (C).** A belief in the existence of witches was *prevalent* during the seventeenth century.

16. **The correct answer is (A).** The defense attorney *contends* that his client was out of town when the crime was committed.

17. **The correct answer is (A).** The action showed her *flagrant* disregard for school rules.

18. **The correct answer is (B).** The storyteller *enthralled* his young audience.

19. **The correct answer is (C).** Vandals *desecrated* the flag by burning it.

20. **The correct answer is (B).** Children often *ostracize* classmates who seem different in any way.

21. **The correct answer is (D).** Some tenants are charged *exorbitant* rents by greedy landlords.

22. **The correct answer is (A).** Civilization could be *obliterated* by an atomic war.

23. **The correct answer is (C).** *Austerity* means self-control, as in "Crude oil shortages make *austerity* a necessity."

24. **The correct answer is (C).** *Corroboration* of the defendant's alibi will be difficult to find.

25. **The correct answer is (B).** A decrease in contagious diseases shows the *salutary* effects of preventive medicine.

26. **The correct answer is (C).** The police were forced to *acquiesce* to the kidnapper's demands.

27. **The correct answer is (A).** Janet's *diffidence* kept her from participating in class discussions.

28. **The correct answer is (A).** *Reprisals* were organized against the terrorists.

29. **The correct answer is (B).** Mr. Jones *capitulated* to his students' demands.

30. **The correct answer is (D).** I knew the history book was a *reputable* source because its author is renowned for accurately reporting events.

SUMMING IT UP

- Synonyms are words with similar meanings, and synonym questions ask you to choose a word with a meaning similar to that of a given word or to complete a sentence.

- Never choose an answer simply because it is the one word you don't recognize. The correct answer may be the easiest and most obvious word.

- Read the question carefully and try using the word in a sentence of your own.

Verbal Analogies (SSAT Only)

chapter 7

OVERVIEW

- **What makes a verbal analogy?**
- **What do verbal analogy questions look like?**
- **How do you solve verbal analogies?**
- **What do smart test-takers know?**
- **Summing it up**

WHAT MAKES A VERBAL ANALOGY?

Verbal analogies are all about relationships. They test your ability to see a relationship between two words and to recognize a similar relationship between two other words. Verbal analogy tests measure not only your understanding of the words themselves but also your mental flexibility and ability to manipulate relationships. The key to analogy success is being able to express the relationship between the words in a pair—not what the words mean, but how they are related.

WHAT DO VERBAL ANALOGY QUESTIONS LOOK LIKE?

An analogy can be written in several different ways. It may be written as a sentence, using only words, or symbols may be substituted for the connecting words. SSAT analogy questions use *only* words.

Q Winter is to summer as cold is to

(A) wet

(B) future

(C) hot

(D) freezing

A **The correct answer is (C).** WINTER and SUMMER are opposites, or antonyms. The antonym for COLD is HOT.

Some analogies supply three of the four necessary words. You must find the relationship between the first two words and then choose a word that is related to the third word in the same way.

> **Q** Spelling is to punctuation as biology is to
>
> **(A)** science
> **(B)** animals
> **(C)** dissection
> **(D)** chemistry
>
> **A** **The correct answer is (D).** SPELLING and PUNCTUATION are two subjects studied in English. BIOLOGY and CHEMISTRY are two subjects studied in the field of science.

Other analogies begin with a pair of words. You must first decide how those words are related. Then, from a list of four or five pairs, you must choose the pair that illustrates the same relationship.

> **Q** Spelling is to punctuation as
>
> **(A)** pajamas is to fatigue
> **(B)** powder is to shaving
> **(C)** bandage is to cut
> **(D)** biology is to chemistry

SSAT verbal analogy questions appear in different formats. Some supply three words, requiring you to choose a fourth that is related to the third in the same way that the first two words are related. Other SSAT verbal analogy questions supply a pair of words and require you to choose another pair with the same relationship to one another.

HOW DO YOU SOLVE VERBAL ANALOGIES?

To solve verbal analogies, follow these five steps:

ANALOGIES: GETTING IT RIGHT

1 Figure out how the first two words are related.

2 Make up a sentence that expresses that relationship.

3 Try out your sentence on each answer choice and eliminate the ones that don't work.

4 If you're left with more than one answer—or no answer at all—go back and make your sentence fit better.

5 Choose the best answer. If none of the choices fit exactly, choose the one that works best.

TIP

What if none of the answers are exactly right? Remember: The directions tell you to choose the best answer. The correct answer won't necessarily be a perfect fit, but it will work better than the other choices.

WHAT DO SMART TEST-TAKERS KNOW?

A Sentence Can Make the Connection

Q Scribble is to write as

(A) inform is to supply

(B) mutter is to listen

(C) nuzzle is to feel

(D) ramble is to play

(E) stagger is to walk

A Summarize each analogy relationship with a sentence. In this case, *scribbling is a bad kind of writing*. Use the same sentence to test connections between the words in the answer choices. When you find one that works, you've found your answer.

(A) *Informing* is a bad kind of *supplying*. (No.)

(B) *Muttering* is a bad kind of *listening*. (No.)

(C) *Nuzzling* is a bad kind of *feeling*. (No.)

(D) *Rambling* is a bad kind of *playing*. (No.)

(E) *Staggering* is a bad kind of *walking*. (Yes!)

The More Precise Your Sentence, the Better

You cannot expect to solve every analogy by simply plugging in a list of common analogy types. Remember that the analogies get more difficult as you work your way through each group. Use the common categories as a starting point, but be prepared to refine the relationship by making your sentence more precise. Consider this example:

Q Grain is to silo as

(A) pilot is to plane

(B) judge is to courtroom

(C) water is to reservoir

(D) clock is to time

(E) automobile is to highway

If you apply the "place where" idea without thinking, here is what happens:

A silo is a place where you would find grain.

(A) A *plane* is a place where you would find a *pilot*.

(B) A *courtroom* is a place where you would find a *judge*.

(C) A *reservoir* is a place where you would find *water*.

(D) A *clock* is a place where you would find *time*.

(E) A *highway* is a place where you would find *automobiles*.

You can eliminate choice (D), but that still leaves you with four possible answers. Now is the time to go back and make your original sentence fit better. How can you express the relationship between silo and grain more precisely?

A silo is a place where grain is stored.

(A) A *plane* is a place where a *pilot* is stored.

(B) A *courtroom* is a place where a *judge* is stored.

(C) A *reservoir* is a place where *water* is stored.

(E) A *highway* is a place where *automobiles* are stored.

A The correct answer is (C).

Know the Most Common Verbal Analogy Categories

The same relationships appear over and over again in verbal analogy questions. Knowing what the categories are and looking for them as you tackle each problem will make your job easier. Some of the most commonly used with SSAT analogy questions are:

Synonym Relationships

Synonyms are words that have similar meanings.

> **Q** Enormous is to huge as muddy is to
>
> **(A)** unclear
> **(B)** clean
> **(C)** rocky
> **(D)** roguish
>
> **A** **The correct answer is (A).** Something that is described as MUDDY is clouded, or UNCLEAR.

Antonym Relationships

Antonyms are words that have opposite meanings.

> **Q** Good is to evil as
>
> **(A)** suave is to blunt
> **(B)** north is to climate
> **(C)** angel is to devil
> **(D)** sorrow is to happiness
>
> **A** **The correct answer is (C).** ANGEL is the opposite of DEVIL.

NOTE: The words that have a positive association, GOOD and ANGEL, are the first words in each pair. The words with a negative association, EVIL and DEVIL, are the second words in each pair. "Sorrow is to happiness" also represents the antonym relationship, but it is an incorrect answer because the terms are in reversed order. A properly completed analogy consists of terms with the same relationship occurring in the same order.

Part-Whole Relationships

In this type of analogy, one of the words in each pair represents a single part of a whole person, place, thing, or idea.

> **Q** Snake is to reptile as
>
> **(A)** patch is to thread
> **(B)** hand is to clock
> **(C)** hand is to finger
> **(D)** struggle is to fight
>
> **A** **The correct answer is (B).** A SNAKE is part of the REPTILE family. A HAND is part of a CLOCK. Choice (C) also shows a similar relationship, but the words are given in the wrong order.

Noun-Verb Relationships

In this type of analogy, one of the words in a pair names a person, place, thing, or idea. The other word represents an action that can be associated with that word.

> **Q** Steak is to broil as
>
> **(A)** food is to sell
> **(B)** wine is to pour
> **(C)** bread is to bake
> **(D)** sugar is to spill
>
> **A** **The correct answer is (C).** One way to cook a STEAK is to BROIL it; similarly, we BAKE BREAD in order to cook it. Choices (B) and (D) both show noun-verb relationships, with the nouns and verbs in the correct sequence, but neither uses a verb that relates to cooking. Therefore, the best answer would be choice (C) because broiling and baking are both forms of cooking food.

Cause-and-Effect Relationships

Two types of cause-and-effect relationships may be used in analogies. In the first type, one word in the pair will sometimes result in the second word.

> **Q** Race is to fatigue as fast is to
>
> **(A)** track
> **(B)** hunger
> **(C)** run
> **(D)** obesity
>
> **A** **The correct answer is (B).** Running a RACE may cause the runner FATIGUE. FASTING may cause HUNGER.

In the second type of cause-and-effect analogy, one word in a pair may produce the other.

> **Q** Cow is to milk as bee is to
>
> **(A)** honey
> **(B)** drone
> **(C)** nest
> **(D)** wasp
>
> **A** **The correct answer is (A).** A COW produces MILK; a BEE produces HONEY.

Purpose Relationships

In this type of analogy, one of the words in each pair is used in a task involving the other word in the pair.

> **Q** Glove is to ball as
>
> **(A)** hook is to fish
> **(B)** winter is to weather
> **(C)** game is to pennant
> **(D)** stadium is to seats
>
> **A** **The correct answer is (A).** A GLOVE is used in baseball to catch a BALL. When fishing, a HOOK is used to catch a FISH.

Association Relationships

In this type of analogy, one word in a pair is commonly thought of in connection with the second word.

> **Q** Young is to lamb as
>
> **(A)** ram is to ewe
> **(B)** old is to mutton
> **(C)** lamb is to chop
> **(D)** wool is to shear
>
> **A** **The correct answer is (B).** The meat of YOUNG sheep is called LAMB. The meat of OLD sheep is called MUTTON.

ALERT!
Don't confuse the order of the words. The relationship of the words in the answer must be in the same order as the relationship of the words in the first pair.

Other Analogy Categories

Other analogy categories with which you should also become familiar are:

"Type of" Analogies

SWORD is to WEAPON	A sword is a type of weapon.
GRIMACE is to EXPRESSION	A grimace is a type of expression.
OAK is to TREE	An oak is a type of tree.
WATERCOLOR is to PAINTING	A watercolor is a type of painting.

"Part of the definition of" Analogies

GENEROSITY is to PHILANTHROPIST	Generosity is part of the definition of a philanthropist.
BRAVERY is to HERO	Bravery is part of the definition of a hero.
FALSE is to LIE	It is part of the definition of a lie that it is false.
INVENTION is to ORIGINAL	It is part of the definition of an invention that it is original.
FACULTY is to TEACH	It is part of the definition of a faculty that it is supposed to teach.

"Lack of something is part of the definition" Analogies

TRAITOR is to LOYALTY	Lack of loyalty is part of the definition of a traitor.
NEGLIGENT is to CARE	It is part of the definition of being negligent that someone lacks care.
ARID is to MOISTURE	Lack of moisture is part of the definition of an arid region.
IGNORANCE is to KNOWLEDGE	Lack of knowledge is part of the definition of ignorance.
POVERTY is to FUNDS	Part of the definition of poverty is a lack of funds.

"Part to whole" Analogies

MOVEMENT is to SONATA	A movement is a part of a sonata.
CHAPTER is to BOOK	A chapter is a part of a book.
ACTOR is to TROUPE	An actor is a part of a troupe.
LION is to PRIDE	A lion is part of a pride.
FINISH is to RACE	The finish is part of a race.

"A place for" Analogies

WITNESS is to COURTROOM	A courtroom is the place for a witness.
ACTOR is to STAGE	A stage is the place for an actor.
GRAIN is to SILO	A silo is a place for storing grain.
PILOT is to AIRPLANE	An airplane is a place where you would find a pilot.
ORE is to MINE	A mine is the place where you would find ore.

"Degree" Analogies

BREEZE is to GALE	A gale is more powerful than a breeze.
TRICKLE is to GUSH	To gush is more forceful than to trickle.
ANNOY is to ENRAGE	To enrage is stronger than to annoy.
MOUNTAIN is to HILL	A mountain is a very large hill.
WASH is to SCRUB	To scrub is stronger than to wash.

Words with Similar Meanings Can Fool You

In analogy questions, what counts is the relationship between the first two words. The words in the correct answer choice must have a similar relationship. There is no need for one or both to be related in meaning to the words. Consider this analogy:

Q Tangled is to knot as

   (A) snarled is to rope

   (B) crumpled is to wrinkle

   (C) mussed is to hair

   (D) empty is to cup

   (E) canned is to preserves

A **The correct answer is (B).** This is a "part of the definition of" analogy. Part of the definition of a *knot* is that it is something *tangled*. Likewise, part of the definition of a *wrinkle* is that it is something *crumpled*. Don't be misled by choice (A). Although *snarled* is similar in meaning to *tangled*, a rope does not have to be snarled.

TIP

Make the sentence connection. Turn the analogy pairs into sentences to help you see the connection. Then fit the answer pairs into the same sentence until you find the one that works best.

ALERT!

Don't be fooled by similar words. In analogy questions, you're looking for similar relationships, not similar words.

Some Analogies Work Better When You Turn Them Around

Sometimes the first two words fall easily into a sentence that expresses their relationship—and sometimes they don't. If you're having trouble making up a sentence that relates the two words, be prepared to shift gears. Try reversing the order of the original word pair. Let's see how this technique works on the following analogy:

Q Ice is to glacier as

    (A) train is to trestle

    (B) sand is to dune

    (C) path is to forest

    (D) feather is to bird

    (E) ocean is to ship

If you can't come up with a sentence relating ICE to GLACIER, try relating GLACIER to ICE:

A *glacier* is made up of *ice*.

Here's the only catch: If you reverse the order of the words, you must also reverse the order of the words in each answer choice. So when you apply your sentence to the answer choices, this is how you'll have to do it:

(A) A *trestle* is made up of a *train*.

(B) A *dune* is made up of *sand*.

(C) A *forest* is made up of a *path*.

(D) A *bird* is made up of a *feather*.

(E) A *ship* is made up of an *ocean*.

A **The correct answer is (B).** Only choice (B) exhibits the same relationship as the original pair.

TEST YOURSELF QUIZZES

Use the following quizzes to help you determine what your weaknesses might be. Answers can be found on pages 159–161.

Test Yourself 1

Directions: Look at the first two words and decide how they are related to each other. Then decide which of the answer choices relate to the third word in the same way that the first two are related. Circle the letter that appears before your answer.

1. Mow is to lawn as prune is to
   (A) plum
   (B) raisin
   (C) tree
   (D) hair
   (E) meadow

2. Antecedent is to precedent as consequent is to
   (A) decadent
   (B) subsequent
   (C) ebullient
   (D) transient
   (E) penitent

3. Bassinet is to crib as car is to
   (A) bus
   (B) airplane
   (C) stroller
   (D) bed
   (E) taxicab

4. Restaurant is to eating as barracks is to
   (A) cleaning
   (B) military
   (C) inspection
   (D) nutrition
   (E) sleeping

5. Flame is to fire as smoke is to
   (A) heat
   (B) ashes
   (C) water
   (D) fire
   (E) match

6. Bludgeon is to spear as lathe is to
   (A) vise
   (B) carpenter
   (C) battle
   (D) curve
   (E) construction

7. Risk is to escapade as age is to
   (A) hilarity
   (B) intemperance
   (C) luminosity
   (D) mayhem
   (E) heirloom

8. Asset is to black as debit is to
   (A) debt
   (B) red
   (C) blue
   (D) left
   (E) ledger

9. Darkness is to eclipse as tidal wave is to
   (A) tsunami
   (B) eruption
   (C) ocean
   (D) beach
   (E) earthquake

10. Hen is to brood as mother is to
    (A) family
    (B) chickens
    (C) children
    (D) shoe
    (E) mom

Test Yourself 2

Directions: Decide how the words in the first pair are related. Choose a pair of words below that shows the same relationship. Circle the letter that appears before your answer.

1. Flood is to drought as
   (A) rich is to poor
   (B) camel is to desert
   (C) drizzle is to downpour
   (D) evening is to night
   (E) gold is to silver

2. Voracious is to gluttonous as
   (A) hungry is to thirsty
   (B) warm is to hot
   (C) potent is to strong
   (D) flight is to fight
   (E) yard is to meter

3. Hurricane is to wind as
   (A) wind is to water
   (B) typhoon is to wind
   (C) tornado is to twister
   (D) tornado is to typhoon
   (E) hurricane is to typhoon

4. Dung is to elephant as
   (A) horse is to manure
   (B) fish is to food
   (C) worm is to soil
   (D) oxygen is to tree
   (E) aquarium is to terrarium

5. Centipede is to spider as
   (A) pentagon is to triangle
   (B) rowboat is to sailboat
   (C) BC is to AD
   (D) percussion is to string
   (E) duet is to trio

6. Head is to hammer as
   (A) tooth is to saw
   (B) nail is to screw
   (C) awl is to punch
   (D) screw is to driver
   (E) beginning is to end

7. Anthem is to inspire as
   (A) aspirin is to pain
   (B) light is to see
   (C) organ is to grind
   (D) ape is to copy
   (E) shuttle is to transport

8. Hook is to eye as
   (A) sleeve is to coat
   (B) button is to hole
   (C) boot is to shoe
   (D) adhesive is to tape
   (E) honey is to bear

9. Actor is to script as
   (A) architect is to design
   (B) painter is to mural
   (C) musician is to score
   (D) judge is to brief
   (E) student is to textbook

10. Goalie is to net as
    (A) hockey is to soccer
    (B) player is to game
    (C) sentry is to fort
    (D) bat is to ball
    (E) ice is to turf

11. Topography is to geography as
    (A) water is to land
    (B) physics is to mathematics
    (C) geography is to history
    (D) mountain is to valley
    (E) biology is to science

12. Rocket is to torpedo as
    (A) fire is to water
    (B) air is to water
    (C) explosion is to hole
    (D) up is to down
    (E) war is to peace

Test Yourself 3

Directions: Look at the first two words and decide how they are related to each other. Then decide which of the answer choices relates to the third word in the same way that the first two are related. Circle the letter that appears before your answer.

1. Vertical is to horizontal as erect is to
   (A) honest
   (B) construct
   (C) prone
   (D) lumber
   (E) proper

2. Oust is to overthrow as molt is to
   (A) melt
   (B) shed
   (C) shape
   (D) weaken
   (E) spoil

3. Inline skates is to motorcycle as skis is to
   (A) snowmobile
   (B) bicycle
   (C) snow
   (D) ice skates
   (E) snow plow

4. Scale is to fish as hide is to
   (A) seek
   (B) tan
   (C) hole
   (D) ride
   (E) horse

5. Wind is to seed as bee is to
   (A) pollen
   (B) honey
   (C) hive
   (D) bear
   (E) flower

6. Glove is to hand as hose is to
   (A) garden
   (B) water
   (C) foot
   (D) nozzle
   (E) shoe

7. Piglet is to pig as islet is to
   (A) pond
   (B) lace
   (C) lake
   (D) rivulet
   (E) island

8. Depressed is to mope as tired is to
   (A) yawn
   (B) cope
   (C) car
   (D) laugh
   (E) suppressed

9. Masticate is to chew as gesticulate is to
   (A) vomit
   (B) digest
   (C) urbanize
   (D) point
   (E) offer

10. Tree is to forest as sand is to
   (A) dune
   (B) details
   (C) hours
   (D) time
   (E) sandwich

11. Seemly is to behavior as gawky is to
   (A) length
   (B) teenager
   (C) volume
   (D) barnyard
   (E) appearance

12. Flit is to dart as foil is to
   (A) fence
   (B) thwart
   (C) aluminum
   (D) change
   (E) surprise

Test Yourself 4

Directions: Decide how the words in the first pair are related. Choose a pair of words below that shows the same relationship. Circle the letter that appears before your answer.

1. Ravenous is to hungry as
   (A) hungry is to thirsty
   (B) stingy is to thrifty
   (C) boil is to bake
   (D) full is to empty
   (E) small is to little

2. Bonanza is to windfall as
   (A) earn is to merit
   (B) western is to eastern
   (C) horse is to apple
   (D) sun is to rain
   (E) gift is to accident

3. Salvage is to wreck as
   (A) bury is to treasure
   (B) paint is to antique
   (C) sink is to vessel
   (D) retrieve is to property
   (E) excavate is to ruin

4. Dimple is to pimple as
   (A) face is to back
   (B) down is to up
   (C) chin is to cheek
   (D) baby is to adolescent
   (E) love is to loathing

5. Filch is to pilfer as
   (A) steal is to squander
   (B) squeal is to wriggle
   (C) pinch is to puff
   (D) fidget is to squirm
   (E) rob is to fence

6. Hindsight is to foresight as
   (A) cure is to prevention
   (B) then is to now
   (C) later is to never
   (D) prediction is to predilection
   (E) vision is to perception

7. Fodder is to cattle as
   (A) water is to fish
   (B) bird is to worm
   (C) restaurant is to people
   (D) silo is to corn
   (E) fuel is to engine

8. Affix is to stamp as
   (A) letter is to postmark
   (B) hammer is to nail
   (C) run is to horse
   (D) glue is to mucilage
   (E) mail is to deliver

9. Leeward is to windward as
   (A) port is to starboard
   (B) meadow is to ocean
   (C) motor is to sail
   (D) pirate is to privateer
   (E) tugboat is to liner

10. Punish is to berate as
    (A) leafy is to green
    (B) deep is to ocean
    (C) jump is to leap
    (D) soak is to dampen
    (E) hike is to trek

11. Tobacco is to cigarette as
    (A) liquor is to drink
    (B) cough is to cold
    (C) wheat is to bread
    (D) cow is to milk
    (E) smoking is to cancer

12. Shun is to embrace as
    (A) shrink is to pounce
    (B) slender is to sloping
    (C) tousle is to muss
    (D) show is to tell
    (E) kiss is to hug

Test Yourself 5

Directions: Look at the first two words and decide how they are related to each other. Then decide which of the answer choices relates to the third word in the same way that the first two are related. Circle the letter that appears before your answer.

1. Comprehensive is to inclusive as apprehensive is to
   (A) exclusive
   (B) misunderstood
   (C) caught
   (D) uneasy
   (E) understanding

2. Chalk is to crayon as bed is to
   (A) chair
   (B) sleep
   (C) bunk
   (D) ladder
   (E) seat

3. Ceremonious is to informal as clerical is to
   (A) typographical
   (B) numerical
   (C) religious
   (D) retail
   (E) secular

4. Desist is to cease as resist is to
   (A) oppose
   (B) give up
   (C) resolve
   (D) remain
   (E) presume

5. Putrid is to garbage as aromatic is to
   (A) smell
   (B) pleasant
   (C) spirits
   (D) spray
   (E) spice

6. Harpoon is to whaling as buffoon is to
   (A) sorcery
   (B) clowning
   (C) badminton
   (D) spelunking
   (E) ballooning

7. Horn is to blow as harp is to
   (A) democracy
   (B) play
   (C) denounce
   (D) pluck
   (E) pants

8. Bald is to hirsute as anemic is to
   (A) tiny
   (B) fat
   (C) robust
   (D) loud
   (E) redundant

9. Green is to youth as gray is to
   (A) age
   (B) hair
   (C) gloom
   (D) mare
   (E) elderly

10. Gridiron is to football as gridlock is to
    (A) waffles
    (B) chess
    (C) prison
    (D) wrestling
    (E) traffic

11. Sow is to reap as crawl is to
    (A) sneak
    (B) harvest
    (C) walk
    (D) cultivate
    (E) wheat

12. Horde is to throng as hurl is to
    (A) thrust
    (B) jump
    (C) throw
    (D) defeat
    (E) smash

Test Yourself 6

Directions: Decide how the words in the first pair are related. Choose a pair of words below that shows the same relationship. Circle the letter that appears before your answer.

1. Salary is to income as
   (A) income is to tax
   (B) money is to evil
   (C) spring is to water
   (D) wage is to work
   (E) dollars is to cents

2. Tree is to climb as
   (A) scale is to mountain
   (B) horse is to ride
   (C) garden is to eat
   (D) gem is to die
   (E) cat is to mouse

3. Consider is to dismiss as
   (A) reflect is to absorb
   (B) wade is to swim
   (C) current is to recent
   (D) help is to assist
   (E) decide is to determine

4. Compost is to fertilizer as
   (A) dentist is to teeth
   (B) ball is to basket
   (C) hole is to drill
   (D) value is to price
   (E) ice is to refrigerant

5. Trance is to hypnosis as
   (A) knowledge is to study
   (B) poison is to ivy
   (C) vaccination is to immunity
   (D) banana is to plantain
   (E) pie is to apple

6. Pianist is to musician as
   (A) organist is to pianist
   (B) violinist is to fiddler
   (C) musician is to writer
   (D) mathematics is to mathematician
   (E) psychiatrist is to physician

7. Poetry is to prose as
   (A) seeing is to hearing
   (B) light is to heavy
   (C) sonata is to étude
   (D) opera is to book
   (E) melody is to rhythm

8. Hull is to strawberry as
   (A) tree is to leaf
   (B) hull is to ship
   (C) puppy is to dog
   (D) milk is to cow
   (E) butter is to bread

9. Poison is to skull and crossbones as
   (A) rope is to gallows
   (B) pirate is to gangplank
   (C) antidote is to poison
   (D) love is to heart
   (E) bow is to arrow

10. Trivial is to grievous as
    (A) acid is to bitter
    (B) light is to heavy
    (C) boring is to sad
    (D) oil is to water
    (E) funny is to hilarious

11. Ax is to hatchet as
    (A) fish is to nursery
    (B) chicken is to egg
    (C) chop is to cut
    (D) hammer is to sickle
    (E) cello is to violin

12. Fortuitous is to luck as
    (A) chivalrous is to manners
    (B) fossil is to fuel
    (C) formula is to milk
    (D) music is to dance
    (E) pool is to swimming

Test Yourself 7

Directions: Look at the first two words and decide how they are related to each other. Then decide which of the answer choices relates to the third word in the same way that the first two are related. Circle the letter that appears before your answer.

1. Hassock is to feet as pillow is to
   (A) cushion
   (B) chair
   (C) boots
   (D) fight
   (E) head

2. Ghost is to haunt as guru is to
   (A) frighten
   (B) teach
   (C) amuse
   (D) adhere
   (E) tempt

3. Nail is to toe as lock is to
   (A) key
   (B) combination
   (C) hair
   (D) hammer
   (E) barrel

4. Sub is to under as super is to
   (A) janitor
   (B) chief
   (C) terrific
   (D) over
   (E) better

5. Deciduous is to leaves as evergreen is to
   (A) needles
   (B) tree
   (C) Christmas
   (D) conifer
   (E) forest

6. Flounder is to shark as tick is to
   (A) clock
   (B) deer
   (C) flea
   (D) insect
   (E) woods

7. Starch is to stiff as bleach is to
   (A) smooth
   (B) soft
   (C) colorful
   (D) dry
   (E) white

8. Shellfish is to lobster as poultry is to
   (A) fowl
   (B) spider
   (C) chicken
   (D) bird
   (E) octopus

9. Oval is to oblong as circle is to
   (A) round
   (B) square
   (C) sphere
   (D) cube
   (E) rectangle

10. Capacious is to cramped as agape is to
    (A) ajar
    (B) painful
    (C) surprised
    (D) empty
    (E) sealed

11. Brood is to litter as peon is to
(A) farmer
(B) slave
(C) migrant
(D) laborer
(E) scatter

12. Anorexia is to bulimia as asthma is to
(A) eating
(B) breathing
(C) allergy
(D) emphysema
(E) headache

Test Yourself 8

Directions: Decide how the words in the first pair are related. Choose a pair of words below that shows the same relationship. Circle the letter that appears before your answer.

1. Felon is to crime as
(A) judge is to jury
(B) courtroom is to trial
(C) physician is to cure
(D) verdict is to sentence
(E) pharmacy is to pharmacist

2. Odor is to stench as
(A) sad is to tragic
(B) rich is to poor
(C) green is to brown
(D) summer is to winter
(E) flower is to animal

3. Overblown is to exaggerated as
(A) warrant is to justify
(B) anachronism is to timely
(C) malapropism is to accurate
(D) requirement is to optional
(E) indefinite is to tomorrow

4. Loom is to appear as
(A) weave is to wool
(B) root is to dig
(C) come is to go
(D) seem is to be
(E) warp is to woof

5. Escape is to flee as
(A) run is to hide
(B) break is to enter
(C) hide is to seek
(D) captive is to captor
(E) dismount is to alight

6. Assent is to dissent as
(A) assert is to desert
(B) compact is to expansive
(C) assist is to desist
(D) obtain is to retain
(E) future is to futility

7. Nature is to nurture as
(A) father is to mother
(B) authentic is to artificial
(C) congenital is to acquired
(D) native is to alien
(E) home is to school

8. Squat is to crouch as
(A) incise is to precise
(B) countenance is to face
(C) lax is to strict
(D) molten is to solid
(E) mongrel is to puppy

9. Rudder is to steering as
   (A) razor is to shaving
   (B) wheel is to turning
   (C) cow is to grazing
   (D) cloud is to raining
   (E) stapling is to stapler

10. Standee is to seat as
    (A) kitty is to litter
    (B) apple is to pie
    (C) salt is to ocean
    (D) acorn is to oak
    (E) nomad is to home

11. Pauper is to poor as
    (A) shoe is to pair
    (B) book is to long
    (C) skyscraper is to high
    (D) bed is to make
    (E) clever is to owl

12. Cursory is to superficial as
    (A) dismal is to cheerful
    (B) approbation is to consecration
    (C) death is to victory
    (D) desultory is to aimless
    (E) heroism is to reward

Test Yourself 9

Directions: Look at the first two words and decide how they are related to each other. Then decide which of the answer choices relates to the third word in the same way that the first two are related. Circle the letter that appears before your answer.

1. Prattle is to baby as discourse is to
   (A) conversation
   (B) scholar
   (C) speech
   (D) subject
   (E) lecture

2. Dose is to medicine as portion is to
   (A) dessert
   (B) serving
   (C) potion
   (D) food
   (E) section

3. Bowl is to soup as plate is to
   (A) cup
   (B) fork
   (C) dinner
   (D) china
   (E) meat

4. Gram is to ounce as meter is to
   (A) mile
   (B) pound
   (C) yard
   (D) weigh
   (E) measure

5. Flower is to seed as seed is to
   (A) plant
   (B) water
   (C) grow
   (D) food
   (E) nut

6. Oil is to earth as salt is to
   (A) shaker
   (B) pepper
   (C) blood pressure
   (D) lick
   (E) sea

7. Pest is to annoying as plateau is to
   (A) level
   (B) calming
   (C) boring
   (D) curved
   (E) hilly

8. Survive is to succumb as swim is to
   (A) sail
   (B) dive
   (C) row
   (D) sink
   (E) float

9. Taunt is to tease as voluble is to
   (A) loud
   (B) large
   (C) talkative
   (D) willing
   (E) loyal

10. Tiara is to jewel as wreath is to
    (A) crown
    (B) flower
    (C) head
    (D) woman
    (E) door

11. Torrid is to extreme as temperate is to
    (A) warm
    (B) hot
    (C) climate
    (D) moderate
    (E) heat

12. Axle is to wheels as chain is to
    (A) necklace
    (B) handcuffs
    (C) door
    (D) gang
    (E) daisies

Test Yourself 10

Directions: Decide how the words in the first pair are related. Choose a pair of words below that shows the same relationship. Circle the letter that appears before your answer.

1. Peacock is to plumage as
   (A) lion is to mane
   (B) friend is to diamonds
   (C) coat is to tails
   (D) shine is to shoes
   (E) dowager is to furs

2. Quagmire is to quarry as
   (A) hunter is to prey
   (B) hide is to seek
   (C) mud is to stone
   (D) sink is to swim
   (E) find is to keep

3. Frog is to tadpole as
   (A) toad is to tree
   (B) mushroom is to toadstool
   (C) moth is to polliwog
   (D) butterfly is to caterpillar
   (E) imago is to earthworm

4. Cotton is to summer as
   (A) rain is to snow
   (B) wool is to winter
   (C) boll is to weevil
   (D) fur is to coat
   (E) leaf is to tree

5. Motion is to queasy as
   (A) itchy is to rash
   (B) unfamiliar is to strange
   (C) round is to dizzy
   (D) fever is to hot
   (E) ocean is to wavy

6. Nay is to yea as
   (A) voices is to hands
   (B) now is to later
   (C) horse is to sleigh
   (D) neither is to nor
   (E) negate is to affirm

7. Knocker is to doorbell as
   (A) pen is to pencil
   (B) sound is to alarm
   (C) strike is to hours
   (D) in is to out
   (E) pleasant is to unpleasant

8. Bullet is to gun as
   (A) blade is to hatchet
   (B) slingshot is to pebble
   (C) arrow is to bow
   (D) sword is to spear
   (E) victim is to target

9. Walrus is to seal as
   (A) cow is to calf
   (B) doe is to deer
   (C) elephant is to lizard
   (D) ram is to ewe
   (E) goose is to duck

10. Freezer is to ice cream as
    (A) safe is to money
    (B) jelly is to jam
    (C) paper is to pencil
    (D) rain is to snow
    (E) coins is to piggybank

11. Hum is to sing as
    (A) speak is to see
    (B) deaf is to mute
    (C) pantomime is to act
    (D) play is to opera
    (E) prose is to poetry

12. Patriarch is to matriarch as
    (A) church is to state
    (B) leader is to follower
    (C) noble is to common
    (D) tailor is to seamstress
    (E) ancient is to modern

Test Yourself 11

Directions: Look at the first two words and decide how they are related to each other. Then decide which of the answer choices relates to the third word in the same way that the first two are related. Circle the letter that appears before your answer.

1. Calligraphy is to precise as scrawl is to
   (A) handwriting
   (B) primitive
   (C) careless
   (D) illegible
   (E) scratchy

2. Agitated is to stoic as sociable is to
   (A) hermit
   (B) socialite
   (C) cheerleader
   (D) friendly
   (E) acrobat

3. Sweat is to perspire as swat is to
   - (A) fly
   - (B) destroy
   - (C) exercise
   - (D) kill
   - (E) hit

4. Nostalgia is to past as anticipation is to
   - (A) excitement
   - (B) future
   - (C) present
   - (D) apprehension
   - (E) past

5. Gleeful is to gloomy as organized is to
   - (A) original
   - (B) neat
   - (C) unintellectual
   - (D) disinterested
   - (E) messy

6. Venison is to deer as veal is to
   - (A) lamb
   - (B) steer
   - (C) cow
   - (D) sheep
   - (E) calf

7. Obedience is to obstinacy as peace is to
   - (A) prosperity
   - (B) patriotism
   - (C) penury
   - (D) war
   - (E) tranquility

8. Traitor is to treason as patriot is to
   - (A) espionage
   - (B) jingoism
   - (C) loyalty
   - (D) heritage
   - (E) sacrifice

9. Rink is to skate as sink is to
   - (A) wash
   - (B) swim
   - (C) fish
   - (D) soap
   - (E) kitchen

10. Gully is to water as furrow is to
    - (A) brow
    - (B) farm
    - (C) erosion
    - (D) rabbit
    - (E) plow

11. Desert is to jungle as dusty is to
    - (A) damp
    - (B) dirty
    - (C) dry
    - (D) hot
    - (E) dark

12. Steam is to boiling as smoke is to
    - (A) heat
    - (B) chimney
    - (C) combustion
    - (D) freezing
    - (E) vapor

Test Yourself 12

Directions: Decide how the words in the first pair are related. Choose a pair of words below that shows the same relationship. Circle the letter that appears before your answer.

1. Till is to cultivate as
   (A) plow is to horse
   (B) tractor is to plow
   (C) plant is to furrow
   (D) farm is to soil
   (E) toil is to work

2. Tooth is to bone as
   (A) tire is to fan belt
   (B) pond is to forest
   (C) fish is to bird
   (D) star is to sun
   (E) house is to home

3. Fry is to stew as
   (A) chicken is to beef
   (B) heat is to fire
   (C) pan is to pot
   (D) dry is to wet
   (E) meat is to potatoes

4. Rustle is to roar as
   (A) water is to wind
   (B) walk is to run
   (C) rain is to snow
   (D) cattle is to coyote
   (E) shout is to yell

5. Fall is to leaf as
   (A) melt is to snow
   (B) build is to house
   (C) shrub is to flower
   (D) sneeze is to cough
   (E) dig is to spade

6. Spa is to health as
   (A) museum is to pictures
   (B) conservation is to zoo
   (C) sport is to stadium
   (D) library is to information
   (E) quiet is to church

7. Exacting is to demanding as
   (A) burrowing is to building
   (B) testing is to proving
   (C) changing is to appearing
   (D) thrilling is to boring
   (E) extracting is to removing

8. Labyrinth is to network as
   (A) weather is to climate
   (B) vein is to blood
   (C) maze is to passages
   (D) epic is to hero
   (E) Greece is to myths

9. Kiss is to cheek as
   (A) cheek is to jowl
   (B) shake is to hand
   (C) hug is to bear
   (D) nose is to rub
   (E) milk is to cookies

10. Ingest is to digest as
    (A) sergeant is to captain
    (B) eat is to drink
    (C) drink is to drive
    (D) spider is to fly
    (E) understand is to study

11. Imp is to horns as
    (A) devil is to angel
    (B) evil is to good
    (C) halo is to wings
    (D) mischief is to elf
    (E) cherub is to wings

12. Knead is to dough as
    (A) rotted is to apple
    (B) fallen is to arches
    (C) soak is to beans
    (D) drifted is to snow
    (E) spent is to money

Test Yourself 13

Directions: Find a relationship between the first two words in each question. To complete the analogy, choose the answer that shows a similar relationship.

1. Light is to dark as wet is to
   (A) snow
   (B) rain
   (C) hinge
   (D) dry

2. Summer is to winter as evening is to
   (A) sunset
   (B) coolness
   (C) darkness
   (D) morning

3. Right is to left as low is to
   (A) high
   (B) bottom
   (C) sorrow
   (D) note

4. Nothing is to everything as whisper is to
   (A) mystery
   (B) something
   (C) shout
   (D) ghost

5. Day is to night as sun is to
   (A) solar
   (B) heat
   (C) universe
   (D) moon

6. Weak is to strong as incapable is to
   (A) clumsy
   (B) cowardly
   (C) adept
   (D) failure

7. Advance is to halt as
   (A) stop is to go
   (B) return is to change
   (C) go is to stop
   (D) conquer is to take

8. Skillful is to clumsy as
   (A) alert is to sleepy
   (B) deft is to awkward
   (C) quick is to swift
   (D) smooth is to slick

9. Enemies is to friends as
   (A) pacify is to quiet
   (B) hate is to dislike
   (C) defeat is to lose
   (D) despise is to esteem

10. Blame is to praise as
    (A) fail is to succeed
    (B) defeat is to condemn
    (C) succeed is to defeat
    (D) emerge is to emanate

Test Yourself 14

Directions: Find a relationship between the first two words in each question. To complete the analogy, choose the answer that shows a similar relationship.

1. Window is to pane as door is to
   (A) panel
   (B) knob
   (C) hinge
   (D) key

2. Paragraph is to sentence as sentence is to
   (A) modifier
   (B) word
   (C) composition
   (D) grammar

3. Nut is to shell as pea is to
   (A) shooter
   (B) soup
   (C) green
   (D) pod

4. Antler is to deer as
   (A) tusk is to husk
   (B) animal is to elephant
   (C) tusk is to elephant
   (D) horn is to antler

5. Jewel is to ring as
   (A) stone is to ruby
   (B) locket is to necklace
   (C) precious is to stone
   (D) iron is to chain

6. Pit is to peach as
   (A) sun is to solar system
   (B) moon is to Earth
   (C) plane is to Earth
   (D) moon is to orbit

7. Page is to book as
   (A) period is to comma
   (B) novel is to book
   (C) word is to page
   (D) library is to story

8. State is to country as
   (A) continent is to world
   (B) world is to continent
   (C) country is to city
   (D) ocean is to shore

9. Hand is to body as star is to
   (A) sky
   (B) universe
   (C) eye
   (D) movie

10. Play is to prologue as constitution is to
    (A) preamble
    (B) Bill of Rights
    (C) preview
    (D) Supreme Court

Test Yourself 15

Directions: Find a relationship between the first two words in each question. To complete the analogy, choose the answer that shows a similar relationship.

1. Letter is to mail as money is to
   (A) bank
   (B) savings
   (C) invest
   (D) account

2. Seal is to float as bird is to
   (A) flap
   (B) wing
   (C) soar
   (D) nest

3. Egg is to scramble as potato is to
   (A) mash
   (B) skin
   (C) butter
   (D) slice

4. Artist is to paint as contractor is to
   (A) agreement
   (B) build
   (C) masonry
   (D) carpentry

5. Scissors is to trim as scales is to
   (A) fish
   (B) weight
   (C) measure
   (D) weigh

6. Bed is to sleep as chair is to
   (A) carry
   (B) sit
   (C) stare
   (D) recline

7. Taste is to tongue as touch is to
   (A) skin
   (B) arms
   (C) feelings
   (D) ears

8. Box is to cover as bottle is to
   (A) glass
   (B) contain
   (C) cork
   (D) break

9. Shoe is to lace as door is to
   (A) hinge
   (B) enter
   (C) swing
   (D) lock

10. Typewriter is to write as calculator is to
   (A) add
   (B) compute
   (C) percentage
   (D) predict

Test Yourself 16

Directions: Find a relationship between the first two words in each question. To complete the analogy, choose the answer that shows a similar relationship.

1. Satisfaction is to good deed as improvement is to
   (A) sin
   (B) fault
   (C) criticism
   (D) kindness

2. Seed is to plant as egg is to
   (A) yolk
   (B) crack
   (C) bird
   (D) shell

3. Wheat is to flour as grape is to
   (A) vintage
   (B) wine
   (C) vine
   (D) vineyard

4. Heat is to fire as cloud is to
   (A) sky
   (B) snow
   (C) sun
   (D) moisture

5. Threat is to insecurity as
   (A) challenge is to fight
   (B) thunder is to lightning
   (C) reason is to anger
   (D) speed is to brake

6. Heat is to radiator as
   (A) sea is to wave
   (B) tree is to breeze
   (C) wind is to trees
   (D) breeze is to fan

7. Medication is to cure as
   (A) drug is to diagnosis
   (B) examination is to treatment
   (C) physician is to relief
   (D) vaccination is to prevention

8. War is to grief as
   (A) joy is to peace
   (B) peace is to happiness
   (C) peace is to finish
   (D) joy is to happiness

9. Moon is to light as
   (A) sunset is to sun
   (B) earth is to orbit
   (C) eclipse is to dark
   (D) gravity is to earth

10. Ignition is to starter as
    (A) radio is to antenna
    (B) brake is to stop
    (C) air is to tire
    (D) shut is to door

Test Yourself 17

Directions: Find a relationship between the first two words in each question. To complete the analogy, choose the answer that shows a similar relationship.

1. Ring is to finger as cuff is to
   (A) arm
   (B) shoulder
   (C) hand
   (D) wrist

2. Gas is to vehicle as wood is to
   (A) tree
   (B) fire
   (C) stove
   (D) heat

3. Refrigerator is to meat as bank is to
   (A) cashier
   (B) combination
   (C) watchman
   (D) money

4. Watchman is to protect as navigator is to
   (A) navy
   (B) guide
   (C) plan
   (D) map

5. Gymnasium is to game as auditorium is to
   (A) production
   (B) script
   (C) cafeteria
   (D) actors

Test Yourself 18

Directions: Find a relationship between the first two words in each question. To complete the analogy, choose the answer that shows a similar relationship.

1. Present is to birthday as reward is to
   (A) accomplishment
   (B) medal
   (C) punishment
   (D) money

2. Guest is to acceptance as host is to
   (A) party
   (B) invitation
   (C) hostess
   (D) refreshments

3. Stick is to puck as bat is to
   (A) cricket
   (B) ball
   (C) touchdown
   (D) bowl

4. Fever is to spring as leaves is to
   (A) October
   (B) season
   (C) autumn
   (D) sadness

5. Honorable is to bravery as guilty is to
   (A) criminal
   (B) peaceful
   (C) important
   (D) productive

ANSWER KEY

Test Yourself 1

1. C	4. E	7. E	9. E
2. B	5. D	8. B	10. C
3. A	6. A		

Test Yourself 2

1. A	4. D	7. E	10. C
2. C	5. A	8. B	11. E
3. B	6. A	9. C	12. B

Test Yourself 3

1. C	4. E	7. E	10. A
2. B	5. A	8. A	11. E
3. A	6. C	9. D	12. B

Test Yourself 4

1. B	4. B	7. E	10. D
2. A	5. D	8. B	11. C
3. E	6. A	9. A	12. A

Test Yourself 5

1. D	4. A	7. D	10. E
2. C	5. E	8. C	11. C
3. E	6. B	9. A	12. C

Test Yourself 6

1. C	4. E	7. C	10. B
2. B	5. A	8. B	11. E
3. A	6. E	9. D	12. A

Test Yourself 7

1. E	4. D	7. E	10. E
2. B	5. A	8. C	11. D
3. C	6. C	9. A	12. D

Test Yourself 8

1. C	4. B	7. C	10. E
2. A	5. E	8. B	11. C
3. A	6. B	9. A	12. D

Test Yourself 9

1. B	4. C	7. A	10. B
2. D	5. A	8. D	11. D
3. E	6. E	9. C	12. B

Test Yourself 10

1. A	4. B	7. A	10. A
2. C	5. D	8. C	11. C
3. D	6. E	9. E	12. D

Test Yourself 11

1. C	4. B	7. D	10. E
2. A	5. E	8. C	11. A
3. E	6. E	9. A	12. C

Test Yourself 12

1. E	4. B	7. E	10. A
2. A	5. A	8. C	11. E
3. C	6. D	9. B	12. C

Test Yourself 13

1. D	4. C	7. C	9. D
2. D	5. D	8. A	10. A
3. A	6. C		

Test Yourself 14

1. A	4. C	7. C	9. B
2. B	5. B	8. A	10. A
3. D	6. A		

Test Yourself 15

1. C	4. B	7. A	9. D
2. C	5. D	8. C	10. B
3. A	6. B		

Test Yourself 16

1. C	4. D	7. D	9. C
2. C	5. A	8. B	10. C
3. B	6. D		

Test Yourself 17

1. D	3. D	5. A
2. C	4. B	

Test Yourself 18

1. A	3. B	5. A
2. B	4. C	

EXERCISES: MIXED RELATIONSHIPS

The analogies in this section are **not** arranged in any particular pattern. You must decide what type of relationship is being used in each item.

Directions: Find a relationship between the first two words in each question. To complete the analogy, choose the answer that shows a similar relationship.

1. Thanksgiving is to November as Christmas is to
   (A) Santa Claus
   (B) December
   (C) snow
   (D) Jingle Bells

2. Remember is to forget as find is to
   (A) locate
   (B) keep
   (C) lose
   (D) return

3. Ship is to anchor as automobile is to
   (A) brake
   (B) wheel
   (C) stop
   (D) accelerator

4. End is to abolish as begin is to
   (A) establish
   (B) finish
   (C) tyranny
   (D) crusade

5. Wood is to decay as iron is to
   (A) dampness
   (B) rust
   (C) steel
   (D) ore

6. Month is to week as week is to
   (A) month
   (B) hour
   (C) year
   (D) day

7. Flour is to wheat as gravel is to
   (A) brick
   (B) rock
   (C) coal
   (D) bread

8. Attack is to protect as offense is to
   (A) combat
   (B) defense
   (C) conceal
   (D) reconcile

9. Divide is to multiply as subtract is to
   (A) plus
   (B) reduce
   (C) multiply
   (D) add

10. Mine is to my as yours is to
    (A) you
    (B) ours
    (C) your
    (D) you're

11. Glasses is to vision as
    (A) glass is to mirror
    (B) light is to vision
    (C) eating is to fork
    (D) hand is to object

12. Flame is to burn as
    (A) insult is to anger
    (B) glass is to crack
    (C) birth is to life
    (D) sun is to orbit

13. Look is to see as
    (A) illuminate is to light
    (B) audition is to speak
    (C) listen is to hear
    (D) follow is to lead

14. Wolf is to pack as
    (A) cow is to herd
    (B) cattle is to farmer
    (C) cow is to graze
    (D) farmer is to farm

15. Leave is to stay as depart is to
    (A) home
    (B) disembark
    (C) run
    (D) remain

16. Car is to mechanic as people is to
    (A) butcher
    (B) lawyer
    (C) spouse
    (D) doctor

17. Forest is to tree as crowd is to
    (A) person
    (B) alone
    (C) men
    (D) many

18. Fiction is to novelist as fact is to
    (A) legend
    (B) story
    (C) historian
    (D) research

19. Stranger is to strange as
    (A) oddest is to odd
    (B) artist is to artistic
    (C) art is to artist
    (D) satirist is to artist

20. Librarian is to library as
    (A) school is to education
    (B) office is to principal
    (C) teacher is to school
    (D) gymnasium is to workout

21. Sickness is to health as death is to
    (A) mortician
    (B) skull
    (C) life
    (D) pirate

22. Inventor is to machine as author is to
    (A) book
    (B) poet
    (C) creator
    (D) computer

23. Weight is to pound as distance is to
    (A) liter
    (B) mile
    (C) ruler
    (D) space

24. Conceal is to reveal as ascend is to
    (A) embark
    (B) descend
    (C) mount
    (D) leave

25. Cape is to continent as
    (A) ocean is to lake
    (B) lake is to reservoir
    (C) reservoir is to water
    (D) gulf is to ocean

26. Vision is to lens as
    (A) mobility is to crutches
    (B) crutch is to legs
    (C) walking is to paralysis
    (D) doctor is to paralysis

27. Bus is to road as
    (A) wheel is to street
    (B) steel is to rails
    (C) locomotive is to track
    (D) locomotive is to steam

28. Year is to July as
    (A) week is to month
    (B) meter is to centimeter
    (C) month is to century
    (D) millimeter is to centimeter

29. Resignation is to sigh as
    (A) hope is to wish
    (B) faith is to pray
    (C) surprise is to gasp
    (D) terror is to fear

30. Lincoln is to Nebraska as
    (A) Washington is to Oregon
    (B) New York is to Kentucky
    (C) Chicago is to New York
    (D) Trenton is to New Jersey

31. Pencil is to sharpen as
    (A) knife is to cut
    (B) carpenter is to build
    (C) wood is to saw
    (D) well is to fill

32. Finger is to hand as
    (A) arm is to sleeve
    (B) shoe is to foot
    (C) strand is to hair
    (D) blouse is to skirt

33. Convex is to concave as
    (A) hill is to hole
    (B) in is to within
    (C) round is to square
    (D) nose is to mouth

34. Cow is to milk as
    (A) rat is to cheese
    (B) bee is to honey
    (C) bird is to wing
    (D) cat is to dog

35. Exercise is to reduce as
    (A) grumble is to resign
    (B) snow is to freeze
    (C) spending is to save
    (D) luck is to win

36. Mountain is to peak as
    (A) wave is to crest
    (B) storm is to ocean
    (C) tide is to ocean
    (D) storm is to hurricane

37. Food is to body as
    (A) fuel is to engine
    (B) bat is to ball
    (C) kite is to tail
    (D) mechanic is to engine

38. Pressure is to barometer as
    (A) temperature is to thermometer
    (B) speedometer is to distance
    (C) meter is to perimeter
    (D) comptometer is to comptroller

39. Famine is to abundance as
    (A) hunger is to starvation
    (B) squalor is to starvation
    (C) poverty is to wealth
    (D) famine is to hunger

40. Study is to studiously as
    (A) work is to learning
    (B) play is to playfully
    (C) book is to bookish
    (D) habit is to habitual

41. Discard is to delete as
    (A) attach is to detach
    (B) contagious is to spread
    (C) farther is to far
    (D) alter is to revise

42. Reject is to aversion as
    (A) think is to consider
    (B) choose is to preference
    (C) impose is to act
    (D) content is to change

43. Measles is to disease as
    (A) felony is to crime
    (B) measles is to mumps
    (C) felony is to misdemeanor
    (D) crime is to law

44. Occasional is to constant as
    (A) intermittent is to incessant
    (B) intramural is to inconsistent
    (C) frequent is to incessant
    (D) inadvertent is to accidental

45. Active is to mobile as
    (A) mobile is to immobile
    (B) inflammable is to extinguished
    (C) sedentary is to immobile
    (D) sensational is to movement

46. Eliminate is to optional as
    (A) maintain is to option
    (B) retain is to essential
    (C) option is to opportunity
    (D) sequential is to order

47. Allude is to refer as
    (A) illusion is to reality
    (B) similar is to disparate
    (C) imply is to state
    (D) conclude is to infer

48. Plane is to charter as
    (A) worker is to use
    (B) assistant is to appoint
    (C) person is to hire
    (D) manager is to salary

49. Superscript is to subscript as
    (A) introvert is to extrovert
    (B) introvert is to convert
    (C) impede is to intercede
    (D) subscription is to prescription

50. Complement is to compliment as
    (A) effect is to affect
    (B) surfeit is to surface
    (C) interface is to surface
    (D) style is to stile

51. Premonition is to prophesy as
    (A) preface is to prologue
    (B) predict is to relate
    (C) prologue is to epilogue
    (D) history is to archives

52. Collaboration is to cooperation as
    (A) collation is to correction
    (B) concentration is to quiet
    (C) coercion is to submission
    (D) compromise is to promise

53. Revert is to reversion as
    (A) interest is to intercession
    (B) invert is to overt
    (C) sympathize is to sympathy
    (D) sympathy is to sympathetic

54. Salesperson is to commission as
    (A) author is to royalty
    (B) agent is to actor
    (C) tip is to waiter
    (D) fee is to charge

55. Harassment is to anger as
    (A) disappointment is to sorrow
    (B) height is to weight
    (C) laughter is to tears
    (D) marriage is to love

56. Divulge is to disclose as
    (A) revise is to create
    (B) appraise is to estimate
    (C) dispel is to collect
    (D) bulge is to close

57. Sodium is to salt as
    (A) torch is to acetylene
    (B) ammonia is to pneumonia
    (C) oxygen is to water
    (D) balloon is to helium

58. Cautious is to impulsive as
    (A) secretive is to candid
    (B) caustic is to biting
    (C) creative is to work
    (D) punish is to behavior

59. Hidden is to obvious as
    (A) reserved is to rambunctious
    (B) emphatic is to vehement
    (C) embezzle is to steal
    (D) open is to door

60. Sword is to dueling as pen is to
    (A) writer
    (B) inkwell
    (C) ink
    (D) writing

61. Reprimand is to disapproval as compliment is to
    (A) flatter
    (B) approval
    (C) affirmation
    (D) improvement

62. Gold is to yellow as royal is to
    (A) black
    (B) purple
    (C) blue
    (D) white

63. Recurrence is to periodic as determination is to
    (A) cowardly
    (B) hopeless
    (C) literary
    (D) persevering

64. Anarchy is to law as discord is to
    (A) difference
    (B) agreement
    (C) adaptation
    (D) confusion

65. Ceiling is to chandelier as puppeteer is to
    (A) puppet
    (B) puppet show
    (C) stage
    (D) ventriloquist

66. Accident is to carelessness as response is to
    (A) answer
    (B) correct
    (C) stimulus
    (D) effect

67. Correction is to erroneous as clarification is to
    (A) criticism
    (B) failure
    (C) amend
    (D) ambiguous

68. Automobile is to horse as telephone is to
    (A) wagon
    (B) telegraph
    (C) communication
    (D) transportation

69. Intimidate is to daunt as dismay is to
    (A) horrify
    (B) destroy
    (C) dismantle
    (D) forego

70. Spontaneous is to calculated as impromptu is to
    (A) ad lib
    (B) scheduled
    (C) verbose
    (D) prolific

71. Critic is to play as reviewer is to
    (A) job
    (B) work
    (C) newspaper
    (D) book

72. Lion is to pride as
    (A) bird is to vanity
    (B) cow is to pasture
    (C) pack is to dog
    (D) fish is to school

73. Referee is to rules as conscience is to
    (A) morality
    (B) thoughts
    (C) regulations
    (D) behavior

74. Money is to steal as idea is to
    (A) lose
    (B) manuscript
    (C) plagiarize
    (D) thief

75. Book is to paper as scroll is to
    (A) cloth
    (B) binding
    (C) roll
    (D) parchment

ANSWER KEY AND EXPLANATIONS

1. B	16. D	31. C	46. B	61. B
2. C	17. A	32. C	47. C	62. C
3. A	18. C	33. A	48. C	63. D
4. A	19. B	34. B	49. A	64. B
5. B	20. C	35. D	50. A	65. A
6. D	21. C	36. A	51. D	66. C
7. B	22. A	37. A	52. B	67. D
8. B	23. B	38. A	53. C	68. B
9. D	24. B	39. C	54. A	69. A
10. C	25. D	40. B	55. A	70. B
11. B	26. A	41. D	56. B	71. D
12. A	27. C	42. B	57. C	72. D
13. C	28. B	43. A	58. A	73. A
14. A	29. C	44. A	59. A	74. C
15. D	30. D	45. C	60. D	75. D

1. **The correct answer is (B).** THANKSGIVING is in NOVEMBER; CHRISTMAS is in DECEMBER.

2. **The correct answer is (C).** Antonym relationships

3. **The correct answer is (A).** ANCHORS stop SHIPS; BRAKES stop AUTOMOBILES. The second word in each pair is the part used to stop the first noun.

4. **The correct answer is (A).** The words in each pair are synonyms.

5. **The correct answer is (B).** WOOD DECAYS; IRON RUSTS. The first word in each pair is a noun. The second is a verb that relates to the first.

6. **The correct answer is (D).** A WEEK is part of a MONTH; a DAY is part of a WEEK.

7. **The correct answer is (B).** FLOUR is ground WHEAT; GRAVEL is broken ROCK.

8. **The correct answer is (B).** The words in each pair are antonyms.

9. **The correct answer is (D).** The words in each pair are antonyms.

10. **The correct answer is (C).** Each pair contains similar possessive pronouns.

11. **The correct answer is (B).** GLASSES and LIGHT enhance a person's VISION.

12. **The correct answer is (A).** A FLAME may cause a BURN; an INSULT may cause ANGER.

13. **The correct answer is (C).** SEEING is the result of LOOKING; HEARING is the result of LISTENING.

14. **The correct answer is (A).** WOLVES gather in PACKS; COWS gather in HERDS.

15. **The correct answer is (D).** The words in each pair are antonyms.

16. **The correct answer is (D).** MECHANICS repair CARS; DOCTORS "repair" PEOPLE.

17. **The correct answer is (A).** A TREE is one part of a FOREST; a PERSON is one part of a CROWD.

18. **The correct answer is (C).** A NOVELIST writes FICTION; a HISTORIAN writes about FACTS.

19. **The correct answer is (B).** STRANGER is the noun form of the adjective STRANGE; ARTIST is the noun form of the adjective ARTISTIC.

20. **The correct answer is (C).** A LIBRARIAN works in a LIBRARY; a TEACHER works in a SCHOOL.

21. **The correct answer is (C).** The words in each pair are antonyms.

22. **The correct answer is (A).** New MACHINES are created by INVENTORS; new BOOKS are created by AUTHORS.

23. **The correct answer is (B).** A POUND is a unit of WEIGHT; a MILE is a unit of DISTANCE.

24. **The correct answer is (B).** The words in each pair are antonyms.

25. **The correct answer is (D).** A CAPE is a geographical part of a CONTINENT; a GULF is part of an OCEAN.

26. **The correct answer is (A).** A LENS is an aid to VISION; CRUTCHES aid MOBILITY.

27. **The correct answer is (C).** A BUS travels along a ROAD; a LOCOMOTIVE moves on a TRACK.

28. **The correct answer is (B).** YEAR is the whole; JULY is the part; METER the whole; CENTIMETER the part. All other part-whole relationships are reversed.

29. **The correct answer is (C).** A SIGH is a kind of breath that expresses RESIGNATION; a GASP is a kind of breath that expresses SURPRISE.

30. **The correct answer is (D).** LINCOLN is the capital of NEBRASKA; TRENTON is the capital of NEW JERSEY.

31. **The correct answer is (C).** SHARPEN a PENCIL; SAW a piece of WOOD.

32. **The correct answer is (C).** A FINGER is part of a HAND; a STRAND of hair is part of a head of HAIR.

33. **The correct answer is (A).** CONVEX, an outward curve, is the antonym of CONCAVE, an indented curve. Similarly, HILL and HOLE are antonyms.

34. **The correct answer is (B).** COWS produce MILK; BEES produce HONEY.

35. **The correct answer is (D).** EXERCISE aids weight REDUCTION; LUCK is an aid to WINNING.

36. **The correct answer is (A).** A PEAK is the top part of a MOUNTAIN; a CREST is the top of a WAVE.

37. **The correct answer is (A).** FOOD enables a BODY to do work; FUEL, such as gasoline, enables an ENGINE to work in a similar way.

38. **The correct answer is (A).** A BAROMETER measures atmospheric PRESSURE; a THERMOMETER measures TEMPERATURE.

39. **The correct answer is (C).** The words in each pair are antonyms.

40. **The correct answer is (B).** STUDIOUSLY is the adverb form of the verb STUDY; PLAYFULLY is the adverb form of the verb PLAY.

41. **The correct answer is (D).** The words in each pair are synonyms.

42. **The correct answer is (B).** Having an AVERSION to something may cause one to REJECT it; a PREFERENCE causes one to CHOOSE it.

43. **The correct answer is (A).** MEASLES is a kind of DISEASE; a FELONY is a kind of CRIME.

44. **The correct answer is (A).** The words in each pair are antonyms.

45. **The correct answer is (C).** The word ACTIVE is associated with MOBILITY, or movement; SEDENTARY is associated with IMMOBILITY, or lack of movement.

46. **The correct answer is (B).** An OPTIONAL item may be ELIMINATED; an ESSENTIAL one must be kept, or RETAINED.

47. **The correct answer is (C).** The words in each pair have similar meanings.

48. **The correct answer is (C).** Charter means to hire; CHARTER a PLANE, HIRE a PERSON.

49. **The correct answer is (A).** The prefixes SUPER- and SUB- have opposite meanings; similarly, INTRO- and EXTRO- are antonyms.

50. **The correct answer is (A).** The words of each pair have related but different meanings and similar pronunciations but different spellings.

51. **The correct answer is (D).** A PREMONITION is a feeling about the future; a PROPHESY is a statement about the future. HISTORY is what has happened in the past; ARCHIVES are the records of those happenings.

52. **The correct answer is (B).** COLLABORATION requires COOPERATION; similarly, QUIET is necessary for CONCENTRATION.

53. **The correct answer is (C).** REVERSION is the noun form of the verb REVERT; SYMPATHY is the noun form of the verb SYMPATHIZE.

54. **The correct answer is (A).** A COMMISSION is a percentage of sales paid to the SALESPERSON; a ROYALTY is a percentage of book sales paid to the AUTHOR.

55. **The correct answer is (A).** HARASSMENT causes ANGER; DISAPPOINTMENT causes SORROW.

56. **The correct answer is (B).** The words in each pair are synonyms.

57. **The correct answer is (C).** SODIUM is an element of SALT; OXYGEN is an element of WATER.

58. **The correct answer is (A).** The words in each pair are antonyms.

59. **The correct answer is (A).** The words in each pair are antonyms.

60. **The correct answer is (D).** A SWORD is the tool used for DUELING; a PEN is a tool used for WRITING.

61. **The correct answer is (B).** A REPRIMAND is a verbal show of DISAPPROVAL; a COMPLIMENT is a verbal show of APPROVAL.

62. **The correct answer is (C).** GOLD is a deep shade of YELLOW; ROYAL is a deep shade of BLUE.

63. **The correct answer is (D).** A PERIODIC event RECURS; a DETERMINED person PERSEVERES.

64. **The correct answer is (B).** ANARCHY occurs in the absence of LAW; DISCORD is the result of a lack of AGREEMENT.

65. **The correct answer is (A).** A CHANDELIER is attached to a CEILING; a PUPPET is held by a PUPPETEER.

66. **The correct answer is (C).** An ACCIDENT may be the result of CARELESSNESS; a RESPONSE may be the result of a STIMULUS.

67. **The correct answer is (D).** Something ERRONEOUS is in error and subject to CORRECTION; something AMBIGUOUS is confusing and subject to CLARIFICATION.

68. **The correct answer is (B).** HORSES were used for transportation before AUTOMOBILES; TELEGRAPHS were used for communication before TELEPHONES.

69. **The correct answer is (A).** The words in each pair are synonyms.

70. **The correct answer is (B).** The words in each pair are antonyms.

71. **The correct answer is (D).** CRITICS criticize PLAYS; REVIEWERS criticize BOOKS.

72. **The correct answer is (D).** A LION is a member of a PRIDE; a FISH is a member of a SCHOOL.

73. **The correct answer is (A).** A REFEREE enforces RULES; a CONSCIENCE enforces MORALITY.

74. **The correct answer is (C).** The second word in each pair refers to the theft of something represented by the first word in the pair.

75. **The correct answer is (D).** BOOKS consist of PAPER pages; SCROLLS are pieces of PARCHMENT.

SUMMING IT UP

- Verbal analogies test your ability to see a relationship between two words and to recognize a similar relationship between two other words.

- The key to analogy success is being able to express the relationship between the words in a pair—not what the words mean, but how they're related.

- Remember that the analogies get more difficult as you work your way through each group.

- Also remember that the relationship of the words in the answer must be in the same order as the relationship of the words in the first pair.

Sentence Completions (ISEE Only)

OVERVIEW

- **What makes a sentence completion?**
- **How do you answer sentence completion questions?**
- **What do smart test-takers know?**
- **Summing it up**

WHAT MAKES A SENTENCE COMPLETION?

Are you drawing a blank? Get used to it, because you'll see a lot of them in the sentence completion questions on the ISEE. In this kind of question, you are given a sentence that has one or more blanks. A number of words or pairs of words are suggested to fill in the blank spaces. It's up to you to select the word or pair of words that will best complete the meaning of the sentence.

Why are there sentence completion questions on the ISEE? Sentence completion questions test your vocabulary as well as your ability to understand what you read. In a typical sentence completion question, several of the choices *could* be inserted into the blank spaces. However, only one answer will make sense and carry out the full meaning of the sentence.

chapter 8

HOW DO YOU ANSWER SENTENCE COMPLETION QUESTIONS?

Are you ready to start filling in some of those blanks? The following six steps will help you answer sentence completion questions:

SENTENCE COMPLETIONS: GETTING IT RIGHT

1 Read the sentence carefully.

2 Guess at the answer.

3 Scan the answer choices for the word you guessed. If it's there, mark it and go on. If it's not, go on to Step 4.

4 Examine the sentence for clues to the missing word.

5 Eliminate any answer choices that are ruled out by the clues.

6 Try the ones that are left and pick whichever is best.

Now, let's try out these steps on a couple of sentence completion questions:

Q Those who feel that war is stupid and unnecessary think that to die on the battlefield is ____.
(A) courageous
(B) pretentious
(C) useless
(D) illegal

Following the steps outlined above:

1 Read the sentence.

2 Think of your own word to fill in the blank. You're looking for a word that completes the logic of the sentence. You might come up with something like *dumb*.

3 Look for *dumb* in the answer choices. It's not there, but *useless* is. That's pretty close, so mark it and go on.

4 If you couldn't guess the word, take your clue from the words *stupid* and *unnecessary* in the sentence. They definitely point toward some negative-sounding word.

5 The clues immediately eliminate choice (A), *courageous*, which is a positive word.

6 Try the remaining choices in the sentence, and you'll see that *useless* fits best.

> **Q** Unruly people may well become ____ if they are treated with ____ by those around them.
>
> **(A)** angry .. kindness
>
> **(B)** calm .. respect
>
> **(C)** peaceful .. abuse
>
> **(D)** interested .. medicine

1 Read the sentence. This time there are two blanks, and the missing words need to have some logical connection.

2 Think of your own words to fill in the blanks. You might guess that the unruly people will become *well-behaved* if they are treated with *consideration*.

3 Now look for your guesses in the answer choices. They're not there, but there are some possibilities.

4 Go back to the sentence and look for clues. *Become* signals that the unruly people will change their behavior. How that behavior changes will depend on how they are treated.

5 You can eliminate choice (A) because a negative behavior change (*angry*) doesn't logically follow a positive treatment (*kindness*). Likewise, you can eliminate choice (C) because a *peaceful* behavior change is not likely to follow from *abuse*. Finally, you can eliminate choice (D) because *interested* and *medicine* have no logical connection.

6 The only remaining choice is (B), which fits the sentence and must be the correct answer.

WHAT DO SMART TEST-TAKERS KNOW?

Thinking Up Your Own Answer Is the Way to Start

> **Q** Robert was extremely ____ when he received a B on the exam, for he was almost certain he had gotten an A.
>
> **(A)** elated
>
> **(B)** dissatisfied
>
> **(C)** fulfilled
>
> **(D)** harmful
>
> **A** **The correct answer is (B).** If you read this sentence carefully, you are likely to come up with the right answer, *dissatisfied*, on your own, But even if you didn't, you'd come up with something close, such as *upset* or *disappointed*. Then when you look at the answer choices, you will immediately see that the closest word is *dissatisfied*.

NOTE

Some words signal blanks that go with the flow:

- and
- also
- consequently
- as a result
- thus
- hence
- so
- for example

Identify Clue Words

If you can't come up with the missing word immediately, look for clue words in the surrounding sentence. Clue words can tell you "where the sentence is going." Is it continuing along one line of thought? If it is, you're looking for a word that supports that thought. Is it changing direction in midstream? Then you're looking for a word that sets up a contrast between the thoughts in the sentence.

Some Blanks Go with the Flow

The missing word may be one that supports another thought in the sentence, so you need to look for an answer that "goes with the flow."

Q The service at the restaurant was so slow that by the time the salad had arrived we were ____.

(A) ravenous

(B) excited

(C) incredible

(D) forlorn

A **The correct answer is (A).** Where is this sentence going? The restaurant service is very slow. That means you have to wait a long time for your food, and the longer you wait, the hungrier you'll get. So the word in the blank should be something that completes this train of thought. Answer choice (A), *ravenous*, which means very hungry, is the best answer. It works because it "goes with the flow."

Q As a teenager, John was withdrawn, preferring the company of books to that of people; consequently, as a young adult John was socially ____.

(A) successful

(B) uninhibited

(C) intoxicating

(D) inept

A **The correct answer is (D).** The word *consequently* signals that the second idea is an outcome of the first; so again, you are looking for a word that completes the train of thought. What might happen if you spent too much time with your nose stuck in a book (except for this one, of course)? Most likely you would be more comfortable with books than with people. Choice (D), *inept*, meaning awkward, is a good description of someone who lacks social graces, making this the right answer.

Q A decision that is made before all of the relevant data are collected can only be called ____.

(A) calculated

(B) laudable

(C) unbiased

(D) premature

A **The correct answer is (D).** The word *called* tells you that the blank is the word that the rest of the sentence describes. A decision that is made before all the facts are collected can only be described as *premature*, choice (D).

Some Blanks Shift Gears

The missing word may be one that reverses a thought in the sentence, so you need to look for an answer that "shifts gears."

Q The advance of science has demonstrated that a fact that appears to contradict a certain theory may actually be ____ a more advanced formulation of that theory.

(A) incompatible with

(B) in opposition to

(C) consistent with

(D) eliminated by

A **The correct answer is (C).** Look at the logical structure of the sentence. The sentence has set up a contrast between what appears to be and what is actually true. This indicates that the correct answer will "shift gears" and be the opposite of *contradict*. The choice *consistent with* provides this meaning. The other choices do not.

Q Although she knew that the artist's work was considered by some critics to be ____, the curator of the museum was anxious to acquire several of the artist's paintings for the museum's collection.

(A) insignificant

(B) important

(C) desirable

(D) successful

A **The correct answer is (A).** The very first word of the sentence, *although*, signals that the sentence is setting up a contrast between the critics and the curator. The critics had one opinion, but the curator had a different one. Since the curator liked the artworks well enough to acquire them, you can anticipate that the critics disliked the artworks. So the blank requires a word with negative connotations, and choice (A), *insignificant*, is the only one that works.

NOTE

Some words sig-
nal blanks that shift
gears:

- but
- yet
- although
- on the other hand
- in contrast
- however
- nevertheless

Q After witnessing several violent interactions between the animals, the anthropologist was forced to revise her earlier opinion that the monkeys were ____.

(A) peaceable

(B) quartersome

(C) insensitive

(D) prosperous

A The correct answer is (A). Where do you begin? The words "forced to revise" clearly signal a shift in the anthropologist's ideas. Her discovery that the monkeys were violent made her abandon an earlier contrasting opinion. Among the answer choices, the only contrast to *violent* is choice (A), *peaceable*.

The Right Answer Must Be Both Logical and Grammatically Correct

When answering sentence completion questions, you can always simply toss out any answer choices that do not make sense in the sentence or that would not be grammatically correct.

Q An advocate of consumer rights, Nader has spent much of his professional career attempting to ____ the fraudulent claims of American business.

(A) expose

(B) immortalize

(C) reprove

(D) import

A The correct answer is (A). What would you do with a fraudulent claim? Immortalize it? Import it? Not likely. These choices are not logical. The only logical answer is (A). You would *expose* a fraudulent claim.

ALERT!

Remember that more
than one answer
can seem to make
sense, but there is
only one correct
answer. Make your
best guess based on
the full meaning of
the sentence.

Q Despite the harsh tone of her comments, she did not mean to ____ any criticism of you personally.

(A) infer

(B) aim

(C) comply

(D) imply

A The correct answer is (D). *Imply* means "suggest indirectly." Choice (A), *infer*, is a word often confused with *imply*. It means "conclude from reasoning or implication." A speaker implies; a listener infers. Choice (C), *comply*, meaning "obey," makes no sense in this context. Choice (B), *aim*, is more likely, but it doesn't work in the sentence as given. You might say, "she did not mean to *aim* any criticism *at* you," but you would not normally say, "she did not mean to *aim* any criticism *of* you."

Two-Blank Questions Give You Two Ways to Get It Right

When there are two blanks in a sentence completion question, you have two ways to eliminate answer choices. You can start with either blank to eliminate choices that don't work. So pick the one that's easier for you. If you can eliminate just one of the words in a two-word answer choice, the whole choice won't work, so you can toss it out and go on.

TEST YOURSELF QUIZZES

Take the following quizzes to help you determine what your weaknesses might be. Answers can be found on page 185.

Test Yourself 1

Directions: Each of the following questions consists of an incomplete sentence followed by four words or pairs of words. Choose that word or pair of words which, when substituted for the blank space or spaces, *best* completes the meaning of the sentence, and circle the letter of your choice.

1. The Spanish dancer stamped her feet and ____ the rhythm with the click of ____.
   (A) ignored .. dice
   (B) kept .. cutlery
   (C) accented .. castanets
   (D) diffused .. a guitar

2. A bustling hospital floor is not ____ to a good night's sleep.
   (A) related
   (B) conducive
   (C) necessary
   (D) productive

3. The job applicant was so ____ as he approached the interview that his hands were ____ and his knees shook.
   (A) confident .. agitated
   (B) impressed .. clean
   (C) unhappy .. stiff
   (D) nervous .. clammy

4. A serious side effect of some drugs is recurrent ____.
   (A) elucidations
   (B) hallucinations
   (C) formulations
   (D) flagellations

5. Disgruntled ____ often become highly effective spies.
   (A) defectors
   (B) officers
   (C) anarchists
   (D) censors

6. I wish I could guarantee that the machine is ____ reliable, but in truth its performance is somewhat ____.
   (A) invariably .. sporadic
   (B) often .. skittish
   (C) serially .. erratic
   (D) consistently .. invincible

7. He extolled the juicy sweet fruit as being nothing less than ____.
   (A) surreal
   (B) saccharine
   (C) cloying
   (D) succulent

8. The military ____ of the burning buildings led the investigator to conclude that the fires had been set in an act of ____.
   (A) location .. arson
   (B) significance .. sabotage
   (C) stance .. sobriety
   (D) discipline .. treason

9. As the name of the prize winner was ____, the runner-up looked totally ____.
   (A) extolled .. exonerated
   (B) awarded .. devastated
   (C) announced .. crestfallen
   (D) proclaimed .. credulous

10. The unexploded device found rusting in the weeds must have been a ____.
    (A) bomb
    (B) decoy
    (C) calamity
    (D) dud

Test Yourself 2

Directions: Each of the following questions consists of an incomplete sentence followed by four words or pairs of words. Choose that word or pair of words which, when substituted for the blank space or spaces, *best* completes the meaning of the sentence, and circle the letter of your choice.

1. The professor ____ had had a long and distinguished career and was held in high ____ by her peers.
   (A) eminent .. stratosphere
   (B) emeritus .. esteem
   (C) lecturing .. tribute
   (D) triumphant .. spirits

2. A famous person will sometimes prepare his own ____ to be engraved on his tombstone.
   (A) epitaph
   (B) elegy
   (C) epithet
   (D) eulogy

3. Common examples of verbal redundancies include expressions such as ____ poor and ____ natives.
   (A) indignant .. indolent
   (B) indulgent .. industrious
   (C) insolvent .. iniquitous
   (D) indigent .. indigenous

4. The teacher's ____ tone of voice ____ that the threat was not to be taken seriously.
   (A) gruff .. belied
   (B) sprightly .. inferred
   (C) jocular .. implied
   (D) languid .. asserted

5. Collecting cans and bottles and redeeming them for the deposit provides a meager ____.
   (A) squalor
   (B) subsistence
   (C) subsidy
   (D) supplement

6. Recent trials of serial murderers reveal ____ behavior, including ____ and cannibalism.
   (A) lunatic .. manipulation
   (B) lethargic .. massacre
   (C) macabre .. torture
   (D) mercurial .. grimaces

7. As the bus rounded the curve, it ____ violently and caused some standees to lose their balance.
   (A) lunged
   (B) overturned
   (C) lurched
   (D) plummeted

8. The elderly gentleman was noticeably shaken when he read his own ____ in the local newspaper.
   (A) editorial
   (B) obituary
   (C) necromancy
   (D) necrology

9. We have narrowed our vacation options to two destinations, ____, the Florida Keys or a Caribbean island.
   (A) in fact
   (B) both
   (C) therefore
   (D) namely

10. The child appeared to be tall and ____, so his frequent absences for illness led the teacher to suspect that he was ____.
   (A) fat .. faking
   (B) ruddy .. sick
   (C) robust .. malingering
   (D) lanky .. truant

Test Yourself 3

Directions: Each of the following questions consists of an incomplete sentence followed by four words or pairs of words. Choose that word or pair of words which, when substituted for the blank space or spaces, *best* completes the meaning of the sentence, and circle the letter of your choice.

1. The speaker rose from his seat, placed his notes on the ____, and began his address.
   (A) platform
   (B) dais
   (C) rostrum
   (D) lectern

2. The senator's attitude so ____ the community that the various groups came to ____ one another.
   (A) energized .. contradict
   (B) antagonized .. respect
   (C) polarized .. despise
   (D) divided .. assist

3. It is ____ to tape record the testimony of a witness so as to have a(n) ____ record.

   (A) advisable .. verbatim

   (B) illegal .. accurate

   (C) permissible .. facsimile

   (D) prudent .. visible

4. The prodigy's grandmother felt ____ pleasure at her grandchild's piano success.

   (A) violent

   (B) vicarious

   (C) virtuous

   (D) vocal

5. Many people offered to adopt the ____ ____ who had been abandoned in the mall.

   (A) rabid .. mongrel

   (B) crippled .. cart

   (C) winsome .. waif

   (D) fluffy .. boa

6. The ____ costumes greatly increased the children's ____ as they witnessed their first ballet performance.

   (A) elaborate .. understanding

   (B) grotesque .. discomfort

   (C) fanciful .. delight

   (D) comfortable .. skill

7. The construction crew unexpectedly unearthed traces of a ____ unknown burial ground.

   (A) historically

   (B) hitherto

   (C) fortunately

   (D) persistently

8. I ____ my grandfather; to me he is the ____ of a gentleman.

   (A) idolize .. epitome

   (B) despise .. prototype

   (C) adore .. antithesis

   (D) excuse .. model

9. The young suspect was released on his own ____ with the ____ that he remains in school.

   (A) volition .. caveat

   (B) recognition .. promise

   (C) signature .. prerequisite

   (D) recognizance .. proviso

10. If a broken leg remains in a cast too long, the muscles may ____ from disuse.

    (A) petrify

    (B) exacerbate

    (C) atrophy

    (D) putrefy

Test Yourself 4

Directions: Each of the following questions consists of an incomplete sentence followed by four words or pairs of words. Choose that word or pair of words which, when substituted for the blank space or spaces, *best* completes the meaning of the sentence, and circle the letter of your choice.

1. The judge ____ the physician to refrain from using too much medical ____ in his statement.
   (A) admonished .. jargon
   (B) ordered .. literature
   (C) permitted .. economics
   (D) implored .. jingoism

2. I am not ____ to walking in the rain, ____ if given the option I will ride.
   (A) accustomed .. however
   (B) opposed .. therefore
   (C) averse .. nonetheless
   (D) agreeable .. moreover

3. The psychiatrist feared that the suspect might commit suicide, so the suspect was kept under 24-hour ____.
   (A) arrest
   (B) constraints
   (C) interrogation
   (D) surveillance

4. The statement "You're only young once" is a(n) ____.
   (A) spoof
   (B) truism
   (C) adage
   (D) motto

5. That rice pudding is most ____; it looks like a(n) ____ mass.
   (A) delicious .. gargantuan
   (B) unappetizing .. glutinous
   (C) cloying .. quivering
   (D) uninspiring .. esoteric

6. With the current rise of ____ feeling, ____ are being kept busy delineating the shifting boundaries.
   (A) entrepreneurial .. artists
   (B) antagonistic .. governments
   (C) cooperative .. economists
   (D) nationalistic .. cartographers

7. I sat in the park and listened to the ____ from the nearby church tower.
   (A) carillon
   (B) harangue
   (C) calliope
   (D) sycophant

8. In the hot summer months, our city's air is often ____ with the ____ murk of pollution.
   (A) endowed .. luminous
   (B) infused .. negligible
   (C) suffused .. oppressive
   (D) alleviated .. aromatic

9. Could you supply some examples to ____ your argument?
   (A) refute
   (B) bolster
   (C) destroy
   (D) exaggerate

10. I fear the discipline in that household is so ____ that the children will grow up without character.
    (A) rigid
    (B) ludicrous
    (C) attainable
    (D) lax

Test Yourself 5

Directions: Each of the following questions consists of an incomplete sentence followed by four words or pairs of words. Choose that word or pair of words which, when substituted for the blank space or spaces, *best* completes the meaning of the sentence, and circle the letter of your choice.

1. That strain of cancer is so ____ that no amount of treatment can ____ it.
   (A) abundant .. describe
   (B) capricious .. enhance
   (C) virulent .. destroy
   (D) arcane .. cure

2. He is a very ____ person, always carrying a rabbit's foot in his pocket as a(n) ____.
   (A) timorous .. omen
   (B) superstitious .. talisman
   (C) gullible .. charm
   (D) conscientious .. key ring

3. Sometimes the effect of a ____ meal is to make the diner very sleepy.
   (A) hearty
   (B) haughty
   (C) healthy
   (D) hasty

4. The ____ garden is ____ and fragrant.
   (A) formal .. overgrown
   (B) artificial .. infested
   (C) public .. forbidding
   (D) vernal .. verdant

5. The ____ vending machine spewed change all over the floor.
   (A) recalcitrant
   (B) zealous
   (C) hulking
   (D) rambunctious

6. The fire trucks arriving at the scene of the ____ created a massive traffic jam.
   (A) convocation
   (B) simulation
   (C) conflagration
   (D) mutiny

7. A ____ tends to rely on ____ evidence.
   (A) visionary .. prodigious
   (B) pragmatist .. empirical
   (C) jury .. spurious
   (D) scientist .. theoretical

8. I am pleased that I will be able to go swimming wearing my ____ watch.
   (A) aquamarine
   (B) digital
   (C) liquefied
   (D) submersible

9. Caring for younger siblings can be a(n) ____ responsibility for the child of a(n) ____.
   (A) onerous .. alcoholic
   (B) preordained .. acrobat
   (C) negligible .. supplicant
   (D) appreciable .. parent

10. The clergyman was so highly respected that no one could believe that he was a(n) ____.
    (A) transgressor
    (B) hemophiliac
    (C) executor
    (D) altruist

ANSWER KEY

Test Yourself 1

1. C	3. D	5. A	7. D	9. C
2. B	4. B	6. A	8. B	10. D

Test Yourself 2

1. B	3. D	5. B	7. C	9. D
2. A	4. C	6. C	8. B	10. C

Test Yourself 3

1. D	3. A	5. C	7. B	9. D
2. C	4. B	6. C	8. A	10. C

Test Yourself 4

1. A	3. D	5. B	7. A	9. B
2. C	4. B	6. D	8. C	10. D

Test Yourself 5

1. C	3. A	5. D	7. B	9. A
2. B	4. D	6. C	8. D	10. A

EXERCISES: SENTENCE COMPLETIONS

Directions: Fill in the correct answer from the choices given.

1. His theory is not ____; it only sounds plausible to the uninformed because he ____ several facts and fails to mention the mountain of evidence that contradicts his ideas.
   (A) tenable .. distorts
   (B) pliable .. pursued
   (C) predominant .. embellished
   (D) sufficient .. invokes

2. That organization ____ its concern for endangered species of wildlife by encouraging congresspeople to pass laws that ____ these animals.
   (A) imposes .. promote
   (B) manipulates .. defend
   (C) manifests .. protect
   (D) supplants .. prohibit

3. His filing system was so ____ that no one else in the department could locate material quickly.
   (A) specific
   (B) appropriate
   (C) intense
   (D) peculiar

4. When the last item on the ____ had been taken care of, the meeting was ____.
   (A) roster .. called to order
   (B) itinerary .. finalized
   (C) table .. sequestered
   (D) agenda .. adjourned

5. It has been predicted that the new ____ barring discrimination in employment on the basis of sexual orientation will dramatically ____ hiring practices.
   (A) morality .. effect
   (B) permissiveness .. reflect
   (C) legislation .. affect
   (D) rulings .. reset

6. The Navy scoured the area for over a month, but the ____ search turned up no clues.
   (A) cursory
   (B) fruitful
   (C) present
   (D) painstaking

7. Although her personality is sometimes ____, she is a conscientious worker and is ____ better treatment than she has received.
   (A) pleasing .. conscious of
   (B) abrasive .. entitled to
   (C) gloomy .. eligible for
   (D) cheerful .. granted

8. ____ manipulation of the stock market and other ____ practices in security sales resulted in the 1933 legislation for the control of security markets.
   (A) Degenerate .. lucrative
   (B) Economic .. useless
   (C) Continual .. productive
   (D) Unscrupulous .. unethical

9. The handbook ____ for beginners was written in an elementary style.
   (A) bound
   (B) intended
   (C) paged
   (D) authored

10. When a job becomes too ____, workers get ____, their attention wanders, and they start to make careless errors.
    (A) diverse .. busy
    (B) hectic .. lazy
    (C) tedious .. bored
    (D) fascinating .. interested

11. Because of her uncompromising stands on divisive issues, she was unable to ____ broad support among the voters; however, the minority who did support her were exceptionally ____.
    (A) alienate .. many
    (B) survey .. divided
    (C) cut across .. quiet
    (D) amass .. loyal

12. His remarks were too ____ to be taken seriously.
    (A) germane
    (B) crucial
    (C) pointed
    (D) insipid

13. No training course can operate to full advantage without job descriptions that ____ those parts of the job that require the most training before the training course is ____.
    (A) list .. improved
    (B) identify .. implemented
    (C) teach .. predicted
    (D) insulate .. finished

14. Since the course was not only ____ but also had a reputation for being extremely difficult, ____ students registered for it.
    (A) enjoyable .. many
    (B) required .. some
    (C) useful .. practical
    (D) optional .. few

15. The new secretary has a more businesslike manner than her ____ in the job.
    (A) precedent
    (B) ancestor
    (C) successor
    (D) predecessor

16. Because of the ____ hazard, regulations forbid the use of highly ____ materials in certain items such as children's pajamas.
    (A) health .. synthetic
    (B) fire .. flammable
    (C) drug .. inflammatory
    (D) chemical .. flame-retardant

17. The ____ report was submitted, subject to such ____ as would be made before the final draft.
    (A) preliminary .. revisions
    (B) ubiquitous .. submissions
    (C) ultimate .. editions
    (D) committee's .. references

18. ____ action on the part of a passerby revived the victim before brain damage could occur.
    (A) Physical
    (B) Prompt
    (C) Violent
    (D) Delayed

exercises

19. As the workload ____, she ____ responsibility for many routine tasks to an assistant.
    (A) evolved .. preserved
    (B) changed .. handled
    (C) increased .. delegated
    (D) steadied .. abased

20. For many years ____ have been recognized as breeding disease, juvenile delinquency, and crime, which not only threaten the health and welfare of people who live there but also ____ the structure of society as a whole.
    (A) prisons .. rebuild
    (B) schools .. disengage
    (C) colonialization .. alienate
    (D) slums .. weaken

21. As citizens we would be ____ if we did not make these facts public.
    (A) entitled
    (B) nominative
    (C) elective
    (D) derelict

22. A ____ in the diplomatic service, she had not yet ____ such a question of protocol.
    (A) success .. dispatched
    (B) volunteer .. avoided
    (C) veteran .. battered
    (D) novice .. encountered

23. Excessive fatigue can ____ be attributed to ____ working conditions such as poor lighting.
    (A) inevitably .. archaic
    (B) occasionally .. inadequate
    (C) always .. obsolete
    (D) never .. demoralizing

24. The company received a ____ from the government to help develop new sources of energy.
    (A) reward
    (B) compendium
    (C) memorandum
    (D) subsidy

25. The ____ with which the agent calmed the anxieties and soothed the tempers of the travelers ____ by the delay was a mark of frequent experience with similar crises.
    (A) evasiveness .. angered
    (B) reverence .. pleased
    (C) facility .. inconvenienced
    (D) mannerism .. destroyed

26. The greater the ____ of a mineral in an ore, the less it costs to refine it.
    (A) expense
    (B) weight
    (C) oxidation
    (D) concentration

27. The church had traditionally served as a ____ for debtors, and those ____ it were safe from prosecution.
    (A) prison .. leaving
    (B) blessing .. obeying
    (C) court .. denying
    (D) sanctuary .. entering

28. Today's students are encouraged to absorb facts rather than to apply ____. Education is becoming ____.
    (A) understanding .. regrettable
    (B) intelligence .. invaluable
    (C) knowledge .. passive
    (D) formulas .. extensive

29. Man's survival is a result of mutual assistance, since he is essentially ____ rather than ____.
    (A) superior .. inferior
    (B) cooperative .. competitive
    (C) individualistic .. gregarious
    (D) selfish .. stingy

30. Ancient Greeks were not only concerned with the development of the ____ but also felt training of the body was of ____ importance.
    (A) muscles .. equal
    (B) psyche .. little
    (C) mind .. prime
    (D) physical .. vital

31. Although for years ____ resources had been devoted to alleviating the problem, a satisfactory solution remained ____.
    (A) natural .. costly
    (B) adequate .. probable
    (C) substantial .. elusive
    (D) capital .. decisive

32. The police department will not accept for ____ a report of a person missing from his or her residence if such ____ is located outside of the city.
    (A) convenience .. location
    (B) control .. report
    (C) filing .. department
    (D) investigation .. residence

33. The treaty cannot go into effect until it has been ____ by the Senate.
    (A) considered
    (B) debated
    (C) ratified
    (D) shelved

34. His ____ of practical experience and his psychological acuity more than ____ his lack of formal academic training.
    (A) claims .. comprise
    (B) background .. educate for
    (C) brief .. account for
    (D) wealth .. compensate for

35. Because I wanted to use a(n) ____, I looked the word up in the ____.
    (A) synonym .. thesaurus
    (B) homonym .. directory
    (C) antonym .. encyclopedia
    (D) pseudonym .. dictionary

36. You will have to speak to the head of the department; I am not ____ to give out that information.
    (A) willing
    (B) authorized
    (C) programmed
    (D) happy

37. Research in that field has become so ____ that researchers on different aspects of the same problem may be ____ each other's work.
    (A) secure .. bombarded with
    (B) partial .. surprised at
    (C) departmental .. inimical to
    (D) specialized .. unfamiliar with

38. She ____ the way things were done, but many of the ____ for which she broke ground were left to be fully realized by others.
    (A) disliked .. provocations
    (B) eliminated .. foundations
    (C) implemented .. buildings
    (D) revolutionized .. innovations

39. A change in environment is very likely to ____ a change in one's work habits.
  (A) affect
  (B) inflict
  (C) propose
  (D) effect

40. A shift to greater use of ____ or inexhaustible resources in the production of power would slow the depletion of ____ fuel materials.
  (A) synthetic .. regional
  (B) natural .. chemical
  (C) renewable .. irreplaceable
  (D) unknown .. fossil

41. A ____ is likely to give you ____ advice.
  (A) fool .. useful
  (B) doctor .. lethal
  (C) friend .. harmful
  (D) charlatan .. unreliable

42. An accident report should be written as soon as possible after the necessary ____ has been obtained.
  (A) bystander
  (B) formulation
  (C) information
  (D) permission

43. To protect the respondents' ____, names and social security numbers are ____ the questionnaires before the results are tabulated.
  (A) privilege .. referred to
  (B) privacy .. deleted from
  (C) information .. retained in
  (D) rights .. appended to

44. While fewer documents are being kept, the usefulness of those ____ is now ____ by an improved cataloging system.
  (A) printed .. documented
  (B) discarded .. concurred
  (C) read .. emblazoned
  (D) retained .. insured

45. The man ____ the speaker at the meeting by shouting false accusations.
  (A) corrected
  (B) argued with
  (C) disconcerted
  (D) interfered with

46. For the sake of public ____, public officials should avoid even the ____ of a conflict of interest.
  (A) confidence .. appearance
  (B) relations .. actuality
  (C) appearances .. apparition
  (D) commotion .. hint

47. A professional journalist will attempt to ____ the facts learned in an interview by independent ____.
  (A) endorse .. questions
  (B) query .. situation
  (C) garnish .. sources
  (D) verify .. investigation

48. The ____ of the award stopped by the financial aid office to pick up his check.
  (A) recipient
  (B) subject
  (C) donor
  (D) sponsor

49. He often, out of modesty, _____ his own contribution; without his efforts, _____, the program would still be in the planning stage.

(A) affirms .. therefore

(B) represses .. notwithstanding

(C) belittles .. however

(D) rescinds .. moreover

50. The committee was so _____ about the legitimate sources of the students' unrest that its recommendations were _____ value.

(A) incensed .. of moderate

(B) uninformed .. devoid of

(C) uninterested .. depreciating in

(D) blasé .. of incontestable

ANSWER KEY AND EXPLANATIONS

1. A	11. D	21. D	31. C	41. D
2. C	12. D	22. D	32. D	42. C
3. D	13. B	23. B	33. C	43. B
4. D	14. D	24. D	34. D	44. D
5. C	15. D	25. C	35. A	45. C
6. D	16. B	26. D	36. B	46. A
7. B	17. A	27. D	37. D	47. D
8. D	18. B	28. C	38. D	48. A
9. B	19. C	29. B	39. D	49. C
10. C	20. D	30. C	40. C	50. B

1. **The correct answer is (A).** The first blank might be filled equally well by the first term of choice (A) or choice (D); however, the coordinating "and" implies that the second blank must be filled with something negative that he does to the facts. DISTORTS is the best word here.

2. **The correct answer is (C).** Choice (D) makes no sense. "Encouraging" is not a coercive type of activity, so choices (A) and (B) would be too forceful as completions in the first blank.

3. **The correct answer is (D).** If no one else could locate the material, you may be pretty sure that his filing system was PECULIAR.

4. **The correct answer is (D).** The list of items for consideration at a meeting is the AGENDA. When the business is completed, one might as well ADJOURN the meeting.

5. **The correct answer is (C).** The barring of discrimination is an official act, so only choice (C) or choice (D) could fill the first blank. The second blank is best filled with the idiomatic "AFFECT hiring practices."

6. **The correct answer is (D).** A search that lasts more than a month is most certainly a PAINSTAKING one.

7. **The correct answer is (B).** The first blank calls for a negative trait to contrast with her conscientiousness. Choices (B) and (C) might both be correct, but ENTITLED TO better fits the informality of the sentence. "Eligible for" implies a legal requirement.

8. **The correct answer is (D).** The coordinating "and" in the compound subject requires that both words have the same connotation. Since these acts led to the imposition of controls, we must assume that they were negative acts.

9. **The correct answer is (B).** The style of a manual must be appropriate to the audience for which it is INTENDED.

10. **The correct answer is (C).** The key here is that the workers' attention wanders. Attention wanders when one is BORED. One becomes BORED when the work is TEDIOUS.

11. **The correct answer is (D).** Only AMASS really makes sense in the first blank.

12. **The correct answer is (D).** Any remarks other than stupid or INSIPID ones should be taken seriously.

13. **The correct answer is (B).** The second blank can be filled only by choice (B) or choice (D). Choice (D) makes no sense in the first blank.

14. **The correct answer is (D).** The "not only .. but also" construction implies two complementary reasons why a classification of students might register for the course. Only choice (D) really fits this requirement. A course that is OPTIONAL and very difficult will draw FEW registrants.

15. **The correct answer is (D).** The person who held this job before the current secretary was her PREDECESSOR.

16. **The correct answer is (B).** Only choice (A) or choice (B) makes sense in the first blank. Synthetics are not in themselves a health hazard.

17. **The correct answer is (A).** The report was submitted before the final draft. Only choice (A) or choice (D) can describe the report. A report is not made subject to references; it is made subject to REVISIONS before the final draft.

18. **The correct answer is (B).** Since the action was taken before brain damage could occur, the best completion implies speed.

19. **The correct answer is (C).** The best thing to do with excess responsibility is to DELEGATE it.

20. **The correct answer is (D).** The second blank must be filled by a negative word. This limits the answer to choices (B), (C), and (D). Of the three first-term choices, only SLUMS are recognized as the breeding grounds of disease, juvenile delinquency, and crime.

21. **The correct answer is (D).** The structure of the sentence leaves only choice (D) as a sensible completion.

22. **The correct answer is (D).** The words "not yet" imply that she was new to or a NOVICE in the diplomatic service.

23. **The correct answer is (B).** Excessive fatigue can often be attributed to factors other than inhospitable working conditions, but OCCASIONALLY, INADEQUATE working conditions are its cause.

24. **The correct answer is (D).** Money helps in the development of new processes and products. A SUBSIDY is money received in advance of the work. Rewards and honoraria follow a service.

25. **The correct answer is (C).** The blanks could be filled with choices (A) or (C). However, frequent experience should lead to FACILITY in soothing INCONVENIENCED travelers, so choice (C) is the best answer.

26. **The correct answer is (D).** It is reasonable to assume that a more CONCENTRATED ore would yield a greater quantity of the mineral and would thus be more cost efficient.

27. **The correct answer is (D).** The word "and" connecting the two clauses implies that safety from prosecution applies to the church. A SANCTUARY is a place for refuge and protection, and all who ENTER it are safe.

28. **The correct answer is (C).** Absorption of facts is PASSIVE, as opposed to the more active mode of education, the application of KNOWLEDGE.

29. **The correct answer is (B).** The sentence, by the words "rather than," requires that the two words filling the blanks be opposites. Only choice (D) does not meet this requirement. However, mutual assistance implies COOPERATION; hence choice (B) is the correct answer.

30. **The correct answer is (C).** The sentence requires that the first blank be filled by a word that contrasts with body. Of the choices, MIND, choice (C), best meets this criterion.

31. **The correct answer is (C).** The construction of the sentence demands that the first blank be filled with a positive word while the second is filled with a less positive word. Choice (C) best fits these requirements.

32. The correct answer is (D). A missing-person report demands INVESTIGATION.

33. The correct answer is (C). All the consideration, amending, and debate will not put a treaty into effect until it is RATIFIED.

34. The correct answer is (D). The words in the blanks should contrast with his lack of formal academic training.

35. The correct answer is (A). The THESAURUS is a book of SYNONYMS.

36. The correct answer is (B). All choices except (C) might be correct, but the imperative of "you will have to" implies that I am not AUTHORIZED.

37. The correct answer is (D). No enmity is implied in this sentence, so choice (D) is a better answer than choice (C).

38. The correct answer is (D). One might break ground for choices (B), (C), or (D), but only INNOVATIONS for which one breaks ground are fully realized by others.

39. The correct answer is (D). To EFFECT is to cause. Inflict has a negative connotation that is uncalled for in this sentence.

40. The correct answer is (C). Fuel materials that could be depleted are either choice (C) or choice (D). Only choice (C) fits into the first blank. The use of RENEWABLE resources would slow the depletion of IRREPLACEABLE fuel materials.

41. The correct answer is (D). The type of advice must be appropriate to the giver. The advice of a CHARLATAN or imposter is likely to be UNRELIABLE.

42. The correct answer is (C). An accident report should be dependent only upon INFORMATION and not upon permission or certificates.

43. The correct answer is (B). DELETION of identification insures PRIVACY.

44. The correct answer is (D). If fewer documents are being kept, we are probably discussing those that are RETAINED. Their usefulness is INSURED by an improved cataloging system.

45. The correct answer is (C). The man would have interfered with the speaker even if he had shouted words of agreement. Since the point is made that the man shouted false accusations, the best answer is that he DISCONCERTED the speaker.

46. The correct answer is (A). The second blank could be filled with choice (A) or choice (D); however, the first term of choice (D) makes no sense in the first blank.

47. The correct answer is (D). VERIFICATION is at the heart of professionalism.

48. The correct answer is (A). Only the RECIPIENT would pick up the check.

49. The correct answer is (C). Modesty would lead one to BELITTLE one's role. The connective HOWEVER makes the best transition between the two clauses.

50. The correct answer is (B). The second blank might be filled by all choices except (C). However, the two terms of choice (D) make no sense in apposition. Choice (A) is not the correct answer. The committee might have been incensed about the students' unrest but it would be unlikely to be incensed about the legitimate causes of that unrest. If it were UNINFORMED of the legitimate causes, its recommendations would be DEVOID OF value.

SUMMING IT UP

Review this page the night before you take your high school entrance exam. It will help you get the answers to verbal ability questions.

Synonyms

- These four steps will help you answer synonym questions:

  1 Read the question carefully. Consider *every* answer choice.

  2 Eliminate obviously wrong responses immediately.

  3 Use word-analysis techniques to help you with difficult words.

  4 Try using the word in a sentence of your own; think about the meaning of the word as you have used it.

- The correct answer may not be a perfect synonym, but it will be the *best* choice.

- The correct choice might be the easiest word. Do *not* choose a word just because you do not know it.

- Synonym questions are arranged from easy to hard.

Verbal Analogies

- These five steps will help you solve analogy questions:

  1 Figure out how the first two words are related.

  2 Make up a sentence that expresses that relationship.

  3 Try out your sentence on each answer choice and eliminate the ones that don't work.

  4 If you're left with more than one answer—or no answer at all—go back and make your sentence fit better.

  5 Choose the best answer.

- Remember the sentence connection. Create a sentence that summarizes the relationship between the original analogy words. Use the sentence to test the answer choices.

- The order of the relationship must be the same in both pairs.

- Some common verbal analogy categories are:
  SYNONYMS
  ANTONYMS
  PART-WHOLE
  NOUN-VERB

CAUSE-AND-EFFECT

PURPOSE

ASSOCIATION

TYPE OF

PART OF THE DEFINITION OF

LACK OF SOMETHING IS PART OF THE DEFINITION

A PLACE FOR

DEGREE

- Analogies are arranged from easy to hard.

Sentence Completions

- These six steps will help you as you work through this section:

  1 Read the sentence carefully.

  2 Guess at the answer.

  3 Scan the answer choices for the word you guessed. If it's there, mark it and go on. If it's not, go on to Step 4.

  4 Examine the sentence for clues to the missing word.

  5 Eliminate any answer choices that are ruled out by the clues.

  6 Try the ones that are left and pick whichever is best.

- Be alert for clues in the sentence. Look for negative words or positive words.

- Sentence completion questions go from easy to hard.

PART V
READING REVIEW

Reading Comprehension (SSAT and ISEE)

chapter 9

OVERVIEW

- **Why is my reading ability being tested?**
- **What kinds of questions will be asked?**
- **How do you answer reading comprehension questions?**
- **What do smart test-takers know?**
- **Summing it up**

WHY IS MY READING ABILITY BEING TESTED?

Reading is a prerequisite to learning, and it is evaluated by all aptitude, admissions, and achievement tests.

WHAT KINDS OF QUESTIONS WILL BE ASKED?

The questions that follow each passage are in the standard multiple-choice format with either four (ISEE) or five (SSAT) answer choices. On high school entrance exams, the questions tend to fall into four categories. These questions ask you to do one of the following:

- Identify the main idea or the author's purpose.
- Locate details that support the main idea.
- Define a word based on its meaning in the passage.
- Draw inferences from ideas in the passage.

Main Idea

This type of question presents several titles or phrases and asks you to choose the one that best expresses the main idea of the passage. Main ideas often can be found in a topic sentence. Topic sentences usually appear in the first paragraph, as part of the introduction, or in the last paragraph, as a summary.

Q The social standing of a wife in colonial days was determined by the standing of her husband as well as by her own ability and resourcefulness. She married not only a husband but also a career. Her position in the community was established in part by the quality of the bread she baked, by the food she preserved for the winter's use, by the whiteness of her washing on the line, by the way her children were clothed, and by her skill in nursing. Doctors were scarce. In case of the illness or death of a neighbor, a woman would put aside her own work to help, and she was honored for what she could do.

The title that best expresses the main idea of this selection is

(A) "Care of Children in Colonial Times."

(B) "Community Spirit."

(C) "Medical Care in Pre-Revolutionary Times."

(D) "The Colonial Housewife."

A **The correct answer is (D).** This selection describes the various home-making duties a colonial woman was expected to perform.

Details

Details are the facts and ideas in a selection that explain and support the main idea.

Q There are many signs by which people predict the weather. Some of these have a true basis, but many have not. There is, for example, no evidence that it is more likely to storm during one phase of the moon than during another. If it happens to rain on Easter, there is no reason to think that it will rain for the next seven Sundays. The groundhog may or may not see his shadow on Groundhog Day, but it probably won't affect the weather anyway.

Which of the following is NOT listed as a predictive weather phenomenon?

(A) Rain on Easter

(B) The phases of the moon

(C) Pain in a person's joints

(D) The groundhog's shadow

A **The correct answer is (C).** The other choices were mentioned in the passage.

Vocabulary

This type of question, sometimes called "words in context," asks you to choose a synonym for one of the words in the passage.

> **Q** The maritime and fishing industries find perhaps 250 *applications* for rope and cordage. There are hundreds of different sizes, constructions, tensile strengths, and weights in rope and twine. Rope is sold by the pound but ordered by length and is measured by circumference rather than by diameter.
>
> In this context, the word *applications* means
>
> **(A)** uses.
>
> **(B)** descriptions.
>
> **(C)** sizes.
>
> **(D)** types.
>
> **A** **The correct answer is (A).** Try it in the sentence in place of the word *application:* "Uses" makes sense in that context and keeps the meaning of the sentence intact.

Inference

An inference is a conclusion that is drawn from the details in a reading selection. The answer to an inferential question will not be found in the passage and is therefore the most difficult type of comprehension question to answer. You must read carefully and think logically in order to draw the correct conclusion from the information given.

> **Q** The facts, as we see them, on drug use and the dangerous behaviors caused by drugs are that some people do get into trouble while using drugs, and some of those drug users are dangerous to others. Sometimes a drug is a necessary element in order for a person to commit a crime, although it may not be the cause of his or her criminality. On the other hand, the use of a drug sometimes seems to be the only convenient explanation by means of which the observer can account for the undesirable behavior.
>
> The author apparently feels that
>
> **(A)** the use of drugs always results in crime.
>
> **(B)** drugs and crime are only sometimes related.
>
> **(C)** the relationship of drug use to crime is purely coincidental.
>
> **(D)** drugs are usually an element in accidents and suicides.
>
> **A** **The correct answer is (B).** The author states that drugs are sometimes a necessary element in a crime, but at other times is just an excuse for criminal behavior.

TIP

Don't go for the ordinary.
Vocabulary-in-context questions seldom test the most common meaning of a word. Look for a meaning that is not the usual one.

HOW DO YOU ANSWER READING COMPREHENSION QUESTIONS?

Success with reading comprehension questions requires both speed in reading and efficiency in answering questions.

Two important techniques that you must master are:

1 Skimming
2 Scanning

Skimming

Skimming is a form of speed-reading that is useful for extracting the main idea and supporting details from a reading selection. As you skim a passage, pay special attention to the first and last sentences or paragraphs. The purpose of skimming is to locate the topic sentence, the main idea, and some of the major supporting details. This overview of the location of information within the passage will help you to answer the more difficult inference questions quickly.

Scanning

Scanning is a method of looking for specific information without truly reading but by looking for key words. The following six steps will help you answer reading comprehension questions.

READING COMPREHENSION: GETTING IT RIGHT

1 Read through the questions quickly. This will guide your reading by showing you what information you will be expected to find. Skip over the answer choices for now.

2 Read the passage.

3 Answer vocabulary questions first. Find the answers by scanning the passage.

4 Answer detail questions next. Pick a key word or two from the question itself and scan the passage until you find it. The sentence in which the word appears probably contains the answer to the question.

5 Answer main-idea questions by reading the first and last sentences of the passage.

6 Leave inference questions for last. Skim the passage. Eliminate choices that are obviously wrong. Take your best guess.

WHAT DO SMART TEST-TAKERS KNOW?

Reading comprehension questions can eat up your time very quickly. Check out these tips for smarter solutions.

You Only Have Time to Read Each Passage Once

Because there's only time to read each passage once, you'll want to answer every question that you can about the passage before moving on. If you skip a question and try to come back to it later, you might have to reread the whole passage to find the answer and you'll be out of time. Guess if you have to, but finish all the questions that you can.

Everything You Need to Know Is Right There in Front of You

The introductory paragraph and the passage have all the information you'll need to answer the questions. Even if the passage is about the price of beans in Bulgaria or the genetic makeup of a wombat, don't worry. It's all right there on the page.

The Passages Are Supposed to Be Unfamiliar

In order to put all candidates on a level playing field, test-makers choose obscure reading passages. ISEE passages draw upon social studies and the sciences; SSAT passages cover more general topics or come from literature. Either way, you probably have not seen the reading material before, and it doesn't matter. Remember, you're not being tested on your knowledge of the topic, but on how well you:

- Figure out the meaning of an unfamiliar word from its context.
- Determine what an author means by noting certain words and phrases.
- Understand the author's assumptions, point of view, and main idea.

Passages That Interest You Are Easier for You to Work On

If there's a choice, it's best to start with the passage that's more interesting to you, whether it's fiction, a science article, or whatever. If the style appeals to you, you will probably go through the passage more quickly and find the questions easier to deal with.

It Pays to Be an Active Reader

Since you've already scanned the questions, you know what to look for as you read. When you find these points, use your pencil to underline or circle them. You'll be able to find them easily when you need them to answer the questions.

ALERT!

Don't let unfamiliar topics throw you. There's no need to worry whether you know anything about a topic in a passage. The answers are based on the information in the passage, not on your knowledge or experience.

NOTE

Reading comprehension takes a lot of time, but there is a way to go faster. Read the questions first so you know what to look for as you read the passage. Then you won't have to read things twice to find the information you need.

Details Can Bog You Down

Remember, you don't have to understand every bit of information. You just have to find the information you need to answer the questions. Don't waste your time on technical details or on information that the questions don't ask for.

What's True Is Not Necessarily the Answer

What does that mean? It means that a certain answer choice may be perfectly true, but it might not be the correct answer to the question that's being asked. Read carefully—and don't be fooled!

You Can Solve Vocabulary-in-Context Questions by Plugging in Choices

For vocabulary-in-context questions, plug the choices into the original sentence and don't be fooled by the obvious synonym.

The Answer to a Main Idea Question Is Neither Too General Nor Too Specific

For a question about the main idea or the author's purpose, look for an answer choice that states it. Don't be too general or too specific.

The Answer to a Main Idea Question Is Often in the First or Last Paragraph

Look in the first or last (or both) paragraph of the passage for answers to main idea/author's purpose questions.

You Have to Read between the Lines

When a reading comprehension question asks for something the author has suggested, implied, or not stated directly, you have to use the information in the passage and draw your own conclusions. Read between the lines to see if the author has given any hints that would lead you to the correct answer.

TEST YOURSELF QUIZZES

Take the following quizzes to help you determine what weaknesses you might have. Answers can be found on pages 221–222.

Test Yourself 1

Directions: Read the following passage and then decide which of the responses is the best answer to each question. Circle the letter that appears before your answer.

Early in the nineteenth century, American youths were playing a game, somewhat like the English game of rounders, which contained
(5) all the elements of modern baseball. It was neither scientifically planned nor skillfully played, but it furnished considerable excitement for players and spectators alike. The playing
(10) field was a sixty-foot square with goals, or bases, at each of its four corners. A pitcher stationed himself at the center of the square, and a catcher and an indefinite number of
(15) fielders supported the pitcher and completed the team. None of these players, usually between eight and twenty on a side, covered the bases. The batter was out on balls caught
(20) on the fly or the first bound, and a base runner was out if he was hit by a thrown ball while off base. The bat was nothing more than a stout paddle with a two-inch-thick handle. The ball
(25) was apt to be an impromptu affair composed of a bullet, cork, or metal slug tightly wound with wool yarn and string. With its simple equipment and only a few rules, this game steadily
(30) increased in popularity during the first half of the century.

1. The title that best expresses the main idea of this selection is
   (A) "Baseball Rules."
   (B) "An English Game."
   (C) "Baseball's Predecessor."
   (D) "American Pastimes."

2. The rules of this game required
   (A) eight fielders.
   (B) a pitcher, a catcher, and one fielder for each base.
   (C) twenty fielders.
   (D) no specific number of players.

3. This selection suggests that
   (A) the game of baseball has grown more complicated over the years.
   (B) the game described was very dangerous.
   (C) baseball originated in the United States.
   (D) the game described required skilled players.

4. The word *impromptu* in line 25 means
   (A) carefully planned.
   (B) careless.
   (C) informal.
   (D) skillful.

Test Yourself 2

Directions: Read the following passage and then decide which of the responses is the best answer to each question. Circle the letter that appears before your answer.

John J. Audubon, a bird watcher, once noticed that a pair of phoebes nested in the same place year after year, and he wondered if they might
(5) be the same birds. He put tiny silver bands on their legs, and the next spring the banded birds returned to the same nesting place.

This pair of phoebes were the first
(10) birds to be banded. Since that time, naturalists, with the aid of the federal government's Fish and Wildlife Department, band birds in an effort to study them. The bands, which are
(15) made of lightweight aluminum so as not to harm the birds, bear a message requesting finders to notify the department. Careful records of these notifications are kept and analyzed.
(20) In this way, naturalists have gained a great deal of knowledge about the nesting habits, migration patterns, and populations of a large variety of bird species. Most importantly, they
(25) are able to identify those species that are in danger of extinction.

1. The title below that best expresses the main idea of this passage is
   (A) "The Migration of Birds."
   (B) "One Method of Studying Birds."
   (C) "The Habits of Birds."
   (D) "The Work of John Audubon."

2. Audubon's purpose in banding the phoebes was to
   (A) satisfy his own curiosity.
   (B) start a government study of birds.
   (C) gain fame as the first birdbander.
   (D) chart the phoebe's migration patterns.

3. Audubon proved his theory that
   (A) silver and aluminum are the best metals for birdbands.
   (B) the government should study birds.
   (C) phoebes are the most interesting birds to study.
   (D) birds return to the same nesting place each spring.

4. The word *habits* in line 22 means
   (A) naturalists.
   (B) living environments.
   (C) behaviors.
   (D) ecosystem.

Test Yourself 3

Directions: Read the following passage and then decide which of the responses is the best answer to each question. Circle the letter that appears before your answer.

A vast stretch of land lies untouched by civilization in the back country of the eastern portion of the African continent. With the occasional excep-
(5) tion of a big-game hunter, foreigners never penetrate this area. Aside from the Wandorobo tribe, even the natives shun its confines because it harbors the deadly tsetse fly. The
(10) Wandorobo nomads depend on the forest for their lives, eating its roots and fruits and making their homes wherever they find themselves at the end of the day.
(15)   One of the staples of their primitive diet, and their only sweet, is honey. They obtain it through an ancient, symbiotic relationship with a bird known as the Indicator. The scien-
(20) tific community finally confirmed the report, at first discredited, that this bird purposefully led the natives to trees containing the honeycombs of wild bees. Other species of honey
(25) guides are also known to take advantage of the foraging efforts of some animals in much the same way that the Indicator uses men.
         This amazing bird settles in a
(30) tree near a Wandorobo encampment and chatters incessantly until the men answer it with whistles. It then begins its leading flight. Chattering, it hops from tree to tree, while the
(35) men continue their musical answering call. When the bird reaches the tree, its chatter becomes shriller and its followers examine the tree carefully. The Indicator usually perches
(40) just over the honeycomb, and the men hear the humming of the bees in the hollow trunk. Using torches, they smoke most of the bees out of the tree, but those that escape the
(45) nullifying effects of the smoke sting

the men viciously. Undaunted, the Wandorobos free the nest, gather the honey, and leave a small offering for their bird guide.

1. The word *symbiotic* is synonymous with
   (A) partnership.
   (B) adversary.
   (C) parasitic.
   (D) opponent.

2. According to the selection, one characteristic of the Wandorobo tribe is that its members
   (A) avoid the country of the tsetse fly.
   (B) have no permanent homes.
   (C) lack physical courage.
   (D) live entirely on a diet of honey.

3. The title that best expresses the topic of this selection is
   (A) "Life in the African Backwoods."
   (B) "The Wandorobo Tribe."
   (C) "Locating a Honeycomb."
   (D) "Men and Birds Work Together."

4. The word *incessantly* in line 31 means
   (A) intermittently.
   (B) loudly.
   (C) constantly.
   (D) strangely.

Test Yourself 4

Directions: Read the following passage and then decide which of the responses is the best answer to each question. Circle the letter that appears before your answer.

The proud, noble American eagle appears on one side of the Great Seal of the United States, which is printed on every dollar bill. The same majestic
(5) bird can be seen on state seals, half dollars, and even in some commercial advertising. In fact, though we often encounter artistic representations of our national symbol, it is rarely seen
(10) alive in its native habitat. It is now all but extinct.

In the days of the founding fathers, the American eagle resided in nearly every corner of the territory now
(15) known as the continental United States. Today the eagle survives in what ornithologists call significant numbers only in two regions. An estimated 350 pairs inhabit Florida,
(20) and perhaps another 150 live in the Chesapeake Bay area of Delaware, Maryland, and Virginia. A few stragglers remain in other states, but in most, eagles have not been sighted
(25) for some time.

A federal law passed in 1940 protects these birds and their nesting areas, but it came too late to save more than a pitiful remnant of the
(30) species' original population.

1. An ornithologist is a person who studies
   (A) geographical regions.
   (B) the history of extinct species.
   (C) the populations of certain areas.
   (D) the habits and habitats of birds.

2. Today eagles are found in the greatest numbers in
   (A) Florida.
   (B) Delaware.
   (C) the Chesapeake Bay region.
   (D) Virginia.

3. The selection implies that
   (A) the number of eagles is likely to increase.
   (B) the eagle population decreased because of a lack of protective game laws.
   (C) there were only two localities where eagles could survive.
   (D) the government knows very little about eagles.

Test Yourself 5

Directions: Read the following passage and then decide which of the responses is the best answer to each question. Circle the letter that appears before your answer.

The Alaska Highway, which runs 1,523 miles from Dawson Creek, British Columbia, to Fairbanks, Alaska, was built by U.S. Army Engineers
(5) to counter a threatened Japanese invasion of Alaska. It was rushed through in an incredibly short period of nine months and was therefore never properly surveyed. Some of
(10) the territory it passes through has not even been explored.

Although the story that the builders followed the trail of a wandering moose is probably not true, the ef-
(15) fect is much the same. The leading bulldozer simply crashed through the brush wherever the going was easiest, avoiding the big trees, swampy hollows, and rocks. The project was
(20) made more complicated by the necessity of following not the shortest or easiest route but one that would serve the string of United States-Canadian airfields that stretch from Montana
(25) to Alaska. Even on flat land, the road twists into hairpin curves. In rough terrain it goes up and down like a roller coaster. In the mountains, sometimes clinging to the sides of
(30) cliffs 400 feet high, it turns sharply, without warning, and gives rear seat passengers the stomach-gripping sensation of taking off into space. There is not a guardrail in its entire
(35) 1,500-mile length. Dust kicks up in giant plumes behind every car and on windless days hovers in the air like a thick fog.

Both the Canadian Army and the
(40) Alaskan Road Commission, which took over from the Army Engineers in 1946, do a commendable but nearly impossible job of maintaining the road. Where it is built on eternally frozen
(45) ground, it buckles and heaves, on

the jellylike muskeg it is continually sinking and must be graveled afresh every month. Bridges thrown across rivers are swept away in flash floods.
(50) Torrential thaws wash out miles of highway every spring. On mountainsides, you can tell the age of the road by counting the remains of earlier roads that have slipped down the slope.

1. The title that best expresses the main idea of this selection is
   (A) "The Alaskan Road Commission."
   (B) "Building and Maintaining the Alaska Highway."
   (C) "Exploring Alaska."
   (D) "Driving Conditions in the Far North."

2. The Alaska Highway was built to
   (A) make the route between Alaska and the States shorter.
   (B) promote trade with Canada.
   (C) meet a wartime emergency.
   (D) aid exploration and surveying efforts.

3. The job of maintaining the road is complicated by the
   (A) threat of invasion.
   (B) forces of nature.
   (C) lack of surveying.
   (D) age of the road.

4. The word *terrain* in line 27 refers to
   (A) geographical features of the land.
   (B) geographical mountains and valleys.
   (C) a specific land area.
   (D) swamps.

Test Yourself 6

Directions: Read the following passage and then decide which of the responses is the best answer to each question. Circle the letter that appears before your answer.

When the first white men came to North America, they found an abundance of valuable natural resources. Forests covered enormous areas; the
(5) soil was extremely fertile; and the forests, prairies, streams, and rivers abounded with wildlife. Later, huge quantities of gas, oil, and minerals were discovered.

(10) These resources were so vast that it seemed they could never be exhausted. The forests were cleared for farmland. Grasslands and prairies were plowed and planted with crops.
(15) Mammals and birds were hunted for food and sport, and eventually factories, mills, and power companies were built on nearly every river. Minerals and oil were used to supply and power
(20) a young industrial nation.

The effects of these actions became apparent within a relatively short period of time. Timber shortages were predicted. The fertile soil was
(25) washed away by rain and blown about in great dust storms by the wind. Several species of birds began to disappear, and some of the great mammals became extinct.

(30) Many rivers were made unfit for fish by the pollution of factories. The seemingly inexhaustible stores of oil and minerals began to show signs of depletion.

(35) Since that time, Americans have sponsored the creation of conservation programs in the hope that future generations may continue to share and enjoy the natural resources that
(40) are part of our heritage.

1. The title that best expresses the main idea of this selection is
   (A) "The First White Men in America."
   (B) "The Loss of America's Natural Resources."
   (C) "Our American Heritage."
   (D) "The Cause of Our Timber Shortages."

2. The word *depletion* in line 34 means
   (A) extinction.
   (B) running out.
   (C) having the quality of being inexhaustible.
   (D) destruction.

3. It seemed to the early settlers that
   (A) there was a shortage of minerals.
   (B) there had been a great deal of soil erosion.
   (C) the natural resources were inexhaustible.
   (D) resources should be carefully used.

Test Yourself 7

Directions: Read the following passage and then decide which of the responses is the best answer to each question. Circle the letter that appears before your answer.

The peopling of the Northwest Territory by companies from the eastern states, such as the Ohio Company under the leadership of Reverend
(5) Manasseh Cutler of Ipswich, Massachusetts, furnishes us with many interesting historical tales.

The first towns to be established were Marietta, Zanesville, Chilli-
(10) cothe, and Cincinnati. After the Ohio Company came the Connecticut Company, which secured all the territory bordering Lake Erie, save a small portion known as fire lands
(15) and another portion known as Congress lands. The land taken up by the Connecticut people was called the Western Reserve and was settled almost entirely by New England
(20) people. The remainder of the state of Ohio was settled by Virginians and Pennsylvanians. Because the British controlled Lakes Ontario and Erie, the Massachusetts and Connecticut
(25) people made their journey into the Western Reserve through the southern part of the state. General Moses Cleaveland, the agent for the Connecticut Land Company, led a body
(30) of surveyors to the tract, proceeding by way of Lake Ontario. He quieted the Indian claims to the eastern portion of the reserve by giving them five hundred pounds, two heads of cattle,
(35) and one hundred gallons of whiskey. Landing at the mouth of the Conneaut River, General Moses Cleaveland and his party of fifty, including two women, celebrated Independence
(40) Day, 1796, with a feast of pork and beans with bread. A little later, a village was established at the mouth of the Cuyahoga River and was given the name of Cleaveland, in honor
(45) of the agent of the company. It is

related that the name was afterward shortened to Cleveland by one of the early editors because he could not get so many letters into the heading of
(50) his newspaper.

1. Reverend Manasseh Cutler
   (A) led the Ohio Company.
   (B) owned the Western Reserve.
   (C) led the Connecticut Land Company.
   (D) settled the Congress lands.

2. The title that best expresses the main idea of this selection is
   (A) "The Settling of the Northwest Territory."
   (B) "Control of the Great Lake Region."
   (C) "The Accomplishments of Reverend Manasseh Cutler."
   (D) "The Naming of Cleveland, Ohio."

3. In the last sentence of the selection, the word *related* is used to mean
   (A) associated with.
   (B) rumored.
   (C) reported.
   (D) thought.

4. The selection suggests that General Cleaveland at first found the Indians to be
   (A) extremely noisy people.
   (B) hostile to his party of strangers.
   (C) starving.
   (D) eager to work with him.

Test Yourself 8

Along the shores of the Indian Ocean, from Africa around to the large islands southeast of Asia, is found a pretty little shellfish that is noted
(5) for furnishing what may have been the first money ever used. Its shell, called a cowrie, is white or light yellow, and is about one inch long. Millions of people around the ocean were
(10) using these cowries, separately or on strings, for money long before furs or cattle or other kinds of money were used anywhere, as far as is known. Cowries have been found in Assyria,
(15) many miles inland, and in China they were used with several other kinds of shells. Tortoise shells had the highest value there, so it might be said that the tortoise shells were
(20) the dollar bills while the cowries were the coins. Now, after thousands of years, there are still some tribes in Africa, India, and the South Seas that use cowries.

1. The author believes that the earliest money may have been in the form of
   (A) cattle.
   (B) furs.
   (C) shells.
   (D) string.

2. It is surprising to learn that cowries were used in Assyria because
   (A) cowries are only one inch long.
   (B) cattle were plentiful in Assyria.
   (C) Assyria is away from the seacoast.
   (D) tortoise shells took the place of dollars.

3. The Chinese used _____ for money.
   (A) cattle.
   (B) tortoise shells.
   (C) shellfish.
   (D) whale's teeth.

Test Yourself 9

From Gettysburg to the Battle of the Bulge, carrier pigeons have winged their way through skies fair and foul to deliver the vital messages of
(5) battle. Today, in spite of electronics and atomic weapons, these feathered heroes are still an important communication link in any army.

No one could be surer of this than
(10) the men at Fort Monmouth, New Jersey, the sole Army pigeon breeding

and training center in this country. On the roosts at Fort Monmouth perch many genuine battle heroes,
(15) among them veteran G.I. Joe.

In 1943, one thousand British troops moved speedily ahead of the Allied advance in Italy to take the small town of Colvi Vecchia. Since
(20) communications could not be established in time to relay the victory to headquarters, the troops were due for

a previously planned Allied bombing raid. Then, one of the men released
(25) carrier pigeon G.I. Joe. With a warning message on his back, he flew 20 miles in 20 minutes, arriving just as the bombers were warming up their motors. For saving the day for the
(30) British, the Lord Mayor of London later awarded G.I. Joe the Dickin Medal, England's highest award to an animal.

Even when regular message chan-
(35) nels are set up, equipment can break or be overloaded or radio silence must be observed. Then, the carrier pigeon comes into his own. Ninety-nine times out of a hundred, he completes his
(40) mission. In Korea, Homer the homing pigeon was flying from the front to a rear command post when he developed wing trouble. Undaunted, Homer made a forced landing, hopped
(45) the last two miles and delivered his message. For initiative and loyalty, Homer was promoted to Pfc.—Pigeon First Class!

1. The writer of this passage evidently believes that carrier pigeons
   (A) have no usefulness in modern warfare.
   (B) should be forced to fly only in emergencies.
   (C) are remarkably reliable as message carriers.
   (D) should receive regular promotions.

2. G.I. Joe was rewarded for
   (A) preventing unnecessary loss of life.
   (B) guiding a bomber's flight.
   (C) returning in spite of an injured wing.
   (D) bringing the news of an allied defeat.

3. G.I. Joe's reward was a
   (A) promotion.
   (B) reception given by the Lord Mayor.
   (C) chance to retire to Fort Monmouth.
   (D) medal.

4. The word *vital* in line 4 means
   (A) extremely important.
   (B) frequent.
   (C) recent.
   (D) written.

Test Yourself 10

Directions: Read the following passage and then decide which of the responses is the best answer to each question. Circle the letter that appears before your answer.

"Sophistication by the reel" is the motto of Peretz Johannes, who selects juvenile films for Saturday viewing at the Museum of the City of New York.
(5) Sampling the intellectual climate of the young fans in this city for the past two years has convinced him that many people underestimate the taste level of young New Yorkers.
(10) Consequently, a year ago he began to show films ordinarily restricted to art movie distribution. The series proved enormously successful, and in September, when the program
(15) commenced for this season, youngsters from the five boroughs filled the theater.

As a student of history, Mr. Johannes has not confined himself to
(20) productions given awards in recent

years, but has spent many hours among dusty reels ferreting out such pre-war favorites as the silhouette films of Lotte Reiniger that were (25) made in Germany. One program included two films based on children's stories, "The Little Red Lighthouse" and "Mike Mulligan and His Steam Shovel." The movies are shown at (30) 11 a.m. and 3 p.m., with a short program of stories and a demonstration of toys presented during the intermission.

1. Mr. Johannes found that the children's taste in motion pictures
   (A) was more varied than had been thought.
   (B) ruled out pictures made before their own day.
   (C) was limited to cartoons.
   (D) was even poorer than adults had suspected.

2. Admission to the program described is
   (A) limited to children in the neighborhood of the museum.
   (B) for Manhattan residents only.
   (C) available for all the city.
   (D) for teenagers only.

3. Mr. Johannes
   (A) followed an established policy in planning his programs.
   (B) has failed so far to secure a good audience.
   (C) limits his programs to the newest award-winning pictures.
   (D) evidently is a good judge of children's tastes.

4. *Ferreting out* (line 22) a picture is
   (A) giving it a trial run.
   (B) searching diligently for it.
   (C) reviving it.
   (D) banning it.

Test Yourself 11

Directions: Read the following passage and then decide which of the responses is the best answer to each question. Circle the letter that appears before your answer.

Today, the theory of "continental drift," which supposes that the earth's great land masses have moved over time, is a basic premise accepted by (5) most geologists. However, this was not always so. Although Alfred Wegener was not the first scientist to propose the idea that the continents have moved, his 1912 outline of the (10) hypothesis was the first detailed description of the concept and the first to offer a respectable mass of supporting evidence for it. It is appropriate, then, that the theory of continental (15) drift was most widely known as "Wegener's hypothesis" during the more than fifty years of debate that preceded its ultimate acceptance by most earth scientists.

(20) In brief, Wegener's hypothesis stated that, in the late Paleozoic era, all of the present-day continents were part of a single giant land mass, Pangaea, which occupied almost (25) half of the earth's surface. About 40 million years ago Pangaea began to break into fragments that slowly moved apart, ultimately forming the various continents we know today. (30) Wegener supported his argument with data drawn from geology, paleontology, zoology, climatology, and other fields. So impressive was his array of evidence that his hypoth-

(35) esis could not be ignored. However, until the 1960s most scientists were reluctant to accept Wegener's ideas. There are several reasons why this was so. First, although Wegener *(40)* showed that continental movement was consistent with much of the geological and other evidence—for example, the apparent family relationships among forms of plants *(45)* and animals now separated by vast expanses of ocean, once geographically united on the hypothetical pangaea—he failed to suggest any causal mechanism for continental *(50)* drift sufficiently powerful and plausible to be convincing. Second, while the period during which Wegener's theory was propounded and debated saw rapid developments in many *(55)* branches of geology and an explosion of new knowledge about the nature of the earth and the forces at work in its formation, little of this evidence seemed to support *(60)* Wegener. For example, data drawn from the new science of seismology, including experimental studies of the behavior of rocks under high pressure suggested that the earth *(65)* has far too much internal strength and rigidity to allow continents to "drift" across its surface. Measurements of the earth's gravitational field made by some of the early *(70)* scientific satellites offered further evidence in support of this view as late as the early 1960s. Third, and perhaps most significant, Wegener's theory seemed to challenge one of the *(75)* most deeply held philosophical bases of geology—the doctrine of uniformitarianism, which states that earth history must always be explained by the operation of essentially unchang- *(80)* ing, continuous forces. Belief in the intervention of unexplained, sporadic, and massive shaping events was considered beyond the pale by mainstream geologists.

(85) Wegener was not, strictly speaking, a catastrophist—he did not suggest that some massive cataclysm had triggered the breakup of Pangaea— but his theory did imply a dramatic *(90)* change in the face of the earth occurring relatively late in geologic history. Such a belief, viewed as tainted with catastrophism, was abhorrent to most geologists throughout the first half of *(95)* the last century.

1. According to the passage, Wegener believed that Pangaea

   (A) was destroyed in a massive cataclysm occurring about 40 million years ago.

   (B) consisted of several large land areas separated by vast expanses of ocean.

   (C) was ultimately submerged by rising oceans at the end of the Paleozoic era.

   (D) has gradually drifted from its original location into its current position.

   (E) contained in a single land mass the basic material of all the continents that exist today.

2. It can be inferred from the passage that, by the end of the Paleozoic era,

   (A) early human beings existed on earth.

   (B) many forms of plant and animal life existed on earth.

   (C) the land mass of Pangaea no longer existed.

   (D) a series of unexplained catastrophes had changed the face of the earth.

   (E) most of today's land forms had taken their current shape.

3. The author refers to the scientific information gathered by satellites in order to suggest the
   (A) philosophical changes that ultimately led to the acceptance of Wegener's hypothesis.
   (B) dramatic advances in earth science during the 1960s.
   (C) differing directions taken by various earth scientists.
   (D) nature of some of the evidence that appeared to refute Wegener.
   (E) need for experimental demonstration before any new geological theory can be accepted.

4. As used in line 89, the word *dramatic* most nearly means
   (A) exciting.
   (B) violent.
   (C) inexplicable.
   (D) large scale.
   (E) rapid.

Test Yourself 12

Directions: Read the following passage and then decide which of the responses is the best answer to each question. Circle the letter that appears before your answer.

Emily B. Ryerson, First-Class Passenger:

At the time of the collision, I was awake and heard the engines
(5) stop, but felt no jar. My husband was asleep, so I rang and asked the steward what was the matter. He said, "There is a talk of an iceberg, ma'am, and they have stopped, not
(10) to run into it." I told him to keep me informed if there were any orders.

It was bitterly cold, so I put on a warm wrapper and looked out the window and saw the stars shining
(15) and a calm sea, but heard no noise. It was 12 o'clock. After about 10 minutes, I went out in the corridor, and saw far off people hurrying on deck. A passenger ran by and called out
(20) "Put on your life belts and come up on the boat deck." I said, "Where did you get these orders?" He said, "From the captain." I went back then and told Miss Bowen and my daughter,
(25) who were in the next room, to dress immediately, roused my husband and the two younger children...and then remembered my maid. By this time my husband was fully dressed, and
(30) we could hear the noise of feet tramping on the deck overhead. He was quite calm and cheerful and helped me put the life belts on the children and on my maid. I was paralyzed
(35) with fear of not all getting on deck together in time, as there were seven of us. My husband cautioned us all to keep together, and we went up to A deck, where we found quite a group
(40) of people we knew. Everyone had on a life belt, and they were very quiet and self-possessed. We stood there for quite a long time—fully half an hour, I should say. Then we were ordered to
(45) the boat deck. My chief thought and that of everyone else was, I know, not to make a fuss and to do as we were told. My husband joked with

some of the women he knew, and I
(50) heard him say, "Don't you hear the
band playing?" I begged him to let
me stay with him, but he said, "You
must obey orders. When they say,
'Women and children to the boats,'
(55) you must go when your turn comes.
I'll stay with John Thayer. We will
be all right."

All this time we could hear the
rockets going up—signals of distress.
(60) Again, we were ordered down to A
deck. We saw people getting into
boats, but we waited our turn. My
boy, Jack, was with me. An officer
at the window said, "That boy can't
(65) go." My husband stepped forward and
said, "Of course, that boy goes with
his mother; he is only 13." So they let
him pass. I turned and kissed my husband, and as we left he and the other
(70) men I knew were all standing there
together very quietly. The decks were
lighted, and as you went through the
window it was as if you stepped out
into the dark. The order was given to
(75) pull away, then they rowed off. Then
suddenly, when we still seemed very
near, I turned to see the great ship
take a plunge toward the bow, the
two forward funnels seemed to lean,
(80) and then she seemed to break in half
as if cut with a knife, and as the bow
went under the lights went out.

1. The upper-class status of the narrator
   of the passage can be inferred from all
   of the following EXCEPT the
   (A) fact that she had a maid.
   (B) way she was addressed by the
       steward.
   (C) fact that her family occupied
       several cabins.
   (D) fact that her husband sent her
       ahead into a lifeboat.
   (E) fact that the officer deferred
       to her husband's judgment
       concerning their son.

2. The words of the steward who first
   advised the narrator of the passage
   about a problem with the ship (lines
   8–10) suggest that he believed that
   the *Titanic* had been
   (A) severely damaged and would
       sink.
   (B) severely damaged but would
       survive.
   (C) slightly damaged and would be
       late in arriving in New York.
   (D) slightly damaged but would
       arrive in New York on schedule.
   (E) not damaged at all.

3. As used in line 42, the word "self-
   possessed" most nearly means
   (A) in control of one's emotions.
   (B) anxious about one's safety.
   (C) ready to obey orders.
   (D) holding all one's personal
       belongings.
   (E) eager to take action.

4. It can be inferred that all of the fol-
   lowing are true about the husband of
   the narrator of the passage EXCEPT
   he
   (A) made every effort to allay his
       wife's fears.
   (B) tried to ensure that his son
       would survive.
   (C) recognized that he would
       probably not survive.
   (D) behaved as he thought was
       expected of him.
   (E) assumed that he would follow
       his wife on another boat.

Test Yourself 13

Directions: Read the following passage and then decide which of the responses is the best answer to each question. Circle the letter that appears before your answer.

On July 1, 1882, a brief notice appeared in the *Portsmouth* (England) *Evening News*. It read simply, "Dr. Doyle begs to notify that he has
(5) removed to 1, Bush Villas, Elm Grove, next to the Bush Hotel." So was announced the newly formed medical practice of a 23-year-old graduate of Edinburgh University—
(10) Arthur Conan Doyle. But the town of Southsea, the Portsmouth suburb in which Doyle had opened his office, already had several well-established physicians, and while he waited for
(15) patients the young Dr. Doyle found himself with a great deal of time on his hands. To fill it, he began writing—short stories, historical novels, whatever would keep him busy and,
(20) hopefully, bring additional funds into his sparsely filled coffers.

By the beginning of 1886, his practice had grown to the point of providing him with a respectable
(25) if not munificent income, and he had managed to have a few pieces published. Although literary success still eluded him, he had developed an idea for a new book, a detective story,
(30) and in March he began writing the tale that would give birth to one of literature's most enduring figures. Although he was familiar with and impressed by the fictional detectives
(35) created by Edgar Allan Poe, Emile Gaboriau, and Wilkie Collins, Doyle believed he could create a different kind of detective, one for whom detection was a science rather than an
(40) art. As a model, he used one of his medical school professors, Dr. Joseph Bell. As Bell's assistant, Doyle had seen how, by exercising his powers of observation and deduction and
(45) asking a few questions, Bell had been able not only to diagnose his patients' complaints but also to accurately determine their professions and backgrounds. A detective who
(50) applied similar intellectual powers to the solving of criminal mysteries could be a compelling figure, Doyle felt. At first titled *A Tangled Skein*, the story was to be told by his de-
(55) tective's companion, a Dr. Ormand Sacker, and the detective himself was to be named Sherrinford Holmes. But by April, 1886, when Doyle finished the manuscript, the title had become
(60) *A Study in Scarlet*, the narrator Dr. John H. Watson, and the detective Mr. Sherlock Holmes.

1. As used in line 44, the word *deduction* most nearly means
   (A) decreasing.
   (B) discounting.
   (C) reducing.
   (D) reasoning.
   (E) subtracting.

2. It can be inferred from the passage that Sherlock Holmes differed from previous fictional detectives in that
   (A) he focused his detective skills on the solving of crimes.
   (B) he conducted his investigations on a scientific basis.
   (C) he used his own background in medicine as a source of detective methods.
   (D) his cases were chronicled by a companion rather than by the detective himself.
   (E) his exploits were based on the experiences of a real individual.

3. In line 52, the word *compelling* most nearly means

(A) forceful.

(B) inescapable.

(C) believable.

(D) fascinating.

(E) insistent.

4. Which of the following titles best summarizes the content of the passage?

(A) "Arthur Conan Doyle and the Creation of the Modern Detective Story"

(B) "A Detective's Reluctant Chronicler: The Birth of Sherlock Holmes"

(C) "Physician and Author: How Arthur Conan Doyle Balanced Two Callings"

(D) "The Many Strands in the Character of Sherlock Holmes"

(E) "Joseph Bell: The Real-Life Inspiration for Sherlock Holmes"

Test Yourself 14

Directions: Read the following passage and then decide which of the responses is the best answer to each question. Circle the letter that appears before your answer.

Leaving the elevated railroad where it dives under the Brooklyn Bridge at Franklin Square, scarce a dozen steps will take us where we wish, yet in our
(5) ears, we have turned the corner from prosperity to poverty. We stand upon the domain of the tenement. In the shadow of the great stone abutments, the old knickerbocker houses linger
(10) like ghosts of a departed day. Down the winding slope of Cherry Street—proud and fashionable Cherry Hill that was—their broad steps, sloping roofs, and dormer windows are easily
(15) made out; all the more easily for the contrast with the ugly barracks that elbow them right and left.

These never had other design than to shelter, at as little outlay as pos-
(20) sible, the greatest crowds out of which rent could be wrung. They were the bad afterthought of a heedless day. The years have brought to the old houses unhonored age, a querulous
(25) second childhood that is out of tune with the time, their tenants, the neighbors, and cries out against them

and against you in fretful protest in every step on their rotten floors
(30) or squeaky stairs. Good cause have they for their fretting. This one, with its shabby front and poorly patched roof—what flowing firesides, what happy children may it once have
(35) owned? Heavy feet, too often with unsteady step, for the saloon is next door—where is it not next door in these slums?—have worn away the brownstone steps since; the broken
(40) columns at the door have rotted away at the base. Of the handsome cornice barely a trace is left. Dirt and desolation reign in the wide hallway, and danger lurks on the stairs. Rough pine
(45) boards fence off the roomy fireplaces; where coal is bought by the pail at the rate of twelve dollars a ton, these have no place.

The arched gateway leads no longer
(50) to a shady bower on the banks of the rushing stream, inviting day-dreams with its gentle repose, but to a dark and nameless alley, shut in by high brick walls, cheerless as the lives of

(55) those they shelter. The wolf knocks loudly at the gate in the troubled dreams that come to this alley, echoes of the day's cares. A horde of dirty children play about the dripping *(60)* hydrant, the only thing in the alley that thinks enough of its chance to make the most of it: it is the best it can do. These are the children of the tenements, the growing generation of *(65)* the slums; this their home. From the great highway overhead, along which throbs the life-tide of two great cities, one might drop a pebble into half a dozen such alleys.

1. This passage serves primarily to

    (A) argue for the demolition of tenement buildings and restoration of the old houses.

    (B) decry the lifestyle and habits of the Cherry Street tenement dwellers.

    (C) describe how previous generations enjoyed their prosperous life on Cherry Street.

    (D) contrast present and past conditions of life on Cherry Street.

    (E) give a detailed accounting of the structural demise of the old knickerbocker houses.

2. In line 19, the word *outlay* most nearly means

    (A) expense.

    (B) inconvenience.

    (C) need.

    (D) danger.

    (E) distance.

3. The author ascribes human feelings to the old houses in lines 23–35 ("The years have brought . . . . what happy children may it once have owned?") primarily in order to

    (A) contrast the graceful houses with the poor tenement dwellers.

    (B) emphasize how time and poverty have ravaged the houses.

    (C) suggest that inanimate objects are capable of feelings and sensations.

    (D) elicit sympathy from readers who may care more for houses than people.

    (E) imply a value judgment about the current residents of the houses.

4. The author implies that the present residents of the Cherry Street houses

    (A) are too unrefined to appreciate the architectural beauty of their houses.

    (B) are too poor to properly maintain the old houses.

    (C) would be better off in the more recently erected barracks nearby.

    (D) are responsible for most of the physical damage to the houses.

    (E) could easily escape the poverty of their surroundings if they so wished.

5. In lines 58–65, the author's description of the children at play suggests that he views them with

    (A) disdain.

    (B) revulsion.

    (C) pity.

    (D) admiration.

    (E) fear.

ANSWER KEY

Test Yourself 1

1. C	2. D	3. A	4. C

Test Yourself 2

1. B	2. A	3. D	4. C

Test Yourself 3

1. A	2. B	3. D	4. C

Test Yourself 4

1. D	2. A	3. B

Test Yourself 5

1. B	2. C	3. B	4. A

Test Yourself 6

1. B	2. B	3. C

Test Yourself 7

1. A	2. A	3. C	4. B

Test Yourself 8

1. C	2. C	3. B

Test Yourself 9

1. C	2. A	3. D	4. A

Test Yourself 10

1. A	2. C	3. D	4. B

Test Yourself 11

| 1. E | 2. B | 3. D | 4. D |

Test Yourself 12

| 1. D | 2. E | 3. A | 4. E |

Test Yourself 13

| 1. D | 2. B | 3. D | 4. B |

Test Yourself 14

| 1. D | 3. B | 5. C |
| 2. A | 4. B | |

EXERCISES: MAIN IDEA

Directions: Read each passage carefully. Then decide which of the possible responses is the best answer to each question. Circle the appropriate answer.

At a distance of approximately 250,000 miles from Earth, the moon is our nearest celestial neighbor. A rugged terrain of mountains, cliffs,
(5) plains, and craters covers this globe of 2,000 miles in diameter, but this landscape contains no water. There is no precipitation of any kind on the moon because it lacks an at-
(10) mosphere. For the same reason, a constant barrage of meteorites and other space debris reaches its surface without hindrance. The beautiful, silvery moon is, in actuality, a
(15) barren desert, suffering from great extremes of temperature and devoid of any life as we know it.

1. The title that best expresses the main idea of this selection is
   (A) "Landscapes in Space."
   (B) "Life on the Moon."
   (C) "The Moon's Atmosphere."
   (D) "Conditions on the Moon."

The more complicated our thoughts and emotions, the less effective is language as a tool of expression. This is not a simple matter of style or elo-
(5) quence, for even the finest speakers and writers, using the most sensitive language, would be incapable of putting certain thoughts into words. For this reason, many people use poetry
(10) and music instead of prose. These two forms of communication convey subtle yet powerful meanings that cannot be expressed with ordinary words.

2. The title that best expresses the theme of this selection is
   (A) "Words, Poetry, and Music."
   (B) "The Hidden Meanings of Words."
   (C) "The Eloquence of Fine Speakers."
   (D) "Limitations of Language."

The Caribbean Sea is to North and South America what the Mediterranean is to the European continent—a central sea. The American body of wa-
(5) ter is not landlocked. Double strings of islands—the Cuba group and the Bahamas—form an arc at the Atlantic entrance, and this arc is now firmly fortified. Since the Mediterranean
(10) of the West is the passage between the Americas, it must be controlled by these countries in order to carry on trade.

This sea is as necessary to the
(15) Caribbean countries as the Mediterranean is to Italy. The countries of this area produce large quantities of oil, tropical fruits, and vegetables. They are also rich in minerals. This
(20) region is capable of supplying the United States with many goods formerly imported from Africa and Asia. In exchange, the countries of this region need the manufactured
(25) goods that can be provided only by an industrial nation.

3. The Caribbean Sea and the Mediterranean are alike with respect to their

   (A) variety of exports.

   (B) epidemics of serious diseases.

   (C) geographical importance.

   (D) living standards.

The dangers to which migratory birds are subjected during their journeys are but little less than those that would befall them if they remained
(5) in unsuitable zones. During long oversea passages, fatigue and hunger weed out the weaklings. Sudden storms and adverse winds strike migrating birds where no land is near,
(10) and they are often carried far from their intended destinations. Predatory birds accompany them, taking a toll en route, and predatory man waits for the tired wanderers with
(15) gun and net.

4. The title that best expresses the main idea of this passage is

   (A) "Dangers of Storms."

   (B) "Perils of Migration."

   (C) "Unsuitable Environment."

   (D) "How Birds Reach Goals."

In his library at Monticello, Jefferson made hundreds of architectural drawings, all of which have been preserved. He must have had a great
(5) gift of concentration and a real love for his subject to be able to work in a room with such an outlook. And what energy he had to find time and will for this precise and exquisite
(10) work was also devoted to riding over his estate, working in his garden, and carrying out correspondence with everyone from the Marquis de Lafayette to his youngest grandchild.
(15) "Something pursued with ardor" was Jefferson's prescription for life, and he got the last ounce of excitement and interest out of everything that came to his notice.

5. The main idea of this selection is expressed in the title
   (A) "The Library at Monticello."
   (B) "The Care of the Estate."
   (C) "A Full Life."
   (D) "Jefferson, the Architect."

Specific types of lighting are required at first-class airports by the Department of Commerce. To identify an airport, there must be a beacon light
(5) of not less than 100,000 candle power, with a beam that properly distributes light up in the air so that it can be seen all around the horizon from an altitude of 500 to 2,000 feet. All
(10) flashing beacons must have a definite Morse code characteristic to aid in identification. Colored lights are required to indicate where the safe area for landing ends, red lights being
(15) used where landing is particularly dangerous.

6. The best title for this selection is
   (A) "Landing Areas."
   (B) "Colored Lights at Airports."
   (C) "Identification of Airports."
   (D) "Airport Lighting Requirements."

ANSWER KEY AND EXPLANATIONS

1. D	3. C	5. C
2. D	4. B	6. D

1. **The correct answer is (D).** The word *conditions* covers all aspects of the moon discussed in this selection: the moon's size, its terrain, its atmosphere, temperature, etc. Choice (A) is incorrect because it suggests discussion of more than one celestial body, but this selection talks only about the moon. Choice (B) is incorrect because there is no life on the moon, and choice (C) is incorrect because the moon's atmosphere is only one of the subtopics—not the main idea—of the selection.

2. **The correct answer is (D)** The selection discusses some of the reasons and remedies for the limitations of language. Choices (A), (B), and (C) are incorrect because, though the topics are mentioned, they are not the theme of the selection.

3. **The correct answer is (C).** Both bodies of water serve the bordering land masses in similar ways.

4. **The correct answer is (B).** Each sentence in the paragraph explains why migration is perilous. Choices (A), (C), and (D) are topics that aren't discussed.

5. **The correct answer is (C).** The selection describes in detail Jefferson's "full life": his architectural drawings, his love of his estate and gardens, his correspondences, and his "prescription for life." Choices (A), (B), and (D) are either not discussed or are only one aspect of the topic.

6. **The correct answer is (D).** The selection describes several lighting requirements for airports. Choices (A), (B), and (C) are incorrect because they refer to only one specific type of lighting or lighting requirement.

EXERCISES: DETAILS

Directions: Read each passage carefully. Then decide which of the possible responses is the best answer to each question. Circle the appropriate answer.

Ants are very interesting insects. There are about 8,000 different kinds with various ways of finding food. There are hunter ants that capture
(5) other insects, shepherd ants that care for aphids from which they get sweet honeydew, thief ants that live by stealing, slave-making ants that kidnap the children of other ant na-
(10) tions, and mighty military ants that live by plundering and destroying, driving even men and elephants before them.

A city of ants includes the queen,
(15) the workers, the baby ants, and their nurses. Ant babies change their form three times. First, they are small, white eggs. When they hatch, they are little, fat, white worms called larvae.
(20) The larvae change into pupae, and the pupae change into adults. The queen is the mother of all the ants in the community. The workers bring food to her and protect her from invaders.

1. Hunter ants
   (A) care for aphids.
   (B) kidnap young ants from other colonies.
   (C) capture other insects.
   (D) plunder and destroy.

2. A colony of ants
   (A) includes a queen, workers, babies, and their nurses.
   (B) may have as many as 8,000 members.
   (C) is built in a hill.
   (D) protects its members.

3. Immediately prior to entering the adult stage, ants
   (A) hatch from eggs.
   (B) come from larvae.
   (C) are all workers.
   (D) come from pupae.

Commercial interests were quick to recognize the great possibilities of presenting by means of radio what is in effect a person-to-person ap-
(5) peal. At first the novelty made people listen to almost anything, but as the audiences became more accustomed to broadcasts, varied methods of capturing and holding the attention
(10) have developed. These vary from the frank interjection of advertising matter in a program of entertainment to the mere sponsoring of the program. Entertainment at first appeared to
(15) have the greatest appeal, and low comedy and jazz music filled the air. There has come, however, the realization that the radio audience is now as complex as the public and that
(20) programs must be set up to attract the attention of as many different types of hearers as possible.

4. When radio was new,
   (A) people would listen to almost anything.
   (B) advertising was poor.
   (C) advertising was interjected into the programming.
   (D) entertainment was limited.

The part of the ear we see is only a cartilage and skin trumpet that catches sound waves. Buried in bone at the base of the skull is the delicate
(5) apparatus that makes hearing possible.
   A passage leads from the outer ear to a membrane called the eardrum. Sound waves striking the eardrum
(10) make it vibrate. On the other side of the eardrum lies a space called the middle ear. Across this a chain of three tiny bones carries sound vibrations to another space called
(15) the inner ear. Sound messages are conducted along the auditory nerve, located in the inner ear, to the brain for interpretation. The middle ear is connected to the throat by the Eu-
(20) stachian tube. This tube ends near the throat opening of the nose, close to the tonsils. The middle ear also communicates with the mastoid, or air cells in the bone behind the ear.

5. The outer ear is made of
   (A) a delicate apparatus.
   (B) a membrane.
   (C) cartilage and skin.
   (D) three tiny bones.

6. The eardrum is a(n)
   (A) membrane.
   (B) piece of thin cartilage.
   (C) air cell.
   (D) short tube.

7. Sound vibrations are carried
   (A) along the auditory nerve.
   (B) through the eardrum.
   (C) to the inner ear across a chain of three tiny bones.
   (D) to the base of the skull.

Track-and-field events are the only modern sports that would be recognizable in their original form. They can be traced back more than 2,500 years
(5) to the ancient civilization of Greece. The Greeks held their athletes in high esteem, and champions were looked upon as national heroes.

The Greeks began the original
(10) Olympic games for the purpose of assembling the greatest athletes of their country. The games were religious pageants as well as peerless athletic events and were held every four years
(15) for more than eight centuries.

8. In ancient Greece, athletes were

   (A) trained as professionals.

   (B) forced to participate in the games.

   (C) usually defeated by the Romans.

   (D) regarded very highly by the public.

9. The present-day Olympics

   (A) have a 2,500-year-old history.

   (B) are religious pageants.

   (C) have been held every four years for eight centuries.

   (D) are completely different from the Greek games.

Observe the people who make an abiding impression of strength and goodness and you will see that their personal attractiveness and force are
(5) rooted in fundamentals of character. They have the physical vitality, endurance, and courage that come from good living. They have the mental stamina and penetration that come
(10) from facing up to one's problems, however difficult, and from keeping one's mind on things that really matter. They have the moral power that comes from an active sense of what is
(15) right, from doing their part to make truth, justice, and beauty prevail in the world. They have the inner peace and grace that are the basics of a truly charismatic personality. People
(20) trust them, like to be with them, and depend on them in emergencies. They are the salt of the earth.

10. A quality NOT mentioned by the author is

    (A) courage.

    (B) dependability.

    (C) tolerance.

    (D) inner grace.

Although you may still enjoy fairy tales, they probably do not engross you to the degree that they might have a few years ago. Fairy tales belong
(5) primarily to a stage in our lives when we are most interested by the world of fantasy. Goblins, wizards, and dwarfs appeal to the young child's wandering imagination and contribute greatly to
(10) the development of creativity, but it is a temporary infatuation.

As we grow older, real challenges begin to interest us more. The imaginary victories brought about by fairy
(15) godmothers lose their power of enchantment, and we become absorbed in the stories of real people, real success, and real accomplishment. The fascination of "Jack the Giant
(20) Killer" gives way to a keen interest in Commander Byrd's Antarctic exploration, Helen Keller's biography, or the harrowing adventures of spelunkers, deep-sea divers, and mountain
(25) climbers. This step marks one of the first great advances in the process of intellectual maturation.

11. Young children are primarily interested in
    (A) fantasy stories.
    (B) horror stories.
    (C) goblins and witches.
    (D) adventure stories.

12. People become interested in real-life stories when they
    (A) are young.
    (B) are adults.
    (C) begin to mature.
    (D) are bored.

ANSWER KEY AND EXPLANATIONS

1. C	4. A	7. C	10. C
2. A	5. C	8. D	11. A
3. D	6. A	9. A	12. C

1. **The correct answer is (C).** See paragraph one, sentence three.

2. **The correct answer is (A).** See paragraph two, sentence one.

3. **The correct answer is (D).** See paragraph two, sentence five.

4. **The correct answer is (A).** See the second sentence.

5. **The correct answer is (C).** See paragraph one, sentence one.

6. **The correct answer is (A).** See paragraph two, sentence one.

7. **The correct answer is (C).** See paragraph two, sentence four. Sound messages are carried along the auditory nerve.

8. **The correct answer is (D).** See paragraph one, sentence three.

9. **The correct answer is (A).** See paragraph one, sentence two.

10. **The correct answer is (C).** The other choices are all mentioned in the passage.

11. **The correct answer is (A).** See the first paragraph.

12. **The correct answer is (C).** See paragraph two, sentences one and two.

answers exercises

EXERCISES: VOCABULARY

Directions: Read each passage carefully. Then decide which of the possible responses is the best answer to each question. Circle the appropriate answer.

In May of each year, the ghost of Mark Twain must hover over Angel's Camp, California, while all eyes in this colorful old mining town turn to
(5) the tailless, leaping *amphibians* of the genus Rana. It was just this sort of event that Twain made famous in his early humorous story, "The Celebrated Jumping Frog of Calaveras
(10) County."

Thousands of spectators gather each year to watch the county's champions hop their way to fame and compete for a $500 first prize. Each
(15) frog must undergo a rigid inspection to insure against foul play, such as the loading of the competitor with buckshot, as happened in Twain's tall tale.

(20) Back in 1944, Alfred Jermy was the proud owner of Flash, a frog that held the world's championship with a fifteen-foot, ten-inch leap. In 1950, a seven-year-old boy's pet, X-100,
(25) stole top honors with three jumps averaging fourteen feet, nine inches. As amazing as these might seem to the *novice*, these are mere puddle jumps.

(30) Half the fun in visiting this Calaveras County contest is to be found in listening to the tales of 600-foot leaps in a favorable wind—well, why not?

1. The *amphibians* mentioned in the first paragraph are the
   (A) storytellers.
   (B) frogs.
   (C) citizens of Calaveras County.
   (D) human contestants.

2. The word *novice* in the third paragraph means
   (A) the judges.
   (B) the spectators.
   (C) the owners of the frogs.
   (D) inexperienced readers.

In the year 1799, an officer of the French Army was stationed in a small fortress on the Rosetta River, a mouth of the Nile, near Alexandria, Egypt.

(5) He was interested in the ruins of the ancient Egyptian civilization and had seen the Sphinx and the pyramids, those mysterious structures that were erected by men of another era.

(10) One day, as a trench was being dug, he found a piece of black slate on which letters had been carved. He had studied Greek in school and knew this was an *inscription* written in

(15) that language. There were two more lines carved into the stone: one in the Egyptian characters he had seen on other ruins, the other in completely unfamiliar characters.

(20) The officer realized the importance of such a find and *relinquished* it to scholars who had been puzzling over Egyptian inscriptions.

In 1802, a French professor by the

(25) name of Champollion began studying the stone in an attempt to *decipher* the two unknown sets of characters using the Greek letters as a key. He worked with the stone for over 20

(30) years and, in 1823, announced that he had discovered the meaning of the fourteen signs and in doing so had unlocked the secret of ancient Egyptian writing. Some 5,000 years

(35) after an unknown person had made those three inscriptions, the Rosetta Stone became a key, unlocking the written records of Egypt and sharing the history of that civilization with

(40) the rest of the world.

3. The word *decipher* is synonymous with
   (A) translate.
   (B) encode.
   (C) transcribe.
   (D) transmit.

4. The word *inscription* means
   (A) a picture carved in stone.
   (B) a relief sculpture.
   (C) letters carved into a hard substance.
   (D) a written message.

5. The word *relinquish* means to
   (A) give up possession of something.
   (B) lend to someone.
   (C) sell an object.
   (D) study an object.

The impressions that an individual gets from his environment are greatly influenced by his emotional state. When he is happy, objects and people

(5) present themselves to him in a favorable aspect; when he is depressed, he views the same things in an entirely different light. It has been said that a person's moods are the lenses that col-

(10) or life with many different hues. Not only does mood affect impression; impression also affects mood. The beauty of a spring morning may *dissipate* the gloom of a great sorrow; the good-

(15) natured chuckle of a child may turn anger into a smile; or a telegram may *transform* a house of mirth into a house of mourning.

6. The word *dissipate* means
   (A) condense.
   (B) draw out.
   (C) melt away.
   (D) inflate.

7. The word *transform* is synonymous with
   (A) convert.
   (B) conclude.
   (C) interpret.
   (D) convey.

ANSWER KEY AND EXPLANATIONS

1. B	3. A	5. A	7. A
2. D	4. C	6. C	

1. **The correct answer is (B).** Frogs are a type of *amphibian*.

2. **The correct answer is (D).** The word choice *novice* means "inexperienced."

3. **The correct answer is (A).** *Decipher* means to break a code and translate the message.

4. **The correct answer is (C).** Other examples of inscriptions are names carved into gravestones and initials inscribed into jewelry. To inscribe is to write into.

5. **The correct answer is (A).** The word *relinquish* means "let go" or "give up."

6. **The correct answer is (C).** Other synonyms for the word *dissipate* are "scatter," "dissolve," and "evaporate."

7. **The correct answer is (A).** When something is changed to something else, it is *transformed*, or converted.

EXERCISES: INFERENCE

Directions: Read each passage carefully. Then decide which of the possible responses is the best answer to each question. Circle the appropriate answer.

Intuition is not a quality everyone can understand. As the unimaginative are miserable about a work of fiction until they discover what flesh-and-
(5) blood individual served as a model for the hero or heroine, so, too, many scientists scoff at the unscientific notion that intuition as a force exists. They cannot believe that a blind man
(10) can see something they cannot see. They rely utterly on the celebrated inductive method of reasoning: expose the facts and conclude from them only what can be proven. Generally
(15) speaking, this is a very sound rule, but can we be certain that the really great accomplishments are initiated in this plodding fashion? Dreams are made of quite different stuff, and if
(20) any are left in the world who does not know that dreams have remade the world, then perhaps there is little we can teach them.

1. The author implies that intuition
   (A) is the product of imagination.
   (B) relies on factual information.
   (C) is an inductive reasoning process.
   (D) is valueless.

It is exceedingly difficult to draw on a canvas the man whose nature is large and central, without cranks or oddities. The very simplicity of such
(5) souls defies an easy summary, for they are as spacious in their effect as daylight or summer. Often we remember friends by a gesture or a trick of expression, or by a favorite phrase.
(10) But with Nelson I do not find myself thinking of such idiosyncrasies. His presence warmed and lit up so big a region of life that in thinking of him one is overwhelmed by the multitude
(15) of things that he made better by simply existing among them. If you remove a fire from the hearth, you will remember the look, not so much of the blaze itself, as of the whole
(20) room in its pleasant glow.

2. The phrase "to draw on a canvas" is used in this context to mean to
   (A) paint a portrait.
   (B) summarize.
   (C) make a collage.
   (D) describe.

3. The last sentence is a metaphor comparing Nelson to
   (A) the blaze in a fireplace.
   (B) a hearth.
   (C) fire.
   (D) a pleasant glow.

4. From the tone of this selection, you might draw the conclusion that the author
   (A) thinks of Nelson as a strange man.
   (B) is describing a man who has died.
   (C) is overwhelmed by Nelson.
   (D) remembers Nelson only by his gestures.

A glass case in the British Museum houses the mummified remains of two Egyptian kings who lived beside the Nile. The exhibit includes a bro-
(5) ken plow, a rusted sickle, and two sticks tied together with a leather strap. These were the "bread tools" of Egyptians who lived 4,000 years ago during the reigns of the two kings.
(10) They are not unlike the tools used by eighteenth-century American farm-ers, and, in fact, similar sickles may be viewed at Mount Vernon, George Washington's Virginia home.

5. We may conclude from this selection that the ancient Egyptians

    (A) had only two important kings.

    (B) taught farming techniques to eighteenth-century Americans.

    (C) were relatively advanced in the use of agricultural tools.

    (D) neglected their equipment.

The horn of an automobile is a valu-able aid to good driving if properly used. When about to pass another car, it is advisable to notify the
(5) driver of the car ahead. Children or animals on the street should be given a warning note. Of course, a courteous driver would not blow his horn unnecessarily in the vicinity of
(10) a hospital or a place of worship. He should also be considerate of schools, where quiet is important. The way in which a driver uses his horn is a fairly accurate index to his character, for
(15) through the sound he expresses his impatience and his good manners, or the lack of them.

6. The place that a good driver would be least likely to use his horn is

    (A) St. James Theater.

    (B) Riverdale Apartments.

    (C) Memorial Convalescent Home.

    (D) Yankee Stadium.

7. The character of a driver who fails to sound his horn when a dog is crossing the street is

    (A) noble.

    (B) impatient.

    (C) uncaring

    (D) bold.

exercises

According to early English history, a small group of people from north-eastern Europe, called Easterlings, came by invitation to England to
(5) devise and develop a new system of coinage. These people lived in towns that were famous for the accuracy of their coins. The coins that they worked out for England were made
(10) of silver and came to be known as the Easterling coins. Later the word *Easterling* was shortened to sterling. The word *sterling* gradually came to be applied to all silver articles of very
(15) fine quality.

8. The passage implies that the Easterlings
   (A) had an excellent reputation.
   (B) used silver exclusively.
   (C) were silversmiths.
   (D) coined the word *sterling*.

9. The word *sterling* began to be used for high-quality silver because
   (A) it was used to make English coins.
   (B) the Easterlings were known for the quality of their work.
   (C) silver is very expensive.
   (D) the Easterlings were the only people who could make silver coins.

ANSWER KEY AND EXPLANATIONS

1. A	3. A	5. C	7. C	9. B
2. D	4. B	6. C	8. A	

1. **The correct answer is (A).** The author likens intuition to "dreams" (line 18) and scoffs at the belief that inductive reasoning initiates all great accomplishments (lines 16–19).

2. **The correct answer is (D).** Lines 4 and 5 further explain the author's assertion that it is not easy to describe Nelson and his affect on her.

3. **The correct answer is (A).** The author describes the "pleasant glow" that comes from Nelson as if he were fire.

4. **The correct answer is (B).** The entire passage is about remembering Nelson, and lines 16–20 make reference (in metaphor) to Nelson's leaving.

5. **The correct answer is (C).** The tools used by Egyptians 4,000 years ago are similar to those tools used by American farmers in the eighteenth century.

6. **The correct answer is (C).** A good (and courteous) driver would not "blow his horn unnecessarily in the vicinity of a hospital" (lines 8–10).

7. **The correct answer is (C).** The paragraph states that "animals on the street should be given a warning note" (lines 6–7). An uncaring or inattentive driver would not blow his or her horn as a warning.

8. **The correct answer is (A).** The passage states that the Easterlings were "invited" by England to develop a new coinage system.

9. **The correct answer is (B).** According to the passage, the Easterlings developed coinage of the highest quality.

SUMMING IT UP

Review this page the night before you take your high school entrance exam. It will help you get the answers to reading comprehension questions.

- When you get to the reading comprehension section, take a deep breath and follow these six steps:

  ❶ Read through the questions quickly, noting what information you will have to find. Skip over the answer choices for now.

  ❷ Read the passage.

  ❸ Scan the passage and answer the vocabulary questions first.

  ❹ Tackle detail questions second. Pick a key word or two from the question and scan the passage for the location of the answer.

  ❺ Read the first and last sentences of the passage to answer main-idea questions.

  ❻ Skim for answers to inference questions. Eliminate wrong answers and make your best guess.

- All the information you need is right in the passage.

- Reading comprehension questions are not arranged in order of difficulty.

- Don't get bogged down in details. Look for important ideas and mark them as you find them.

- Answer every question for a passage before starting the next passage.

PART VI

MATHEMATICS REVIEW

Mathematics (SSAT and ISEE)

OVERVIEW

- **What mathematics must I know?**
- **How do I estimate the answer?**
- **When must I calculate?**
- **Summing it up**

WHAT MATHEMATICS MUST I KNOW?

The answer to this question is a question. What grade are you in? If you are in eighth grade, you must know basic arithmetic, fundamental operations using fractions and decimals, percents, and very basic algebra and geometry. If you are in twelfth grade seeking an extra year before college, you should be thoroughly familiar with complex algebra and geometry and with roots and exponents.

Remember that scoring of your high school entrance exam is based upon your grade. You do not need to know what you have not yet been taught. But you must have mastered all the mathematics appropriate to your grade level. Use your math textbook to help you limit the extent of your study in this chapter. Don't try to learn ahead. Concentrate on doing well on the math that a person your age must know.

The Fundamental Operations

Addition, subtraction, multiplication, and division are the basic operations upon which the structure of mathematics is based. There is no substitute for having good skills in computation to achieve success on one of the high school entrance examinations. Proceed through this section carefully, being honest with yourself about the accuracy and speed with which you solve these problems. Note problems that are difficult for you as well as those that are easy. Adjust your study plans accordingly.

chapter 10

The Number Line

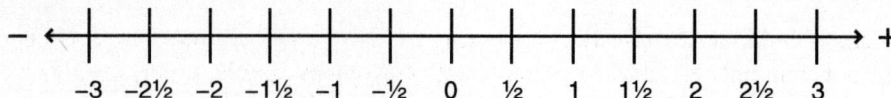

$$-3 \quad -2\tfrac{1}{2} \quad -2 \quad -1\tfrac{1}{2} \quad -1 \quad -\tfrac{1}{2} \quad 0 \quad \tfrac{1}{2} \quad 1 \quad 1\tfrac{1}{2} \quad 2 \quad 2\tfrac{1}{2} \quad 3$$

A number line is a convenient concept to use as a mental picture. The number line above shows whole numbers and fractions greater than zero and less than zero. Numbers increase in size as you move to the right and decrease in size as you move to the left. The number line above has an arrow at each end, meaning that the number line goes on infinitely in both positive and negative directions.

Number lines can be drawn to aid in basic mathematical calculations. Either fractions, whole numbers, or decimals can be used to name the intervals on the line. We suggest that you use number lines when dealing with signed (+, –) numbers and inequalities.

Addition

In the process of addition, we add together numbers, which we call addends, to result in a sum. Addends may be added in any order (commutative property).

Example: $\underbrace{203+155+80}_{\text{addends}} = \underbrace{438}_{\text{sum}}$

Example: $\underbrace{17.4+6.2+2.2}_{\text{addends}} = \underbrace{25.8}_{\text{sum}}$

Example: $\underbrace{\tfrac{3}{4}+1\tfrac{1}{2}+\tfrac{5}{8}}_{\text{addends}} = \underbrace{2\tfrac{7}{8}}_{\text{sum}}$

Example: $\underbrace{\tfrac{3}{5}+1.25+2}_{\text{addends}} = 3.85$ (decimal notation)

$$= 3\tfrac{17}{20} \text{ (fractional notation)}$$

Simple addition problems may consist of only whole number addends (as in Example 1), of only decimal or fractional addends (as in Examples 2 and 3), or of a mixture of all three (as in Example 4).

WHOLE NUMBER ADDITION

To add whole numbers as in Example 1, line up the addends in a column. Add each column of numbers carefully, making sure to carry tens to the next column:

TIP

Remember:
Line the numbers up underneath each other carefully.

```
  203
  155
+  80
-----
  438
```

HOW DO I ESTIMATE THE ANSWER?

In multiple-choice math questions, the answer is in front of you. You don't need to calculate it; you only need to recognize it. The problem may be much simpler than it looks or reads. In fact, if it looks as if the calculation will be very long or complicated, you are probably heading down the wrong track. High school entrance exams are not meant to be tests of your computational skills; they are testing your understanding of concepts and ability to apply that understanding. Leave your pencil on the desk for a moment and start with common sense:

Q $3.01 + 10.73 + 2.01 + .781 =$

(A) 13.522

(B) 16.531

(C) 20.860

(D) 36.036

Note that in this case it is best not to proceed by writing down the numbers to be added, adding them, and then checking your answer against those supplied. Calculating the answer in this way would waste valuable time that could be used later on.

A The correct answer is (B).

ESTIMATING THE ANSWER: GETTING IT RIGHT

1. Read the question, and note that it is a decimal addition problem. DON'T CALCULATE YET.

2. Read the possible answers; notice the range they cover.

3. Estimate the sum of the four numbers as $3 + 11 + 2 + 1 = 17$.

4. Note that choice (B) is the only answer anywhere near a sum of 17. Choose it as the correct answer.

Or, even simpler:

1. Read the question and note that it is a decimal addition problem. DON'T CALCULATE YET.

2. Look at the four addends. Note that three have digits two places to the right of the decimal point and that only one has a digit in the thousandths place. That digit is a "1."

3. Look at the four answer choices. Concentrate on the digit in the thousandths place.

4. Choose (B) as the only possible correct answer, and move on quickly to the next question.

WHEN MUST I CALCULATE?

There will be some problems that will require you to use a pencil and paper (no calculators, alas!). You may be able to estimate an answer to those questions, but the choices given will make estimating too risky.

We suggest you calculate the answer when:

- The answer choices differ only very slightly.
- The problem requires three or more steps, making it difficult to remember accurately your intermediate steps.
- You have to change larger units into smaller ones, or vice versa, for purposes of calculation. It is easy to lose track of units within the English system of measurements when working with time, units of measurement, and so on.

TEST YOURSELF QUIZZES

Take the following quizzes to help you determine your weaknesses. Answers can be found on pages 326–335.

8/3/08

Test Yourself 1

> **Directions:** Try these problems. The answers are on page 326. Aim for 100 percent accuracy and note your errors.

1. 463 + 729 + 36
2. 257 + 32
3. 174 + 20,962
4. 1,732 + 32,629
5. 33 + 472 + 8

6. 138 + 76 + 82 + 1,224
7. 59 + 732 + 111
8. 137,921 + 29 + 71
9. 393 + 462 + 1,701 + 733
10. 145 + 66 + 78

DECIMAL ADDITION

Decimals are a way of writing fractions using tenths, hundredths, thousandths, and so forth. If you can count money, make change, or understand a batting average, decimals should present no problem.

When writing decimals, the most important step is placing the decimal point. The whole system is based upon its location. Remember the decimal places?

Example: 1, 2 3 6, 5 4 0 . 1 3 2 4 5 6

MILLIONS | HUNDRED THOUSANDS | TEN THOUSANDS | THOUSANDS | HUNDREDS | TENS | ONES | DECIMAL POINT | TENTHS | HUNDREDTHS | THOUSANDTHS | TEN THOUSANDTHS | HUNDRED THOUSANDTHS | MILLIONTHS

Test Yourself 2

Directions: If you need practice reading decimals, try the exercises below.

1. .0076
2. 11.3
3. 1,402.639
4. $7,222.93
5. 0.50

6. 0.05
7. 16.2163
8. .00029
9. 3.0006
10. 62.391

Test Yourself 3

Directions: If you did well on Quiz 2, try to determine which of these pairs of numbers is larger.

1. .5 or .05
2. 5.12 or 5.012
3. 0.007 or 0.07
4. 16.20 or 16.2

5. 10.7 or 1.70
6. 0.762 or 7.62
7. 3.009 or 3.0009
8. .143 or .1430

Adding decimals is no harder than adding whole numbers, as long as you pay attention to the decimal point. To add a group of decimals, place them in a column, being certain to line up the decimal points.

Example: $17.4 + 6.2 + 2.2 = 25.8$

Solution:
```
 17.4
  6.2
+ 2.2
 25.8
```

Notice that the decimal point is brought straight down! Now, try the next example for practice. Where decimal places may be "missing," fill in with zeros if you need to.

Example: Add 22.0061 + 7.003 + 2.1 + .001 + 100.01

Solution:
```
  22.0061
  07.0030
  02.1000
  00.0010
+ 100.0100
  131.1201
```

The underlined numbers show where you may fill in with zeros if you want.

Test Yourself 4

Directions: Try these problems.

1. 7.223 + 60.1
2. .0792 + 5.06
3. 100.23 + 9.7962
4. 82.48 + 21.2417
5. .0323 + .06

6. 9623.2 + 43.788
7. 14.1414 + .044
8. .02 + 3.63 + 92.003
9. 720.72 + 69.58
10. 4.7 + 3.2 + .9 + 1.2

Fractions

Fractions are used when we want to indicate parts of things. A fraction consists of a numerator and a denominator.

$$3 \leftarrow \text{numerator} \rightarrow 7$$
$$4 \leftarrow \text{denominator} \rightarrow 8$$

The *denominator* tells you how many equal parts the object or number has been divided into, and the *numerator* tells how many of those parts we are concerned with.

Examples:

Divide a baseball game, a football game, and a hockey game into convenient numbers of parts.

Write a fraction to answer each question.

1. If a pitcher played two innings, how much of the whole baseball game did (s)he play?

2. If a quarterback played three quarters of a football game, how much of the whole game did (s)he play?

3. If a goalie played two periods of a hockey game, how much of the whole game did (s)he play?

Solutions:

1. A baseball game is conveniently divided into nine parts (each an inning). The pitcher pitched two innings. Therefore, (s)he played $\frac{2}{9}$ of the game.

   The denominator represents the nine parts the game is divided into; the numerator, the two parts we are concerned with.

2. Similarly, there are four quarters in a football game, and a quarterback playing three of those quarters plays in $\frac{3}{4}$ of the game.

3. There are three periods in hockey, and the goalie played in two of them. Therefore, (s)he played in $\frac{2}{3}$ of the game.

Simplest Form and Equivalence

Fractions having different denominators and numerators may actually represent the same amount. Such fractions are equivalent fractions.

For example, the circle below is divided into two equal parts. Write a fraction to indicate that half of the circle is shaded.

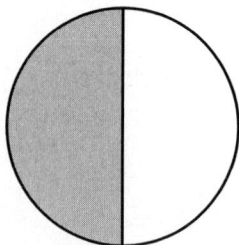

$$\frac{1 \text{ shaded}}{2 \text{ parts}} = \frac{1}{2} \text{ of circle is shaded.}$$

The circle below is divided into four equal parts. Write a fraction to indicate how much of the circle is shaded.

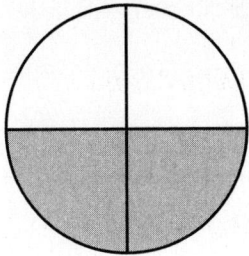

$$\frac{2 \text{ shaded}}{4 \text{ parts}} = \frac{2}{4} \text{ of circle is shaded.}$$

This circle is divided into eight equal parts. Write a fraction to indicate how much of the circle is shaded.

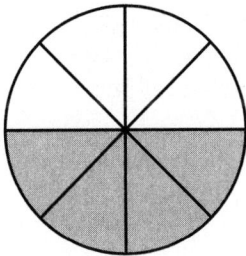

$$\frac{4 \text{ shaded}}{8 \text{ parts}} = \frac{4}{8} \text{ of the circle is shaded.}$$

In each circle the same amount was shaded. This shows you that there is more than one way to indicate one half of something.

The fractions $\frac{1}{2}$, $\frac{2}{4}$, and $\frac{4}{8}$ that you wrote are *equivalent fractions*, because they all represent the same amount. Notice that the denominator is twice as large as the numerator in *every* case. Any fraction you write that has a denominator that is exactly twice as large as the numerator will be equivalent to $\frac{1}{2}$.

Example: Write other fractions equivalent to $\frac{1}{2}$.

Solution: Any fraction that has a denominator that is *twice* as large as the numerator: $\frac{3}{6}$, $\frac{5}{10}$, $\frac{6}{12}$, $\frac{32}{64}$, etc.

Example: Write other fractions equivalent to $\frac{1}{4}$.

Solution: Any fraction that has a denominator that is *four* times as large as the numerator: $\frac{2}{8}$, $\frac{4}{16}$, $\frac{5}{20}$, $\frac{15}{60}$, etc.

Example: Write other fractions equivalent to $\frac{2}{3}$.

Solution: Any fraction that has a denominator that is *one-and-one-half* times as large as the numerator:

$$\frac{4}{6}, \frac{10}{15}, \frac{14}{21}, \frac{16}{24}, \text{ etc.}$$

When the numerator and denominator of a fraction cannot be divided evenly by the same whole number (other than 1), the fraction is said to be in simplest form. In the examples above, $\frac{1}{2}$, $\frac{1}{4}$, and $\frac{2}{3}$ are in simplest form.

Test Yourself 5

Directions: Indicate which of the following fractions are in *simplest form*. For those fractions that are not, try to simplify them.

1. $\frac{13}{42}$

2. $\frac{12}{18}$

3. $\frac{8}{48}$

4. $\frac{21}{26}$

5. $\frac{6}{9}$

6. $\frac{42}{48}$

7. $\frac{9}{24}$

8. $\frac{17}{32}$

9. $\frac{9}{108}$

10. $\frac{4}{24}$

To write equivalent fractions where the numerator is not 1 requires one more step:

Example: What is the equivalent fraction for $\dfrac{4}{5}$ using 10 as a denominator?

Solution: Each $\dfrac{1}{5}$ is equivalent to $\dfrac{2}{10}$; therefore, $\dfrac{4}{5}$ is equivalent to $\dfrac{8}{10}$.

The quickest way to find an equivalent fraction is to divide the denominator of the fraction you know into the denominator you want. Take the result and multiply it by the numerator of the fraction you know. This becomes the numerator of the equivalent fraction.

Example: Change $\dfrac{3}{8}$ to an equivalent fraction having 16 as a denominator.

Solution: $16 \div 8 = 2; 2 \times 3 = 6$. Answer: $\dfrac{6}{16}$

Example: Change $\dfrac{3}{4}$ into equivalent fractions having 8, 12, 24, and 32 as

denominators.

Solution: $\dfrac{3}{4} = \dfrac{6}{8}$ $(8 \div 4 = 2; 2 \times 3 = 6)$

$\dfrac{3}{4} = \dfrac{9}{12}$ $(12 \div 4 = 3; 3 \times 3 = 9)$

$\dfrac{3}{4} = \dfrac{18}{24}$ $(24 \div 4 = 6; 6 \times 3 = 18)$

$\dfrac{3}{4} = \dfrac{24}{32}$ $(32 \div 4 = 8; 8 \times 3 = 24)$

Test Yourself 6

Directions: Try the problems below.

1. $\dfrac{5}{8} = \dfrac{?}{32}, \dfrac{?}{40}, \dfrac{?}{16}$

2. $\dfrac{7}{9} = \dfrac{?}{36}, \dfrac{?}{81}$

3. $\dfrac{4}{5} = \dfrac{?}{15}, \dfrac{?}{20}, \dfrac{?}{45}$

4. $\dfrac{2}{3} = \dfrac{?}{6}, \dfrac{?}{27}, \dfrac{?}{33}$

5. $\dfrac{1}{14} = \dfrac{?}{28}, \dfrac{?}{42}, \dfrac{?}{84}$

6. $\dfrac{5}{6} = \dfrac{?}{18}, \dfrac{?}{24}, \dfrac{?}{36}$

7. $\dfrac{1}{2} = \dfrac{?}{52}, \dfrac{?}{76}$

8. $\dfrac{4}{7} = \dfrac{?}{21}, \dfrac{?}{35}, \dfrac{?}{49}$

9. $\dfrac{3}{11} = \dfrac{?}{22}, \dfrac{?}{88}$

10. $\dfrac{2}{13} = \dfrac{?}{26}, \dfrac{?}{52}$

A fraction that has a numerator larger than the denominator is called an *improper fraction*. A number expressed as an integer together with a proper fraction is called a mixed number.

Examples of improper fractions include $\dfrac{3}{2}$, $\dfrac{12}{7}$, and $\dfrac{9}{5}$. Note that each is in *simplest*

form because the numerator and denominator cannot be divided evenly by a number other than 1.

Examples of mixed numbers include $1\dfrac{1}{2}$, $1\dfrac{5}{7}$, and $1\dfrac{4}{5}$. These are called *mixed numbers*

because they have a whole number part and a fractional part. These mixed numbers are equivalent to the improper fractions given above.

To rename a mixed number as an improper fraction is easy:

Example: Rename $2\dfrac{1}{4}$ as an improper fraction.

Solution: The whole number 2 contains 8 fourths. Add to it the $\dfrac{1}{4}$ to create

the equivalent fraction $\dfrac{9}{4}$.

An alternative way of figuring this is to multiply the denominator of the fraction by the whole number and add the numerator:

Example: Rename $2\frac{1}{4}$ as an improper fraction.

Solution: $4 \times 2 = \frac{8}{4} + \frac{1}{4} = \frac{9}{4}$

To rename an improper fraction as a mixed number, just proceed backward.

Example: Rename $\frac{9}{4}$ as a mixed number.

Solution: Divide the denominator into the numerator and use the remainder as the fraction:

$$9 \div 4 = 2; \text{R1} = 2\frac{1}{4}$$

Test Yourself 7

Directions: Try these, renaming each as its equivalent form.

1. $3\frac{7}{8}$

2. $2\frac{9}{10}$

3. $11\frac{14}{15}$

4. $7\frac{2}{3}$

5. $1\frac{3}{4}$

6. $\frac{22}{7}$

7. $\frac{16}{3}$

8. $\frac{45}{8}$

9. $\frac{9}{2}$

10. $\frac{61}{12}$

Addition of Fractions

To add fractions you must first be sure that the addends have the same denominators.

Example: Add: $\dfrac{1}{4}+\dfrac{3}{4}+\dfrac{3}{4}$

Solution: The denominators are the same, so just add the numerators to arrive at the answer, $\dfrac{7}{4}$, or $1\dfrac{3}{4}$.

In most cases, denominators will be different, so you will have to find a *common denominator*.

Example: Add: $\dfrac{1}{4}+\dfrac{1}{2}$

Solution: $\dfrac{1}{2}$ is equivalent to $\dfrac{2}{4}$, so $\dfrac{1}{4}+\dfrac{2}{4}=\dfrac{3}{4}$.

Example: Add: $\dfrac{1}{4}+\dfrac{1}{3}$

Solution: This problem is trickier. It requires the writing of *equivalent fractions* in a common denominator to which 4 and 3 can easily be connected.

$\dfrac{1}{4}$ is equivalent to $\dfrac{3}{12}$.

$\dfrac{1}{3}$ is equivalent to $\dfrac{4}{12}$.

We can now add the fractions because we have written equivalent fractions in a common denominator.

$$\frac{3}{12}+\frac{4}{12}=\frac{7}{12}$$

Therefore, $\dfrac{1}{4}+\dfrac{1}{3}=\dfrac{7}{12}$.

Seven-twelfths is in simplest form, because 7 and 12 do not have a whole number (other than 1) that divides into both evenly.

How to Find a Common Denominator

You can *always* find a common denominator by multiplying the denominators together.

Example: Find a common denominator for $\dfrac{3}{4}$ and $\dfrac{3}{8}$.

Solution: Multiply 4×8; 32 is a common denominator. However, 16 and 24 are also common denominators for 4 and 8.

Don't worry about finding the *lowest* common denominator when you are adding fractions. When you see the sum, you will probably notice that the fraction can be simplified to simplest form. When you have simplified the fraction as far as you can, you have probably found the lowest common denominator.

Test Yourself 8

Directions: Try the following problems. Find a common denominator, then simplify the answer to its simplest form.

1. $\dfrac{3}{4}+\dfrac{9}{10}+\dfrac{1}{5}$

2. $\dfrac{3}{8}+\dfrac{1}{4}$

3. $5\dfrac{5}{7}+\dfrac{1}{3}$

4. $\dfrac{1}{9}+\dfrac{3}{4}+\dfrac{5}{6}$

5. $\dfrac{7}{9}+\dfrac{5}{8}+1\dfrac{1}{12}$

6. $\dfrac{2}{3}+\dfrac{9}{13}$

7. $\dfrac{6}{7}+\dfrac{6}{9}$

8. $\dfrac{1}{2}+\dfrac{3}{4}+\dfrac{5}{8}$

9. $2\dfrac{2}{3}+\dfrac{5}{6}$

10. $\dfrac{3}{11}+\dfrac{2}{13}$

Subtraction

To subtract one number from another means to find the *difference* between them on the number line. The number being subtracted is called the *subtrahend*; the number being subtracted from is the *minuend*.

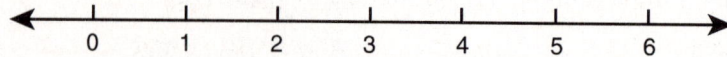

A number line, such as the one above, lets you see the difference between numbers before subtracting. For example, the difference between six and two is four units; therefore, $6 - 2 = 4$. Or, the difference between six and zero is six units; therefore, $6 - 0 = 6$. If you remember that when subtracting numbers you are interested in the difference between them on the number line, you will understand subtraction easily.

Subtraction *cannot* occur in any order, as can addition. For example, $6 - 3$ is not the same as $3 - 6$, nor is $100 - 1$ the same as $1 - 100$.

Subtracting Whole Numbers

To find the difference between a pair of whole numbers, write the smaller beneath the larger. Borrow a group from the next larger column when you are subtracting a larger numeral from a smaller one.

Example: Find the difference between 6,937 and 4,178.

Solution:
$$\begin{array}{r} 6,937 \\ -\ 4,178 \\ \hline 2,759 \end{array}$$

Step 1:   Begin by borrowing a group from the 3 (leaving 2) to make 17. Eight from 17 is 9.

Step 2:   Next, borrow a group from the 9 (leaving 8) to make 12. Seven from 12 is 5.

Step 3:   Subtract 1 from 8, giving 7.

Step 4:   Subtract 4 from 6, giving 2.

The correct difference, 2,759, can be checked by adding it to the number you first subtracted, 4,178. You should end with 6,937 again.

Test Yourself 9

Directions: Practice subtraction with the problems below.

1. $703 - 98$
2. $1,762 - 983$
3. $429 - 108$
4. $63,921 - 4,930$
5. $278 - 88$

6. $9,000 - 699$
7. $13,706 - 4,838$
8. $863 - 92$
9. $7,333 - 6,444$
10. $290,723 - 176,731$

Subtracting Decimals

If necessary, review the basics of decimal notation that you studied earlier under decimal addition. Most of the same guidelines apply to the subtraction of decimals.

When finding the difference between two numbers written in decimal notation, be sure to arrange the smaller beneath the larger, keeping the decimal points in line. Then proceed just as if you were subtracting whole numbers.

As with addition, you may want to write in zeros to "fill in" those decimal places having no numerals in them.

Example: Subtract 22.02 from 23.001.

Solution:
$$\begin{array}{r} 23.001 \\ -\ 22.020 \\ \hline 00.981 \end{array}$$

Remember that the decimal point in the answer is placed directly below the decimal points of the subtrahend and minuend.

Test Yourself 10

Directions: Try the following problems as practice.

1. $16.17 - .9902$
2. $.83 - .0624$
3. $.918 - .759$
4. $.360 - .204$
5. $6.57 - 2.43$

6. $28.47 - 3.622$
7. $809.03 - 24.9$
8. $37.94 - .4223$
9. $38.83 - 9.003$
10. $67.2115 - 3.79$

Subtracting Fractions

To find the difference between two fractions that have the same denominators, simply subtract the numerators, leaving the denominators alone.

Example: Find the difference between $\frac{7}{8}$ and $\frac{3}{8}$.

Solution: $\frac{7}{8} - \frac{3}{8} = \frac{4}{8}$. Simplified to simplest form: $\frac{4}{8} = \frac{1}{2}$.

When subtracting mixed numbers that have the same denominators, one more step is required:

Example: Subtract $2\frac{3}{4}$ from $9\frac{1}{4}$.

Solution: *Step 1:* Rename the mixed numbers as improper form:

$$2\frac{3}{4} = \frac{11}{4} \ (4 \times 2 + 3 = 11)$$

$$9\frac{1}{4} = \frac{37}{4} \ (4 \times 9 + 1 = 37)$$

Step 2: Subtract the numerators, leaving the denominators alone:

$$\frac{37}{4} - \frac{11}{4} = \frac{26}{4} \quad \text{Simplified to simplest form} = \frac{13}{2}$$

$$\text{Renamed as a mixed number} = 6\frac{1}{2}$$

Before trying to subtract mixed numbers having different denominators, review the procedure for writing equivalent fractions as it was explained earlier in the book. Finding the difference between two mixed numbers is easy after you find common denominators and equivalent fractions:

Example: Subtract $3\dfrac{3}{4}$ from $6\dfrac{3}{8}$.

Solution: *Step 1:* Rename each mixed number as its improper form:

$$3\frac{3}{4} = \frac{15}{4} \ (4 \times 3 + 3 = 15)$$

$$6\frac{3}{8} = \frac{51}{8} \ (8 \times 6 + 3 = 51)$$

Step 2: Find a common denominator. For fourths and eighths, eighths are a good choice.

Step 3: Write the equivalent fractions:

$$\frac{15}{4} = \frac{30}{8} \ (8 \div 4 = 2; \ 2 \times 15 = 30)$$

$$\frac{51}{8} = \frac{51}{8}$$

Step 4: $\dfrac{51}{8} - \dfrac{30}{8} = \dfrac{21}{8}$, or $2\dfrac{5}{8}$

Test Yourself 11

Directions: Practice the following problems.

1. $\dfrac{15}{16} - \dfrac{2}{8}$

2. $\dfrac{7}{9} - \dfrac{2}{3}$

3. $1\dfrac{7}{10} - \dfrac{9}{16}$

4. $9\dfrac{5}{8} - \dfrac{6}{32}$

5. $3\dfrac{7}{12} - 1\dfrac{2}{3}$

6. $\dfrac{4}{7} - \dfrac{1}{4}$

7. $7\dfrac{9}{10} - \dfrac{19}{20}$

8. $\dfrac{3}{4} - \dfrac{2}{3}$

9. $2\dfrac{2}{3} - \dfrac{4}{5}$

10. $4\dfrac{2}{3} - \dfrac{3}{4}$

Multiplication

Multiplication is a shortcut for addition. For example, rather than add a number 12 times, we simply multiply it by 12. The result of multiplying two numbers is called the *product*. The numbers that are multiplied are called *factors*.

Most errors in multiplication result from not having memorized the multiplication tables. One of the best ways to improve your mathematics ability is to practice reciting the multiplication tables until you know them thoroughly. You can find these tables in any arithmetic textbook.

Multiplication of Whole Numbers

The following examples show the procedures used in multiplying whole numbers. Note the care with which the partial products are written in columns before being added. You should aim to be just as careful.

Example: Multiply 435 by 253.

Solution:

$$
\begin{array}{r}
435 \\
\times\ 253 \\
\hline
1305 \leftarrow \\
2175\ \leftarrow \\
870 \\
\hline
\end{array}
$$

Each line is a *partial product*.

product → 110,055

Test Yourself 12

Directions: Practice your multiplication using the following examples, and time yourself. Then make up ten similar problems and try again, emphasizing speed and accuracy.

1. 726×29
2. 33×14
3. $1,064 \times 397$
4. 512×136
5. $3,112 \times 223$

6. $11,550 \times 32$
7. $4,619 \times 550$
8. 217×118
9. $1,214 \times 104$
10. $64,397 \times 1,472$

Multiplication of Decimals

Multiplication of decimals is no harder than multiplication of whole numbers. However, you must remember one more step: to count off the correct number of decimal places in the product.

The rule for counting off the correct number of decimal places is: *The number of decimal places in the product is equal to the total number of decimal places in both factors.*

The following three problems should make this rule clear:

Example:

$$
\begin{array}{r}
3.11 \leftarrow 2\ \text{decimal places} \\
\times\ \ 2 \leftarrow 0\ \text{decimal places} \\
\hline
6.22 \leftarrow 2\ \text{decimal places}
\end{array}
$$

Example:

$$
\begin{array}{r}
3.11 \leftarrow 2\ \text{decimal places} \\
\times\ .2 \leftarrow 1\ \text{decimal place} \\
\hline
.622 \leftarrow 3\ \text{decimal places}
\end{array}
$$

Example:

$$
\begin{array}{r}
.311 \leftarrow 3\ \text{decimal places} \\
\times\ .2 \leftarrow 1\ \text{decimal place} \\
\hline
.0622 \leftarrow 4\ \text{decimal places (A zero was added to make a fourth place)}
\end{array}
$$

When multiplying larger decimals, line up the partial products carefully, count up the total number of decimal places in the factors, and place the decimal point in the product the same number of places from the last numeral.

Example: 2.301← 3 decimal places
            ×18.73← 2 decimal places
               6903
           16107
           18408
            2301
         43.09773← 5 decimal places from right

Test Yourself 13

Directions: Practice the following.

1. $7{,}209 \times .3741$
2. 103.2×97.1
3. 638.63×83.6
4. $29.10 \times .04$
5. $7.720 \times .34$
6. 8143.6×20.13
7. $.0034 \times .276$
8. 93.2×1.26
9. $103.621 \times .43$
10. 72.7×63.8

Multiplication of Fractions

The multiplication of fractions is simple and straightforward. It consists of two steps:

1 Multiplying the numerator by the numerator and the denominator by the denominator

2 Simplifying the product (answer) to the simplest form

Example: Multiply $\dfrac{3}{8}$ by $\dfrac{2}{3}$.

Solution: We multiply straight across.

Step 1: $\dfrac{3}{8} \bullet \dfrac{2}{3} = \dfrac{6}{24}$

Step 2: Simplify $\dfrac{6}{24}$ to simplest form.

$$\dfrac{6}{24} = \dfrac{1}{4}$$

There is no need to find common denominators when multiplying (or dividing) fractions. Simply remember to multiply straight across and simplify the product if necessary.

In some problems, one factor may be a mixed number and the other a proper fraction. In that case, proceed as follows:

Example: Multiply $\frac{7}{8}$ by $2\frac{1}{2}$.

Solution: Write the fractions as before, renaming $2\frac{1}{2}$ as an improper fraction.

Multiply straight across:

Step 1: $\frac{7}{8} \cdot \frac{5}{2} = \frac{35}{16}$

Step 2: Because the product is in simplest form, leave it that way or rewrite it as the mixed number $2\frac{3}{16}$.

Test Yourself 14

Directions: Practice on the following problems.

1. $\frac{3}{8} \cdot 3\frac{1}{6}$

2. $\frac{4}{7} \cdot \frac{9}{10}$

3. $\frac{2}{5} \cdot 60$

4. $1\frac{2}{11} \cdot 16\frac{1}{2}$

5. $2\frac{2}{3} \cdot \frac{9}{11}$

6. $100 \cdot \frac{3}{5}$

7. $\frac{6}{25} \cdot \frac{8}{45}$

8. $7\frac{7}{8} \cdot 6\frac{5}{9}$

9. $\frac{3}{4} \cdot \frac{1}{2} \cdot \frac{2}{3}$

10. $1\frac{1}{5} \cdot 5 \cdot \frac{3}{8}$

Squares and Square Roots

Squares

The product of a number times itself is called the *square* of that number. For example, 9 is the square of 3; 16 is the square of 4; and 25 is the square of 5. Any number we work with has a square; we simply multiply the number by itself to find it.

Examples: Find the squares of the following numbers:

(A) 15

(B) 3.22

(C) $\dfrac{3}{4}$

(D) .01

(E) 125

(F) $\dfrac{7}{6}$

Solutions: (A) $15 \times 15 = 225$

(B) $3.22 \times 3.22 = 10.3684$

(C) $\dfrac{3}{4} \times \dfrac{3}{4} = \dfrac{9}{16}$

(D) $.01 \times .01 = .0001$

(E) $125 \times 125 = 15{,}625$

(F) $\dfrac{7}{6} \times \dfrac{7}{6} = \dfrac{49}{36}$ *or* $1\dfrac{13}{36}$

The word *square* is also used as a verb to describe the process used to find the product of a number times itself. To *square a number* means to multiply it by itself. Special notation is used when working with squares. Rather than write $15 \times 15 = 225$, we use an exponent, $15^2 = 225$.

There is further discussion and practice in using exponents in the section "Exponents" on page 284.

You will find that test-makers and mathematics textbook writers rely on easily recognized squares in many problems. For this reason, we think it is very important that you learn to recognize certain common numbers as squares of other numbers.

The table on pages 268 and 269 lists numbers and their squares. Note that once you learn the link between a number and its square, you can apply that knowledge regardless of where the decimal point is located. For example, if you know that $15^2 = 225$, you also know that $1.5^2 = 2.25$, and $.15^2 = .0225$, and $150^2 = 22{,}500$.

Study the table carefully. It is a good idea to memorize the squares of the numbers 1 through 25, 30, 40, 50, 60, 70, 80, 90, and 100, although you should not spend a great deal of time on it. The important thing is to understand the relationships in the table and to link in your mind a whole number with its square.

Square Roots

Every number that is a square has a *square root*. In the table on pages 268 and 269, for example, you can see that the number multiplied by itself to find the square is the *square root* of the square.

For example, 15 is the square root of 225, 1.5 is the square root of 2.25, and .15 is the square root of .0225.

Test Yourself 15

Directions: Try these, using the table of squares. Find the square root of the following.

1. 32,400
2. 1.96
3. 225
4. 441

5. 5.29
6. 625
7. 6.25
8. 900

A special notation called a *radical* ($\sqrt{\ }$) is used when working with square roots. For example, $\sqrt{9} = 3$ is read: "The square root of nine equals three." The radical over the number nine is read "square root of."

If you are asked to find the square root of a fraction, simply consider the numerator and denominator as separate numbers, and find the square root of each.

Example: Find: $\sqrt{\dfrac{9}{16}}$

Solution: $\dfrac{\sqrt{9}}{\sqrt{16}} = \dfrac{3}{4}$. The square root of $\dfrac{9}{16}$ is $\dfrac{3}{4}$.

Check: $\left(\dfrac{3}{4}\right)^2 = \dfrac{3}{4} \cdot \dfrac{3}{4} = \dfrac{9}{16}$

No doubt you have learned ways of finding square roots of numbers that don't fit so neatly into a table such as the one below. However, because such problems occur so rarely on high school entrance examinations, we will not review those methods in this book. In most cases, you will be able to estimate the square root of a number accurately enough to select the correct answer. That is why we suggest you study the table closely and learn to recognize those numbers and their squares and square roots.

Test Yourself 16

Directions: Try the following problems without using the table.

1. $14^2 =$

2. $\sqrt{169} =$

3. $\sqrt{\dfrac{121}{81}} =$

4. $\sqrt{5.76} =$

5. $100^2 =$

6. $25^2 =$

7. $20^2 =$

8. $\sqrt{\dfrac{1}{4}} =$

9. $\sqrt{144} =$

10. $2.5^2 =$

You will find further work with exponents and other roots in the section entitled "Exponents" page 284.

Related Numbers and Their Squares

$1 = 1$	$.1^2 = .01$	$10^2 = 100$
$2 = 4$	$.2^2 = .04$	$20^2 = 400$
$3 = 9$	$.3^2 = .09$	$30^2 = 900$
$4 = 16$	$.4^2 = .16$	$40^2 = 1,600$
$5 = 25$	$.5^2 = .25$	$50^2 = 2,500$
$6 = 36$	$.6^2 = .36$	$60^2 = 3,600$
$7 = 49$	$.7^2 = .49$	$70^2 = 4,900$
$8 = 64$	$.8^2 = .64$	$80^2 = 6,400$
$9 = 81$	$.9^2 = .81$	$90^2 = 8,100$
$10 = 100$	$1.0^2 = 1$	$100^2 = 10,000$
$11 = 121$	$1.1^2 = 1.21$	$110^2 = 12,100$
$12 = 144$	$1.2^2 = 1.44$	$120^2 = 14,400$
$13 = 169$	$1.3^2 = 1.69$	$130^2 = 16,900$
$14 = 196$	$1.4^2 = 1.96$	$140^2 = 19,600$
$15 = 225$	$1.5^2 = 2.25$	$150^2 = 22,500$

Related Numbers and Their Squares

$16 = 256$	$1.6^2 = 2.56$	$160^2 = 25,600$
$17 = 289$	$1.7^2 = 2.89$	$170^2 = 28,900$
$18 = 324$	$1.8^2 = 3.24$	$180^2 = 32,400$
$19 = 361$	$1.9^2 = 3.61$	$190^2 = 36,100$
$20 = 400$	$2.0^2 = 4$	$200^2 = 40,000$
$21 = 441$	$2.1^2 = 4.41$	$210^2 = 44,100$
$22 = 484$	$2.2^2 = 4.84$	$220^2 = 48,400$
$23 = 529$	$2.3^2 = 5.29$	$230^2 = 52,900$
$24 = 576$	$2.4^2 = 5.76$	$240^2 = 57,600$
$25 = 625$	$2.5^2 = 6.25$	$250^2 = 62,500$

You can refer to the table to find the square roots of some commonly used numbers.

Division

The process of division is used to determine the number of parts into which another number can be divided. A division problem is made up of the number that is being divided, called the *dividend*; the number that is doing the dividing, called the *divisor*; and the answer, called the *quotient*.

Division of Whole Numbers

The following examples show how long division is used when one whole number is divided into another. Note that in two cases the remainder is expressed as the numerator of a fraction having the divisor as the denominator. An alternative way to express the remainder is by continuing the long division and creating a quotient having a decimal remainder instead.

Study these examples carefully. Note that the decimal point in the quotient is located directly above the decimal point in the dividend. Note also that the first numeral of the quotient is placed very carefully in the correct decimal place.

Example:

$$15\frac{5}{8}$$
$$8\overline{)125}$$
$$\underline{8}$$
$$45$$
$$\underline{40}$$
$$5$$

or

$$15.625 \leftarrow \text{quotient}$$
$$\text{divisor} \rightarrow 8\overline{)125.000} \leftarrow \text{dividend}$$
$$\underline{8}$$
$$45$$
$$\underline{40}$$
$$50$$
$$\underline{48}$$
$$20$$
$$\underline{16}$$
$$40$$
$$\underline{40}$$
$$0$$

Example:

$$20.571$$
$$35\overline{)720.000}$$
$$\underline{70}$$
$$200$$
$$\underline{175}$$
$$250$$
$$\underline{245}$$
$$50$$
$$\underline{35}$$
$$15$$
$$STOP$$

or

$$20\frac{20}{35} = 20\frac{4}{7}$$
$$35\overline{)720}$$
$$\underline{70}$$
$$20$$

Example:

$$122\overline{)98}$$
$$= \frac{98}{122}$$
$$= \frac{49}{61}$$

or

$$.8032$$
$$122\overline{)98.0000}$$
$$\underline{976}$$
$$400$$
$$\underline{366}$$
$$340$$
$$\underline{244}$$
$$96$$
$$STOP$$

When using decimal quotients and remainders, it is usually allowable to stop after three or four decimal places have been calculated. Note that you *can* continue to divide—in some cases, forever. Your goal should be to divide only as far as is necessary for you to come up with an answer that corresponds to the answer choices given in a particular question.

Test Yourself 17

Directions: Try the following problems for practice.

1. $3,867 \div 47$
2. $935 \div 22$
3. $103 \div 272$
4. $5,760 \div 139$
5. $5,015 \div 462$

6. $4,211 \div 104$
7. $76 \div 93$
8. $2,200 \div 1,113$
9. $678 \div 803$
10. $1,930 \div 48$

Division of Decimals

When the divisor is not a whole number but has tenths, hundredths, thousandths, and so forth as part of it, one additional step is required to solve the problem. For example:

$$12.5\overline{)250}$$

Here, we move the decimal point in the divisor as many places to the right as necessary to make the divisor a whole number. Then we add that same number of places to the dividend. In the example above:

$$12.5\overline{)2500.}$$

Now, the problem becomes one of simple whole number long division:

$$
\begin{array}{r}
20. \\
125\overline{)2500.} \\
\underline{250} \\
00
\end{array}
$$

Thus, $250 \div 12.5 = 20$.

Example: Divide .666 into .333.

Solution: $.666\overline{)333}$ Move the decimal point, and add zeros.

$$666\overline{)333.00}^{\,.50}$$ The answer is .5.
$$\underline{333\ 0}$$
$$0$$

or $666\overline{)333}$

$$=\frac{333}{666}=\frac{1}{2}$$

In those cases in which the divisor is not a whole number, be sure to move the decimal point the correct number of places in the divisor and dividend. Then, place the decimal point in the quotient directly above its new place.

Test Yourself 18

Directions: Try the problems below for practice.

1. $.396 \div 1.3$
2. $493.2 \div 85.63$
3. $1{,}034.62 \div 7.88$
4. $972.1 \div .0543$
5. $42.678 \div 501.3$
6. $45.776 \div 62.11$
7. $9.1494 \div 933.06$
8. $203.4 \div 38.32$
9. $280.420 \div 1.980$
10. $.092 \div 47.4284$

Division of Fractions

If you multiply fractions accurately, you can divide them just as easily. For example, to divide $\frac{3}{4}$ by $\frac{5}{8}$, multiply by the reciprocal of the divisor. The problem $\frac{3}{4} \div \frac{5}{8}$ thus becomes $\frac{3}{4} \times \frac{8}{5}$.

Simply multiply straight across, and simplify the resulting fraction:

$$\frac{3}{4} \times \frac{8}{5} = \frac{24}{20} = \frac{6}{5} \text{ or } 1\frac{1}{5}$$

This procedure works whether both numbers are fractions or not. If a whole number is to be inverted, you should change it to a fraction first. For example $\frac{3}{16} \div 2$ becomes $\frac{3}{16} \div \frac{2}{1}$. To divide, multiply by the reciprocal of the divisor:

$$\frac{3}{16} \times \frac{1}{2} = \frac{3}{32}$$

Another example is $3\frac{1}{2} \div \frac{3}{8}$, which becomes $\frac{7}{2} \div \frac{3}{8}$.

To divide, multiply by the reciprocal of the divisor:

$$\frac{7}{2} \times \frac{8}{3} = \frac{56}{6} = 9\frac{2}{6} = 9\frac{1}{3}$$

Test Yourself 19

Directions: When dividing fractions, estimating the quotient can be an important help. Try the following problems to practice dividing fractions.

1. $\frac{7}{8} \div \frac{2}{3} =$

2. $4\frac{3}{4} \div 2\frac{1}{2} =$

3. $\frac{6}{16} \div \frac{9}{13} =$

4. $\frac{9}{14} \div 9\frac{4}{8} =$

5. $\frac{3}{5} \div 6\frac{3}{8} =$

6. $20\frac{1}{3} \div \frac{1}{51} =$

7. $\frac{4}{5} \div 6 =$

8. $\frac{4}{21} \div \frac{3}{4} =$

9. $\frac{3}{8} \div 2 =$

10. $\frac{4}{15} \div \frac{2}{5} =$

Operations Using Fractions and Decimals

It is not uncommon to have fractions and decimals appear in the same problem. However, because they are different forms of notation, one must be renamed as the other before you can perform any of the basic operations with them. *You may not add, subtract, multiply, or divide using both kinds of notation at once.*

For example, to add $3\frac{1}{2}$ and 1.35, you must rename either $3\frac{1}{2}$ to decimal notation or 1.35 to fractional notation. The examples below will show you both ways.

To rename a fraction as its equivalent decimal, simply divide the denominator into the numerator.

Example: Find the decimal equivalent of $\frac{3}{8}$.

Solution:
$$8\overline{)3.000} \qquad \frac{3}{8} = .375$$

.375
$$\begin{array}{r} 24 \\ \hline 60 \\ 56 \\ \hline 40 \\ 40 \\ \hline 0 \end{array}$$

This process will always work, regardless of the fraction. It will be useful to memorize the decimal fractional equivalents on page 273. Remember, though, that you can always find a decimal equivalent of a fraction by dividing its denominator into its numerator.

To rename a decimal as a fraction requires a similar method. Simply write the decimal as a fraction, and simplify it as necessary.

Example: Rename .125 as a fraction.

Solution: .125 is read "one hundred twenty-five thousandths."

Write it as $\frac{125}{1,000}$, and simplify it by dividing the numerator and denominator by 125.

$$\frac{125}{1,000} = \frac{1}{8} \ or \ .125 = \frac{1}{8}$$

Test Yourself 20

> **Directions:** Practice the problems below. Rename fractions as decimals and decimals as fractions.

1. $\dfrac{4}{5}$

2. .75

3. $\dfrac{7}{25}$

4. $\dfrac{333}{1,000}$

5. .435

6. .18

7. $\dfrac{3}{10}$

8. .45

9. .125

10. $\dfrac{13}{50}$

It may be a good idea to review the fractional and decimal equivalents on page 281.

Combining Operations

Frequently, more than one operation must be used to arrive at an answer to a problem. That is, a series of calculations may have to be strung together to produce the correct answer. Problems of this type are no more complicated than the ones you have done already, but require one additional piece of knowledge.

For example, how would you approach this problem?

$$2\dfrac{1}{2} + 10 \div 1\dfrac{1}{4} - 3.125 \times .80$$

Which operations would you do first? Fortunately, the answer is clear, if you observe the following two rules:

1 Do multiplication and division first, in order, from left to right.

2 Do addition and subtraction second, in order, from left to right.

Therefore, the first step is to put parentheses around the multiplication and division operations.

$$2\dfrac{1}{2} + \left(10 \div 1\dfrac{1}{4}\right) - (3.125 \times .80)$$

Then, do the operations inside the parentheses, and simplify.

$$2\frac{1}{2} + 8 - 2.5 = 8$$

Another example is a problem that looks simple but may be confusing, unless you understand the order of operations described above.

$$2 \div 3 + 1 \div 2 + 2 \times 3 + 1$$

To solve this problem, put parentheses around the multiplication and division operations. Then, perform the operations inside the parentheses, and simplify.

$$(2 \div 3) + (1 \div 2) + (2 \times 3) + 1 =$$

$$\frac{2}{3} + \frac{1}{2} + 6 + 1 = 8\frac{1}{6}$$

Solve the following problems, interchanging fractional and decimal notation when necessary. It is up to you to decide, based upon whichever is easier, whether to rename the decimals as fractions or to rename the fractions as decimals. For example, when adding $5\frac{3}{4}$ and .6157, it is easier to rename $5\frac{3}{4}$ as 5.750 and add it to .6157 rather than the other way around. You must make the same choice when multiplying or dividing fractions with decimals.

Test Yourself 21

Directions: Now, go on to the problems that follow.

1. $7\frac{1}{100} \times .467$ 6. $2\frac{3}{8} \times 10.65$

2. $3.27 - 2\frac{1}{4}$ 7. $1\frac{1}{5} + .05$

3. $13\frac{2}{5} - 5.2$ 8. $1\frac{1}{2} - .789$

4. $6\frac{3}{4} \div .375$ 9. $4\frac{1}{7} \times .9$

5. $9\frac{1}{8} \div 2.76$ 10. $6\frac{3}{10} + 15.65$

Percentage

It is a good idea to have studied all of the previous sections about decimals in this book before starting this section. If you can work easily with decimals, percentages should present no difficulty for you.

One percent is one one-hundredth of something. The last syllable of the word *percent*, *-cent*, is the name we give to one one-hundredth of a dollar.

One percent of $1, then, is one cent. Using decimal notation, we can write one cent as $.01, five cents as $.05, twenty-five cents as $.25, and so forth.

Twenty-five cents represents twenty-five one-hundredths of a dollar. Rather than say that something is so many one-hundredths of something else, we use the word *percent*. Twenty-five cents, then, is twenty-five *percent* of a dollar. We use the symbol % to stand for *percent*.

Percentage ("hundredths of") is a convenient and widely used way of measuring all sorts of things. By measuring in hundredths, we can be very precise and notice very small changes.

Test Yourself 22

Directions: Suppose Jane drove a car 100 miles on Monday, and 101 miles on Tuesday. Notice that she drove *one percent farther* on Tuesday than on Monday. For the days listed below, by how much percent more, or less, did she drive compared to Monday, if she drove the following distances?

1. Wednesday 110 miles
2. Thursday 140 miles
3. Friday 100 miles
4. Saturday 99 miles
5. Sunday 90 miles

Test Yourself 23

Directions: By what percent is the second number of each pair listed below larger or smaller than the first number?

1. 100, 150
2. 100, 73
3. 100, 80
4. 100, 1

5. 100, .5
6. 100, 200
7. 100, 450
8. 100, .01

Percentage is not limited to comparing other numbers to 100. You can divide *any* number into hundredths and talk about percentage.

Example: Find 1% of 200.

Solution: 1% of 200 is one one-hundredth of 200.

$$200 \div 100 = 2$$

Using decimal notation we can calculate one percent of 200 by:

$$200 \times .01 = 2$$

Similarly, we can find a percentage of any number we choose by multiplying it by the correct decimal notation. For example:

Five percent of fifty: $.05 \times 50 = 2.5$

Three percent of 150: $.03 \times 150 = 4.5$

Ten percent of 60: $.10 \times 60 = 6$

Test Yourself 24

Directions: Do the following problems for practice.

1. Ten percent of eight
2. Twenty-five percent of sixty
3. Eleven percent of ten
4. One percent of three hundred fifty

5. Ninety-nine percent of eighty
6. Thirty-three percent of thirty-three
7. Seventy-five percent of one hundred twelve
8. Fifty percent of two hundred

All percentage measurements are not between one percent and one-hundred percent. We may want to consider less than one percent of something, especially if it is very large.

For example, if you were handed a book one thousand pages long and were told to read one percent of it in five minutes, how much would you have to read?

$$1,000 \times .01 = 10 \text{ pages}$$

Quite an assignment! You might bargain to read one-half of one percent, or one-tenth of one percent, in the five minutes allotted to you.

Using decimal notation, we write one-tenth of one percent as .001, the decimal number for one one-thousandth. If you remember that a percent is one one-hundredth of something, you can see that one-tenth of that percent is equivalent to one one-thousandth of the whole.

In percent notation, one-tenth of one percent is written as .1%. On high school entrance exams, students often mistakenly think that .1% is equal to .1. As you now know, .1% is really equal to .001.

Test Yourself 25

Directions: For practice, rename the following percents as decimal notation and vice versa.

1. 1%   6. .003
2. 1.2%   7. 1.5%
3. .5%   8. .015
4. .05   9. 15%
5. .001   10. .0001

Sometimes we are concerned with more than 100% of something. But, you may ask, if 100% constitutes all of something, how can we speak of *more* than all of it?

Where things are growing, or increasing in size or amount, we may want to compare their new size to the size they once were. For example, suppose we measured the heights of three plants to be 6 inches, 9 inches, and 12 inches one week, and discover a week later that the first plant is still 6 inches tall but the second and third ones are now 18 inches tall.

- The six-inch plant grew *zero percent*, because it didn't grow at all.
- The second plant *added 100%* to its size. It doubled in height.
- The third plant *added 50%* to its height.

We can also say:

- The first plant is 100% of its original height.
- The second plant grew to 200% of its original height.
- The third plant grew to 150% of its original height.

Test Yourself 26

Directions: Practice the following problems. For each pair of numbers, tell (1) what percentage of the first number would have to be added to get the second number, and (2) what percentage of the first number is the second number.

Example: 100, 150

Solution: *Step 1:* Fifty percent of 100 would have to be added to 100 to get 150.

Step 2: 150 represents 150% of 100.

1. 50, 75   6. 1, 1.5

2. 50, 100   7. .5, .75

3. 10, 15   8. 33, 44

4. 100, 132   9. 55, 55

5. 20, 24   10. 100, 1,000

You may want to know a certain percentage of a fraction.

Example: What is 50% of $\frac{2}{3}$?   *or*   What is 20% of $1\frac{1}{2}$?

Solution: Rename 50% as its equivalent fraction and multiply $\frac{1}{2} \cdot \frac{2}{3} = \frac{2}{6} = \frac{1}{3}$, or

rename $\frac{2}{3}$ and 50 to decimal notation and multiply:

$.50 \times .666 = .333$

Similarly, the second example can be calculated as:

$\frac{1}{5} \times \frac{3}{2} = \frac{3}{10}$ *or* $.20 \times 1.5 = .30$

Here are some common percentage and fractional equivalents you should remember:

- Ten percent (10%) = one-tenth (.10), *or* $\left(\dfrac{1}{10}\right)$.

- Twelve and one-half percent (12.5%) = one-eighth (.125), *or* $\left(\dfrac{1}{8}\right)$.

- Sixteen and two-thirds percent $\left(16\dfrac{2}{3}\%\right)$ = one-sixth (0.166666̄), *or* $\left(\dfrac{1}{6}\right)$.

- Twenty percent (20%) = one-fifth (.20), *or* $\left(\dfrac{1}{5}\right)$.

- Twenty-five percent (25%) = one quarter or one-fourth (.25), *or* $\left(\dfrac{1}{4}\right)$.

- Thirty-three and one-third percent $\left(33\dfrac{1}{3}\%\right)$ = one-third (.33̄3), *or* $\left(\dfrac{1}{3}\right)$.

- Thirty-seven and one-half percent (37.5%) = three-eighths (.375), *or* $\left(\dfrac{3}{8}\right)$.

- Fifty percent (50%) = one-half (.50), *or* $\left(\dfrac{1}{2}\right)$.

- Sixty-two and one-half percent (62.5%) = five-eighths (.625), *or* $\left(\dfrac{5}{8}\right)$.

- Sixty-six and two-thirds percent $\left(66\dfrac{2}{3}\%\right)$ = two-thirds (.66̄6), *or* $\left(\dfrac{2}{3}\right)$.

- Seventy-five percent (75%) = three quarters or three-fourths (.75), *or* $\left(\dfrac{3}{4}\right)$.

- Eighty-three and one-third percent $\left(83\dfrac{1}{3}\right)$ = five-sixths (.83̄3), *or* $\left(\dfrac{5}{6}\right)$.

- Eighty-seven and one-half percent (87.5%) = seven-eighths (.875), *or* $\left(\dfrac{7}{8}\right)$.

Test Yourself 27

Directions: Do the following for practice.

1. What is 75% of $\frac{7}{8}$?

2. What is 10% of $3\frac{3}{4}$?

3. What is 40% of $\frac{2}{3}$?

4. What is 27% of $4\frac{1}{2}$?

5. What is $33\frac{1}{3}$ % of $6\frac{2}{3}$?

6. What is 16% of $7\frac{5}{8}$?

Types of Percentage Problems

There are three types of percentage problems:

① The problem asks you to find a percentage of a certain number.

Example: Find 22% of 50.

Solution: $.22 \times 50 = 11$

② The problem gives you a number and then asks you to find another number, of which the first is a certain percentage.

Example: 30 is 20% of what number?

Solution: If 30 is 20% of a number, it is one-fifth of it. Thirty is one-fifth of 150. Or, 30 = .20 of the number. Long division leads to the answer: 150.

$$
\begin{array}{r}
150 \\
.20\overline{)30.00} \\
\underline{20} \\
100 \\
\underline{100} \\
0
\end{array}
$$

Problems like this are easily solved using a short algebraic sentence. We know that 30 equals 20% of an unknown number. Thus, 30 = .20n. Dividing both sides by .20, we get the answer, $n = 150$.

3   The problem asks you to find what percent one number is of another.

Example: 15 is what percent of 60?

Solution: This is a simple division problem in long division.

$$\frac{15}{60} = 60\overline{)15.000}$$

$$
\begin{array}{r}
0.250 \\
60\overline{)15.000} \\
\underline{120} \\
300 \\
\underline{300} \\
0
\end{array}
$$

$$.250 = 25\%$$

An alternative method is to simplify the fraction $\frac{15}{60}$ to its simplest form, $\frac{1}{4}$. The percentage equivalent of $\frac{1}{4}$ is 25%.

Final Words on Percentage

When solving problems involving percentages, be careful of common errors:

- **Read the notation carefully.** .50% is *not* fifty percent, but one half of one percent.

- When solving problems for percentage increases or decreases in size, **read the problem carefully**.

- **Use common sense.** If you want to find less than 100% of a number, your result will be smaller than the number you started with. For example, 43% of 50 is less than 50.

- **Using common sense works in the other direction as well.** For example, 70 is 40% of what number? The number you are looking for must be larger than 70, because 70 is only $\frac{40}{100}$ of it. Moreover, you can estimate that the number you are looking for will be a little more than twice as large as 70, because 70 is almost half (50%) of that number.

Test Yourself 28

Directions: Solve these problems.

1. 28% of 45 is ____.

2. $\frac{1}{4}$ % of 75 is ____.

3. $2\frac{1}{2}$ % of ____ is 75.

4. 35 is ____% of 70.

5. 50 is ____% of 12.5.

6. 1.5 is ____% of 9.

7. 3% of 1.75 is ____.

8. 12 is 5% of ____.

9. 130% of 60 is ____.

10. 180 is 200% of ____.

11. 2.5% of 50 is ____.

12. 60 is ____% of 90.

13. 30 is 20% of ____.

14. $66\frac{2}{3}$ % of ____ is 104.

Exponents

It is frequently beneficial to use shorthand methods of writing numbers in mathematics. One of the most common is the use of *exponents*.

An exponent is a number that tells you how many times the number it refers to (called the *base*) is used as a factor in a given calculation.

For example,

$$10^3 \leftarrow \text{exponent}$$
$$\uparrow$$
$$\text{base}$$

is a shorthand way of writing $10 \cdot 10 \cdot 10$, or 1,000. Note that the exponent is written to the right and above the base, and, to avoid confusion, the numeral is smaller in size.

Test Yourself 29

Directions: Take a minute to write out the following numbers as was done earlier. There is no need to calculate the actual product. For example: $5^4 = 5 \cdot 5 \cdot 5 \cdot 5$.

1. 10^7
2. 1^3
3. 3^2
4. $\left(\dfrac{1}{2}\right)^4$
5. $(.45)^5$

6. 11^2
7. 0^2
8. x^3
9. b^8
10. $(ab)^5$

Exponents are most useful in certain scientific realms in which very large or very small numbers are involved. For example, it is much easier to write 10^9 rather than 1,000,000,000.

Geometry is another subject that has frequent use for exponents. Area and surface area are measured in *square* units such as square feet, square inches, and so forth. Volume is measured in cubic feet, cubic inches, or in other *cubic* units.

For example, the area of a floor might be 200 square feet. Using an exponent, we can write 200 ft.^{2}. The volume of a cube might be 8 cubic feet. We can write this as 8 ft.^{3}.

The exponent "2" is read "square" or "squared." The exponent "3" is read "cube" or "cubed."

For exponents other than 2 and 3, we use the phrase "to the ____ power." For example, 5^6 would be read "five to the sixth power."

When the exponent is not written, as when we write most numbers, the exponent is understood to be equal to 1. Any number to the first power is equivalent to itself.

For example, $10 = 10^1$. We do not write 1 as an exponent.

There are two major rules to help you calculate numbers written in exponential form. Both require that the bases of the numbers be the same.

The *first rule* involves **multiplying numbers in exponential form having the same base.** In such instances, the product may be found by adding the exponents as shown on the next page:

Example: Multiply 10^3 by 10^5.

Solution: $10^3 \cdot 10^5 = 10^{3+5} = 10^8$

Example: Multiply 2^3 by 2^4.

Solution: $2^3 \cdot 2^4 = 2^{3+4} = 2^7$

Example: Multiply x^2 by x^3.

Solution: $x^2 \cdot x^3 = x^{2+3} = x^5$

Example: Multiply 3^3 by 3.

Solution: $3^3 \cdot 3 = 3^{3+1} = 3^4$

It is very important to note that the bases were equal in each of the preceding problems. The exponents may be different.

The *second rule* involves **division of numbers in exponential form having the same base**. In finding the product of numbers in exponential form, we added the exponents. To find their quotient, we subtract the exponent of the divisor from that of the dividend as shown below:

Example: Divide 10^3 by 10^2.

Solution: $10^3 \div 10^2 = 10^{3-2} = 10^1 = 10$

Example: Divide 5^6 by 5^3.

Solution: $5^6 \div 5^3 = 5^{6-3} = 5^3$

Example: Divide x^4 by x^2.

Solution: $x^4 \div x^2 = x^{4-2} = x^2$

Example: Divide a^3 by a.

Solution: $\dfrac{a^3}{a} = a^{3-1} = a^2$

For each of the preceding examples, you may want to calculate the problem in standard fashion to prove to yourself that it works.

Test Yourself 30

Directions: Practice the problems below.

1. $1^3 \div 1^2$
2. $6^{10} \div 6^8$
3. 15^5 times 15^3
4. M^3 times M^3
5. $10^{10} \div 10^8$
6. 3^6 times 3^2
7. a^2 times a^3

8. $100^{10} \div 100^9$
9. $\left(\dfrac{3}{4}\right)^3$ times $\left(\dfrac{3}{4}\right)^2$
10. $8^5 \div 8^4$
11. $a^5 \div a^3$
12. $\left(\dfrac{1}{2}\right)^5 \div \left(\dfrac{1}{2}\right)^4$
13. x^2 times x^2

Zero and Negative Exponents

You may have noticed while practicing that you can divide numbers written in exponential notation and end up with an exponent that is negative or equal to zero. Both results are perfectly acceptable; they will be mentioned only briefly because you will probably not encounter them on the high school entrance examination you take.

Example: Divide 5^3 by 5^3.

Solution: $5^3 \div 5^3 = 5^{3-3} = 5^0$

You may have realized that when we divide a number by itself, the result is 1. Therefore, any number (or variable representing a number) having zero as an exponent is equal to 1. For example:

$$10^6 \div 10^6 = 10^{6-6} = 10^0 = 1$$
$$x^3 \div x^3 = x^{3-3} = x^0 = 1$$

What happens if we divide 5^3 by 5^4?

$$5^3 \div 5^4 = 5^{3-4} = 5^{-1}$$

Notice that the exponent becomes negative. A negative exponent is the symbol for a reciprocal. For example:

$$\frac{5^3}{5^4} = \frac{5 \cdot 5 \cdot 5}{5 \cdot 5 \cdot 5 \cdot 5} = \frac{1}{5} = 5^{-1}$$

$$\frac{4^2}{4^5} = \frac{4 \cdot 4}{4 \cdot 4 \cdot 4 \cdot 4 \cdot 4} = \frac{1}{4^3} = 4^{-3}$$

$$\frac{10^3}{10^5} = \frac{10 \cdot 10 \cdot 10}{10 \cdot 10 \cdot 10 \cdot 10 \cdot 10} = \frac{1}{10^2} = 10^{-2}$$

You may want to multiply these examples out to convince yourself of their truth.

Algebra

If you are finishing the eighth grade this year, you may not yet have had a formal algebra class. Nevertheless, you have probably used algebraic terms and expressions, and you have probably solved simple equations. This section reviews the skills you have acquired so far and shows you the kinds of questions you can expect to find on a high school entrance examination.

This section contains a review of:

- Signed numbers
- Variables and coefficients
- Operations with algebraic expressions
- Evaluating algebraic expressions
- Solving equations

Signed Numbers

The number line exists to both sides of zero. Each positive number to the right of zero has a negative counterpart to the left of zero. The number line below shows the location of some pairs of numbers (+4, −4; +2, −2; +1, −1).

Because each number of a pair is located the same distance from zero (although in different directions), each has the same absolute value. Two vertical bars symbolize absolute value:

$$|+4| = |-4| = 4$$

The absolute value of +4 equals the absolute value of −4. Both are equivalent to 4. If you think of absolute value as distance from zero, regardless of direction, you will understand it more easily. The absolute value of any number, positive or negative, is always expressed as a positive number.

ADDITION OF SIGNED NUMBERS

When two oppositely signed numbers having the same absolute value are added, the sum is zero:

Example: $+10 + (-10) = 0$ **Example:** $-1.5 + (+1.5) = 0$

Example: $-.010 + (+.010) = 0$ **Example:** $+\frac{3}{4} + \left(-\frac{3}{4}\right) = 0$

If one of the two oppositely signed numbers is larger in absolute value, the sum is equal to the amount of that excess and carries the same sign as the number having the larger absolute value:

Example: $+2 + (-1) = +1$ **Example:** $-2.5 + (+2.0) = -.5$

Example: $+8 + (-9) = -1$ **Example:** $-\frac{3}{4} + \left(+\frac{1}{2}\right) = -\frac{1}{4}$

Test Yourself 31

Directions: Add the following groups of numbers.

1. −2, +4, −10, and −3

2. −1.2, 2.6, and −.0005

3. 9.001, −9.002, and 1.0

4. 125, −130, −27, and 63

5. $1\frac{3}{5}$, $6\frac{2}{3}$, −2, and −4

6. $-3\frac{1}{2}$, −1.25, and −6

7. $-\frac{5}{8}, 1\frac{3}{4}$, and $-2\frac{1}{2}$

8. −100.1, −62.35, and 42.2

9. .0002, −3.6, and 1.85

10. 68.25, −74.35. and 6.10

SUBTRACTION OF SIGNED NUMBERS

Subtraction is the operation that finds the difference between two numbers, including the difference between signed numbers.

When subtracting signed numbers, it is helpful to refer to the number line:

For example, if we want to subtract +2 from +5, we can use the number line to see that the difference is +3. We give the sign to the difference that represents the direction we are moving along the number line, from the number being subtracted to the number from which we are subtracting. In this case, because we are subtracting +2 from +5, we count three units in a positive direction from +2 to +5 on the number line.

When subtracting signed numbers:

- The distance between the two numbers gives you the absolute value of the difference.
- The direction you have to move from the number being subtracted to get to the number from which you are subtracting gives you the sign of the difference.

Example: Subtract −3 from +5.

Solution: Distance on number line between −3 and +5 is 8 units. Direction is from negative to positive—a positive direction. Answer is +8.

Example: Subtract −6 from −8.

Solution: Distance on number line between −6 and −8 is 2 units. Direction is from −6 to −8—a negative direction. Answer is −2.

Example: Subtract +1.30 from −2.70.

Solution: Distance between them on the number line is 4.0. Direction is from +1.30 to −2.70—a negative direction. Answer is −4.0.

Test Yourself 32

Directions: Try these subtraction problems. Think before you answer!

1. −2 from −3

2. $-\dfrac{3}{5}$ from $1\dfrac{2}{5}$

3. 6.8 from 2.2

4. −3.6 from 5.5

5. −7.65 from .002

6. −1 from 1

7. .0019 from −.0010

8. 102 from 96.5

9. $-2\dfrac{1}{2}$ from $7\dfrac{2}{3}$

10. $-\dfrac{9}{10}$ from $-\dfrac{9}{10}$

A quick way to subtract signed numbers accurately involves placing the numbers in columns, reversing the sign of the number being subtracted, and then adding the two.

Example: Subtract +26 from +15.

Solution:
$$\begin{array}{r} +15 \\ -\ +26 \\ \hline \end{array} = \begin{array}{r} +15 \\ +\ -26 \\ \hline -11 \end{array}$$

Example: Subtract −35 from +10.

Solution:
$$\begin{array}{r} +10 \\ -\ -35 \\ \hline \end{array} = \begin{array}{r} +10 \\ +\ +35 \\ \hline +45 \end{array}$$

Notice that in each of the examples, the correct answer was found by reversing the sign of the number being subtracted and then adding.

MULTIPLICATION OF SIGNED NUMBERS

Signed numbers are multiplied as any other numbers would be, with the following exceptions:

- The product of two negative numbers is positive.
- The product of two positive numbers is positive.
- The product of a negative number and a positive number is negative.

Example: $-3 \times -6 = +18$

Example: $-3.05 \times +6 = -18.30$

Example: $+4\dfrac{1}{2} \times -3 = -13\dfrac{1}{2}$

Example: $+1 \times -1 \times +1 = -1$

Test Yourself 33

Directions: Practice with the following examples. Remember, the only way to get a negative product is with a pair of oppositely signed factors.

1. -5×-6

2. -2.5×-1.3

3. $-\dfrac{3}{4} \times 1\dfrac{1}{2}$

4. $+\dfrac{2}{7} \times -\dfrac{2}{3}$

5. $-1.2 \times -.75 \times -.1$

6. $-\dfrac{2}{3} \times -\dfrac{1}{2} \times -\dfrac{5}{4}$

7. $-10.6 \times 3.3 \times -1.01$

8. $-2\dfrac{1}{2} \times 5.5 \times 7\dfrac{3}{10}$

9. $+.001 \times -3.25 \times 10$

10. $\dfrac{5}{9} \times 3 \times -\dfrac{1}{3}$

DIVISION OF SIGNED NUMBERS

As with multiplication, the division of signed numbers requires you to observe three simple rules:

- When dividing a positive number by a negative number, the result is negative.
- When dividing a negative number by a positive number, the result is negative.
- When dividing a negative number by a negative number, or a positive number by a positive number, the result is positive.

Example: $+6 \div -3 = -2$

Example: $-6 \div +3 = -2$

Example: $-6 \div -3 = +2$

Example: $+6 \div +3 = +2$

Test Yourself 34

Directions: Try the following problems.

1. $120 \div -8$

2. $-\dfrac{2}{3} \div +\dfrac{1}{3}$

3. $.43 \div -.2$

4. $-.063 \div +9$

5. $+122 \div -10$

6. $-1\dfrac{1}{2} \div -3$

7. $-\dfrac{7}{25} \div +\dfrac{1}{25}$

8. $-2.0002 \div -.01$

9. $\dfrac{1}{10} \div -.10$

10. $-100 \div -.25$

Variables and Coefficients

Algebra uses letters to stand for numbers. Letters of this kind having several possible values are called *variables*. The most commonly used variables are the letters x and y, although all other letters of the alphabet are also used.

The variable x looks very similar to the multiplication sign used in arithmetic. For this reason, it is a good idea to use a dot or parentheses to indicate multiplication, rather than the $\times$ symbol.

For example, if you want to write "six times five," write it like this $6 \bullet 5$ or $6(5)$, rather than 6×5.

Numbers used in front of variables to indicate how many of each variable you are working with are called *coefficients*. Coefficients may be whole numbers, decimals, fractions, or even Greek letters.

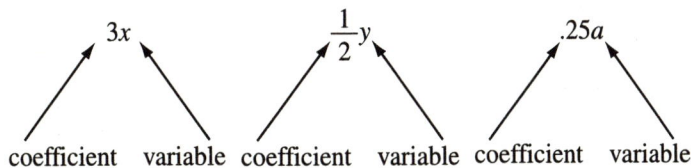

$$3x \qquad \frac{1}{2}y \qquad .25a$$

coefficient   variable   coefficient   variable   coefficient   variable

Example 1 indicates a number three times the size of x; Example 2, a number one half the size of y; and Example 3, a number one fourth the size of a.

Where you see no coefficient written, the coefficient is assumed to be 1.

Coefficients include negative numbers as well. For example, the examples below have coefficients of 1 or −1.

$$\underset{\text{coefficient} = 1}{\overset{x}{\uparrow}} \qquad \underset{\text{coefficient} = -1}{\overset{-a}{\uparrow}} \qquad \underset{\text{coefficient} = -1}{\overset{-y}{\uparrow}} \qquad \underset{\text{coefficient} = 1}{\overset{b}{\uparrow}}$$

Adding and Subtracting Algebraic Expressions

Addition of algebraic expressions or terms such as the ones described above is quite easy. You can add expressions only if the variables are identical, and you do that by adding the coefficients together.

Example: Add $2x$ and $3x$.

Solution: $5x$

Example: Add $\frac{1}{2}y$ and $2y$.

Solution: $2\frac{1}{2}y$

Example: Add $.50a$ and $.75a$.

Solution: $1.25a$

Example: Add b and b.

Solution: $2b$

Test Yourself 35

Directions: In the exercises below, add the expressions together to find an answer. Some cannot be combined because the variables are not identical. Others have negative coefficients, so be careful.

1. $a, 3a, 5a$

2. $10x, 4x, 20x$

3. $3m, 4r, 3s$

4. $-2b, -3b, 6b$

5. $-1.5r, 2r, 3s,$ and $-2s$

6. $\frac{3}{4}t, \frac{2}{3}m, -1\frac{1}{4}t, \frac{2}{5}m$

7. $0.001S, .210S, -1.25S$

8. $-20k, 2.5k, 1\frac{3}{4}k$

9. $-2x, -3y, 4x, -4z$

10. $1.02p, -.62p, -40r$

Subtracting algebraic expressions is accomplished by simply subtracting the coefficients. You must be careful if the coefficients are negative numbers, however. Use what you learned about signed numbers earlier in this book.

Example: Subtract x from $4x$.

Solution: $4x - x = 3x$

Example: Subtract $-2x$ from $4x$.

Solution: $4x - (-2x) = 6x$ (Remember the number line!)

Test Yourself 36

Directions: Try the following subtraction problems. Some have fractional coefficients, some have decimal coefficients, and others cannot be subtracted because the variables are not identical.

1. $3d$ from $4d$

2. $-1\frac{1}{2}x$ from $2x$

3. $6y$ from $-2b$

4. $-a$ from $-a$

5. $1.25m$ from $-2.25m$

6. $-.001x$ from $-.002x$

7. $2.483f$ from $-5.0f$

8. $-\frac{7}{16}r$ from $-\frac{9}{16}r$

9. $3p$ from $-2r$

10. $-16x$ from $-14x$

Multiplying Algebraic Expressions

First, review the section in this book about exponents. Pay particular attention to operations involving multiplication and division of numbers expressed with exponents.

When multiplying algebraic expressions, multiply the coefficients as you would any numbers and then add the exponents of the identical variables to find the product.

Example: Multiply $2x \cdot 3x$.

Solution: Multiply the coefficients and add the exponents of the identical variables: $2x \cdot 3x = 6x^2$.

Remember that where an exponent is not written, it is equivalent to 1.

Example: $\frac{1}{2}x \cdot 3x = \frac{3}{2}x^2$

Example: $-5y \cdot 2y = -10y^2$

Example: $-2a^2 \cdot 2a = -4a^3$

Example: $.25m^3 \cdot -.25m^3 = -.0625m^6$

Test Yourself 37

Directions: Try the following problems.

1. $3x \cdot 2x$

2. $-\dfrac{2}{3}y \cdot -2y$

3. $-1.5a \cdot 3.2a$

4. $-2z^2 \cdot 3z$

5. $1.021r \cdot 1.010r^2$

6. $-3.65f \cdot 1.60f^3$

7. $\dfrac{5}{7}z \cdot \dfrac{1}{3}z$

8. $-\dfrac{5}{16}m \cdot \dfrac{1}{4}m^2$

9. $2.02x^2 \cdot -1.1x^2$

10. $-7.1b \cdot 10.1b^3$

Any two expressions can be multiplied together and rewritten as one expression. The same multiplication rules apply.

Example: Multiply $2x \cdot 3y$.

Solution: Multiply the coefficients and add the exponents of identical variables. Because the variables are not identical in this problem, we simply multiply them together. The product is thus $6xy$.

Example: $-2a \cdot 3b = -6ab$

Example: $.35m \cdot 2f = .70fm$

Example: $-2x^2 \cdot -4y = 8x^2y$

Example: $4a^2b \cdot -3ab^2 = -12a^3b^3$ (The exponents of the identical variables were added together.)

Test Yourself 38

Directions: Try the following problems.

1. $7x \cdot 2y$

2. $\dfrac{3}{2}a^2 \cdot \dfrac{3}{2}b^2$

3. $1.2d \cdot 1.3f$

4. $-45x^2 \cdot .50y$

5. $-6.9a^2 \cdot 3.2b$

6. $100abc \cdot -a$

7. $-5q \cdot 1\dfrac{3}{10}r^2$

8. $-x^2 \cdot -y^2 \cdot -z^2$

9. $-2x^2 \cdot 4y^2 \cdot -3z$

10. $-3a \cdot 5b \cdot 2c$

Dividing Algebraic Expressions

Division is a process that reverses multiplication. When dividing algebraic expressions, divide the coefficients and subtract the exponents of the identical variables. You must also obey the rules governing division of signed numbers if the coefficients are signed.

Review the section on exponents if you cannot follow these examples:

Example: Divide $6x$ by 2.

Solution: $6x \div 2 = 3x$

Example: Divide $4a^2$ by $2a$.

Solution: $4a^2 \div 2a = 2a$

Example: Divide $-3b^2$ by $.5b$.

Solution: $-3b^2 \div .5b = -6b$

Example: Divide $2x^2y^2$ by $.4xy$.

Solution: $2x^2y^2 \div .4xy = 5xy$

Example: Divide $-6x^3y^4$ by $-x^2y$.

Solution: $-6x^3y^4 \div -x^2y = 6xy^3$

Test Yourself 39

Directions: Try the following problems for practice.

1. $100c^2 \div 10c$

2. $-3.5x \div .7x$

3. $2.20y^2 \div -1.1y$

4. $-4a^2b \div 2a$

5. $22ab^2 \div -11b$

6. $-5.1abc \div 1.7bc$

7. $4\frac{1}{2}\, ax^2 \div -1\frac{1}{2}\, a$

8. $-.001y^3 \div .01y^2$

9. $-2.8r^2s \div -.7rs$

10. $70xy^2 \div -35xy^2$

Removing Grouping Symbols

Mathematics uses parentheses and brackets to group numbers for various reasons. When calculations have to be made, it is necessary to remove the grouping symbols and combine as many of the numbers as you can.

Example 1: $6(3 + 5) = 6 \cdot 8 = 48$

Example 2: $-6(1 + 2) = -6 \cdot 3 = -18$

Example 3: $-2(a + b) = -2a + -2b = -2a - 2b$

In Examples 1 and 2, the operation inside the parentheses was carried out first, with the result then multiplied with the number outside the parentheses. In Example 3, the letters inside the parentheses could not be added, so −2 was multiplied by both a and b. In some cases, additional steps are required.

Example: Simplify: $2 - [4 - (3 - 1) + 6]$

Solution: Begin by working with the innermost parentheses, removing one set of grouping symbols at each step.

$2 - [4 - (3 - 1) + 6]$

$= 2 - [4 - 2 + 6]$

$= 2 - [8]$

$= 2 - 8$

$= -6$

This same procedure can be used with variables.

Example: Simplify: $a - [b - (a - 2b) + 3a]$

Solution: Begin with the innermost group and work outward.

$$= a - [b - (a - 2b) + 3a]$$

$$= a - (b - a + 2b + 3a)$$

$$= a - (3b + 2a)$$

$$= a - 3b - 2a$$

$$= -a - 3b$$

In the example above, it is important to note that the negative sign in front of the grouping symbol reverses the sign of the numbers within. A positive sign changes nothing.

Test Yourself 40

Directions: Try the following problems. Remember to remove the grouping symbols in order, beginning with the innermost.

1. $2 + (3 - 2) - 2$

2. $-2 - [1 + (6 - 2)]$

3. $[a + (1 - 2) + b - 3]$

4. $-1 + 2 - (3 - 4)$

5. $-5 - [(6 - 3) - (1 - 2)]$

6. $a - [3 - (b - 2) - (a - 1)]$

Evaluating Algebraic Expressions

It is often necessary to determine the value of an algebraic expression if its variables are given precise numerical values. You have done this when finding the areas, perimeters, and volumes of geometric figures. When given a formula for the area of a triangle, for example, you can find the area if you know the base and the height. The same procedure is used in evaluating algebraic expressions.

Example: Find the value of $10x$ if $x = 2$.

Solution: Substitute 2 for x, and multiply $10 \cdot 2 = 20$.

Example: Evaluate $3a^2$ if $a = 5$.

Solution: Substitute 5 for a, and multiply $3 \cdot 5^2 = 3 \cdot 25 = 75$.

Example: Evaluate $-2x^2y^2$ if $x = 2$ and $y = 3$.

Solution: $-2 \cdot 2^2 \cdot 3^2 = -2 \cdot 4 \cdot 9 = -72$

Example: Evaluate $\dfrac{2}{x^3}$ if $x = \dfrac{1}{2}$.

Solution: $\dfrac{2}{\left(\dfrac{1}{2}\right)^3} = \dfrac{2}{\left(\dfrac{1}{8}\right)} = 16$

Test Yourself 41

Directions: Try the following problems.

1. $3(x + y)$ if $x = 2, y = -1$

2. $a^2 - b^2$ if $a = 3, b = 4$

3. $4m^2n^2$ if $m = \dfrac{1}{2}, n = 1$

4. $\dfrac{1}{2}ax^2$ if $a = 32, x = 4$

5. $(b + c)(d + 2)$ if $b = \dfrac{3}{4}, c = 2, d = 0$

6. $\dfrac{1}{x^2}$ if $x = \dfrac{1}{a}$

7. $\dfrac{7y}{3}$ if $y = \dfrac{1}{3}$

8. $\dfrac{1}{2}(a + b)h$ if $a = 4, b = 3, h = 1.5$

9. $\dfrac{m_1 m_2}{r^2}$ if $m_1 = 32, m_2 = 320, r = 10$

10. $\dfrac{by^2}{c}$ if $b = 4.8, c = 1.2, y = 1$

Solving Simple Equations

Much of the work in algebra consists of finding precise values for variables. To find these precise values, variables are set equal to known quantities in *equations*. For example, the simplest equation possible is $x = 2$. This equation says, "The variable x is equal to two."

One step further is: $2y = 2$. This says, "Two times y equals two."

In the equation $2y = 2$, let's find what y equals. If 2 times y equals 2, we know y equals 1.

Example: $a + 1 = 3$

Solution: Because the variable a plus 1 equals 3, 3 is 1 larger than a. $a = 2$.

Example: $Z - 3 = 6$

Solution: The variable Z minus 3 equals 6. Z is 3 larger than 6, so $Z = 9$.

Test Yourself 42

Directions: Try the following examples. Solve the equation for the variable.

1. $a + 3 = 6$
2. $2x - 1 = 7$
3. $-2x = 6$
4. $r - 3 = -1$

5. $3b - 6 = 6$
6. $100y - 1 = 99$
7. $10 + x = 5$

Solving More Difficult Equations

Equations may have variables with fractional and decimal coefficients. Variables may also appear on both sides of the equal sign. The following examples should help to review how to solve these kinds of equations:

Example 1: $2x - 3 = x + 2$

Example 2: $\frac{3}{4}y = 15$

Example 3: $.25a = a - 1.5$

Example 4: $6(x - 2) = 12$

When working with equations such as those above, it is necessary to work on the left side of the equal sign as well as the right side.

To make equations easier to work with, elements of the equation must be moved across the equal sign from one side to the other. The goal is to place all of the terms having a variable on one side of the equation and all of the terms not having a variable on the other. In doing this, obey one simple rule: *When moving a term to the other side of the equation, reverse its sign.*

Example 1 would be solved like this:

Solution 1: Solve for x: $2x - 3 = x + 2$

1 Put all terms containing x on the left side of the equal sign. The others go on the right. Reverse the signs of those terms moved from one side to the other.

2 $2x - x = 2 + 3$

3 Simplify: $x = 5$. The equation is thus solved.

In some cases, multiplication and division may be involved, as in Example 2. Example 2 would be solved like this:

Solution 2: Solve for y: $\frac{3}{4}y = 15$.

1 The term having the variable is already on the left, and the other is already on the right.

2 Divide both sides of the equation by the coefficient of the variable: $\dfrac{\frac{3}{4}y}{\frac{3}{4}} = \dfrac{15}{\frac{3}{4}}$

3 $y = 20$

You may have been able to solve this problem without calculations. By thinking about what number 15 was three quarters of, you may have figured out that y was equal to 20.

Example 3 would be solved like this:

Solution 3: Solve for a: $.25a = a - 1.5$

1 Put the terms with the variable on the left; those without, on the right. Reverse the sign of those that cross the equal sign.

2 $.25a - a = -1.5$

3 Combine: $-.75a = -1.5$

4 Divide both sides by the coefficient of the variable:

$$\frac{-.75a}{-.75} = \frac{-1.5}{-.75}$$

$$a = 2$$

Example 4 would be solved like this:

Solution 4: Solve for x: $6(x - 2) = 12$

1 Remove the grouping symbol by multiplying by 6: $6x - 12 = 12$

2 Move -12 to the right and change its sign: $6x = 12 + 12$

3 Combine: $6x = 24$

4 Divide both sides by the coefficient of the variable:

$$\frac{6x}{6} = \frac{24}{6}$$

$$x = 4$$

Test Yourself 43

Directions: Try the following problems. You may be able to solve some of them in your head without calculating on paper.

1. $\frac{1}{4}x - 1 = 2$

2. $\frac{1}{x-2} = 1$

3. $2x - 2 = 4x - 10$

4. $\frac{7}{x} = 14$

5. $3.2x = 64$

6. $5(x - 3) = x + 9$

7. $\frac{3}{4}x = 20$

8. $4a + 3 = 3a - \frac{1}{2}$

9. $3b = b$

10. $6m - 1 = m + 4$

Geometry

Geometry is that part of mathematics that studies lines, curves, and angles and the various shapes they create when placed together in different ways. Usually, geometry is divided into two subgroups: *plane geometry* and *solid geometry*.

Plane geometry studies any shapes and angles that can be drawn in one plane. This means that shapes that can be measured in only one or two dimensions, or directions, are studied. For example:

- A line has only one dimension, its length.
- A triangle, a square, or a circle drawn on a piece of paper can he measured in only two directions, or dimensions: length and width.

Solid geometry studies shapes that have three dimensions: length, width, and thickness. For example:

- An object such as a brick or a shoebox is a rectangular solid that can be measured in three directions or dimensions: length, width, and height.
- Cubes, cones, spheres, cylinders, pyramids, or tetrahedrons are examples of shapes that are three dimensional and as such require the use of the principles of solid geometry.

First we will review some basics of plane geometry.

Points, Lines, and Angles

A *point* is an exact location and has no dimensions.

By placing lots of points in a row, we build a line. A line has infinite length in both directions, and has a symbol like this:

The arrowhead at each end indicates that the line is infinite. Usually, we select two points on the line, give them names, and name the line the same way:

$= \overleftrightarrow{AB}$ read: "line *AB*"

Note that we need a minimum of two points to make a line. There is no *maximum* number of points on a line, however.

A *ray* is a line that has one endpoint, and goes infinitely in one direction. We refer to a ray by its endpoint and one other point along it.

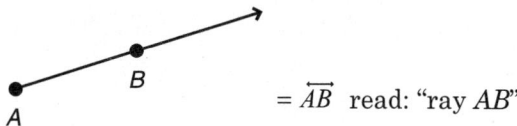

$= \overrightarrow{AB}$ read: "ray *AB*"

A *line segment* is a piece of a line having two endpoints. We name it by naming the endpoints:

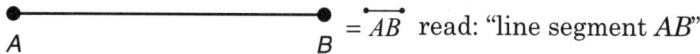

$= \overline{AB}$ read: "line segment *AB*"

Because their length is infinite, lines and rays cannot be measured. Line segments, on the other hand, are finite and *can* be measured.

ANGLES

Where lines, line segments, or rays meet or cross each other, *angles* are formed. The simplest angle is that formed by two rays having the same endpoint but going in different directions. The endpoint that these two rays share is called the *vertex* of the angle.

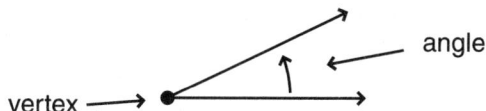

Angles are measured in units called *degrees*. A degree is $\frac{1}{360}$ of a complete revolution around the point called the vertex.

For example, the drawings below show one ray of an angle going through one complete revolution around the vertex. In each case, the measure of the angle is shown.

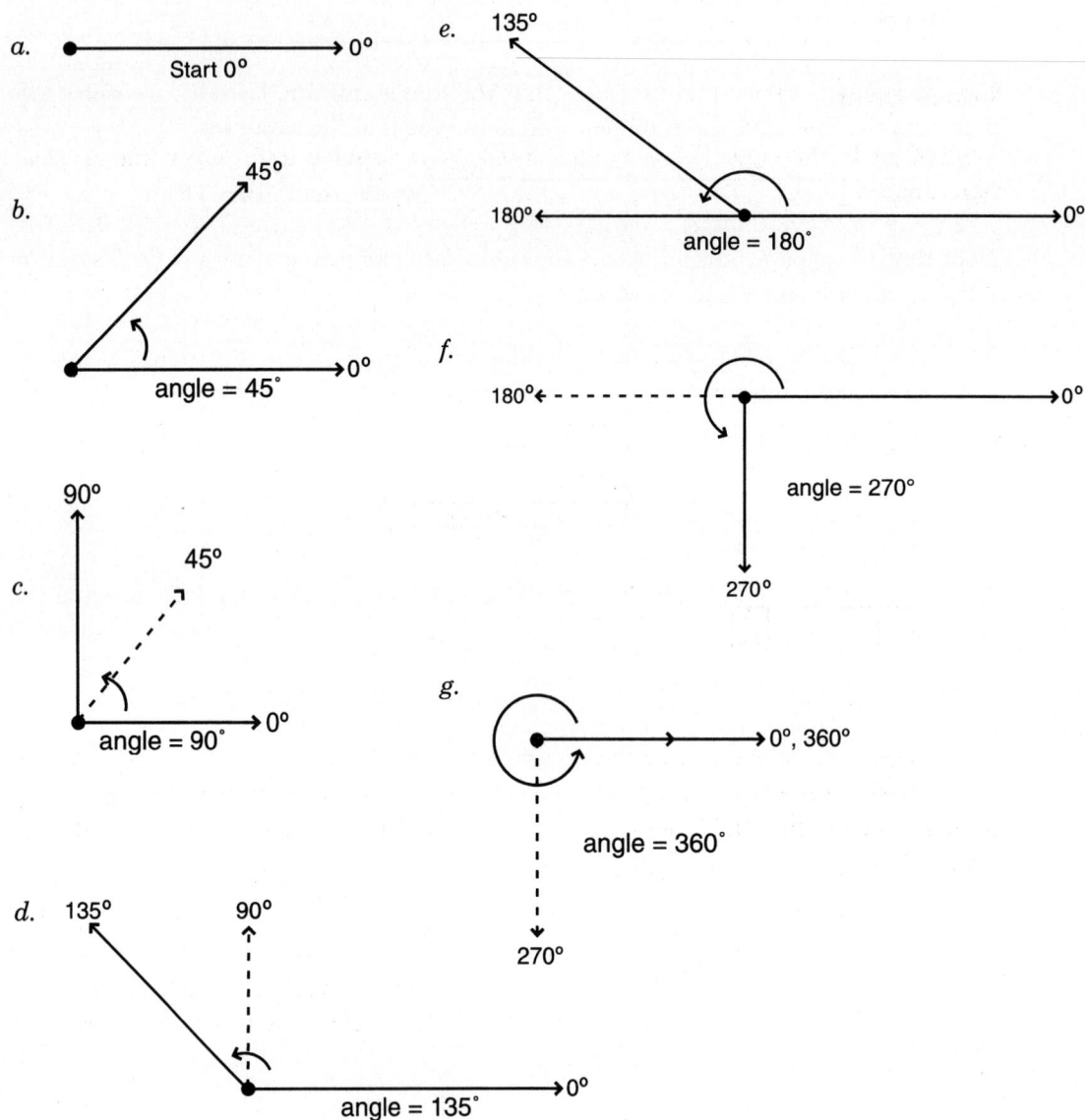

a.

Start 0° → 0°

b.

45°

angle = 45˚ → 0°

c.

90°

45°

angle = 90˚ → 0°

d.

135°   90°

angle = 135˚ → 0°

e.

135°

180° ←   → 0°

angle = 180˚

f.

180° ←   → 0°

angle = 270°

270°

g.

→ 0°, 360°

angle = 360˚

270°

The sequence on the previous page should remind you of a number of rules:

- Each complete revolution around the vertex creates an angle of 360°.
- Angles are measured counterclockwise.
- The measure of the angle is the same, no matter how long the rays are. The tips of each ray have the same angle between them as do two points closer to the vertex.

KINDS OF ANGLES

A 90° angle is also called a *right angle*. Squares, rectangles, and some triangles have right angles.

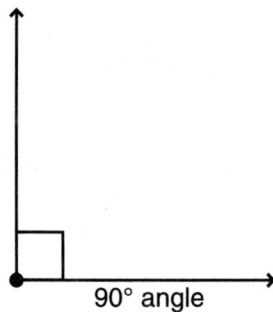

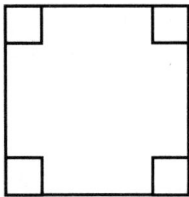

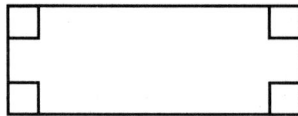

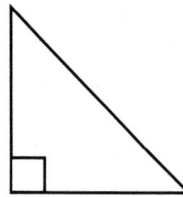

90° angle

Angles smaller than 90° are called *acute angles*. The measure of an acute angle is greater than zero, but less than 90°.

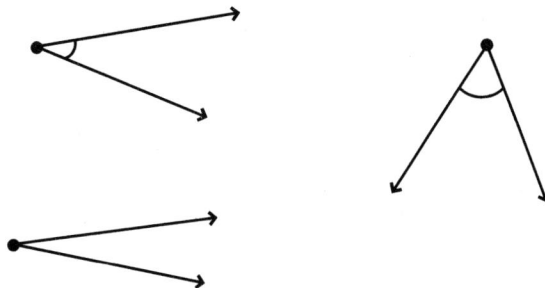

An angle that measures greater than 90° but less than 180° is called an *obtuse angle*.

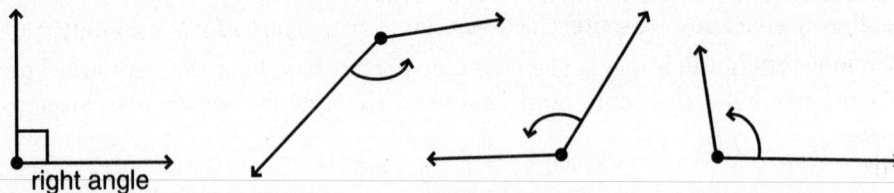

right angle

An angle equivalent to 180° is a *straight angle*. Lines may be thought of as straight angles.

Angles whose sum is 180° are *supplementary angles*. For example, the sum of 60° and 120° is 180°. Each angle is a supplement of the other.

A line intersecting a straight angle cuts it into supplementary angles.

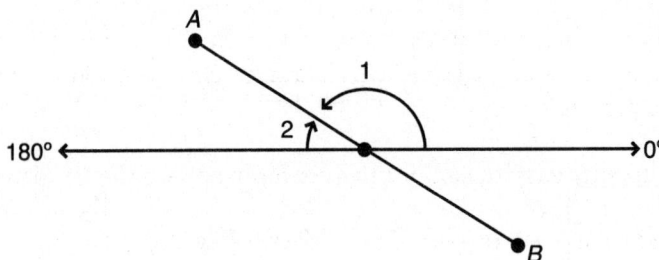

Angle 1 and angle 2 are supplementary angles.

Angles whose sum is 90° are *complementary angles*. For example, the sum of 60° and 30° is 90°. Each angle is a complement of the other.

Test Yourself 44

Directions: For the following problems, state whether the angle is acute or obtuse. If it is obtuse, name its supplement. If it is acute, name its supplement and complement.

1. 170°

2. 30°

3. 142°

4. 60°

5. 90°

6. 27°

7. 135°

8. 95°

9. 57°

10. 45°

Perimeter

The perimeter of an object is the distance around it. For example, if you walked all the way around the "outside" of a football field, a track, or a building, you would have walked along its perimeter.

Perimeters are usually easy to compute. We simply add up the lengths of the sides.

For example, what is the perimeter of the object below?

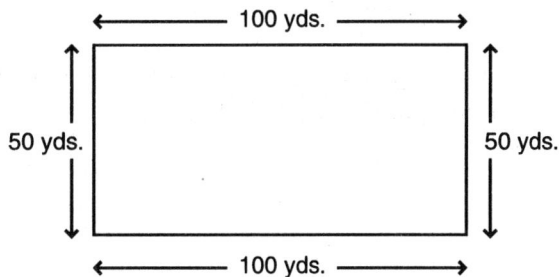

Just add the length of each side:

100 yards

100 yards

50 yards

+ 50 yards
_____

300 yards = perimeter

Frequently, objects are much more irregular than the one shown above. For an object such as the one below, for example, you must find the length of each small segment of the perimeter. Then add the lengths together to find the perimeter.

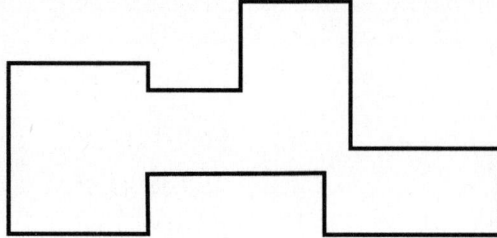

The perimeter of a circle is called its *circumference*, which is computed in a special way.

Ancient Greek mathematicians discovered an important fact about circles. No matter how large the circle was, they found that its circumference (perimeter) was almost exactly 3.14 times its diameter. They named the number by which they multiplied a circle's diameter to get its circumference *pi*. We use the value 3.14, or the fraction $\frac{22}{7}$, to represent pi, although its value is slightly larger. The symbol π stands for pi.

To find the perimeter (circumference) of this circle:

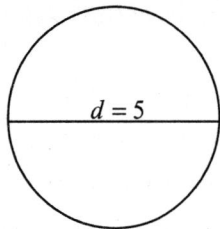

diameter = 5"

$d = 5$

$$\text{circumference} = \text{pi} \times 5"$$
$$= 3.14 \times 5"$$
$$= 15.70"$$

We can also work backward to find the diameter of a circle from its circumference. For example, if the circumference of a circle is 21.98 inches, what is its diameter?

Because the circumference is the product of π and the diameter, divide the circumference by π to find the diameter.

$$21.98 \div 3.14 = 7" \text{ (diameter)}$$

Test Yourself 45

Directions: For each circle, use the given information, diameter (d) or circumference (c), to find the other quantity.

1. $d = 3.5"$

2. $d = 5.0"$

3. $c = 22"$

4. $d = 2\frac{1}{2}"$

5. $c = 31.4"$

6. $c = 15.7"$

Area of Plane Figures

When a plane figure such as a rectangle, triangle, or circle lies flat, it covers a certain amount of area. When it is necessary to buy carpeting, grass seed, paint, and many other things, the area of the place to be covered must be calculated.

Area is always measured in square units, such as square inches, square feet, square yards, or square miles. Metric system units for area include square centimeters, square meters, and square kilometers. Generally, the unit of measurement to be used is based upon the area of the object being measured.

For example:

- The area of a city would be measured in square miles or square kilometers.
- The area of a football field would be measured in square yards or square meters.
- The area of this page would be measured in square inches or square centimeters.

When calculating area, it is most important to remember that you are dealing with square units. Area is always given in square inches, square meters, and so on.

AREA OF SQUARES AND RECTANGLES

The area of squares and rectangles is found by multiplying the length of any one side by the length of the side adjoining it.

For example:

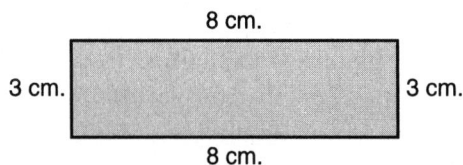

The area of this rectangle is the product of 8 cm. × 3 cm. = 24 sq. cm.

The area of any rectangle can be found by multiplying the length of its longest side by the length of its shortest side.

Area of a rectangle = length times width

$$A = l \times w$$

The area of squares is calculated the same way. You just have to remember that the sides of a square are all the same length. If you know the length of one side, you know the lengths of all the sides.

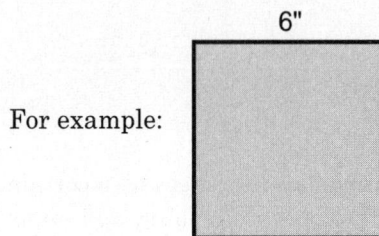

6"

For example: The area of the square is 6 in. × 6 in. = 36 sq. in.

Test Yourself 46

Directions: Find the area of the rectangles or squares having the following dimensions.

1. 3" long, 2" wide

2. 3 feet 6" long, 2 feet wide

3. 10 cm. long, 10 cm. wide

4. $1\frac{1}{2}$ miles long, $\frac{3}{5}$ miles wide

5. 12" long, 12" wide*

6. 3' long, 3' wide**

7. $\frac{1}{2}$" wide, 10" long

8. $\frac{3}{4}$" wide by $\frac{3}{4}$" long

    *144 sq. in. equals 1 sq. ft.

    **9 sq. ft. equals 1 sq. yd.

AREA OF TRIANGLES

Triangles may be:

- *Acute*, if each of their angles is less than 90°:

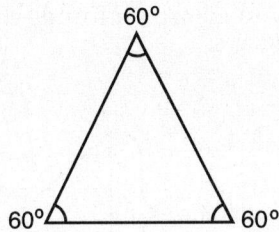

If each angle is 60°, the triangle is called *equilateral*, because all angles are equal in measure.

- *Right*, if one angle is 90°:

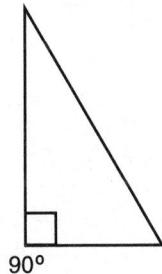

- *Obtuse*, if one angle is larger than 90°:

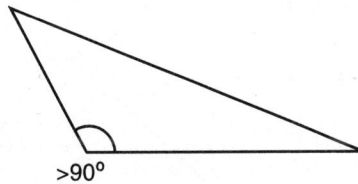

Familiarize yourself with these kinds of triangles, because finding their area requires you to be very careful about one thing: *measuring the altitude correctly.*

We find the area of triangles by using the following formula:

Area = one-half the product of the base and the altitude

$$A = \frac{1}{2} \times b \times a \text{ or } A = \frac{1}{2}ba$$

The *altitude* of a triangle is the distance from a vertex to the line containing the opposite side (base). The altitude is always perpendicular to the base.

These drawings show how to measure altitude correctly.

In a right triangle:

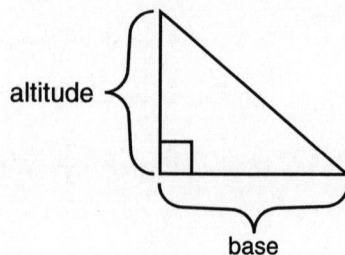

In an obtuse triangle:

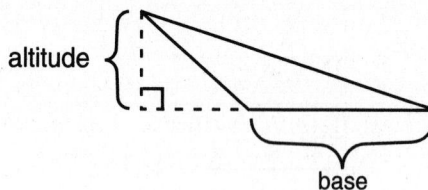

In an acute triangle:

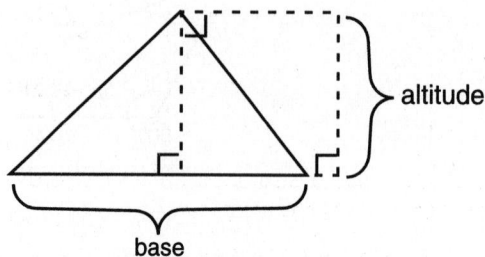

Notice that in each case, the altitude or height of a triangle must be measured along a line that makes a right angle with the base.

Example: Find the area of the triangle shown below.

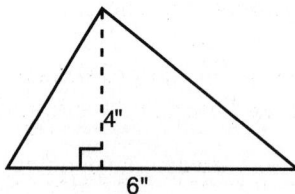

Solution: $A = \dfrac{1}{2}ba$

$A = \dfrac{1}{2} \cdot 4" \cdot 6"$

$A = 12\,\text{sq.in.}$

Test Yourself 47

Directions: Find the areas of the triangles whose dimensions are given below.

1. $b = 16"$, $a = 8"$

2. $b = 4\frac{1}{2}$ feet, $a = 2$ feet

3. $b = 11.5$ cm., $a = 4.5$ cm.

4. $b = 2.4$ feet, $a = 6.3$ feet

5. $b = 8$ inches, $a = 2.5$ feet

6. $b = 1\frac{2}{3}$ yds., $a = 3\frac{1}{4}$ yds.

AREA OF PARALLELOGRAMS AND TRAPEZOIDS

A *parallelogram* is a four-sided figure with opposite sides parallel to each other. The area of a parallelogram can be found by multiplying the length of the base by the altitude.

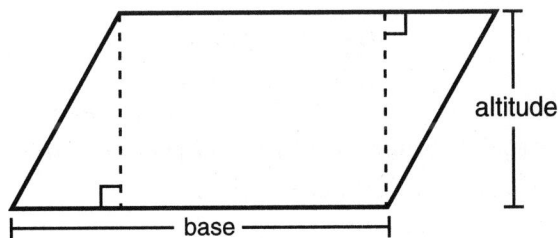

Area = base × altitude

$$A = b \times a \text{ or } A = ba$$

Here again, you *must* be careful to measure the altitude perpendicular to the base, just as you did when finding the areas of triangles.

A *trapezoid* is a four-sided figure with one pair of sides parallel, and one pair nonparallel. The parallel sides are called the *bases*, and we find the area as follows:

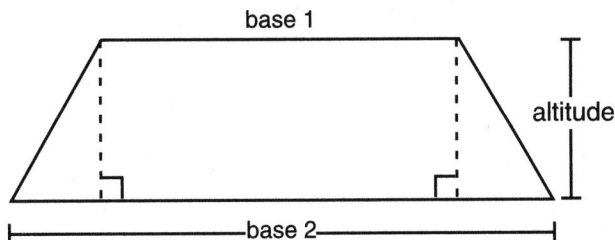

$$\text{Area} = \frac{1}{2} \times \text{altitude} \times (\text{length of base 1} + \text{length of base 2})$$

$$A = \frac{1}{2} \times a \times (b1 + b2) \text{ or } A = \frac{1}{2}a(b1 + b2)$$

Be sure to measure the altitude of the trapezoid along a line that makes a right angle with the base.

Test Yourself 48

Directions: Find the areas of the following parallelograms and trapezoids. "P" means parallelogram; "T" means trapezoid.

1. P: $b = 6"$, $a = 4"$

2. P: $b = 5"$, $a = 2"$

3. T: $b1 = 10"$, $b2 = 15"$, $a = 3"$

4. T: $b1 = 20$ cm., $b2 = 40$ cm., $a = 6$ cm.

5. P: $b = 4.125$ ft., $a = 3.34$ ft.

6. T: $b1 = 5"$, $b2 = 7"$, $a = 3"$

AREA OF A CIRCLE

The area of a circle is easily calculated, if you remember two things:

1 Use the number pi ($\pi = 3.14$, or $\frac{22}{7}$).

2 Use the radius of the circle in the calculation instead of the diameter. The radius is one half of the diameter: $r = \frac{d}{2}$.

To find the area of a circle, use the following formula:

Area = $\pi \times$ length of radius $\times$ length of radius

$A = \pi r^2$

For example, this circle has a radius of 3".

Thus, its area is:

$$A = \pi r^2$$

$$= 3.14 \times 3" \times 3"$$

$$= 28.26 \text{ sq. in.}$$

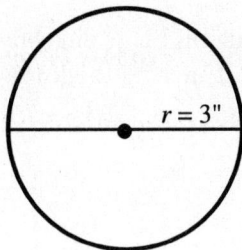

Sometimes, to avoid the extra calculation, areas of circles are written in pi. In the example above, we would write:

$$A = \pi \times 3" \times 3"$$

$$= 9\pi \text{ sq. in.}$$

Test Yourself 49

Directions: Practice finding the areas of the circles below. Remember to use the length of the radius in the calculation. Write your answers in terms of pi, as well as multiplied out.

1. $r = 2.17$ inches

2. $r = 3.5$ cm.

3. $d = 10$ feet

4. $d = 20$ yds.

5. $r = 22$ inches

6. $d = 11$ inches

7. $r = \dfrac{1}{2}$ cm.

8. $d = 100$ cm.

9. $c = 31.4$ inches

10. $c = 125.6$ miles

Volume of Solid Figures

Three-dimensional figures such as cubes, cones, spheres, and rectangular solids take up space. The amount of space an object or substance takes up is called its *volume*.

Because we purchase items and plan the sizes of buildings, homes, ships, and so forth according to our needs for a certain volume of something, volume is one of the most important measurements that we make. In this section, you will review how to calculate the volume of certain easy-to-measure shapes.

VOLUME OF RECTANGULAR SOLIDS

A familiar rectangular solid is a shoe box. Its volume is calculated by multiplying its length times its width times its thickness or depth. The formula is:

volume $= l \times w \times h$ **or** $V = lwh$

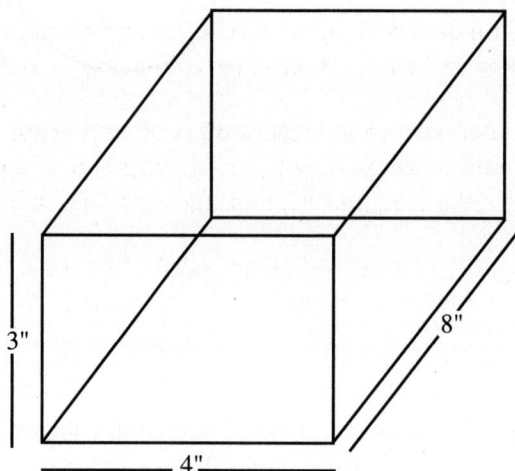

For example, the box shown below has the volume:

$$V = 3" \times 4" \times 8"$$

$$= 96 \text{ cu. in.}$$

Notice that we multiplied the measurement of each dimension of the box only once. The units that we use in measuring volume are *cubic* units.

A special rectangular solid is a *cube*. A cube has all of its dimensions the same length, so you need only the length of one edge to find its volume.

For example, the drawing below shows a cube with an edge 4" long.

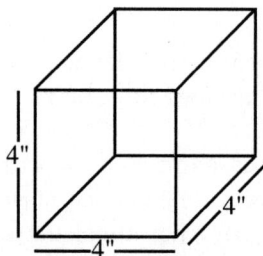

Its volume is calculated:

$$V = 4" \times 4" \times 4"$$
$$= 64 \text{ cu. in.}$$

When you are calculating the volume of rectangular solids, shoe boxes, rooms, and so forth, be certain that you have measurements for each dimension before you calculate.

VOLUME OF A CYLINDER

Cylinders are objects we deal with all the time. Soft drink cans and many other containers, as well as pipes and smokestacks, are cylinders.

In many ways, a cylinder resembles a stack of coins, or a stack of round, thin objects such as cocktail coasters, or slices of bologna. By thinking of a cylinder as a stack of slices or coins, it is easy to remember how to calculate its volume.

The volume of a cylinder can be calculated by first finding the area of the circular base, and multiplying that value by the height.

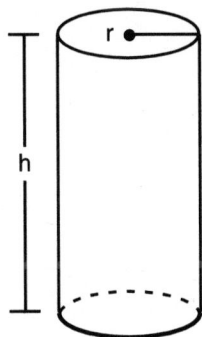

$$\text{Volume} = \underset{\text{area of base}}{\pi\,r^2} \quad \times \quad \underset{\substack{\text{height or length} \\ \text{of cylinder}}}{h}$$

By finding the area of the base, you are finding the area of one "slice" of the cylinder. When you multiply that by the height or length, you are calculating volume by counting all of the "slices" that you could make.

For example, find the volume of the cylinder below:

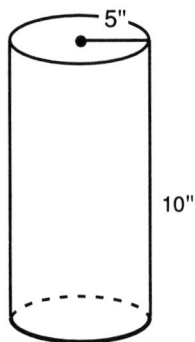

The radius of the base is 5". The height, or length, is 10".

$$
\begin{aligned}
V &= \pi\,r^2 h \\
V &= \pi \times 5" \times 5" \times 10" \\
V &= \pi \times 250 \text{ cu. in.} \\
  &= 3.14 \times 250 \text{ cu. in.}
\end{aligned}
$$
Volume = 785 cu. in.

As with area, you may find that the answer can be left in terms of pi. That is, it may not be necessary to multiply by 3.14. In the previous example, the answer $V = 250\pi$ *cubic inches* is acceptable.

Test Yourself 50

Directions: Find the volumes of the cylinders. Volume = $\pi r^2 h$. State your answers in terms of pi, as well as multiplied out.

1. $r = 1"$, $h = 1"$

2. $r = 2"$, $h = 2"$

3. $r = 3.5"$, $h = 6.20"$

4. $r = 1$ ft., $h = 2$ ft.

5. $r = 1.1$ cm., $h = 3.2$ cm.

6. $r = 10"$, $h = 1"$

7. $r = .25"$, $h = 1"$

8. $r = 20$ cm., $h = 70$ cm.

9. $r = .5"$, $h = 1.0"$

10. $r = x"$, $h = y"$

Word Problems

Two very common kinds of word problems that you will encounter on high school entrance examinations are rate, time, and distance problems and work problems.

Rate, Time, and Distance Problems

The basic formula used in solving problems for distance is:

$$d = rt \text{ (distance = rate} \times \text{time)}$$

Use this form when you know rate (speed) and time.

To find rate, use:

$$r = \frac{d}{t} \text{ (rate = distance} \div \text{time)}$$

To find time, use:

$$t = \frac{d}{r} \text{ (time = distance} \div \text{rate)}$$

Study the following problems:

Example: Two hikers start walking from the city line at different times but in the same direction. The second hiker, whose speed is 4 miles per hour, starts 2 hours after the first hiker, whose speed is 3 miles per hour. Determine the amount of time and distance that will be consumed before the second hiker catches up with the first.

Solution: Because the first hiker has a 2-hour head start and is walking at the rate of 3 miles per hour, that hiker is 6 miles from the city line when the second hiker starts.

$$\text{Rate} \times \text{Time} = \text{Distance}$$

Subtracting 3 miles per hour from 4 miles per hour gives us 1 mile per hour, or the difference in the rates of speed of the two hikers. In other words, the second hiker gains 1 mile on the first hiker in every hour.

Since there is a 6-mile difference to cover and it is decreased 1 mile every hour, it is clear that the second hiker will need 6 hours to overtake the first.

In this time, the second hiker will have traveled $4 \times 6 = 24$, or 24 miles. The first hiker will have been walking 8 hours, because of the 2-hour head start, $8 \times 3 = 24$, or 24 miles.

Example: The same two hikers start walking toward each other along a road connecting two cities that are 60 miles apart. Their speeds are the same as in the preceding problems, 3 and 4 miles per hour, respectively. How much time will elapse before they meet?

Solution: In each hour of travel toward each other, the hikers will cover a distance equal to the sum of their speeds, $3 + 4 = 7$ miles per hour. To meet they must cover 60 miles, and at 7 miles per hour this would be:

$$\frac{D}{R} = T \qquad \frac{60}{7} = 8\frac{4}{7}\text{hours}$$

The problem might also have asked: "How much distance must the slower hiker cover before the two hikers meet?" In such a case we should have gone through the same steps plus one additional step:

The time consumed before meeting was $8\frac{4}{7}$ hours. To find the distance covered by the slower hiker, we merely multiply his rate by the time elapsed:

$$R \times T = D \qquad 3 \times 8\frac{4}{7} = 25\frac{5}{7}$$

Test Yourself 51

Directions: Solve the problems below, using the formula for rate, time, and distance problems.

1. Matt walked 3 miles in $\frac{3}{4}$ of an hour.

   At what rate of speed did he walk in miles per hour?

2. A commuter train travels the distance from Acton to Boston in 1 hour and 10 minutes. If the train is traveling at an average speed of 48 miles per hour, what is the distance between the two cities?

3. Paddling 7 miles upstream, Sarah and her brother averaged 2 miles per hour. On the way back, their rate of speed was $3\frac{1}{2}$ miles per hour. How long did it take them to make the round trip?

4. Two cars begin driving toward each other from towns that are 150 miles apart. The first car is traveling 45 miles per hour, and the second is traveling 55 miles per hour. If each leaves at 2:15 p.m., when will the two cars pass on the road?

Work Problems

Work problems generally involve two or more workers doing a job at different rates. The aim of work problems is to predict how long it will take to complete a job if the number of workers is increased or decreased. Work problems may also involve determining how fast pipes can fill or empty tanks. Study the examples in this section carefully.

Example: If *A* does a job in six days, and *B* does the same job in three days, how long will it take the two of them, working together, to do the job?

Solution: Problems of this sort can be done using fractions.

Step 1: Write the amount of the job each worker does each day as a fraction.

A does $\frac{1}{6}$ of the job in one day.

B does $\frac{1}{3}$ of the job in one day.

Step 2: Write the amount of the job completed by both workers in one day.

$$A \; \frac{1}{6} \text{ of job}$$

$$B \; \frac{1}{3} \text{ of job}$$

$$A + B = \frac{1}{6} + \frac{1}{3} = \frac{1}{2}$$

One-half of the job is completed in one day by both workers working together.

Step 3: Compare the result from Step 2 to how much work has to be done. Because one-half of the job is finished in one day, it will take two days for both workers to finish the job working together.

In general, if you are given the amount of time that a job takes, you must find the reciprocal of that time to find out how much of the job is completed in one day, 1 hour, and so on.

For example, if a job takes $2\frac{1}{2}$, or $\frac{5}{2}$ days, you could do $\frac{2}{5}$ of the job in one day.

If a job takes $4\frac{1}{2}$ hours, you could do $\frac{2}{9}$ of the job in 1 hour.

If you are given the fraction of the job completed in one day, find the reciprocal of the fraction to determine how long the whole job will take.

For example, if $\frac{2}{3}$ of a lawn can be mowed in an hour, the whole lawn will take $\frac{3}{2}$, or $1\frac{1}{2}$, hours to mow.

If $\frac{3}{4}$ of a job can be done in one day, the whole job can be done in $\frac{4}{3}$, or $1\frac{1}{3}$, days.

Example: *A* and *B*, working together, do a job in $4\frac{1}{2}$ days. *B*, working alone, is able to do the job in ten days. How long would it take *A* to do the job working alone?

Solution: *Step 1:* The whole job takes $4\frac{1}{2}$, or $\frac{9}{2}$, days. *B*, working alone, can do $\frac{1}{10}$ of the job in one day.

Step 2: To find the work done by *A* in one day, subtract *B*'s work from the amount of work done by the two workers together in one day:

$$\frac{2}{9} - \frac{1}{10} = \frac{20-9}{90} = \frac{11}{90}$$

$\frac{11}{90}$ represents the portion of the total job done by A in one day.

Step 3: Taking the reciprocal, find how long it would take A to do the entire job.

$$\frac{90}{11} = 8\frac{2}{11} \text{ days}$$

Example: A can do a job in 6 days that B can do in $5\frac{1}{2}$ days and C can do in $2\frac{1}{5}$ days. How long will the job take if A, B, and C were working together?

Solution: A does the job in 6 days: $\frac{1}{6}$ of the job in one day.

B does the job in $5\frac{1}{2}$ days: $\frac{2}{11}$ of the job in one day.

C does the job in $2\frac{1}{5}$ days: $\frac{5}{11}$ of the job in one day.

Add the work done by A, B, and C in one day to find the work done by all three in one day:

$$\frac{1}{6} + \frac{2}{11} + \frac{5}{11} = \frac{11}{66} + \frac{12}{66} + \frac{30}{66} = \frac{53}{66}$$

Find the reciprocal of $\frac{53}{66}$ in order to find how long the total job would take:

$$\frac{66}{53} = 1\frac{13}{53} \text{ days}$$

Example: One pipe can fill a pool in 20 minutes, a second can fill the pool in 30 minutes, and a third can fill it in 10 minutes. How long would it take the three together to fill the pool?

Solution: First pipe fills the pool in 20 minutes: $\frac{1}{20}$ of pool in 1 minute.

Second pipe fills the pool in 30 minutes: $\frac{1}{30}$ of pool in 1 minute.

Third pipe fills the pool in 10 minutes: $\frac{1}{10}$ of pool in 1 minute.

Add the three fractions together to determine what part of the pool will be filled in one minute when the three pipes are working together.

$$\frac{1}{20} + \frac{1}{30} + \frac{1}{10} = \frac{3}{60} + \frac{2}{60} + \frac{6}{60} = \frac{11}{60}$$

If $\frac{11}{60}$ of the pool is filled in one minute, the reciprocal of the fraction will tell us how many minutes will be required to fill the whole pool.

$$\frac{60}{11} = 5\frac{5}{11} \text{ min.}$$

Test Yourself 52

Directions: Solve the problems below using the solution steps shown for work problems.

1. Michelle and Barb can complete a job in 2 hours when working together. If Michelle requires 6 hours to do the job alone, how many hours does Barb need to do the job alone?

2. If John can do $\frac{1}{4}$ of a job in $\frac{3}{4}$ of a day, how many days will it take him to do the entire job?

3. It takes $1\frac{3}{4}$ hours to fill a new underground gasoline storage tank. What part of the tank would be full if the gasoline had been shut off after 1 hour?

4. Mary can clean the house in 6 hours. Her younger brother Jim can do the same job in 9 hours. In how many hours can they do the job if they work together?

ANSWERS

Test Yourself 1

1. 1,228	3. 21,136	5. 513	7. 902	9. 3,289
2. 289	4. 34,361	6. 1,520	8. 138,021	10. 289

Test Yourself 2

1. Seventy-six ten-thousandths

2. Eleven and three-tenths

3. One thousand four hundred two and six hundred thirty-nine thousandths

4. Seven thousand two hundred twenty-two dollars and ninety-three cents

5. Fifty one-hundredths (five-tenths)

6. Five one-hundredths

7. Sixteen and two thousand one hundred sixty-three ten-thousandths

8. Twenty-nine hundred-thousandths

9. Three and six ten-thousandths

10. Sixty-two and three hundred ninety-one thousandths

Test Yourself 3

1. .5	3. .07	5. 10.7	7. 3.009
2. 5.12	4. equal	6. 7.62	8. equal

Test Yourself 4

1. 67.323	3. 110.0262	5. .0923	7. 14.1854	9. 790.3
2. 5.1392	4. 103.7217	6. 9,666.988	8. 95.653	10. 10.0

Test Yourself 5

1. Simplest form

2. $\dfrac{2}{3}$

3. $\dfrac{1}{6}$

4. Simplest form

5. $\dfrac{2}{3}$

6. $\dfrac{7}{8}$

7. $\dfrac{3}{8}$

8. Simplest form

9. $\dfrac{1}{12}$

10. $\dfrac{1}{6}$

Test Yourself 6

1. $\dfrac{20}{32}, \dfrac{25}{40}, \dfrac{10}{16}$ 3. $\dfrac{12}{15}, \dfrac{16}{20}, \dfrac{36}{45}$ 5. $\dfrac{2}{28}, \dfrac{3}{42}, \dfrac{6}{84}$ 7. $\dfrac{26}{52}, \dfrac{38}{76}$ 9. $\dfrac{6}{22}, \dfrac{24}{88}$

2. $\dfrac{28}{36}, \dfrac{63}{81}$ 4. $\dfrac{4}{6}, \dfrac{18}{27}, \dfrac{22}{33}$ 6. $\dfrac{15}{18}, \dfrac{20}{24}, \dfrac{30}{36}$ 8. $\dfrac{12}{21}, \dfrac{20}{35}, \dfrac{28}{49}$ 10. $\dfrac{4}{26}, \dfrac{8}{52}$

Test Yourself 7

1. $\dfrac{31}{8}$ 3. $\dfrac{179}{15}$ 5. $\dfrac{7}{4}$ 7. $5\dfrac{1}{3}$ 9. $4\dfrac{1}{2}$

2. $\dfrac{29}{10}$ 4. $\dfrac{23}{3}$ 6. $3\dfrac{1}{7}$ 8. $5\dfrac{5}{8}$ 10. $5\dfrac{1}{12}$

Test Yourself 8

1. C.D. $= 20;\ \dfrac{37}{20} = 1\dfrac{17}{20}$

2. C.D. $= 8;\ \dfrac{5}{8}$

3. C.D. $= 21;\ \dfrac{127}{21} = 6\dfrac{1}{21}$

4. C.D. $= 36;\ \dfrac{61}{36} = 1\dfrac{25}{36}$

5. C.D. $= 72;\ \dfrac{179}{72} = 2\dfrac{35}{72}$

6. C.D. $= 39;\ \dfrac{53}{39} = 1\dfrac{14}{39}$

7. C.D. $= 63;\ \dfrac{96}{63} = \dfrac{32}{21} = 1\dfrac{11}{21}$

8. C.D. $= 8;\ \dfrac{15}{8} = 1\dfrac{7}{8}$

9. C.D. $= 6;\ \dfrac{21}{6} = 3\dfrac{3}{6} = 3\dfrac{1}{2}$

10. C.D. $= 143;\ \dfrac{61}{143}$

Test Yourself 9

1. 605   3. 321   5. 190   7. 8,868   9. 889

2. 779   4. 58,991   6. 8,301   8. 771   10. 113,992

Test Yourself 10

1. 15.1798   3. .159   5. 4.14   7. 784.13   9. 29.827

2. .7676   4. .156   6. 24.848   8. 37.5177   10. 63.4215

Test Yourself 11

1. $\dfrac{11}{16}$

2. $\dfrac{1}{9}$

3. $\dfrac{91}{80} = 1\dfrac{11}{80}$

4. $\dfrac{302}{32} = 9\dfrac{14}{32} = 9\dfrac{7}{16}$

5. $\dfrac{23}{12} = 1\dfrac{11}{12}$

6. $\dfrac{9}{28}$

7. $\dfrac{139}{20} = 6\dfrac{19}{20}$

8. $\dfrac{1}{12}$

9. $\dfrac{28}{15} = 1\dfrac{13}{15}$

10. $\dfrac{47}{12} = 3\dfrac{11}{12}$

Test Yourself 12

1. 21,054

2. 462

3. 422,408

4. 69,632

5. 693,976

6. 369,600

7. 2,540,450

8. 25,606

9. 126,256

10. 94,792,384

Test Yourself 13

1. 2,696.8869

2. 10,020.72

3. 53,389.468

4. 1.164

5. 2.6248

6. 163,930.668

7. .0009384

8. 117.432

9. 44.55703

10. 4,638.26

Test Yourself 14

1. $\dfrac{57}{48} = 1\dfrac{9}{48} = 1\dfrac{3}{16}$

2. $\dfrac{36}{70} = \dfrac{18}{35}$

3. $\dfrac{120}{5} = 24$

4. $\dfrac{429}{22} = 19\dfrac{11}{22} = 19\dfrac{1}{2}$

5. $\dfrac{72}{33} = 2\dfrac{6}{33} = 2\dfrac{2}{11}$

6. $\dfrac{300}{5} = 60$

7. $\dfrac{48}{1125} = \dfrac{16}{375}$

8. $\dfrac{3717}{72} = 51\dfrac{45}{72} = 51\dfrac{5}{8}$

9. $\dfrac{6}{24} = \dfrac{1}{4}$

10. $\dfrac{90}{40} = 2\dfrac{1}{4}$

Test Yourself 15

1. 180

2. 1.4

3. 15

4. 21

5. 2.3

6. 25

7. 2.5

8. 30

Test Yourself 16

1. 196

2. 13

3. $\dfrac{11}{9}$

4. 2.4

5. 10,000

6. 625

7. 400

8. $\dfrac{1}{2}$

9. 12

10. 6.25

Test Yourself 17

1. 82.277 or $82\frac{13}{47}$

2. 42.50 or $42\frac{1}{2}$

3. .379 or $\frac{103}{272}$

4. 41.439 or $41\frac{61}{139}$

5. 10.855 or $10\frac{395}{462}$

6. 40.49 or $40\frac{51}{104}$

7. .817 or $\frac{76}{93}$

8. 1.977 or $1\frac{1087}{1113}$

9. .844 or $\frac{678}{803}$

10. 40.208 or $40\frac{5}{24}$

Test Yourself 18

1. .305

2. 5.760

3. 131.297

4. 17,902.394

5. .085

6. .737

7. .0098

8. 5.308

9. 141.626

10. .0019

Test Yourself 19

1. $\frac{21}{16} = 1\frac{5}{16}$

2. $\frac{38}{20} = 1\frac{18}{20} = 1\frac{9}{10}$

3. $\frac{78}{144} = \frac{13}{24}$

4. $\frac{72}{1,064} = \frac{9}{133}$

5. $\frac{24}{255} = \frac{8}{85}$

6. $\frac{3,111}{3} = 1,037$

7. $\frac{4}{30} = \frac{2}{15}$

8. $\frac{16}{63}$

9. $\frac{3}{16}$

10. $\frac{20}{30} = \frac{2}{3}$

Test Yourself 20

1. .80

2. $\dfrac{3}{4}$

3. .28

4. .333

5. $\dfrac{87}{200}$

6. $\dfrac{9}{50}$

7. .30

8. $\dfrac{9}{20}$

9. $\dfrac{1}{8}$

10. .26

Test Yourself 21

1. 3.27

2. 1.02

3. 8.2

4. $\dfrac{216}{12} = 18$

5. 3.31

6. 25.294

7. 1.25

8. .711

9. $\dfrac{261}{70} = 3\dfrac{51}{70}$

10. 21.95

Test Yourself 22

1. Wednesday, 10 miles farther, 10% farther

2. Thursday, 40 miles farther, 40% farther

3. Friday, 0 miles farther, 0% farther

4. Saturday, 1 mile less, 1% less

5. Sunday, 10 miles less, 10% less

Test Yourself 23

1. 50% larger

2. 27% smaller

3. 20% smaller

4. 99% smaller

5. 99.5% smaller

6. 100% larger

7. 350% larger

8. 99.99% smaller

Test Yourself 24

1. $.10 \times 8 = .8$

2. $.25 \times 60 = 15$

3. $.11 \times 10 = 1.1$

4. $.01 \times 350 = 3.50$

5. $.99 \times 80 = 79.2$

6. $.33 \times 33 = 10.89$

7. $.75 \times 112 = 84$

8. $.50 \times 200 = 100$

Test Yourself 25

1. .01

2. .012

3. .005

4. 5%

5. .1% or $\dfrac{1}{10}$ of one percent

6. .3% or $\dfrac{3}{10}$ of one percent

7. .015

8. 1.5%

9. .15

10. .01% or $\dfrac{1}{100}$ of one percent

Test Yourself 26

1. 50%; 150%
2. 100%; 200%
3. 50%; 150%
4. 32%; 132%
5. 20%; 120%

6. 50%; 150%
7. 50%; 150%
8. $33\frac{1}{3}$%; $133\frac{1}{3}$%
9. 0%; 100%
10. 900%; 1000%

Test Yourself 27

1. $\frac{21}{32}$ or .656
2. $\frac{3}{8}$ or .375
3. $\frac{4}{15}$ or .267

4. $\frac{243}{200}$ or 1.215
5. $2\frac{2}{9}$ or 2.22
6. $1\frac{11}{50}$ or 1.22

Test Yourself 28

1. 12.6	4. 50%	7. .0525	10. 90	13. 150
2. .1875	5. 400%	8. 240	11. 1.25	14. 156
3. 3,000	6. $16\frac{2}{3}$%	9. 78	12. $66\frac{2}{3}$%	

Test Yourself 29

1. $10\cdot10\cdot10\cdot10\cdot10\cdot10\cdot10$
2. $1\cdot1\cdot1$
3. $3\cdot3$
4. $\frac{1}{2}\cdot\frac{1}{2}\cdot\frac{1}{2}\cdot\frac{1}{2}$
5. $(.45)\,(.45)\,(.45)\,(.45)\,(.45)$

6. $11\cdot11$
7. $0\cdot0$
8. $x\cdot x\cdot x$
9. $b\cdot b\cdot b\cdot b\cdot b\cdot b\cdot b$
10. $(ab)\,(ab)\,(ab)\,(ab)\,(ab)$

Test Yourself 30

1. $1^{3-2} = 1$
2. $6^{10-8} = 6^2$
3. $15^{5+3} = 15^8$
4. $M^{3+3} = M^6$
5. $10^{10-8} = 10^2$
6. $3^{6+2} = 3^8$
7. $a^{2+3} = a^5$

8. $100^{10-9} = 100^1 = 100$
9. $\left(\dfrac{3}{4}\right)^{3+2} = \left(\dfrac{3}{4}\right)^5$
10. $8^{5-4} = 8^1 = 8$
11. $a^{5-3} = a^2$
12. $\left(\dfrac{1}{2}\right)^{5-4} = \left(\dfrac{1}{2}\right)^1 = \dfrac{1}{2}$
13. $x^{2+2} = x^4$

Test Yourself 31

1. -11
2. 1.3995
3. $.999$
4. 31
5. $2\dfrac{4}{15}$
6. -10.75
7. $-1\dfrac{3}{8}$
8. -120.25
9. -1.7498
10. 0

Test Yourself 32

1. -1
2. 2
3. -4.6
4. 9.1
5. 7.652
6. 2
7. $-.0029$
8. -5.5
9. $10\dfrac{1}{6}$
10. 0

Test Yourself 33

1. 30
2. 3.25
3. $-\dfrac{9}{8} = -1\dfrac{1}{8}$
4. $-\dfrac{4}{21}$
5. $-.09$
6. $-\dfrac{5}{12}$
7. 35.3298
8. $-100\dfrac{3}{8}$
9. $-.0325$
10. $-\dfrac{5}{9}$

Test Yourself 34

1. -15
2. -2
3. -2.15
4. $-.007$
5. -12.2
6. $\dfrac{1}{2}$ or $.5$
7. -7
8. 200.02
9. -1
10. 400

Test Yourself 35

1. $9a$

2. $34x$

3. $3m + 4r + 3s$

4. b

5. $.5r + s$

6. $1\frac{1}{15}m - \frac{1}{2}t$

7. $-1.039S$

8. $-15.75k$ or $-15\frac{3}{4}k$

9. $2x - 3y - 4z$

10. $.4p - 40r$

Test Yourself 36

1. d

2. $3\frac{1}{2}x$

3. $-2b - 6y$

4. 0

5. $-3.50m$

6. $-.001x$

7. $-7.483f$

8. $-\frac{1}{8}r$

9. $-2r - 3p$

10. $2x$

Test Yourself 37

1. $6x^2$

2. $1\frac{1}{3}y^2$

3. $-4.8a^2$

4. $-6z^3$

5. $1.03121r^3$

6. $-5.84f^4$

7. $\frac{5}{21}z^2$

8. $-\frac{5}{64}m^3$

9. $-2.222x^4$

10. $-71.71b^4$

Test Yourself 38

1. $14xy$

2. $2\frac{1}{4}a^2b^2$

3. $1.56df$

4. $-22.5x^2y$

5. $-22.08a^2b$

6. $-100a^2bc$

7. $-6\frac{1}{2}qr^2$

8. $-x^2y^2z^2$

9. $24x^2y^2z$

10. $-30abc$

Test Yourself 39

1. $10c$

2. -5

3. $-2y$

4. $-2ab$

5. $-2ab$

6. $-3a$

7. $-3x^2$

8. $-.1y$

9. $4r$

10. -2

Test Yourself 40

1. 1

2. -7

3. $a + b - 4$

4. 2

5. -9

6. $2a + b - 6$

Test Yourself 41

1. 3
2. −7
3. 1
4. 256
5. $5\frac{1}{2}$
6. a^2
7. $\frac{7}{9}$
8. 5.25
9. 102.4
10. 4

Test Yourself 42

1. $a = 3$
2. $x = 4$
3. $x = -3$
4. $r = 2$
5. $b = 4$
6. $y = 1$
7. $x = -5$

Test Yourself 43

1. $x = 12$
2. $x = 3$
3. $x = 4$
4. $x = \frac{1}{2}$
5. $x = 20$
6. $x = 6$
7. $x = 26\frac{2}{3}$
8. $a = -3\frac{1}{2}$
9. $b = 0$
10. $m = 1$

Test Yourself 44

1. Obtuse; 10°
2. Acute; 150°, 60°
3. Obtuse; 38°
4. Acute; 120°, 30°
5. Right; 90°, no complement
6. Acute; 153°, 63°
7. Obtuse; 45°
8. Obtuse; 85°
9. Acute; 123°, 33°
10. Acute; 135°, 45°

Test Yourself 45

1. 10.99"
2. 15.7"
3. 7"
4. $7\frac{6}{7}$"
5. 10"
6. 5"

Test Yourself 46

1. 6 sq. in.
2. 7 sq. ft.
3. 100 sq. cm.
4. $\frac{9}{10}$ sq. mi.
5. 144 sq. in., or 1 sq. ft.
6. 9 sq. ft., or 1 sq. yd.
7. 5 sq. in.
8. $\frac{9}{16}$ sq. in.

Test Yourself 47

1. 64 sq. in.

2. $4\frac{1}{2}$ sq. ft.

3. 25.875 sq. cm.

4. 7.56 sq. ft.

5. $\frac{5}{6}$ sq. ft. or 120 sq. in.

6. $2\frac{17}{24}$ sq. yd.

Test Yourself 48

1. 24 sq. in.

2. 10 sq. in.

3. $37\frac{1}{2}$ sq. in.

4. 180 sq. cm.

5. 13.7775 sq. ft.

6. 18 sq. in.

Test Yourself 49

1. 4.71 π sq. in., or 14.79 sq. in.

2. 12.25 π sq. cm., or 38.47 sq. cm.

3. 25 π sq. ft., or 78.5 sq. ft.

4. 100 π sq. yds., or 314 sq. yds.

5. 484 π sq. in., or 1,519.76 sq. in.

6. 30.25 π sq. in., or 94.985 sq. in.

7. $\frac{1}{4}$ π sq. cm. or .785 sq. cm.

8. 2,500 π sq. cm., or 7,850 sq. cm.

9. $r = 5$; $A = 25$ π sq. in., or 78.5 sq. in.

10. $r = 20$; $A = 400$ π sq. mi., 1,256 sq. mi.

Test Yourself 50

1. π cu. in.; 3.14 cu. in.

2. 8 π cu. in.; 25.12 cu. in.

3. 75.95 π cu. in.; 238.48 cu. in.

4. 2 π cu. ft.; 6.28 cu. ft.

5. 3.872 π cu. cm.; 12.158 cu. cm.

6. 100 π cu. in.; 314 cu. in.

7. .0625 π cu. in.; .19625 cu. in.

8. 28000 π cu. cm.; 87,920 cu. cm.

9. .25 π cu. in.; .785 cu. in.

10. π x^2y cu. in; 3.14x^2y cu. in.

Test Yourself 51

1. 4 miles per hour

2. 56 miles

3. $5\frac{1}{2}$ hours

4. 3:45 p.m.

Test Yourself 52

1. 3 hours

2. 3 days

3. $\frac{4}{7}$

4. $3\frac{3}{5}$ hours

EXERCISES: MATHEMATICS

Directions: Solve the following questions and choose the correct answer.

1. Where $x = 1\frac{2}{3}$, the reciprocal of x equals

   (A) $\frac{2}{3}$

   (B) $\frac{5}{3}$

   (C) $\frac{3}{5}$

   (D) $\frac{1}{x^2}$

2. The product of $\frac{7}{16}$ and a number x is 1. The number is

   (A) $1\frac{7}{16}$

   (B) $\frac{16}{7}$

   (C) $\frac{33}{14}$

   (D) 1

3. $\dfrac{\frac{1}{x}+1}{1+\frac{1}{x}}$ is equivalent to

   (A) 1

   (B) $\frac{1}{x}$

   (C) $\frac{1}{x}+2$

   (D) $1 + x$

4. $\dfrac{\frac{2}{3}+\frac{3}{8}}{\frac{1}{4}-\frac{3}{16}}$ equals

   (A) $15\frac{2}{3}$

   (B) $\frac{25}{16}$

   (C) $\frac{13}{32}$

   (D) $\frac{50}{3}$

5. In the formula $L = \frac{3}{4} bxh$, if $b = 2$, $x = 7$, and $h = \frac{1}{2}$, L equals

   (A) $\frac{21}{2}$

   (B) $\frac{21}{4}$

   (C) $\frac{21}{8}$

   (D) $\frac{7x}{4}$

6. Two angles of a triangle are 45° and 75°. What is the measure of the third angle?

   (A) 60°

   (B) 35°

   (C) 180°

   (D) 45°

7.

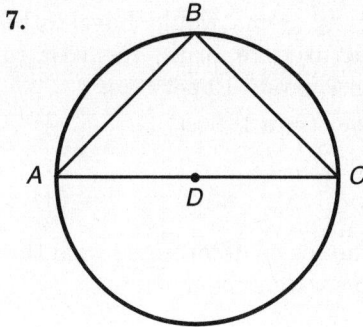

Isosceles △ABC is inscribed in circle D that has a diameter of 10 centimeters. The area of the triangle is

(A) 78.5 sq. cm.

(B) 12.5 sq. cm.

(C) 25 sq. cm.

(D) 50 sq. cm.

8. The volume of a small warehouse measuring 75 feet long, 50 feet wide, and 30 feet high is

(A) 1,112,500 cubic feet.

(B) 112,500 square feet.

(C) 112,500 feet.

(D) 112,500 cubic feet.

9. A department store marks up its clothing 80% over cost. If it sells blue jeans for $14, how much did the store pay for them?

(A) $7.78

(B) $17.50

(C) $11.20

(D) $1.12

10. The same store puts the same $14 jeans on sale at a 25% discount. What is the new selling price?

(A) $13.75

(B) $10.50

(C) $3.50

(D) $13.65

11. If $y = .25$, the value of $y^2 + \sqrt{y}$ is

(A) 1.125

(B) .1125

(C) .6750

(D) .5625

12. The monthly finance charge on a charge account is $1\frac{1}{2}$ % on the unpaid amount up to $500, and 1% on the unpaid amount over $500. What is the finance charge on an unpaid amount of $750?

(A) $22.50

(B) $1

(C) $10

(D) $100

13. Simplify: $1 - [5 + (3 - 2)]$

(A) −3

(B) −5

(C) 6

(D) 0

14. Simplify: $-3 - [-2 + (5 - 6) - 3]$

(A) +3

(B) −1

(C) +1

(D) −3

15.

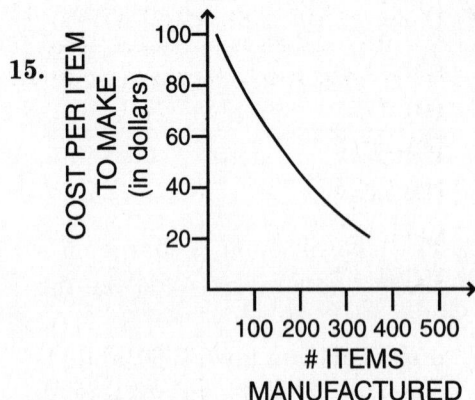

The graph above shows

(A) more items cost more money to make.

(B) by making more items, the production cost per item is lower.

(C) there is a limit to the number of items that can be made.

(D) None of the above

16. Based upon the graph above, what is the cost per item if 300 items are manufactured?

(A) $40

(B) $28

(C) $20

(D) >$20

17. If the company produced only 100 items, approximately how much would each item cost?

(A) $100

(B) $75

(C) $10

(D) $60

18. How many items would have to be manufactured to bring the cost to between $5 and $10 per item?

(A) Fewer than 100

(B) 1,000

(C) 2,000

(D) It cannot be determined with the information given.

19. $.6 + 1\frac{1}{2} + \frac{3}{4} =$

(A) 2.31

(B) 2.52

(C) 2.85

(D) $2\frac{13}{20}$

20. $\frac{2}{3} \cdot \frac{3}{2} + \frac{1}{4} \div \frac{1}{3} - \frac{7}{12} =$

(A) $\frac{7}{6}$

(B) $2\frac{2}{3}$

(C) $\frac{19}{6}$

(D) None of the above

21. $6 \div .0006 =$

(A) .0036

(B) 10,000

(C) 60,000

(D) 100,000

22.

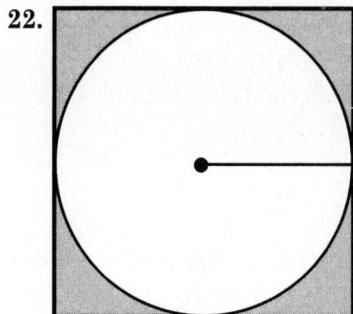

The square above has a side 4" long. The area of the shaded portion is

(A) $\frac{22}{7}$ sq. in.

(B) 16 sq. in.

(C) $3\frac{3}{7}$ sq. in.

(D) $4\frac{4}{7}$ sq. in.

23. Evaluate: $\frac{100^4}{10^8}$

(A) 10^2

(B) 1,000

(C) 1

(D) 10^{12}

24. What is the value of x^5, if $x = 3$?

(A) 81

(B) 243

(C) 15

(D) 35

25. The ratio of teachers to students in a certain school is 1:14. If there are fourteen teachers in the school, how many students are there?

(A) 14

(B) 196

(C) 206

(D) 176

26. Of 27 people in a certain group, 15 are men and 12 are women. What is the ratio of men to women in simplest form?

(A) 15:12

(B) 12:15

(C) 5:4

(D) 27:12

27.

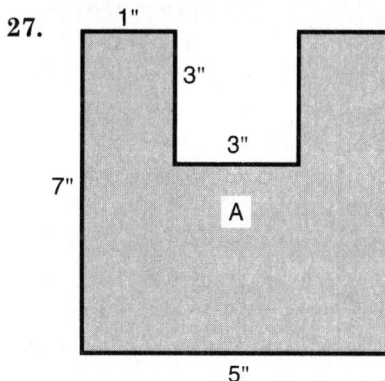

The perimeter of figure A is

(A) 19 in.

(B) 30 in.

(C) 23 sq. in.

(D) 19 sq. in.

28. The area of figure A is

(A) 26 sq. in.

(B) 19 sq. in.

(C) 44 sq. in.

(D) 30 sq. in.

29. The surface area of a brick with the dimensions 6" × 3" × 2" is

(A) 36 sq. in.

(B) 72 sq. in.

(C) 128 sq. in.

(D) 72 in.

30. The ratio of surface area to volume of a cube having an edge of two inches is

(A) 2:3

(B) 1:3

(C) 6:1

(D) 3:1

31.

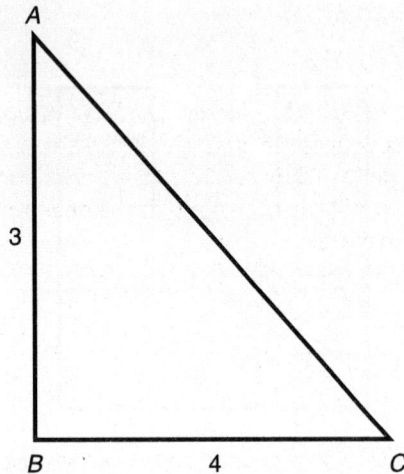

The length of $\overline{AC}$ in the triangle above is

(A) 4.5

(B) 3.5

(C) 5

(D) 4

32.

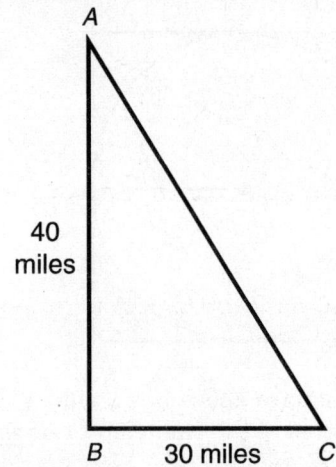

Two drivers begin at point C simultaneously. One drives from C to B to A. The other drives directly to A at 50 mph. How fast must the first person drive to get to A first?

(A) Less than 50 mph

(B) Less than 60 mph

(C) Less than 70 mph

(D) More than 70 mph

33. If $x = .25$, $\dfrac{1}{x} =$

(A) $\dfrac{1}{25}$

(B) 4

(C) $\dfrac{1}{4}$

(D) 1

34.

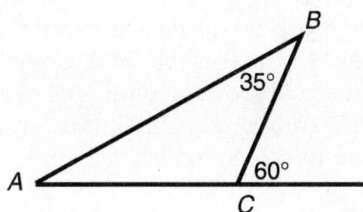

The measure of angle A is

(A) 15°

(B) 20°

(C) 25°

(D) 35°

35. A boy M years old has a brother six years older and a sister four years younger. The combined age of the three is

(A) $M + 10$

(B) $3M + 2$

(C) $3M - 2$

(D) $2M - 6$

36. If A number of people each make L things, the total number of things made is

(A) $A \div L$

(B) $A + L$

(C) $A - L$

(D) AL

37. If a man runs M miles in T hours, his speed is

(A) $M \div T$

(B) $M + T$

(C) $M - T$

(D) MT

38. How many square inches are there in R rooms, each having S square feet?

(A) RS

(B) $144RS$

(C) $9 \div RS$

(D) $S + R$

39. The drawing of a wheel in a book is done at $\frac{1}{16}$ scale. If the drawing is 1.8 inches in diameter, what is the true diameter of the wheel?

(A) 32"

(B) 28.8"

(C) 24"

(D) .1125"

40. One of the scales used in drawing topographic maps is 1:24,000. On a scale of this sort, one inch on the map would equal how much distance on the ground?

(A) One inch

(B) 2,000 feet

(C) 24,000 feet

(D) One mile

41. On a blueprint, two inches represent 24 feet. How long must a line be to represent 72 feet?

(A) 36 inches

(B) 12 inches

(C) 6 inches

(D) 4 inches

42. $\dfrac{5^5}{5^3} =$

(A) 25

(B) $1\frac{2}{3}$

(C) 3,000

(D) None of the above

43. $X^3 \bullet X^2 =$

(A) X^6

(B) X^5

(C) $2X^5$

(D) $2X^6$

44. Event A occurs every 14 minutes and event B every 12 minutes. If they both occur at 1 p.m., when will be the next time that both occur together?

(A) 2:12 p.m.

(B) 1:48 p.m.

(C) 2:24 p.m.

(D) 3:48 p.m.

45. Event A occurs every 4 years, event B every 11 years, and event C every 33 years. If they last occurred together in 1950, when will they next occur simultaneously?

(A) 3402

(B) 1983

(C) 2082

(D) 6804

46. If x is an odd whole number, which of the following also represents an odd number?

(A) $2x + 1$

(B) $x - 2$

(C) $4x - 3$

(D) All of the above

47. The sum of 4 hours 17 minutes, 3 hours 58 minutes, 45 minutes, and 7 hours 12 minutes is

(A) 15 hr. 32 min.

(B) 17 hr. 32 min.

(C) 16 hr. 12 min.

(D) 14 hr. 50 min.

48. If 8 lb. 12 oz. of fruit were to be divided among 8 people, how much would each receive?

(A) 1 lb. 1.5 oz.

(B) 10.5 oz.

(C) 2. lbs.

(D) 13.5 oz.

49. How much faster does a runner who finishes a marathon in 2 hours 12 minutes 38 seconds complete the race than a runner who finishes in 3 hours 2 minutes 24 seconds?

(A) 48 min. 56 sec.

(B) 49 min. 46 sec.

(C) 1 hr. 51 min. 22 sec.

(D) 1 hr. 26 min. 12 sec.

50. In the number 6,000,600,000, there are

(A) 6 billions and 6 hundred thousands.

(B) 6 millions and 6 thousands.

(C) 6 billions and 6 millions.

(D) 6 millions and 60 thousands.

51.

The graph above shows

(A) x increasing faster than y.

(B) y increasing faster than x.

(C) x increasing as fast as y.

(D) no relationship between x and y.

52. The difference between 1,001,000 and 999,999 is

(A) 101,001

(B) 1,999

(C) 10,001

(D) 1,001

53. If $3x - 6 = 2$, find x.

(A) $\dfrac{8}{3}$

(B) 8

(C) $-\dfrac{4}{3}$

(D) $\dfrac{2}{3}$

54. If $-3(y + 2) = 9$, find y.

(A) -3

(B) 15

(C) -5

(D) 3

55. Evaluate $-4xy^2z^3$ if $x = \dfrac{1}{3}$, $y = -2$, and $z = 1$.

(A) $-\dfrac{16}{3}$

(B) -16

(C) $\dfrac{16}{3}$

(D) $4\dfrac{2}{3}$

56. What is the value of the expression $A = \dfrac{1}{2}\,bh$, when $h = 2$ and $b = \dfrac{1}{4}$?

(A) $A = \dfrac{1}{3}$

(B) $A = \dfrac{1}{4}$

(C) $A = \dfrac{1}{6}$

(D) $A = \dfrac{2}{5}$

57. Simplify: $-6 - [2 - (3a - b) + b] + a$

(A) $4 - 3a + 2b$

(B) $-6 + 3a + b$

(C) $-8 + 4a - 2b$

(D) $-8 + 3a - b$

58. Simplify: $-2[-4(2 - 1) + (3 + 2)]$

(A) 18

(B) 2

(C) -18

(D) -2

59. $5:6$ as $15:$

(A) 25

(B) 16

(C) 18

(D) 12

60. The ratio of the six inches to six feet is

(A) $1:6$

(B) $12:1$

(C) $1:12$

(D) $24:1$

ANSWER KEY AND EXPLANATIONS

1. C	13. B	25. B	37. A	49. B
2. B	14. A	26. C	38. B	50. A
3. A	15. B	27. B	39. B	51. C
4. D	16. B	28. A	40. B	52. D
5. B	17. B	29. B	41. C	53. A
6. A	18. D	30. D	42. A	54. C
7. C	19. C	31. C	43. B	55. A
8. D	20. A	32. D	44. C	56. B
9. A	21. B	33. B	45. C	57. C
10. B	22. C	34. C	46. D	58. D
11. D	23. C	35. B	47. C	59. C
12. C	24. B	36. D	48. A	60. C

1. **The correct answer is (C).** The reciprocal of a fraction is the fraction "turned upside down." $1\frac{2}{3}$ is equivalent to $\frac{5}{3}$. The reciprocal of $\frac{5}{3}$ is $\frac{3}{5}$. Choice (D) is a distractor. Because x has a precise value in the problem, we must choose an answer having a precise value.

2. **The correct answer is (B).** The product of any number and its reciprocal is 1. Therefore, $\frac{7}{16} \bullet \frac{16}{7} = 1$, and choice (B) is the correct choice. Even if you didn't know this rule, you could have examined the answers and eliminated both choice (A), because the product was greater than 1, and choice (D), because the product was less than 1.

3. **The correct answer is (A).** This problem looks much harder than it really is. The numerator of this complex fraction is the same as the denominator. When numerator and denominator are equivalent, the fraction is equal to 1. Choice (A) is the correct answer.

4. **The correct answer is (D).** This is a complex fraction requiring all of your skills in working with fractions. To estimate the correct answer, note that the numerator is slightly larger than $1\left(\frac{2}{3}+\frac{3}{8}>1\right)$, and the denominator is equivalent to $\frac{4}{16}-\frac{3}{16}$, or $\frac{1}{16}$. Therefore, a number slightly larger than 1 divided by $\frac{1}{16}$ is slightly larger than 16. The closest answer is choice (D), $\frac{50}{3}$, which is equivalent to $16\frac{2}{3}$. To solve the problem by calculation, simplify the numerator and denominator, and then divide.

5. **The correct answer is (B).** This is a problem in which you must substitute the values given into the formula. Once you do that, it is a simple problem.

$$L = \frac{3}{4} \cdot 2 \cdot 7 \cdot \frac{1}{2}$$

$$= \frac{3 \cdot 2 \cdot 7 \cdot 1}{4 \cdot 2} = \frac{42}{8} = \frac{21}{4}$$

Therefore, (B) is the correct answer. The other answers would have resulted if you had forgotten to multiply one of the numbers in the numerator. Choice (D) might have been chosen by someone who didn't know what to do but thought the most difficult-looking answer would be the best.

6. **The correct answer is (A).** The sum of the angles of a triangle is always 180°. The correct answer, therefore, is (A), because 45° + 75° + 60° = 180°. Choices (B), (C), and (D) give sums larger or smaller than 180° when added to 45° and 75°.

7. **The correct answer is (C.)** Note that the base of the triangle is the same as the diameter of the circle. Because △ABC is isosceles, its altitude is the same length as the radius of the circle. Use the formula for the area of a triangle, and substitute the correct values:

$$A = \frac{1}{2} ba$$

$$= \frac{1}{2} \cdot 10 \cdot 5$$

$$= 25 \text{ cm}^2$$

The correct answer, then, is choice (C). Choice (A) is the area of the circle.

8. **The correct answer is (D).** These measurements describe a large rectangular room 30 feet high. Use the formula $V = l \cdot w \cdot h$ to find the volume:

V = 75 feet • 50 feet • 30 feet

= 112,500 cubic feet

Choices (B) and (C) use the wrong units. Volume is always measured in cubic units.

9. **The correct answer is (A).** A store markup of 100% would exactly double the price. An 80% markup almost doubles the price. The $14 jeans are priced at almost double their cost to the store. By estimation, the best answer is choice (A). To figure precisely, remember that an 80% markup is the equivalent of multiplying the cost by 180%, or 1.80.

cost • 1.80 = 14

cost = 14 ÷ 1.80

cost = $7.78

10. **The correct answer is (B).** Reduce the $14 price by 25%.

25% of 14 = $14 × .25 = $3.50

$14 − 3.50 = $10.50 (new price)

Therefore, choice (B) is the correct answer. Choice (A) indicates a reduction of only twenty-five cents. Choice (C) represents a reduction to 25% of the original price, or a 75% decrease in price.

11. **The correct answer is (D).** Substitute .25 into the problem.

$$= (.25)^2 + \sqrt{.25}$$

$$= .0625 + .5$$

$$= .5625$$

This might be a good time to review the table of squares and square roots on pages 260 and 261. Choice (A) would have resulted if you had squared .25, gotten .625, and added it to .5. $(.25)^2 = .0625$. Choice (B) would have resulted if you had squared .25 correctly, but thought the square root of .25 was .05. Choice (C) would have resulted if you had made errors in both steps.

12. **The correct answer is (C).** The finance charge will be the sum of $1\frac{1}{2}$% of $500, plus 1% of $250. You can write this as follows:

$(.015 \bullet 500) + (.01 \bullet 250)$

$= \$7.50 + \$2.50 = \$10$

You can estimate the answer if you remember that percent means "hundredths of." One one-hundredth of $500 is $5.00; one one-hundredth of $250 is $2.50. The only answer near this sum is choice (C). Choices (B) and (D) would have resulted if you had misplaced a decimal point.

13. **The correct answer is (B).** Begin removing the innermost grouping symbols, rewriting each time a set of symbols is removed:

Step 1: $1 - [5 + (3 - 2)]$

Step 2: $2 - [5 + 1]$

Step 3: $1 - [6]$

Step 4: $1 - 6 = -5$

A minus sign in front of a bracket or parenthesis reverses the sign of the number inside. A positive sign does not.

14. **The correct answer is (A).**

Step 1: $-3 - [-2 + (5 - 6) - 3]$

Step 2: $-3 - [-2 + (-1) - 3]$

Step 3: $-3 - [-2 - 1 - 3]$

Step 4: $-3 - [-6]$

Step 5: $-3 + 6 = +3$

A minus sign in front of a bracket or parenthesis reverses the sign of the number inside. A positive sign does not.

15. **The correct answer is (B).** Each point on the line has a coordinate on the horizontal axis and one on the vertical axis. The coordinates of points located at the lower right part of the graph are low cost per item and large numbers of items manufactured. Therefore, interpret this graph to mean that where larger numbers of items are manufactured, the cost per item is lower.

16. **The correct answer is (B).** Find 300 on the horizontal axis. Draw a vertical line upward until you touch the line. Move horizontally from this point on the line to the vertical axis. Note that you touch the vertical axis at a point roughly equivalent to $28. We suggest you use a straight edge to sketch your line.

17. **The correct answer is (B).** Find 100 on the horizontal axis and follow the same procedure as above. The coordinate on the vertical axis is approximately $75.

18. **The correct answer is (D).** Find the approximate location of $5–$10 on the vertical axis. Try to follow a horizontal path across until you hit the line of the graph. Note that your path does not intersect the line. Therefore, the graph does not predict the information asked for.

19. **The correct answer is (C).** By far the easiest way to solve this problem is to change the fractions to decimals: $.6 + 1.5 + .75 = 2.85$. If you were to convert to fractions, the correct answer would be $2\frac{17}{20}$.

20. **The correct answer is (A).** Be careful to use the correct process. First use multiplication, division, addition, and finally subtraction. To simplify, change the fractions to decimals.

21. **The correct answer is (B).** Be careful in counting places and in positioning the decimal point.

22. **The correct answer is (C).** The area of the shaded portion is equal to the area of the square, less the area of the circle. The length of the side of the square is equal to the diameter of the circle. Therefore, using $\frac{22}{7}$ for pi: (4" × 4") − $(\pi 2^2)$ = 16 sq. in. − $\frac{88}{7}$ sq. in. = $3\frac{3}{7}$ sq. in. If you answered choice (D), $4\frac{3}{7}$, check your skills in subtracting fractions from whole numbers.

23. **The correct answer is (C).** The long way to solve this problem is to multiply both the numerator and denominator out, and then divide. If you notice that 100^4 can also be written as 10^8, the answer is obviously choice (C).

$100^4 = (10^2)^4 = 10^2 \cdot 10^2 \cdot 10^2 \cdot 10^2 = 10^8$

24. **The correct answer is (B).** Substitute 3 for x. The problem, then, is to compute 3^5.

$3^5 = 3 \cdot 3 \cdot 3 \cdot 3 \cdot 3$

$= 243$

Choice (C) would have resulted if you had multiplied 5 × 3, instead of 3 times itself 5 times.

25. **The correct answer is (B).** For each teacher, there are 14 students. Because there are 14 teachers, there must be 14 ×14, or 196, students.

26. **The correct answer is (C).** The ratio of men to women is 15:12, but this ratio must be expressed in simplest form. Because 15 and 12 have 3 as a common factor, the ratio expressed correctly is 5:4. Choice (C) is the correct choice.

27. **The correct answer is (B).** To find the perimeter, we add up the dimensions of all of the sides. Note that there are some parts that have not been assigned measurements, so we have to infer that they are the same as those corresponding parts whose measurements have been designated. Beginning at the bottom and moving clockwise, the dimensions are:

5" + 7" + 1" + 3" + 3" + 3" + 1" + 7"

These equal 30 inches. If you chose choices (A), (D), or (C), you failed to add up all of the segments.

28. **The correct answer is (A).** The area is most easily found by multiplying the length of the figure by its width, and then subtracting the area of the small 3" × 3" square.

(7" × 5") − (3" × 3") = Area

35 sq. m. − 9 sq. in. = 26 sq. in.

Shapes such as this are often used for irregular pieces of carpeting or covering.

29. **The correct answer is (B).** The surface of a rectangular solid such as a brick is found by calculating the area of each face of the brick and finding the sum of the areas of the faces. The brick has six faces:

Two faces 6" × 3"; Total 36 sq. in.

Two faces 6" × 2"; Total 24 sq. in.

Two faces 3" × 2"; Total <u>12 sq. in.</u>

Total 72 sq. in.

Choice (D) is wrong because it is not written in square units.

30. **The correct answer is (D).** Calculate the surface area of the cube. It has six faces, each 2" × 2". Its surface area, then, is 6 × 4 sq. in. or 24 sq. in. Its volume is found by multiplying its length × width × height, or 2" × 2" × 2" = 8 cu. in. The ratio of surface area to volume is 24:8, or 3:1.

31. The correct answer is (C). The Pythagorean Theorem is used to find the length of the sides of right triangles. The square of the length of the longest side (the hypotenuse) is equal to the sum of the squares of the other two sides. Once we know the square of the length of the longest side, it is easy to find the length.

$$(AC)^2 = (AB)^2 + (BC)^2$$
$$(AC)^2 = 3^2 + 4^2$$
$$(AC)^2 = 25$$
$$(AC) = \sqrt{25} = 5$$

32. The correct answer is (D). This is a two-step problem. First, find the length of the hypotenuse, so you know how far the other person is driving.

$$(AC)^2 = (AB)^2 + (BC)^2$$
$$= (40)^2 + (30)^2$$
$$= 1,600 + 900$$
$$(AC) = \sqrt{2,500} = 50 \text{ miles}$$

The person driving from C to A must drive 50 miles at 50 mph. He or she will get there in 1 hour. The other must drive 70 miles. To get there first, he or she must drive faster than 70 miles per hour.

33. The correct answer is (B). This is a simple division problem. Divide 1.0 by .25. Here is another way to solve this problem. Since $.25 = \dfrac{1}{4}$, the reciprocal of $\dfrac{1}{4}$ is 4.

34. The correct answer is (C). A straight line represents a "straight angle" of 180°. An angle of 60° is given, so $\angle C$ must be 120° to complete the line. Knowing that all the angles in a

triangle added together equal 180°, therefore:

$$m\angle A + m\angle B + m\angle C = 180°$$
$$m\angle A + 35° + 120° = 180°$$
$$m\angle A = 180° - 155°$$
$$m\angle A = 25°$$

35. The correct answer is (B). The boy's age is M years. His older brother is $M + 6$ years old, and his younger sister is $M - 4$ years old. Adding the three ages together,

$$M + (M + 6) + (M - 4) = 3M + 2$$

36. The correct answer is (D). This is a literal problem requiring you to "think without numbers." Creating mental pictures may help you solve this type of problem. If each person in a group makes L number of things, the group's output will be the product of the number of people in the group and the number of things each makes. Choice (D) represents the product and is the correct choice.

37. The correct answer is (A). This problem asks you to find speed or rate. Speed or rate is found by dividing the distance traveled by the time required. The choice in which distance is divided by time is choice (A).

38. The correct answer is (B). R rooms each with S square feet contain a total of RS square feet. Because there are 144 square inches in each square foot, the rooms contain $144RS$ square inches.

39. The correct answer is (B). If the drawing is at $\dfrac{1}{16}$ scale, it means that the drawing is $\dfrac{1}{16}$ the size of the

actual wheel. Therefore, multiply the size of the drawing by 16.
$1.8 \times 16 = 28.8$ inches

40. **The correct answer is (B).** A scale of 1:24,000 means that 1 inch on the map equals 24,000 inches on the ground. 24,000 inches equal 2,000 feet.

41. **The correct answer is (C).** If two inches equal 24 feet, one inch equals 12 feet. A line representing 72 feet, therefore, must be six inches long ($72 \div 12 = 6$).

42. **The correct answer is (A).** In this problem, the bases are the same, so you must subtract the exponent of the divisor from that of the dividend to find the answer:

$$5^5 \div 5^3 = 5^{5-3} = 5^2 = 25$$

Therefore, choice (A) is the correct answer. Note that the bases must be identical and the exponents must be subtracted. You can check this answer by multiplying each number out and dividing.

$$\frac{5^5}{5^3} = \frac{3{,}125}{125} = 25$$

43. **The correct answer is (B).** When multiplying, if the bases are identical, add the exponents:

$$X^3 \bullet X^2 = X^5$$

Note that because we are multiplying, the coefficient remains 1.

44. **The correct answer is (C).** This problem requires two steps. First, find the smallest number divisible by 14 and 12 (the least common multiple, or LCM). Secondly, add that number to 1 and convert to time of day. The LCM of 14 and 12 is 84. Both events will occur simultaneously 84 minutes past 1:00 or 2:24 p.m.

45. **The correct answer is (C).** Here, three events occur periodically, so we must find the LCM of 4, 11, and 33, and add that number to 1950. That year will be the next common occurrence. The LCM of 4, 11, and 33 is 132. 1950 + 132 = 2082. Therefore, choice (C) is correct.

46. **The correct answer is (D).** In the whole number system, every other number is odd, and every other is even. If x is odd, $x + 1$ is even, $x + 2$ is odd, $x + 3$ is even, and so forth. Also, if x is odd, $x - 1$ is even, $x - 2$ is odd, and $x - 3$ is even. If an even or odd number is doubled, the outcome is even. Therefore, if x is odd, $2x + 1$ is odd, $x - 2$ is odd, and $4x - 3$ is odd.

47. **The correct answer is (C).** Arrange the periods of time in columns and add as you would add whole numbers:

   4 hr. 17 min.

   3 hr. 58 min.

        45 min.

+ 7 hr. 12 min.

  14 hr. 132 min.

We know there are 60 minutes in each hour. Therefore, 132 minutes equals 2 hours 12 minutes. The correct answer for this addition is 16 hours 12 minutes, or choice (C). When working with units that measure time, volume, and length, it is usually best to represent the answer using as many larger units as possible. That's why 16 hours 12 minutes is preferable to 14 hours 132 minutes as an answer.

48. **The correct answer is (A).** You do not have to calculate this answer. If 8 people are sharing equally of 8 pounds and some ounces of fruit, each person would receive 1 pound and a few ounces.

49. The correct answer is (B). This is a subtraction problem. You must find the difference between the lengths of time required to finish the race. As with other problems involving units of measurement, you must work carefully.

    3 hr. 2 min. 24 sec.

    − 2 hr. 12 min. 38 sec.

Because 38 seconds is larger than 24 seconds and 12 minutes is larger than 2 minutes, borrow from the minute's column and the hour column and rewrite the problem as follows:

    2 hr. 61 min. 84 sec.

    − 2 hr. 12 min. 38 sec.

    0 hr. 49 min. 46 sec.

50. The correct answer is (A). The first 6 is in the billions place; the second, in the hundred thousands place. If you had trouble with this problem, review the sections on how to read numbers and determine place values in your math textbook.

51. The correct answer is (C). This graph contains a line that has points with coordinates (1, 1), (2, 2), (3, 3), and (4, 4). From one point to another the value of the x-coordinate changes just as much as the value of the y-coordinate. Therefore, choice (C) is the correct answer. This line is at a 45° angle from the x-axis and will be created whenever the x- and y-coordinates are equal.

52. The correct answer is (D). This is a simple subtraction problem designed to test how carefully you can subtract. It is possible to calculate the correct answer without pencil and paper. 999,999 is only 1 less than a million, and 1,001,000 is 1,000 greater than a million. The difference, then, is 1,000 + 1, or 1,001. Or, you may figure the problem in the following way:

$$1,001,000$$
$$\underline{-\ 999,999}$$
$$1,001$$

53. The correct answer is (A). This equation can be solved in two steps:

Step 1:   Move −6 to the right side and change the sign.

$3x = 2 + 6$

$3x = 8$

Step 2:   Divide by the coefficient of the variable.

$\dfrac{3x}{3} = \dfrac{8}{3}$

$x = \dfrac{8}{3}$

54. The correct answer is (C).

Step 1:   First, remove the grouping parentheses:

$-3(y + 2) = 9$

$-3y - 6 = 9$

Step 2:   Then move −6 to the right side, change its sign, and combine:

$-3y = 9 + 6$

$-3y = 15$

Step 3:   Divide through by the coefficient of the variable:

$\dfrac{-3y}{-3} = \dfrac{15}{-3} \quad y = -5$

55. The correct answer is (A). To solve this problem, simply plug in the values given and multiply:

Step 1: $-4xy^2z^3$

Step 2: $-4\left(\dfrac{1}{3}\right)(-2)^2(1)^3$

Step 3: $\quad -4\left(\dfrac{1}{3}\right)(4)(1)$

Step 4: $\quad \left(-\dfrac{4}{3}\right)(4) = -\left(\dfrac{16}{3}\right)$

56. The correct answer is (B). Here again, simply plug in the values and multiply the fractions:

Step 1: $\quad A = \dfrac{1}{2}bh$

Step 2: $\quad A = \dfrac{1}{2} \bullet \dfrac{1}{4} \bullet 2$

Step 3: $\quad A = \dfrac{2}{8} = \dfrac{1}{4}$

If you had trouble with these fractions, review multiplication of fractions.

57. The correct answer is (C). When simplifying, begin with the innermost grouping symbols first, and work your way outward:

Step 1: $\quad -6 - [2 - (3a - b) + b] + a$

Step 2: $\quad -6 - [2 - 3a + b + b] + a$

Step 3: $\quad -6 - [2 - 3a + 2b] + a$

Step 4: $\quad -6 - 2 + 3a - 2b + a$

Step 5: $\quad -8 + 4a - 2b$

58. The correct answer is (D.) Begin with the innermost parentheses and work your way outward. Note that a minus sign in front of a grouping symbol reverses the signs of all numbers within:

Step 1: $\quad -2[-4(2 - 1) + (3 + 2)]$

Step 2: $\quad -2[-4(1) + (5)]$

Step 3: $\quad -2[-4 + 5]$

Step 4: $\quad -2[+ 1] = -2$

59. The correct answer is (C). This proportion asks you to find the missing element. A proportion is a statement of equality between two ratios, so we know that 5 bears the same relationship to 15 as 6 does to the unknown number. Because 3 × 5 equals 15, we know 3 × 6 equals the unknown number. The number, thus, is 18. The completed proportion should read: 5:6 as 15:18. Proportions may also be written with a set of two colons replacing the word "as." In this case, the proportion would read: 5:6 :: 15:18.

60. The correct answer is (C).

Step 1: To find the correct ratio, write it as:

$$\dfrac{6 \text{ inches}}{6 \text{ feet}}$$

Step 2: Rewrite each quantity in inches:

$$\dfrac{6 \text{ inches}}{72 \text{ inches}}$$

Step 3: Simplify the ratio:

$$\dfrac{6}{72} = \dfrac{1}{12} = 1:12$$

SUMMING IT UP

- If you're in the 8th grade, you must know basic arithmetic, fundamental operations using fractions and decimals, percents, and very basic algebra and geometry.

- If you're in the 12th grade seeking an extra year before college, you should be thoroughly familiar with complex algebra and geometry.

- Remember that scoring your high school entrance exam is based on your grade. You do not need to know what you have not yet been taught, but you must have mastered all of the math appropriate to your grade level.

- Addition, subtraction, multiplication, and division are the basic operations upon which the structure of mathematics is based.

- Make sure you note the problems that were difficult for you, as well as those that were easy, and adjust your study plans.

Quantitative Ability (SSAT and ISEE)

OVERVIEW

- What makes multiple-choice math easier?
- How do you solve multiple-choice Quantitative Ability questions?
- What do smart test-takers know?
- Summing it up

WHAT MAKES MULTIPLE-CHOICE MATH EASIER?

How can one kind of quantitative ability question possibly be easier than another? Well, multiple-choice math is easier than the math tests you take in school. Why? Simple. Because it's multiple choice, the correct answer is always on the page in front of you. So even if you are estimating, you'll be able to narrow down the choices and improve your guessing odds.

Some multiple-choice questions require no calculation at all; the correct answer is based upon your grasp of the concepts introduced by the question. Some questions are straight calculations; others are presented in the form of word problems. Some include graphs, charts, or tables that you will be asked to interpret. All the questions have either four (ISEE) or five (SSAT) answer choices. These choices are arranged in order by size from smallest to largest or from largest to smallest.

HOW DO YOU SOLVE MULTIPLE-CHOICE QUANTITATIVE ABILITY QUESTIONS?

Although it sounds quite official, Quantitative Ability is really just a fancy way to say "math." Keeping that in mind, walk through the following steps and firm up your attack plan for handling the math problems you'll find on your test.

chapter 11

MULTIPLE-CHOICE MATH: GETTING IT RIGHT

1 Read the question carefully and determine what's being asked.

2 Decide which math principles apply and use them to solve the problem.

3 Look for your answer among the choices. If it's there, mark it and go on.

4 If the answer you found is not there, recheck the question and your calculations.

5 If you still can't solve the problem, eliminate obviously wrong answers and take your best guess.

Now let's try out these steps on a couple of multiple-choice math questions.

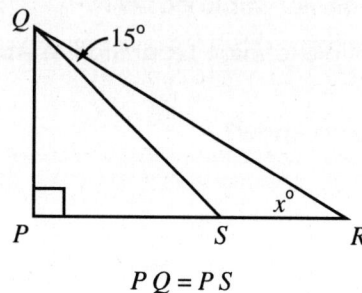

$PQ = PS$

In the figure above, $x =$

(A) 15°

(B) 30°

(C) 40°

(D) 60°

(E) 75°

1 The problem asks you to find the measure of one angle of right triangle PQR.

2 Two math principles apply: (1) the sum of the measures, in degrees, of the angles of a triangle is 180°, and (2) 45°-45°-90° right triangles have certain special properties. Because $PQ = PS$, triangle PQS is a 45°-45°-90° right triangle. Therefore, angle $PQS = 45°$ and angle $PQR = 45° + 15° = 60°$. Therefore, angle $x = 180° - 90° - 60° = 30°$.

3 **The correct answer is (B).**

If x and y are negative numbers, which of the following is negative?

(A) xy

(B) $(xy)^2$

(C) $(x-y)^2$

(D) $x + y$

(E) $\dfrac{x}{y}$

1 The problem asks you to pick an answer choice that is a negative number.

2 The principles that apply are those governing operations with signed numbers. Because x and y are negative, both choices (A) and (E) must be positive. As for choices (B) and (C), so long as neither x nor y is zero, those expressions must be positive. (Any number other than zero squared gives a positive result.) Choice (D), however, is negative because it represents the sum of two negative numbers.

3 By applying the rules governing signed numbers to each answer choice, you can determine that choices (A), (B), (C), and (E) can only be positive numbers.

Therefore, the correct answer must be choice (D). If you have trouble working with letters, try substituting easy numbers for x and y in each choice.

TIP

Look for shortcuts. Math problems test your math reasoning, not your ability to make endless calculations. If you find yourself calculating too much, you've probably missed a shortcut that would have made your work easier.

WHAT DO SMART TEST-TAKERS KNOW?

Some of these you've heard before, some will be new to you. Whatever the case, read them, learn them, love them. They will help you.

The Question Number Tells You How Hard the Question Will Be

Just as in most of the other test sections, the questions go from easy to hard as you work toward the end. The first third of the questions are easy, the middle third are average but harder, and the final third get more and more difficult. Take a look at these three examples. Don't solve them yet (you'll be doing that in a couple of minutes), just get an idea of how the level of difficulty changes from Question 1 to Question 12 to Question 25.

1. If $x - 2 = 5$, then $x =$

(A) -10

(B) -3

(C) $\dfrac{5}{2}$

(D) 3

(E) 7

12. For how many integers x is $-7 < 2x < -5$?

(A) None

(B) One

(C) Two

(D) Three

(E) Indefinite number

25. In a set of 5 books, no two of which have the same number of pages, the longest book has 150 pages and the shortest book has 130 pages. If x pages is the average (arithmetic mean) of the number of pages in the 5-book set, which of the following best indicates all possible values of x?

(A) $130 < x < 150$

(B) $131 < x < 149$

(C) $133 < x < 145$

(D) $134 < x < 145$

(E) $135 < x < 145$

Can you see the difference? You can probably do Question 1 with your eyes closed. For Question 12 you probably have to open your eyes and do some calculations on scratch paper. Question 25 may cause you to wince a little, and then get started on some heavy-duty thinking.

Easy Questions Have Easy Answers; Difficult Questions Don't

Duh, but with an explanation. The easy questions are straightforward and don't have any hidden tricks. The obvious answer is almost always the correct answer. So for Question 1 the answer is indeed choice (E).

When you hit the difficult stuff, you have to think harder. The information is not straightforward and the answers aren't obvious. You can bet that your first-choice, easy answer will be wrong. If you don't believe it, let's take a closer look at the difficult solution for Question 25.

25. In a set of 5 books, no two of which have the same number of pages, the longest book has 150 pages and the shortest book has 130 pages. If x pages is the average (arithmetic mean) of the number of pages in the 5-book set, which of the following best indicates all possible values of x and only possible values of x?

(A) $130 < x < 150$

(B) $131 < x < 149$

(C) $133 < x < 145$

(D) $134 < x < 145$

(E) $135 < x < 145$

Yes, it's difficult mostly because the process you have to use to find the solution is difficult. Let's start by eliminating answer choices. Choice (A) is a bad guess. You see the same info as you see in the word problem so you figure it's got to be right. Wrong. All it does is say that the shortest book is 130 pages, the longest book is 150 pages, and the average is between 130 and 150. Simple and wrong.

Choice (B) illustrates the reasoning that "no two books have the same number of pages, so the average must be one page more than the shortest book and one page less than the longest." Remember, it's a difficult question, it's just not that easy an answer.

OK then, let's skip to the correct answer, which is choice (E), and find out how we got there. First, you want to find the minimum value for x so you assume that the other three books contain 131, 132, and 133 pages. So the average would be:

$$\frac{130+131+132+133+150}{5} = \frac{676}{5} = 135.2$$

So x must be more than 135. Now assume that the other three books contain 149, 148, and 147 pages. Then the average length of all five books would be:

$$\frac{150+149+148+147+130}{5} = \frac{724}{5} = 144.8$$

Then x would be greater than 135 but less than 145.

When Guessing at Hard Questions, You Can Toss Out Easy Answers

Now that you know the difficult questions won't have easy or obvious answers, use a guessing strategy. (Use all the help you can get!) When you have less than a clue about a difficult question, scan the answer choices and eliminate the ones that seem easy or obvious, such as any that just restate the information in the question. Ditch those and then take your best guess.

Questions of Average Difficulty Won't Have Trick Answers

Let's look again at Question 12:

12. For how many integers x is $-7 < 2x < -5$?
   (A) None
   (B) One
   (C) Two
   (D) Three
   (E) Indefinite number

This is a bit more difficult than Question 1, but it's still pretty straightforward. There is only one integer between -7 and -5, and that's -6. There's also only one value for integer x so that $2x$ equals -6, and that is -3. Get it? $2(-3) = -6$. So, choice (B) is the correct answer. Trust your judgment and your reasoning; no tricks here.

It's Smart to Test Answer Choices

Every standard multiple-choice math problem includes four (ISEE) or five (SSAT) answer choices. One of them has to be correct; the others are wrong. This means that it's always possible to solve a problem by testing each of the answer choices. Just plug each choice into the problem and sooner or later you'll find the one that works! Testing answer choices can often be a much easier and surer way of solving a problem than attempting a lengthy calculation.

When Testing Choices, It's Smart to Start Near the Middle

Remember, the answer is somewhere right in front of you. If you test all the answer choices, you'll find the right one. However, the smart place to start is always as close to the middle as possible. Why? Because the quantities in the choices are always arranged in order, either from smallest to largest or the other way around. If you start at the middle and it's too large, you'll just have to concentrate on the smaller choices. There, you've knocked off some choices in a heartbeat. Let's give it a "test" run, so to speak...

> If a rectangle has sides of $2x$ and $3x$ and an area of 24, what is the value of x?
>
> **(A)** 2
>
> **(B)** 3
>
> **(C)** 4
>
> **(D)** 5
>
> **(E)** 6
>
> You know that one of these is right. Get started by testing choice (C), and assume that $x = 4$. Then the sides would have lengths 2 (4) = 8 and 3 (4) = 12 and the rectangle would have an area of 8 × 12 = 96. Because 96 is larger than 24 (the area in the question), start working with the smaller answer choices. [Which means, of course, that you can immediately forget about choices (D) and (E). Great!] When you plug 3 into the figuring, you get 2 (3) = 6 and 3 (3) = 9 and 6 × 9 = 54; still too large. The only choice left is choice (A), and it works.

Now try this testing business with a more difficult question:

> A farmer raises chickens and cows. If her animals have a total of 120 heads and a total of 300 feet, how many chickens does the farmer have?
>
> **(A)** 50 chickens
>
> **(B)** 60 chickens
>
> **(C)** 70 chickens
>
> **(D)** 80 chickens
>
> **(E)** 90 chickens

Here goes—starting with choice (C). If the farmer has 70 chickens, she has 50 cows. (You know the farmer has 120 animals, because they each have only one head, right?) So now you're talking about 70 × 2 = 140 chicken feet and 50 × 4 = 200 cow feet, for a grand total of 340 animal feet. Well, that's more than the 300 animal feet in the question. How will you lose some of those feet? First, assume that the farmer has more chickens and fewer cows (cows have more feet than chickens do). Give choice (D)—80—a try. Test 80 × 2 = 160 and 40 × 4 = 160; your total is 320 feet, which is closer but not quite right. The only answer left is choice (E), and that's the correct one. Check it out:

90 × 2 = 180 and 30 × 4 = 120 and the total is . . . 300!

It's Easier to Work with Numbers than with Letters

Because numbers are more meaningful than letters, try plugging them into equations and formulas in place of variables. This technique can make problems much easier to solve. Here are some examples:

If $x - 4$ is 2 greater than y, then $x + 5$ is how much greater than y?

(A) 1

(B) 3

(C) 7

(D) 9

(E) 11

Choose any value for x. Let's say you decide to make $x = 4$.

All right, $4 - 4 = 0$, and 0 is 2 greater than y. So $y = -2$. If $x = 4$, then $x + 5 = 4 + 5 = 9$, and so $x + 5$ is 11 more than y. Therefore, the correct answer is choice (E).

The unit cost of pens is the same regardless of how many pens are purchased. If the cost of p pens is d dollars, what is the cost, in dollars, of x pens?

(A) xd

(B) xpd

(C) $\dfrac{xd}{p}$

(D) $\dfrac{xp}{d}$

(E) $\dfrac{pd}{x}$

Time to plug in some real numbers, because you need real money to buy anything, including pens. Say that four pens (p) cost $2 ($d$), so each pen would cost 50 cents. And say that you really only need one pen (x), so you're spending only \$0.50. Then $p = 4$, $d = 2$, and $x = 1$, and the right answer would be 0.5. Now, start using these numbers with the answer choices:

(A) $xd = (1)(2) = 2$ (Nope.)

(B) $xpd = (1)(4)(2) = 8$ (Nope, again.)

(C) $\dfrac{xd}{p} = \dfrac{(1)(2)}{4} = 0.5$ (Yes, there it is.)

(D) $\dfrac{xp}{d} = \dfrac{(1)(4)}{2} = 2$ (Nope.)

(E) $\dfrac{pd}{x} = \dfrac{(4)(2)}{1} = 8$ (Nope.)

If a question asks for an odd integer or an even integer, go ahead and pick any odd or even integer you like.

It's Okay to Write in Your Test Booklet, So Use It for Scratch Work

The test booklet is yours, so feel free to use it for your scratch work. Also, go ahead and mark up any diagrams with length or angle information; it helps. But don't waste time trying to redraw diagrams; it's just not worth it.

A Reality Check Can Help You Eliminate Answers That Can't Possibly Be Right

Knowing whether your calculations should produce a number that's larger or smaller than the quantity you started with can point you toward the right answer. It's also an effective way of eliminating wrong answers. Here's an example:

> Using his bike, Daryl can complete a paper route in 20 minutes. Jennifer, who walks the route, can complete it in 30 minutes. How long will it take the two kids to complete the route if they work together, one starting at each end of the route?
>
> **(A)** 8 minutes
>
> **(B)** 12 minutes
>
> **(C)** 20 minutes
>
> **(D)** 30 minutes
>
> **(E)** 45 minutes

Immediately you can see that choices (C), (D), and (E) are impossible because the two kids working together will have to complete the job in less time than either one of them working alone. In fact, the correct answer is choice (B), 12 minutes.

	Daryl	Jennifer
Time actually spent	x	x
Time needed to do entire job alone	20	30

$$\frac{x}{20} + \frac{x}{30} = 1$$

Multiply by 60 to clear fractions:

$$3x + 2x = 60$$
$$5x = 60$$
$$x = 12$$

Your Eye Is a Good Estimator

Figures in the standard multiple-choice math section are always drawn to scale unless you see the warning "Note: Figure not drawn to scale." That means you can sometimes solve a problem just by looking at the picture and estimating the answer. Here's how this works:

In the rectangle $PQRS$ shown, TU and WV are parallel to SR. If $PS = 6$, $UV = 1$, and PR (not shown) = 10, what is the area of rectangle $TUVW$?

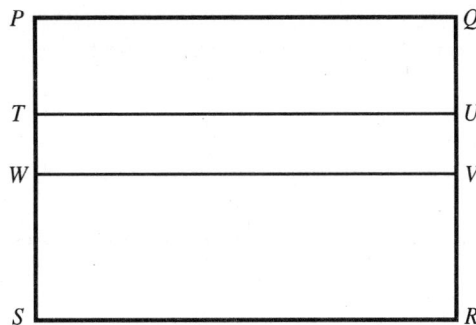

(A) 8
(B) 12
(C) 16
(D) 24
(E) 32

To solve the problem, you will need to find the length of TU. You can do this by using the Pythagorean Theorem. The triangle PSR has sides of 6 and 10, so $SR = 8$. Because $TU = SR$, $TU = 8$, so the area of the small rectangle is equal to $1 \times 8 = 8$.

As an alternative, you could simply estimate the length of TU. TU appears to be longer than PS (6), and TU must be shorter than PR (10). Therefore, TU appears to be approximately 8. And the area must be approximately $1 \times 8 = 8$. Is that sufficiently accurate to get the right answer? Look at the choices. Choice (A) is 8, and it's the only choice that is even close to 8.

TIP

Circle what's asked. For multiple-choice math questions, circle what's being asked so that you don't pick a wrong answer by mistake. That way, for example, you won't pick an answer that gives a perimeter when the question asks for an area.

If Some Questions Always Give You Trouble, Save Them for Last

You know which little demons haunt your math skills. If you find questions that you know will give you nightmares, save them for last. They will take up a lot of your time, especially if you're panicking, and you can use that time to do more of the easier questions.

TEST YOURSELF QUIZZES

Take the following quizzes to help you determine what your weaknesses might be. Answers can be found on pages 386–387.

Test Yourself 1

Directions: Each of the following questions has four suggested answers. Decide which one is best. Circle the letter that appears before your answer.

1. In the simplest form, $-11 - (-2)$ is
   - **(A)** 7
   - **(B)** 9
   - **(C)** -9
   - **(D)** -11

2. Find the average of 6.47, 5.89, 3.42, .65, and 7.09.
   - **(A)** 3.920
   - **(B)** 4.704
   - **(C)** 4.705
   - **(D)** 5.812

3. Change 0.03125 to a common fraction.
   - **(A)** $\dfrac{3}{64}$
   - **(B)** $\dfrac{1}{16}$
   - **(C)** $\dfrac{1}{64}$
   - **(D)** $\dfrac{1}{32}$

4. A roll of carpeting will cover 224 square feet of floor space. How many rolls will be needed to carpet a room 36' × 8' and another 24' × 9'?
   - **(A)** 2.25
   - **(B)** 2.50
   - **(C)** 4.25
   - **(D)** 4.50

5. After deducting a discount of 30%, the price of a coat was $35. The regular price of the coat was
   - **(A)** $24.50
   - **(B)** $42
   - **(C)** $50
   - **(D)** $116.67

6. Find the sum of -16, 14, -38, 26, and 20.
   - **(A)** 6
   - **(B)** 4
   - **(C)** 0
   - **(D)** -6

7. The number of cubic feet of soil needed for a flower box 3 feet long, 8 inches wide, and 1 foot deep is

   (A) 24

   (B) 12

   (C) $4\frac{2}{3}$

   (D) 2

8. Using exponents, write 359 in expanded form.

   (A) $(3 \times 10^2) + (5 \times 10) + 9$

   (B) $(3^2 \times 10) + (5^2 \times 10) + 9$

   (C) $(3 \times 10^2) + (5 \times 10 \times 3^2)$

   (D) $(3 \times 10^3) + (5 \times 10 + 3^2)$

9. The scale of a certain map is 4 inches = 32 miles. The number of inches that would represent 80 miles is

   (A) 16

   (B) 12

   (C) 10

   (D) 8

10. 15 is 20% of

    (A) 3

    (B) 18

    (C) 35

    (D) 75

11. The bar graph below shows the population of a town during a 30-year period. By what number of people did the population decrease between 1960 and 1970?

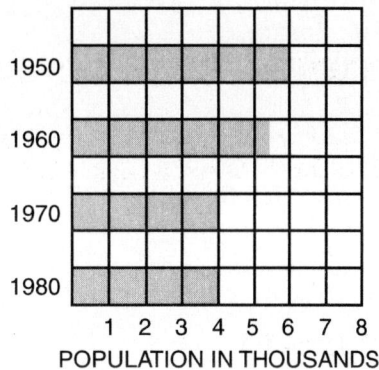

1 2 3 4 5 6 7 8
POPULATION IN THOUSANDS

    (A) 1,000

    (B) 1,500

    (C) 2,500

    (D) 15,000

12. Which of these fractions is greater than $\frac{9}{17}$?

    (A) $\frac{6}{13}$

    (B) $\frac{13}{25}$

    (C) $\frac{11}{20}$

    (D) $\frac{1}{2}$

13. If $y = x - 4$, then $y - 2 =$

    (A) $x - 6$

    (B) $x + 2$

    (C) $x - 2$

    (D) $x + 6$

14. $19\frac{2}{3} - 7\frac{1}{4} =$

(A) $12\frac{1}{4}$

(B) $12\frac{1}{3}$

(C) $12\frac{5}{12}$

(D) $12\frac{3}{4}$

15. If $a - b = 7$ and a and b are both positive integers, what is the minimum possible value of $a + b$?

(A) 11

(B) 9

(C) 8

(D) 0

Test Yourself 2

Directions: Each of the following questions has four suggested answers. Decide which one is best. Circle the letter that appears before your answer.

1. The sum of $\frac{2}{3}, \frac{1}{8}, \frac{5}{6}$, and $3\frac{1}{2}$ is

(A) $4\frac{1}{3}$

(B) $4\frac{3}{4}$

(C) $5\frac{1}{8}$

(D) $5\frac{3}{8}$

2. A store sold suits for $65 each. The suits cost the store $50 each. The percentage of increase of selling price over cost is

(A) 40%

(B) $33\frac{1}{2}$%

(C) $33\frac{1}{3}$%

(D) 30%

3. 72 divided by .0009 =

(A) .125

(B) 80

(C) 800

(D) 80,000

4. What is the simple interest on $460 for two years at $2\frac{1}{2}$%?

(A) $20

(B) $23

(C) $25

(D) $28

5. A house plan uses the scale $\frac{1}{4}$ inch = 1 foot, and, in the drawing, the living room is 7 inches long. If the scale is changed to 1 inch = 1 foot, what will the length of the living room be in the new drawing?

    (A) 18 in.

    (B) 28 in.

    (C) 30 in.

    (D) 36 in.

6. During his summer vacation, a boy earned $14.50 per day and saved 60% of his earnings. If he worked 45 days, how much did he save?

    (A) $287.93

    (B) $391.50

    (C) $402.75

    (D) $543.50

7. $\frac{27}{64}$ expressed as a percent is

    (A) 40.625%

    (B) 42.188%

    (C) 43.750%

    (D) 45.313%

8. If the formula for the area of a circle is πr^2, find the area of a circle that has a diameter 8 inches long.

    (A) 50.24 sq. in.

    (B) 100.48 sq. in.

    (C) 102.34 sq. in.

    (D) 200.96 sq. in.

9. If $8 > x > 5$ and $3 > y > -2$, then

    (A) $x < y$

    (B) $x \le y$

    (C) $x \ge y$

    (D) $x > y$

10. $5^3 \times 3^4 =$

    (A) $5 \times 3 \times 3 \times 4$

    (B) $5 \times 5 \times 5 \times 3 \times 3 \times 3$

    (C) $5 \times 5 \times 5 \times 3 \times 3 \times 3 \times 3$

    (D) $5 \times 5 \times 5 \times 5 \times 3 \times 3 \times 3$

11. If $a + b = 200°$, and $c + d + e + f = 140°$, what is the number of degrees in angle g?

    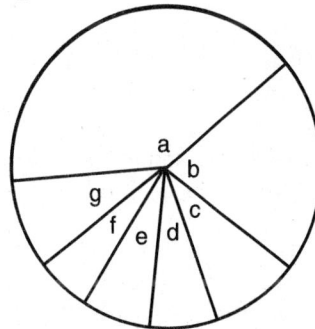

    (A) 10°

    (B) 20°

    (C) 30°

    (D) 45°

12. If a steel bar is 0.39 feet long, its length in *inches* is

    (A) less than 4.

    (B) between 4 and $4\frac{1}{2}$.

    (C) between $4\frac{1}{2}$ and 5.

    (D) between 5 and 6.

13. The graph below shows the number of hours in each 8-hour working day that Mr. Smith spent on the telephone last week. What fraction represents the average of the part of the day Mr. Smith spends on the telephone?

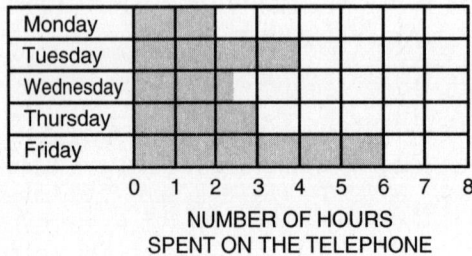

Monday								
Tuesday								
Wednesday								
Thursday								
Friday								

0 1 2 3 4 5 6 7 8
NUMBER OF HOURS
SPENT ON THE TELEPHONE

(A) $\frac{3}{8}$

(B) $\frac{7}{16}$

(C) $\frac{4}{5}$

(D) $\frac{72}{24}$

14. Multiply: $(10a^3)(5a)$.
    (A) $14a^3$
    (B) $50a^4$
    (C) $40a^3$
    (D) $15a^4$

15. The formula for the area of a triangle is $A = \frac{1}{2}bh$. Find A if $b = 12$ and $h = 10$.
    (A) 22
    (B) 32
    (C) 50
    (D) 60

Test Yourself 3

Directions: Each of the following questions has four suggested answers. Decide which one is best. Circle the letter that appears before your answer.

1. Find the hypotenuse of a right triangle if the legs are 6 and 8.
   (A) 8
   (B) 9
   (C) 10
   (D) 11

2. One man earns $24,000 per year. Another earns $1,875 per month. How much more does the first man make in a year than the second man?
   (A) $2,500
   (B) $2,000
   (C) $1,500
   (D) $1,000

3. The square root of 53 is closest to
   (A) 8
   (B) 7
   (C) 6.5
   (D) 6

4. Solve for x: $4x - 8 = 16$
   (A) 4
   (B) 6
   (C) 8
   (D) 10

5. A library contains 60 books on arts and crafts. If this is .05% of the total number of books on the shelves, how many books does the library own?
   (A) 1,200
   (B) 12,000
   (C) 120,000
   (D) 1,200,000

6. The graph below represents Ms. Lawson's monthly budget. What percentage of her salary does she spend on things other than housing costs?

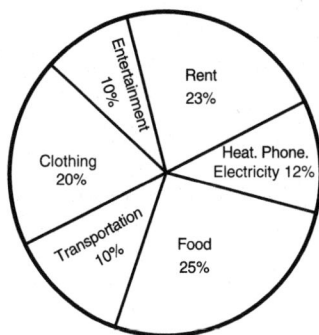

   (A) 35%
   (B) 40%
   (C) 52%
   (D) 65%

7. Find the length in inches of diagonal *DB* in the rectangle below:

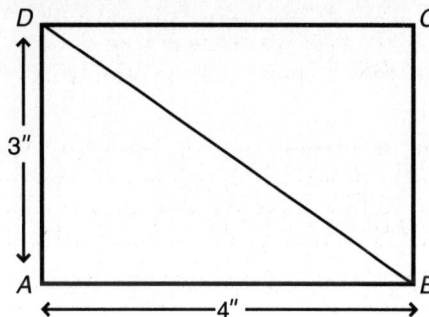

   (A) 5
   (B) 7
   (C) 9
   (D) 11

8. A woman borrowed $5,000 and agreed to pay $11\frac{1}{2}$ % simple interest. If she repaid the loan in 6 months, how much interest would she pay?
   (A) $287.50
   (B) $575
   (C) $2,875
   (D) $5,750

9. Solve for x: $2x^2 - 6 = 44$
   (A) ± 4
   (B) ± 5
   (C) ± 12.5
   (D) ± 25

10. At an annual rate of $.40 per $100, what is the annual fire insurance premium for a house that is insured for $80,000?
    (A) $3.20
    (B) $32
    (C) $320
    (D) $3,200

11. Simplify: $\dfrac{2}{3}+\left(\dfrac{3}{4}\times\dfrac{2}{9}\right)-\dfrac{1}{6}$

   (A) $\dfrac{3}{4}$

   (B) $\dfrac{1}{2}$

   (C) $\dfrac{1}{3}$

   (D) $\dfrac{2}{3}$

12. Which of the following is true?

   (A) $\dfrac{2}{3}>\dfrac{7}{10}$

   (B) $\dfrac{2}{7}>\dfrac{1}{3}$

   (C) $\dfrac{5}{7}<\dfrac{8}{9}$

   (D) $\dfrac{2}{9}<\dfrac{1}{5}$

13. Find the missing term in the proportion x: 5 = 24:30.

   (A) 3

   (B) 4

   (C) 6

   (D) 8

14. A distance of 25 miles is represented on a map by $2\dfrac{1}{2}$ inches. On the map, how many miles are represented by one inch?

   (A) 6

   (B) 8

   (C) 10

   (D) 12

15. If the school tax rate in a community is \$33.50 per \$1,000 of assessed valuation, find the amount of tax on property assessed at \$50,000.

   (A) \$167.50

   (B) \$420.02

   (C) \$1,675.00

   (D) \$4,200.02

Test Yourself 4

Directions: Each of the following questions has four suggested answers. Decide which one is best. Circle the letter that appears before your answer.

1. A junior high school established a school savings account, and the eighth grade saved $990. If this was 45% of the total amount saved by the school, find the total amount.
   (A) $220
   (B) $1,210
   (C) $2,100
   (D) $2,200

2. A team won 25 games and lost 8. What is the ratio of the number of games won to the number of games played?
   (A) 33:25
   (B) 25:33
   (C) 58:25
   (D) 25:58

3. A circular flower garden has a diameter of 21 feet. How many feet of fencing will be required to enclose this garden?
   (A) 72
   (B) 66
   (C) 60
   (D) $20\frac{1}{12}$

4. Solve for x: $7x - 4 = 115$
   (A) 17
   (B) 19
   (C) 21
   (D) 22

5. The best approximate answer for $1.2507623 \times 72.964896$ is
   (A) 100
   (B) 90
   (C) 70
   (D) 9

6. $3\frac{1}{2} \times 2\frac{1}{4} =$
   (A) $5\frac{3}{4}$
   (B) $6\frac{1}{8}$
   (C) $6\frac{2}{8}$
   (D) $7\frac{7}{8}$

7. The area of a rectangular room is 1,000 square feet. If the width of the room is 25 feet, what is the length of the room?
   (A) 30 feet
   (B) 35 feet
   (C) 40 feet
   (D) 45 feet

8. An order for 345 machine bolts at $4.15 per hundred will cost
   (A) $.1432
   (B) $1.14
   (C) $14.32
   (D) $143.20

9. On the first day of its drive, a junior high school raised $40, which was $33\frac{1}{3}$ % of its quota. How much was the quota?

   (A) $120
   (B) $100
   (C) $80
   (D) $68

10. According to the 1950 census, 14,830,192 people were then living in New York State. Round this number off to the nearest thousand.

    (A) 14,000
    (B) 148,300
    (C) 1,483,000
    (D) 14,830,000

11. Simplify: $x - [8 - (x - 2)]$

    (A) -10
    (B) $2x - 10$
    (C) $2x + 10$
    (D) $2x - 6$

12. Sharon made a circle graph and drew an angle of 45° to show the number of pupils in her grade who had earned an A in mathematics. What percent of her grade earned an A?

    (A) 10%
    (B) $12\frac{1}{2}$ %
    (C) $16\frac{2}{3}$%
    (D) 20%

QUESTIONS 13–15 REFER TO THE GRAPH BELOW.

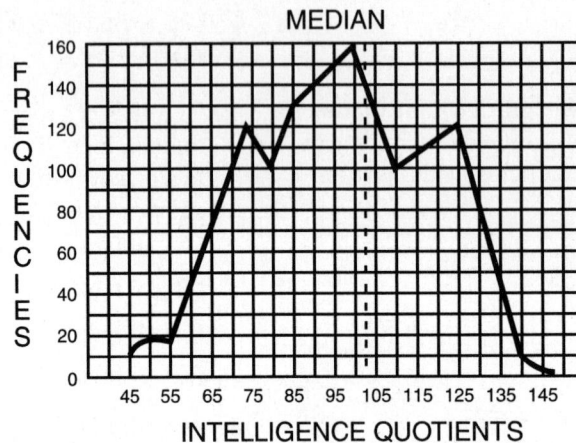

13. The number of pupils having the highest intelligence quotient (I.Q.) is about

    (A) 5
    (B) 20
    (C) 145
    (D) 160

14. The number of pupils having an I.Q. of 80 is identical with the number of pupils having an I.Q. of

    (A) 68
    (B) 100
    (C) 110
    (D) 128

15. The intelligence quotient that has the greatest frequency is

(A) 95

(B) 100

(C) 105

(D) 160

Test Yourself 5

Directions: Each of the following questions has four suggested answers. Decide which one is best. Circle the letter that appears before your answer.

1. You roll a fair, six-sided die twice. What is the probability that the die will land with the same side facing up both times?

(A) $\dfrac{1}{6}$

(B) $\dfrac{1}{12}$

(C) $\dfrac{2}{36}$

(D) $\dfrac{1}{36}$

2. The area of the shaded portion of the rectangle below is

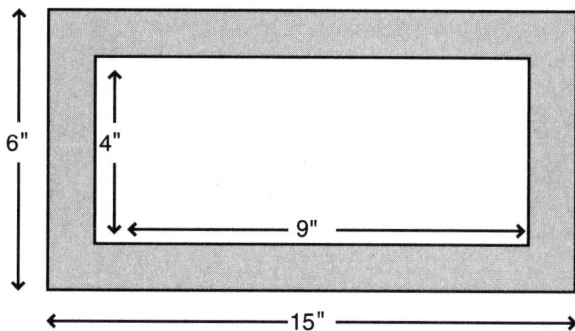

(A) 90 sq. in.

(B) 54 sq. in.

(C) 45 sq. in.

(D) 36 sq. in.

3. The ratio of 16:36 is ?

(A) 3:5

(B) 3:21

(C) 4:8

(D) 4:9

4. 595 written in expanded form with exponents is

(A) $(5 \times 10) + (9 \times 10) + (5 \times 1)$

(B) $(5 \times 10^2) + (9 \times 10) + 5$

(C) $(5 \times 10^2) + (9 \times 10) + (5 \times 5)$

(D) $(5 \times 10^2) + (3 \times 10) + 5$

5. Jane saved $5 by buying a jacket at a sale where a 25% discount was given. What was the original price of the jacket
   (A) $14
   (B) $16
   (C) $18
   (D) $20

6. How many square yards are there in the area of a rug that is 15 feet long and 12 feet wide?
   (A) 18
   (B) 20
   (C) 22
   (D) 24

7. Solve for x: $3x^2 + 15 = 90$
   (A) ± 75
   (B) ± 60
   (C) ± 25
   (D) ± 5

8. A scale drawing of a bird is $\frac{1}{8}$ actual size. If the drawing is $\frac{3}{4}$ inches high, find in inches the height of the real bird.
   (A) 2
   (B) 4
   (C) 6
   (D) 8

9. Find the sum of –8, 17, 29, –12, –3, and 5.
   (A) –18
   (B) 28
   (C) 29
   (D) 33

10. If a man walks $\frac{2}{5}$ mile in 5 minutes, what is his average rate of walking in miles per hour?
    (A) 4
    (B) $4\frac{1}{2}$
    (C) $4\frac{4}{5}$
    (D) $5\frac{1}{5}$

11. Solve for x: $\frac{x}{2} + 3 = 15$
    (A) 18
    (B) 20
    (C) 22
    (D) 24

12. On a map, 1 inch represents 500 miles. How many miles apart are two places that are $1\frac{1}{2}$ inches apart on the map?
    (A) 750
    (B) 1,000
    (C) 1,250
    (D) 1,500

13. $(6 \times 10^3) + (8 \times 10^2) + (7 \times 10) + 3$ is equal to
    (A) 6,873
    (B) 60,873
    (C) 68,730
    (D) 600,873

14. A salesman received a salary of $150 a week plus 5% commission on his total weekly sales. During one week his total sales amounted to $1,800. How much did he earn that week?

   (A) $90

   (B) $240

   (C) $330

   (D) $340

15. If a car averages 18 miles to a gallon of gasoline, how many gallons of gasoline will be used on a trip of 369 miles?

   (A) 18

   (B) $20\frac{1}{2}$

   (C) $21\frac{3}{4}$

   (D) 22

Test Yourself 6

Directions: Each question below has five suggested answers. Decide which one is best. Circle the letter that appears before your answer.

1. A boy's quarterly test marks were 67, 74, 86, and 89. What was the average of his test marks?

   (A) 75

   (B) 79

   (C) 81

   (D) 84

   (E) 85

2. What fraction is equal to 2.5%?

   (A) $\frac{1}{400}$

   (B) $\frac{1}{40}$

   (C) $\frac{1}{4}$

   (D) $2\frac{1}{4}$

   (E) $2\frac{1}{2}$

3. To the nearest tenth, find the square root of 48.

   (A) 5.9

   (B) 6.5

   (C) 6.9

   (D) 7.2

   (E) 7.3

4. Solve for x: $x + 2\frac{1}{2} = 5$

   (A) $-2\frac{1}{2}$

   (B) 2

   (C) $2\frac{1}{2}$

   (D) 3

   (E) $7\frac{1}{2}$

5. Simplify: $\dfrac{68}{204}$

    (A) $\dfrac{1}{6}$

    (B) $\dfrac{2}{9}$

    (C) $\dfrac{4}{12}$

    (D) $\dfrac{1}{3}$

    (E) $\dfrac{3}{8}$

6. Using a scale of $\dfrac{1}{8}$ inch = 1 foot, what length line would be needed to represent 23 feet?

    (A) $2\dfrac{3}{8}$

    (B) $2\dfrac{7}{8}$

    (C) 3

    (D) $3\dfrac{1}{8}$

    (E) $3\dfrac{3}{8}$

7. Which of these fractions is equal to $\dfrac{1}{4} - \dfrac{2}{3}$?

    (A) $\dfrac{5}{12}$

    (B) $\dfrac{3}{10}$

    (C) $-\dfrac{3}{10}$

    (D) $-\dfrac{5}{12}$

    (E) $-\dfrac{7}{12}$

8. The formula for finding the area of a triangle is $A = \dfrac{1}{2}bh$. Find the area of the triangle below:

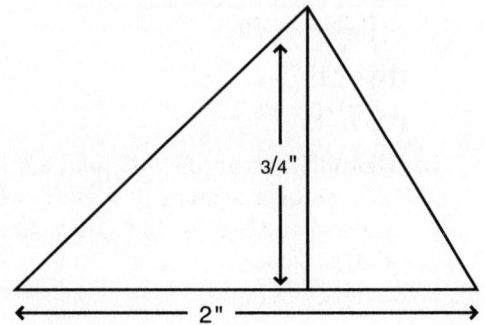

    (A) 3 sq. in.

    (B) $2\dfrac{1}{2}$ sq. in.

    (C) $1\dfrac{1}{2}$ sq. in.

    (D) 1 sq. in.

    (E) $\dfrac{3}{4}$ sq. in.

9. Solve for x: $\dfrac{x}{9} = 27$

    (A) 272

    (B) 243

    (C) 181

    (D) 81

    (E) 3

10. A salesperson gets a commission of 4% on her sales. If she wants her commission to amount to $40, she will have to sell merchandise totaling

    (A) $10

    (B) $100

    (C) $160

    (D) $1,000

    (E) $10,000

11. Using the formula $A = \pi r^2$, find the area of a circle whose diameter is 14 feet.

    (A) 154 sq. ft.

    (B) 256 sq. ft.

    (C) 286 sq. ft.

    (D) 544 sq. ft.

    (E) 615.4 sq. ft.

12. Using the formula $V = lwh$, find the volume of a rectangular solid whose dimensions are $l = 46$ ft., $w = 38$ ft., $h = 40$ ft.

    (A) 89,176 cu. ft.

    (B) 79,507 cu. ft.

    (C) 75,380 cu. ft.

    (D) 69,920 cu. ft.

    (E) 7,538 cu. ft.

13. The standing of a seventh grade baseball team that won ten games and lost five games is

    (A) .667

    (B) .500

    (C) .333

    (D) .250

    (E) .200

14. If $x = 10$, which of the following statements is true?

    (A) $x^2 < 2x$

    (B) $x^2 = 15x - 50$

    (C) $3x > x^3$

    (D) $x^3 = x^2 + 2x$

    (E) $x^3 < x^2 + x^2$

15. 921 written in expanded exponential form is

    (A) $(9 \times 10^2) + (2 \times 10) + 21$

    (B) $(9 \times 100) + (2 \times 10) + 1$

    (C) $(9 \times 10^2) + (2 \times 10) + 1$

    (D) $(9 \times 10^3) + (2 \times 10^2) + 1$

    (E) $(9 \times 10^3) + (2 \times 10) + 1$

Test Yourself 7

Directions: Each question below has five suggested answers. Decide which one is best. Circle the letter that appears before your answer.

1. How many degrees are in angle A of the triangle below?

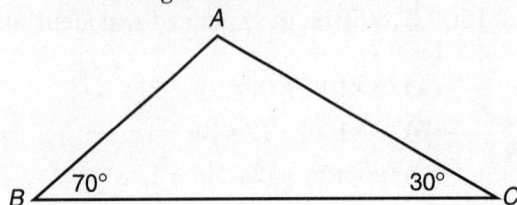

   (A) 60°

   (B) 70°

   (C) 80°

   (D) 90°

   (E) 100°

2. What is the cost of nine ounces of cheese at $.80 per pound?

   (A) $.36

   (B) $.45

   (C) $.48

   (D) $.52

   (E) $.55

3. A man borrowed $3,600 for one month at an annual rate of 5%. How much interest did he owe?

   (A) $5

   (B) $7.50

   (C) $12.50

   (D) $15

   (E) $30

4. One piece of wire is 25 feet 8 inches long and another is 18 feet 10 inches long. What is the difference in length?

   (A) 6 ft. 10 in.

   (B) 6 ft. 11 in.

   (C) 7 ft. 2 in.

   (D) 7 ft. 4 in.

   (E) 7 ft. 5 in.

5. The ratio of 24 to 64 is ?

   (A) 8:3

   (B) 24:100

   (C) 3:8

   (D) 64:100

   (E) 8:12

6. Express algebraically the perimeter of the figure below:

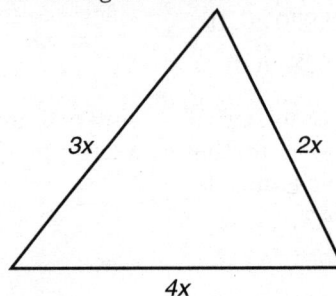

   (A) $3x$

   (B) $5x$

   (C) $7x$

   (D) $9x$

   (E) $24x$

7. If three times a certain number increased by 4 is equal to 19, what is the number?

   (A) 10

   (B) 8

   (C) 7

   (D) 6

   (E) 5

QUESTIONS 8–10 REFER TO THE FOLLOWING GRAPH.

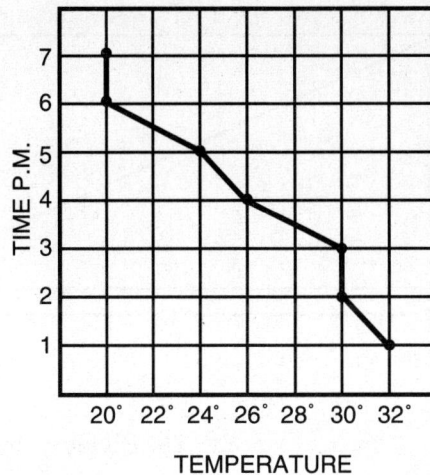

8. What was the approximate temperature at 3:30 p.m.?
   (A) 26°
   (B) 27°
   (C) 28°
   (D) 29°
   (E) 30°

9. What was the percent of decrease in temperature between 2 and 5 p.m.?
   (A) 50%
   (B) 45%
   (C) 38%
   (D) 25%
   (E) 20%

10. The ratio of the rate of temperature decrease between 1–3 p.m. and 4–7 p.m. is
   (A) 2:3
   (B) 3:4
   (C) 1:4
   (D) 1:2
   (E) 3:5

11. If a box of 24 candy bars is bought for $.80, and the bars are sold for $.05 each, what is the percent of profit on the cost?
   (A) 25%
   (B) 30%
   (C) 45%
   (D) 50%
   (E) 75%

12. Find the length of the diagonal in the rectangle below:

(A) 12"

(B) 13"

(C) 16"

(D) 17"

(E) 20"

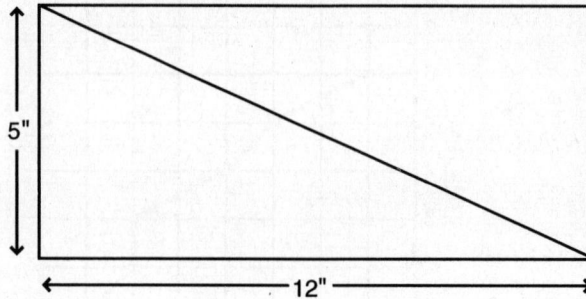

13. Multiply: $(-8)(+6)$

(A) -2

(B) -14

(C) -48

(D) $+24$

(E) $+48$

14. If $x > 9$, then

(A) $x^2 > 80$

(B) $x^2 - 2 = 47$

(C) $x^2 < 65$

(D) $x^2 - 2 > 90$

(E) $x^2 + x < 90$

15. Divide $\frac{7}{8}$ by $\frac{7}{8}$.

(A) $\frac{64}{49}$

(B) 1

(C) $\frac{7}{8}$

(D) $\frac{49}{64}$

(E) 0

Test Yourself 8

Directions: Each question below has five suggested answers. Decide which one is best. Circle the letter that appears before your answer.

1. If the scale on a map indicates that $1\frac{1}{2}$ inches equal 500 miles, 5 inches on that map represent approximately
   (A) 1,800 miles.
   (B) 1,700 miles.
   (C) 1,300 miles.
   (D) 700 miles.
   (E) 350 miles.

2. Change 0.03125 to a common fraction.
   (A) $\frac{1}{8}$
   (B) $\frac{1}{16}$
   (C) $\frac{3}{64}$
   (D) $\frac{1}{32}$
   (E) $\frac{1}{64}$

3. Solve for x: $2x^2 - 5 = 93$
   (A) ± 7
   (B) ± 9
   (C) ± 12
   (D) ± 36
   (E) ± 49

4. Find the area of the shaded portion of the figure below:

   (A) 18.50 sq. in.
   (B) 23.98 sq. in.
   (C) 25.72 sq. in.
   (D) 28.86 sq. in.
   (E) 32.24 sq. in.

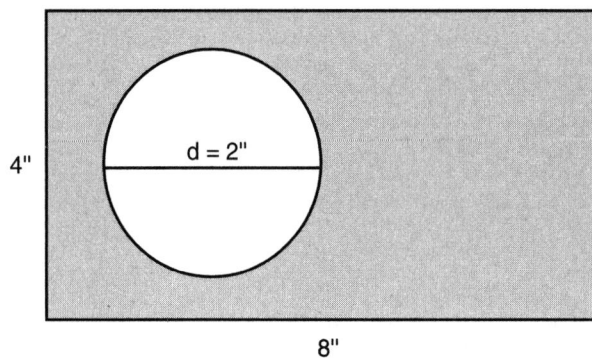

5. What is the simple interest on a loan of $20,000 taken for five years at 12% interest?
   (A) $240
   (B) $1,200
   (C) $2,400
   (D) $6,000
   (E) $12,000

6. The sum of $(10^3 + 2) + (3 \times 10^2)$ is
   (A) 13,002
   (B) 3,102
   (C) 1,302
   (D) 312
   (E) 132

7. A woman whose salary is $225 per week has 12% deducted for taxes and 5% deducted for Social Security. What is her take-home salary?
   (A) $213.75
   (B) $198
   (C) $186.75
   (D) $112.80
   (E) $39.25

8. Find the volume of a cube whose side measures 5 yds.
   (A) 25 cu. yd.
   (B) 100 cu. yd.
   (C) 125 cu. yd.
   (D) 225 cu. yd.
   (E) 625 cu. yd.

9. $42 \div .06 =$
   (A) .07
   (B) .7
   (C) 7
   (D) 70
   (E) 700

10. Solve for x: $x - 62 = -18$
    (A) 124
    (B) 80
    (C) 44
    (D) −44
    (E) −80

11. On a mathematics test, $12\frac{1}{2}$% of a class received marks of D, $37\frac{1}{2}$% received C's, 25% marks of B, and the remainder received A's. What percent of the class received a mark of A?
    (A) 20%
    (B) 25%
    (C) 28%
    (D) 30%
    (E) $33\frac{1}{3}$%

12. The scale on a blueprint is $\frac{1}{4}$" = 1 foot. A room whose actual dimensions are 28 feet by 14 feet would be what size in the drawing?
    (A) 14" × 7"
    (B) $8\frac{1}{4}$" × $4\frac{1}{2}$"
    (C) $7\frac{1}{2}$" × 3"
    (D) 7" × $3\frac{1}{2}$"
    (E) 7" × $3\frac{1}{4}$"

13. $(2 \times 10^4 + 1) - (10^3 + 9) =$
    (A) 18,992
    (B) 16,540
    (C) 1,892
    (D) 1,654
    (E) 992

14. Find the approximate area of a circle whose radius is 21 inches.

(A) 138 sq. in.

(B) 795 sq. in.

(C) 989 sq. in.

(D) 1,385 sq. in.

(E) 3,725 sq. in.

15. If $x = 3.5$, then

(A) $x^2 < 10$

(B) $4x + 6 = 18$

(C) $x^3 - 5 < 4$

(D) $x^2 + x^2 = 15.75$

(E) $x^3 + x < 50$

Test Yourself 9

Directions: Each question below has five suggested answers. Decide which one is best. Circle the letter that appears before your answer.

1. One man earns $21,000 per year. Another man earns $1,675 per month. How much more does the first man earn in a year than the second man?

(A) $19

(B) $90

(C) $190

(D) $900

(E) $1,900

2. Solve for x: $2x^2 - 2 = 30$

(A) ± 2

(B) ± 4

(C) ± 5

(D) ± 16

(E) ± 32

3. By purchasing her coat on sale, Jan saved $25, a savings of $33\frac{1}{3}\%$. What was the original price of the coat?

(A) $120

(B) $100

(C) $90

(D) $75

(E) $60

4. Find the volume of a cube whose edge is 4 inches long.

(A) 32 cu. in.

(B) 48 cu. in.

(C) 64 cu. in.

(D) 84 cu. in.

(E) 96 cu. in.

5. Which of the following has the same value as .5%?

(A) $\frac{1}{2}\%$

(B) $\frac{1}{5}\%$

(C) $\frac{1}{20}\%$

(D) $\frac{1}{50}\%$

(E) $\frac{1}{500}\%$

6. On a map, $1\frac{1}{2}$ inches represent 25 miles. How many miles apart are two places that are $3\frac{3}{4}$ inches apart on the map?

   (A) 50 miles

   (B) 55.5 miles

   (C) 60 miles

   (D) 62.5 miles

   (E) 67.5 miles

7. Find the sum of −11, −22, 60, 2, and −36.

   (A) −131

   (B) −7

   (C) 0

   (D) 7

   (E) 131

8. A certain department store arrives at its retail prices by adding a 150% mark-up to wholesale prices. If a dress cost the store $30 wholesale, what will its retail price be?

   (A) $75

   (B) $70

   (C) $65

   (D) $60

   (E) $45

9. Find the difference between $(3^4 + 4)$ and $(4^3 + 1)$.

   (A) 21

   (B) 20

   (C) 18

   (D) 14

   (E) 3

10. Solve for x: $\frac{x}{12} = 7.5$

    (A) 78

    (B) 80

    (C) 84

    (D) 90

    (E) 102

11. A woman bought groceries totaling $22.73 and gave the clerk three ten-dollar bills and three pennies. How much change did she receive?

    (A) $8.30

    (B) $8.20

    (C) $7.30

    (D) $7.27

    (E) $7.20

12. Find the total surface area for a rectangular solid with these dimensions: $l = 8"$, $w = 4"$, $h = 8"$.

    (A) 64 sq. in.

    (B) 128 sq. in.

    (C) 256 sq. in.

    (D) 320 sq. in.

    (E) 512 sq. in.

13. A woman bought a lamp for $16.75. She returned it the next day and chose a lamp that cost $18.95. She gave the clerk a five-dollar bill to pay the difference in price. How much change did she get?

    (A) $2.10

    (B) $2.30

    (C) $2.40

    (D) $2.60

    (E) $2.80

14. A boy sold $60 worth of magazine subscriptions, for which he was paid $18. What rate of commission was he paid?

(A) 20%

(B) 30%

(C) 40%

(D) 50%

(E) 60%

15. Which consecutive integers for x and y would make this statement true?

$$x < \sqrt{200} < y$$

(A) 100 and 101

(B) 40 and 50

(C) 27 and 33

(D) 14 and 15

(E) 10 and 11

Test Yourself 10

Directions: Each question below has five suggested answers. Decide which one is best. Circle the letter that appears before your answer.

1. Last year the enrollment in a kindergarten was 150 pupils. This year the enrollment is 180 pupils. What was the percent of the increase in enrollment?

(A) 10%

(B) 15%

(C) 20%

(D) 25%

(E) 30%

2. The dimensions of a room are: $l = 15$ feet, $w = 12$ feet, and $h = 8$ feet. How many square feet of wallpaper will be required to cover the walls of this room?

(A) 192 sq. ft.

(B) 216 sq. ft.

(C) 240 sq. ft.

(D) 432 sq. ft.

(E) 648 sq. ft.

3. If $a = 8$ and $b = 3$, find the value of $4a + 3b^2$.

(A) 39

(B) 41

(C) 59

(D) 66

(E) 70

4. Model trains are built on a scale of 1 inch = 1 foot. If a particular model train is 3 feet 7 inches long, how many yards long would the actual train be?

(A) 14.3

(B) 28

(C) 36

(D) 43.5

(E) 57.75

5. A recipe calls for $1\frac{1}{2}$ cups of sugar. It is necessary to make eight times the recipe for a church supper. If 2 cups of sugar equal one pound, how many pounds of sugar will be needed to make the recipe for the supper?

(A) 4

(B) 6

(C) 8

(D) 10

(E) 12

6. The tax rate, in decimal form, for a certain community was .029 of the assessed valuation. Express this tax rate in dollars per $1,000 of the assessed valuation.

    (A) $25 per $1,000

    (B) $29 per $1,000

    (C) $32 per $1,000

    (D) $34 per $1,000

    (E) $290 per $1,000

7. Which of the following is a member of the solution set of $x - y > 10$?

    (A) $(8, -3)$

    (B) $(6, -3)$

    (C) $(3, -7)$

    (D) $(-3, 7)$

    (E) $(-6, 3)$

8. Find the area of the triangle pictured below:

    (A) 72 sq. in.

    (B) 40 sq. in.

    (C) 36 sq. in.

    (D) 32 sq. in.

    (E) 18 sq. in.

9. Solve for x: $\dfrac{x^2}{2} = 18$

    (A) ± 72

    (B) ± 36

    (C) ± 9

    (D) ± 8

    (E) ± 6

10. The daily almanac report for one day during the summer stated that the sun rose at 6:14 a.m. and set at 6:06 p.m. Find the number of hours and minutes in the time between the rising and setting of the sun on that day.

    (A) 11 hr. 2 min.

    (B) 11 hr. 48 min.

    (C) 11 hr. 52 min.

    (D) 12 hr. 8 min.

    (E) 12 hr. 48 min.

11. Express 894 in expanded form, using exponents.

    (A) $(8 \times 10^2) + (9 \times 10) + 4$

    (B) $(8 \times 10) + (9 \times 10) + 4$

    (C) $(9^2 + 8) + 4$

    (D) $(8 \times 10^3) + (9 \times 10^2) + 4$

    (E) $(8^2 + 3^3) + 2^2$

12. The price of eggs increased from 50 cents to 60 cents a dozen. What was the percent of increase in price?

    (A) 10%

    (B) 15%

    (C) 20%

    (D) 25%

    (E) 30%

13. Tom spent 2 hours and 30 minutes studying for three classes. What was the average time in minutes that he spent in studying for each class?

    (A) 30

    (B) 40

    (C) 45

    (D) 50

    (E) 55

14. Find the perimeter of a parallelogram whose dimensions are $l = 16$ inches, $w = 12$ inches.

    (A) 24 in.

    (B) 28 in.

    (C) 38 in.

    (D) 56 in.

    (E) 63 in.

15. Approximate the square root of 91 to the nearest tenth.

    (A) 9.9

    (B) 9.5

    (C) 9.1

    (D) 8.9

    (E) 8.5

ANSWER KEY

Test Yourself 1

1. C	4. A	7. D	10. D	13. A
2. B	5. C	8. A	11. B	14. C
3. D	6. A	9. C	12. C	15. B

Test Yourself 2

1. C	4. B	7. B	10. C	13. B
2. D	5. B	8. A	11. B	14. B
3. D	6. B	9. D	12. C	15. D

Test Yourself 3

1. C	4. B	7. A	10. C	13. B
2. C	5. C	8. A	11. D	14. C
3. B	6. D	9. B	12. C	15. C

Test Yourself 4

1. D	4. A	7. C	10. D	13. A
2. B	5. B	8. C	11. B	14. C
3. B	6. D	9. A	12. B	15. B

Test Yourself 5

1. A	4. B	7. D	10. C	13. A
2. B	5. D	8. C	11. D	14. B
3. D	6. B	9. B	12. A	15. B

Test Yourself 6

1. B	4. C	7. D	10. D	13. A
2. B	5. D	8. E	11. A	14. B
3. C	6. B	9. B	12. D	15. C

Test Yourself 7

1. C	4. A	7. E	10. D	13. C
2. B	5. C	8. C	11. D	14. A
3. D	6. D	9. E	12. B	15. B

Test Yourself 8

1. B	4. D	7. C	10. C	13. A
2. D	5. E	8. C	11. B	14. D
3. A	6. C	9. E	12. D	15. E

Test Yourself 9

1. D	4. C	7. B	10. D	13. E
2. B	5. A	8. A	11. C	14. B
3. D	6. D	9. B	12. C	15. D

Test Yourself 10

1. C	4. A	7. A	10. C	13. D
2. D	5. B	8. E	11. A	14. D
3. C	6. B	9. E	12. C	15. B

EXERCISES: QUANTITATIVE ABILITY

> **Directions:** Following each problem in this section, there are five suggested answers. Work each problem in your head or in the space provided (there will be space for scratchwork in your test booklet). Then look at the five suggested answers and decide which is best.

1. A gas tank is $\frac{1}{3}$ empty. When full, the tank holds 18 gallons. How many gallons are in the tank now?
   (A) 3
   (B) 6
   (C) 8
   (D) 12
   (E) 18

2. Which of the following is the least?
   (A) $\frac{1}{4} + \frac{2}{3}$
   (B) $\frac{3}{4} - \frac{1}{3}$
   (C) $\frac{1}{12} \div \frac{1}{3}$
   (D) $\frac{3}{4} \times \frac{1}{3}$
   (E) $\frac{1}{12} \times 2$

3. If the sum of x and $x + 3$ is greater than 20, which is a possible value for x?
   (A) -10
   (B) -8
   (C) -2
   (D) 8
   (E) 10

4. If a square has a perimeter of 88, what is the length of each side?
   (A) 4
   (B) 11
   (C) 22
   (D) 44
   (E) 110

5. If a Set R contains four positive integers whose average is 9, what is the greatest number Set R could contain?
   (A) 4
   (B) 9
   (C) 24
   (D) 33
   (E) 36

6. Which of the following is NOT a multiple of 4?
   (A) 20
   (B) 30
   (C) 36
   (D) 44
   (E) 96

QUESTIONS 7 AND 8 REFER TO THE FOLLOWING DEFINITION: FOR ALL REAL NUMBERS m, $*m = 10m - 10$.

7. $*7 =$
   (A) 70
   (B) 60
   (C) 17
   (D) 7
   (E) 0

8. If $*m = 120$, then $m =$
   (A) 11
   (B) 12
   (C) 13
   (D) 120
   (E) 130

9. At the Shop Here, an item that usually sells for $9 is on sale for $6. What approximate discount does that represent?

(A) 10%

(B) 25%

(C) 33%

(D) 50%

(E) 66%

10. In Linda's golf club, 8 of the 12 members are right-handed. What is the ratio of left-handed members to right-handed members?

(A) 1:2

(B) 2:1

(C) 2:3

(D) 3:4

(E) 4:3

11. The sum of five consecutive positive integers is 35. What is the square of the greatest of these integers?

(A) 5

(B) 9

(C) 25

(D) 81

(E) 100

12. $2^2 \times 2^3 \times 2^3 =$

(A) 24

(B) 64

(C) 2^8

(D) 2^{10}

(E) 2^{18}

13. If the area of a square is $100s^2$, what is the length of one side of the square?

(A) $100s^2$

(B) $10s^2$

(C) $100s$

(D) $10s$

(E) 10

14. If 10 books cost d dollars, how many books can be purchased for 4 dollars?

(A) $\dfrac{4d}{10}$

(B) $40d$

(C) $\dfrac{d}{40}$

(D) $\dfrac{40}{d}$

(E) $\dfrac{10d}{4}$

15. If g is an even integer, h is an odd integer, and j is the product of g and h, which of the following must be true?

(A) j is a fraction.

(B) j is an odd integer.

(C) j is divisible by 2.

(D) j is between g and h.

(E) j is greater than 0.

16. If a class of 6 students has an average grade of 78 before a seventh student joins, what must the seventh student get as a grade in order to raise the class average to 80?

(A) 80

(B) 84

(C) 88

(D) 92

(E) 96

17. If 6 is a factor of a certain number, what must also be factors of that number?

(A) 1, 2, 3, and 6

(B) 2 and 3 only

(C) 6 only

(D) 2 and 6 only

(E) 1, 2, and 3

18.

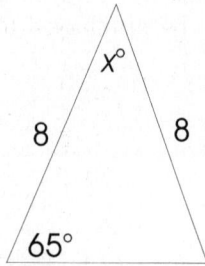

$x =$

(A) 8

(B) 30

(C) 50

(D) 65

(E) 70

19. For what priced item does 40% off equal a $2.00 discount?

(A) $5.00

(B) $4.00

(C) $10.00

(D) $80.00

(E) $40.00

20. On Monday, Gerri ate $\frac{1}{4}$ of an apple pie. On Tuesday, she ate $\frac{1}{2}$ of what was left of the pie. What fraction of the entire pie did Gerri eat on both days?

(A) $\frac{3}{8}$

(B) $\frac{1}{2}$

(C) $\frac{5}{8}$

(D) $\frac{3}{4}$

(E) $\frac{7}{8}$

21. If the area of a square is equal to its perimeter, what is the length of one side of that square?

(A) 1

(B) 2

(C) 4

(D) 8

(E) 10

ANSWER KEY AND EXPLANATIONS

1. D	6. B	10. A	14. D	18. C
2. E	7. B	11. D	15. C	19. A
3. E	8. C	12. C	16. D	20. C
4. C	9. C	13. D	17. A	21. C
5. D				

1. **The correct answer is (D).** If the tank is $\frac{1}{3}$ empty, it must be $\frac{2}{3}$ full. $\frac{2}{3}$ the total capacity of 18 gallons is 12.

2. **The correct answer is (E).** The value of choice (A) is $\frac{11}{12}$; the value of choice (B) is $\frac{5}{12}$; the value of choice (C) is $\frac{1}{4}$ or $\frac{3}{12}$; the value of choice (D) is $\frac{1}{4}$ or $\frac{3}{12}$; and the value of choice (E) is $\frac{1}{6}$ or $\frac{2}{12}$. Therefore, choice (E) has the least value.

3. **The correct answer is (E).** If $x + (x + 3) > 20$, then $2x > 17$. So $x > 8.5$. The only answer that is appropriate is 10.

4. **The correct answer is (C).** The perimeter of a square is found by summing the lengths of each side. Because the lengths are equal on a square, you can multiply one side by 4 to get the perimeter. Therefore, $4s = 88$, so $s = 22$.

5. **The correct answer is (D).** To find the greatest value of the four, assume the remaining three values are the least possible positive integer, 1. The average then is $\frac{1+1+1+x}{4} = 9$. Solve for x. $3 + x = 36$, so $x = 33$.

6. **The correct answer is (B).** Multiples of 4 include: 4, 8, 12, 16, 20, 24, 28, 32, 36, 40, 44, etc. Comparing these with the answers provided, notice that the number 30 is not a multiple of 4.

7. **The correct answer is (B).** Substitute 7 for m. *7 = 10(7) – 10 = 70 – 10 = 60.

8. **The correct answer is (C).** If *m = $10m - 10$ and *m = 120, then $10m - 10 = 120$. Solve for m: $10m = 130$, $m = 13$.

9. **The correct answer is (C).** The total discounted amount is $3 or ($9 – $6). The original amount × the discounted percent = the total discounted amount.

   $9 × discounted percent = $3.

   The discounted percent =

   $\frac{3}{9} = \frac{1}{3} \approx 33\%$.

10. **The correct answer is (A).** The number of left-handed members is equal to $12 - 8$, or 4. The ratio of left-handers to right-handers is 4:8, which simplifies to 1:2.

11. **The correct answer is (D).** Let the five consecutive integers be: x, $x + 1$, $x + 2$, $x + 3$, and $x + 4$.

    Then $x + x + 1 + x + 2 + x + 3 + x + 4 = 35$; $5x + 10 = 35$; $5x = 25$; $x = 5$

    Since the least of the five integers is 5, the greatest is $5 + 4$, or 9. $9^2 = 81$.

12. The correct answer is (C). When multiplying like values raised to a power, add the exponents.

$$2^2 \times 2^3 \times 2^3 = 2^{2+3+3} = 2^8$$

13. The correct answer is (D). The area of a square is equal to the (length of the side)^2, or L^2.

$$100s^2 = L^2$$
$$\sqrt{100s^2} = \sqrt{L^2}$$
$$10s = L$$

14. The correct answer is (D). Set up a ratio for this problem and solve:

Let x represent the number of books purchased with 4 dollars.

$$\frac{10}{d} = \frac{x}{4}$$

$10 \times 4 = d \times x$ (using cross-multiplication)

$$\frac{40}{d} = x$$

15. The correct answer is (C). Since integers can be both positive and negative, and the product of a positive and negative integer is always negative, choice (E) must be false. Looking further at the answers, notice that choices (B) and (C) are opposites of one another. Therefore, one of those must be true and the other false. Substitute two numbers for g and h and see which of the two is true. If $g = -4$ and $h = 5$, $g \times h = -4 \times 5 = -20$. Since -20 is even, choice (C) is correct.

16. The correct answer is (D). The sum of the first six grades is $78 \times 6 = 468$. (To find the average grade of 78, divide the sum of the six grades by 6.)

The average with seven students is $468 + x = 80 \times 7$.

$468 + x = 560$; $x = 92$

17. The correct answer is (A).

All factors of 6 are factors of the number. The factors of 6 are:

1×6

2×3

18. The correct answer is (C). Since this is an isosceles triangle, the angles opposite the congruent sides are also congruent. The sum of the angles in a triangle equal 180°. So 65° + 65° + x° = 180° and $x = 50$°.

19. The correct answer is (A).

Let p equal the price of the item.

Price × Discount Rate = Discount Amount

$$p \times 40\% = \$2.00$$
$$p \times .40 = 2.00$$

So $$p = \frac{2.00}{.40} = 5$$

20. The correct answer is (C). On Monday, $\frac{1}{4}$ of the pie was eaten. On Tuesday, there was $\frac{3}{4}$ of the pie left.

$$\frac{1}{2} \times \frac{3}{4} = \frac{3}{8} \text{ and } \frac{1}{4} + \frac{3}{8} = \frac{5}{8}$$

21. The correct answer is (C). The perimeter of a square equals $4s$. The area of a square equals s^2. Setting them equal will determine the length of one side, s.

$$\frac{1}{2} \times \frac{3}{4} = \frac{3}{8} \text{ and } \frac{1}{4} + \frac{3}{8} = \frac{5}{8}$$

Since it would make no sense for the length to be 0, the correct answer is 4.

SUMMING IT UP

- With multiple-choice questions, the correct answer is always on the page in front of you. So even if you're estimating, you'll be able to narrow down the choices.

- Some multiple-choice questions require no calculations—the correct answer is based on how well you know the concepts in the question.

- Some multiple-choice questions include graphs, charts, or tables for you to interpret.

- The answer choices are arranged in order by size from smallest to largest or from largest to smallest.

- The question number usually tells you how hard the question will be since the questions go from easy to hard as you work toward the end.

- For multiple-choice math questions, circle what's being asked so you don't pick a wrong answer by mistake. For example, you won't pick an answer that gives a perimeter when the question asks for an area.

- Quantitative Ability is really a fancy way to say "math."

Quantitative Comparisons (ISEE Only)

chapter 12

OVERVIEW

- What are these strange-looking questions?
- How do you solve Quantitative Comparisons?
- What do smart test-takers know?
- Summing it up

WHAT ARE THESE STRANGE-LOOKING QUESTIONS?

You picked up this book. You flipped through some pages. You got to this chapter and thought, "What the heck am I supposed to do with these weird questions? What do they want from me now?" Well, quantitative comparisons are not quite as wacky as they look. You can recognize quantitative comparison questions easily because they look very different from other math questions. Each one has two side-by-side boxes containing quantities that you must compare. Then you choose the correct answers from choices (A) through (D).

There are some good things to remember about these. First, the choices are always the same (check out the sample directions on page 396). Second, you don't actually have to solve a problem. The questions are really testing knowledge of mathematical principles rather than your calculating skills. Third, sometimes the testing folks give you a little help and provide a diagram or other information centered above the boxes with the information you are comparing.

HOW DO YOU SOLVE QUANTITATIVE COMPARISONS?

Your estimating and comparison skills, as well as the following four steps, will help you cope with these questions. Once you get used to the choices, things can move pretty quickly.

Quantitative Comparisons: Getting It Right

① Memorize the answer choices.

② For each question, compare the boxed quantities.

③ Consider all possibilities for any variables.

④ Choose your answer.

Now let's look at these steps in more detail:

① Don't just learn the directions; try to memorize the answer choices. (Remember, they are always the same.) Then you can save time because you won't need to refer to them for every question.

② Even though there are two quantities in each question, deal with one at a time. If there is extra information above the boxes, see how each quantity relates to it. Then do any figuring you need to do. (There won't be much.)

③ Consider all possibilities for any unknowns. Think what would happen if special numbers such as 0, negative numbers, or fractions were put into play.

④ Choose your answer. You shouldn't have to do involved calculations to get to the answer. If you're calculating endlessly, you've probably missed the mathematical principle the question is asking about.

Column A	**Column B**

The price of a pound of cheese
increased from $2 to $2.50.

The percent increase in the price of cheese	25%

① Memorize the answer choices.

② The centered information tells you that cheese increased in price from $2 to $2.50 per pound. Column A asks for the percent increase, which is $\frac{\$0.50}{\$2} = 25\%$. Column B requires no calculation, and it's equal to Column A.

③ There are no variables, so go on to Step 4.

④ Since the two columns are equal, the answer is choice (C).

⑤ Mark choice (C) on the answer sheet.

Column A	Column B
$x^2 + y^2$	$(x + y)^2$

TIP

Variables stay constant. A variable that appears in both columns has the same meaning in each column.

1 Memorize the answer choices.

2 The expression in Column B is $(x + y)^2 = x^2 + 2xy + y^2$. This is the same as the expression in Column A with the addition of the middle term $2xy$.

3 The terms x and y are variables that can be positive or negative or zero. For example, if x were 1 and y were 2, Column A would be $1^2 + 2^2 = 5$ and Column B would be $(1 + 2)^2 = 9$. The correct answer would then be choice (B). But if x were −1 and y were 2, Column A would be $−1^2 + 2^2 = 5$ and Column B would be $(−1 + 2)^2 = 1^2 = 1$. This time the correct answer would be choice (A).

4 Any time more than one answer can be true for a comparison—as is the case here— then the answer to that question must be choice (D), "the relationship cannot be determined from the information given."

5 Mark choice (D) on the answer sheet.

Remember that many quantitative comparisons can be solved without doing any calculating at all. In many cases, you should be able to arrive at the correct answer simply by applying your knowledge of basic math rules and principles. Look at these examples:

Column A	Column B

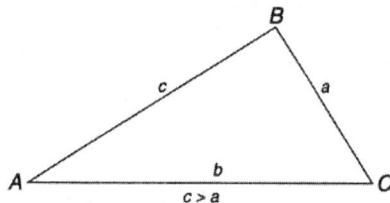

c > a

	Column A	Column B
1.	$\angle A$	$\angle C$
2.	$\angle A$	$\angle B$
3.	$a + b$	c

ALERT!

Figures can be deceiving. If a figure carries a warning that it is not drawn to scale, don't depend on estimating or measuring to help you solve the problem.

1 If two sides of a triangle are unequal, the angles opposite them are unequal, and the larger angle is opposite the longer side. So, the answer for this question is choice (B).

2 Because we can't really tell whether a or b is greater, we can't tell which angle is greater, so choice (D) is the correct answer.

3 The sum of any two sides of a triangle must always be greater than the length of the third side. The only answer for this question is choice (A).

WHAT DO SMART TEST-TAKERS KNOW?

Quantitative comparisons may look complex, but if you come at them from the right angle (pardon the pun), you can streamline the answering process.

A Comparison Is Forever

In quantitative comparisons, choice (A) is correct only if the quantity is *always* greater than that in Column B. The reverse is true of choice (B); it must *always* be greater than the information in Column A. If you choose (C), it means that the two quantities are *always* equal. The condition must hold true regardless of what number you plug in for a variable.

The Higher the Number, the Tougher the Choice

Just like the other sets of questions, quantitative comparisons go from easy to difficult as you progress through the section.

Quantitative Comparisons Are Not About Calculating

If you find yourself calculating up a storm on a quantitative comparison, you've probably missed the boat. There's sure to be a simpler, shorter way to solve the problem. Find a way to reduce the amount of actual math you need to do. Take a look at these examples:

Column A	Column B
$31 \times 32 \times 33 \times 34 \times 35$	$32 \times 33 \times 34 \times 35 \times 36$

You don't have to do any calculations to get the answer. You would be comparing the product of five consecutive integers, but notice that the integers in Column B are larger. Therefore, the product of those numbers would be greater than the product of those in Column A. So, the correct answer is (B), and you didn't have to multiply a thing.

Column A	Column B

The formula for the volume of a
right circular cylinder is $V = \pi r^2 h$

The volume of a right circular cylinder with $r = 3$ and $h = 6$	The volume of a right circular cylinder with $r = 6$ and $h = 3$

You might think that for this question you absolutely have to do the complete calculations to find the volume of each cylinder. But you don't! Take a look at how simply this problem can be solved.

Volume $A = \pi(3^2)(6) = (3.14)(3)(3)(6)$

Volume $B = \pi(6^2)(3) = (3.14)(6)(6)(3)$

Since you're doing the same operation for both formulas—multiplying by 3.14—that cancels out. So the problem then shifts to the other factors: Which is larger, $(3^2)(6)$ or $(6^2)(3)$? At this point you should be able to see that the second one is larger. If you still need to take it another step, multiply $(3^2)(6) = (9)(6) = 54$ and then $(6^2)(3) = (36)(3)$. You don't have to finish because you can see that $(36)(3)$ is larger than 54.

If the Math Is Not Difficult, You Should Do It

Column A	Column B
$(0.6)\,(0.6)$	$\dfrac{36}{100}$

The correct answer is (C). Do this simple math and you've got a guaranteed correct answer. They both equal 0.36, so your choice is (C).

When the Centered Information Has Unknowns, You Should Solve for the Unknowns

Column A	Column B
$3x = 12$	
$4y = 20$	
x	y

The correct answer is (B). You need to know what each of the unknowns is, so you have to solve for both.

It Pays to Simplify

$$\frac{(8)(45)(17)}{(462)(8)} \qquad\qquad \frac{(17)(9)(42)}{(231)(16)}$$

There are a couple of things to notice here that will help you simplify the problem. First, both denominators are really the same: 462 is 231×2, so the denominators become $(231)(2)(8)$. Next, the (17)'s in both numerators cancel each other out. Now, all you have to do is figure out the results of $(8)(45)$ and $(9)(42)$, compare, and mark the correct answer. (It's choice (B), by the way.)

NOTE

For most of the questions you can estimate, or use your knowledge of basic mathematical principles to make your comparisons.

You Can Simplify by Adding or Subtracting the Same Value in Each Column

Column A	Column B
$4x + 5$	$3x + 6$

The correct answer is (D). You might not see that right away, so we'll show you why it's true. The first thing you do is subtract 5 from both sides. The result is $4x$ and $3x + 1$. Now subtract $3x$ from both sides; you end up with x and 1. Since you don't know what x is, you can't know if it is larger or smaller than 1. That's why choice (D) is the correct answer.

You Can Simplify by Multiplying or Dividing Each Side by the Same Positive Number

Column A	Column B
$9^{99} - 9^{98}$	9^{98}

You begin to simplify by dividing both sides by 9^{98}.

Column A	Column B
$\dfrac{9^{99} - 9^{98}}{9^{98}}$	$\dfrac{9^{98}}{9^{98}}$
$9^1 - 9^0$	9^0
$9 - 1$	1
8	1

The correct answer is (A). This proves that the quantity in Column A is larger, even though you haven't solved for the exact quantity.

You Have to Consider All the Possibilities

When there are unknowns in the quantities being compared, you have to remember to consider all possibilities for what those unknowns might be. For example, an unknown might be 1, 0, a fraction, or a negative number. In each of these cases, the number has special properties that will affect your calculations. Or, unless otherwise stated, two unknowns could even be equal.

An Unknown Might Be a Zero

Zero has special properties that come into play when you plug it in for an unknown.

Column A	Column B

$$x > 0, y > 0, z = 0$$

$3z(2x + 5y)$	$3x(2z + 5y)$

The correct answer is (B). If $z = 0$, then $3z = 0$ and the product of Column A is 0. In Column B, though, $2z = 0$, so it comes out of the expression. The product will be $(3x)(5y)$, which will be a positive number.

Column A	Column B

$$x < 0, y > 0, z = 0$$

$3z(2x + 5y)$	$3x(z + 5y)$

The correct answer is (A). Again, the product of Column A is 0, because $3z$ still equals 0. The change comes in Column B. Because x is less than 0, $3x$ will be negative and $5y$ will be positive, so the product will be a negative number.

An Unknown Might Be a Negative Number

Column A	Column B

$$3x = 4y$$

x	y

The correct answer is (D). Don't think that choice (A) is the correct answer, even though if x and y are positive, x is greater than y. What if x and y are negative, as in $3(-4) = 4(-3)$; then y is greater than x. And if x and y are both zero, both columns are equal. Since you have no way of knowing what the values are, the correct answer is (D).

An Unknown Might Be a Fraction

Column A	Column B

$$x > 0 \text{ and } x \neq 1$$

x^2	x

The correct answer is (D). If x is larger than 1, then x^2 is larger than x. But if x is between 0 and 1—a fraction—then x^2 is smaller than x.

Fractions Can Play Tricks

Remember that a proper fraction raised to a positive power is smaller than the fraction itself.

Column A	Column B
$\dfrac{27}{41}$	$\left(\dfrac{27}{41}\right)^{15}$

The correct answer is (A). If you keep the math principle in mind, you don't even have to think about doing these calculations. Since each successive multiplication would result in a smaller fraction, Column A will always be larger than Column B, so your answer is choice (A).

In Quantitative Comparisons, Figures Are Not Necessarily Drawn to Scale

Column A	Column B

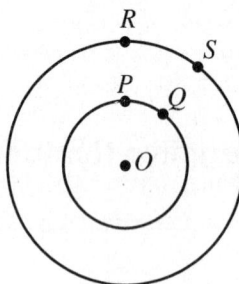

Minor arcs PQ and RS have equal length and each circle has center O.

NOTE: Figure not drawn to scale.

Degree measure of angle POQ	Degree measure of angle ROS

In the figure, angles POQ and ROS seem to be equal, but remember the warning. You're told that the figure is not drawn to scale, so don't be fooled.

The correct answer is (A). You can prove this by the figure below that is drawn to scale.

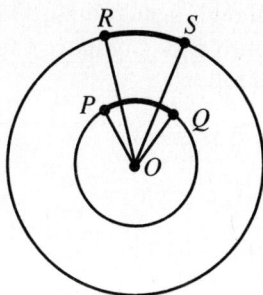

Plugging in Numbers Can Help

If you're stuck on a comparison with unknowns, try substituting numbers. Choose the numbers at random and plug them into the equations. Do this with three different substitutions and see if there is any consistent result. It's not a guarantee, but it's definitely worth a shot.

Strategic Guessing Can Raise Your Score

When all else fails, call up your guessing skills. Here's how you can tip the scales in your favor, even if it's only a little bit:

- If a comparison involves only numbers without any unknowns, chances are that you'll be able to figure out the quantities and make a comparison. So in this situation, don't guess choice (D).

- If the comparison does contain an unknown or a figure, as a last resort guess choice (D).

TEST YOURSELF QUIZZES

Take the following quizzes to help you determine what your weaknesses might be. The answers are on page 409.

Test Yourself 1

Directions: For each of the following questions, two quantities are given—one in Column A, the other in Column B. Compare the two quantities and write your answer in the margin as follows:

(A) if the quantity in Column A is greater

(B) if the quantity in Column B is greater

(C) if the quantities are equal

(D) if the relationship cannot be determined from the information given

Notes

- In some questions, information concerning one or both of the quantities to be compared is centered above the entries in the two columns.

- A symbol that appears in any column represents the same value in Column A as it does in Column B.

- All numbers used are real numbers; letters such as x, y, and t stand for real numbers.

- Assume that the position of points, angles, regions, and so forth are in the order shown and that all figures lie in a plane unless otherwise indicated.

- Figures are not necessarily drawn to scale.

	Column A	Column B
1.	The average of 18, 20, 22, 24, 26	The average of 19, 21, 23, 25
2.	$8 + 14 (8 - 6)$	$14 + 8 (8 - 6)$
3.	6% of 30	The number 30 is 6% of
4.	$\left(\dfrac{1}{5}\right)^3$	$\left(\dfrac{1}{5}\right)^2$
5.	2^2	$\sqrt[3]{64}$
6.	$(8 - 6)(2 + 7)$	$\dfrac{9+12}{4-6}$

Column A	Column B

The ratio of girls to boys in a math class is 3:1

7. | Ratio of boys to the entire class | $\dfrac{1}{3}$ |

A sport jacket priced $48 after a 20% discount

8. | Original price of the sport jacket | $60 |

9. | 1^{17} | 17^1 |

10. | Price of package of meat weighing 1.8 lbs. (unit price 92.6¢ per lb.) | Price of package of meat weighing 2.3 lbs. (unit price 67.5¢ per lb.) |

$$x - y = -6$$

$$x + y = -2$$

11. | x | y |

$$(x - 6)(x + 4) = 0$$

12. | The smallest root of the equation | The negative of the greatest root of the equation |

$$\dfrac{x}{4} = y^2$$

13. | x | y |

$$x = -1$$

14. | $3x^2 - 2x + 4$ | $2x^3 + x^2 + 4$ |

$$6 > y > -2$$

15. | $\dfrac{y}{4}$ | $\dfrac{4}{y}$ |

Test Yourself 2

Directions: For each of the following questions, two quantities are given—one in Column A, the other in Column B. Compare the two quantities and write your answer in the margin as follows:

(A) if the quantity in Column A is greater

(B) if the quantity in Column B is greater

(C) if the quantities are equal

(D) if the relationship cannot be determined from the information given

Notes

- In some questions, information concerning one or both of the quantities to be compared is centered above the entries in the two columns.

- A symbol that appears in any column represents the same value in Column A as it does in

- All numbers used are real numbers; letters such as x, y, and t stand for real numbers.

- Assume that the position of points, angles, regions, and so forth are in the order shown and that all figures lie in a plane unless otherwise indicated.

- Figures are not necessarily drawn to scale.

Column A	Column B
$x < 0$	
$y < 0$	

1.

Column A	Column B
$x + y$	$x - y$

$t < 0$

2.

Column A	Column B
t^3	t^2

$$\frac{a}{b} = \frac{c}{d}$$

3.

Column A	Column B
$a + b$	$c + d$

Column A	Column B

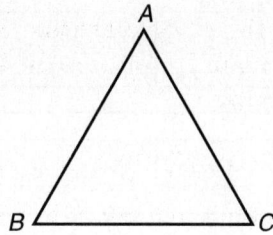

$$AB = AC$$

$$\angle A < \angle B$$

4.

BC	AB

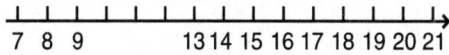 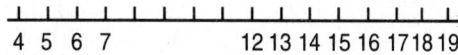

5.

Sum of the missing numbers on the number line	Sum of the missing numbers on the number line

6.

$0.41	Sum of one quarter, two nickels, and three pennies

7.

$\dfrac{8}{6}\ \dfrac{14}{6}\ \dfrac{18}{6}\ \dfrac{20}{6}$ The whole number in this group of fractions	$\dfrac{13}{5}\ \dfrac{15}{5}\ \dfrac{17}{5}\ \dfrac{22}{5}$ The whole number in this group of fractions

8.

The largest number that can be written by rearranging the digits in 263	The largest number that can be written by rearranging the digits in 192

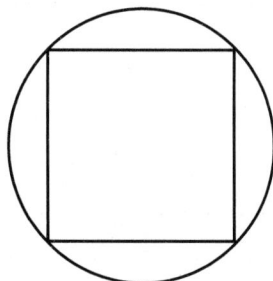

9.

Circumference of the circle	Perimeter of the square

	Column A	Column B
10.	2 more than $\frac{1}{3}$ of 63	2 less than $\frac{1}{3}$ of 66
11.	Two eights plus three	Eight twos plus three
12.	$4 \times 4 \times 6$	$6 \times 6 \times 4$
13.	The average of the numbers 2, 7, 9	The average of the numbers 3, 5, 9

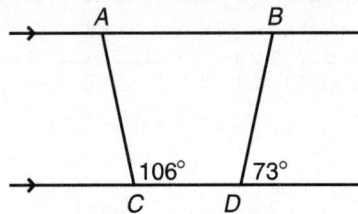

	Column A	Column B
14.	AC	BD

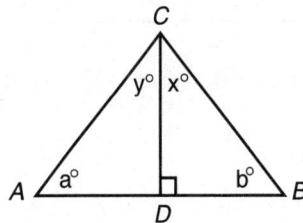

$$a > b$$

	Column A	Column B
15.	x	y

ANSWER KEY

Test Yourself 1

1. C	4. B	7. B	10. A	13. D
2. A	5. C	8. C	11. B	14. A
3. B	6. A	9. B	12. A	15. D

Test Yourself 2

1. B	4. B	7. C	10. A	13. A
2. B	5. B	8. B	11. C	14. B
3. D	6. A	9. A	12. B	15. A

EXERCISES: QUANTITATIVE COMPARISONS

Directions: For each of the following questions, two quantities are given—one in Column A, the other in Column B. Compare the two quantities and write your answer in the margin as follows:

(A) if the quantity in Column A is greater

(B) if the quantity in Column B is greater

(C) if the quantities are equal

(D) if the relationship cannot be determined from the information given

Notes

- In some questions, information concerning one or both of the quantities to be compared is centered above the entries in the two columns.

- A symbol that appears in any column represents the same value in Column A as it does in Column B.

- All numbers used are real numbers; letters such as x, y, and t stand for real numbers.

- Assume that the position of points, angles, regions, and so forth are in the order shown and that all figures lie in a plane unless otherwise indicated.

- Figures are not necessarily drawn to scale.

Column A	Column B
	$a > 0$
	$x > 0$

1. $\boxed{a - x}$ $\boxed{a + x}$

2. $\boxed{\begin{array}{c}\text{The average of}\\ \text{18, 20, 22, 24}\end{array}}$ $\boxed{\begin{array}{c}\text{The average of}\\ \text{17, 19, 21, 23}\end{array}}$

3. $\boxed{\text{5\% of 34}}$ $\boxed{\begin{array}{c}\text{The number}\\ \text{34 is 5\% of}\end{array}}$

$$s = 1$$
$$t = 3$$
$$a = -2$$

4. $\boxed{[5a(4t)]^3}$ $\boxed{[4a(5s)]^2}$

Column A	Column B

$$a < b$$

5. $\boxed{KR}$ $\boxed{KT}$

$$4 > x > -3$$

6. $\boxed{\dfrac{x}{3}}$ $\boxed{\dfrac{3}{x}}$

Column A	Column B
7. $\dfrac{2}{3}+\dfrac{3}{7}$	$\dfrac{16}{21}-\dfrac{3}{7}$

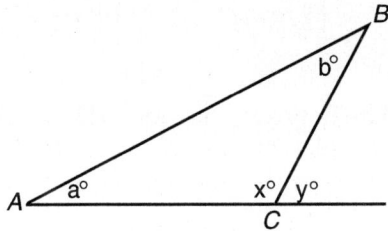

$a > b$

$x < a + b$

Column A	Column B
8. $a + b$	y

$y =$ an odd integer

Column A	Column B
9. The numerical value of y^2	The numerical value of y^3

Column A	Column B
10. $(8 + 6) \div [3 - 7(2)]$	$(6 + 8) \div [2 - 7(3)]$

Column A	Column B
11. three-fourths of $\dfrac{9}{9}$	$\dfrac{9}{9} \bullet \dfrac{3}{4}$

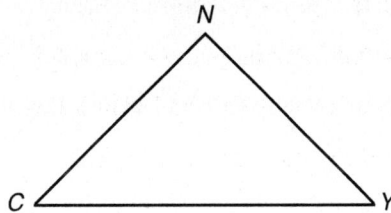

$NC = NY$

$\angle N > \angle C$

Column A	Column B
12. NC	CY

Column A	Column B
13. A given chord in a given circle.	The radius of the same circle.

Column A	Column B
14. $\dfrac{1}{\sqrt{9}}$	$\dfrac{1}{3}$

Column A	Column B
15. $5\left(\dfrac{2}{3}\right)$	$\left(\dfrac{5}{3}\right)2$

ANSWER KEY AND EXPLANATIONS

1. B	4. B	7. A	10. B	13. D
2. A	5. A	8. C	11. C	14. C
3. B	6. D	9. D	12. B	15. C

1. **The correct answer is (B).** The given information, $a > 0$ and $x > 0$, informs us that both a and x are positive numbers. The sum of two positive numbers is always greater than their difference.

2. **The correct answer is (A).** The numbers in Column A are respectively larger than the numbers in Column B; therefore, their average must be greater.

3. **The correct answer is (B).**

$$\frac{5}{100} = \frac{x}{34} \qquad\qquad \frac{5}{100} = \frac{34}{x}$$
$$100x = 170 \qquad\qquad 5x = 3400$$
$$x = 1.7 \qquad\qquad x = 680$$

4. **The correct answer is (B).**

$$[5a(4t)]^3 = [-10(12)]^3$$
$$= (-120)^3$$
$$= \text{negative answer}$$
$$[4a(5s)]^2 = [-8(5)]^2$$
$$= (-40)^2$$
$$= \text{positive answer}$$

∴ A positive product is greater than a negative one.

5. **The correct answer is (A).**

$b > a$ (given)
∴ $KR > KT$ (in a triangle, the greater side lies opposite the greater angle)

6. **The correct answer is (D).** Because x could be any integer from 4 to −3, the values of the fractions are impossible to determine.

7. **The correct answer is (A).**

$$\frac{2}{3} + \frac{3}{7} = \frac{14}{21} + \frac{9}{21} \qquad \frac{16}{21} - \frac{3}{7} = \frac{16}{21} - \frac{9}{21}$$
$$= \frac{23}{21} \qquad\qquad\qquad = \frac{7}{21}$$

8. **The correct answer is (C).**

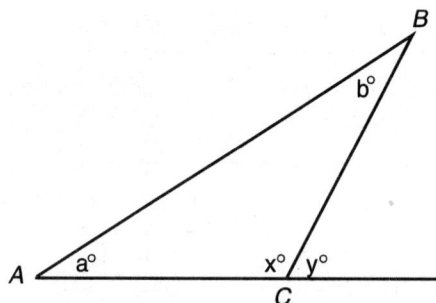

$y = a + b$ (an exterior angle of a triangle is equal to the sum of the two interior remote angles)

9. **The correct answer is (D).** There is not enough information, as y could equal 1, which would make both quantities equal; or y could be greater than 1, which would make y^3 greater than y^2. If y were a negative integer, then y^2 would be greater that y^3.

10. The correct answer is (B).

$(8 + 6) \div [3 - 7(2)]$

$= 14 \div -11 = \dfrac{14}{-11}$

$(6 + 8) \div [2 - 7(3)]$

$= 14 \div -19 = \dfrac{14}{-19}$

11. The correct answer is (C).

$\dfrac{3}{4} \times \dfrac{9}{9} = \dfrac{3}{4}$ $\qquad$ $\dfrac{9}{9} \times \dfrac{3}{4} = \dfrac{3}{4}$

12. The correct answer is (B).

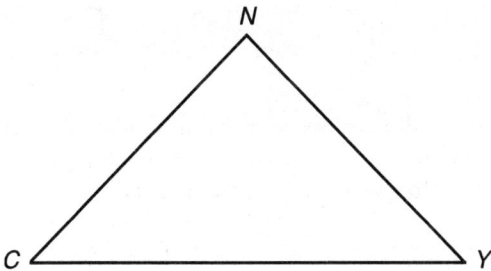

$NC = NY$ $\qquad$ (given)

$\angle C \cong \angle Y$ $\qquad$ (angles opposite equal sides are equal)

$\angle N > \angle C$ $\qquad$ (given)

$\angle N > \angle Y$ $\qquad$ (substitution)

$CY > NC$ $\qquad$ (the greater side lies opposite the greater angle)

13. The correct answer is (D). The radius could be less than, equal to, or greater than the chord.

14. The correct answer is (C). $\dfrac{1}{\sqrt{9}} = \dfrac{1}{3}$

15. The correct answer is (C).

$5\left(\dfrac{2}{3}\right) = \dfrac{5}{1} \cdot \dfrac{2}{3} = \dfrac{10}{3}$ $\qquad$ $\left(\dfrac{5}{3}\right)2 = \dfrac{5}{3} \cdot \dfrac{2}{1} = \dfrac{10}{3}$

SUMMING IT UP

Review this page the night before you take your high school entrance exam. It will help you get the answers to your math questions.

Multiple-Choice Questions—Both Exams

- These six steps will help you solve multiple-choice math questions:
  1. Read the question carefully and determine what's being asked.
  2. Decide which math principles apply, and use them to solve the problem.
  3. Look for your answer among the choices. If it's there, mark it and go on.
  4. If the answer you found is not there, recheck the question and your calculations.
  5. If you still can't solve the problem, eliminate obviously wrong answers and take your best guess.
  6. The questions in the multiple-choice math section go from easy to hard, and the answer choices generally go from smallest to largest or from largest to smallest.

- If a certain kind of math question always gives you trouble, save it for last.

Quantitative Comparison Questions—ISEE Only

- Remember these four steps as you work through the questions in this section:
  1. Memorize the answer choices.
  2. For each question, compare the boxed quantities.
  3. Consider all possibilities for any variables.
  4. Choose your answer.

- The quantitative comparison questions usually require less reading and computation than the standard multiple-choice questions.

- You don't actually have to solve the problem; you just need to determine which expression, if any, is greater.

- Quantitative comparison questions go from easy to hard.

PART VII
WRITING SAMPLE REVIEW

Writing Mechanics (SSAT and ISEE)

chapter 13

OVERVIEW

- **What are writing mechanics?**
- **What are the rules of spelling?**
- **Spelling demons**
- **What are the rules of punctuation?**
- **What are the rules for capitalization?**
- **What are the rules of grammar?**
- **What is correct English usage?**
- **How can I improve my writing?**
- **Summing it up**

WHAT ARE WRITING MECHANICS?

The mechanics of writing are spelling, capitalization, punctuation, grammar, and usage. Neither the SSAT nor the ISEE includes test questions that directly measure any of these topics, although some of the Catholic high school entrance exams and other less commonly used private secondary school admissions tests do.

You won't have to take a test of your knowledge of writing mechanics, but you will have to submit a writing sample in the form of an essay on an assigned topic. The essay tests far more than mechanics. It shows your ability to organize and convey your thoughts. Your essay will not be scored. It will be photocopied and sent to the schools to which you apply. The essay will give the school an overall impression of your maturity and power of self-expression.

Clear thinking and a good vocabulary are important aspects of a well-written essay. Correct spelling, capitalization, punctuation, grammar, and English usage also do much for the quality of an essay. This chapter gives you some of the most important rules to help you through the mechanics of your essay writing and some practical exercises to help you put to use the information you are learning.

WHAT ARE THE RULES OF SPELLING?

Rule 1

If a one-syllable word ends with a short vowel and one consonant,

- DOUBLE THE FINAL CONSONANT before adding a suffix that begins with a vowel.
- DO NOT DOUBLE THE FINAL CONSONANT before adding a suffix that begins with a consonant or if the word has two vowels before the consonant or ends in two consonants.

Double the Final Consonant

-er	-er, -est	-y	-en	-ing	-ed
blotter	biggest	baggy	bidden	budding	nodded
chopper	dimmer	blurry	bitten	clipping	plotted
clipper	fattest	funny	fatten	dropping	rubbed
fitter	flatter	furry	flatten	fanning	scarred
hopper	gladdest	muddy	gladden	fretting	skipped
plotter	grimmer	sloppy	hidden	grinning	stabbed
quitter	hottest	starry	madden	gripping	stepped
shipper	madder	stubby	sadden	hopping	stopped
shopper	reddest	sunny	trodden	quitting	tanned

Do NOT Double the Final Consonant

-ing, -ed, -er	-ly	-ness	-ful	-y
acting	badly	baseness	baleful	dirty
burned	dimly	bigness	boastful	dusky
climber	gladly	coldness	doleful	fishy
coasted	madly	dimness	fitful	frosty
cooked	manly	fatness	fretful	leafy
farmer	nearly	grimness	masterful	misty
feared	sadly	redness	sinful	rainy
feasting	thinly	sadness		soapy
quoted	trimly	wetness		weedy

Rule 2

If a word of more than one syllable ends with a short vowel and one consonant,

- DOUBLE THE FINAL CONSONANT before adding a suffix that begins with a vowel if the accent is on the last syllable.
- DO NOT DOUBLE THE FINAL CONSONANT if the accent is not on the last syllable or if the suffix begins with a consonant.

Double the Final Consonant

-ing, -ed	-ence, -ent	-ance	-al
befitting	abhorrence	acquittance	acquittal
befogged	concurrent	admittance	transmittal
committing	excellence	remittance	noncommittal
compelled	intermittent	transmittance	
controlling	occurrence		
impelling	recurrent		
incurred			
omitting	**-er**	**-en**	**-able**
permitted	beginner	forbidden	controllable
propelling	propeller	forgotten	forgettable
regretted	transmitter		regrettable
submitting			

Do NOT Double the Final Consonant

ENDING IN TWO CONSO-NANTS	TWO VOWELS BEFORE THE CONSONANT	ACCENT NOT ON THE FINAL SYLLABLE	SUFFIX BEGINS WITH A CONSONANT
-ing, -ed	-ing, -ed	-ing, -ed	-ment
consenting	concealing	benefiting	allotment
converted	contained	blossomed	annulment
demanding	detaining	differed	commitment
diverted	disdained	gathered	deferment
requesting	refraining	limiting	equipment
subsisted	remounted	profited	interment
supplanting	restraining	quarreling	preferment
supported	retained	soliciting	
transcending	revealing	summoned	

Rule 3

If a word ends with a silent *e*,

- DROP THE *E* before adding a suffix that begins with a vowel.
- DO NOT DROP THE *E* before a suffix that begins with a consonant.

Drop the Silent *E*

-ing, -ed	-able	-ation	-ive
achieving	believable	admiration	abusive
balanced	debatable	continuation	appreciative
believing	desirable	declaration	creative
capsized	endurable	derivation	decorative
relieved	excitable	duplication	exclusive
revolving	imaginable	exhalation	expensive
telephoned	measurable	inclination	illustrative
trembled	observable	inhalation	intensive
trembling	pleasurable	quotation	repulsive

Do NOT Drop the Silent *E*

-ful	-ment	-ly	-ness
careful	achievement	accurately	completeness
disgraceful	amusement	affectionately	cuteness
distasteful	announcement	bravely	fineness
fateful	engagement	extremely	genuineness
hopeful	enlargement	genuinely	lameness
prideful	enslavement	immediately	lateness
tasteful	entanglement	intensely	likeness
vengeful	management	intimately	ripeness
wasteful	replacement	sincerely	wideness

EXCEPTIONS

acknowledgment	changeable	judgment	peaceable
acreage	chargeable	manageable	pronounceable
advantageous	duly	noticeable	replaceable
argument	dyeing (color)	outrageous	serviceable
awful	exchanging		

Rule 4

To make a word plural,

- ADD -*ES* to words ending in *s, x, l, ch,* or *sh.*
- ADD -*S* to all other words.

ADD -*S*		ADD -*ES*	
advantages	croutons	annexes	fizzes
angles	distances	birches	hoaxes
beacons	effects	brushes	marshes
briquets	rings	caresses	witnesses
candles		coaches	

Rule 5

If a word ends with a *y* that has a vowel sound,

- CHANGE THE *Y* TO *I* before adding any suffix EXCEPT one that begins with the letter *i*.
- DO NOT CHANGE THE *Y* if it is preceded by another vowel, or if the suffix begins with *i*.

Change the Y to I

-er, -est, -ly, -ness	-ous	-ance, -ant	-able, -ful
craftier	ceremonious	alliance	beautiful
daintiest	harmonious	appliance	fanciful
healthier	industrious	compliant	justifiable
heavily	injurious	defiant	merciful
moldiness	luxurious	pliant	pitiable
moodiest	melodious	reliance	pliable
murkiness	mysterious		
sleepiness	studious		
steadily	victorious		

Do NOT Change the Y		EXCEPTIONS
-ing	**-ly, -ness**	**-ous**
allying	dryly	beauteous
applying	dryness	bounteous
complying	shyly	duteous
defying	shyness	miscellaneous
fortifying	slyly	piteous
justifying	slyness	plenteous
multiplying	spryly	
pitying	wryly	
supplying		

Rule 6

Put *i* before *e*,

Except after *c*,

Or when sounded like *a*,

As in *neighbor* or *weigh*.

I BEFORE *E*	EXCEPT AFTER *C*	OR SOUNDS LIKE *A*	EXCEPTIONS
achieve	ceiling	deign	ancient
believe	conceit	eight	conscience
fiend	conceive	freight	deficient
fierce	deceit	inveigh	efficient
grief	deceive	neighbor	foreign
relieve	perceive	reign	glacier
reprieve	receipt	skein	heifer
retrieve	receive	vein	leisure
sieve		weigh	proficient
			weird

Rule 7

The suffix *-ful* never has two *l*'s. When *-ful* is added to a word, the spelling of the base word does not change.

Examples

careful	disdainful	distasteful
forceful	grateful	hopeful
masterful	powerful	sorrowful

Rule 8

When the suffix *-ly* is added to a word, the spelling of the base word does not change.

Examples

coyly	quickly	frankly	swiftly	forcefully

EXCEPTIONS

When *-ly* is added to a word ending with *-le*, the *e* is replaced by a *y*.

forcibly	despicably	illegibly
indelibly	probably	suitably

When the base word ends with a *y* following a consonant, the *y* is changed to *i* before *-ly*.

busily	daintily	heavily
luckily	merrily	sleepily

Rule 9

When a syllable ends in a long vowel sound, that sound is made by the vowel alone: OPEN SYLLABLE.

A long vowel sound occurring in a one-syllable word, or in a syllable that ends with a consonant, is usually spelled by a vowel team: CLOSED SYLLABLE.

OPEN SYLLABLE	CLOSED SYLLABLE
recent	sublime
premium	infantile
sequence	crayon
stationary	attainment
fatality	cavalcade

OPEN SYLLABLE	CLOSED SYLLABLE
abrasion	genteel
motivate	intercede
custodian	sincere
component	ridicule
proprietor	vestibule
microbe	clapboard
cyclone	disclose
cucumber	telescope
humane	growth

SPELLING DEMONS

aberration	correlation	hearth
abscess	crystallized	heritage
abundance	currency	hindrance
accumulation	deferred	imminent
acquaint	derogatory	impartiality
adjunct	desecrated	incongruous
aggravate	dilapidated	indict
alleged	disappearance	inimitable
amendment	dissatisfied	irreparably
ancient	distinguished	jeopardy
anecdote	ecstasy	journal
annoyance	embarrass	judgment
apparatus	eminent	laboratory
arraignment	emphasis	lacquer
ascertain	emphatically	liquidate
assessment	essential	maneuver
beleaguered	exaggerate	masquerade
bureau	exceed	matinee
character	exhortation	mechanical
column	existence	medieval
committal	fascinated	memoir
committee	feudal	mischievous
community	financier	negligible
confectionery	harassment	nickel

occasionally	regrettable	staunch
occur	rehearsal	subversive
official	relevant	surgeon
pamphlet	repetitious	symmetrical
panicky	resilience	temperamental
parliamentary	rhetorical	thorough
patient	rhythm	tomorrow
peculiar	sacrilegious	transient
picnic	scissors	vacillate
pneumonia	separate	vacuum
possession	sophomore	vengeance
precious	source	whether
presumptuous	sovereign	wholly
publicity	specialized	wield
punctilious	specifically	yacht

WHAT ARE THE RULES OF PUNCTUATION?

Apostrophe (')

The apostrophe is used:

- To indicate possession:

    Bob's hat; Burns' poems

    NOTE: Use *apostrophe only* (without the *s)* for certain words that end in *s:*

a. When *s* or *z* sound comes before the final *s:*

    Moses' journey

    Cassius' plan

b. After a plural noun:

    girls' shoes

    horses' reins

Where to Place the Apostrophe

Example:

These (ladie's, ladies') blouses are on sale.

The apostrophe means *belonging to everything to the* left *of the apostrophe.*

ladie's means *belonging to ladie* (no such word)

ladies' means *belonging to ladies* (correct)

Example:

These (childrens', children's) coats are size 8.

One cannot say *belonging to childrens* (childrens'); therefore, children's (belonging to children) is correct.

NOTE:

a. When two or more names comprise one firm, possession is indicated in the last name:

    Lansdale, Jackson, and Roosevelt's law firm

    Sacks and Company's sale

b. In a compound noun, separated by hyphens, the apostrophe belongs in the last syllable—father-in-law's.

Note that the *plurals* of compound nouns are formed by adding the *s* (no apostrophe, of course) to the *first* syllable: I have three *brothers-in-law.* The apostrophe has two other uses besides indicating possession:

- For plurals of letters and figures: three d's; five 6's
- To show that a letter has been left out: let's (for let us)

NOTE A: ours, yours, his, hers, its, theirs, and whose—all are possessive but have no apostrophe.

NOTE B: The apostrophe is omitted occasionally in titles: Teachers College, Actors Equity Association.

Colon (:)

The colon is used:

- After such expressions as "the following," "as follows," and their equivalents:
  The sciences studied in high schools are as follows: biology, chemistry, and physics.
- After the salutation in a business letter:

    Gentlemen:

    Dear Mr. Jones:

NOTE: A comma (see below) is used after the salutation in a friendly letter:

Dear Ted,

The semicolon is *never* used in a salutation.

Comma (,)

In general, the comma is used in writing just as you use a pause in speaking. Here are the specific situations in which commas are used:

- Direct address:

  Mr. Adams, has the report come in yet?

- Apposition:

  Sam, our buyer, gave us some good advice.

- Parenthetical expression:

  We could not, however, get him to agree.

- Complimentary closing of a letter:

  Sincerely,

  Truly yours,

- Date, address:

  November 11, 2008

  Cleveland, Ohio

- Series:

  We had soup, salad, ice cream, and milk for lunch.

- Phrase or clause at the beginning of a sentence (if longer than four words):

  As I left the room to go to school, my mother called me.

- Separating two independent clauses joined by a conjunction:

  We asked for Mr. Smith, but he had already left for home.

- Clarity:

  After planting, the farmer had his supper.

- Direct quotation:

  Mr. Arnold blurted out, "This is a fine mess!"

- Modifier expressions that do not restrict the meaning of the thought that is modified:

  Air travel, which may or may not be safe, is an essential part of our way of life.

  NOTE: Travel that is on the ground is safer than air travel. (NO COMMAS)

EM Dash (—)

The dash is about twice as long as the hyphen. The dash is used:

- To break up a thought:

  There are five—remember I said five—good reasons to refuse their demands.

- Instead of parentheses:

  A beautiful horse—Black Beauty is its name—is the hero of the book.

Exclamation Mark (!)

The exclamation mark is used after an expression of strong feeling:

Ouch! I hurt my thumb.

Hyphen (-)

The hyphen divides a word:

mother-in-law

NOTE: When written out, numbers from twenty-one through ninety-nine are hyphenated.

Parentheses ( )

- Parentheses set off that part of the sentence that is not absolutely necessary to the completeness of the sentence:

  I was about to remark (this may be repetition) that we must arrive there early.

- Parentheses are also used to enclose or to set off figures, letters, signs, and dates:

  Shakespeare (1564–1616) was a great dramatist.

  The four forms of discourse are (a) narration, (b) description, (c) exposition, (d) argument.

Period (.)

The period is used:

- After a complete thought unit:

  The section manager will return shortly.

- After an abbreviation:

  Los Angeles, Calif.; Mr.; Mrs.; Dr.

Question Mark (?)

The question mark is used after a request for information:

When do you leave for lunch?

Quotation Marks (" ")

Quotation marks are used:

- To enclose what a person says directly:

  "No one could tell," she said, "that it would occur."

  He exclaimed, "This is the end!"

  "Don't leave yet," the boss told her.

- To enclose a title of short work:

  I have just finished reading the poem "The Road Not Taken."

Semicolon (;)

The semicolon is not used much. The following, however, are the common uses of the semicolon:

- To avoid confusion with numbers:

  Add the following: $1.25; $7.50; and $12.89.

- Before explanatory words or abbreviations—namely, e.g., etc.:

  We are able to supply you with two different gauges of nylon stockings; namely, 45 and 51.

  NOTE: The semicolon goes before the expression "namely." A comma follows the expression.

- To separate short statements of contrast:

  War is destructive; peace is constructive.

WHAT ARE THE RULES FOR CAPITALIZATION?

Capitalize:

- The first word of a sentence:

    With cooperation, a depression can be avoided.

- All proper names:

    America, Sante Fe Chief, General Motors, Abraham Lincoln

- Days of the week and months:

    The check was mailed on *Thursday*.

  NOTE: The seasons are not capitalized.

  Example: In Florida, *winter* is mild.

- The word *dear* when it is the first word in the salutation of a letter:

    Dear Mr. Jones:

    but—My *dear* Mr. Jones:

- The first word of the complimentary close of a letter:

    Truly yours,

    Very truly yours,

- The first and all other important words in a title:

    The Art of Salesmanship

- A word used as part of a proper name:

    William *Street* (but—That *street* is narrow.)

    Morningside *Terrace* (but—We have a *terrace* apartment.)

- Titles, when they refer to a particular official or family member:

  The report was read by *Secretary* Marshall.

  (but—Miss Shaw, our *secretary*, is ill.)

  Let's visit *Uncle* Harry.

  (but—I have three *uncles*.)

- Points of a compass, when they refer to particular regions of a country:

  We're going to the *South* next week. (but—New York City is *south* of Albany.)

  NOTE: Write: the Far West, the Pacific Coast, the Middle East, etc.

- The first word of a direct quotation:

  It was Alexander Pope who wrote, "A little learning is a dangerous thing."

  NOTE: When a direct quotation sentence is broken, the first word of the second half of the sentence is not capitalized.

  "Don't phone," Lilly told me, "because they're not in yet."

WHAT ARE THE RULES OF GRAMMAR?

The rules of grammar govern the ways in which parts of speech are organized in a sentence. There are rules concerning word endings, word order, and which words may be used together. You must know the parts of speech in order to follow the rules of grammar.

Parts of Speech

A **NOUN** is the name of a person, place, thing, or idea:

teacher	city	desk	democracy

PRONOUNS substitute for nouns:

he	they	ours	those

An **ADJECTIVE** describes a noun:

warm	quick	tall	blue

A **VERB** expresses action or a state of being:

yell	interpret	feel	are

An **ADVERB** modifies a verb, an adjective, or another adverb:

fast	slowly	friendly	well

CONJUNCTIONS join words, sentences, and phrases:

and	but	or

A **PREPOSITION** shows position in time or space:

in	during	after	behind

Nouns

There are different kinds of nouns.

Common nouns are general:

house   girl   street   city

Proper nouns are specific:

White House   Jane   Main Street   New York

Collective nouns name groups:

team   crowd   organization   Congress

Nouns have *cases*:

Nominative—the subject, noun of address, or predicate noun

Objective—the direct object, indirect object, or object of the preposition

Possessive—the form that shows possession

Pronouns

The **antecedent of the pronoun** is the noun to which a pronoun refers. A pronoun must agree with its antecedent in gender, person, and number.

There are several kinds of pronouns. (Pronouns *also* have cases.)

Demonstrative pronoun: this, that, these, those

Indefinite pronoun: all, any, nobody

Interrogative pronoun: who, which, what

Personal pronoun:

		NOMINATIVE	OBJECTIVE	POSSESSIVE
SINGULAR	1st person	I	me	my, mine
	2nd person	You	you	your, yours
	3rd person	he, she, it	him, her, it	his, hers
PLURAL	1st person	We	us	our, ours
	2nd person	You	you	your, yours
	3rd person	They	them	their, theirs

Adjectives

Adjectives answer the questions:

"Which one?"

"What kind?"

"How many?"

There are three uses of adjectives:

A **noun modifier** is usually placed directly before the noun it describes: He is a *tall* man.

A **predicate adjective** follows an inactive verb and modifies the subject: She is *happy*. I feel *terrible*.

Article or **noun marker** are other names for these adjectives: *the, a, an*.

Adverbs

Adverbs answer the questions:

"Why?"

"How?"

"Where?"

"When?"

"To what degree?"

Adverbs should not be used to modify nouns.

Twenty Principles of Grammar

1 The subject of a verb is in the nominative case even if the verb is understood and not expressed.

2 The word *who* is in the nominative case. *Whom* is in the objective case.

3 The word *whoever* is in the nominative case. *Whomever* is in the objective case.

4 Nouns or pronouns connected by a form of the verb *to be* should always be in the nominative case.

5 The object of a preposition or of a transitive verb should use a pronoun in the objective case.

6 It is unacceptable to use the possessive case in relation to inanimate objects.

7 A pronoun agrees with its antecedent in person, number, gender, and case.

8 A noun or pronoun linked with a gerund should be in the possessive case.

9 *Each, every, everyone, everybody, anybody, either, neither, no one, nobody,* and similar words are singular and require the use of singular verbs and pronouns.

10 When modifying the words *kind* and *sort*, the words *this* and *that* always remain in the singular.

11. The word *don't* is not used with third-person singular pronouns or nouns.

12. A verb agrees in number with its subject. A verb should not be made to agree with a noun that is part of a phrase following the subject.

13. The number of the verb is not affected by the addition to the subject of words introduced by *with, together with, no less than, as well as*, and so on.

14. Singular subjects joined by the words *nor* and *or* take a singular verb.

15. A subject consisting of two or more nouns joined by the word *and* takes a plural verb.

16. A verb should agree in number with the subject, not with the predicate noun.

17. In *there is* and *there are*, the verb should agree in number with the noun(s) that follow(s) it.

18. An adjective should not be used to modify a verb.

19. Statements equally true in the past and in the present are usually expressed in the present tense.

20. The word *were* is used to express a condition contrary to fact or a wish.

WHAT IS CORRECT ENGLISH USAGE?

Correct English usage refers to word choice. Correct English usage means using the right word with the specific meaning intended. Many English words are easily confused and misused. Here is a list of commonly misused words and examples of how to use them correctly.

accede—means to agree with.

concede—means to yield, but not necessarily in agreement.

exceed—means to be more than.

> We shall accede to your request for more evidence.

> To avoid delay, we shall concede that more evidence is necessary.

> Federal expenditures now exceed federal income.

access—means availability.

excess—means too much.

> The lawyer was given access to the grand jury records.

> The expenditures this month are far in excess of income.

accept—means to take when offered.

except—means excluding. (preposition)

except—means to leave out. (verb)

> The draft board will accept all seniors as volunteers before graduation.

> All eighteen-year-olds except seniors will be called.

> The draft board will except all seniors until after graduation.

adapt—means to adjust or change.

adopt—means to take as one's own.

adept—means skillful.

> Children can adapt to changing conditions very easily.

> The war orphan was adopted by the general's family.

> Proper instruction makes children adept in various games.

> **NOTE:** adapt to, adopt by, adept in or at.

adapted to—implies original or natural suitability.

> The gills of the fish are adapted to underwater breathing.

adapted for—implies created suitability.

> Atomic energy is constantly being adapted for new uses.

adapted from—implies changed to be made suitable.

> Many of Richard Wagner's opera librettos were adapted from old Norse sagas.

addition—means the act or process of adding.

edition—means a printing of a publication.

> In addition to a dictionary, she always used a thesaurus.

> The first edition of Shakespeare's plays appeared in 1623.

advantage—means a superior position.

benefit—means a favor conferred or earned (as a profit).

> He had an advantage in experience over his opponent.

> The rules were changed for his benefit.

> **NOTE:** to take advantage of, to have an advantage over.

adverse—(pronounced AD-verse) means unfavorable.

averse—(pronounced a-VERSE) means disliking.

> He took the adverse decision in poor taste.

> Many students are averse to criticism by their classmates.

advise—means to give advice. Advise is losing favor as a synonym for notify.

Acceptable: The teacher will advise the student in habits of study.

Unacceptable: We are advising you of a delivery under separate cover. (SAY: notifying)

affect—means to influence. (verb)

effect—means an influence. (noun)

effect—means to bring about. (verb)

> Your education must affect your future.

> The effect of the last war is still being felt.

> A diploma effected a tremendous change in her attitude.

> **NOTE:** Affect also has a meaning of pretend.

> She had an affected manner.

after—is unnecessary with the past participle.

> SAY: After checking the timetable, I left for the station.

> DON'T SAY: After having checked (omit after) the timetable, I left for the station.

ain't—is an unacceptable contraction for am not, are not, or is not.

aisle—is a passageway between seats.

isle—is a small island. (Both words rhyme with pile.)

all ready—means everybody or every thing ready.

already—means previously.

> They were all ready to write when the teacher arrived.

> They had already begun writing when the teacher arrived.

alright—is unacceptable.

all right—is acceptable.

all-round—means versatile or general.

all around—means all over a given area.

> Rafer Johnson, decathlon champion, is an all-round athlete.

> The police were lined up for miles all around.

all together—means everybody or everything together.

altogether—means completely.

> The boys and girls sang all together.

> This was altogether strange for a person of that type.

all ways—means in every possible way.

always—means at all times.

> She was in all ways acceptable to the voters.

> His reputation had always been spotless.

allude—means to make a reference to.

elude—means to escape from.

> Only incidentally does Coleridge allude to Shakespeare's puns.

> It is almost impossible for one to elude tax collectors.

allusion—means a reference.

illusion—means a deception of the eye or mind.

> The student made allusions to his teacher's habits.

> Illusions of the mind, unlike those of the eye, cannot be corrected with glasses.

alongside of—means side by side with.

alongside—means parallel to the side.

> Bill stood alongside of Barb.

> Park the car alongside the curb.

alot—is unacceptable. It should always be written as two words: a lot.

among—is used with more than two persons or things.

> **NOTE:** Amongst should be avoided.

between—is used with two persons or things.

> The inheritance was equally divided among the four children.

> The business, however, was divided between the oldest and the youngest one.

amount—applies to quantities that cannot be counted one by one.

number—applies to quantities that can be counted one by one.

> A large amount of grain was delivered to the storehouse.

> A large number of bags of grain were delivered.

annual—means yearly.

biannual—means twice a year. (Semi-annual means the same.)

biennial—means once in two years or every two years.

anywheres—is unacceptable.

anywhere—is acceptable.

> SAY: We can't find it anywhere.

> ALSO SAY nowhere (NOT nowheres), somewhere (NOT somewheres).

aren't I—is colloquial. Its use is to be discouraged.

> SAY: Am I not entitled to an explanation? (preferred to Aren't I …)

as—(used as a conjunction) is followed by a verb.

like—(used as a preposition) is NOT followed by a verb.

Do as I do, not as I say.

Try not to behave like a child.

Unacceptable: He acts like I do.

as far as—expresses distance.

so far as—indicates a limitation.

We hiked as far as the next guest house.

So far as we know, the barn was adequate for a night's stay.

as good as—should be used for comparisons only.

This motel is as good as the next one.

NOTE: As good as does NOT mean practically.

Unacceptable: They as good as promised us a place in the hall.

Acceptable: They practically promised us a place in the hall.

as if—is correctly used in the expression, "He talked as if his jaw hurt him."

Unacceptable: "He talked like his jaw hurt him."

ascared—no such word. It is unacceptable for scared.

The child was scared of ghosts. (NOT ascared).

ascent—is the act of rising.

assent—means approval.

The ascent to the top of the mountain was perilous.

Congress gave its assent to the President's emergency directive.

assay—means to analyze or examine.

essay—means a short literary composition.

The chemist assayed the content of the ore.

The candidate expressed her views in an essay.

attend to—means to take care of.

tend to—means to be inclined to.

One of the clerks will attend to mail in my absence.

Inactive people tend to gain weight.

back—should NOT be used with such words as refer and return since the prefix *re* means back.

Unacceptable: Refer back to the text, if you have difficulty recalling the facts.

backward ⎫
backwards ⎭ Both are acceptable and may be used interchangeably as an adverb.

We tried to run backward. (or backwards)

Backward as an adjective means slow in learning. (DON'T say backwards in this case.)

A backward pupil should be given every encouragement.

berth—is a resting place.

birth—means the beginning of life.

The new liner was given a wide berth in the harbor.

He was a fortunate man from birth.

beside—means close to.

besides—refers to something that has been added.

He lived beside the stream.

He found wild flowers and weeds besides.

better—means recovering.

well—means completely recovered.

> She is better now than she was a week ago. In a few more weeks, she will be well.

both—means two considered together.

each—means one of two or more.

> Both of the applicants qualified for the position.
>
> Each applicant was given a generous reference.
>
> **NOTE:** Avoid using such expressions as the following:
>
> Both girls had a new computer. (Use each girl instead.)
>
> Both girls tried to outdo the other. (Use each girl instead.)
>
> They are both alike (OMIT both).

breath—means an intake of air.

breathe—means to draw air in and give it out.

breadth—means width.

> Before you dive in, take a very deep breath. It is difficult to breathe under water.
>
> In a square, the breadth should be equal to the length.

bring—means to carry toward the person who is speaking.

take—means to carry away from the speaker.

> Bring the books here.
>
> Take your raincoat with you when you go out.

broke—is the past tense of break.

broke—is unacceptable for without money.

> He broke his arm.

> "Go for broke" is a slang expression widely used in gambling circles.

bunch—refers to things.

group—refers to people or things.

> This looks like a delicious bunch of bananas.
>
> What a well-behaved group of children!
>
> **NOTE:** The colloquial use of bunch applied to people is to be discouraged.
>
> A bunch of the boys were whooping it up. (Number is preferable.)

certainly—(and surely) is an adverb.

sure—is an adjective.

> He was certainly learning fast.
>
> *Unacceptable*: He sure was learning fast.

cite—means to quote.

sight—refers to vision or appearance.

site—means a place for a building.

> He was fond of citing from the Scriptures.
>
> The sight of the wreck was appalling.
>
> The Board of Education is seeking a site for the new school.

coarse—means vulgar or harsh.

course—means a path or a study.

> We were shunned because of his coarse behavior.
>
> The ship took its usual course.
>
> Which course in English are you taking?

come to be—should NOT be replaced with the expression become to be, since become means come to be.

True freedom will come to be when all tyrants have been overthrown.

comic—means intentionally funny.

comical—means unintentionally funny.

A clown is a comic figure.

The peculiar hat she wore gave her a comical appearance.

conscience—means sense of right.

conscientious—means faithful.

conscious—means aware.

People's conscience prevents them from becoming completely selfish.

We all depend on him because he is conscientious.

The injured woman was completely conscious.

considerable—is properly used only as an adjective, NOT as a noun.

cease—means to end.

seize—means to take hold of.

Will you please cease making those sounds?

Seize him by the collar as he comes around the corner.

cent—means a coin.

scent—means an odor.

sent—is the past tense of send.

The one-cent postal card is a thing of the past.

The scent of roses is pleasing.

We were sent to the rear of the balcony.

calendar—is a system of time.

calender—is a smoothing and glazing machine.

colander—is a kind of sieve.

In this part of the world, most people prefer the twelve-month calendar.

In ceramic work, the potting wheel and the calender are indispensable.

Garden-picked vegetables should be washed in a colander before cooking.

can—means physically able.

may—implies permission.

I can lift this chair over my head.

You may leave after you finish your work.

cannot help—must be followed by an *-ing* form.

We cannot help feeling (NOT feel) distressed about this.

NOTE: *cannot help but* is unacceptable.

can't hardly—is a double negative. It is unacceptable.

SAY: The child can hardly walk in those shoes.

capital—is the city.

capitol—is the building.

Paris is the capital of France.

The Capitol in Washington is occupied by the Congress.

(The Washington Capitol is capitalized.)

NOTE: Capital also means wealth.

compare to—means to liken to something that has a different form.

compare with—means to compare persons or things with each other when they are of the same kind.

contrast with—means to show the difference between two things.

A minister is sometimes compared to a shepherd.

Shakespeare's plays are often compared with those of Marlowe.

The writer contrasted the sensitivity of the dancer with the grossness of the pugilist.

complement—means a completing part.

compliment—is an expression of admiration.

Her wit was a complement to her beauty.

He complimented her sense of humor.

consul—means a government representative.

council—means an assembly that meets for deliberation.

counsel—means advice.

Americans abroad should keep in touch with their consuls.

The City Council enacts local laws and regulations.

The defendant heeded the counsel of his friends.

convenient to—should be followed by a person.

convenient for—should be followed by a purpose.

Will these plans be convenient to you?

You must agree that they are convenient for the occasion.

copy—is an imitation of an original work. (NOT necessarily an exact imitation)

facsimile—is an exact imitation of an original work.

The counterfeiters made a crude copy of the hundred-dollar bill.

The official government engraver, however, prepared a facsimile of the bill.

could of—is unacceptable. (Should of is also unacceptable.)

could have—is acceptable. (Should have is acceptable.)

Acceptable: You could have done better with more care.

Unacceptable: I could of won.

ALSO AVOID: must of, would of.

decent—means suitable.

descent—means going down.

dissent—means disagreement.

The decent thing to do is to admit your fault.

The descent into the cave was treacherous.

Two of the nine justices filed a dissenting opinion.

deduction—means reasoning from the general (laws or principles) to the particular (facts).

induction—means reasoning from the particular (facts) to the general (laws or principles).

All humans are mortal. Since John is human, he is mortal. (deduction)

There are 10,000 oranges in this truckload. I have examined 100 from various parts of the load and find them all of the same quality. I conclude that the 10,000 oranges are of this quality. (induction)

delusion—means a wrong idea that will probably influence action.

illusion—means a wrong idea that will probably not influence action.

People were under the delusion that the earth was flat.

It is just an illusion that the earth is flat.

desert—(pronounced DEZZ-ert) means an arid area.

desert—(pronounced di-ZERT) means to abandon; also a reward or punishment.

dessert—(pronounced di-ZERT) means the final course of a meal.

The Sahara is the world's most famous desert.

A husband must not desert his wife.

Execution was a just desert for his crime.

We had plum pudding for dessert.

different from—is acceptable.

different than—is unacceptable.

Acceptable: Jack is different from his brother.

Unacceptable: Florida's climate is different than New York's climate.

doubt that—is acceptable.

doubt whether—is unacceptable.

Acceptable: I doubt that you will pass this term.

Unacceptable: We doubt whether you will succeed.

dual—means relating to two.

duel—means a contest between two people.

Dr. Jekyl had a dual personality.

Alexander Hamilton was fatally injured in a duel with Aaron Burr.

due to—is unacceptable at the beginning of a sentence. Use because of, on account of, or some similar expression instead.

Unacceptable: Due to the rain, the game was postponed.

Acceptable: Because of the rain, the game was postponed.

Acceptable: The postponement was due to the rain.

each other—refers to two people.

one another—refers to more than two people.

The two girls have known each other for many years.

Several of the girls have known one another for many years.

either . . . or—is used when referring to choices.

neither . . . nor—is the negative form.

Either you or I will win the election.

Neither Bill nor Barb is expected to have a chance.

eliminate—means to get rid of.

illuminate—means to supply with light.

Let us try to eliminate the unnecessary steps.

Several lamps were needed to illuminate the corridor.

emerge—means to rise out of.

immerge—means to sink into. (ALSO immerse)

The swimmer emerged from the pool.

The launderer immerged the dress in the tub of water.

emigrate—means to leave one's country for another.

immigrate—means to enter another country.

The Norwegians emigrated from Norway in the mid-1860s.

Many of the Norwegian immigrants settled in the Middle West.

everyone—is written as one word when it is a pronoun.

every one—(two words) is used when each individual is stressed.

Everyone present voted for the proposal.

Every one of the voters accepted the proposal.

NOTE: Everybody is written as one word.

everywheres—is unacceptable.

everywhere—is acceptable.

We searched everywhere for the missing book.

NOTE: Everyplace (one word) is likewise unacceptable.

feel bad—means to feel ill.

feel badly—means to have a poor sense of touch.

I feel bad about the accident I saw.

The numbness in his limbs caused him to feel badly.

feel good—means to be happy.

feel well—means to be in good health.

I feel very good about my recent promotion.

Spring weather always made me feel well.

flaunt—means to make a display of.

flout—means to insult.

Hester Prynne flaunted her scarlet "A."

Mary flouted the authority of the principal.

formally—means in a formal way.

formerly—means at an earlier time.

The letter of reference was formally written.

Max was formerly a delegate to the convention.

former—means the first of two.

latter—means the second of two.

The former half of the book was in prose.

The latter half of the book was in poetry.

forth—means forward.

fourth—comes after third.

They went forth like warriors of old.

The Fourth of July is our Independence Day.

NOTE: spelling of forty (40) and fourteen (14).

get—is a verb that strictly means to obtain.

Please get my bag.

There are many slang forms of GET that should be avoided:

AVOID: Do you get me? (SAY: Do you understand me?)

AVOID: You can't get away with it. (SAY: You won't avoid punishment if you do it.)

AVOID: Get wise to yourself. (SAY: Use common sense.)

AVOID: We didn't get to go. (SAY: We didn't manage to go.)

got—means obtained.

He got the tickets yesterday.

AVOID: You've got to do it. (SAY: You have to do it.)

AVOID: We have got no sympathy for them. (SAY: We have no sympathy for them.)

AVOID: They have got a great deal of property. (SAY: They have a great deal of property.)

hanged—is used in reference to a person.

hung—is used in reference to a thing.

The prisoner was hanged at dawn.

The picture was hung above the fireplace.

however—means nevertheless.

how ever—means in what possible way.

We are certain, however, that you will like this class.

We are certain that, how ever you decide to study, you will succeed.

if—introduces a condition.

whether—introduces a choice.

I shall go to Europe if I win the prize.

He asked me whether I intended to go to Europe. (not if)

if it was—implies that something might have been true in the past.

if it were—implies doubt, or indicates something that is contrary to fact.

If your book was there last night, it is there now.

If it were summer now, we would all go swimming.

in—usually refers to a state of being. (no motion)

into—is used for motion from one place to another.

The records are in that drawer.

I put the records into that drawer.

NOTE: "We were walking in the room" is correct even though there is motion. The motion is not from one place to another.

irregardless—is unacceptable.

regardless—is acceptable.

Unacceptable: Irregardless of the weather, I am going to the game.

Acceptable: Regardless of his ability, he is not likely to win.

its—means belonging to it.

it's—means it is.

The house lost its roof.

It's an exposed house, now.

kind of
sort of } are unacceptable for rather.

SAY: We are rather disappointed in you.

last—refers to the final member in a series.

latest—refers to the most recent in time.

latter—refers to the second of two.

This is the last bulletin. There won't be any other bulletins.

This is the latest bulletin. There will be other bulletins.

Of the two most recent bulletins, the latter is more encouraging.

lay—means to place.

lie—means to recline.

Note the forms of each verb:

Tense	Lay (Place)
Present	The chicken is laying an egg.
Past	The chicken laid an egg.
Pres. Perf.	The chicken has laid an egg.

Tense	Lie (Recline)
Present	The child is lying down.
Past	The child lay down.
Pres. Perf.	The child has lain down.

lightening—is the present participle of to lighten.

lightning—means the flashes of light accompanied by thunder.

Leaving the extra food behind resulted in lightening the pack.

Summer thunderstorms produce startling lightning bolts.

many—refers to a number.

much—refers to a quantity in bulk.

How many inches of rain fell last night?

I don't know, but I would say much rain fell last night.

may—is used in the present tense.

might—is used in the past tense.

We are hoping that they may come today.

He might have done it if you had encouraged him.

it's I—is always acceptable.

it's me—is acceptable only in colloquial speech or writing.

It's him
This is her } always *unacceptable*
It was them

It's he
This is she } always *acceptable*
It was they

noplace—as a solid word, is unacceptable for no place or nowhere.

Acceptable: You now have nowhere to go.

number—is singular when the total is intended.

The number (of pages in the book) is 500.

number—is plural when the individual units are referred to.

A number of pages (in the book) were printed in italic type.

of any—(and of anyone) is unacceptable for of all.

SAY: Hers was the highest mark of all.

(NOT of any or of anyone)

off of—is unacceptable.

SAY: He took the book off the table.

out loud—is unacceptable for aloud.

SAY: Jane read aloud to her family every evening.

outdoor—(and out-of-door) is an adjective.

outdoors—is an adverb.

We spent most of the summer at an outdoor music camp.

Most of the time we played string quartets outdoors.

NOTE: Out-of-doors is acceptable in either case.

people—comprise a united or collective group of individuals.

persons—are individuals that are separate and unrelated.

The people of New York City have enthusiastically accepted "Shakespeare-in-the-Park" productions.

Only five persons remained in the theater after the first act.

persecute—means to make life miserable for someone. (Persecution is illegal.)

prosecute—means to conduct a criminal investigation. (Prosecution is legal.)

Some people insist upon persecuting other ethnic groups.

The District Attorney is prosecuting the racketeers.

precede—means to come before.

proceed—means to go ahead. (Procedure is the noun.)

supersede—means to replace.

What were the circumstances that preceded the attack?

We can then proceed with our plan for resisting a second attack.

It is then possible that Plan B will supersede Plan A.

principal—means chief or main (as an adjective); a leader (as a noun).

principle—means a fundamental truth or belief.

His principal supporters came from among the peasants.

The principal of the school asked for cooperation from the staff.

Humility was the guiding principle of Buddha's life.

NOTE: Principal may also mean a sum placed at interest.

Part of her monthly payment was applied as interest on the principal.

sit—means take a seat. (intransitive verb)

set—means place. (transitive verb)

Note the forms of each verb:

Tense	Sit (Take a Seat)
Present	He sits on a chair.
Past	He sat on the chair.
Pres. Perf.	He has sat on the chair.

Tense	Set (Place)
Present	He sets the lamp on the table.
Past	He set the lamp on the table.
Pres. Perf.	He has set the lamp on the table.

some time—means a portion of time.

sometime—means at an indefinite time in the future.

sometimes—means occasionally.

I'll need some time to make a decision.

Let us meet sometime after noon.

Sometimes it is better to hesitate before signing a contract.

somewheres—is unacceptable.

somewhere—is acceptable.

stationary—means standing still.

stationery—means writing materials.

In ancient times people thought the earth was stationary.

We bought writing paper at the stationery store.

stayed—means remained.

stood—means remained upright or erect.

The army stayed in the trenches for five days.

The soldiers stood at attention for one hour.

sure—for surely is unacceptable.

SAY: You surely (NOT sure) are not going to write that!

take in—is unacceptable in the sense of deceive or attend.

SAY: We were deceived (NOT taken in) by his oily manner.

We should like to attend (NOT take in) a few plays during our vacation.

their—means belonging to them.

there—means in that place.

they're—means they are.

We took their books home with us.

You will find your books over there on the desk.

They're going to the ballpark with us.

theirselves—is unacceptable for themselves.

SAY: Most children of school age are able to care for themselves in many ways.

these kind—is unacceptable.

this kind—is acceptable.

I am fond of this kind of apple.

NOTE: These kinds would also be acceptable.

through—meaning finished or completed is unacceptable.

SAY: We'll finish (NOT be through with) the work by five o'clock.

try to—is acceptable.

try and—is unacceptable.

Try to come (NOT try and come).

NOTE: *plan on going* is unacceptable; *plan to go* is acceptable.

two—is the numeral 2.

to—means in the direction of.

too—means more than or also.

There are two sides to every story.

Three twos (or 2's) equal six.

We shall go to school.

We shall go, too.

The weather is too hot for school.

was } If something is contrary to fact
were } (not a fact), use were in every instance.

I wish I were in Bermuda.

Unacceptable: If he was sensible, he wouldn't act like that.

(SAY: If he were...)

ways—is unacceptable for way.

SAY: We climbed a little way (NOT ways) up the hill.

went and took—(went and stole, and so on) is unacceptable.

SAY: They stole (NOT went and stole) our tools.

when (and where)—should NOT be used to introduce a definition of a noun.

SAY: A tornado is a twisting, high wind on land (NOT is when a twisting, high wind is on land).

A pool is a place for swimming. (NOT is where people swim)

whereabouts—is unacceptable for where.

SAY: Where (NOT whereabouts) do you live?

NOTE: Whereabouts as a noun meaning a place is acceptable.

Do you know his whereabouts?

whether—should NOT be preceded by of or as to.

SAY: The President will consider the question whether (NOT of whether) it is better to ask for or demand higher taxes now.

He inquired whether (NOT as to whether) we were going or not.

which—is used incorrectly in the following expressions:

He asked me to stay, which I did.
(CORRECT: He asked me to stay and I did.)

It has been a severe winter, which is unfortunate.
(CORRECT: Unfortunately, it has been a severe winter.)

You did not write, besides which you have not telephoned.
(CORRECT: Omit which)

while—is unacceptable for *and* or *though.*

SAY: The library is situated on the south side; (OMIT while) the laboratory is on the north side.

Though (NOT while) I disagree with you, I shall not interfere with your right to express your opinion.

Though (NOT while) I am in my office every day, you do not attempt to see me.

who
whom } The following is a method

(without going into grammar rules) for determining when to use WHO or WHOM:

"Tell me (Who, Whom) you think should represent our company?"

Step 1: Change the "who, whom" part of the sentence to its natural order.

"You think (who, whom) should represent our company?"

Step 2: Substitute HE for WHO, HIM for WHOM.

"You think (he, him) should represent our company?"

You would say HE in this case.

THEREFORE: "Tell me WHO you think should represent the company?" is correct.

who is
who am } Note these constructions:

It is I who am the most experienced.

It is he who is . . .

It is he or I who am . . .

It is I or he who is . . .

It is he and I who are . . .

whose—means of whom.

who's—means who is.

Whose is the notebook?

Who's in the next office?

would have—is unacceptable for had.

SAY: I wish you had (NOT would have) called earlier.

you all—is unacceptable for you (plural).

SAY: We welcome *you*, the delegates from Ethiopia.

You are all welcome, delegates of Ethiopia.

HOW CAN I IMPROVE MY WRITING?

Written communication starts with the sentence. A group of related sentences forms a paragraph. A series of connected paragraphs becomes a composition.

The first step in improving your writing is to know what makes a good sentence.

What Is a Sentence?

A sentence must have a subject and an action word or verb. In addition, a sentence must express a complete thought.

EXAMPLES OF SENTENCES: Bob walks.

                            Eric swims.

Other words can be added to make these sentences more descriptive.

IMPROVED SENTENCES: Bob walks briskly.

                         Eric swims rapidly.

Adding phrases that tell more about the subject or the verb can make these same two sentences even more interesting.

GOOD SENTENCES: Bob walks briskly down the road.

                     Eric swims rapidly across the pool.

The addition of another phrase at either the beginning or the end of these sentences provides an even clearer picture of Bob and Eric.

BETTER SENTENCES: In a hurry to get to school on time, Bob walks briskly down the road.

                       Eric swims rapidly across the pool, attempting to overtake his opponent.

The more you can practice writing clear, descriptive sentences, the better you will become at writing them.

The second step in improving your writing is to learn what makes a good paragraph.

What Is a Paragraph?

A paragraph is a group of sentences that develops one main idea. Usually this main idea or topic is slated in the first sentence of the paragraph. The rest of the paragraph can provide details about the topic or it can clarify the topic by providing specific examples.

There are no rules for determining the length of a paragraph. However, it is a good idea to make most paragraphs in a composition or report at least three sentences long.

Example of a Paragraph Developed by Details:

The man opened the door cautiously and slipped quietly into the crowded waiting room. He was dressed in a clean but well-worn overcoat and sneakers that had seen better days. On his head was a black knitted cap, pulled down to cover his forehead and ears.

Every sentence in this paragraph provides additional details about the topic—the man.

Example of a Paragraph Developed by Examples:

Intramural sports are a valuable part of the high school curriculum. A sports program provides a constructive outlet for the energy that has been stored up during the school day. Practice sessions or games take up the time that might otherwise be spent hanging out on street corners looking for trouble. Tossing a basketball around the gym provides an acceptable alternative to tossing rocks at street lights or store windows.

Each sentence in this paragraph provides a specific example of the value of intramural sports.

A new paragraph indicates a change. Start a new paragraph to show a change in:

- The **time**, the **place**, or the **action** in a story
- The **mood** or **point of view** in a description
- **Ideas** or **steps** in an explanation
- **Speakers** in a conversation

Connecting Paragraphs

Just as you must provide for an orderly flow of sentences within a paragraph, you must also provide for a logical transition from paragraph to paragraph in any composition or report.

The three most common means of connecting paragraphs are:

1. **Repetition of a key word or phrase** introduced in one paragraph and expanded upon in the next paragraph.
2. **Use of pronouns** that refer to a person or an idea mentioned in the previous paragraph.
   Examples of pronouns: he, she, they, this, that, these, those, such, both, all.
3. **Use of transitional words and phrases** to illustrate the relationship of one topic to another.

Examples of transitional words and phrases: although, as a result, consequently, for example, in comparison, in contrast, in fact, nevertheless, therefore, thus.

Example of Paragraphs Connected by Repetition of a Key Word

Last summer our whole family piled into the car and drove to Disney World in Florida. Although we had heard about the amusement park from friends who had already been there, this would be our first experience at a Disney park. We were all eager to get there, but we really did not know what to expect.

Our first day at Disney World went beyond any expectations we might have had…

These paragraphs are connected by the use of forms of the same word. *Expect* in paragraph 1 is repeated as *expectations* in paragraph 2, allowing one thought to flow from the first paragraph to the second. The second paragraph will continue with specific things the family did at Disney World.

Example of Paragraphs Connected by Transitional Words

Teenage alcoholism is a serious problem today. It is a problem that affects young people of all types, regardless of ethnic background or socio-economic level. Alcoholism shows no discrimination in choosing its victims.

Although the problem is far from being solved, steps are being taken by both families and schools to deal with alcoholism among teens…

These paragraphs are connected by the use of the transitional word *although* and the repetition of the key word *problem*. The second paragraph will continue by detailing some of the steps that are being taken to combat alcoholism.

EXERCISES: SPELLING

Directions: Each of the following exercises contains a group of four words. Only one of these words is spelled correctly. Circle the letter of the correctly spelled word. You will find the correct answer and a reference to one of the spelling rules you have just learned in the answer explanations.

1. **(A)** transient
   (B) transeint
   (C) transent
   (D) transint

2. **(A)** heratage
   (B) heritage
   (C) heiritage
   (D) heretage

3. **(A)** retreivable
   (B) retrievable
   (C) retrievible
   (D) retreivible

4. **(A)** foriegn
   (B) foreign
   (C) foureign
   (D) fouriegn

5. **(A)** witneses
   (B) wittnesses
   (C) witnesses
   (D) wittneses

6. **(A)** priceing
   (B) pricing
   (C) priseing
   (D) prising

7. **(A)** intermittent
   (B) intermitant
   (C) intermittant
   (D) intermitent

8. **(A)** disgracefully
   (B) disgracefull
   (C) disgracful
   (D) disgracefuly

9. **(A)** complyeing
   (B) complieing
   (C) complying
   (D) compling

10. **(A)** acheivment
    (B) achievment
    (C) acheivement
    (D) achievement

Directions: In each of the following exercises you find a group of three words, plus choice (D), NO ERROR. You have to decide whether one of the three words is misspelled. The incorrectly spelled word is spelled correctly in the answer explanation. You are referred back to the spelling rules, if necessary.

11. **(A)** nuisanse
    (B) obedience
    (C) nonsense
    (D) NO ERROR

12. **(A)** confidential
    (B) initial
    (C) marsial
    (D) NO ERROR

13. **(A)** Saturday
    (B) Thursday
    (C) Wendsday
    (D) NO ERROR

14. **(A)** confessing
    (B) aroussing
    (C) caressing
    (D) NO ERROR

15. **(A)** medicine
    (B) feminine
    (C) paraffin
    (D) NO ERROR

16. **(A)** pleasure
    (B) measure
    (C) liesure
    (D) NO ERROR

17. **(A)** libary
    (B) contemporary
    (C) canary
    (D) NO ERROR

18. **(A)** prosperity
    (B) university
    (C) susceptibility
    (D) NO ERROR

19. **(A)** immaterial
    (B) immeasurable
    (C) implicit
    (D) NO ERROR

20. **(A)** ocassionaly
    (B) necessarily
    (C) recommended
    (D) NO ERROR

21. **(A)** feudal
    (B) fugitive
    (C) muetiny
    (D) NO ERROR

22. **(A)** donkies
    (B) territories
    (C) secretaries
    (D) NO ERROR

23. **(A)** squashes
    (B) shelfs
    (C) lenses
    (D) NO ERROR

24. **(A)** blamless
    (B) nervous
    (C) immensity
    (D) NO ERROR

25. (A) concurence
    (B) remittance
    (C) appearance
    (D) NO ERROR

26. (A) gracefully
    (B) intimately
    (C) steadyly
    (D) NO ERROR

27. (A) deficient
    (B) wierd
    (C) financier
    (D) NO ERROR

28. (A) forcible
    (B) irascible
    (C) tyrannical
    (D) NO ERROR

29. (A) driest
    (B) dryly
    (C) driness
    (D) NO ERROR

30. (A) embargos
    (B) topazes
    (C) sheaves
    (D) NO ERROR

Directions: In each of the following exercises you find a group of four words. One of these four is spelled incorrectly. You are to find the incorrectly spelled word. It is spelled correctly in the answer explanation. You are referred back to the spelling rules, if necessary.

31. (A) heinous
    (B) arrainment
    (C) bureau
    (D) repetitious

32. (A) corrugated
    (B) regrettable
    (C) deliberasion
    (D) yacht

33. (A) posession
    (B) blamable
    (C) bookkeeping
    (D) whether

34. (A) mediocrity
    (B) dilapidated
    (C) derogatory
    (D) irelevant

35. (A) soverein
    (B) mischievous
    (C) harassment
    (D) masquerade

36. (A) anemia
    (B) equilibrium
    (C) presumptious
    (D) baccalaureate

37. (A) vengance
    (B) punctilious
    (C) vacillation
    (D) resilience

38. (A) beatitude
    (B) aggravation
    (C) description
    (D) beleagered

39. (A) inimitable

   (B) iminent

   (C) eminent

   (D) impartial

40. (A) recognizeable

   (B) incongruity

   (C) temperamentally

   (D) complacency

exercises

ANSWER KEY AND EXPLANATIONS

1. A	9. C	17. A	25. A	33. A
2. B	10. D	18. D	26. C	34. D
3. B	11. A	19. D	27. B	35. A
4. B	12. C	20. A	28. D	36. C
5. C	13. C	21. C	29. C	37. A
6. B	14. B	22. A	30. A	38. D
7. A	15. D	23. B	31. B	39. B
8. A	16. C	24. A	32. C	40. A

1. **The correct answer is (A).** See Rule 6 and the Demons list.

2. **The correct answer is (B).** See the Demons list.

3. **The correct answer is (B).** See Rule 6.

4. **The correct answer is (B).** See Rule 6, Exceptions.

5. **The correct answer is (C).** See Rule 4.

6. **The correct answer is (B).** See Rule 3.

7. **The correct answer is (A).** See Rule 1.

8. **The correct answer is (A).** See Rule 7.

9. **The correct answer is (C).** See Rule 5.

10. **The correct answer is (D).** See Rules 3 and 6.

11. **The correct answer is (A).** nuisance

12. **The correct answer is (C).** martial

13. **The correct answer is (C).** Wednesday

14. **The correct answer is (B).** arousing. See Rule 3.

15. **The correct answer is (D).** No error.

16. **The correct answer is (C).** leisure. See Rule 6.

17. **The correct answer is (A).** library

18. **The correct answer is (D).** No error.

19. **The correct answer is (D).** No error.

20. **The correct answer is (A).** occasionally. See the Demons List.

21. **The correct answer is (C).** mutiny. See Rule 9.

22. **The correct answer is (A).** donkeys. See Rule 5.

23. **The correct answer is (B).** Shelves is the plural form of the word shelf.

24. **The correct answer is (A).** blameless. See Rule 3.

25. **The correct answer is (A).** concurrence. See Rule 2.

26. **The correct answer is (C).** steadily. See Rule 8, Exceptions.

27. **The correct answer is (B).** weird. See Rule 6, Exceptions.

28. **The correct answer is (D).** No error.

29. **The correct answer is (C).**
    dryness. See Rule 5.

30. **The correct answer is (A).**
    embargoes

31. **The correct answer is (B).**
    arraignment. See the Demons List.

32. **The correct answer is (C).**
    deliberation

33. **The correct answer is (A).**
    possession. See the Demons List.

34. **The correct answer is (D).**
    irrelevant

35. **The correct answer is (A).**
    sovereign. See the Demons List.

36. **The correct answer is (C).**
    presumptuous. See the Demons List.

37. **The correct answer is (A).**
    vengeance. See the Demons List.

38. **The correct answer is (D).**
    beleaguered. See the Demons List.

39. **The correct answer is (B).**
    imminent. See the Demons List.

40. **The correct answer is (A).** recognizable. See Rule 3.

answers exercises

EXERCISES: PRINCIPLES OF GRAMMAR

Directions: Each of the sentences below is grammatically incorrect. Rewrite each sentence correctly. The answer explanations refer to the Principle of Grammar that governs each sentence.

1. They are as old as us.
2. Whom do you suppose paid us a visit?
3. Punish whomever is guilty.
4. It is me.
5. Can it be them?
6. It would be impossible for you and I.
7. He had difficulty with the store's management.
8. I, who's older, know better than you.
9. Is there any criticism of Arthur going?
10. Everybody tried their hardest.
11. I do not like these sort of cakes.
12. She don't like to engage in such activity.
13. The use of liquors are dangerous.
14. The district attorney, as well as many of his aides, have been involved in the investigation.
15. Either the fifth or the seventh of the courses they had laid open are to be accepted.
16. The fighting and wrestling of the two men is excellent.
17. The worst feature of the play were the abominable actors.
18. There is present a child and two dogs.
19. He spoke slow and careful.
20. He said that Venus was a planet.
21. I wish I was a clown.

ANSWER EXPLANATIONS

1. They are as old as *we* (are). See Principle 1.

2. *Who* do you suppose paid us a visit? See Principle 2.

3. Punish *whoever* is guilty. See Principle 3.

4. It is *I*. See Principle 4.

5. Can it be *they*? See Principle 4.

6. It would be impossible for you and *me*. See Principle 5.

7. He had difficulty with the *management of the store*. See Principle 6.

8. I, *who am* older, know better than you. See Principle 7.

9. Is there any criticism of *Arthur's* going? See Principle 8.

10. Everybody tried *his* (or *her*) hardest. See Principle 9.

11. I do not like *this sort* of cake. See Principle 10.

12. She *doesn't* like to engage in such activity. See Principle 11.

13. The use of liquors *is* dangerous. See Principle 12.

14. The district attorney, as well as many of his aides, *has* been involved in the investigation. See Principle 13.

15. Either the fifth or the seventh of the courses they *have* laid open *is* to be accepted. See Principle 14.

16. The fighting and wrestling of the two men *are* excellent. See Principle 15.

17. The worst feature of the play *was* the abominable actors. See Principle 16.

18. There *are* present a child and two dogs. See Principle 17.

19. He spoke *slowly* and *carefully*. See Principle 18.

20. He said that Venus *is* a planet. See Principle 19.

21. I wish I *were* a clown. See Principle 20.

SUMMING IT UP

- The mechanics of writing are

    —Spelling

    —Capitalization

    —Punctuation

    —Grammar

    —Usage

- The SSAT and the ISEE do not include test questions that directly measure the mechanics of writing, but you will have to submit a writing sample.

- The writing sample shows your ability to organize and convey your thoughts.

- Correct spelling, capitalization, punctuation, grammar, and English usage contribute to the quality of an essay.

The Essay (SSAT and ISEE)

chapter 14

OVERVIEW

- **What is the purpose of the essay?**
- **How do you write an essay under time pressure?**
- **What do smart test-takers know?**
- **Summing it up**

WHAT IS THE PURPOSE OF THE ESSAY?

The essay on your high school entrance exam serves as a writing sample. Its purpose is to show the school admissions committee how well you express yourself in writing. The school is interested in how you organize your thoughts and how you convey those thoughts to a reader. The essay is not graded and does not count toward your test score. Each school that receives your test score also receives a copy of your essay.

The SSAT Essay

The SSAT essay is the first part of the SSAT exam. You have 25 minutes to read the essay topic, choose a position, organize your essay, and write.

The ISEE Essay

The ISEE essay is the last part of the ISEE exam. You will be given 30 minutes to read and consider the topic, decide what to say, organize your thoughts, and write the essay.

NOTE

The essay does not count toward your score at all. In fact, the essay is not even graded. The essay does count toward the impression you make on the school. Admissions officers read your essay to learn about how well you express yourself in writing.

HOW DO YOU WRITE AN ESSAY UNDER TIME PRESSURE?

To write a coherent, correct essay in 25 or 30 minutes, follow these six steps:

Essay Writing: Getting It Right

1. Read the question to find out exactly what it asks you to do.
2. Choose a point of view or decide how to answer the question.
3. Outline your essay. You will probably want four paragraphs: an introduction, two paragraphs for two supporting ideas or illustrations, and a conclusion.
4. Write the essay.
5. Proofread. Correct errors in punctuation, spelling, grammar, and word choice.
6. If needed, make phrasing changes as neatly as possible.

Now let's try these steps on a couple of sample topics:

Topic: Every student should be required to complete 60 hours of community service during his or her high school years. Do you agree or disagree?

1. This question is asking you to choose sides, then support your position.
2. You must now decide whether you want to write in favor or in opposition. Choose the side that you will find easier to defend with strong examples; which side you choose does not matter. The question is not really seeking your opinion. For this exercise, let's disagree.
3. Introduction: Community service should not be compulsory.

    Point 1:   Involuntary activities are never performed well.

    A. Beneficiaries suffer from half-hearted service.

    B. Student is resentful and gains no satisfaction.

    Point 2:   Teenagers must learn to arrange priorities and manage their time for their own benefit.

    A. Some poor students cannot afford to give up so much study time.

    B. Many beneficial extracurricular activities compete for precious time.

    C. Some students must hold part-time jobs to help their families.

    Conclusion: Community service should be encouraged, not compulsory.
4. Write the essay.
5. Proofread. Ask yourself these questions:
    - Does each paragraph have a topic sentence? Is the topic sentence well developed within the paragraph?
    - Is my language colorful and descriptive? Have I varied my sentence structure?

- Do I make a convincing argument for my position?
- How is my spelling? Is my punctuation correct? What about my grammar?

6 Refine the essay if necessary. Remember: neatness counts.

Topic: If you were in charge of planning your family's next two-week vacation, where would you go and what would you do? Why?

1 This question is asking you to tell about a place you want to see or an activity you especially enjoy and to explain why this appeals to you.

2 You must name a place to which you would like to go or, if yours will be a stay-close-to-home vacation, an activity, or series of activities. If you have an ideal vacation in mind, describe it. You might also describe a vacation you have already taken. The readers are not interested in the vacation you choose; they want to know how you write about it. For this exercise, let's choose a summer vacation in eastern Canada.

3 Introduction: Canada is a nearby neighbor with much to offer in terms of culture and vacation activities.

Paragraph: We should know more about our closest neighbor and trading partner.

    A. People speak English; easy to learn about lifestyles and ideas.

    B. Easy to get to, can drive.

Paragraph: Canada offers scenic beauty, recreational activities, and foreign culture.

    A. Nova Scotia, Prince Edward Island, and Laurentians all scenic.

    B. Hiking and water sports available.

    C. Montreal and Quebec offer food, architecture, general feel of French cities.

Conclusion: Summer vacation in Canada will be interesting, fun, and not too expensive.

4 Write the essay.

5 Proofread. Ask yourself these questions:

- Does each paragraph have a topic sentence? Is the topic sentence well developed within the paragraph?
- Is my language colorful and descriptive? Have I varied my sentence structure?
- Do I make a convincing argument? Does my vacation sound appealing?
- How is my spelling? Is my punctuation correct? What about my grammar?

6 Refine the essay if necessary. Remember: neatness counts. Be certain your writing is legible.

TIP

Answer the question you are being asked to address. You get no credit for an essay that does not do what is asked for.

TIP

Organize your thoughts before you begin. Your first draft is your only draft. There is no time to rewrite.

WHAT DO SMART TEST-TAKERS KNOW?

Planning Comes First

Allow yourself 2 to 3 minutes for planning.

Do not even think about beginning to write until you have carefully read the essay topic and have answered these questions for yourself:

- *What* must I prove?
- *How many* things am I being asked to do?
- *How many paragraphs* will I need for this?

If you are asked to discuss advantages and disadvantages, you must represent both sides.

If you are asked for your opinion, you must state it clearly and must support your position with good reasons.

If you are asked to support your statements with a specific number of examples from your own experience, from history, or from literature, you must provide the requested number of examples from the appropriate sources.

Jot down your ideas on the topic. Think of what you want to say, and sketch out your points and supporting statements. As good descriptive words or phrases pop into your head, write them down on the same scratch paper. Don't let any thoughts get away. You'll want to refer to your list of ideas as you write so that you don't have to squeeze ideas between the lines after you have written your essay.

Outlines Are Important

Spend 3 to 5 minutes drafting your outline.

No matter how little time you have, an outline will save you time in the end. The outline is a framework for your essay to hang on. Your outline consists of specific details in the order in which you would like them to appear in the essay. Your outline will not be sent to the schools, so you do not need to be concerned with complete sentences, with spelling and punctuation, nor with legibility for anyone but yourself.

The following is a typical outline plan, but you may use any format that works well for you. Include as many paragraph outlines as you need to cover the points you must make in your essay.

I. Introductory paragraph
   A. Topic sentence (rephrase or state your position on the question)
   B. Sentence that introduces second paragraph
   C. Sentence that introduces third paragraph
   D. Optional sentence leading into second paragraph

II. The first point you have to make

   A. Topic sentence

   B. First idea that supports this point

       1. Detail or illustration—experience, citing of example

       2. Detail or illustration

   C. Second idea supporting first point

       1. Detail or illustration

       2. Detail or illustration

Finish your essay with a summary statement.

Topic Sentences Are a Must

Thoughtful topic sentences will keep your writing on target and help you prove your points.

A Well-Targeted Topic Sentence Is Crucial

Remember: A topic sentence has an idea that can be fully proven in one paragraph. For example, the sentence "You can learn a lot about human nature just by observing people" is so broad that it cannot be proven in one single paragraph. But if we write:

"You can learn a lot about human nature by watching people at a bus station"

or

"You can learn a lot about human nature by watching people at the beach," we have a topic that we can prove in one paragraph.

Another way to look at topic sentences is through the controlling idea. This is a key word or group of words that expresses the basic idea of the sentence. When the controlling idea is clear, the entire sentence will be specific and clear.

    Example: An encyclopedia is a handy book for students.

      "Handy" is the controlling idea. In the paragraph that follows, you will explain *how* the encyclopedia is handy.

    Example: Traveling by train has several advantages over traveling by car.

      "Several advantages" is the controlling idea. The paragraph will detail these advantages.

    Example: Good English is clear, appropriate, and vivid.

      "Clear, appropriate, and vivid" is the controlling idea. The paragraph will offer illustrations of clear, appropriate, and vivid English.

Descriptive Words Make Writing Interesting

To prove your point and make your writing interesting, you have to use specific words and phrases:

His face was _____ with fright.

colorless   scarlet   chalky   pale

"Chalky" is the best word for in addition to color—a pale, dry white—it implies a texture—dry and lifeless. "Scarlet" is incorrect because your face does not become scarlet (red) when you are afraid. "Colorless" and "pale" are too vague. "Chalky" is the most descriptive word and the one that makes this sentence most effective.

The sun is high and hot, the air is sultry; it is _____ time.

siesta   sleep   nap   rest

"Siesta" describes a nap that is taken when it is very warm during the middle of the day and is thus the most precise word. Then would come:

nap (a short sleep)

sleep (a type of rest)

rest (any sitting down and relaxing)

Proofreading Will Improve Your Essay

Writing your essay should take you about 15 minutes. Allow at least 3 minutes to proofread and make corrections. Check for the following:

- Did I answer the question?
- Did I provide good, specific details to support my ideas?
- Did I organize my answer in the best possible way to make my point clearly?
- Did I make any errors in spelling, grammar, punctuation, or word use?

Proofreading time is time well spent. Check over what you said, being sure to read what is really there and not what you think is there. Do not read too quickly or you may miss obvious errors. If you find that a sentence might be improved by different phrasing or that a line is illegible, rewrite more clearly at the bottom of the page, cross out the offending portion neatly, and indicate by arrows where the substitution should be inserted.

TIP

Keep your handwriting legible. If they can't read it, it won't count.

EXERCISES: ESSAY WRITING 1

Directions: Choose the essay topic appropriate to your exam and write an essay. Sample responses begin on the next page.

SSAT-Style Topic

25 Minutes

Topic: Some educators suggest that all elementary, middle school, and high school students should be required to wear school uniforms. What do you think?

ISEE-Style Topic

30 Minutes

Topic: Tell about a time when you felt a very strong emotion. What was it? Why did you feel it?

EXERCISES: ESSAY WRITING 2

Directions: You are already familiar with the following essay topics, what they require of you, and how they might be organized. Choose the topic appropriate to your exam and write your own essay.

SSAT-Style Topic

25 Minutes

Topic: Every student should be required to complete 60 hours of community service during his or her high school years. Do you agree or disagree?

ISEE-Style Topic

30 Minutes

Topic: If you were in charge of planning your family's next two-week vacation, where would you go and what would you do? Why?

SAMPLE RESPONSES 1

SSAT-Style Topic

Many people have suggested that all students be required to wear uniforms to school. Some students object to this idea because it takes away their individuality, but I think there are a number of reasons why school uniforms might be a good idea.

Over the past few years, there have been no dress guidelines and no dress codes in our schools. Some students just naturally dress neatly and appropriately, but others are truly sloppy. When people dress in sloppy clothing, they tend to be too relaxed. This leads to sloppy thinking. Pretty soon they lose respect for school and teachers and the whole learning process. School uniforms would remind these students that they are in school for a purpose. I think that if everyone were dressed in the same uniform there would be more school spirit too. Students would all feel as if they were part of something important.

Some students, especially girls, worry too much about their clothes and how they look. They bother their parents to spend too much on clothes, often more than their families can afford, and are always trying to compete. I have heard about boys fighting over "status" clothes. There have been cases of stealing fancy jackets and sneakers and even some knifings. School uniforms might cost more, but each student needs only two or three of them. This would take the pressure off poorer families. If everyone dressed alike, there would be no competition. A special benefit that educators probably haven't thought of is that of extra sleep. With no choice of what to wear, it will be much quicker to dress and get out in the morning.

I think we should try out school uniforms. I expect that discipline, paying attention, and school spirit will go up while squabbles about appearance and fights over clothing will go down. And I think that many students will be happier without the competition, and parents will be happier too.

ISEE-Style Topic

On October 15th of last year my grandmother died. Grandmother had been sick and in pain for some months, so her death was not a surprise and in some ways it was a relief and a blessing. But I was unbelievably saddened when she died. I had never felt this type or degree of sadness before.

My grandmother was an extraordinary woman. Her own parents died when she was a teenager, and she raised two younger sisters alone. Then her husband died while she was still in her thirties, leaving her with my mother, then only seven years old, and my uncle, then only nine. Still, she maintained a sense of humor and great dignity. As I grew up, my grandmother was always there for me. She listened to my joys and problems and always gave me good advice. She was never judgmental but always gave me unconditional love and much warmth. I will miss her a lot.

Part of my sadness, I think, was sadness for my mother who is now an orphan herself. She and my grandmother were always very close. Grandmother was the last family member of her generation. There is now a void in the family, and celebrations will always have an empty place.

I loved my grandmother very much, and now she is gone. I was very, very sad when she died. I have overcome that sadness by now, but many little things remind me of her. Every once in a while something happens and I first think that I must tell Grandma—that she will be interested or amused. Then I remember that Grandma is gone, and I feel a twinge of sadness again.

SAMPLE RESPONSES 2

SSAT-Style Topic

The school board has been debating about a proposed new graduation requirement. They are suggesting that every student be required to complete 60 hours of community service during the high school years. I think that community service is a noble concept but that it should not be compulsory.

A student who is forced to perform an activity against his or her will is unlikely to perform it well. The very fact of the coercion almost guarantees a half-hearted approach. Community service not done well is hardly service at all. Yet, someone thinks that service is being performed. Then the intended beneficiaries suffer from the lack of service. Community service is supposed to be ennobling. Yet the student who is forced to perform this service is resentful and gains no satisfaction from it.

There are more downsides to compulsory community service. Students must learn to arrange their own priorities and to manage their own time. Some poor students can not afford to give up so much study time, yet they are not permitted to devote the study time they would like because of the required community service. Other students must hold part-time paid jobs to help out their families or to have any spending money for themselves. Community service to the extent proposed would be a hardship for them. Still other students are so deeply into extracurriculars—sports, music, drama, or religious studies—that compulsory community service would cut into study time or sleep time.

Community service is certainly a worthwhile goal, and all students should be encouraged to engage in some service that suits their interests, abilities, and time schedule. However, I don't think that compulsory community service is a good idea. School administrators and teachers should instead help students devise creative forms of community service that the students will want to fit into their busy lives.

ISEE-Style Topic

Canada is a foreign country, yet it is only an automobile drive away from many states in the northern part of the United States. In Canada, there are rivers, lakes, mountains, and seacoast along with interesting cities. It should be easy to plan a Canadian vacation.

The United States shares its borders with only two countries—Mexico to the south and Canada to the north. We really should know more about these neighbors. Since I live in New England, Canada is easier for my family to visit. We can drive to Canada's northeast in one day. Best of all, nearly all Canadians speak English so it should be easy to get around and easy to learn about lifestyles and ideas.

Because Canada is so big, it offers every kind of vacation. Nova Scotia and Prince Edward Island are filled with quaint fishing villages and spectacular seacoast scenery. They are probably cold for ocean swimming, but great for hiking. The Laurentian Mountains are known for skiing, but their lakes offer all sorts of water sports and we might camp in the mountains. And to vary the vacation, we should visit the cities of Montreal and Quebec, which retain much French influence. I am looking forward to real French food.

For a summer vacation that will be fun, not too expensive, and educational besides, Canada can't be beat. It should not be too hard to convince my family.

SUMMING IT UP

Review this page the night before you take your exam. It will help you write an impressive essay:

- The essay does not count toward your score, but it does influence the admissions committee.

- Follow these six steps:
  1. Read the question to find out exactly what it asks you to do.
  2. Choose a point of view or decide how to answer the question.
  3. Outline your essay. Sketch in and organize the ideas that you want to include in each paragraph.
  4. Write the essay, paying attention to mechanics.
  5. Proofread. Correct errors in punctuation, spelling, grammar, and word choice.
  6. Make changes and refinements as neatly as possible.

- Remember: Your essay must be legible.

PART VIII

FOUR PRACTICE TESTS

ANSWER SHEET PRACTICE TEST 2: SSAT (Upper Level)

Part I: Writing Sample

_____

_____

_____

_____

_____

_____

_____

_____

_____

_____

_____

_____

_____

_____

_____

_____

_____

_____

answer sheet

Part II: Multiple-Choice

Section 1: Verbal

1 Ⓐ Ⓑ Ⓒ Ⓓ Ⓔ	16 Ⓐ Ⓑ Ⓒ Ⓓ Ⓔ	31 Ⓐ Ⓑ Ⓒ Ⓓ Ⓔ	46 Ⓐ Ⓑ Ⓒ Ⓓ Ⓔ
2 Ⓐ Ⓑ Ⓒ Ⓓ Ⓔ	17 Ⓐ Ⓑ Ⓒ Ⓓ Ⓔ	32 Ⓐ Ⓑ Ⓒ Ⓓ Ⓔ	47 Ⓐ Ⓑ Ⓒ Ⓓ Ⓔ
3 Ⓐ Ⓑ Ⓒ Ⓓ Ⓔ	18 Ⓐ Ⓑ Ⓒ Ⓓ Ⓔ	33 Ⓐ Ⓑ Ⓒ Ⓓ Ⓔ	48 Ⓐ Ⓑ Ⓒ Ⓓ Ⓔ
4 Ⓐ Ⓑ Ⓒ Ⓓ Ⓔ	19 Ⓐ Ⓑ Ⓒ Ⓓ Ⓔ	34 Ⓐ Ⓑ Ⓒ Ⓓ Ⓔ	49 Ⓐ Ⓑ Ⓒ Ⓓ Ⓔ
5 Ⓐ Ⓑ Ⓒ Ⓓ Ⓔ	20 Ⓐ Ⓑ Ⓒ Ⓓ Ⓔ	35 Ⓐ Ⓑ Ⓒ Ⓓ Ⓔ	50 Ⓐ Ⓑ Ⓒ Ⓓ Ⓔ
6 Ⓐ Ⓑ Ⓒ Ⓓ Ⓔ	21 Ⓐ Ⓑ Ⓒ Ⓓ Ⓔ	36 Ⓐ Ⓑ Ⓒ Ⓓ Ⓔ	51 Ⓐ Ⓑ Ⓒ Ⓓ Ⓔ
7 Ⓐ Ⓑ Ⓒ Ⓓ Ⓔ	22 Ⓐ Ⓑ Ⓒ Ⓓ Ⓔ	37 Ⓐ Ⓑ Ⓒ Ⓓ Ⓔ	52 Ⓐ Ⓑ Ⓒ Ⓓ Ⓔ
8 Ⓐ Ⓑ Ⓒ Ⓓ Ⓔ	23 Ⓐ Ⓑ Ⓒ Ⓓ Ⓔ	38 Ⓐ Ⓑ Ⓒ Ⓓ Ⓔ	53 Ⓐ Ⓑ Ⓒ Ⓓ Ⓔ
9 Ⓐ Ⓑ Ⓒ Ⓓ Ⓔ	24 Ⓐ Ⓑ Ⓒ Ⓓ Ⓔ	39 Ⓐ Ⓑ Ⓒ Ⓓ Ⓔ	54 Ⓐ Ⓑ Ⓒ Ⓓ Ⓔ
10 Ⓐ Ⓑ Ⓒ Ⓓ Ⓔ	25 Ⓐ Ⓑ Ⓒ Ⓓ Ⓔ	40 Ⓐ Ⓑ Ⓒ Ⓓ Ⓔ	55 Ⓐ Ⓑ Ⓒ Ⓓ Ⓔ
11 Ⓐ Ⓑ Ⓒ Ⓓ Ⓔ	26 Ⓐ Ⓑ Ⓒ Ⓓ Ⓔ	41 Ⓐ Ⓑ Ⓒ Ⓓ Ⓔ	56 Ⓐ Ⓑ Ⓒ Ⓓ Ⓔ
12 Ⓐ Ⓑ Ⓒ Ⓓ Ⓔ	27 Ⓐ Ⓑ Ⓒ Ⓓ Ⓔ	42 Ⓐ Ⓑ Ⓒ Ⓓ Ⓔ	57 Ⓐ Ⓑ Ⓒ Ⓓ Ⓔ
13 Ⓐ Ⓑ Ⓒ Ⓓ Ⓔ	28 Ⓐ Ⓑ Ⓒ Ⓓ Ⓔ	43 Ⓐ Ⓑ Ⓒ Ⓓ Ⓔ	58 Ⓐ Ⓑ Ⓒ Ⓓ Ⓔ
14 Ⓐ Ⓑ Ⓒ Ⓓ Ⓔ	29 Ⓐ Ⓑ Ⓒ Ⓓ Ⓔ	44 Ⓐ Ⓑ Ⓒ Ⓓ Ⓔ	59 Ⓐ Ⓑ Ⓒ Ⓓ Ⓔ
15 Ⓐ Ⓑ Ⓒ Ⓓ Ⓔ	30 Ⓐ Ⓑ Ⓒ Ⓓ Ⓔ	45 Ⓐ Ⓑ Ⓒ Ⓓ Ⓔ	60 Ⓐ Ⓑ Ⓒ Ⓓ Ⓔ

Section 2: Quantitative (Math)

1 Ⓐ Ⓑ Ⓒ Ⓓ Ⓔ	8 Ⓐ Ⓑ Ⓒ Ⓓ Ⓔ	15 Ⓐ Ⓑ Ⓒ Ⓓ Ⓔ	22 Ⓐ Ⓑ Ⓒ Ⓓ Ⓔ
2 Ⓐ Ⓑ Ⓒ Ⓓ Ⓔ	9 Ⓐ Ⓑ Ⓒ Ⓓ Ⓔ	16 Ⓐ Ⓑ Ⓒ Ⓓ Ⓔ	23 Ⓐ Ⓑ Ⓒ Ⓓ Ⓔ
3 Ⓐ Ⓑ Ⓒ Ⓓ Ⓔ	10 Ⓐ Ⓑ Ⓒ Ⓓ Ⓔ	17 Ⓐ Ⓑ Ⓒ Ⓓ Ⓔ	24 Ⓐ Ⓑ Ⓒ Ⓓ Ⓔ
4 Ⓐ Ⓑ Ⓒ Ⓓ Ⓔ	11 Ⓐ Ⓑ Ⓒ Ⓓ Ⓔ	18 Ⓐ Ⓑ Ⓒ Ⓓ Ⓔ	25 Ⓐ Ⓑ Ⓒ Ⓓ Ⓔ
5 Ⓐ Ⓑ Ⓒ Ⓓ Ⓔ	12 Ⓐ Ⓑ Ⓒ Ⓓ Ⓔ	19 Ⓐ Ⓑ Ⓒ Ⓓ Ⓔ	
6 Ⓐ Ⓑ Ⓒ Ⓓ Ⓔ	13 Ⓐ Ⓑ Ⓒ Ⓓ Ⓔ	20 Ⓐ Ⓑ Ⓒ Ⓓ Ⓔ	
7 Ⓐ Ⓑ Ⓒ Ⓓ Ⓔ	14 Ⓐ Ⓑ Ⓒ Ⓓ Ⓔ	21 Ⓐ Ⓑ Ⓒ Ⓓ Ⓔ	

answer sheet

Section 3: Reading Comprehension

1 Ⓐ Ⓑ Ⓒ Ⓓ Ⓔ   11 Ⓐ Ⓑ Ⓒ Ⓓ Ⓔ   21 Ⓐ Ⓑ Ⓒ Ⓓ Ⓔ   31 Ⓐ Ⓑ Ⓒ Ⓓ Ⓔ
2 Ⓐ Ⓑ Ⓒ Ⓓ Ⓔ   12 Ⓐ Ⓑ Ⓒ Ⓓ Ⓔ   22 Ⓐ Ⓑ Ⓒ Ⓓ Ⓔ   32 Ⓐ Ⓑ Ⓒ Ⓓ Ⓔ
3 Ⓐ Ⓑ Ⓒ Ⓓ Ⓔ   13 Ⓐ Ⓑ Ⓒ Ⓓ Ⓔ   23 Ⓐ Ⓑ Ⓒ Ⓓ Ⓔ   33 Ⓐ Ⓑ Ⓒ Ⓓ Ⓔ
4 Ⓐ Ⓑ Ⓒ Ⓓ Ⓔ   14 Ⓐ Ⓑ Ⓒ Ⓓ Ⓔ   24 Ⓐ Ⓑ Ⓒ Ⓓ Ⓔ   34 Ⓐ Ⓑ Ⓒ Ⓓ Ⓔ
5 Ⓐ Ⓑ Ⓒ Ⓓ Ⓔ   15 Ⓐ Ⓑ Ⓒ Ⓓ Ⓔ   25 Ⓐ Ⓑ Ⓒ Ⓓ Ⓔ   35 Ⓐ Ⓑ Ⓒ Ⓓ Ⓔ
6 Ⓐ Ⓑ Ⓒ Ⓓ Ⓔ   16 Ⓐ Ⓑ Ⓒ Ⓓ Ⓔ   26 Ⓐ Ⓑ Ⓒ Ⓓ Ⓔ   36 Ⓐ Ⓑ Ⓒ Ⓓ Ⓔ
7 Ⓐ Ⓑ Ⓒ Ⓓ Ⓔ   17 Ⓐ Ⓑ Ⓒ Ⓓ Ⓔ   27 Ⓐ Ⓑ Ⓒ Ⓓ Ⓔ   37 Ⓐ Ⓑ Ⓒ Ⓓ Ⓔ
8 Ⓐ Ⓑ Ⓒ Ⓓ Ⓔ   18 Ⓐ Ⓑ Ⓒ Ⓓ Ⓔ   28 Ⓐ Ⓑ Ⓒ Ⓓ Ⓔ   38 Ⓐ Ⓑ Ⓒ Ⓓ Ⓔ
9 Ⓐ Ⓑ Ⓒ Ⓓ Ⓔ   19 Ⓐ Ⓑ Ⓒ Ⓓ Ⓔ   29 Ⓐ Ⓑ Ⓒ Ⓓ Ⓔ   39 Ⓐ Ⓑ Ⓒ Ⓓ Ⓔ
10 Ⓐ Ⓑ Ⓒ Ⓓ Ⓔ   20 Ⓐ Ⓑ Ⓒ Ⓓ Ⓔ   30 Ⓐ Ⓑ Ⓒ Ⓓ Ⓔ   40 Ⓐ Ⓑ Ⓒ Ⓓ Ⓔ

Section 4: Quantitative (Math)

1 Ⓐ Ⓑ Ⓒ Ⓓ Ⓔ   8 Ⓐ Ⓑ Ⓒ Ⓓ Ⓔ   15 Ⓐ Ⓑ Ⓒ Ⓓ Ⓔ   22 Ⓐ Ⓑ Ⓒ Ⓓ Ⓔ
2 Ⓐ Ⓑ Ⓒ Ⓓ Ⓔ   9 Ⓐ Ⓑ Ⓒ Ⓓ Ⓔ   16 Ⓐ Ⓑ Ⓒ Ⓓ Ⓔ   23 Ⓐ Ⓑ Ⓒ Ⓓ Ⓔ
3 Ⓐ Ⓑ Ⓒ Ⓓ Ⓔ   10 Ⓐ Ⓑ Ⓒ Ⓓ Ⓔ   17 Ⓐ Ⓑ Ⓒ Ⓓ Ⓔ   24 Ⓐ Ⓑ Ⓒ Ⓓ Ⓔ
4 Ⓐ Ⓑ Ⓒ Ⓓ Ⓔ   11 Ⓐ Ⓑ Ⓒ Ⓓ Ⓔ   18 Ⓐ Ⓑ Ⓒ Ⓓ Ⓔ   25 Ⓐ Ⓑ Ⓒ Ⓓ Ⓔ
5 Ⓐ Ⓑ Ⓒ Ⓓ Ⓔ   12 Ⓐ Ⓑ Ⓒ Ⓓ Ⓔ   19 Ⓐ Ⓑ Ⓒ Ⓓ Ⓔ
6 Ⓐ Ⓑ Ⓒ Ⓓ Ⓔ   13 Ⓐ Ⓑ Ⓒ Ⓓ Ⓔ   20 Ⓐ Ⓑ Ⓒ Ⓓ Ⓔ
7 Ⓐ Ⓑ Ⓒ Ⓓ Ⓔ   14 Ⓐ Ⓑ Ⓒ Ⓓ Ⓔ   21 Ⓐ Ⓑ Ⓒ Ⓓ Ⓔ

Practice Test 2: SSAT (Upper Level)

PART I: WRITING SAMPLE

25 Minutes

Directions: Write a convincing, legible essay supporting your opinion on the topic that follows. Use the answer sheet provided.

Topic: To reduce the accident rate, the state legislature should pass a proposal to raise the minimum driving age from 16 to 18.

Do you agree or disagree with this statement? Support your position with specific examples.

PART II: MULTIPLE-CHOICE

Section 1: Verbal

60 Questions • 30 Minutes

The Verbal section consists of two different types of questions. There are directions for each type of question.

> **Directions:** Each question shows a word in capital letters followed by five words or phrases. Choose the word or phrase whose meaning is most similar to the word in capital letters. Mark the appropriate space on your answer sheet.

1. DETER
   - (A) halt
   - (B) steer
   - (C) sting
   - (D) turn
   - (E) hinder

2. HOSTILE
   - (A) friendly
   - (B) unfriendly
   - (C) suspicious
   - (D) indifferent
   - (E) doubtful

3. UTILIZE
   - (A) make use of
   - (B) utilities
   - (C) modernize
   - (D) sing
   - (E) undo

4. ABDICATE
   - (A) resign
   - (B) explain
   - (C) remorse
   - (D) disprove
   - (E) control

5. PROMINENT
   - (A) disturbing
   - (B) secret
   - (C) outstanding
   - (D) extravagant
   - (E) surreptitious

6. BOUNDARY
   - (A) hovel
   - (B) limit
   - (C) ceiling
   - (D) map
   - (E) seam

7. ILLITERATE
   - (A) unable to vote
   - (B) unmanageable
   - (C) sickly
   - (D) unable to read
   - (E) unclean

8. ORATOR
   - (A) professor
   - (B) poet
   - (C) speaker
   - (D) ear
   - (E) student

9. CORROBORATE
   (A) confirm
   (B) understand
   (C) cooperate
   (D) agree
   (E) disagree

10. RATIFY
    (A) delete
    (B) consider
    (C) approve
    (D) examine
    (E) assess

11. PERILOUS
    (A) careless
    (B) conniving
    (C) irregular
    (D) estranged
    (E) hazardous

12. STATIONARY
    (A) paper
    (B) moving
    (C) immobile
    (D) position
    (E) mobile

13. TRANSCRIBE
    (A) copy
    (B) illustrate
    (C) circulate
    (D) request
    (E) author

14. PROFICIENT
    (A) well-known
    (B) professional
    (C) adept
    (D) practice
    (E) prolific

15. DECEIVE
    (A) rearrange
    (B) mislead
    (C) pretend
    (D) stun
    (E) examine

16. AGILE
    (A) strong
    (B) similar
    (C) anxious
    (D) rested
    (E) nimble

17. DURATION
    (A) area
    (B) temptation
    (C) term
    (D) wait
    (E) former

18. AMBIGUOUS
    (A) unclear
    (B) adhere
    (C) aspire
    (D) afflict
    (E) certain

19. PREROGATIVE
    (A) command
    (B) choice
    (C) prerequisite
    (D) conviction
    (E) haggard

20. INTRIGUING
    (A) business
    (B) furtive
    (C) mystery
    (D) fascinating
    (E) boorish

practice test

21. CLANDESTINE
- **(A)** overt
- **(B)** dated
- **(C)** exclusive
- **(D)** fortunate
- **(E)** secret

22. BOUNTEOUS
- **(A)** elastic
- **(B)** industrious
- **(C)** abundant
- **(D)** mutinous
- **(E)** energetic

23. DIVERGE
- **(A)** annoy
- **(B)** change course
- **(C)** stay
- **(D)** analyze
- **(E)** distract

24. BENIGN
- **(A)** gentle
- **(B)** blessed
- **(C)** initial
- **(D)** virulent
- **(E)** malignant

25. CAUCUS
- **(A)** dispersal
- **(B)** corpse
- **(C)** meeting
- **(D)** partnership
- **(E)** cosmetic

26. DISSEMINATE
- **(A)** collate
- **(B)** strip
- **(C)** collect
- **(D)** disagree
- **(E)** spread

27. CHAGRIN
- **(A)** delight
- **(B)** alter
- **(C)** embarrass
- **(D)** wreck
- **(E)** anger

28. VALOR
- **(A)** courage
- **(B)** disclosure
- **(C)** treason
- **(D)** hate
- **(E)** foreboding

29. NONCHALANT
- **(A)** interested
- **(B)** caring
- **(C)** impoverished
- **(D)** indifferent
- **(E)** persecuted

30. LIAISON
- **(A)** permission
- **(B)** laziness
- **(C)** scarf
- **(D)** remedy
- **(E)** association

Directions: The following questions ask you to find relationships between words. Read each question, and then choose the answer that best completes the meaning of the sentence. Mark the appropriate space on your answer sheet.

31. Beg is to borrow as offer is to
    (A) lender
    (B) bank
    (C) lend
    (D) repay
    (E) security

32. Lazy is to inert as resist is to
    (A) refuse
    (B) reply
    (C) respond
    (D) active
    (E) insist

33. Cylinder is to circle as pyramid is to
    (A) sphere
    (B) point
    (C) triangle
    (D) angle
    (E) height

34. Crocodile is to reptile as kangaroo is to
    (A) amphibian
    (B) marsupial
    (C) opossum
    (D) canine
    (E) tail

35. Milliliter is to quart as
    (A) pound is to gram
    (B) millimeter is to yard
    (C) inch is to yard
    (D) pint is to quart
    (E) foot is to yard

36. Destroy is to demolish as
    (A) win is to lose
    (B) candid is to secret
    (C) amend is to change
    (D) establish is to abolish
    (E) attempt is to succeed

37. Plaintiff is to defendant as
    (A) plain is to ordinary
    (B) lawyer is to courtroom
    (C) professor is to college
    (D) complain is to complainant
    (E) prosecute is to defend

38. Fundamental is to frivolous as
    (A) fantasy is to fiction
    (B) nonfiction is to fact
    (C) regulation is to rule
    (D) truth is to nonsense
    (E) strange is to common

39. Wild is to wolf as domestic is to
    (A) dog
    (B) coyote
    (C) pet
    (D) cat
    (E) animal

40. Hammer is to carpenter as
    (A) awl is to cobbler
    (B) computer is to printer
    (C) saw is to timber
    (D) author is to typewriter
    (E) scale is to musician

41. Subject is to predicate as senator is to
    (A) congress
    (B) president
    (C) capitol
    (D) representative
    (E) senate

42. Pungent is to odor as
    (A) intense is to emotion
    (B) pervade is to atmosphere
    (C) infect is to spread
    (D) proverb is to paragraph
    (E) resent is to denial

43. Exploit is to adventure as
    (A) rule is to governor
    (B) safari is to expedition
    (C) school is to field trip
    (D) attack is to hunt
    (E) chase is to escape

44. Spread is to scatter as separate is to
    (A) integrate
    (B) distribute
    (C) reap
    (D) group
    (E) displace

45. Exuberant is to mood as adroit is to
    (A) proficient
    (B) adept
    (C) hand
    (D) dexterous
    (E) movement

46. Defiance is to opposition as exertion is to
    (A) expert
    (B) vigor
    (C) endeavor
    (D) restraint
    (E) challenge

47. Food is to nutrition as light is to
    (A) watt
    (B) bulb
    (C) electricity
    (D) reading
    (E) vision

48. Perpetuity is to impermanence as interminable is to
    (A) impertinent
    (B) brief
    (C) incessant
    (D) eternal
    (E) occasional

49. Erratic is to predictable as exorbitant is to
    (A) reasonable
    (B) productive
    (C) absorbent
    (D) small
    (E) implicit

50. Comment is to speech as
    (A) question is to answer
    (B) exclamation is to statement
    (C) written is to spoken
    (D) prose is to essay
    (E) note is to letter

51. Flammable is to inflammable as
    (A) persistent is to important
    (B) opportune is to inopportune
    (C) relevant is to incoherent
    (D) truculent is to intrusion
    (E) impartial is to disinterested

52. Tailor is to pattern as builder is to
    (A) architect
    (B) contractor
    (C) foundation
    (D) construct
    (E) blueprint

53. Impeach is to dismiss as
(A) arraign is to indict
(B) accuse is to charge
(C) imprison is to jail
(D) plant is to sow
(E) absent is to present

54. Speedy is to greyhound as
(A) wool is to lamb
(B) shark is to voracious
(C) clever is to fox
(D) mammal is to whale
(E) fin is to fish

55. Exhale is to lung as
(A) exhume is to corpse
(B) pump is to heart
(C) think is to brain
(D) perspire is to skin
(E) taste is to tongue

56. Celebrate is to birth as
(A) grieve is to death
(B) announce is to birthday
(C) crime is to penalty
(D) joy is to lament
(E) party is to graduation

57. Recommend is to urge as
(A) request is to plead
(B) refuse is to deny
(C) harass is to bother
(D) cajole is to insult
(E) apply is to receive

58. Weeping is to tears as breathing is to
(A) air
(B) lungs
(C) nose
(D) mouth
(E) carbon dioxide

59. Plane is to air pocket as
(A) vehicle is to rut
(B) hangar is to airport
(C) ground is to sky
(D) safety is to danger
(E) horse is to reins

60. Arbitrate is to dispute as
(A) solve is to mystery
(B) regard is to problem
(C) exacerbate is to problem
(D) organize is to labor
(E) management is to union

STOP END OF SECTION 1. IF YOU HAVE ANY TIME LEFT, GO OVER YOUR WORK IN THIS SECTION ONLY. DO NOT WORK IN ANY OTHER SECTION OF THE TEST.

Section 2: Quantitative (Math)

25 Questions • 30 Minutes

Directions: Calculate the answer to each of the following questions. Select the answer choice that is best, and mark the appropriate letter on your answer sheet.

1. $1\frac{1}{2}$ + .750 + .1010 =

   (A) 1.001

   (B) 2.051

   (C) 2.055

   (D) 2.351

   (E) 2.551

2. Evaluate: $\dfrac{2^{12}}{2^8}$

   (A) 2^{20}

   (B) 16

   (C) 8

   (D) 2

   (E) 1^{20}

3. 503.384 ÷ 62.3 =

   (A) 7.08

   (B) 7.68

   (C) 8.08

   (D) 9.08

   (E) 10.08

4. Evaluate: $\dfrac{1\frac{3}{4} - \frac{1}{8}}{\frac{1}{8}}$

   (A) 1

   (B) 2

   (C) 12

   (D) 13

   (E) 14

5. 2.01 ÷ 1.02 =

   (A) .507

   (B) 1.83

   (C) 1.97

   (D) 2.0001

   (E) 3.03

6. $-3 - [(2 - 1) - (3 + 4)] =$

   (A) 12

   (B) 6

   (C) 3

   (D) −6

   (E) −9

7. 3,003 − 699 =

   (A) 2,294

   (B) 2,304

   (C) 2,314

   (D) 2,404

   (E) 2,414

8. If $a = 5$ and $b = \frac{1}{5}$, then the value of a, expressed in terms of b, is

   (A) $25b$

   (B) $20b$

   (C) $5\frac{1}{5}\,b$

   (D) $5b$

   (E) $\frac{1}{25}\,b$

9. 140% of 70 is
   - (A) .98
   - (B) 9.8
   - (C) 98
   - (D) 150
   - (E) 9,800

10.
$$\begin{array}{ll} & \text{5 gallons} \quad \text{2 quarts} \quad \text{1 pint} \\ - & \text{1 gallon} \quad \text{3 quarts} \\ \hline \end{array}$$

   - (A) 2 gal. 2 qt. 1 pt.
   - (B) 2 gal. 6 qt. 2 pt.
   - (C) 3 gal. 3 qt. 1 pt.
   - (D) 4 gal. 3 qt. 1 pt.
   - (E) 4 gal. 9 qt. 1 pt.

11. In the fraction $\dfrac{xy}{z}$, if the value of z is doubled and the value of x is halved, the value of the fraction is
   - (A) multiplied by four.
   - (B) decreased by $\dfrac{1}{2}$.
   - (C) increased by $\dfrac{1}{2}$.
   - (D) doubled.
   - (E) divided by four.

12. 20 is 8 percent of
   - (A) 1.60
   - (B) 160
   - (C) 200
   - (D) 250
   - (E) 400

13. How much larger than 80 is 100?
   - (A) 18%
   - (B) 20%
   - (C) 25%
   - (D) 35%
   - (E) 40%

14. If $\dfrac{3}{8}$ ″ on a scale drawing is equivalent to one foot at full scale, what distance on the drawing will stand for forty inches?
   - (A) $\dfrac{1}{8}$ inches
   - (B) $\dfrac{7}{8}$ inches
   - (C) $1\dfrac{1}{4}$ inches
   - (D) $2\dfrac{1}{3}$ inches
   - (E) $8\dfrac{8}{9}$ inches

15. $6 \div \dfrac{1}{3} + \dfrac{2}{3} \times 9 =$
   - (A) $\dfrac{2}{3}$
   - (B) 11
   - (C) 24
   - (D) 54
   - (E) 168

16. If $x - 3 < 12$, x may be
   - (A) less than 15.
   - (B) greater than 16.
   - (C) equal to 15.
   - (D) less than 18.
   - (E) equal to 18.

17. If $a = 9$, $b = 2$, and $c = 1$, the value of $\sqrt{a + 3b + c}$ is
   - (A) 16
   - (B) 7
   - (C) 6
   - (D) 4
   - (E) 2

18. The average of −10, 6, 0, −3, and 22 is
   (A) 4
   (B) 3
   (C) 2
   (D) −3
   (E) −6

19. In the fraction $\dfrac{1}{\Delta - 2}$, Δ can be replaced by all of the following EXCEPT
   (A) +3
   (B) +2
   (C) 0
   (D) −1
   (E) −2

20. .10101 ÷ 10 is equivalent to
   (A) .0010101
   (B) .0100
   (C) .010101
   (D) .1001
   (E) 1.0101

21. David walked from his home to town, a distance of 5 miles, in 1 hour. The return trip took 2 hours because he made several stops along the way. What was his average rate of speed (in miles per hour) for the entire walk?

   (A) $\dfrac{3}{10}$ mph

   (B) $1\dfrac{1}{2}$ mph

   (C) $1\dfrac{2}{3}$ mph

   (D) $3\dfrac{1}{3}$ mph

   (E) 4 mph

22. 7 is to 21 as $\dfrac{2}{3}$ is to
   (A) 3
   (B) 2
   (C) $\dfrac{4}{3}$
   (D) 1
   (E) $\dfrac{5}{9}$

23. If $n = \sqrt{85}$, then
   (A) $9 > n > 8$
   (B) $n = 9.5$
   (C) $10 > n > 9$
   (D) $8 < n < 9$
   (E) $n^2 > 100$

24.

   The sum of which points on the number line above would be equal to zero?
   (A) B, D, E, I
   (B) C, D, G, H
   (C) A, C, F, I
   (D) D, E, F, G
   (E) B, C, H, I

25. How many fourths are there in $\dfrac{5}{6}$?

   (A) $\dfrac{5}{24}$

   (B) $\dfrac{7}{12}$

   (C) $1\dfrac{1}{2}$

   (D) 2

   (E) $3\dfrac{1}{3}$

STOP   END OF SECTION 2. IF YOU HAVE ANY TIME LEFT, GO OVER YOUR WORK IN THIS
SECTION ONLY. DO NOT WORK IN ANY OTHER SECTION OF THE TEST.

Section 3: Reading Comprehension

40 Questions • 40 Minutes

Directions: Read each passage carefully. Then decide which of the possible responses is the best answer to each question. Mark the appropriate space on your answer sheet.

As recently as the 1860s, most people believed that the earth, and humanity with it, was created a mere 6,000 to 7,000 years ago. For centuries, beauti-
(5) fully worked flints were regarded as the work of elves, a notion once far more plausible than the idea that humans roamed the world's wilder-nesses in small bands long before
(10) the days of the Greek and Roman Empires. Even when these stones were accepted as man-made tools, they were attributed to the Romans or Early Britons.
(15)   Today, we think in wider terms, but the older ideas about humanity's beginnings faded slowly. During the late eighteenth and early nineteenth centuries, excavators, mainly enthu-
(20) siastic amateurs, began to associate fossil remains of men and extinct animals with the stone tools. Still, most geologists continued to think in Biblical terms, maintaining that these
(25) associations were merely coincidental. They believed the Flood had mixed the bones of ancient animals with the tools and remains of recent humans. These theories finally crumbled as
(30) archaeologists began to find bones and tools together in unflooded, undis-turbed deposits, including a number of important sites on the banks of the Sommes River. British investigators
(35) came to check the French deposits, were convinced that the bones and tools had not collected as a result of flooding, and announced their conclu-sions in 1859. This was the same year
(40) that Darwin published *On the Origin of Species*, the date that marks the beginning of modern research into human evolution.

1. All of the following types of archaeo-logical evidence were mentioned EXCEPT
   (A) carbon dating.
   (B) fossils.
   (C) extinct animal remains.
   (D) man-made objects.
   (E) flint.

2. The turning point in scientific theories about the age of humanity's existence on earth was
   (A) the discovery in France of the remains of extinct animals and humans together in an unflooded area.
   (B) the publication of Darwin's *On the Origin of Species*.
   (C) new theological research of the Bible.
   (D) new theories about the Flood and its effects on humanity.
   (E) evidence left by the Greeks, Romans, and early Britons.

3. In the early nineteenth century
   (A) elves made flints in caves.
   (B) small bands of Romans roamed the earth.
   (C) geologists dated humanity's early existence to 1859.
   (D) stones were accepted as ancient tools and artifacts of 20,000-year-old man.
   (E) most people believed that humanity's existence was 6,000 to 7,000 years old.

Next morning, I saw for the first time an animal that is rarely encountered face to face. It was a wolverine. Though relatively small, rarely
(5) weighing more than 40 pounds, he is, above all animals, the one most hated by the Indians and trappers. He is a fine tree climber and a relentless destroyer. Deer, reindeer, and even
(10) moose succumb to his attacks. We sat on a rock and watched him come, a bobbing rascal in blackish-brown. Because the male wolverine occupies a very large hunting area and fights
(15) to the death any male that intrudes on his domain, wolverines are always scarce, and in order to avoid extinction need all the protection that humans can give. As a trapper, Henry wanted
(20) me to shoot him, but I refused, for this is the most fascinating and little known of all our wonderful predators. His hunchback gait was awkward and ungainly, lopsided yet tireless.

4. Wolverines are very scarce because
   (A) they suffer in the survival of the fittest.
   (B) they are afraid of all humankind.
   (C) they are seldom protected by man.
   (D) trappers take their toll of them.
   (E) their food supply is limited.

5. The author of this selection is most probably a(n)
   (A) conscious naturalist.
   (B) experienced hunter.
   (C) inexperienced trapper.
   (D) young Indian.
   (E) farmer.

6. The word *succumb* as used in the fifth sentence means
   (A) outmaneuver.
   (B) surrender.
   (C) overcome.
   (D) invite.
   (E) repel.

When Jason, the son of the dethroned king of Solcus, was a little boy, he was sent away from his parents and placed under the queerest schoolmaster that (5) ever you heard of. This learned person was one of the people, or *quadrupeds*, called Centaurs. He lived in a cavern and had the body and legs of a white horse, with the head and shoulders (10) of a man. His name was Chiron; and, in spite of his odd appearance, he was a very excellent teacher and had several scholars who afterward did him credit by making great figures (15) in the world. The famous Hercules was one, and so was Achilles, and Philoctetes, likewise, and Aesculapius, who acquired immense repute as a doctor. The good Chiron taught his (20) pupils how to play upon the harp and how to cure diseases and how to use the sword and shield, together with various other branches of education in which the lads of those days used (25) to be instructed, instead of writing and arithmetic.

—from *The Golden Fleece* by Nathaniel Hawthorne

7. The main purpose of this passage is to
   (A) describe Jason.
   (B) describe Chiron.
   (C) describe Jason's education.
   (D) explain Jason's family relationships.
   (E) name the scholars taught by Chiron.

8. The word *quadruped* probably means a(n)
   (A) creature with four feet.
   (B) creature with two feet.
   (C) strange schoolmaster.
   (D) educated person.
   (E) scholar.

9. Chiron
   (A) taught writing and arithmetic to his pupils.
   (B) acquired a reputation as a doctor.
   (C) instructed the Centaurs.
   (D) was the son of Solcus.
   (E) had the body and legs of a horse and the head and shoulders of a man.

practice test

The kangaroo is found nowhere in the world but in Australasia. Ages ago, when that part of our earth was cut off from the Asian mainland, this
(5) fantastic animal from nature's long-ago was also isolated. There are about two dozen species distributed through Australia, southward to Tasmania and northward to New Guinea and
(10) neighboring islands. Some are no bigger than rabbits; some can climb trees. They are known by a variety of picturesque names: wallabies, wallaroos, potoroos, boongaries, and
(15) paddymelons. But the kangaroo—the one that is Australia's national symbol—is the great gray kangaroo of the plains, admiringly known throughout the island continent as
(20) the Old Man, and also as Boomer, Forester, and Man of the Woods. His smaller mate, in Australian talk, is called a flyer. Their baby is known as Joey.
(25)   A full-grown kangaroo stands taller than a man, and commonly weighs 200 pounds. Even when he sits in his favorite position, reposing on his haunches and tilting back on
(30) the propping support of his "third leg"—his tail—his head is five feet or more above the ground. His huge hind legs, with steel-spring power, can send him sailing over a ten-foot
(35) fence with ease, or in a fight can beat off a dozen dogs. A twitch of his tail can break someone's leg like a match stick.
  Kangaroos provide an endless sup-
(40) ply of tall tales to which wide-eyed visitors are treated in the land Down Under. The beauty of the tall tales about the kangaroo is that they can be almost as tall as you please and
(45) still be close to fact.

10. Kangaroos are found only
   (A) in Australia.
   (B) in Australasia.
   (C) on the Asian mainland.
   (D) in Tasmania.
   (E) on New Guinea.

11. A female kangaroo is called
   (A) a wallaby.
   (B) a potoroo.
   (C) a Joey.
   (D) a flyer.
   (E) the Old Man.

12. The amazing jumping power of the kangaroo is chiefly due to the
   (A) power of the hind legs.
   (B) support of the tail.
   (C) kangaroo's size.
   (D) kangaroo's weight.
   (E) kangaroo's tilted sitting position.

13. Which statement is true according to the passage?
   (A) The name "Old Man" shows the people's dislike of kangaroos.
   (B) Visitors to Australia hear very little about kangaroos.
   (C) A kangaroo's tail is a powerful weapon.
   (D) The most widely known species of kangaroo is no larger than a rabbit.
   (E) Kangaroos have three legs.

14. The author believes that the stories told about kangaroos are generally
   (A) harmful.
   (B) true.
   (C) suspicious.
   (D) beautiful.
   (E) ancient.

What is a cord of wood? Some people say the cord is the most elastic unit of measure ever devised by the mind of humans. A "standard" cord is a pile (5) of stacked wood 4 × 4 × 8 feet; that's 128 cubic feet. How much of this is wood? That depends on what kind of wood, the size and straightness of the sticks, and who does the pil- (10) ing. Small crooked sticks, cut from hardwood limbs and piled by one of those cordwood artists who know how to make air spaces, may contain less than 30 cubic feet of solid wood per (15) cord. Smooth, round wood such as birch or spruce, in sizes eight inches and better, will average 100 cubic feet or more per cord. That's with the bark on. Peeled wood will make (20) 10 to 12 percent more cubic volume in the same sized stack.

The heating value of wood varies enormously with the kind of tree. Black locust, white oak, hickory, (25) black birch, and ironwood are the best. A cord of any of these woods, when seasoned, is worth approximately a ton of coal. Beech, yellow birch, sugar maple, ash, and red (30) oak are next. White birch, cherry, soft maple, sycamore, and elm are comparatively poor fuel woods, with basswood, butternut, poplar, and the softwoods at the bottom of the (35) scale.

15. The title that best expresses the main idea of this selection is
    (A) "Fuels."
    (B) "The Value of a Cord of Wood."
    (C) "Kinds of Trees."
    (D) "Standard Measures."
    (E) "Modern Heating."

16. A standard cord of wood
    (A) always contains 128 cubic feet of wood.
    (B) will average 100 cubic feet of wood.
    (C) contains less than 30 cubic feet of solid wood.

    (D) is stacked wood in a pile 4 × 4 × 8 feet.
    (E) is measured by weight of the wood per foot.

17. Removal of the bark before stacking
    (A) increases the cubic volume of wood in a cord.
    (B) makes the stacking easier.
    (C) allows more air spaces in a cord of wood.
    (D) prevents seasoning of wood.
    (E) decreases the measurements of the wood.

18. The amount of heat supplied by wood depends upon the
    (A) person who has piled the wood.
    (B) type of tree from which the wood came.
    (C) way the wood was cut.
    (D) straightness of the sticks.
    (E) amount of bark left on the wood.

19. The most valuable fuel woods come from
    (A) all kinds of birches and oaks.
    (B) any kind of wood that is well-seasoned.
    (C) home-grown beech, maple, cherry, and elm trees.
    (D) hickory, ironwood, black birch, black locust, and white oak.
    (E) sycamore, ash, butternut, and poplar that have been sprayed.

Eight of the city's twelve workers in Venetian glass recently finished one of the most unusual murals ever made for a New York skyscraper. It
(5) is an abstract, the creation of Hans Hofmann, a 77-year-old German-born painter.

The mural covers 1,200 square feet of the outer wall of the elevator shaft
(10) in the William Kaufman Building at 711 Third Avenue. More than a half-million tiles in close to 500 shades of color have gone into it. Blue, red, and yellow are the chief colors. Each tile
(15) was made in Venice and is somewhat less than postage-stamp size. Each is beaten into a special everlasting concrete with a kind of flat wooden hand tool used for nothing else.
(20) Mr. Hofmann did the original color sketch about one-sixth of the final size. This was photographed, and from the negative an enlargement was hand-colored by the artist,
(25) cut into sections, and sent in that form to the Vincent Foscato plant in Long Island City, which specializes in Venetian glass tile, or mosaic. There the Venetian specialists, whose
(30) trade has been handed down through families through the centuries, set each mosaic into place on the cartoon section, with painstaking fidelity to Mr. Hofmann's color rendering.
(35) Although Mr. Foscato's plant keeps 1,400 shades of the glass mosaic, it had to have twelve additional shades specially made in Venice to match the sketch coloring for perfect blending.
(40) When all the sections had been filled and approved, they were carried by truck to the building lobby, the walls were covered with a special cement, and the workers carefully beat each
(45) bit into place.

20. The best title for this selection would be
(A) "Picture by German Artist to Hang in New York."
(B) "New Mosaic Designed by Vincent Foscato."
(C) "Unusual Photograph Decorates New York Building."
(D) "Venetian-Glass Mural Installed in Skyscraper."
(E) "The William Kaufman Building."

21. The original design was
(A) painted on the wall of the Kaufman building.
(B) a fraction of the size of the finished mural.
(C) imported from Venice.
(D) larger than the finished mural.
(E) projected on a large sheet of paper.

22. Mr. Hofmann
(A) learned from his father how to do mosaic work.
(B) is a native of New York.
(C) is a painter.
(D) lives in Long Island City.
(E) is a Venetian-glass specialist.

23. In making the mural
(A) the shades of tile that the Foscato plant had in stock were not adequate.
(B) 1,412 shades were needed.
(C) half a million colors were used.
(D) over 500 shades of color were used.
(E) 1,400 specialists were consulted.

24. Mr. Hofmann
    (A) took a color photograph of his painting.
    (B) used only the most unusual shades of red, blue, and green.
    (C) had no further connection with the work after making the original sketch.
    (D) died shortly before the mural was completed.
    (E) colored the enlarged reproduction of the original.

25. Of the tiles used
    (A) some were made of special colors by Mr. Foscato.
    (B) all were made by the workers who put the mural in place.
    (C) all were made in Italy.
    (D) all were made in New York.
    (E) many were made by a wooden hand tool.

26. The mosaic was assembled by
    (A) Hans Hofmann.
    (B) an artist specializing in Venetian glass.
    (C) Vincent Foscato of Long Island.
    (D) workers in the Foscato plant.
    (E) Venetian workers.

The history of modern pollution problems shows that most have resulted from negligence and ignorance. We have an appalling tendency to (5) interfere with nature before all of the possible consequences of our actions have been studied in-depth. We produce and distribute radioactive substances, *synthetic* chemicals, and (10) many other potent compounds before fully comprehending their effects on living organisms. Our education is dangerously incomplete.

It is often argued that the purpose (15) of science is to move into unknown territory, to explore, and to discover. It can be said that similar risks have been taken before, and that these risks are necessary to technological (20) progress.

These arguments overlook an important element. In the past, risks taken in the name of scientific progress were restricted to a small (25) place and a brief period of time. The effects of the processes we now strive to master are neither localized nor brief. Air pollution covers vast urban areas. Ocean pollutants have (30) been discovered in nearly every part of the world. Synthetic chemicals spread over huge stretches of forest and farmland may remain in the soil for decades. Radioactive pollutants (35) will be found in the biosphere for generations. The size and persistence of these problems have grown with the expanding power of modern science.

(40) One might also argue that the hazards of modern pollutants are small compared to the dangers associated with other human activity. No estimate of the actual harm done (45) by smog, fallout, or chemical residues can obscure the reality that the risks are being taken before being fully understood.

The importance of these issues (50) lies in the failure of science to predict and control human intervention into natural processes. The true measure of the danger is represented by the hazards we will encounter if we enter (55) the new age of technology without first evaluating our responsibility to the environment.

27. According to the author, the major cause of pollution is the result of

    (A) designing synthetic chemicals to kill living organisms.

    (B) a lack of understanding of the history of technology.

    (C) scientists who are too willing to move into unknown territory.

    (D) changing our environment before understanding the effects of these changes.

    (E) not passing enough laws.

28. The author believes that the risks taken by modern science are greater than those taken by earlier scientific efforts because

    (A) the effects may be felt by more people for a longer period of time.

    (B) science is progressing faster than ever before.

    (C) technology has produced more dangerous chemicals.

    (D) the materials used are more dangerous to scientists.

    (E) the problems are greater.

29. The author apparently believes that the problem of finding solutions to pollution depends on

    (A) the removal of present hazards to the environment.

    (B) the removal of all potential pollutants from their present uses.

    (C) overcoming technical difficulties.

    (D) the willingness of scientists to understand possible dangers before using new products in the environment.

    (E) a new age of science that will repair the faults of our present technology.

30. The author seems to feel that the attitude of scientists toward pollution has been

    (A) naïve.

    (B) concerned.

    (C) confused.

    (D) ignorant.

    (E) nonchalant.

31. The word *synthetic* means

    (A) new.

    (B) unsafe.

    (C) polluting.

    (D) man-made.

    (E) progressive.

A third of our lives is spent in the mysterious state of sleep. Throughout our history, we have attempted to understand this remarkable ex-
(5) perience. Many centuries ago, for example, sleep was regarded as a type of anemia of the brain. Alemaeon, a Greek scientist, believed that blood retreated into the veins, and the
(10) partially starved brain went to sleep. Plato supported the idea that the soul left the body during sleep, wandered the world, and woke up the body when it returned.

(15) Recently, more scientific explanations of sleep have been proposed. According to one theory, the brain is put to sleep by a chemical agent that accumulates in the body when it is
(20) awake. Another theory is that weary branches of certain nerve cells break connections with neighboring cells. The flow of impulses required for staying awake is then disrupted. These
(25) more recent theories have had to be subjected to laboratory research.

Why do we sleep? Why do we dream? Modern sleep research is said to have begun in the 1950s, when Eu-
(30) gene Aserinsky, a graduate student at the University of Chicago, and Nathaniel Kleitman, his professor, observed periods of rapid eye movements (REMs) in sleeping subjects.
(35) When awakened during these REM periods, subjects almost always remembered dreaming. On the other hand, when awakened during non-REM phases of sleep, the subjects
(40) rarely could recall their dreams.

Guided by REMs, it became possible for investigators to "spot" dreaming from outside and then awaken the sleepers to collect dream stories. They
(45) could also alter the dreamers' experiences with noises, drugs, or other *stimuli* before or during sleep.

Since the mid-1950s, researchers have been drawn into sleep labora-
(50) tories. There, bedrooms adjoin other rooms that contain recorders known as electroencephalograph (EEG) machines.

The EEG amplifies signals from
(55) sensors on the face, head, and other parts of the body, which together yield tracings of respiration, pulse, muscle tension, and changes of electrical potential in the brain that are
(60) sometimes called brain waves. These recordings supply clues to the changes of the sleeping person's activities.

32. The main purpose of this passage is to
(A) describe early beliefs about sleep.
(B) compare modern scientific theories to early ideas about sleep.
(C) point out the importance of REMs in human sleep.
(D) describe modern research techniques.
(E) give a short history of human's interest in sleep.

33. This passage implies that the importance of the research of Aserinsky and Kleitman was mainly in the
(A) reports they published.
(B) problems they attacked.
(C) information they observed and recorded.
(D) understandings they uncovered.
(E) conclusions they drew for treatment of sleep disorders.

34. All of the following were mentioned as possible causes of sleep EXCEPT

(A) exhausted nerve endings.

(B) a build-up of certain body chemicals.

(C) recurrent periods of rapid eye movement.

(D) the absence of the conscious spirit.

(E) the departure of the soul from the body.

35. In paragraph 4, the word *stimuli* means

(A) substances that make a person more alert.

(B) drugs.

(C) sleep inducing.

(D) comatose.

(E) things that cause the body to react in a certain way.

As he threw his head back in the chair, his glance happened to rest upon a bell, a disused bell, that hung in the room and communicated, for
(5) some purpose now forgotten, with a chamber in the highest story of the building. It was with great astonishment, and with a strange *inexplicable* dread, that, as he looked, he
(10) saw this bell begin to swing. Soon it rang out loudly, and so did every bell in the house.

This was succeeded by a clanking noise, deep down below as if some
(15) person were dragging a heavy chain over the casks in the wine merchant's cellar. Then he heard the noise much louder on the floors below; then coming up the stairs; then coming
(20) straight toward his door.

It came in through the heavy door, and a *specter* passed into the room before his eyes. And upon its coming in, the dying flame leaped
(25) up, as though it cried, "I know him! Marley's ghost!"

—from *A Christmas Carol* by Charles Dickens

36. The word *inexplicable* means

(A) explaining in simple terms.

(B) not able to be taken out of.

(C) without an expressed reason.

(D) eerie.

(E) incapable.

37. The bell that began ringing

(A) was large and heavy.

(B) did so by itself.

(C) could be rung from another room.

(D) was attached to every bell in the house.

(E) rested first on his glance.

38. The man who was listening to the bell
    (A) dragged a chain across the wine casks.
    (B) sat perfectly still.
    (C) was apparently very frightened.
    (D) was Marley's ghost.
    (E) was quite curious.

39. The word *specter* probably means
    (A) a long-handled sword.
    (B) a bright light.
    (C) a hazy, recognizable vision.
    (D) strange noises.
    (E) clanking chains.

40. The man in the story
    (A) first heard noises in his room.
    (B) is probably a wine merchant.
    (C) had been asleep.
    (D) recognized Marley's ghost.
    (E) set the room on fire.

STOP END OF SECTION 3. IF YOU HAVE ANY TIME LEFT, GO OVER YOUR WORK IN THIS SECTION ONLY. DO NOT WORK IN ANY OTHER SECTION OF THE TEST.

Section 4: Quantitative (Math)

25 Questions • 30 Minutes

Directions: Each question below is followed by five possible answers. Select the one that is best, and mark the appropriate letter on your answer sheet.

1. In 2 hours, the minute hand of a clock rotates through an angle of

    (A) 60°

    (B) 90°

    (C) 180°

    (D) 360°

    (E) 720°

2. Which of the following fractions is less than one third?

    (A) $\dfrac{22}{63}$

    (B) $\dfrac{4}{11}$

    (C) $\dfrac{15}{46}$

    (D) $\dfrac{33}{98}$

    (E) $\dfrac{102}{303}$

3.

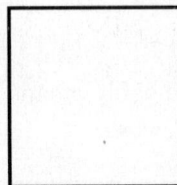

The length of each side of the square above is $\dfrac{2x}{3} + 1$. The perimeter of the square is

(A) $\dfrac{8x}{3} + 4$

(B) $\dfrac{8x+4}{3}$

(C) $\dfrac{2x}{3} + 4$

(D) $\dfrac{2x}{3} + 16$

(E) $\dfrac{4x}{3} + 2$

4.

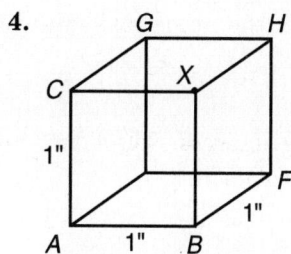

The diagram shows a cube.

The distance from A to X is

(A) 2 inches

(B) $\sqrt{3}$ inches

(C) $\sqrt{2}$ inches

(D) 1 inch

(E) $\frac{1}{\sqrt{2}}$ inches

5. A motorist travels 120 miles to his destination at an average speed of 60 miles per hour and returns to the starting point at an average speed of 40 miles per hour. His average speed for the entire trip is

(A) 53 miles per hour.

(B) 52 miles per hour.

(C) 50 miles per hour.

(D) 48 miles per hour.

(E) 45 miles per hour.

6. A snapshot measures $2\frac{1}{2}$ inches by $1\frac{7}{8}$ inches. It is to be enlarged so that the longer dimension will be 4 inches. The length of the enlarged shorter dimension will be

(A) $2\frac{1}{2}$ inches.

(B) $2\frac{5}{8}$ inches.

(C) 3 inches.

(D) $3\frac{3}{8}$ inches.

(E) $3\frac{5}{8}$ inches.

7. From a piece of tin in the shape of a square 6 inches on a side, the largest possible circle is cut out. Of the following, the ratio of the area of the circle to the area of the original square is closest in value to

(A) $\frac{4}{5}$

(B) $\frac{2}{3}$

(C) $\frac{3}{5}$

(D) $\frac{7}{9}$

(E) $\frac{3}{4}$

8. If the outer diameter of a metal pipe is 2.84 inches and the inner diameter is 1.94 inches, the thickness of the metal is

(A) .45 in.

(B) .90 in.

(C) 1.42 in.

(D) 1.94 in.

(E) 2.39 in.

9. A sportswriter claims that her football predictions are accurate 60% of the time. During football season, a fan kept records and found that the writer was inaccurate for a total of 16 games, although she did maintain her 60% accuracy. For how many games was the sportswriter accurate?

(A) 5

(B) 15

(C) 24

(D) 40

(E) 60

10. In a certain boys' camp, 30% of the boys are from New York State and 20% of these are from New York City. What percent of the boys in the camp are from New York City?

(A) 60%

(B) 50%

(C) 33%

(D) 10%

(E) 6%

11.

A unit block for construction is $1 \times 2 \times 3$ inches. What is the number of whole blocks required to cover an area 1 foot long by $1\frac{1}{4}$ feet wide with *one layer* of blocks?

(A) 30 blocks

(B) 60 blocks

(C) 72 blocks

(D) 90 blocks

(E) 180 blocks

12. If the number of square inches in the area of a circle is equal to the number of inches in its circumference, the diameter of the circle is

(A) 4 inches.

(B) 2 inches.

(C) 1 inch.

(D) π inches.

(E) 2π inches.

13. The least common multiple of 20, 24, and 32 is

(A) 240

(B) 480

(C) 960

(D) 1,920

(E) 15,360

14. If $9x + 5 = 23$, the numerical value of $18x + 5$ is

(A) 46

(B) 41

(C) 38

(D) 36

(E) 32

15. When the fractions $\frac{2}{3}$, $\frac{5}{7}$, $\frac{8}{11}$, and $\frac{9}{13}$ are arranged in ascending order of size, the result is

(A) $\frac{8}{11}, \frac{5}{7}, \frac{9}{13}, \frac{2}{3}$

(B) $\frac{5}{7}, \frac{8}{11}, \frac{2}{3}, \frac{9}{13}$

(C) $\frac{2}{3}, \frac{8}{11}, \frac{5}{7}, \frac{9}{13}$

(D) $\frac{2}{3}, \frac{9}{13}, \frac{5}{7}, \frac{8}{11}$

(E) $\frac{9}{13}, \frac{2}{3}, \frac{8}{11}, \frac{5}{7}$

16. If a cubic inch of a metal weighs 2 pounds, a cubic foot of the same metal weighs

(A) 8 pounds.

(B) 24 pounds.

(C) 96 pounds.

(D) 288 pounds.

(E) 3,456 pounds.

17. A micromillimeter is defined as one millionth of a millimeter. A length of 17 micromillimeters may be represented as

(A) .00017 mm.

(B) .000017 mm.

(C) .0000017 mm.

(D) .00000017 mm.

(E) .000000017 mm.

18. To find the radius of a circle whose circumference is 60 inches,

    (A) multiply 60 by π.

    (B) divide 60 by 2π.

    (C) divide 30 by 2π.

    (D) divide 60 by π and extract the square root of the result.

    (E) multiply 60 by $\dfrac{\pi}{2}$.

19. A carpenter needs four boards, each 2 feet 9 inches long. If wood is sold only by the foot, how many feet must he buy?

    (A) 9

    (B) 10

    (C) 11

    (D) 12

    (E) 13

20. The approximate distance, S, in feet that an object falls in t seconds when dropped from a height can be found by using the formula $S = 16t^2$. In 8 seconds the object will fall

    (A) 256 feet.

    (B) 1,024 feet.

    (C) 1,084 feet.

    (D) 2,048 feet.

    (E) 15,384 feet.

QUESTIONS 21 AND 22 REFER TO THE FOLLOWING GRAPH.

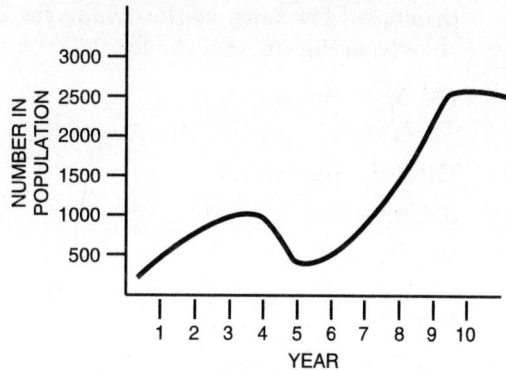

21. During which years did the population increase at the fastest rate?

    (A) Years 5–7

    (B) Years 1–3

    (C) Years 4–5

    (D) Years 7–9

    (E) Years 9–10

22. During which year did the size of the population decrease the most?

    (A) Years 4–5

    (B) Years 3–4

    (C) Years 9–10

    (D) Years 1–2

    (E) Years 4–6

23. The number of telephones in Adelaide, Australia is 48,000. If this represents 12.8 telephones per 100 people, the population of Adelaide to the nearest thousand is

    (A) 128,000

    (B) 375,000

    (C) 378,000

    (D) 556,000

    (E) 575,000

24. One person can load a truck in 25 minutes, a second can load it in 50 minutes, and a third can load it in 10 minutes. How long would it take the three together to load the truck?

(A) $5\frac{3}{11}$ minutes

(B) $6\frac{1}{4}$ minutes

(C) $8\frac{1}{3}$ minutes

(D) 10 minutes

(E) $28\frac{1}{3}$ minutes

25. Event A occurs every 4 minutes, event B every 6 minutes, and event C every 15 minutes. If they occur simultaneously at noon, when is the next time all three events will occur together again?

(A) 1 p.m.

(B) 1:30 p.m.

(C) 3 p.m.

(D) 6 p.m.

(E) 12 a.m.

STOP END OF SECTION 4. IF YOU HAVE ANY TIME LEFT, GO OVER YOUR WORK IN THIS SECTION ONLY. DO NOT WORK IN ANY OTHER SECTION OF THE TEST.

ANSWER KEY AND EXPLANATIONS

Part I: Writing Sample

Example of a well-written essay.

The proposal to raise the minimum licensing age from 16 to 18 should be rejected for a number of reasons. There are no solid statistics proving that youths cause the accidents that they are involved in, so the 16- and 17-year-old age group should not be penalized for those accidents. Also, for many young people, use of a car is an absolute necessity.

Legislators should ask themselves why 16- to 18-year-old drivers tend to be involved in accidents. I think that the main cause of these accidents is lack of experience. If a study were made, I suspect that it would show that new drivers of any age tend to have accidents. Raising the licensing age would only raise the age of drivers involved in accidents. A better cure might be driving education programs that stress judgment on the road and a requirement for a longer period of driving under supervision before licensing.

Raising the driving age would create a real financial hardship for some teenagers and their families. Many working parents count on their high schoolers to transport younger children in the afternoon and to run errands. Other teens have part-time jobs in locations that can be reached only by car. Attempting to solve the accident problem by creating financial problems does not seem logical.

Raising the licensing age could actually lead to a higher accident rate. Teenagers who have to drive would drive anyway, but without benefit of driver education or the testing that is required for getting that license. Untrained, untested teenage drivers would be a menace on the roads. The 16-year minimum should be retained for the safety of all.

Part II: Multiple-Choice

Section 1: Verbal

1. E	13. A	25. C	37. E	49. A
2. B	14. C	26. E	38. D	50. E
3. A	15. B	27. C	39. A	51. E
4. A	16. E	28. A	40. A	52. E
5. C	17. C	29. D	41. D	53. A
6. B	18. A	30. E	42. A	54. C
7. D	19. B	31. C	43. B	55. D
8. C	20. D	32. A	44. B	56. A
9. A	21. E	33. C	45. E	57. A
10. C	22. C	34. B	46. E	58. E
11. E	23. B	35. B	47. E	59. A
12. C	24. A	36. C	48. B	60. A

1. **The correct answer is (E).** To DETER is to *discourage* a person or group from doing something. Fear of retaliation may deter our enemies from attacking.

2. **The correct answer is (B).** HOSTILE means *antagonistic* or *unfriendly*. It is the nature of cats to be hostile to dogs.

3. **The correct answer is (A).** To UTILIZE is to *make practical use of*. You can utilize the microwave for quick defrosting.

4. **The correct answer is (A).** To ABDICATE is to *give up formally* or to *resign*. King Edward abdicated from the English throne to marry a divorced woman.

5. **The correct answer is (C).** PROMINENT means *sticking out*, *noticeable*, or *outstanding*. Jimmy Durante had a prominent nose.

6. **The correct answer is (B).** A BOUNDARY is a *border*. Mexico shares a boundary with the state of Texas.

7. **The correct answer is (D).** ILLITERATE means *unable to read*. One who is literate is educated and is able to read. The prefix *il-* creates the negative. Many of the homeless are unemployable because they are illiterate.

8. **The correct answer is (C).** An ORATOR is *one who speaks*. (Can you see the root *oral*?) The keynote speaker at the convention was a superb orator.

9. **The correct answer is (A).** To CORROBORATE is to *strengthen*, to *support*, or to *confirm*. The bloody knife served to corroborate the eyewitness's testimony.

10. **The correct answer is (C).** To RATIFY is to *give official sanction to* or to *approve*. If three more states

ratify the proposed amendment, it will become a part of our Constitution.

11. **The correct answer is (E).** PERILOUS means *risky* or *dangerous*. Construction of skyscrapers is perilous work.

12. **The correct answer is (C).** STATIONARY means *not moving* or *not movable*. It is the adjective form of the noun *station*. Choice (A) refers to the homophone *stationery*. Unlike Easter, Christmas is a stationary holiday; it always occurs on the same date.

13. **The correct answer is (A).** To TRANSCRIBE is to *write out in full* or to *make a recording*. The court stenographer transcribed the full proceedings of the trial.

14. **The correct answer is (C).** PROFICIENT means *highly skilled*, *competent*, or *adept*. The concert pianist is proficient at the art.

15. **The correct answer is (B).** To DECEIVE is to *make a person believe what is not true*. The purpose of a lie is to deceive.

16. **The correct answer is (E).** AGILE means *deft*, *active*, and *lively*. Prize-winning gymnasts are always agile.

17. **The correct answer is (C).** The DURATION is the *time that a thing continues or lasts*. The duration of a school semester is a four-month term.

18. **The correct answer is (A).** AMBIGUOUS means *having two meanings* or *being vague and uncertain*. The prefix *ambi-* means *both* and implies that both possible interpretations might be correct and therefore neither is clear. Her ambiguous answer left us uncertain as to whether she meant "Yes" or "No."

19. **The correct answer is (B).** A PRE-ROGATIVE is a *right*, *privilege*, or

special advantage. The aged and the disabled have the prerogative of sitting at the front of the bus.

20. **The correct answer is (D).** That which is INTRIGUING excites *interest* and *curiosity* and is *fascinating*. His interpretation of the event presents an intriguing new theory.

21. **The correct answer is (E).** CLANDESTINE means *surreptitious* or *secret*, usually for some illicit reason or purpose. The married man had clandestine meetings with his mistress.

22. **The correct answer is (C).** BOUNTEOUS means *plentiful, generous*, and *abundant*. At the end of a favorable growing season, we had a bounteous harvest.

23. **The correct answer is (B).** To DIVERGE is to *move off in different directions* or to *become different*. Parallel lines do not diverge.

24. **The correct answer is (A).** BENIGN means *good-natured*, *kindly*, or *harmless*. When applied to a tumor, *benign* means harmless as opposed to *malignant*, which implies *life-threatening*. The Pope faced his audience with a benign smile.

25. **The correct answer is (C).** A CAUCUS is a *meeting of people with similar goals*, usually a group of people within a larger group. The Black Congressional caucus meets periodically to discuss minority issues.

26. **The correct answer is (E).** To DISSEMINATE is to *scatter widely*. It is important that we disseminate information about the transmission of AIDS.

27. **The correct answer is (C).** CHAGRIN is *embarrassment* or *humiliation*. The bettor was chagrined that the horse he had praised so loudly came in last.

28. **The correct answer is (A).** VALOR is *high value*, *courage*, or *bravery*. The soldiers defended the Alamo with valor.

29. **The correct answer is (D).** NONCHALANT means *without enthusiasm* or *indifferent*. The student was so nonchalant about her award that she did not even tell her parents.

30. **The correct answer is (E).** A LIAISON is a *linking up* or a *connection*. The liaison of allies from a number of countries led to defeat of the enemy forces.

31. **The correct answer is (C).** The relationship is not of precise synonyms, but it is close. Both *beg* and *borrow* have to do with *ask for* and *take*. Both *offer* and *lend* have to do with *give*. *Repay* also has to do with *give* but it implies a previous activity not implied in the relationship of *beg* and *borrow*.

32. **The correct answer is (A).** One who is *lazy* is *inert*. One who *resists*, *refuses*. The relationship is one of characteristics or even synonyms.

33. **The correct answer is (C).** A *circle* is the base of a *cylinder*; a *triangle* is the base of a *pyramid*. We have explained this as a part-to-whole relationship. The actual statement of the analogy is whole-to-part.

34. **The correct answer is (B).** This is a true part-to-whole analogy. A *crocodile* is part of a larger group, *reptiles*. A *kangaroo* is part of a larger group, *marsupials*.

35. **The correct answer is (B).** This is another part-to-whole relationship. A *quart* is roughly equivalent to a liter, and a *milliliter* is $\frac{1}{1,000}$ of a liter. A *yard* is roughly equivalent to a meter, and a *millimeter* is $\frac{1}{1,000}$ of a meter.

Choice (A) reverses the relationship. The other choices do not move from metric to American measures.

36. **The correct answer is (C).** These are true synonyms.

37. **The correct answer is (E).** These are true antonyms.

38. **The correct answer is (D).** In neither set are the terms true antonyms, but they clearly have opposite connotations. Choice (E) also offers opposite connotations, but the order of the terms is reversed.

39. **The correct answer is (A).** *Wild* is a characteristic of *wolf* as *domestic* is a characteristic of both *dog* and *cat*. You must narrow further to choose the best answer. *Dog* is the domestic counterpart of *wolf*, so *dog* creates the best analogy.

40. **The correct answer is (A).** This is a purpose relationship. A *hammer* is a tool used by a *carpenter*; an *awl* is a tool used by a *cobbler*. Choice (D) reverses the order of tool and its user.

41. **The correct answer is (D).** This is a part-to-part relationship. Both *subject* and *predicate* are parts of a sentence; both *senator* and *representative* are parts of the congress. (A) is an incorrect answer because a senator's relationship to congress is that of part-to-whole.

42. **The correct answer is (A).** This is an association relationship. *Pungent* is an adjective used to describe a degree of *odor*. *Intense* is an adjective used to describe a degree of *emotion*.

43. **The correct answer is (B).** The analogy is based on synonyms.

44. **The correct answer is (B).** All four terms are synonyms.

45. The correct answer is (E). The relationship is one of association or characteristic. *Exuberant* is an adjective used to describe *mood*; *adroit* is an adjective used to describe *movement*.

46. The correct answer is (E). *Opposition* leads to *defiance*; *challenge* leads to *exertion*. The actual statement of the analogy is effect and its cause.

47. The correct answer is (E). This is a true cause-and-effect relationship. *Food* promotes *nutrition*; *light* promotes *vision*. Light does not promote any of the other choices.

48. The correct answer is (B). The relationship is that of true antonyms. The false choices are synonyms or partial antonyms, making this a very difficult analogy question.

49. The correct answer is (A). This antonym relationship is easier to see at a glance.

50. The correct answer is (E). This may be either a part-to-whole relationship or an analogy of degree. Either a *comment* is part of a *speech* and a *note* is part of a *letter* or a *comment* is much shorter than a *speech* and a *note* is much shorter than a *letter*.

51. The correct answer is (E). Be careful. *Flammable* and *inflammable* are synonyms; both mean *easily inflamed*. *Disinterested* means *impartial*.

52. The correct answer is (E). This is a purpose relationship. A *tailor* follows a *pattern* to construct a piece of clothing; a *builder* follows a *blueprint* to construct a building.

53. The correct answer is (A). The relationship is sequential. *Impeachment* (accusation) comes before *dismissal*. *Arraignment* (accusation) comes before *indictment* (placement of charges).

54. The correct answer is (C). The relationship is of characteristic to animal. Choice (B) reverses the relationship.

55. The correct answer is (D). All choices except (A) involve the activity of a bodily organ, so you must think further. Both *exhalation* and *perspiration* involve giving off something from within the body.

56. The correct answer is (A). You *celebrate* a *birth*; you *grieve* over a *death*. The analogy states the effect and its cause.

57. The correct answer is (A). This is an analogy of degree. To *urge* is to *recommend strongly*; to *plead* is to *request strongly*. Choice (B) offers synonyms of equal degree; choice (C) reverses the order.

58. The correct answer is (E). This is a cause-and-effect relationship. When one *weeps*, one gives off *tears*; when one *breathes*, one gives off *carbon dioxide*.

59. The correct answer is (A). The relationship is hard to categorize but easy to spot. An *air pocket* makes a *plane* bounce; a *rut* has the same effect on a *vehicle*.

60. The correct answer is (A). This is a verb-to-noun relationship. *Arbitrate* is what one does to a *dispute*; *solve* is what must be done to a *mystery*.

Section 2: Quantitative (Math)

1. D	6. C	11. E	16. A	21. D
2. B	7. B	12. D	17. D	22. B
3. C	8. A	13. C	18. B	23. C
4. D	9. C	14. C	19. B	24. A
5. C	10. C	15. C	20. C	25. E

1. **The correct answer is (D).** Rename $1\frac{1}{2}$ as the decimal 1.5 and add.

$$\begin{array}{r} 1.5 \\ .750 \\ .1010 \\ \hline 2.351 \end{array}$$

2. **The correct answer is (B).** When dividing numbers having the same base, simply subtract the exponents.

$$\frac{2^{12}}{2^8} = 2^{12-8} = 2^4 = 16$$

3. **The correct answer is (C).**

$$\begin{array}{r} 8.08 \\ 62.3\overline{)503.384} \\ \underline{4984} \\ 4984 \\ \underline{4984} \\ 0 \end{array}$$

4. **The correct answer is (D).** Simplify the numerator of the fraction, and then divide.

$$\frac{1\dfrac{3}{4}-\dfrac{1}{8}}{\dfrac{1}{8}} = \frac{1\dfrac{6}{8}-\dfrac{1}{8}}{\dfrac{1}{8}}$$

$$= \frac{1\dfrac{5}{8}}{\dfrac{1}{8}} = 1\frac{5}{8}\cdot\frac{8}{1}$$

$$= \frac{13}{8}\cdot\frac{8}{1} = 13$$

5. **The correct answer is (C).**

$$\begin{array}{r} 1.970 \\ 1.02\overline{)2.010000} \\ \underline{102} \\ 990 \\ \underline{918} \\ 720 \\ \underline{714} \\ 60 \end{array}$$

6. **The correct answer is (C).** Begin working with the innermost parentheses and work your way out.

$$-3-[(2-1)-(3+4)]$$
$$=-3-[(1)-(7)]$$
$$=-3-[1-7]$$
$$=-3-[-6]$$
$$=-3+6$$
$$=3$$

7. **The correct answer is (B).** This is a good problem to do in your head. Mentally subtract 700 from 3,003 and get 2,303. Then look at the answers carefully and note that only choice (B) is close to your estimate.

$$3,003$$
$$-\ \ \ 699$$
$$2,304$$

8. **The correct answer is (A).** The problem states that $a = 5$ and $b = \frac{1}{5}$; $\frac{1}{5}$ is $\frac{1}{25}$ of 5. Therefore, the value of a expressed in terms of b is $25 \times \frac{1}{5} =$ 5, or $25b$.

9. **The correct answer is (C).** This is a good problem to do in your head. Note that 10% of 70 is 7. 140%, then, is 14×7, or 98.

10. **The correct answer is (C).** Borrow a gallon and add it to 2 quarts. Rewrite the problem. Remember that you borrowed.

4 gallons	6 quarts	1 pint
− 1 gallon	3 quarts	0 pints
3 gallons	3 quarts	1 pint

11. **The correct answer is (E).** By doubling the denominator of a fraction, we actually divide it by two. By halving one of the factors in the numerator, we also halve the value of the fraction. By

doing both, we have actually divided the original value by four. Plug in some values for x, y, and z, and try this.

12. **The correct answer is (D).** This is a good problem to estimate. Since 8% is slightly less than $\frac{1}{12}$, you can multiply 20 by 12 to approximate the answer. Note that 250 is close enough to your 240 estimate. To be precise:

$$20 \div .08 =$$

$$\begin{array}{r} 250. \\ .08\overline{)20.00} \\ \underline{16} \\ 40 \\ \underline{40} \\ 0 \end{array}$$

13. **The correct answer is (C).** 100 is 20 larger than 80. 20 is one fourth, or 25%, of 80. Therefore, 125% of 80 is equivalent to 100.

14. **The correct answer is (C).** Forty inches equals $3\frac{1}{3}$ feet. Since $\frac{3}{8}$ " on the drawing equals 1 foot at full scale,

$$3\frac{1}{3}\text{ feet} = 3\frac{1}{3} \cdot \frac{3}{8}$$
$$= \frac{10}{3} \cdot \frac{3}{8}$$
$$= \frac{10}{8}$$
$$= 1\frac{1}{4}"$$

15. **The correct answer is (C).** Bracket the multiplication and division first, and solve the problem.

$$\left(6 \div \frac{1}{3}\right) + \left(\frac{2}{3} \times 9\right)$$
$$= 18 + 6$$
$$= 24$$

16. **The correct answer is (A).** Since $x - 3 < 12$, x can be any number less than 15.

17. **The correct answer is (D).** Substitute the values into the expression.

$$\sqrt{9 + 3(2) + 1}$$
$$= \sqrt{9 + 6 + 1}$$
$$= \sqrt{16}$$
$$= 4$$

18. **The correct answer is (B).** To find the average, find the sum of the addends and divide that sum by the number of addends.

$$-10 + 6 + 0 + -3 + 22 = 15$$
$$15 \div 5 = 3$$

19. **The correct answer is (B).** By substituting +2 for the triangle, the denominator of the fraction becomes zero. A denominator of zero is undefined in mathematics.

20. **The correct answer is (C).** Simply move the decimal point one place to the left and insert a zero in the newly created decimal place.

$$.10101 \div 10 = .010101$$

21. **The correct answer is (D).** The formula for rate is rate = distance ÷ time. In this problem, rate = 10 miles ÷ 3 hours, or $3\frac{1}{3}$ miles per hour.

22. **The correct answer is (B).** 7 is one third of 21, and $\frac{2}{3}$ is one third of 2. As a proportion:

$$\frac{7}{21} = \frac{\frac{2}{3}}{x}$$

23. **The correct answer is (C).** The square root of 85 is between 9, whose square is 81, and 10, whose square is 100.

24. **The correct answer is (A).** $-6 + -2 + 0 + 8 = 0$

25. **The correct answer is (E).** Simply divide $\frac{5}{6}$ by $\frac{1}{4}$.

$$\frac{5}{6} \div \frac{1}{4} = \frac{5}{6} \cdot \frac{4}{1}$$
$$= \frac{20}{6} = 3\frac{1}{3}$$

Section 3: Reading Comprehension

1. A	9. E	17. A	25. C	33. C
2. A	10. B	18. B	26. D	34. C
3. E	11. D	19. D	27. D	35. E
4. A	12. A	20. D	28. A	36. C
5. A	13. C	21. B	29. D	37. B
6. B	14. B	22. C	30. E	38. C
7. B	15. B	23. A	31. D	39. C
8. A	16. D	24. E	32. E	40. D

1. **The correct answer is (A).** This is a detail question that you answer through a process of elimination. Choices (D) and (E) are mentioned in the first paragraph, whereas (B) and (C) may be found in the second sentence of the second paragraph.

2. **The correct answer is (A).** Careful reading will find this detail in lines 27–32.

3. **The correct answer is (E).** See the first sentence.

4. **The correct answer is (A).** You must infer this answer from the information given. Because "the male wolverine .. fights to the death any male that intrudes on his domain . . ." only the fittest, the best fighters, survive, and numbers are held down.

5. **The correct answer is (A).** The writer's total fascination with and expertise on the subject of the wolverine leads us to infer that he is a naturalist. The fact that he is carrying a gun in wild country does not necessarily imply that he is a hunter. Prudent naturalists may carry guns for self-defense in the wilderness.

6. **The correct answer is (B).** The wolverine is a destroyer, and even large animals succumb to his attacks.

The large animals *are overcome* by the wolverine, but the word *succumb* is an active verb; therefore, what the animals who are overcome do is *surrender*.

7. **The correct answer is (B).** This is a main-idea question. The paragraph describes Chiron.

8. **The correct answer is (A).** The paragraph states that Chiron had the legs of a horse; a horse has four legs. From basic etymology, you know that "quad" means "four" and that "ped" refers to feet.

9. **The correct answer is (E).** Read carefully. The physical description is the only choice supported by the paragraph. The last sentence specifically states that Chiron did *not* teach writing and arithmetic.

10. **The correct answer is (B).** See the first sentence.

11. **The correct answer is (D).** See the next-to-last sentence of the first paragraph.

12. **The correct answer is (A).** Lines 32–36 provide this information.

13. **The correct answer is (C).** You certainly can infer this from the last sentence of the second paragraph.

14. **The correct answer is (B).** This is the author's meaning in the last sentence, in which the author states that the tall tales are close to fact.

15. **The correct answer is (B).** This is a main-idea question, and you must choose the most inclusive title for the entire selection. The selection discusses the value of a cord of wood—the volume value in the first paragraph and the heating value in the second paragraph.

16. **The correct answer is (D).** This detail question is answered in the third sentence.

17. **The correct answer is (A).** See the last sentence of the first paragraph.

18. **The correct answer is (B).** See the first sentence of the second paragraph.

19. **The correct answer is (D).** See the second sentence of the second paragraph.

20. **The correct answer is (D).** The selection is all about the mural.

21. **The correct answer is (B).** The first sentence of the third paragraph gives this information.

22. **The correct answer is (C).** The second sentence tells us that Mr. Hofmann is a painter. All the other choices confuse other information.

23. **The correct answer is (A).** This is a difficult question requiring concentration on the meanings of statements. The selection tells us that the Foscato plant had 1,400 shades in stock yet had to send to Italy for 12 special shades, but it does not say that all 1,400 shades in stock were used.

24. **The correct answer is (E).** Find the answer to this question by means of elimination and inference. The passage tells us that Mr. Hofmann colored the enlarged reproduction of the original. None of the other choices can be supported by the text.

25. **The correct answer is (C).** The next-to-last sentence of the second paragraph states that each tile was made in Venice. Venice is in Italy.

26. **The correct answer is (D).** In the middle of the third paragraph we learn that the mosaic was assembled—each mosaic was set into place—by specialists in the Foscato plant.

27. **The correct answer is (D).** Read carefully the second sentence of the first paragraph.

28. **The correct answer is (A).** You can infer this answer from the third paragraph in which the author states that "The effects of the processes .. are neither localized nor brief."

29. **The correct answer is (D).** This answer can be inferred from the whole tone of the selection. None of the other choices can be supported by the selection.

30. **The correct answer is (E).** *Nonchalant* means *casually indifferent*. Negligence and ignorance on the part of scientists certainly implies nonchalance.

31. **The correct answer is (D).** *Synthetic* means *not natural* or *man-made*.

32. **The correct answer is (E).** The approach of the entire selection is historical. Each of the other choices focuses on one paragraph, one phase of this history.

33. **The correct answer is (C).** Aserinsky and Kleitman observed, recorded, and reported; they did not explain. Their observations opened lines for future research.

34. The correct answer is (C). Rapid eye movement is mentioned as a part of sleep, not as a cause.

35. The correct answer is (E). A stimulus is anything that produces some kind of reaction, physical or mental. *Stimuli* is the plural of this Latin word.

36. The correct answer is (C). Use word arithmetic. *In* = not; *able* = able to be; *explic* = explained; in other words, without an expressed reason.

37. The correct answer is (B). If a disused bell suddenly began to swing, it must have done so all by itself.

38. The correct answer is (C). Great astonishment and inexplicable dread certainly imply fright.

39. The correct answer is (C). You can get this definition from the last paragraph. A specter is a ghost.

40. The correct answer is (D). This is the only choice supported by the selection. The answer is in the last sentence. Choice (A) is incorrect because the man first saw the bell begin to move, and then he heard noises.

Section 4: Quantitative (Math)

1. E	6. C	11. A	16. E	21. D
2. C	7. D	12. A	17. B	22. A
3. A	8. A	13. B	18. B	23. B
4. C	9. C	14. B	19. C	24. B
5. D	10. E	15. D	20. B	25. A

1. The correct answer is (E). In one hour, the minute hand of a clock goes around in a complete circle. In two hours, it revolves through two circles. Because each circle consists of 360°, two revolutions equal 720°.

2. The correct answer is (C). A fraction is less than $\frac{1}{3}$ if three times the numerator is less than the denominator. Of the fractions listed, only $\frac{15}{46}$ has a numerator that is less than $\frac{1}{3}$ of the denominator.

3. The correct answer is (A). The figure is a square, so all four sides are equal in length. The perimeter is the sum of the lengths of the four sides.

Each side is $\frac{2x}{3} + 1$.

The sum, then, is $\left(\frac{2x}{3}+1\right) + \left(\frac{2x}{3}+1\right) + \left(\frac{2x}{3}+1\right) + \left(\frac{2x}{3}+1\right) = \frac{8x}{3} + 4.$

You could also multiply $\frac{2x}{3} + 1$ by 4 for the same result.

4. The correct answer is (C). The face of the cube is a square, 1" by 1". Use the Pythagorean Theorem to find the length of the diagonal of the square.

$$c^2 = a^2 + b^2$$
$$c^2 = 1^2 + 1^2$$
$$c^2 = 2$$
$$c = \sqrt{2}$$

5. **The correct answer is (D).** The average speed for the entire trip is the total distance (240 miles) divided by the total time (5 hours), which yields 48 mph.

6. **The correct answer is (C).** This is a proportion problem. Set up the proportion as follows:

$$\frac{2\frac{1}{2}}{4} = \frac{1\frac{7}{8}}{?}$$

Substitute x for ?: $\dfrac{2\frac{1}{2}}{4} = \dfrac{1\frac{7}{8}}{x}$

Cross-multiply: $\dfrac{2\frac{1}{2}}{4} \bowtie \dfrac{1\frac{7}{8}}{x}$

$$2\frac{1}{2}x = 4 \cdot 1\frac{7}{8}$$

Divide both sides by the coefficient of x and calculate:

$$\frac{5}{2}x = \frac{60}{8}$$

$$x = \frac{60}{8} \div \frac{5}{2}$$

$$x = \frac{60}{8} \times \frac{2}{5}$$

$$x = 3$$

7. **The correct answer is (D).** To find the ratio of the circle to the area of the square, first find the area of each. Note that the diameter of the circle equals the width of the square.

Area of the square = 6" × 6" = 36 sq. in.

Area of circle = $\pi 3^2 = 9\pi = 9 \cdot \dfrac{22}{7}$ =

$\dfrac{198}{7}$ = 28 sq. in., approximately.

Ratio of the area of the circle to the area of the square: $\dfrac{28}{36} = \dfrac{7}{9}$

8. **The correct answer is (A).** The difference is .90 inches, but the outside diameter consists of two thicknesses of metal (one on each side). Therefore, the thickness of the metal is .90 ÷ 2 = .45 inches.

9. **The correct answer is (C).** If 60% of the games were predicted accurately, 40% of the games were predicted inaccurately.

Let x = games played

$.40x = 16$

$x = 40$ games played

40 − 16 = 24 games won

Therefore, the sportswriter was accurate for 24 games.

10. **The correct answer is (E).** Thirty percent of the boys are from New York State, and 20% of them (.20 of them) are from New York City. Therefore, 6% (.20 × .30) of the boys in the camp are from New York City.

11. **The correct answer is (A).** An area 1 foot long by $1\frac{1}{4}$ feet wide is 12" × 15", or 180 square inches in area. Each block is 6 square inches in area. Therefore, the number of blocks needed is $\dfrac{180}{6}$ = 30 blocks. The height of each block is irrelevant to the solution of the problem.

12. **The correct answer is (A).** The area of a circle is equal to πr^2. The circumference of a circle is equal to πd. If the number of inches in each are equal, then $\pi d = \pi r^2$, or the diameter equals the square of the radius. The only value for which the diameter can equal the square of the radius is a diameter of 4".

13. **The correct answer is (B).** The LCM is found by rewriting each number in prime factorization and finding the product of each unique prime factor. 2^2 and 2^3 are not selected because each is a factor of 2^5.

    $20 = 2^2 \cdot 5$

    $24 = 2^3 \cdot 3$

    $32 = 2^5$

    LCM $= 5 \cdot 3 \cdot 2^5 = 480$

    Trial and error can also give you this answer.

14. **The correct answer is (B).** If $9x + 5 = 23$, then $9x = 18$, and $x = 2$. Therefore, $18x + 5$ equals $18(2) + 5 = 41$.

15. **The correct answer is (D).** Fractions are most easily compared by comparing cross-products. Start by comparing $\frac{2}{3}$ with $\frac{5}{7}$. The product of 3 and 5 is 15. The product of 7 and 2 is 14. Therefore, $\frac{5}{7}$ is larger than $\frac{2}{3}$.

    Continue this process with the other fractions to be compared.

    $\frac{5}{7} \diagtimes \frac{8}{11}$, note $\frac{8}{11} > \frac{5}{7}$ and also $\frac{8}{11} > \frac{2}{3}$

    $\frac{8}{11} \diagtimes \frac{9}{13}$, note $\frac{8}{11} > \frac{9}{13}$

    $\frac{2}{3} \diagtimes \frac{9}{13}$, note $\frac{9}{13} > \frac{2}{3}$ and also $\frac{9}{13} < \frac{5}{7}$

    Therefore, $\frac{2}{3} < \frac{9}{13} < \frac{5}{7} < \frac{8}{11}$.

16. **The correct answer is (E).** A cubic foot contains $12'' \times 12'' \times 12''$ or 1,728 cubic inches. If each cubic inch weighs two pounds, the substance weighs $2 \cdot 1,728$, or 3,456 pounds.

17. **The correct answer is (B).** 17 millionths in decimals is .000017. The number of places to the right of the decimal point is equal to the number of zeros in the whole number. 17,000,000 has six zeros.

18. **The correct answer is (B).** Because the circumference of a circle is equivalent to π times the diameter, the circumference is also equal to π times twice the radius. Divide the circumference by 2π.

19. **The correct answer is (C).** Four boards, each 2'9" long, total 11 feet. The carpenter must buy 11 feet of wood.

20. **The correct answer is (B).** Find the answer to this problem by substituting the values given into the formula.

    $S = 16t^2$

    $S = 16(8)^2 = 16(64) = 1,024$ feet

21. **The correct answer is (D).** The graph is steepest between years 7 and 9. The population was approximately 1,000 in year 7 and increased to over 2,500 by year 9.

22. **The correct answer is (A).** The size of the population was quite constant from year 3 to year 4 and decreased from year 4 to year 5 from almost 1,000 to 500. Notice that the population was the same in year 3 as in year 7.

23. **The correct answer is (B).** By knowing how many telephones are in Adelaide (48,000), and how many serve each group of 100 in the population (12.8), we can find how many groups of 100 are in the population.

    48,000 telephones ÷ 12.8 telephones per 100 of population = 3,750 groups of 100 in the population.

    $3,750 \times 100 = 375,000$ people

24. The correct answer is (B). The first person does $\frac{1}{25}$ of the job in 1 minute. The second person does $\frac{1}{50}$ of the job in 1 minute. The third person does $\frac{1}{10}$ of the job in 1 minute. Together: $\frac{1}{25}$ + $\frac{1}{50}$ + $\frac{1}{10}$ = $\frac{8}{50}$ or $\frac{4}{25}$ of the job in 1 minute = $\frac{25}{4}$ minutes for the entire job, or $6\frac{1}{4}$ minutes.

25. The correct answer is (A). To find the number of minutes that must pass before the events next occur simultaneously, calculate the least common multiple of 4, 6, and 15. The LCM is 60 minutes. If the events last occurred together at noon, the next occurrence will thus be 60 minutes later, or at 1 p.m.

SCORE YOURSELF

Check your answers against the answer keys. Count up the number of answers you got right and the number you got wrong.

Section	No. Right	No. Wrong
Quantitative (Math)		
Reading Comprehension		
Verbal		

Now calculate your raw scores:

Quantitative (Math): $(\underline{\hspace{2cm}}) - \left(\dfrac{1}{4}\right) (\underline{\hspace{2cm}}) = (\underline{\hspace{2cm}})$

No. Right   No. Wrong   Raw Score

Reading Comprehension: $(\underline{\hspace{2cm}}) - \left(\dfrac{1}{4}\right) (\underline{\hspace{2cm}}) = (\underline{\hspace{2cm}})$

No. Right   No. Wrong   Raw Score

Verbal: $(\underline{\hspace{2cm}}) - \left(\dfrac{1}{4}\right) (\underline{\hspace{2cm}}) = (\underline{\hspace{2cm}})$

No. Right   No. Wrong   Raw Score

Now check your Raw Score against the conversion chart to get an idea of the range in which your test scores:

Raw Score	Quantitative (Math)	Reading Comprehension	Verbal
60			350
55			350
50	350		343
45	344		334
40	335	348	325
35	325	324	316
30	316	314	307
25	306	304	298
20	297	294	289
15	288	284	280
10	278	274	271
5	269	264	261
0	260	254	252
−5 or lower	250	250	250

Remember:

- The same exam is given to students in grades 8 through 11. You are not expected to know what you have not been taught.
- You will be compared only to students in your own grade.

Use your scores to plan further study if you have time.

ANSWER SHEET PRACTICE TEST 3: SSAT (Upper Level)

Part I: Writing Sample

_____

_____

_____

_____

_____

_____

_____

_____

_____

_____

_____

_____

_____

_____

_____

_____

_____

_____

answer sheet

_____

_____

_____

_____

_____

_____

_____

_____

_____

_____

_____

_____

_____

_____

_____

_____

_____

_____

_____

_____

_____

Part II: Multiple-Choice

Section 1: Verbal

1 (A) (B) (C) (D) (E)	16 (A) (B) (C) (D) (E)	31 (A) (B) (C) (D) (E)	46 (A) (B) (C) (D) (E)
2 (A) (B) (C) (D) (E)	17 (A) (B) (C) (D) (E)	32 (A) (B) (C) (D) (E)	47 (A) (B) (C) (D) (E)
3 (A) (B) (C) (D) (E)	18 (A) (B) (C) (D) (E)	33 (A) (B) (C) (D) (E)	48 (A) (B) (C) (D) (E)
4 (A) (B) (C) (D) (E)	19 (A) (B) (C) (D) (E)	34 (A) (B) (C) (D) (E)	49 (A) (B) (C) (D) (E)
5 (A) (B) (C) (D) (E)	20 (A) (B) (C) (D) (E)	35 (A) (B) (C) (D) (E)	50 (A) (B) (C) (D) (E)
6 (A) (B) (C) (D) (E)	21 (A) (B) (C) (D) (E)	36 (A) (B) (C) (D) (E)	51 (A) (B) (C) (D) (E)
7 (A) (B) (C) (D) (E)	22 (A) (B) (C) (D) (E)	37 (A) (B) (C) (D) (E)	52 (A) (B) (C) (D) (E)
8 (A) (B) (C) (D) (E)	23 (A) (B) (C) (D) (E)	38 (A) (B) (C) (D) (E)	53 (A) (B) (C) (D) (E)
9 (A) (B) (C) (D) (E)	24 (A) (B) (C) (D) (E)	39 (A) (B) (C) (D) (E)	54 (A) (B) (C) (D) (E)
10 (A) (B) (C) (D) (E)	25 (A) (B) (C) (D) (E)	40 (A) (B) (C) (D) (E)	55 (A) (B) (C) (D) (E)
11 (A) (B) (C) (D) (E)	26 (A) (B) (C) (D) (E)	41 (A) (B) (C) (D) (E)	56 (A) (B) (C) (D) (E)
12 (A) (B) (C) (D) (E)	27 (A) (B) (C) (D) (E)	42 (A) (B) (C) (D) (E)	57 (A) (B) (C) (D) (E)
13 (A) (B) (C) (D) (E)	28 (A) (B) (C) (D) (E)	43 (A) (B) (C) (D) (E)	58 (A) (B) (C) (D) (E)
14 (A) (B) (C) (D) (E)	29 (A) (B) (C) (D) (E)	44 (A) (B) (C) (D) (E)	59 (A) (B) (C) (D) (E)
15 (A) (B) (C) (D) (E)	30 (A) (B) (C) (D) (E)	45 (A) (B) (C) (D) (E)	60 (A) (B) (C) (D) (E)

Section 2: Quantitative (Math)

1 (A) (B) (C) (D) (E)	8 (A) (B) (C) (D) (E)	15 (A) (B) (C) (D) (E)	22 (A) (B) (C) (D) (E)
2 (A) (B) (C) (D) (E)	9 (A) (B) (C) (D) (E)	16 (A) (B) (C) (D) (E)	23 (A) (B) (C) (D) (E)
3 (A) (B) (C) (D) (E)	10 (A) (B) (C) (D) (E)	17 (A) (B) (C) (D) (E)	24 (A) (B) (C) (D) (E)
4 (A) (B) (C) (D) (E)	11 (A) (B) (C) (D) (E)	18 (A) (B) (C) (D) (E)	25 (A) (B) (C) (D) (E)
5 (A) (B) (C) (D) (E)	12 (A) (B) (C) (D) (E)	19 (A) (B) (C) (D) (E)	
6 (A) (B) (C) (D) (E)	13 (A) (B) (C) (D) (E)	20 (A) (B) (C) (D) (E)	
7 (A) (B) (C) (D) (E)	14 (A) (B) (C) (D) (E)	21 (A) (B) (C) (D) (E)	

Section 3: Reading Comprehension

1 Ⓐ Ⓑ Ⓒ Ⓓ Ⓔ   11 Ⓐ Ⓑ Ⓒ Ⓓ Ⓔ   21 Ⓐ Ⓑ Ⓒ Ⓓ Ⓔ   31 Ⓐ Ⓑ Ⓒ Ⓓ Ⓔ
2 Ⓐ Ⓑ Ⓒ Ⓓ Ⓔ   12 Ⓐ Ⓑ Ⓒ Ⓓ Ⓔ   22 Ⓐ Ⓑ Ⓒ Ⓓ Ⓔ   32 Ⓐ Ⓑ Ⓒ Ⓓ Ⓔ
3 Ⓐ Ⓑ Ⓒ Ⓓ Ⓔ   13 Ⓐ Ⓑ Ⓒ Ⓓ Ⓔ   23 Ⓐ Ⓑ Ⓒ Ⓓ Ⓔ   33 Ⓐ Ⓑ Ⓒ Ⓓ Ⓔ
4 Ⓐ Ⓑ Ⓒ Ⓓ Ⓔ   14 Ⓐ Ⓑ Ⓒ Ⓓ Ⓔ   24 Ⓐ Ⓑ Ⓒ Ⓓ Ⓔ   34 Ⓐ Ⓑ Ⓒ Ⓓ Ⓔ
5 Ⓐ Ⓑ Ⓒ Ⓓ Ⓔ   15 Ⓐ Ⓑ Ⓒ Ⓓ Ⓔ   25 Ⓐ Ⓑ Ⓒ Ⓓ Ⓔ   35 Ⓐ Ⓑ Ⓒ Ⓓ Ⓔ
6 Ⓐ Ⓑ Ⓒ Ⓓ Ⓔ   16 Ⓐ Ⓑ Ⓒ Ⓓ Ⓔ   26 Ⓐ Ⓑ Ⓒ Ⓓ Ⓔ   36 Ⓐ Ⓑ Ⓒ Ⓓ Ⓔ
7 Ⓐ Ⓑ Ⓒ Ⓓ Ⓔ   17 Ⓐ Ⓑ Ⓒ Ⓓ Ⓔ   27 Ⓐ Ⓑ Ⓒ Ⓓ Ⓔ   37 Ⓐ Ⓑ Ⓒ Ⓓ Ⓔ
8 Ⓐ Ⓑ Ⓒ Ⓓ Ⓔ   18 Ⓐ Ⓑ Ⓒ Ⓓ Ⓔ   28 Ⓐ Ⓑ Ⓒ Ⓓ Ⓔ   38 Ⓐ Ⓑ Ⓒ Ⓓ Ⓔ
9 Ⓐ Ⓑ Ⓒ Ⓓ Ⓔ   19 Ⓐ Ⓑ Ⓒ Ⓓ Ⓔ   29 Ⓐ Ⓑ Ⓒ Ⓓ Ⓔ   39 Ⓐ Ⓑ Ⓒ Ⓓ Ⓔ
10 Ⓐ Ⓑ Ⓒ Ⓓ Ⓔ   20 Ⓐ Ⓑ Ⓒ Ⓓ Ⓔ   30 Ⓐ Ⓑ Ⓒ Ⓓ Ⓔ   40 Ⓐ Ⓑ Ⓒ Ⓓ Ⓔ

Section 4: Quantitative (Math)

1 Ⓐ Ⓑ Ⓒ Ⓓ Ⓔ   8 Ⓐ Ⓑ Ⓒ Ⓓ Ⓔ   15 Ⓐ Ⓑ Ⓒ Ⓓ Ⓔ   22 Ⓐ Ⓑ Ⓒ Ⓓ Ⓔ
2 Ⓐ Ⓑ Ⓒ Ⓓ Ⓔ   9 Ⓐ Ⓑ Ⓒ Ⓓ Ⓔ   16 Ⓐ Ⓑ Ⓒ Ⓓ Ⓔ   23 Ⓐ Ⓑ Ⓒ Ⓓ Ⓔ
3 Ⓐ Ⓑ Ⓒ Ⓓ Ⓔ   10 Ⓐ Ⓑ Ⓒ Ⓓ Ⓔ   17 Ⓐ Ⓑ Ⓒ Ⓓ Ⓔ   24 Ⓐ Ⓑ Ⓒ Ⓓ Ⓔ
4 Ⓐ Ⓑ Ⓒ Ⓓ Ⓔ   11 Ⓐ Ⓑ Ⓒ Ⓓ Ⓔ   18 Ⓐ Ⓑ Ⓒ Ⓓ Ⓔ   25 Ⓐ Ⓑ Ⓒ Ⓓ Ⓔ
5 Ⓐ Ⓑ Ⓒ Ⓓ Ⓔ   12 Ⓐ Ⓑ Ⓒ Ⓓ Ⓔ   19 Ⓐ Ⓑ Ⓒ Ⓓ Ⓔ
6 Ⓐ Ⓑ Ⓒ Ⓓ Ⓔ   13 Ⓐ Ⓑ Ⓒ Ⓓ Ⓔ   20 Ⓐ Ⓑ Ⓒ Ⓓ Ⓔ
7 Ⓐ Ⓑ Ⓒ Ⓓ Ⓔ   14 Ⓐ Ⓑ Ⓒ Ⓓ Ⓔ   21 Ⓐ Ⓑ Ⓒ Ⓓ Ⓔ

Practice Test 3: SSAT (Upper Level)

PART I: WRITING SAMPLE

25 Minutes

Directions: Write a convincing, legible essay supporting your opinion on the topic that follows. Use the answer sheet provided.

> **Topic:** High schools should require students to maintain a certain grade point level in order to play on competitive sports teams.
>
> Do you agree or disagree with this statement? Support your position with specific examples.

PART II: MULTIPLE-CHOICE

Section 1: Verbal

60 Questions • 30 Minutes

The Verbal section consists of two different types of questions. There are directions for each type of question.

> **Directions:** Each question shows a word in capital letters followed by five words or phrases. Choose the word or phrase whose meaning is most similar to the word in capital letters. Mark the appropriate space on your answer sheet.

1. AGENDA
   - **(A)** receipt
   - **(B)** agent
   - **(C)** combination
   - **(D)** correspondence
   - **(E)** schedule

2. CREDIBLE
   - **(A)** believable
   - **(B)** untrue
   - **(C)** correct
   - **(D)** suitable
   - **(E)** fortunate

3. PLACID
   - **(A)** explosive
   - **(B)** quiet
   - **(C)** public
   - **(D)** lenient
   - **(E)** crystalline

4. INTERVENE
   - **(A)** induce
   - **(B)** invert
   - **(C)** interfere
   - **(D)** solve
   - **(E)** intermediary

5. MUNDANE
   - **(A)** stupid
   - **(B)** extraordinary
   - **(C)** weekly
   - **(D)** immense
   - **(E)** common

6. DEHYDRATED
   - **(A)** airless
   - **(B)** deflated
   - **(C)** pointless
   - **(D)** worthless
   - **(E)** waterless

7. PREVALENT
   - **(A)** predating
   - **(B)** predominant
   - **(C)** preeminent
   - **(D)** prior
   - **(E)** predictive

8. SUCCINCT
   - **(A)** concise
   - **(B)** superfluous
   - **(C)** alert
   - **(D)** despicable
   - **(E)** fearful

9. NOCTURNAL
   (A) by night
   (B) by day
   (C) revolving
   (D) alternating
   (E) frequent

10. EQUITABLE
    (A) preferential
    (B) fair
    (C) unreasonable
    (D) biased
    (E) prejudiced

11. EXPEDITE
    (A) hinder
    (B) harm
    (C) send
    (D) hasten
    (E) block

12. TURBULENT
    (A) authentic
    (B) tranquil
    (C) tamed
    (D) fatal
    (E) violent

13. TENACIOUS
    (A) timid
    (B) thin
    (C) unyielding
    (D) divisive
    (E) stranded

14. PERTINENT
    (A) applicable
    (B) prudent
    (C) irreverent
    (D) irrelevant
    (E) truthful

15. DOGMATIC
    (A) bovine
    (B) canine
    (C) opinionated
    (D) individualistic
    (E) traditional

16. UNSCRUPULOUS
    (A) filthy
    (B) honest
    (C) austere
    (D) unprincipled
    (E) unresolved

17. WILY
    (A) crooked
    (B) narrow
    (C) cunning
    (D) blunt
    (E) broken

18. BLATANT
    (A) insipid
    (B) obvious
    (C) shining
    (D) closed
    (E) secret

19. PRETEXT
    (A) excuse
    (B) reason
    (C) preface
    (D) fit
    (E) doubt

20. ACUMEN
    (A) beauty
    (B) poise
    (C) keenness
    (D) illness
    (E) courtesy

practice test

21. EVASION
    (A) attack
    (B) displeasure
    (C) enjoyment
    (D) avoidance
    (E) fatigue

22. INDISPENSABLE
    (A) incontrovertible
    (B) essential
    (C) impetuous
    (D) ungovernable
    (E) confused

23. OBLITERATE
    (A) obligate
    (B) subjugate
    (C) exhibit
    (D) maintain
    (E) erase

24. AMIABLE
    (A) allied
    (B) disjointed
    (C) indignant
    (D) friendly
    (E) introverted

25. WRITHE
    (A) strangle
    (B) topple
    (C) trouble
    (D) slide
    (E) twist

26. ABATE
    (A) let up
    (B) continue
    (C) forego
    (D) placate
    (E) intimidate

27. ENDORSEMENT
    (A) inscription
    (B) approval
    (C) standard
    (D) editorial
    (E) article

28. CONVERT
    (A) reform
    (B) predict
    (C) weave
    (D) transform
    (E) translate

29. ERUDITE
    (A) knowledgeable
    (B) meddlesome
    (C) eroded
    (D) careless
    (E) intrusion

30. ENDEAVOR
    (A) expectation
    (B) attempt
    (C) tack
    (D) necessity
    (E) ability

Directions: The following questions ask you to find relationships between words. Read each question, and then choose the answer that best completes the meaning of the sentence. Mark the appropriate space on your answer sheet.

31. None is to little as never is to
    (A) nothing
    (B) infrequently
    (C) negative
    (D) much
    (E) often

32. Receive is to admit as settle is to
    (A) resist
    (B) anger
    (C) remain
    (D) adjust
    (E) mediate

33. Dishonesty is to distrust as
    (A) violin is to bow
    (B) hand is to paper
    (C) money is to thief
    (D) strange is to odd
    (E) carelessness is to accident

34. Sociologist is to group as
    (A) psychologist is to individual
    (B) doctor is to nurse
    (C) children is to pediatrician
    (D) biologist is to frog
    (E) mathematician is to algebra

35. Generous is to frugal as
    (A) wasteful is to squander
    (B) philanthropist is to miser
    (C) tasteful is to garish
    (D) gratify is to desire
    (E) important is to nonessential

36. Transparent is to translucent as
    (A) water is to milk
    (B) glass is to crystal
    (C) translucent is to opaque
    (D) muddy is to clear
    (E) suspension is to mixture

37. Discontent is to rebellion as
    (A) friction is to spark
    (B) complacent is to revolt
    (C) success is to study
    (D) employment is to retirement
    (E) surgeon is to operation

38. Beaker is to chemist as hammer is to
    (A) nails
    (B) geologist
    (C) construction
    (D) architect
    (E) noise

39. Follow is to lead as dependent is to
    (A) subservient
    (B) supportive
    (C) child
    (D) autonomous
    (E) anonymous

40. State is to country as country is to
    (A) island
    (B) capitol
    (C) continent
    (D) planet
    (E) ocean

41. Accelerator is to motion as
    (A) catalyst is to change
    (B) inertia is to immobile
    (C) ignition is to speed
    (D) automobile is to vehicle
    (E) experiment is to hypothesis

42. Probable is to certain as
    (A) approach is to reproach
    (B) steady is to rocky
    (C) correct is to accurate
    (D) save is to record
    (E) plausible is to definite

43. Obstruct is to impede as impenetrable is to
    (A) impervious
    (B) hidden
    (C) merciful
    (D) porous
    (E) transparent

44. Include is to omit as acknowledge is to
    (A) notice
    (B) ignore
    (C) recognize
    (D) greet
    (E) know

45. Nucleus is to electron as
    (A) Earth is to satellite
    (B) Earth is to Sun
    (C) constellation is to Sun
    (D) neutron is to proton
    (E) atom is to neutron

46. Sculptor is to statue as
    (A) actor is to play
    (B) paint is to artist
    (C) composer is to music
    (D) orchestra is to conductor
    (E) programmer is to computer

47. Dreary is to happy as
    (A) light is to graceful
    (B) close is to narrow
    (C) dearth is to surplus
    (D) curtain is to play
    (E) interdict is to expect

48. Allow is to restrict as
    (A) gain is to success
    (B) seeing is to believing
    (C) heart is to soul
    (D) encourage is to prevent
    (E) terrible is to worse

49. Interrupt is to speak as
    (A) telephone is to telegraph
    (B) interfere is to assist
    (C) shout is to yell
    (D) intercede is to interfere
    (E) intrude is to enter

50. Modesty is to arrogance as
    (A) debility is to strength
    (B) cause is to purpose
    (C) hate is to emotion
    (D) finance is to poverty
    (E) agility is to stamina

51. Adversity is to happiness as
    (A) fear is to misfortune
    (B) solace is to sorrow
    (C) graduation is to superfluous
    (D) vehemence is to serenity
    (E) troublesome is to petulant

52. Extortionist is to blackmail as
    (A) kleptomaniac is to steal
    (B) criminal is to arrest
    (C) kidnapper is to crime
    (D) businessman is to profit
    (E) clerk is to stock

53. Monsoon is to rain as
    (A) hurricane is to destruction
    (B) tornado is to wind
    (C) sun is to spring
    (D) famine is to drought
    (E) morning is to dew

54. Introspective is to withdrawn as
    (A) hesitant is to hasty
    (B) quick is to feelings
    (C) introvert is to extrovert
    (D) import is to export
    (E) gregarious is to social

55. Equator is to world as
    (A) boundary is to country
    (B) capital is to state
    (C) fur is to animal
    (D) waist is to man
    (E) latitude is to longitude

56. Superficial is to surface as
    (A) probing is to deep
    (B) subway is to subterranean
    (C) crust is to Earth
    (D) tepid is to warm
    (E) internal is to external

57. Stagnant is to pond as
    (A) sandy is to river
    (B) noisy is to sheep
    (C) flowing is to stream
    (D) oceanic is to tide
    (E) tidal is to wave

58. Sanctuary is to fortress as
    (A) sanctum is to inner
    (B) shelter is to house
    (C) violent is to peaceful
    (D) guns is to fort
    (E) sanction is to assassinate

59. Mentor is to professor as
    (A) advisor is to counselor
    (B) child is to parent
    (C) learning is to teacher
    (D) mental is to physical
    (E) tooth is to dentist

60. Lucid is to clear as
    (A) sullen is to gloomy
    (B) furtive is to clever
    (C) potent is to weak
    (D) droll is to serious
    (E) pensive is to hanging

STOP END OF SECTION 1. IF YOU HAVE ANY TIME LEFT, GO OVER YOUR WORK IN THIS SECTION ONLY. DO NOT WORK IN ANY OTHER SECTION OF THE TEST.

Section 2: Quantitative (Math)

25 Questions • 30 Minutes

Directions: Calculate the answer to each of the following questions. Select the answer choice that is best, and mark the appropriate letter on your answer sheet.

1. $\frac{3}{5} + 1.25 + .004 =$

   (A) 1.750
   (B) 1.854
   (C) 1.9
   (D) 2.25
   (E) 2.35

2. Evaluate: $\frac{10^6}{10^3}$

   (A) 1 billion
   (B) 1 million
   (C) 1,000
   (D) 100
   (E) 1^3

3. $71.4 \times 98.2 =$
   (A) 4,011.38
   (B) 5,321.48
   (C) 6,921.38
   (D) 7,011.48
   (E) 8,231.48

4. $\dfrac{4\frac{2}{3} + \frac{1}{6}}{\frac{1}{3}} =$

   (A) 9
   (B) $10\frac{1}{3}$
   (C) $12\frac{3}{24}$
   (D) $14\frac{1}{2}$
   (E) 23

5. $(.25)^2 =$
   (A) .00625
   (B) .0625
   (C) .625
   (D) 1.625
   (E) 16.25

6. $(3 + 1) + [(2 - 3) - (4 - 1)] =$
   (A) 6
   (B) 2
   (C) 0
   (D) −2
   (E) −4

7. $10,001 - 8,093 =$
   (A) 1,908
   (B) 1,918
   (C) 2,007
   (D) 18,094
   (E) 20,007

8. The ratio of 3 quarts to 3 gallons is
   (A) 3:1
   (B) 1:4
   (C) 6:3
   (D) 4:1
   (E) 1:3

9. 10% of $\frac{1}{5}$ of $50 is

   (A) $100
   (B) $5
   (C) $1
   (D) 103
   (E) $\frac{3}{5}$

10.   4 hours 12 minutes 10 sec
   −2 hours 48 minutes 35 sec.

   (A) 2 hr. 23 min. 25 sec.
   (B) 2 hr. 12 min. 40 sec.
   (C) 1 hr. 23 min. 35 sec.
   (D) 1 hr. 23 min. 25 sec.
   (E) 1 hr. 12 min. 35 sec.

11.   If we double the value of a and c in the fraction $\dfrac{ab}{c}$, the value of the fraction is

   (A) doubled.
   (B) tripled.
   (C) multiplied by 4.
   (D) halved.
   (E) unchanged.

12.   What percentage of 220 is 24.2?
   (A) 909%
   (B) 99%
   (C) 40%
   (D) 27%
   (E) 11%

13.   98 reduced by $\dfrac{5}{7}$ is equivalent to

   (A) 28
   (B) 33
   (C) 66
   (D) 70
   (E) 85

14.   How long should an object $6\dfrac{1}{2}$ feet long be drawn, if according to the scale, $\dfrac{1}{4}$ inch in the drawing equals 1 foot?

   (A) $1\dfrac{3}{4}$ inches
   (B) $1\dfrac{5}{8}$ inches
   (C) $\dfrac{7}{8}$ inches
   (D) $\dfrac{5}{8}$ inches
   (E) $\dfrac{17}{32}$ inches

15. $12\dfrac{1}{2} \div \dfrac{1}{2} + \dfrac{3}{2} \times 4 - 3 =$

   (A) 1
   (B) $4\dfrac{3}{4}$
   (C) 20
   (D) 28
   (E) $32\dfrac{1}{2}$

16.   If $y + 2 > 10$, then y may be
   (A) larger than 8.
   (B) larger than 6.
   (C) larger than 0.
   (D) equal to 0.
   (E) unknown.

17.   The shadow of a man six feet tall is 12 feet long. How tall is a tree that casts a 50-foot shadow?
   (A) 100'
   (B) 50'
   (C) 25'
   (D) 15'
   (E) 10'

18. In the fraction $\dfrac{1}{\Delta}$, Δ could be replaced by all of the following EXCEPT
    (A) 0
    (B) 1
    (C) 4.2
    (D) 9
    (E) 10

19. $.0515 \times 100$ is equivalent to
    (A) $5,150 \div 100$
    (B) 5.15×10
    (C) $.00515 \times 1,000$
    (D) $510,000 \div 10$
    (E) $5,150 \div 10,000$

20.

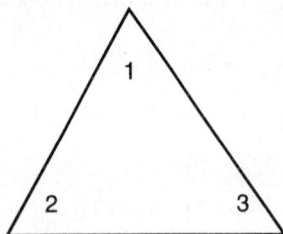

$m\angle 2 = 60°$

NOTE: Figure not drawn to scale.

Which of the following is true?
    (A) $m\angle + m\angle 3 > 180°$
    (B) $m\angle 1 > m\angle 3$
    (C) $m\angle 1 = m\angle 3$
    (D) $m\angle 1 - m\angle 3 > m\angle 2$
    (E) $m\angle 1 + m\angle 3 = 120°$

21. 45 is to _____ as 90 is to .45.
    (A) .225
    (B) .900
    (C) 4.50
    (D) 9.00
    (E) 22.5

22. If $n = \sqrt{20}$, then
    (A) $\sqrt{5} > n > \sqrt{3}$
    (B) $3 > n > 2$
    (C) $n = 4.5$
    (D) $4 < n < 5$
    (E) $n > 5$

23.

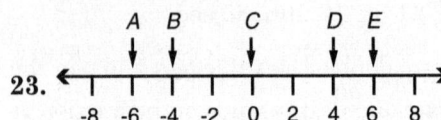

How would you move along the number line above to find the difference between 4 and −6?
    (A) From E to B
    (B) From A to D
    (C) From B to D
    (D) From D to A
    (E) From B to E

24. How many sixths are there in $\dfrac{4}{5}$?
    (A) $2\dfrac{3}{8}$
    (B) 3
    (C) $4\dfrac{4}{5}$
    (D) $5\dfrac{1}{5}$
    (E) 6

25. Four games drew an average of 36,500 people per game. If the attendance at the first three games was 32,000, 35,500, and 38,000, how many people attended the fourth game?
    (A) 36,500
    (B) 37,000
    (C) 39,000
    (D) 40,500
    (E) 43,000

STOP END OF SECTION 2. IF YOU HAVE ANY TIME LEFT, GO OVER YOUR WORK IN THIS SECTION ONLY. DO NOT WORK IN ANY OTHER SECTION OF THE TEST.

Section 3: Reading Comprehension

40 Questions • 40 Minutes

Directions: Read each passage carefully. Then decide which of the possible responses is the best answer to each question. Mark the appropriate space on your answer sheet.

Back in the seventeenth century, when Abraham Rycken owned it, Rikers Island was a tiny spit of land in the East River. It became part
(5) of New York City in the 1890s and was used as a convenient place to deposit the rock and soil debris of subway construction. Later, the island became the end of the line for
(10) the discards of city households, in a landfill operation that went on until Rikers Island reached its present size of 400 acres.

Robert Moses, then New York's
(15) Park Commissioner, was looking for ways to supply city parks with shade trees and eliminate the expense of buying them from commercial nurseries. He noted that weeds grew prodi-
(20) giously in the landfill, thought that trees and plants might do the same, and arranged to clear a few acres for a trial planting. In 1944, the first 287 shrubs and trees were transplanted
(25) from the fledgling nursery to the city's parks. The nursery now covers some 115 acres of the island, and several hundred thousand of its shrubs and trees have been planted along city
(30) streets, in parks, around housing projects, and around the malls and paths of the United Nations.

1. To obtain plantings for New York City, authorities
   (A) buy them from the United Nations.
   (B) purchase them from commercial nurseries.
   (C) transplant them from city-owned property.
   (D) buy them from Robert Moses.
   (E) grow them in Central Park.

2. Rikers Island is currently
   (A) 115 acres in area.
   (B) a landfill operation.
   (C) owned by Abraham Rycken.
   (D) 400 acres in area.
   (E) a dumping ground for subway debris.

3. The soil of the island
   (A) is volcanic.
   (B) was enriched by discarded rubbish.
   (C) was brought in from commercial nurseries.
   (D) is a combination of mud and rock.
   (E) was brought in on subways.

4. The first plantings were taken from Rikers Island
   (A) a decade ago.
   (B) about 1890.
   (C) in the seventeenth century.
   (D) quite recently.
   (E) in 1944.

America's national bird, the bald eagle, which has flown high since the Revolutionary War, may soon be grounded. The eagle population
(5) of the United States is decreasing at an alarming rate, and the National Audubon Society has just launched a full-scale survey to find out how many bald eagles are left and what
(10) measures are necessary to protect them from extinction. The survey, a year-long project, focuses attention on the bird chosen to appear on the Great Seal of the United States.

(15) When it gained its official status over 200 years ago, the bald eagle was undisputed king of America's skies. Many thousands of the great birds roamed the country, and both the
(20) sight of the bald eagle and its piercing scream were familiar to almost every American. Today, naturalists fear that there are less than a thousand of them still in this country.

(25) Nature is partly to blame. Our severe hurricanes have destroyed many eggs, fledglings, and aeries, the eagles' mammoth nests. But man is the chief culprit. Despite legislation
(30) passed by Congress in 1940 to protect the *emblematic birds*, thousands of them have been gunned out of the skies by over-eager shooters who perhaps mistook them for large hawks.

(35) The bald eagle was known as the bald-headed eagle when Congress began the search for a seal in 1776. The archaic meaning of bald—white or streaked with white—refers to his
(40) head, neck, and tail coloring rather than to any lack of plumage in our fine-feathered friend.

5. The Audubon Society is trying to
   (A) rid the country of the bald eagle.
   (B) have the bald eagle chosen as the national bird of the United States.
   (C) prevent the extinction of the bald eagle in this country.
   (D) have Congress pass a law forbidding the shooting of eagles.
   (E) band more eagles.

6. There are now
   (A) more eagles in this country than in 1776.
   (B) fewer eagles here than there were over 200 years ago.
   (C) many thousands of bald eagles.
   (D) eagles whose scream is familiar to every American.
   (E) too many eagles.

7. *Aeries* are
   (A) fledglings.
   (B) eggs.
   (C) young mammoths.
   (D) nests.
   (E) mating areas.

8. The eagle is called an *emblematic bird* because it is
   (A) bald.
   (B) decreasing.
   (C) handsome and powerful.
   (D) prized by hunters.
   (E) a symbol of a nation.

9. The design for the Great Seal of the United States was first considered
   (A) in 1776.
   (B) in 1783.
   (C) in 1840.
   (D) in 1876.
   (E) at an unknown date.

You know, of course, that in China the Emperor is a Chinaman, and all the people around him are Chinamen too. It happened a good many years ago,
(5) but that's just why it's worthwhile to hear the story, before it is forgotten. The Emperor's palace was the most splendid in the world; entirely and altogether made of porcelain, so costly,
(10) but so brittle, so difficult to handle that one had to be terribly careful. In the garden were to be seen the strangest flowers, and to the most splendid of them silver bells were tied, which
(15) tinkled so that nobody should pass by without noticing the flowers. Oh, the Emperor's garden had been laid out very smartly, and it extended so far that the gardener himself didn't
(20) know where the end was. If you went on and on, you came into the loveliest forest with high trees and deep lakes. The forest went right down to the sea, which was blue and deep; tall ships
(25) could sail right in under the branches of the trees; and in the trees lived a nightingale, which sang so sweetly that even the poor fisherman, who had many other things to do, stopped
(30) still and listened when he had gone out at night to take up his nets and then heard the nightingale.

—from *The Nightingale* by
Hans Christian Andersen

10. The author wants to tell this story
(A) because he can't forget the nightingale.
(B) before it is forgotten.
(C) to teach us about China.
(D) because he is a writer and storyteller.
(E) in order to describe the garden.

11. The Emperor's palace was made of
(A) brick.
(B) silver bells.
(C) high trees.
(D) large stones and boulders.
(E) porcelain.

12. Silver bells were tied to flowers in the garden to
(A) draw attention to their beauty.
(B) frighten birds and mice away.
(C) play soft melodies.
(D) remind the gardener not to pick them.
(E) sparkle in the sun.

13. The Emperor's garden
(A) was very strange.
(B) was too large to care for.
(C) led into a lovely forest.
(D) housed a rare nightingale.
(E) was a source of pleasure for all in the kingdom.

14. The forest
(A) was dark and threatening.
(B) contained many rare animals.
(C) was an easy place in which to get lost.
(D) housed the nightingale.
(E) was a fisherman's hiding place.

An excerpt from a Dead Sea Scroll describing Abraham's *sojourn* in Egypt and the beauty of Sarah, his wife, was recently made public for the
(5) first time. The 2,000-year-old scroll, badly preserved and extremely brittle, is the last of seven scrolls found in 1947 in the caves of the Judean desert south of Jericho. Scholars say
(10) that this scroll enlarges on the hitherto known Biblical tales of Lamech, Enoch, Noah, and Abraham.

This document of Hebrew University yielded *decipherable* contents
(15) only after months of exposure to controlled humidity. The centuries had compressed the leather scroll into a brittle, glued-together mass. After it had been rendered flexible,
(20) the scroll was folded into pages. Four complete pages, each with 34 lines of writing, resulted. Besides this, scholars had for their studies large sections of the decipherable writing
(25) on five other pages, and readable lines and words on additional pages. Scholars were delighted, for they had almost despaired of recovering the scroll as a readable document. The
(30) work of giving new life to the desiccated parchment and of unrolling it was done by an old German expert on ancient materials, under the supervision of two Israeli scholars.

15. The word *sojourn* means
  (A) servitude.
  (B) stay.
  (C) congruent.
  (D) flight.
  (E) difficulties.

16. *Decipherable* as used in the second paragraph means
  (A) intelligible.
  (B) durable.
  (C) exciting.
  (D) scholarly.
  (E) practical.

17. The scroll
  (A) was found in Egypt.
  (B) gives new details about people already known of.
  (C) is limited to an account of Abraham and Sarah.
  (D) tells of Abraham's life in the Judean desert.
  (E) is the first of seven found in 1947.

18. The scroll
  (A) belongs to an Israeli university.
  (B) is in Germany.
  (C) was deciphered by a German specialist.
  (D) was taken to Jericho.
  (E) was beautifully preserved.

19. The writing on the scroll
  (A) was finally legible throughout the document.
  (B) was legible on only four pages.
  (C) could be read on several pages.
  (D) was too damaged by age to be deciphered.
  (E) was irreparable.

The police department of New York City has one branch that many do not know about, although it was established almost a century ago.
(5) This is the harbor precinct's 14-boat fleet of police launches, which patrols 578 miles of waters around the city, paying particular attention to the areas containing 500 piers and some
(10) 90 boat clubs.

The boats are equipped for various jobs. One boat is an ice-breaker; another is equipped to render aid in the event of an airplane crash at La
(15) Guardia Airport. All of the boats are equipped with lifeline guns, heavy grappling irons to raise sunken automobiles, and lasso-sticks to rescue animals in the water. They have
(20) power pumps to bail out sinking craft, first-aid kits, extra life preservers, signal flags, and searchlights.

The force of 183 officers have all had previous experience with boats.
(25) Some of the officers are Navy and Coast Guard veterans. Many of the harbor police officers have ocean-going Master's or Harbor Captain's licenses. All are highly trained in the
(30) care and handling of engines and in navigation. All are skilled in giving first aid, and each officer is a qualified radio operator and a trained marksman with a revolver.

(35) The work of the police includes many tasks. One duty of this force is to check the operation of the fleet of 43 junk boats that ply their trade in the harbor, buying scrap, rope, and
(40) other items for resale ashore. These boats could just as easily be used to smuggle narcotics, gems, aliens, or spies into the country, so they are watched closely by the city's harbor
(45) police force. During the last summer, the police launches towed 450 disabled boats and gave some kind of help to thousands of others. The officers also arrest those who break
(50) navigation laws or who endanger the safety of bathers by approaching too near the shore in speed boats.

20. The harbor police were
(A) introduced by order of the mayor.
(B) first used in the twentieth century.
(C) in use before the Civil War.
(D) introduced by veterans of World War II.
(E) in full force almost 100 years ago.

21. The boats used
(A) are uniform in design.
(B) can all serve as ice-breakers.
(C) are all equipped with deck guns.
(D) work at Kennedy Airport.
(E) vary in function.

22. The harbor police
(A) arrest any man found on a junk boat.
(B) prevent the resale of scrap material.
(C) regulate the admission of spies.
(D) ensure legal traffic in junk.
(E) regulate disabled boats.

23. Their services include
(A) towing, life-saving, and salvage.
(B) customs collection, towing, and the sending of radio messages.
(C) first aid, the rescue of animals, and fire patrol.
(D) ice-breaking, the collection of junk, and the transportation of aliens.
(E) smuggling, first aid, and rescue.

24. The police boats
(A) have no responsibility for bathers.
(B) unload ships at the piers.
(C) assist boats of all kinds.
(D) warn offenders but do not make arrests.
(E) cannot detain other boats.

"There are many things from which I might have derived good, by which I have not profited, I dare say, Christmas among the rest. But I am sure I
(5) have always thought of Christmas-time, when it has come round—apart from the *veneration* due to its sacred origin, if anything belonging to it *can* be apart from that—as a good time; a
(10) kind, forgiving, charitable, pleasant time; the only time I know of, in the long calendar of the year, when men and women seem by *one consent* to open their shut-up hearts freely and
(15) to think of people below them as if they really were fellow travelers to the grave, and not another race of creatures bound on other journeys. And therefore, Uncle, though it has
(20) never put a scrap of gold or silver in my pocket, I believe that it *has* done me good, and *will* do me good; and I say, God bless it!"

The clerk in the tank involuntarily
(25) applauded.

"Let me hear another sound from *you*," said Scrooge, "and you'll keep your Christmas by losing your situa-tion! You're quite a powerful speaker,
(30) sir," he added, turning to his nephew. "I wonder you don't go into Parlia-ment."

—from *A Christmas Carol* by Charles Dickens

25. The word *veneration* probably means
- **(A)** worship.
- **(B)** disapproval.
- **(C)** agreement.
- **(D)** love.
- **(E)** participation.

26. The first speaker
- **(A)** is a very religious person.
- **(B)** enjoys and celebrates Christmas.
- **(C)** is defending Christmas.
- **(D)** has been fired by Scrooge.
- **(E)** is obviously frightened of Scrooge.

27. The first speaker believes that Christmas
- **(A)** is a pleasant nuisance.
- **(B)** is an excuse for people to throw wild parties.
- **(C)** has been separated from its religious origin.
- **(D)** could be a profitable time of year.
- **(E)** brings out the best in people.

28. The phrase "by one consent" is syn-onymous with
- **(A)** affirmation.
- **(B)** reaffirmation.
- **(C)** partially.
- **(D)** unanimously.
- **(E)** contractual.

29. Scrooge probably is angry with
- **(A)** the speaker and the clerk.
- **(B)** only the speaker.
- **(C)** only the clerk.
- **(D)** people who celebrate Christmas.
- **(E)** no one.

One day recently, a man in a ten-gallon hat appeared at the gate of New York's famous Bronx Zoo. "Just stopped by on my way through
(5) town," he told zoo officials. "I've got an animal outside I think you might like to see."

The officials raised their eyebrows and looked at each other meaning-
(10) fully, but the man in the hat didn't seem to notice. He went on to introduce himself as Gene Holter. "I call it a Zonkey," he said calmly, "because it's a cross between a donkey and a
(15) zebra. I've got his parents out there, too."

The zoo officials didn't wait to hear about the parents. They left their desks and started for the gate.
(20) Outside, Mr. Holter opened the side door of a huge truck and reached inside. Calmly, he pulled out a gibbon, and hung it, by its tail, from a tree. Then he walked past five ostriches
(25) and carried out the baby Zonkey.

Just three weeks old, the only Zonkey in the world had long ears, a face and legs covered with candy stripes, and a body covered with brown baby
(30) fuzz. The parents were on hand, too. The father was no ordinary zebra. He was broken to ride, and one of the zoo officials realized a lifelong dream when he jumped on the zebra's back
(35) and cantered around.

When last seen, Mr. Holter and his caravan were on their way to Dayton and then to Anaheim, California, where they live year-round.

30. Mr. Holter's manner was
   (A) boastful.
   (B) excitable.
   (C) demanding.
   (D) matter-of-fact.
   (E) personable.

31. When Mr. Holter first approached the zoo officials, they
   (A) were excited about his announcement.
   (B) thought he was telling a tall tale.
   (C) thought he was an interesting person.
   (D) couldn't wait to realize a lifelong dream.
   (E) laughed behind his back.

32. Mr. Holter probably made a living
   (A) as a veterinarian.
   (B) traveling and showing his animals.
   (C) breeding animals for scientific experiments.
   (D) working as a zoo official.
   (E) filming animals.

There is evidence that the usual variety of high blood pressure is, in part, a familial disease. Since families have similar genes as well as similar (5) environment, familial diseases could be due to shared genetic influences, to shared environmental factors, or both. For some years, the role of one environmental factor commonly (10) shared by families, namely dietary salt, has been studied at Brookhaven National Laboratory. The studies suggest that excessive ingestion of salt can lead to high blood pressure in man (15) and animals. Some individuals and some rats, however, consume large amounts of salt without developing high blood pressure. No matter how strictly all environmental factors (20) were controlled in these experiments, some salt-fed animals never developed hypertension, whereas a few rapidly developed very severe hypertension followed by early death. (25) These marked variations were interpreted to result from differences in genetic makeup.

33. The main idea of this article is that

(A) research is desperately needed in the field of medicine.

(B) a cure for high blood pressure is near.

(C) research shows salt to be a major cause of high blood pressure.

(D) a tendency toward high blood pressure may be inherited.

(E) some animals never develop high blood pressure.

34. According to the article, high blood pressure is

(A) strictly a genetic disease.

(B) strictly an environmental disease.

(C) due to both genetic and environmental factors.

(D) caused only by dietary salt.

(E) a more severe form of hypertension.

The dark and the sea are full of dangers to the fishermen of Norway. A whale may come and destroy the floating chain of corks that edge the
(5) nets, break it, and carry it off. Or a storm may come suddenly, unexpectedly, out of the night. The sea seems to turn somersaults. It opens and closes immense caverns with terrible
(10) clashes, chasing boats and men who must flee from their nets and the expected catch. Then the men may lift their nets as empty as they set them. At other times the herring
(15) may come in such masses that the lines break from the weight when lifted, and the men must return home empty-handed, without lines, nets, or the herring.
(20)   But often the nets are full of herring that shine and glisten like silver. Once in a while, a couple of men will venture in their boats along the net lines to see whether the herring are
(25) coming, and when the corks begin to bob and jerk, as if something were hitting the nets to which they are attached, then they know that the herring are there. The nets are being
(30) filled, and all the men sit in quiet excitement. They dare only to whisper to each other, afraid to disturb, and quite overcome by the overwhelming generosity of the sea. Eyes shine in
(35) happy anticipation; hands are folded in thanks. Then muscles strain with power. It is as though the strength of the body doubled. They can work day and night without a thought of
(40) weariness. They need neither food nor rest; the thought of success keeps their vigor up almost endlessly. They will take food and rest when it is all over.

35. The best title for this passage is
   (A) "Whaling in Norway."
   (B) "The Perils and Rewards of Fishing."
   (C) "Hard Work in Norway."
   (D) "Risky Business."
   (E) "The Generosity of the Sea."

36. The fishermen's difficulties include
   (A) the eating of the herring by whales.
   (B) becalming.
   (C) an attack on the men by the herring.
   (D) the jerking of the corks.
   (E) interference by rough seas.

37. At the first indication that herring are entering the nets, the men
   (A) try not to frighten the fish away.
   (B) strain every muscle to haul in the catch.
   (C) glisten like silver.
   (D) collect the nets quickly.
   (E) row quickly along the edge of the nets.

38. Which quality of the sea is NOT mentioned?
   (A) Its sudden changes
   (B) Its generosity
   (C) Its beauty
   (D) Its power
   (E) Its destroying strength

39. The fishermen are described as
   (A) patient, brave, and cautious.
   (B) angry, weary, and sickly.
   (C) strong, angry, and reckless.
   (D) skillful, impatient, and weary.
   (E) hardworking, surly, and excitable.

practice test

40. Which is NOT mentioned as a problem
to fishermen?

(A) Destruction of the nets

(B) Too large a catch

(C) Rough seas

(D) Unexpected storms

(E) Theft of the nets by other
fishermen

STOP   END OF SECTION 3. IF YOU HAVE ANY TIME LEFT, GO OVER YOUR WORK IN THIS
SECTION ONLY. DO NOT WORK IN ANY OTHER SECTION OF THE TEST.

Section 4: Quantitative (Math)

25 Questions • 30 Minutes

Directions: Each question below is followed by five possible answers. Select the one that is best, and mark the appropriate letter on your answer sheet.

1. In two days a point on the earth's surface rotates through an angle of approximately

   (A) 90°

   (B) 180°

   (C) 360°

   (D) 480°

   (E) 720°

2. Which of the following groups is arranged in order from smallest to largest?

   (A) $\dfrac{3}{7}, \dfrac{11}{23}, \dfrac{15}{32}, \dfrac{1}{2}, \dfrac{9}{16}$

   (B) $\dfrac{3}{7}, \dfrac{15}{32}, \dfrac{11}{23}, \dfrac{1}{2}, \dfrac{9}{16}$

   (C) $\dfrac{11}{23}, \dfrac{3}{7}, \dfrac{15}{32}, \dfrac{1}{2}, \dfrac{9}{16}$

   (D) $\dfrac{15}{32}, \dfrac{1}{2}, \dfrac{3}{7}, \dfrac{11}{23}, \dfrac{9}{16}$

   (E) $\dfrac{1}{2}, \dfrac{5}{32}, \dfrac{3}{7}, \dfrac{11}{23}, \dfrac{9}{16}$

3. The rectangle below has a length twice as long as its width. If its width is x, its perimeter is

   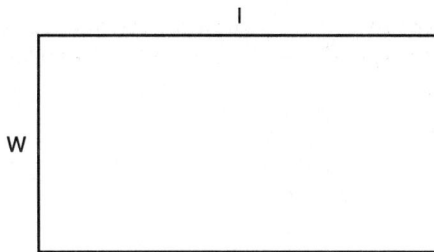

   (A) 6

   (B) $2x^2$

   (C) $4x$

   (D) $6x$

   (E) $8x$

4. This square has a side of 1". The diagonal distance from one corner to another is

   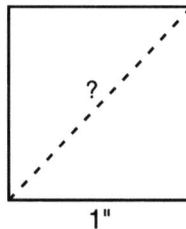

   (A) 1 inch.

   (B) $\sqrt{2}$ inches.

   (C) $\sqrt{3}$ inches.

   (D) 2 inches.

   (E) 3 inches.

5. A plumber needs eight sections of pipe, each 3'2" long. If pipe is sold only by the 10' section, how many sections must he buy?

 (A) 1
 (B) 2
 (C) 3
 (D) 4
 (E) 5

6. The ratio of the area of the shaded part to the unshaded part is

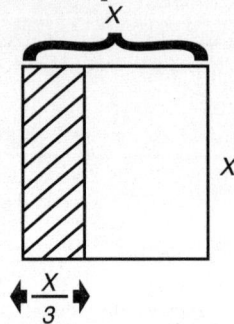

 (A) $x : \dfrac{x}{3}$

 (B) 2:1

 (C) 1:3

 (D) 1:2

 (E) 3:1

7. An airplane on a transatlantic flight took 4 hours 20 minutes to get from New York to its destination, a distance of 3,000 miles. To avoid a storm, however, the pilot went off his course, adding a distance of 200 miles to the flight. Approximately how fast did the plane travel?

 (A) 640 mph
 (B) 710 mph
 (C) 738 mph
 (D) 750 mph
 (E) 772 mph

8. A photograph measuring 5" wide × 7" long must be reduced in size to fit a space four inches long in an advertising brochure. How wide must the space be so that the picture remains in proportion?

 (A) $1\dfrac{4}{7}$"

 (B) $2\dfrac{6}{7}$"

 (C) $4\dfrac{3}{5}$"

 (D) $5\dfrac{3}{5}$"

 (E) $8\dfrac{3}{4}$"

9. The total area of the shaded part of the figure is

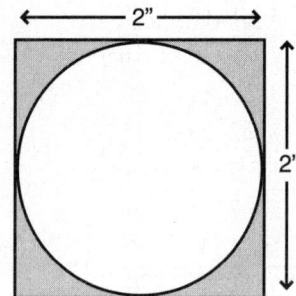

 (A) $\dfrac{2}{7}$ in.^{2}

 (B) $\dfrac{1}{2}$ in.^{2}

 (C) $\dfrac{6}{7}$ in.^{2}

 (D) $1\dfrac{3}{7}$ in.^{2}

 (E) $2\dfrac{1}{3}$ in.^{2}

10. A certain population of microbes grows according to the formula $P = A \times 2^n$, where P is the final size of the population, A is the initial size of the population, and n is the number of times the population reproduces itself. If each microbe reproduces itself every 20 minutes, how large would a population of only one microbe become after 4 hours?

(A) 16

(B) 64

(C) 128

(D) 1,028

(E) 4,096

11. If x is a positive number and $y = \dfrac{1}{x}$, as x increases in value, what happens to y?

(A) y increases

(B) y decreases

(C) y is unchanged

(D) y increases then decreases

(E) y decreases then increases

12. A box was made in the form of a cube. If a second cubical box has inside dimensions three times those of the first box, how many times as much does it contain?

(A) 3

(B) 9

(C) 12

(D) 27

(E) 33

13. Mr. Adams has a circular flower bed with a diameter of 4 feet. He wishes to increase the size of this bed so that it will have four times as much planting area. What must be the diameter of the new bed?

(A) 6 feet

(B) 8 feet

(C) 12 feet

(D) 16 feet

(E) 20 feet

14. A train left Albany for Buffalo, a distance of 290 miles, at 10:10 a.m. The train was scheduled to reach Buffalo at 3:45 p.m. If the average rate of the train on this trip was 50 mph, it arrived in Buffalo

(A) about 5 minutes early.

(B) on time.

(C) about 5 minutes late.

(D) about 13 minutes late.

(E) more than 15 minutes late.

15. If $3x - 2 = 13$, the value of $12x + 20$ is

(A) 5

(B) 20

(C) 30

(D) 37

(E) 80

16. A bakery shop sold three kinds of cake. The prices of these were 25¢, 30¢, and 35¢ per pound. The income from these sales was $36. If the number of pounds of each kind of cake sold was the same, how many pounds were sold?

(A) 120 pounds

(B) 90 pounds

(C) 60 pounds

(D) 45 pounds

(E) 36 pounds

17. How many more 9" × 9" linoleum tiles than 1' × 1' tiles will it take to cover a 12' × 12' floor?

(A) 63

(B) 98

(C) 112

(D) 120

(E) 144

18. If p pencils cost c cents, n pencils at the same rate will cost

(A) $\dfrac{pc}{n}$ cents.

(B) $\dfrac{cn}{p}$ cents.

(C) npc cents.

(D) $\dfrac{np}{c}$ cents.

(E) $n + p + c$ cents.

19. Which, if any, of the following statements is always true?

(A) If the numerator and denominator of a fraction are increased or decreased by the same amount, the value of the fraction is unchanged.

(B) If the numerator and denominator of a fraction are squared, the value of the fraction is unchanged.

(C) The square of any number is greater than that number.

(D) If unequal quantities are added to unequal quantities, the sums are unequal.

(E) None of the above

20. If the length and width of a rectangle are each doubled, by what percent is the area increased?

(A) 50%

(B) 75%

(C) 100%

(D) 300%

(E) 400%

21. If one pipe can fill a tank in $1\dfrac{1}{2}$ hours, and another can fill the same tank in 45 minutes, how long will it take for the two pipes to fill the tank together?

(A) $\dfrac{1}{3}$ hour

(B) $\dfrac{1}{2}$ hour

(C) $\dfrac{5}{6}$ hour

(D) 1 hour

(E) $1\dfrac{1}{2}$ hours

22. A baseball team has won 50 games out of 75 played. It has 45 games still to play. How many of these must the team win to make its record for the season 60%?

(A) 20

(B) 22

(C) 25

(D) 30

(E) 35

DAILY OIL CONSUMPTION

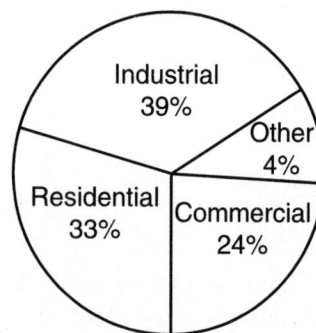

23. If nine million barrels of oil are consumed daily in the United States, how many barrels are required to meet commercial and industrial needs?

(A) 2,840,000

(B) 3,420,000

(C) 4,750,000

(D) 5,670,000

(E) 7,400,000

24. A real estate investor buys a house and lot for $44,000. He pays $1,250 to have it painted, $1,750 to fix the plumbing, and $1,000 for grading a driveway. At what price must he sell the property in order to make a 12% profit?

(A) $53,760

(B) $52,800

(C) $52,000

(D) $49,760

(E) $44,480

25. If $a = 1$, $b = 2$, $c = 3$, and $d = 5$, the value of $\sqrt{b(d+a) - b(c+a)}$ is

(A) 2

(B) 3.5

(C) 4

(D) $\sqrt{20}$

(E) 50

STOP   END OF SECTION 4. IF YOU HAVE ANY TIME LEFT, GO OVER YOUR WORK IN THIS SECTION ONLY. DO NOT WORK IN ANY OTHER SECTION OF THE TEST.

practice test

ANSWER KEY AND EXPLANATIONS

Part I: Writing Sample

Example of a well-written essay.

I can understand why some schools require students to maintain their grades if they want to be in sports. Sports are time consuming and cut into study time. But, I think that less competent students should not be deprived of the benefits of sports participation.

The argument that students should keep up their grades if they want to be in sports is worth listening to. After all, the purpose of going to school is to get an education. And sports practice and games do take a lot of time. The grades of a few students might in fact suffer from sports participation, but I think that more students will work harder and will learn to manage time better if they are allowed to play on the team. Learning to organize time is also an important lesson to be gained from school. Happy people tend to reach to meet expectations, and less capable students may even do better in school to prove that being in sports did not do them any harm.

An equally good argument is that everyone must succeed at something. If a poor student can excel at sports, that student will develop self-esteem. Once that student feels good about himself or herself, the student may transfer that confidence to schoolwork and actually get better grades. The old adage that success breeds success applies here.

While the attitude that schoolwork comes first does make a good point, I think that permitting a student to participate in sports and to develop a good self-image is more important. The school should give extra help to the less competent student, especially help in learning time management. Then it should let that student contribute to school spirit on the playing fields as well as in the classroom.

Part II: Multiple-Choice

Section 1: Verbal

1. E	13. C	25. E	37. A	49. E
2. A	14. A	26. A	38. B	50. A
3. B	15. C	27. B	39. D	51. D
4. C	16. D	28. D	40. C	52. A
5. E	17. C	29. A	41. A	53. B
6. E	18. B	30. B	42. E	54. E
7. B	19. A	31. B	43. A	55. D
8. A	20. C	32. C	44. B	56. A
9. A	21. D	33. E	45. A	57. C
10. B	22. B	34. A	46. C	58. B
11. D	23. E	35. B	47. C	59. A
12. E	24. D	36. C	48. D	60. A

1. **The correct answer is (E).** The AGENDA is the *program of things to be done* or the *schedule*. Preparation of next year's budget was the top item on the agenda for the meeting.

2. **The correct answer is (A).** CREDIBLE means *plausible*, *reliable*, or *believable*. The presence of many squirrels in my yard is a credible explanation for the many holes.

3. **The correct answer is (B).** PLACID means *tranquil*, *calm*, or *peaceful*. Lake Placid in New York is so placid that its waters are seldom stormy.

4. **The correct answer is (C).** To INTERVENE is to *come between two people or things* either to *interfere* or to influence positively. *Intervene* is a verb. An *intermediary* (noun) may intervene in a dispute.

5. **The correct answer is (E).** MUNDANE means *commonplace*, *earthly*, or *ordinary*. Every morning I perform the mundane tasks of brushing my teeth and making my bed.

6. **The correct answer is (E).** To dehydrate is to remove water, therefore DEHYDRATED means *waterless*. The root *hydr-* refers to water, and the prefix *de-* is a negative prefix. Dehydrated foods are lightweight and are easy to store for long periods of time.

7. **The correct answer is (B).** PREVALENT means *widely existing*, *prevailing*, or *generally accepted*. *Preeminent* means *excelling*. The prevalent mood among the Boy Scouts was one of eager anticipation.

8. **The correct answer is (A).** SUCCINCT means *brief* and *to the point*. The legislator gave a succinct background of the reasons for the proposed law.

9. **The correct answer is (A).** That which is NOCTURNAL *happens at night*. Bats do not fly about in the daytime because they are nocturnal creatures.

10. **The correct answer is (B).** EQUITABLE means *fair* and *just*. You should see the root *equal* in this word. The will provided for an equitable distribution of the property.

11. **The correct answer is (D).** To EXPEDITE is to *speed up the action* or to *send quickly*. The Latin derivation of this word is "to free one caught by the feet." You can expedite the delivery of mail by using ZIP Code plus four.

12. **The correct answer is (E).** TURBULENT means *unruly* or *agitated*. As the airplane passed through turbulent air we all felt rather queasy.

13. **The correct answer is (C).** TENACIOUS means *holding on tightly* or persistent. The tenacious salesman calls twice a week between 5 and 7 p.m.

14. **The correct answer is (A).** PERTINENT means *relevant*. Testimony is admitted in court only if it is pertinent to the charges in the case.

15. **The correct answer is (C).** DOGMATIC means *dictatorial* or *opinionated*. The word has to do with *doctrine* or *dogma*, not with *dogs*. My uncle is so dogmatic that he refuses to even listen to my point of view.

16. **The correct answer is (D).** One who is UNSCRUPULOUS is *not restrained by ideas of right and wrong*. The unscrupulous stockbroker used inside information to sell before the stock price plummeted.

17. **The correct answer is (C).** WILY means *crafty* or *sly*. The wily wolf outwitted Red Riding Hood.

18. **The correct answer is (B).** BLATANT means *loud* and *obtrusive*. The misspelling in the address was a blatant error in an otherwise excellent letter.

19. **The correct answer is (A).** A PRETEXT is a *false reason* or *an excuse*. Illness was his pretext for absence from school; actually he went to the beach.

20. **The correct answer is (C).** ACUMEN is *keenness and quickness in understanding and dealing with a situation*. Acumen with respect to foreign cultures is a great asset in the diplomatic corps.

21. **The correct answer is (D).** EVASION is *subterfuge* or *avoidance*. His manner of evasion of embarrassing questions was to make a long speech on another topic.

22. **The correct answer is (B).** That which is INDISPENSABLE *cannot be dispensed with*, that is, it is *absolutely essential*. The president of the company refused to take a vacation because he had the mistaken notion that his presence was indispensable.

23. **The correct answer is (E).** To OBLITERATE is to *destroy without leaving a trace*. The washing waves obliterated our footsteps in the sand.

24. **The correct answer is (D).** AMIABLE means *pleasant, friendly,* and *good-natured*. The amiable shopkeeper allowed us to continue trying on shoes even though it was already past closing time.

25. **The correct answer is (E).** To WRITHE is to *twist, squirm,* or *contort*, usually in discomfort. The skier writhed in pain when she broke her ankle.

26. **The correct answer is (A).** To ABATE is to *diminish*. We will stay tied up in port until the winds abate.

27. **The correct answer is (B).** An ENDORSEMENT is a *statement of approval*. The governor gave his endorsement to the candidate for mayor of the city.

28. **The correct answer is (D).** To CONVERT is to *change* from one form to another. Use a transformer to convert DC current to AC current.

29. **The correct answer is (A).** ERUDITE means *learned* or *scholarly*. He has little information, but his beautiful command of the English language makes him appear to be erudite.

30. The correct answer is (B). To ENDEAVOR is to *attempt* or to *try*. The expedition endeavored to reach the mountaintop before the thunderstorm.

31. The correct answer is (B). The relationship of the terms is one of degree. *None* is the ultimate, the empty set, of *little*; *never* bears the same relationship to *infrequently*.

32. The correct answer is (C). If you think in terms of a house, you can see that the terms on each side of the relationship are synonymous. You can *receive* a person into your home or *admit* the person. Once the person decides to *remain*, that person *settles* in.

33. The correct answer is (E). Here the cause-and-effect relationship is clear. Recognized *dishonesty* leads to *distrust*; *carelessness* leads to *accidents*.

34. The correct answer is (A). The relationship is that of actor to object. A *sociologist* studies *groups*; a *psychologist* studies *individuals*. The relationship of the children to the pediatrician is in reverse order.

35. The correct answer is (B). The terms are antonyms. *Generous* is the opposite of *frugal*; a *philanthropist* is truly the opposite of a *miser*. The terms in choices (C) and (E) are also antonyms. When faced with questions in which the same relationship is maintained by a number of the choices, you must look for a relationship among all four terms. In this case, the theme to be carried through among the choices of the correct analogy is "money."

36. The correct answer is (C). The relationship is one of degree. *Translucent* is denser than *transparent*, that is, one can actually see through something that is transparent whereas only light passes through a translucent medium. Carrying on to the next degree, *opaque* is denser than *translucent*. Not even light can pass through something

that is opaque. Choice (A) is incorrect because it skips a degree and jumps from transparent to opaque. Choice (D) reverses the order. Glass and crystal, choice (B), may both be transparent.

37. The correct answer is (A). This is a classic cause-and-effect relationship. *Discontent* leads to *rebellion*; *friction* creates a *spark*.

38. The correct answer is (B). The relationship is that of worker to tool. A *chemist* uses a *beaker* in the laboratory; a *geologist* uses a *hammer* to chip at rocks in the field or laboratory. Avoid the "trap" of choice (C). A hammer is certainly used in construction, but the relationship of the first two terms requires that a person be involved to complete the analogy.

39. The correct answer is (D). The basis of the analogy is antonyms.

40. The correct answer is (C). This is a part-to-whole analogy. A *state* is part of a *country*; a *country* is part of a *continent*.

41. The correct answer is (A). Cause and effect. An *accelerator* causes the motion of the *car*; a *catalyst* causes the chemical *change*.

42. The correct answer is (E). The relationship is one of degree. *Probable* is likely, but less likely than *certain*; *plausible* is possible, but less likely than *definite*.

43. The correct answer is (A). The relationship is one of true synonyms.

44. The correct answer is (B). This analogy involves true antonyms.

45. The correct answer is (A). The relationship is that of object to actor. The *nucleus* is the object that is orbited by an *electron*; the *earth* is the object that is orbited by a *satellite*. Choice (B) reverses the order of the relationship.

46. **The correct answer is (C).** Here the relationship is that of actor to object. A *sculptor* creates a *statue*; a *composer* creates *music*. An actor performs in a play but does not create it. A programmer creates a program while working at a computer.

47. **The correct answer is (C).** The analogy is based on an antonym relationship.

48. **The correct answer is (D).** This analogy is also based on antonyms.

49. **The correct answer is (E).** It is hard to categorize this relationship. One *interrupts* by *speaking* out of turn; one *intrudes* by *entering* out of turn. The relationship in choice (B) might be that of opposites.

50. **The correct answer is (A).** The first two terms are true opposites. Only choice (A) offers true opposites. *Financial stability* is the opposite of *poverty*, but finance bears no relationship to poverty at all.

51. **The correct answer is (D).** This analogy is best understood as a negative cause and effect. *Adversity* leads to a lack of *happiness*; *vehemence* leads to a lack of *serenity*.

52. **The correct answer is (A).** The relationship is that of actor to action. An *extortionist blackmails*; a *kleptomaniac steals*.

53. **The correct answer is (B).** This is a whole-to-part relationship. A *monsoon* is a major storm of which *rain* is a crucial component; a *tornado* is a major storm of which *wind* is a crucial component.

54. **The correct answer is (E).** The relationship between the two sets of words is that the words in each half of the analogy are synonyms. Don't worry that the words in the first half are antonyms of the second. You aren't looking at how all four words relate to one another in this analogy, just at how the words in each half relate to one another.

55. **The correct answer is (D).** You needn't categorize an analogy; you only need to understand it. The *equator* is the midline that circles the *world*; the *waist* is the midline that circles the *man*.

56. **The correct answer is (A).** On each side of the analogy, the first term is a characteristic of the second.

57. **The correct answer is (C).** This analogy is based on characteristics of bodies of water. A *pond* may be *stagnant*; a *stream* is likely to *flow*. Sheep may be noisy but since there are two choices that involve characteristics, you must choose the one that is closest in other aspects to the first set of terms, that is, the one involving *water*.

58. **The correct answer is (B).** This is a purposeful or functional relationship. A *fortress* gives *sanctuary*; a *house* gives *shelter*.

59. **The correct answer is (A).** The terms are synonyms.

60. **The correct answer is (A).** This analogy is also based on synonyms. Choice (E) is incorrect because pensive means thoughtful. If you made this choice, you were mistaking pensive for pendant, which does mean hanging.

Section 2: Quantitative (Math)

1. B	6. C	11. E	16. A	21. A
2. C	7. A	12. E	17. C	22. D
3. D	8. B	13. A	18. A	23. B
4. D	9. C	14. B	19. C	24. C
5. B	10. C	15. D	20. E	25. D

1. **The correct answer is (B).** Rename $\frac{3}{5}$ as a decimal: $\frac{3}{5} = .6$.

   $.6 + 1.25 + .004 = 1.854$

2. **The correct answer is (C).**

   $\frac{10^6}{10^3} = 10^{6-3} = 1,000$

   or $10^6 = 1,000,000$ and $10^3 = 1,000$

   Therefore, $1,000,000 \div 1,000 = 1,000$

3. **The correct answer is (D).**

$$
\begin{array}{r}
71.4 \\
\times\ 98.2 \\
\hline
1428 \\
5712 \\
6426 \\
\hline
7,011.48
\end{array}
$$

4. **The correct answer is (D).** Simplify the numerator.

   $$\frac{4\frac{2}{3}+\frac{1}{6}}{\frac{1}{3}} = \frac{4\frac{4}{6}+\frac{1}{6}}{\frac{1}{3}} = \frac{4\frac{5}{6}}{\frac{1}{3}}$$

   Proceed as you would to divide any fraction:

   $$4\frac{5}{6} \div \frac{1}{3} = \frac{29}{2\!\!\!\!/6} \cdot \frac{\cancel{3}^1}{1} = 14\frac{1}{2}$$

5. **The correct answer is (B).** $(.25)^2 = .25 \times .25 = .0625$

6. **The correct answer is (C).** Begin with the innermost group and work outward:

   $(3 + 1) + [(2 - 3) - (4 - 1)]$

   $= (3 + 1) + [(-1) - (3)]$

   $= (3 + 1) + [-1 -3]$

   $= (3 + 1) + [-4]$

   $= 4 + -4$

   $= 0$

7. **The correct answer is (A).** Try to estimate the answer rather than calculate:

$$
\begin{array}{r}
10,001 \\
-\ 8,093 \\
\hline
1,908
\end{array}
$$

8. **The correct answer is (B).** Three gallons contain 12 quarts. The ratio is 3 quarts : 12 quarts, or, in simplest form, 1:4.

9. **The correct answer is (C).** One fifth of $50 is $10. Ten percent, or $\frac{1}{10}$, of $10 is $1.

10. **The correct answer is (C).** Borrow one minute from the minutes column, and one hour from the hours column. Then subtract:

$$
\begin{array}{r}
3\text{hr. }71\text{min. }70\text{sec.} \\
-\ 2\text{hr. }48\text{min. }35\text{sec.} \\
\hline
1\text{hr. }23\text{min. }35\text{sec.}
\end{array}
$$

11. **The correct answer is (E).** By doubling the size of one of the factors of the numerator and the size of the denominator, we do not change the value of the fraction. We are actually writing an equivalent fraction. Try this with fractions having numerical values for the numerator and denominator.

12. **The correct answer is (E).** This is a good problem for estimation. Note that 10% of 220 = 22. One percent of 220 = 2.2 and 24.2 = 22 (10 percent) + 2.2 (1 percent). Or, $\frac{24.2}{200} = .11$.

13. **The correct answer is (A).** Be careful. This problem asks you to reduce 98 by $\frac{5}{7}$. In other words, find $\frac{2}{7}$ of 98. $98 \cdot \frac{2}{7} = \frac{98^{14}}{1} \cdot \frac{2}{7_1} = 28$

14. **The correct answer is (B).** Since one foot corresponds to $\frac{1}{4}$ inch in the drawing, the drawing should be $6\frac{1}{2} \cdot \frac{1}{4}$ inches long.

$$6\frac{1}{2} \cdot \frac{1}{4} =$$
$$= \frac{13}{2} \cdot \frac{1}{4}$$
$$= \frac{13}{8} = 1\frac{5}{8}"$$

15. **The correct answer is (D).** Bracket the multiplication and division operations from left to right. Then calculate.

$$\left[12\frac{1}{2} \div \frac{1}{2}\right] + \left[\frac{3}{2} \times 4\right] - 3$$
$$= [25] + [6] - 3$$
$$= 28$$

16. **The correct answer is (A).** Since $y + 2 > 10$, $y > 10 - 2$, or $y > 8$.

17. **The correct answer is (C).** This is a simple proportion. A man casts a shadow twice as long as his height. Therefore, so does the tree. Therefore, a tree that casts a shadow 50' long is 25' high.

18. **The correct answer is (A).** The denominator of a fraction can never be equivalent to zero. Division by zero is undefined in mathematics.

19. **The correct answer is (C).** $.0515 \times 100 = 5.15$, and so does $.00515 \times 1,000$. You should be able to do this problem by moving decimal points and not by multiplying out. To divide by 10, move the decimal point one place to the left. Move it two places to the left to divide by 100, three places to divide by 1,000, and so forth. To multiply by 10, 100, 1,000 and so forth, move the decimal point the corresponding number of places to the right. This is an important skill to review.

20. **The correct answer is (E).** This is a tricky problem. Choices (B), (C), and (D) might be true in some cases, depending upon the exact measurements of $\angle 1$ and $\angle 3$. The only answer that is true no matter what the measures of $\angle 1$ and $\angle 3$ is the one in which their sum is equal to 120°.

21. **The correct answer is (A).** This can be set up as a proportion where x is the unknown number:

$$\frac{45}{x} = \frac{90}{.45}$$

This is a good problem for estimation. Study the numerators of the fractions and note that 45 is one half of 90. Therefore, the denominators of the fractions must have the same relationship. One half of .45 is .225.

22. **The correct answer is (D).** The square root of 20 is less than the square root of 25, which is 5, and greater than the square root of 16, which is 4. Therefore, n is between 4 and 5.

23. **The correct answer is (B).** To find the difference, we subtract –6 from 4 and move from –6 to 4, a distance of +10 units.

24. **The correct answer is (C).** Simply divide $\frac{4}{5}$ by $\frac{1}{6}$ to find the answer.

$$\frac{4}{5} \div \frac{1}{6} = \frac{4}{5} \bullet \frac{6}{1} = \frac{24}{5} = 4\frac{4}{5}$$

25. **The correct answer is (D).** Four games averaging 36,500 people per game total 146,000 attendance. The total for the first three games was 105,500. The fourth game attracted 40,500 people.

Section 3: Reading Comprehension

1. C	9. A	17. B	25. A	33. D
2. D	10. B	18. A	26. C	34. C
3. B	11. E	19. C	27. E	35. B
4. E	12. A	20. E	28. D	36. E
5. C	13. C	21. E	29. A	37. A
6. B	14. D	22. D	30. D	38. C
7. D	15. B	23. A	31. B	39. A
8. E	16. A	24. C	32. B	40. E

1. **The correct answer is (C).** You will find the answer to this detail question in the last two sentences of the selection.

2. **The correct answer is (D).** This detail is given in the last sentence of the first paragraph. All the other answer choices were true of the history of Riker's Island but are not true at the present time.

3. **The correct answer is (B).** You can infer that the discards of city households included garbage. Decayed garbage is an excellent fertilizer.

4. **The correct answer is (E).** See the next-to-last sentence of the selection.

5. **The correct answer is (C).** This is the meaning of the second sentence of the first paragraph.

6. **The correct answer is (B).** Since the thrust of the selection is the threatened extinction of the bald eagle, you really do not need to search for the precise words that answer this question. However, you can find them in the second paragraph.

7. **The correct answer is (D).** This definition is given in the second sentence of the third paragraph: " .. aeries, the eagles' mammoth nests."

8. **The correct answer is (E).** The selection tells us that the bald eagle appears on the Great Seal of the United States, our national emblem. An *emblem* is a symbol. *Emblematic* is the adjective form of the noun, *emblem*.

9. **The correct answer is (A).** This detail may be found in the first sentence of the last paragraph.

10. The correct answer is (B). The author tells you his reason in the second sentence.

11. The correct answer is (E). See the third sentence.

12. The correct answer is (A). The fourth sentence gives this detail.

13. The correct answer is (C). The sixth sentence tells that the garden led to a forest. The selection says that the garden extended so far that the gardener did not know where it ended, but it does not say that he was unable to care for it because of its size.

14. The correct answer is (D). In the last sentence we learn that the forest went down to the sea, and in the trees of the forest at seaside lived a nightingale.

15. The correct answer is (B). This really is a vocabulary question. A *sojourn* is a visit or a temporary stay.

16. The correct answer is (A). The context of the second paragraph should help you to figure out the meaning of this word. In other contexts, *decipher* may mean to *decode*. Here it means to *make out the meaning of ancient, nearly illegible, inscriptions or writings.*

17. The correct answer is (B). See the last sentence of the first paragraph. By enlarging on hitherto known tales of the named persons, the scroll is giving new details about persons already known of. The scroll is the last of the seven found in 1947, not the first. It tells of Abraham's stay in Egypt, but it was found in the Judean desert of Israel.

18. The correct answer is (A). The second paragraph opens by telling us that the scroll belongs to Hebrew University. If you were not certain that Hebrew University is an Israeli university, the statement that the work is being done under the supervision of Israeli scholars (last sentence) should confirm this.

19. The correct answer is (C). If this question gives you trouble, reread the middle of the second paragraph. The readable material included: four full pages, legible parts of five other pages, and some lines and words on additional pages.

20. The correct answer is (E). See the first sentence. A century ago was 100 years ago.

21. The correct answer is (E). The first sentence of the second paragraph says that the boats are equipped for various jobs, which means that they vary in function.

22. The correct answer is (D). By checking on the operation of the junk boats, the harbor police ensure that their activities are legal.

23. The correct answer is (A). The other choices all include some activity that is not mentioned as an activity of the harbor police.

24. The correct answer is (C). The 450 disabled boats that were towed and the thousands that needed some sort of help (next-to-last sentence) could not possibly have all been of the same kind.

25. The correct answer is (A). Context should help you here. " .. veneration due to its sacred origin .. " implies something religious and related to worship.

26. The correct answer is (C). This is an inferential question. The speaker probably enjoys and celebrates Christmas, choice (B) as well, but the primary reason for this speech is defending the holiday to his Uncle Scrooge by listing its advantages to mankind.

27. The correct answer is (E). This is the whole point of the first paragraph.

28. The correct answer is (D). Again, use of the word in context should lead you to its meaning. The paragraph speaks of good will among all men and women. This *one consent* therefore is *unanimous* good feeling.

29. **The correct answer is (A).** Read the last paragraph carefully. Scrooge is first reacting to the clerk who has just applauded the speech in defense of Christmas. Scrooge threatens the clerk with firing. He then turns and makes a sarcastic remark to his nephew. It can be assumed that he is angry with both characters.

30. **The correct answer is (D).** "Just stopped by .." is quite a matter-of-fact way of speaking.

31. **The correct answer is (B).** The raised eyebrows of the first sentence of the second paragraph imply disbelief.

32. **The correct answer is (B).** Mr. Holter had a caravan of animals; was in New York on his way to Dayton, Ohio; and actually lived in Anaheim, California. You can infer that he made his living traveling and showing his animals.

33. **The correct answer is (D).** The article discusses high blood pressure as a familial disease, a disease that runs in families. It goes on to discuss the role of genetic makeup in determining reaction to dietary factors. Genetic makeup refers to hereditary factors.

34. **The correct answer is (C).** This is a main-idea question. The main point of the selection is that there is an interplay of genetic and environmental factors influencing the development of high blood pressure.

35. **The correct answer is (B).** The first paragraph speaks of the perils of fishing, the second about its rewards.

36. **The correct answer is (E).** The middle of the first paragraph discusses the problems created by rough seas. None of the other choices is a mentioned difficulty.

37. **The correct answer is (A).** In the middle of the second paragraph we learn that when the fishermen note that herring are entering the nets they sit in quiet excitement so as not to frighten the fish away. They row along the net, choice (E), in order to find out if the net is filling, and haul in the nets, choices (B) and (D), when the nets are full. It is the fish that glisten, not the fishermen.

38. **The correct answer is (C).** Everything is mentioned except the beauty of the sea.

39. **The correct answer is (A).** All other choices contain at least one trait that is not ascribed to the fishermen.

40. **The correct answer is (E).** One might add honesty to the traits of the fishermen. Theft is not mentioned as a problem.

Section 4: Quantitative (Math)

1. E	6. D	11. B	16. A	21. B
2. B	7. C	12. D	17. C	22. B
3. D	8. B	13. B	18. B	23. D
4. B	9. C	14. D	19. E	24. A
5. C	10. E	15. E	20. D	25. A

1. **The correct answer is (E).** Any point on the surface rotates once each day relative to a point in space. Each revolution is an angle of 360°. In two days, two revolutions take place, 360° × 2 = 720°.

2. **The correct answer is (B).** $\frac{3}{7}$, $\frac{15}{32}$, and $\frac{11}{23}$ are all less than $\frac{1}{2}$; $\frac{9}{16}$ is larger than $\frac{1}{2}$. Compare the size of fractions this way.

$$\frac{3}{7} \times \frac{15}{32}$$

Because the product of 7 and 15 is larger than the product of 32 and 3, $\frac{15}{32}$ will be found to be larger. Using the same method, $\frac{5}{32} < \frac{11}{23}$.

3. **The correct answer is (D).** If the width is x, the length, which is twice as long, is $2x$. The perimeter is equal to the sum of the four sides: $2x + 2x + x + x = 6x$.

4. **The correct answer is (B).** Use the Pythagorean Theorem $c^2 = a^2 + b^2$ to find the length of the diagonal:

$c^2 = 1^2 + 1^2$

$c^2 = 2$

$c = \sqrt{2}$

5. **The correct answer is (C).** Eight sections, each 3'2" long, is equivalent to 8 × 38" = 304".

$304" = 25\frac{1}{3}$ feet, therefore three 10-foot sections are needed.

6. **The correct answer is (D).** The width of the shaded area is $\frac{1}{3}$ of the width of the square. Therefore, the area of the shaded part is $\frac{1}{3}$ the area of the whole square. The unshaded part is twice as large as the shaded part. The ratio of the shaded part to the unshaded, therefore, is 1:2.

7. **The correct answer is (C).** Since distance = rate × time, rate = distance ÷ time. Total distance traveled is 3,200 miles. Total time is 4 hours 20 minutes.

Rate = 3,200 miles ÷ 4 hours 20 minutes

$= 3{,}200$ miles $\div 4\frac{1}{3}$ hours

$= 739$ mph, approximately

8. **The correct answer is (B).** This is a simple proportion: $\frac{7}{4} = \frac{5}{x}$. x is the unknown width. Cross-multiply:

$7x = 20$

$x = \frac{20}{7}$, or $2\frac{6}{7}$"

9. **The correct answer is (C).** Subtract the area of the circle from the area of the square to find the area of just the shaded part.

Note that the diameter of the circle equals the width of the square.

Area of square = s^2 = 4 sq. in.

Area of circle = πr^2 = $\pi(1)^2$ = π sq. in.

Area of square – Area of circle

= 4 sq. in. – $\dfrac{22}{7}$ sq. in.

= $\dfrac{6}{7}$ sq. in., or $\dfrac{6}{7}$ in.²

10. **The correct answer is (E).** The population would reproduce 12 times in 4 hours. The size then is $P = 1 \times 2^{12}$

= 2 • 2 • 2 • 2 • 2 • 2 • 2 • 2 • 2 • 2 • 2 • 2

= 4,096

11. **The correct answer is (B).** The larger the number of the denominator of a fraction, the smaller the quantity represented. For example, $\dfrac{1}{4}$ represents a lesser quantity than $\dfrac{1}{2}$.

Therefore, as x becomes greater, y becomes smaller.

12. **The correct answer is (D).** If the second box has each dimension 3 times that of the first box, then its volume is $3 \times 3 \times 3 = 27$ times as great.

13. **The correct answer is (B).** The area of the flower bed is 4π sq. ft. ($A = \pi r^2$). The area of the new bed is to be four times as great, or 16π sq. ft. A bed with an area of 16π sq. ft. must have a diameter of 8', and a radius of 4', since $A = \pi r^2$.

14. **The correct answer is (D).** Use the formula D = R × T to find the time it actually took to get to Buffalo: time = distance ÷ rate. Travel time of trip was equal to 290 miles ÷ 50 mph.

Travel time = $5\dfrac{4}{5}$ hours, or 5 hours 48 minutes. Scheduled travel time was between 10:10 a.m and 3:45 p.m, an interval of 5 hours 35 minutes. Therefore, the train took about 13 minutes longer than scheduled.

15. **The correct answer is (E).** Solve the equation for x:

$3x - 2 = 13$

$3x = 15$

$x = 5$

If $x = 5$, then $12x + 20 = 12(5) + 20 = 80$.

16. **The correct answer is (A).** Since the number of pounds of each kind of cake sold was the same, we can say that a pound of cake sold for an average price of 30¢ per pound.

25¢ + 30¢ + 35¢ = 90¢ ÷ 3 = 30¢ per lb.

Divide the total sales income of $36 by 30¢ to find how many pounds were sold.

$36 ÷ .30 = 120

17. **The correct answer is (C).** A floor 12' × 12' is 144 sq. ft. in area, and would require 144 tiles that are each one foot by one foot. Twelve tiles would be placed along the width and length of the room. If 9" tiles are used, it requires 16 of them placed end to end to cover the length of the room. Therefore, it requires 16 × 16 tiles to cover the floor, or 256 tiles. It requires 112 more 9" tiles than 12" tiles to cover the floor.

18. **The correct answer is (B).** If p pencils cost c cents, the cost of each pencil is $\dfrac{c}{p}$ cents. To find the cost of n pencils, we multiply the cost of each times n:

$\dfrac{c}{p} \bullet n = \dfrac{cn}{p}$

19. The correct answer is (E). If necessary, try each of the answers for yourself, to see that each is false. Choice (C) is untrue for the number 1.

20. The correct answer is (D). Think of a rectangle with the dimensions 1" by 2". Its area is 2 square inches. If we double each dimension, to 2" by 4", the area becomes 8 square inches, which is four times the area of the first rectangle. This is equal to an increase of 300%.

21. The correct answer is (B). The first pipe can fill the tank in $1\frac{1}{2}$, or $\frac{3}{2}$, hours; that is, it can do $\frac{2}{3}$ of the job in 1 hour. The second pipe can fill the tank in 45 minutes, or $\frac{3}{4}$ of an hour, or it can do $\frac{4}{3}$ of the job in 1 hour. Together the pipes can complete $\frac{4}{3} + \frac{2}{3} = \frac{6}{3}$ of the job in one hour. $\frac{6}{3} =$ 2, or twice the job in one hour. Therefore, together the two pipes could fill the tank in $\frac{1}{2}$ hour.

22. The correct answer is (B). The whole season consists of 120 games. For a season record of 60%, the team must win 72 games. Since it has already won 50, it must win 22 more games out of those left.

23. The correct answer is (D). Commercial and industrial needs total 63% of daily oil consumption. Since consumption is 9 million barrels, 63% of 9 million is 5,670,000 barrels.

24. The correct answer is (A). Add the cost of the house, driveway, painting, and plumbing:

$44,000 + $1,250 + $1,750 + 1,000 = $48,000

If he wants to make a 12% profit when reselling the house, he should increase the total cost by 12% to find the new selling price:

12% of $48,000 = $5,760

$48,000 + $5,760 = $53,760

25. The correct answer is (A). This is a problem that must be done carefully.

$a = 1, b = 2, c = 3, d = 5$

$$\sqrt{b(d+a) - b(c+a)}$$
$$= \sqrt{2(5+1) - 2(3+1)}$$
$$= \sqrt{2(6) - 2(4)}$$
$$= \sqrt{12 - 8}$$
$$= \sqrt{4}$$
$$= 2$$

SCORE YOURSELF

Check your answers against the answer key. Count up the number of answers you got right and the number you got wrong.

Section	No. Right	No. Wrong
Quantitative (Math)		
Reading Comprehension		
Verbal		

Now calculate your raw scores:

Quantitative (Math): (_____) − $\left(\frac{1}{4}\right)$ (_____) = (_____)

                      No. Right   No. Wrong   Raw Score

Reading Comprehension: (_____) − $\left(\frac{1}{4}\right)$ (_____) = (_____)

                      No. Right   No. Wrong   Raw Score

Verbal: (_____) − $\left(\frac{1}{4}\right)$ (_____) = (_____)

                      No. Right   No. Wrong   Raw Score

Now check your Raw Score against the conversion chart to get an idea of the range in which your test scores:

Raw Score	Quantitative (Math)	Reading Comprehension	Verbal
60			350
55			350
50	350		343
45	344		334
40	335	348	325
35	325	324	316
30	316	314	307
25	306	304	298
20	297	294	289
15	288	284	280
10	278	274	271
5	269	264	261
0	260	254	252
−5 or lower	250	250	250

Remember:

- The same exam is given to students in grades 8 through 11. You are not expected to know what you have not been taught.
- You will be compared only to students in your own grade.

Use your scores to plan further study if you have time.

ANSWER SHEET PRACTICE TEST 4: ISEE (Upper Level)

Section 1: Verbal

1 Ⓐ Ⓑ Ⓒ Ⓓ	11 Ⓐ Ⓑ Ⓒ Ⓓ	21 Ⓐ Ⓑ Ⓒ Ⓓ	31 Ⓐ Ⓑ Ⓒ Ⓓ
2 Ⓐ Ⓑ Ⓒ Ⓓ	12 Ⓐ Ⓑ Ⓒ Ⓓ	22 Ⓐ Ⓑ Ⓒ Ⓓ	32 Ⓐ Ⓑ Ⓒ Ⓓ
3 Ⓐ Ⓑ Ⓒ Ⓓ	13 Ⓐ Ⓑ Ⓒ Ⓓ	23 Ⓐ Ⓑ Ⓒ Ⓓ	33 Ⓐ Ⓑ Ⓒ Ⓓ
4 Ⓐ Ⓑ Ⓒ Ⓓ	14 Ⓐ Ⓑ Ⓒ Ⓓ	24 Ⓐ Ⓑ Ⓒ Ⓓ	34 Ⓐ Ⓑ Ⓒ Ⓓ
5 Ⓐ Ⓑ Ⓒ Ⓓ	15 Ⓐ Ⓑ Ⓒ Ⓓ	25 Ⓐ Ⓑ Ⓒ Ⓓ	35 Ⓐ Ⓑ Ⓒ Ⓓ
6 Ⓐ Ⓑ Ⓒ Ⓓ	16 Ⓐ Ⓑ Ⓒ Ⓓ	26 Ⓐ Ⓑ Ⓒ Ⓓ	36 Ⓐ Ⓑ Ⓒ Ⓓ
7 Ⓐ Ⓑ Ⓒ Ⓓ	17 Ⓐ Ⓑ Ⓒ Ⓓ	27 Ⓐ Ⓑ Ⓒ Ⓓ	37 Ⓐ Ⓑ Ⓒ Ⓓ
8 Ⓐ Ⓑ Ⓒ Ⓓ	18 Ⓐ Ⓑ Ⓒ Ⓓ	28 Ⓐ Ⓑ Ⓒ Ⓓ	38 Ⓐ Ⓑ Ⓒ Ⓓ
9 Ⓐ Ⓑ Ⓒ Ⓓ	19 Ⓐ Ⓑ Ⓒ Ⓓ	29 Ⓐ Ⓑ Ⓒ Ⓓ	39 Ⓐ Ⓑ Ⓒ Ⓓ
10 Ⓐ Ⓑ Ⓒ Ⓓ	20 Ⓐ Ⓑ Ⓒ Ⓓ	30 Ⓐ Ⓑ Ⓒ Ⓓ	40 Ⓐ Ⓑ Ⓒ Ⓓ

Section 2: Quantitative (Math)

1 Ⓐ Ⓑ Ⓒ Ⓓ	10 Ⓐ Ⓑ Ⓒ Ⓓ	19 Ⓐ Ⓑ Ⓒ Ⓓ	28 Ⓐ Ⓑ Ⓒ Ⓓ
2 Ⓐ Ⓑ Ⓒ Ⓓ	11 Ⓐ Ⓑ Ⓒ Ⓓ	20 Ⓐ Ⓑ Ⓒ Ⓓ	29 Ⓐ Ⓑ Ⓒ Ⓓ
3 Ⓐ Ⓑ Ⓒ Ⓓ	12 Ⓐ Ⓑ Ⓒ Ⓓ	21 Ⓐ Ⓑ Ⓒ Ⓓ	30 Ⓐ Ⓑ Ⓒ Ⓓ
4 Ⓐ Ⓑ Ⓒ Ⓓ	13 Ⓐ Ⓑ Ⓒ Ⓓ	22 Ⓐ Ⓑ Ⓒ Ⓓ	31 Ⓐ Ⓑ Ⓒ Ⓓ
5 Ⓐ Ⓑ Ⓒ Ⓓ	14 Ⓐ Ⓑ Ⓒ Ⓓ	23 Ⓐ Ⓑ Ⓒ Ⓓ	32 Ⓐ Ⓑ Ⓒ Ⓓ
6 Ⓐ Ⓑ Ⓒ Ⓓ	15 Ⓐ Ⓑ Ⓒ Ⓓ	24 Ⓐ Ⓑ Ⓒ Ⓓ	33 Ⓐ Ⓑ Ⓒ Ⓓ
7 Ⓐ Ⓑ Ⓒ Ⓓ	16 Ⓐ Ⓑ Ⓒ Ⓓ	25 Ⓐ Ⓑ Ⓒ Ⓓ	34 Ⓐ Ⓑ Ⓒ Ⓓ
8 Ⓐ Ⓑ Ⓒ Ⓓ	17 Ⓐ Ⓑ Ⓒ Ⓓ	26 Ⓐ Ⓑ Ⓒ Ⓓ	35 Ⓐ Ⓑ Ⓒ Ⓓ
9 Ⓐ Ⓑ Ⓒ Ⓓ	18 Ⓐ Ⓑ Ⓒ Ⓓ	27 Ⓐ Ⓑ Ⓒ Ⓓ	

answer sheet

Section 3: Reading Comprehension

1 Ⓐ Ⓑ Ⓒ Ⓓ	11 Ⓐ Ⓑ Ⓒ Ⓓ	21 Ⓐ Ⓑ Ⓒ Ⓓ	31 Ⓐ Ⓑ Ⓒ Ⓓ
2 Ⓐ Ⓑ Ⓒ Ⓓ	12 Ⓐ Ⓑ Ⓒ Ⓓ	22 Ⓐ Ⓑ Ⓒ Ⓓ	32 Ⓐ Ⓑ Ⓒ Ⓓ
3 Ⓐ Ⓑ Ⓒ Ⓓ	13 Ⓐ Ⓑ Ⓒ Ⓓ	23 Ⓐ Ⓑ Ⓒ Ⓓ	33 Ⓐ Ⓑ Ⓒ Ⓓ
4 Ⓐ Ⓑ Ⓒ Ⓓ	14 Ⓐ Ⓑ Ⓒ Ⓓ	24 Ⓐ Ⓑ Ⓒ Ⓓ	34 Ⓐ Ⓑ Ⓒ Ⓓ
5 Ⓐ Ⓑ Ⓒ Ⓓ	15 Ⓐ Ⓑ Ⓒ Ⓓ	25 Ⓐ Ⓑ Ⓒ Ⓓ	35 Ⓐ Ⓑ Ⓒ Ⓓ
6 Ⓐ Ⓑ Ⓒ Ⓓ	16 Ⓐ Ⓑ Ⓒ Ⓓ	26 Ⓐ Ⓑ Ⓒ Ⓓ	36 Ⓐ Ⓑ Ⓒ Ⓓ
7 Ⓐ Ⓑ Ⓒ Ⓓ	17 Ⓐ Ⓑ Ⓒ Ⓓ	27 Ⓐ Ⓑ Ⓒ Ⓓ	37 Ⓐ Ⓑ Ⓒ Ⓓ
8 Ⓐ Ⓑ Ⓒ Ⓓ	18 Ⓐ Ⓑ Ⓒ Ⓓ	28 Ⓐ Ⓑ Ⓒ Ⓓ	38 Ⓐ Ⓑ Ⓒ Ⓓ
9 Ⓐ Ⓑ Ⓒ Ⓓ	19 Ⓐ Ⓑ Ⓒ Ⓓ	29 Ⓐ Ⓑ Ⓒ Ⓓ	39 Ⓐ Ⓑ Ⓒ Ⓓ
10 Ⓐ Ⓑ Ⓒ Ⓓ	20 Ⓐ Ⓑ Ⓒ Ⓓ	30 Ⓐ Ⓑ Ⓒ Ⓓ	40 Ⓐ Ⓑ Ⓒ Ⓓ

Section 4: Quantitative (Math)

1 Ⓐ Ⓑ Ⓒ Ⓓ	10 Ⓐ Ⓑ Ⓒ Ⓓ	19 Ⓐ Ⓑ Ⓒ Ⓓ	28 Ⓐ Ⓑ Ⓒ Ⓓ
2 Ⓐ Ⓑ Ⓒ Ⓓ	11 Ⓐ Ⓑ Ⓒ Ⓓ	20 Ⓐ Ⓑ Ⓒ Ⓓ	29 Ⓐ Ⓑ Ⓒ Ⓓ
3 Ⓐ Ⓑ Ⓒ Ⓓ	12 Ⓐ Ⓑ Ⓒ Ⓓ	21 Ⓐ Ⓑ Ⓒ Ⓓ	30 Ⓐ Ⓑ Ⓒ Ⓓ
4 Ⓐ Ⓑ Ⓒ Ⓓ	13 Ⓐ Ⓑ Ⓒ Ⓓ	22 Ⓐ Ⓑ Ⓒ Ⓓ	31 Ⓐ Ⓑ Ⓒ Ⓓ
5 Ⓐ Ⓑ Ⓒ Ⓓ	14 Ⓐ Ⓑ Ⓒ Ⓓ	23 Ⓐ Ⓑ Ⓒ Ⓓ	32 Ⓐ Ⓑ Ⓒ Ⓓ
6 Ⓐ Ⓑ Ⓒ Ⓓ	15 Ⓐ Ⓑ Ⓒ Ⓓ	24 Ⓐ Ⓑ Ⓒ Ⓓ	33 Ⓐ Ⓑ Ⓒ Ⓓ
7 Ⓐ Ⓑ Ⓒ Ⓓ	16 Ⓐ Ⓑ Ⓒ Ⓓ	25 Ⓐ Ⓑ Ⓒ Ⓓ	34 Ⓐ Ⓑ Ⓒ Ⓓ
8 Ⓐ Ⓑ Ⓒ Ⓓ	17 Ⓐ Ⓑ Ⓒ Ⓓ	26 Ⓐ Ⓑ Ⓒ Ⓓ	35 Ⓐ Ⓑ Ⓒ Ⓓ
9 Ⓐ Ⓑ Ⓒ Ⓓ	18 Ⓐ Ⓑ Ⓒ Ⓓ	27 Ⓐ Ⓑ Ⓒ Ⓓ	

Practice Test 4: ISEE (Upper Level)

SECTION 1: VERBAL REASONING

40 Questions • 20 Minutes

Directions: Each question is made up of a word in CAPITAL letters followed by four choices. Choose the one word that is most nearly the same in meaning as the word in CAPITAL letters, and mark its letter on your answer sheet.

1. FEINT
   (A) fool
   (B) proclaim
   (C) penalize
   (D) scavenge

2. PEER
   (A) officer
   (B) beginner
   (C) equal
   (D) patient

3. TRITE
   (A) unskilled
   (B) common
   (C) unlikely
   (D) ignorant

4. AMIABLE
   (A) forgetful
   (B) friendly
   (C) strange
   (D) great

5. GRIMACE
   (A) sneer
   (B) grindstone
   (C) journal
   (D) treasure

6. COMPELLED
   (A) calculated
   (B) combined
   (C) collected
   (D) forced

7. ALLY
   (A) opponent
   (B) passage
   (C) friend
   (D) preference

8. SOLICIT
   (A) consent
   (B) comfort
   (C) request
   (D) help

9. REFUTE
   (A) demolish
   (B) postpone
   (C) disprove
   (D) assist

10. EXPLICIT
    (A) ambiguous
    (B) clearly stated
    (C) give information about
    (D) to blow out

11. RETAIN
    (A) pay out
    (B) play
    (C) keep
    (D) inquire

12. CORRESPONDENCE
    (A) letters
    (B) files
    (C) testimony
    (D) response

13. LEGITIMATE
    (A) democratic
    (B) legal
    (C) genealogical
    (D) underworld

14. DEDUCT
    (A) conceal
    (B) understand
    (C) subtract
    (D) terminate

15. EGRESS
    (A) extreme
    (B) extra supply
    (C) exit
    (D) high price

16. HORIZONTAL
    (A) marginal
    (B) in a circle
    (C) left and right
    (D) up and down

17. CONTROVERSY
    (A) publicity
    (B) debate
    (C) revolution
    (D) revocation

18. PREEMPT
    (A) steal
    (B) empty
    (C) preview
    (D) appropriate

19. PER CAPITA
    (A) for an entire population
    (B) by income
    (C) for each person
    (D) for every adult

20. OPTIONAL
    (A) not required
    (B) infrequent
    (C) choosy
    (D) for sale

Directions: Each of the following questions is made up of a sentence containing one or two blanks. The sentences with one blank indicate that one word is missing. Sentences with two blanks have two missing words. Each sentence is followed by four choices. Choose the one word or pair of words that will best complete the meaning of the sentence as a whole, and mark the letter of your choice on your answer sheet.

21. Custom has so _____ our language that we can _____ only what has been said before.
    (A) improved .. repeat
    (B) changed .. understand
    (C) enslaved .. say
    (D) dominated .. hear

22. A few of the critics _____ the play, but in general they either disregarded or ridiculed it.
    (A) discredited
    (B) criticized
    (C) denounced
    (D) appreciated

23. Politicians are not the only ones who have made _____; being human, we have all blundered at some time in our lives.
    (A) explanations
    (B) arguments
    (C) errors
    (D) excuses

24. Because of his _____ nature, he often acts purely on impulse.
    (A) stoic
    (B) reflective
    (C) passionate
    (D) wistful

25. A system of education should be _____ by the _____ of students it turns out, for quality is preferred to quantity.
    (A) controlled .. intelligence
    (B) justified .. number
    (C) examined .. wealth
    (D) judged .. caliber

26. We seldom feel _____ when we are allowed to speak freely, but any _____ of our free speech brings anger.
    (A) angry .. defense
    (B) blessed .. restriction
    (C) scholarly .. understanding
    (D) enslaved .. misuse

27. The worst team lost because it had many players who though not completely _____ were also not really _____.
    (A) qualified .. agile
    (B) clumsy .. incompetent
    (C) inept .. proficient
    (D) ungraceful .. amateurish

28. Although the _____ of the legislature become law, the exact _____ of the law is the result of judicial interpretation.
    (A) ideas .. enforcement
    (B) bills .. wording
    (C) works .. punishment
    (D) words .. meaning

29. Since movies have become more _____, many people believe television to be _____.
    (A) helpful .. utilitarian
    (B) expensive .. necessary
    (C) common .. inadequate
    (D) costly .. useless

30. Spores are a form of life that remain _____ until environmental conditions exist in which they can become _____.
    (A) inactive .. vibrant
    (B) hidden .. dangerous
    (C) suppressed .. visible
    (D) controlled .. rampant

31. The spirit of science is always trying to lead people to the study of _____ and away from the spinning of fanciful theories out of their own minds.
    (A) tradition
    (B) order
    (C) legalities
    (D) literature

32. The _____ child thought old people should be polite to him!
    (A) submissive
    (B) impertinent
    (C) alternate
    (D) classless

33. The fame of the author does not _____ the quality of his or her works. We must avoid equating success with infallibility.
    (A) prejudice
    (B) assure
    (C) dignify
    (D) extol

34. The mechanisms that develop hatred in man are most potent, since there is more _____ than _____ in the world.
    (A) tolerance .. prejudice
    (B) joy .. rapture
    (C) love .. hatred
    (D) strife .. tranquility

35. Mining is often called the _____ industry, since it neither creates nor replenishes what it takes.
    (A) robber
    (B) ecology
    (C) natural
    (D) evil

36. The racial problem is of such _____ that it makes going to the moon seem _____.
    (A) complexity .. helpful
    (B) certainty .. problematic
    (C) magnitude .. child's play
    (D) docility .. effortless

37. To be _____ a theatrical setting must resemble _____.
    (A) believable .. home
    (B) effective .. reality
    (C) reasonable .. beauty
    (D) respectable .. ideas

38. The _____ mob roamed through the streets of the city, shouting their _____ of law and order.
    (A) influential .. fear
    (B) indifferent .. horror
    (C) disciplined .. disrespect
    (D) hysterical .. hatred

39. Errors in existing theories are discovered, and the theories are either _____ or _____.
    (A) improved .. obeyed
    (B) removed .. followed
    (C) altered .. discarded
    (D) explained .. excused

40. In observing the _____ society of the ant, the scientist can learn much about the more _____ society of man.
    (A) hostile .. evil
    (B) elementary .. complicated
    (C) plain .. homogeneous
    (D) unadorned .. unsophisticated

STOP   END OF SECTION 1. IF YOU HAVE ANY TIME LEFT, GO OVER YOUR WORK IN THIS SECTION ONLY. DO NOT WORK IN ANY OTHER SECTION OF THE TEST.

SECTION 2: QUANTITATIVE REASONING

35 Questions • 35 Minutes

Note: You may assume that all figures accompanying Quantitative Reasoning questions have been drawn as accurately as possible EXCEPT when it is specifically stated that a particular figure is not drawn to scale. Letters such as x, y, and n stand for real numbers. The Quantitative Reasoning Test includes two types of questions. There are separate directions for each type of question.

Directions: For questions 1–17 work each problem in your head or in the margins of the test booklet. Mark the letter of your answer choice on the answer sheet.

1. Which pair of values for x and $\square$ will make the following statement true?
   $2x\square 8$
   - **(A)** $(6, <)$
   - **(B)** $(4, >)$
   - **(C)** $(0, <)$
   - **(D)** $(-3, >)$

2. Complete the following statement:
   $7(3 \times \underline{\hspace{1cm}}) + 4 = 2,104$
   - **(A)** 10
   - **(B)** $10 + 2$
   - **(C)** 10^2
   - **(D)** 10^3

3. .5% is equal to
   - **(A)** .005
   - **(B)** .05
   - **(C)** $\dfrac{1}{2}$
   - **(D)** .5

4. A scalene triangle has
   - **(A)** two equal sides.
   - **(B)** two equal sides and one right angle.
   - **(C)** no equal sides.
   - **(D)** three equal sides.

5. A millimeter is what part of a meter?
   - **(A)** $\dfrac{1}{10}$
   - **(B)** $\dfrac{1}{100}$
   - **(C)** $\dfrac{1}{1,000}$
   - **(D)** $\dfrac{1}{10,000}$

6. What is the least common denominator for $\dfrac{2}{3}$, $\dfrac{1}{2}$, $\dfrac{5}{6}$, and $\dfrac{7}{9}$?
   - **(A)** 36
   - **(B)** 32
   - **(C)** 24
   - **(D)** 18

7. Find the area of a triangle whose dimensions are: $b = 14$ inches, $h = 20$ inches.
   - **(A)** 140 square inches
   - **(B)** 208 square inches
   - **(C)** 280 square inches
   - **(D)** 288 square inches

8. What is the difference between $(4 \times 10^3) + 6$ and $(2 \times 10^3) + (3 \times 10) + 8$?
   - **(A)** 168
   - **(B)** 1,968
   - **(C)** 3,765
   - **(D)** 55,968

9. The set of common factors for 30 and 24 is
   (A) {1, 2, 3, 6}
   (B) {1, 2, 3, 4, 6}
   (C) {1, 2, 4, 6}
   (D) {1, 2, 4, 6, 12}

10.

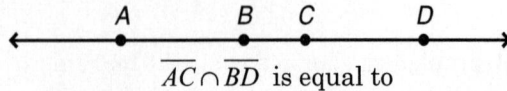

$\overline{AC} \cap \overline{BD}$ is equal to

   (A) $\overline{BC}$
   (B) $\overline{BD}$
   (C) $\overline{AC}$
   (D) $\overline{AD}$

11. The board shown below is six feet long, four inches wide, and two inches thick. One-third of it will be driven into the ground. How much surface area remains above ground?

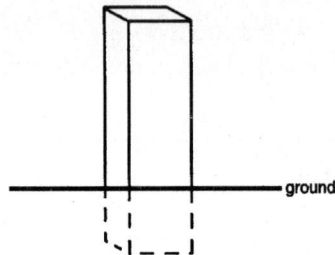

   (A) About 4 sq. ft.
   (B) Slightly less than 5 sq. ft.
   (C) Slightly more than 5 sq. ft.
   (D) About 8 sq. ft.

12. One runner can run M miles in H hours. Another faster runner can run N miles in L hours. The difference in their rates can be expressed as
   (A) $\dfrac{M-N}{H}$
   (B) $MH - HL$
   (C) $\dfrac{HN}{M-L}$
   (D) $\dfrac{N}{L} - \dfrac{M}{H}$

13. If Mary is x years old now and her sister is 3 years younger, then 5 years from now her sister will be what age?
   (A) $x + 5$ years
   (B) $x + 3$ years
   (C) $x + 2$ years
   (D) 8 years

14. In the figure below, the largest possible circle is cut out of a square piece of tin. The area of the remaining piece of tin is approximately (in square inches)

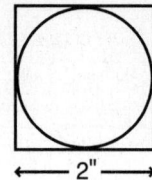

   (A) .14
   (B) .75
   (C) .86
   (D) 3.14

15. A square has an area of 49 sq. in. The number of inches in its perimeter is
   (A) 7
   (B) 14
   (C) 28
   (D) 98

16. If an engine pumps G gallons of water per minute, then the number of gallons pumped in half an hour may be found by
   (A) taking one-half of G.
   (B) dividing 60 by G.
   (C) multiplying G by 30.
   (D) dividing 30 by G.

17. Two cars start from the same point at the same time. One drives north at 20 miles an hour and the other drives south on the same straight road at 36 miles an hour. How many miles apart are they after 30 minutes?

(A) Less than 10

(B) Between 10 and 20

(C) Between 20 and 30

(D) Between 30 and 40

Directions: For questions 18–35, two quantities are given—one in Column A and the other in Column B. In some questions, additional information concerning the quantities to be compared is centered above the entries in the two columns. Compare the quantities in the two columns, and mark your answer sheet as follows:

(A) if the quantity in Column A is greater

(B) if the quantity in Column B is greater

(C) if the quantities are equal

(D) if the relationship cannot be determined from the information given

Column A	Column B

18.

$$s = 1$$
$$t = 3$$
$$a = -2$$

$[5a(4t)]^3$	$[4a(5s)]^2$

19.

$$4 > x > -3$$

$\dfrac{x}{3}$	$\dfrac{3}{x}$

Column A	Column B

20.

$$a < b$$

KR	KT

21.

$\dfrac{2}{3} + \dfrac{3}{7}$	$\dfrac{16}{21} - \dfrac{3}{7}$

22.

$$a > b$$

$$x < a + b$$

$a + b$	y

23. y = an odd integer

The numerical value of y^2	The numerical value of y^3

24.

$(8 + 6) \div [3 - 7(2)]$	$(6 + 8) \div [2 - 7(3)]$

25.

three-fourths of $\dfrac{9}{9}$	$\dfrac{9}{9} \bullet \dfrac{3}{4}$

Column A	Column B

26.

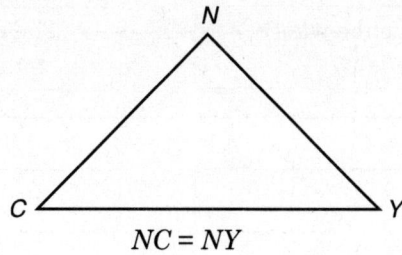

$$NC = NY$$

$$\angle N > \angle C$$

NC	CY

27.

$\dfrac{1}{\sqrt{9}}$	$\dfrac{1}{3}$

28.

$5\left(\dfrac{2}{3}\right)$	$\left(\dfrac{5}{3}\right)2$

29.

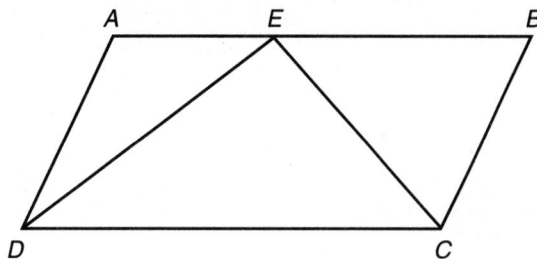

Parallelogram $ABCD$

E is a point on AB

Area of $\triangle DEC$	Area of $\triangle AED +$ Area $\triangle EBC$

30.

$$x = -1$$

$x^3 + x^2 - x + 1$	$x^3 - x^2 + x - 1$

	Column A	Column B

31.

The edge of a cube whose volume is 27	The edge of a cube whose total surface area is 54

32.

$\dfrac{\dfrac{1}{2}+\dfrac{1}{3}}{\dfrac{2}{3}}$	$\dfrac{\dfrac{2}{3}}{\dfrac{1}{2}+\dfrac{1}{3}}$

33.

Area of a circle whose radius is x^3	Area of a circle whose radius is $3x$

34.

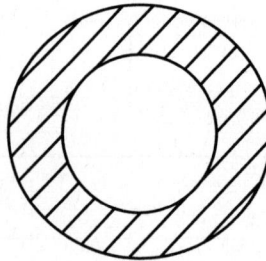

Radius of larger circle = 10

Radius of smaller circle = 7

Area of shaded portion	Area of smaller circle

35.

$$a < 0 < b$$

a^2	$\dfrac{b}{2}$

STOP END OF SECTION 2. IF YOU HAVE ANY TIME LEFT, GO OVER YOUR WORK IN THIS SECTION ONLY. DO NOT WORK IN ANY OTHER SECTION OF THE TEST.

SECTION 3: READING COMPREHENSION

40 Questions • 40 Minutes

Directions: Each reading passage is followed by questions based on its content. Answer the questions on the basis of what is stated or implied in the passage. On your answer sheet, mark the letter of the answer you choose.

When we say a snake "glides," we have already persuaded ourselves to shiver a little. If we say that it "slithers," we are as good as undone. To avoid
(5) unsettling ourselves, we should state the simple fact—a snake walks.

A snake doesn't have any breast-bone. The tips of its ribs are free-moving and amount, so to speak, to
(10) its feet. A snake walks along on its rib tips, pushing forward its ventral scutes at each "step," and it speeds up this mode of progress by undulating from side to side and by taking
(15) advantage of every rough "toehold" it can find in the terrain. Let's look at it this way: A human or other animal going forward on all fours is using a sort of locomotion that's familiar
(20) enough to all of us and isn't at all dismaying. Now: Suppose this walker is enclosed inside some sort of pliable encasement like a sacking. The front "feet" will still step forward, the "hind
(25) legs" still hitch along afterward. It will still be a standard enough sort of animal walking, only all we'll see now is a sort of wiggling of the sacking without visible feet. That's the
(30) snake way. A snake has its covering outside its feet, as an insect has its skeleton on its outside with no bones in the interior. There's nothing more "horrid" about the one arrangement
(35) than about the other.

1. The title below that expresses the main idea of this selection is
   (A) "Snake's Legs."
   (B) "Comparing Snakes to People."
   (C) "The Movement of a Snake."
   (D) "A Slimy Animal."

2. A snake's "feet" are its
   (A) toes.
   (B) ribs.
   (C) side.
   (D) breastbone.

3. The word *terrain* means
   (A) terraced.
   (B) rocky ledge.
   (C) vertical hole.
   (D) ground areas.

4. We may conclude that the author
   (A) raises reptiles.
   (B) dislikes snakes.
   (C) is well informed about snakes.
   (D) thinks snakes move better than humans.

When a luxury liner or a cargo ship nudges into her slip after an ocean crossing, her first physical contact with land is a heaving line. These (5) streamers with a weight at the end called a "monkey fist" arch gracefully from deck to pier. On board the ship the heaving lines are tied to heavy, golden yellow manila mooring lines. (10) Longshoremen quickly pull in the heaving lines until they can fasten the mooring lines to iron bollards (posts). Soon the ship is strung to her pier by four, eight, or as many (15) as twenty-one nine-inch or ten-inch manila lines with perhaps a few wire ropes to stay motion fore and aft. The ship is secure against even the wrath of the storm or hurricane. A ship could (20) dock without the aid of tugboats—and may have in New York in maritime strikes—but not without the lines to moor her to her berth.

The maritime and the related (25) fishing industry find perhaps 250 applications for rope and cordage. There are hundreds of different sizes, constructions, tensile strengths, and weights in rope and twine. Rope is sold (30) by the pound but ordered by length, and is measured by circumference rather than by diameter. The maritime variety is made chiefly from fiber of the abaca, or manila plant, which (35) is imported from the Philippines and Central America. Henequen from Mexico and Cuba, and sisal from Africa, the Netherlands East Indies, and other areas, are also used, but (40) chiefly for twine. Nylon is coming into increasing use, particularly by towing companies. But it is six times more expensive than manila. However, nylon is much stronger, lighter in weight, (45) and longer-wearing than manila. It is also more elastic and particularly adaptable for ocean towing.

5. In docking a ship, rope is
(A) only a little less important than a tugboat.
(B) essential.
(C) helpful but not necessary.
(D) seldom used.

6. A *monkey fist* is a
(A) device for weaving rope.
(B) slang term for a longshoreman.
(C) rope streamer.
(D) weight at the end of a rope.

7. Mooring ropes are
(A) ten inches in diameter.
(B) twenty-one inches in circumference.
(C) six times thicker than heaving ropes.
(D) nine inches in circumference.

8. Which of the following are NOT correctly paired?
(A) Sisal from the Philippines
(B) Henequen from Cuba
(C) Abaca from Central America
(D) Sisal from the Netherlands East Indies

In August of 1814, when news came that the British were advancing on Washington, three State Department clerks stuffed all records and valuable
(5) papers—including the Articles of Confederation, the Declaration of Independence, and the Constitution—into coarse linen sacks and smuggled them in carts to an unoccupied gristmill
(10) on the Virginia side of the Potomac. Later, fearing that a cannon factory nearby might attract a raiding party of the enemy, the clerks procured wagons from neighboring farmers, took
(15) the papers 35 miles away to Leesburg, and locked them in an empty house. It was not until the British fleet had left the waters of the Chesapeake that it was considered safe to return the
(20) papers to Washington.

On December 26, 1941, the five pages of the Constitution together with the single leaf of the Declaration of Independence were taken from the
(25) Library of Congress, where they had been kept for many years and were stored in the vaults of the United States Bullion Depository at Fort Knox, Kentucky. Here they "rode out
(30) the war" safely.

Since 1952, visitors to Washington may view these historic documents at the Exhibition Hall of the National Archives. Sealed in bronze and glass
(35) cases filled with helium, the documents are protected from touch, light, heat, dust, and moisture. At a moment's notice, they can be lowered into a large safe that is bombproof,
(40) shockproof, and fireproof.

9. Before the War of 1812, the Constitution and the Declaration of Independence were apparently kept in
   (A) Independence Hall.
   (B) Fort Knox, Kentucky.
   (C) an office of the State Department.
   (D) a gristmill in Virginia.

10. Nowadays, these documents are on view in the
    (A) National Archives Exhibition Hall.
    (B) Library of Congress.
    (C) United States Bullion Depository.
    (D) United States Treasury Building.

11. An important reason for the installation of a device to facilitate the quick removal of the documents is the
    (A) possibility of a sudden disaster.
    (B) increasing number of tourists.
    (C) need for more storage space.
    (D) lack of respect for the documents.

12. The documents have been removed from Washington at least twice in order to preserve them from
    (A) dust, heat, and moisture.
    (B) careless handling.
    (C) possible war damage.
    (D) sale to foreign governments.

On a population map of the world, deserts are shown as great blank spaces, but in fact, these areas contribute many things to our lives.

(5)   When you go to the market to buy a box of dates, you are buying a bit of sunshine and dry air from the oases of the Sahara Desert or the Coachella Valley. Fresh peas or a lettuce salad
(10) for your winter dinner might be the product of an irrigation farmer in the Salt River Valley or the Imperial Valley. That fine broadcloth shirt you received for your birthday was made
(15) from silky, long-fibered cotton grown in Egypt. A half-wool, half-cotton sweater might contain Australian wool and Peruvian cotton, which are steppe and desert products.

(20)   These are only a few of the contributions these desert areas make to the quality of our lives. They have also made important cultural contributions.

(25)   Our number system is derived from the system used by the ancient civilizations of Arabia. The use of irrigation to make farming of dry areas possible was developed by the
(30) inhabitants of desert regions. The necessity of measuring water levels and noting land boundaries following flooding by the Nile River led to the development of mathematics and the
(35) practice of surveying and engineering. The desert people were also our early astronomers. They studied the locations of the stars in order to find their way across the limitless expanse
(40) of the desert at night.

13. The population of the world's deserts is
(A) scattered.
(B) starving.
(C) large.
(D) small.

14. The Imperial Valley produces
(A) vegetables.
(B) winter dinners.
(C) shirts.
(D) irrigation.

15. According to this passage, broadcloth is made of
(A) wool.
(B) cotton.
(C) silk.
(D) half wool, half cotton.

16. Culturally, desert civilizations have
(A) made no contributions.
(B) made important contributions.
(C) not influenced western civilizations.
(D) been blank spaces.

17. Surveying was developed because people needed to
(A) study astronomy.
(B) find their way across the deserts.
(C) determine land boundaries after floods.
(D) irrigate their crops.

Residents of Montana laughingly refer to the small, windblown settlement of Ekalaka in the Eastern badlands as "Skeleton Flats," but as
(5) curious as it may sound, the name is appropriate.

So many fossils have been dug up in this otherwise unremarkable town that it has become a paradise
(10) for paleontologists, scientists who use fossils to study prehistoric life forms. In fact, dinosaur bones are so plentiful in this area that ranchers have been known to use them as
(15) doorstops!

Ekalaka's fame began to grow more than 50 years ago when Walter H. Peck, whose hobby was geology, found the bones of a Stegosaurus,
(20) a huge, plant-eating dinosaur. The entire community soon became infected with Peck's enthusiasm for his find, and everyone began digging for dinosaur bones. Led by the local sci-
(25) ence teacher, groups of people would go out looking for new finds each weekend, and they rarely returned empty-handed. It would seem there is no end to the fossil riches to be
(30) found in Ekalaka.

Among the most prized finds were the remains of a Brontosaurus, an 80-foot-long monster that probably weighed 40 tons. The skeleton of
(35) a Triceratops was also found. The head of this prehistoric giant alone weighed more than 1,000 pounds. Careful searching also yielded small fossilized fish, complete with stony
(40) scales, and the remains of a huge sea reptile.

The prize find was a *Pachycephalosaurus*, a dinosaur whose peculiar skull was several inches thick. When
(45) descriptions of it reached scientific circles in the east, there was great excitement because this particular prehistoric animal was then completely unknown to scientists.

18. In the first sentence, the author places "Skeleton Flats" in quotation marks to show that this phrase is
(A) a nickname given to the town by Montana residents, not the actual name of the town.
(B) spelled incorrectly.
(C) being spoken by someone other than the author.
(D) a scientific term.

19. This article is primarily about
(A) paleontology.
(B) products of the state of Montana.
(C) fossil finds in Ekalaka.
(D) the *Pachycephalosaurus*.

20. According to this passage, a paleontologist is
(A) someone whose hobby is geology.
(B) a paradise.
(C) a plant-eating dinosaur.
(D) someone who studies fossils.

21. In the third paragraph, the author is describing the
(A) bones of a Stegosaurus.
(B) discovery of the first fossil finds in Ekalaka.
(C) town of Ekalaka.
(D) people of Ekalaka.

22. Discovery of the *Pachycephalosaurus* caused excitement because
(A) its skull was several inches thick.
(B) it was the first evidence of this creature ever found and reported to scientists.
(C) news of it reached eastern scientific circles.
(D) it received a prize.

Powdered zirconium is more fiery and violent than the magnesium powder that went into wartime incendiary bombs. Under some conditions, it
(5) can be ignited with a kitchen match, and it cannot be extinguished with water. Munitions makers once tried to incorporate it into explosives, but turned it down as too dangerous for
(10) even them to handle.

But when this strange metal is transformed into a solid bar or sheet or tube, as lustrous as burnished silver, its temper changes. It is so
(15) docile that it can be used by surgeons as a safe covering plate for sensitive brain tissues. It is almost as strong as steel, and it can be exposed to hydrochloric acid or nitric acid without
(20) corroding.

Zirconium is also safe and stable when it is bound up with other elements to form mineral compounds which occur in abundant deposits in
(25) North and South America, India, and Australia. Although it is classified as a rare metal, it is more abundant in the earth's crust than nickel, copper, tungsten, tin, or lead. Until
(30) a few years ago, scarcely a dozen people had ever seen zirconium in pure form, but today it is the wonder metal of a fantastic new industry, a vital component of television, radar,
(35) and radio sets, an exciting structural material for chemical equipment and for superrockets and jet engines, and a key metal for atomic piles.

23. The title that best expresses the main idea of this selection is
   (A) "A Vital Substance."
   (B) "A Safe, Stable Substance."
   (C) "Zirconium's Uses in Surgery."
   (D) "Characteristics of Zirconium."

24. The word *docile* in line 15 means
   (A) calm.
   (B) pliable.
   (C) strong.
   (D) profuse.

25. The selection emphasizes that
   (A) zirconium rusts easily.
   (B) chemists are finding uses for zirconium.
   (C) keys are often made of zirconium nowadays.
   (D) zirconium is less abundant in the earth's crust than lead.

26. Zirconium is *not* safe to handle when it is
   (A) lustrous.
   (B) powdered.
   (C) in tubes.
   (D) in bar form.

27. The selection tells us that zirconium
   (A) is a metal.
   (B) is fireproof.
   (C) dissolves in water.
   (D) is stronger than steel.

28. Zirconium is likely to be useful in all of these fields EXCEPT
   (A) surgery.
   (B) television.
   (C) atomic research.
   (D) the manufacture of fireworks.

About the year 1812 two steam fer-ryboats were built under the direc-tion of Robert Fulton for crossing the Hudson River, and one of the same
(5) description was built for service on the East River. These boats were what are known as twin boats, each of them having two complete hulls united by a deck or bridge. Because these boats
(10) were pointed at both ends and moved equally well with either end foremost, they crossed and recrossed the river without losing any time in turning about. Fulton also contrived, with
(15) great ingenuity, floating docks for the reception of the ferryboats and a means by which they were brought to the docks without a shock. These boats were the first of a fleet that has
(20) since carried hundreds of millions of passengers to and from New York.

29. The title that best expresses the main idea of this selection is
    (A) "Crossing the Hudson River by Boat."
    (B) "Transportation of Passengers."
    (C) "The Invention of Floating Docks."
    (D) "The Beginning of Steam Ferryboat Service."

30. The steam ferryboats were known as twin boats because
    (A) they had two complete hulls united by a bridge.
    (B) they could move as easily forward as backward.
    (C) each ferryboat had two captains.
    (D) two boats were put into service at the same time.

31. Which statement is *true* according to the selection?
    (A) Boats built under Fulton's direction are still in use.
    (B) Fulton planned a reception to celebrate the first ferryboat.
    (C) Fulton piloted the first steam ferryboats across the Hudson.
    (D) Fulton developed a satisfactory way of docking the ferryboats.

32. Robert Fulton worked in the
    (A) seventeenth century.
    (B) eighteenth century.
    (C) nineteenth century.
    (D) twentieth century.

33. In line 18, the word *shock* is used to mean an
    (A) unpleasant surprise.
    (B) impact.
    (C) illness following an accident.
    (D) electrical impulse.

Between 1780 and 1790, in piece-meal fashion, a trail was established between Catskill on the Hudson and the frontier outpost, Ithaca, in the
(5) Finger Lakes country. This path, by grace of following the valleys, managed to thread its way through the mountains by what are on the whole surprisingly easy grades. Ultimately,
(10) this route became the Susquehanna Turnpike, but in popular speech it was just the Ithaca Road. It was, along with the Mohawk Turnpike and the Great Western Turnpike, one of
(15) the three great east-west highways of the state. Eventually it was the route taken by thousands of Yankee farmers, more especially Connecticut Yankees, seeking new fortunes in
(20) southwestern New York. Along it, the tide of pioneer immigration flowed at flood crest for a full generation.

As the road left Catskill, there was no stream that might not be
(25) either forded or crossed on a crude bridge until the traveler reached the Susquehanna, which was a considerable river and a real obstacle to his progress. The road came down out
(30) of the Catskills via the valley of the Ouleout Creek and struck the Susquehanna just above the present village of Unadilla. Hither about the year 1784 came a Connecticut man, Nathaniel
(35) Wattles. He provided both a skiff and a large flat-bottomed scow so that the homeseeker, his family, team, and household baggage, and oftentimes a little caravan of livestock, might
(40) be set across the river dry-shod and in safety. Wattles here established an inn where one might find lodging and entertainment, and a general store where might be purchased such
(45) staples as were essential for the journey. So it was that Wattles' Ferry became the best known landmark on the Ithaca Road.

34. The author indicates that the Susquehanna Turnpike
   (A) began as a narrow trail.
   (B) was the most important north-south highway in the state.
   (C) furnished travelers with surprising obstacles.
   (D) went out of use after a generation.

35. The western end of the Susquehanna Turnpike was located at
   (A) the Hudson River.
   (B) the Connecticut border.
   (C) Ithaca.
   (D) Catskill.

36. The Susquehanna Turnpike was also known as
   (A) the Ithaca Road.
   (B) Wattles' Ferry.
   (C) the Catskill Trail.
   (D) the Mohawk Turnpike.

37. According to this selection, Nathaniel Wattles was prepared to offer travelers all of the following EXCEPT
   (A) guides.
   (B) a place to sleep.
   (C) entertainment.
   (D) groceries.

As of December, 1983, there were 391 species listed as endangered. Today over 650 have been listed including 282 mammals, 214 birds, 59 reptiles,
(5) 49 fish, 26 mollusks, 16 amphibians, and 8 insects. We hope to provide protection to another 600 species by the end of 1988. Although only four species of plants have been designated as
(10) endangered, with the establishment of five botanist positions in 1985, it is expected that 200 will be listed by the end of 1987.

Success should not be measured by
(15) the number of species listed; the goal is to return the species to the point where they are no longer endangered. This Depart would be just as negligent in the performance of its duties under
(20) the Act for not delisting a species that has recovered as it would be for not listing a critical species. We have not had the staffing or funding to review all of the species listed at the time of
(25) the 1983 Act.

38. It can be inferred that very few plants had been listed by 1983 because

(A) very few are close to extinction.

(B) the Department doesn't classify plants.

(C) no botanists were on the staff at the time.

(D) some endangered mammals eat plants.

39. Which of the following is NOT stated in the passage?

(A) Eight insects have been listed as endangered.

(B) By the end of 1987, many plants will be added to the list.

(C) The Department considers listing species more important than delisting them.

(D) The Department lacked staffing to review all listed species.

40. "Success should not be measured by the number . . ." What is a reasonable inference concerning the purpose of this statement?

(A) To avoid mentioning that the computer that kept count malfunctioned

(B) Because measurement is always statistically difficult

(C) Because the concept of success has been abused in recent years

(D) To counteract criticism that the Department was not listing enough species

STOP END OF SECTION 3. IF YOU HAVE ANY TIME LEFT, GO OVER YOUR WORK IN THIS SECTION ONLY. DO NOT WORK IN ANY OTHER SECTION OF THE TEST.

SECTION 4: MATHEMATICS ACHIEVEMENT

45 Questions • 40 Minutes

Directions: Each question is followed by four answer choices. Choose the correct answer to each question, and mark its letter on your answer sheet.

1. A square measures 8 inches on one side. By how much will the area be increased if its length is increased by 4 inches and its width decreased by 2 inches?
   - **(A)** 14 sq. in.
   - **(B)** 12 sq. in.
   - **(C)** 10 sq. in.
   - **(D)** 8 sq. in.

2. $r = 35 - (3 + 6)(-n)$

   $n = 2$

   $r =$
   - **(A)** 53
   - **(B)** 17
   - **(C)** −17
   - **(D)** −53

3. $(3 + 4)^3 =$
   - **(A)** 21
   - **(B)** 91
   - **(C)** 343
   - **(D)** 490

4. Aluminum bronze consists of copper and aluminum, usually in the ratio of 10:1 by weight. If an object made of this alloy weighs 77 pounds, how many pounds of aluminum does it contain?
   - **(A)** 7
   - **(B)** 7.7
   - **(C)** 10
   - **(D)** 70

5. How many boxes 2 inches × 3 inches × 4 inches can fit into a carton 2 feet × 3 feet × 4 feet?
   - **(A)** 100
   - **(B)** 144
   - **(C)** 1,000
   - **(D)** 1,728

6. A clerk can add 40 columns of figures an hour by using an adding machine and 20 columns of figures an hour without using an adding machine. What is the total number of hours it will take the clerk to add 200 columns of figures if $\frac{3}{5}$ of the work is done by machine and the rest without the machine?
   - **(A)** 6 hours
   - **(B)** 7 hours
   - **(C)** 8 hours
   - **(D)** 9 hours

7. Mr. Lawson makes a weekly salary of $150 plus 7% commission on his sales. What will his income be for a week in which he makes sales totaling $945?
   - **(A)** $196.15
   - **(B)** $206.15
   - **(C)** $216.15
   - **(D)** $226.15

8. Solve for x: $x^2 + 5 = 41$
   - **(A)** ± 6
   - **(B)** ± 7
   - **(C)** ± 8
   - **(D)** ± 9

9. Two rectangular boards each measuring 5 feet by 3 feet are placed together to make one large board. How much shorter will the perimeter be if the two long sides are placed together than if the two short sides are placed together?

    (A) 2 feet

    (B) 4 feet

    (C) 6 feet

    (D) 8 feet

10. If a plane travels 1,000 miles in 5 hours 30 minutes, what is its average speed in miles per hour?

    (A) $181\dfrac{9}{11}$

    (B) $191\dfrac{1}{2}$

    (C) 200

    (D) 215

11. Two years ago a company purchased 500 dozen pencils at 40 cents per dozen. This year only 75 percent as many pencils were purchased as were purchased two years ago, but the price was 20 percent higher than the old price. What was the total cost of pencils purchased by the company this year?

    (A) $180

    (B) $187.50

    (C) $240

    (D) $257.40

12. An adult's ski lift ticket costs twice as much as a child's. If a family of three children and two adults can ski for $49, what is the cost of an adult ticket?

    (A) $7

    (B) $10

    (C) $12

    (D) $14

13. Solve for x: $\dfrac{x}{2} + 36 = 37.25$

    (A) 2.5

    (B) 3.5

    (C) 12.5

    (D) 18.5

14. A group of 6 people raised $690 for charity. One of the people raised 35% of the total. What was the amount raised by the other 5 people?

    (A) $448.50

    (B) $241.50

    (C) $89.70

    (D) $74.75

15. If the scale on a blueprint is $\dfrac{1}{4}$ inch = 1 foot, give the blueprint dimensions of a room that is actually 29 feet long and 23 feet wide.

    (A) $6\dfrac{3}{4}" \times 6"$

    (B) $7\dfrac{1}{4}" \times 5\dfrac{1}{2}"$

    (C) $7\dfrac{1}{4}" \times 5\dfrac{3}{4}"$

    (D) $7\dfrac{1}{2}" \times 5\dfrac{1}{2}"$

16. Find the area of a rectangle with a length of 176 feet and a width of 79 feet.

    (A) 13,904 sq. ft.

    (B) 13,854 sq. ft.

    (C) 13,804 sq. ft.

    (D) 13,304 sq. ft.

17. $63 \div \dfrac{1}{9} =$

    (A) 7

    (B) 56

    (C) 67

    (D) 567

18. With an 18% discount, John was able to save $13.23 on a coat. What was the original price of the coat?
    (A) $69.75
    (B) $71.50
    (C) $73.50
    (D) $74.75

19. If it takes three men 56 minutes to fill a trench 4' × 6' × 5', and two of the men work twice as rapidly as the third, the number of minutes that it will take the two faster men alone to fill this trench is
    (A) 70 minutes.
    (B) 60 minutes.
    (C) 50 minutes.
    (D) 40 minutes.

20. Population figures for a certain area show there are $1\frac{1}{2}$ times as many single men as single women in the area. The total population is 18,000. There are 1,122 married couples, with 756 children. How many single men are there in the area?
    (A) 3,000
    (B) 6,000
    (C) 9,000
    (D) It cannot be determined from the information given.

21. If a vehicle is to complete a 20-mile trip at an average rate of 30 miles per hour, it must complete the trip in
    (A) 20 minutes.
    (B) 30 minutes.
    (C) 40 minutes.
    (D) 50 minutes.

22. Solve for x: $2x^2 + 3 = 21$
    (A) ± 3
    (B) ± 5
    (C) ± 9
    (D) ± 10

23. Find the area of a circle whose diameter is 6".
    (A) 29.26
    (B) 28.26
    (C) 27.96
    (D) 27.26

24. The scale on a map is $\frac{1}{8}$" = 25 miles. If two cities are $3\frac{7}{8}$" apart on the map, what is the actual distance between them?
    (A) 31 miles
    (B) 56 miles
    (C) 675 miles
    (D) 775 miles

25. A house was valued at $83,000 and insured for 80% of that amount. Find the yearly premium if it is figured at $.45 per hundred dollars of value.
    (A) $83.80
    (B) $252.63
    (C) $298.80
    (D) $664

26. If a certain job can be performed by 18 clerks in 26 days, the number of clerks needed to perform the job in 12 days is
    (A) 24 clerks.
    (B) 30 clerks.
    (C) 39 clerks.
    (D) 52 clerks.

27. $72.61 \div .05 =$
    (A) 1.45220
    (B) 14.522
    (C) 145.220
    (D) 1,452.20

28. A car dealer sold three different makes of cars. The price of the first make was $4,200, the second $4,800, and the third $5,400. The total sales were $360,000. If three times as many of the third car was sold as the first, and twice as many of the second make were sold than the first, how many cars of the third make were sold?

    (A) 15

    (B) 24

    (C) 36

    (D) It cannot be determined by the information given.

29. One third of the number of people attending a football game were admitted at the normal price of admission. How many people paid full price, if the gate receipts were $42,000?

    (A) 2,800 people

    (B) 3,500 people

    (C) 5,000 people

    (D) It cannot be determined by the information given.

30. 7 days 3 hours 20 minutes − 4 days 9 hours 31 minutes =

    (A) 2 days 17 hours 49 minutes

    (B) 2 days 17 hours 69 minutes

    (C) 3 days 10 hours 49 minutes

    (D) 3 days 10 hours 69 minutes

31. Find the area of a triangle whose dimensions are $b = 12'$, $h = 14'$.

    (A) 168 sq. ft.

    (B) 84 sq. ft.

    (C) 42 sq. ft.

    (D) 24 sq. ft.

32. Increased by 150%, the number 72 becomes

    (A) 108

    (B) 170

    (C) 180

    (D) 188

33. Which equation represents the statement four times a certain number divided by three, minus six, equals two?

    (A) $\dfrac{4n}{3} - 6 = 2$

    (B) $4n^2 - 6 = 2$

    (C) $4n^2 \div 3 - 6 = 2$

    (D) $\left(\dfrac{1}{4}n \div 3\right) - 6 = 2$

34. If $14x - 2y = 32$ and $x + 2y = 13$, then $x =$

    (A) 8

    (B) 5

    (C) 4

    (D) 3

35. An ordinary die is thrown. What are the odds that it will come up 1?

    (A) $\dfrac{1}{4}$

    (B) $\dfrac{1}{6}$

    (C) $\dfrac{1}{8}$

    (D) $\dfrac{1}{12}$

36. Which is the longest time?

    (A) 25 hours

    (B) 1,440 minutes

    (C) A day

    (D) 3,600 seconds

37. Two cars are 550 miles apart, both traveling on the same straight road. If one travels at 50 miles per hour, the other at 60 miles per hour, and they both leave at 1 p.m., what time will they meet?

    (A) 4 p.m.

    (B) 4:30 p.m.

    (C) 5:45 p.m.

    (D) 6 p.m.

38. Write 493 in expanded form, using exponents.

(A) $(4 \times 10^3) + (9 \times 10^2) + (3 \times 10)$

(B) $(4 \times 10^2) + (9 \times 10) + 3$

(C) $(4 \times 10^2) + (9 \times 10) - 7$

(D) $(4 \times 10^1) + (9 \times 10) + 3$

39. If 10 workers earn $5,400 in 12 days, how much will 6 workers earn in 15 days?

(A) $10,500

(B) $5,400

(C) $4,050

(D) $2,025

40. The scale of a particular map is $\frac{3}{8}'' =$ 5 miles. If the distance between points A and B is $4\frac{1}{2}''$ on the map, what is the distance in actuality?

(A) 12 miles

(B) 36 miles

(C) 48 miles

(D) 60 miles

41. Find the diameter of a circle whose area is 78.5 sq. in.

(A) 25 feet

(B) 10 feet

(C) 25 inches

(D) 10 inches

42. If $ab + 4 = 52$, and $a = 6$, $b =$

(A) 4

(B) 8

(C) 21

(D) 42

43. If $\frac{2}{3}$ of a jar is filled with water in 1 minute, how many minutes longer will it take to fill the remainder of the jar?

(A) $\frac{1}{4}$

(B) $\frac{1}{3}$

(C) $\frac{1}{2}$

(D) $\frac{2}{3}$

44. A group left on a trip at 8:50 a.m. and reached its destination at 3:30 p.m. How long, in hours and minutes, did the trip take?

(A) 3 hours 10 minutes

(B) 4 hours 40 minutes

(C) 5 hours 10 minutes

(D) 6 hours 40 minutes

45. A square is changed into a rectangle by increasing its length 10% and decreasing its width 10%. Its area

(A) remains the same.

(B) decreases by 10%.

(C) increases by 1%.

(D) decreases by 1%.

STOP   END OF SECTION 4. IF YOU HAVE ANY TIME LEFT, GO OVER YOUR WORK IN THIS SECTION ONLY. DO NOT WORK IN ANY OTHER SECTION OF THE TEST.

SECTION 5: ESSAY

30 Minutes

Directions: Write a legible, coherent, and correct essay on the following topic.

Topic: If you could spend an afternoon with any author, living or dead, with whom would you spend it? What would you talk about?

_____

_____

_____

_____

_____

_____

_____

_____

_____

_____

_____

_____

_____

_____

_____

_____

_____

_____

_____

ANSWER KEY AND EXPLANATIONS

Section 1: Verbal Reasoning

1. A	9. C	17. B	25. D	33. B
2. C	10. B	18. D	26. B	34. D
3. B	11. C	19. C	27. C	35. A
4. B	12. A	20. A	28. D	36. C
5. A	13. B	21. C	29. B	37. B
6. D	14. C	22. D	30. A	38. D
7. C	15. C	23. C	31. B	39. C
8. C	16. C	24. C	32. B	40. B

1. **The correct answer is (A).** To FEINT is *to deceive* or *make a pretense of.* One of the skills our soccer coach taught us was how to elude opponents by feinting in the opposite direction of where we planned to pass the ball.

2. **The correct answer is (C).** A PEER is *someone* or something that is of equal standing to another. In a democratic society, each citizen is the peer of all of the other citizens.

3. **The correct answer is (B).** TRITE means *boring from too much use.* Her essay was riddled with trite expressions, such as "a penny saved is a penny earned" and "all good things come to those who wait."

4. **The correct answer is (B).** AMIABLE means *good-natured* and *loveable.* The amiable dog wagged its tail at the letter carrier.

5. **The correct answer is (A).** A GRIMACE is *a facial expression of disgust or displeasure.* The first time the baby ate spinach, she screwed up her mouth in a grimace and spit out the food.

6. **The correct answer is (D).** To COMPEL is *to force.* Our government compels us to pay income taxes each year on April 15th.

7. **The correct answer is (C).** An ALLY is *another with a common purpose, an associate,* or *a helper.* The word meaning "passage" is "alley." Great Britain was our ally during World War II.

8. **The correct answer is (C).** To SOLICIT means *to approach with a request or plea.* Our teacher wants us to solicit help from her whenever we don't understand the math concepts she presents to the class.

9. **The correct answer is (C).** To REFUTE is *to show something to be false.* The lawyer refuted the witness's testimony by presenting contradictory evidence.

10. **The correct answer is (B).** EXPLICIT means *distinct, observable,* or *clearly stated.* The explicit instructions on the package left no opportunity for misunderstanding or error.

11. **The correct answer is (C).** To RETAIN is *to hold on to* or *to keep*. Retain the receipt as proof of payment.

12. **The correct answer is (A).** CORRESPONDENCE is *an exchange of letters* or the *letters* themselves. I save all my correspondence with the schools to which I have applied in an envelope marked "High Schools."

    NOTE: "Correspondence" can also mean "agreement" or "conformity." Your exam will never offer you a choice of two correct meanings for the same word.

13. **The correct answer is (B).** LEGITIMATE means *conforming to the law* or *abiding by the rules*. Since his name is on the deed, he has a legitimate claim to ownership of the property.

14. **The correct answer is (C).** To DEDUCT is to *subtract*. The word with a meaning close to "understand" is "deduce." Each week, my employer deducts social security taxes from my paycheck.

15. **The correct answer is (C).** The EGRESS is the *way out*. The egress is marked with a red "EXIT" sign.

16. **The correct answer is (C).** HORIZONTAL, parallel to the horizon, means *left-to-right* as opposed to "vertical." Place the large books horizontally on the shelf so that they do not topple over.

17. **The correct answer is (B).** CONTROVERSY is *exchange of opposing* opinions or argument. The choice of new wallpaper is a subject of controversy.

18. **The correct answer is (D).** To PREEMPT is to *seize before anyone else can* or to *appropriate*. No dishonesty is implied, just speed or privilege. The president's speech will preempt the time slot usually taken by my favorite game show.

19. **The correct answer is (C).** PER CAPITA literally means *for each head*, therefore *for each person*, one-by-one, with age irrelevant. The per capita consumption of red meat has dropped to 2 pounds per week.

20. **The correct answer is (A).** That which is OPTIONAL is *left to one's choice* and is therefore *not required*. You must study English and history, but study of a musical instrument is optional.

21. **The correct answer is (C).** The sense of the sentence calls for a word with a negative connotation in the first blank; therefore, we need consider only choices (C) and (D). Of these choices, ENSLAVED . . . SAY, choice (C), is clearly the better completion.

22. **The correct answer is (D).** Since it is stated that most critics disregarded or ridiculed the play, the few critics remaining must have done the opposite, or APPRECIATED the work.

23. **The correct answer is (C).** The word that is needed must be a synonym for blunder (a stupid or gross mistake). That word is ERROR.

24. **The correct answer is (C).** One who acts purely on impulse is most likely to have a PASSIONATE (emotional or intense) nature.

25. **The correct answer is (D).** If "quality is preferred to quantity" in an educational system, then the measure by which that system should be JUDGED is the CALIBER (degree of ability or merit) of the students it produces.

26. **The correct answer is (B).** Freedom of speech is something we take for granted, so we do not feel BLESSED when allowed to exercise this freedom; however, we do become angry when any RESTRICTION (limit) is imposed on our right to speak freely.

27. **The correct answer is (C).** The qualities attributed to the players on the worst team must be opposites for comparison and adjectives for parallelism within the sentence. INEPT, which means awkward, and PROFICIENT, which means skilled, comprise the only choice that meets both requirements.

28. **The correct answer is (D).** It is the function of the legislature to write laws (their WORDS become law). It is the function of the judiciary to interpret the words of the law (to determine their MEANING).

29. **The correct answer is (B).** Movies and television are both media of entertainment. The sentence compares the two media in terms of their cost, stating that many people believe television (which is free after the initial investment in the set) is NECESSARY because movies have become so EXPENSIVE (and therefore out of reach for many people).

30. **The correct answer is (A).** The sense of the sentence calls for two words that are opposites and that can both be applied to life forms. Spores are the tiny particles in certain plants that act as seeds in the production of new plants. These spores remain dormant or INACTIVE until the proper conditions exist to render them vigorous or VIBRANT, thus creating a new generation of plants.

31. **The correct answer is (B).** The completion needed is a word that is opposite in meaning to "the spinning of fanciful theories." Of the choices given, the study of ORDER best fulfills this requirement.

32. **The correct answer is (B).** This sentence describes a rebellious attitude. Impertinence means "insolence."

33. **The correct answer is (B).** The second sentence provides the clue to the meaning of the first. If success does not mean infallibility (certainty), then the fame of an author does not ASSURE the quality of his or her work.

34. **The correct answer is (D).** The completion here demands words that are opposites. In addition, the first blank requires a word that would promote hatred. Only STRIFE, meaning conflict, and TRANQUILITY, meaning peace, fulfill these requirements and complete the meaning of the sentence.

35. **The correct answer is (A).** Since mining takes away without replacing what it takes, it may be called a ROBBER industry. With these characteristics, mining might also be considered to be evil, but ROBBER is the most specific completion. It is the adjective that best describes an industry that does not replenish what it takes.

36. **The correct answer is (C).** This sentence presents two problems that are being compared in terms of the ease of their solution. The only choices that fulfill the requirements of such a comparison are MAGNITUDE and CHILD'S PLAY.

37. **The correct answer is (B).** A theatrical setting serves to create a mood or a feeling of being in another time or place. If the setting is to be EFFECTIVE (to make the desired impression on the audience), it must have some semblance of REALITY.

38. **The correct answer is (D).** The word "mob" has a negative connotation and requires an adjective that is also negative. HYSTERICAL (emotional and unmanageable) best meets this requirement. The emotion that a shouting mob is most likely to show is HATRED of law and order.

39. The correct answer is (C). When errors are discovered in existing theories, those theories must either be ALTERED (changed) in the light of the new information or they must be DISCARDED altogether, if the new information renders the old theories false.

40. The correct answer is (B). The sentence compares two different societies and therefore requires completions that are both parallel and opposite. ELEMENTARY (simple) and COMPLICATED (intricate) best meet these requirements.

Section 2: Quantitative Reasoning

1. C	8. B	15. C	22. C	29. C
2. C	9. A	16. C	23. D	30. A
3. A	10. A	17. C	24. B	31. C
4. C	11. A	18. B	25. C	32. A
5. C	12. D	19. D	26. B	33. D
6. D	13. C	20. A	27. C	34. A
7. A	14. C	21. A	28. C	35. D

1. **The correct answer is (C).** If $x = 0$, then $2x < 8$ because $2(0) < 8$. None of the other pairs result in a true statement.

2. **The correct answer is (C).** Substitute n for the blank space.

$$7(3 \times n) + 4 = 2{,}104$$
$$7(3n) + 4 = 2{,}104$$
$$21n + 4 = 2{,}104$$
$$21n = 2{,}100$$
$$n = 100, \text{ or } 10^2$$

3. **The correct answer is (A).** Since 1% = .01, one half of one percent is written .005. Refer to the percentage review section for help if necessary.

4. **The correct answer is (C).** A scalene triangle has no equal sides.

5. **The correct answer is (C).** There are 1,000 millimeters in a meter.

6. **The correct answer is (D).** Choice (A) is also a common denominator, but it is not the least common denominator.

7. **The correct answer is (A).** The area of a triangle is found by using

$$A = \frac{1}{2}bh$$
$$A = \frac{1}{2} \bullet 14 \bullet 20$$
$$= 140 \text{ sq. in.}$$

8. **The correct answer is (B).** $(4 \times 10^3) + 6 = 4{,}006$

$$(2 \times 10^3) + (3 \times 10) + 8 = 2{,}038$$

The difference is 1,968.

9. **The correct answer is (A).** The set of factors for 24 is:

$\{1,2,3,4,6,8,12,24\}$

The set of factors for 30 is:

$\{1,2,3,5,6,10,15,30\}$

The set of common factors is:

$\{1,2,3,6\}$

10. **The correct answer is (A).** The intersection of the two line segments is the place they overlap. Note that they overlap in the interval marked $\overline{BC}$.

11. **The correct answer is (A).** One third of the board will be driven into the ground, leaving 4 feet exposed. The exposed part of the board has 5 faces: two faces 4 feet long by 4 inches wide; two faces 4 feet long by 2 inches wide; and one face (the end) 2 inches by 4 inches. Because the answer choices are in units of square feet, we will calculate in square feet:

$2 \bullet 4 \bullet \dfrac{1}{3} = \dfrac{8}{3}$ or $2\dfrac{2}{3}$ sq. ft.

$2 \bullet 4 \bullet \dfrac{1}{6} = \dfrac{8}{6}$ or $1\dfrac{1}{3}$ sq. ft.

$1 \bullet \dfrac{1}{3} \bullet \dfrac{1}{6} = \dfrac{1}{18}$ sq. ft.

The sum is $4\dfrac{1}{18}$ sq. ft. of board remaining above ground.

12. **The correct answer is (D).** The rate of the first runner is $\dfrac{M}{H}$ miles per hour. The rate of the second is $\dfrac{N}{L}$ miles per hour. The second runner is faster, so the difference in their rates is written $\dfrac{N}{L} - \dfrac{M}{H}$.

13. **The correct answer is (C).** Mary's age now $= x$.

Her sister's age now $= x - 3$.

In five years her sister's age will be $x - 3 + 5 = x + 2$.

14. **The correct answer is (C).** The area of a square $= s^2$.

The area of this square $= 2^2 = 4$.

The area of a circle $= \pi \bullet r^2$

$$\left(r = \dfrac{1}{2}d\right)(\pi = 3.14)$$

The area of this circle $\pi \bullet 1^2 = \pi \bullet 1 = \pi$

The difference between the area of this square and the area of this circle is

$$4 - 3.14 = .86.$$

15. **The correct answer is (C).** Area of a square $= s^2$

$49 = 7^2$

one side $= 7$ inches

$P = 4s$

$P = 4 \times 7" = 28$ inches

16. **The correct answer is (C).** One half hour $= 30$ minutes

Amount $=$ rate $(G) \times$ time $(30$ minutes$)$

17. **The correct answer is (C).** One car went 20 mph for $\dfrac{1}{2}$ hour $= 10$ miles. The other car went 36 mph for $\dfrac{1}{2}$ hour $= 18$ miles.

Since they went in opposite directions, add the two distances to find the total number of miles apart. $10 + 18 = 28$

18. The correct answer is (B).

$$[5a(4t)]^3 = [-10(12)]^3$$
$$= (-120)^3$$
$$= \text{negative answer}$$
$$[4a(5s)]^2 = [-8(5)]^2$$
$$= (-40)^2$$
$$= \text{positive answer}$$

A positive product is greater than a negative one.

19. The correct answer is (D). Since x could be any non-zero value from 4 to -3, the values of the fractions are impossible to determine.

20. The correct answer is (A).

$a < b \therefore b > a$ (given).

$\therefore KR > KT$ (in a triangle the greater side lies opposite the greater angle)

21. The correct answer is (A).

$$\frac{2}{3} + \frac{3}{7} = \frac{14}{21} + \frac{9}{21} \quad \bigg| \quad \frac{16}{21} - \frac{3}{7} = \frac{16}{21} - \frac{9}{21}$$
$$= \frac{23}{21} \qquad\qquad = \frac{7}{21}$$

22. The correct answer is (C).

$y = a + b$ (an exterior angle of a triangle is equal to the sum of the two interior remote angles)

23. The correct answer is (D). There is not enough information, as y could equal 1, which would make both quantities equal; or y could be greater than 1, which would make y^3 greater than y^2. If y were a negative integer, then y^2 would be greater than y^3.

24. The correct answer is (B).

$$(8 + 6) \div [3 - 7(2)]$$
$$= (14) \div (-11) = \frac{14}{-11}$$
$$(6 + 8) \div [2 - 7(3)]$$
$$= (14) \div (-19) = \frac{14}{-19}$$

25. The correct answer is (C).

$$\frac{3}{4} \times \frac{9}{9} = \frac{3}{4} \qquad \frac{9}{9} \times \frac{3}{4} = \frac{3}{4}$$

26. The correct answer is (B).

$NC = NY$ (given)

$\angle C = \angle Y$ (angles opposite equal sides are equal)

$\angle N > \angle C$ (given)

$\angle N > \angle Y$ (substitution)

$CY > NC$ (the greater side lies opposite the greater angle)

27. The correct answer is (C). $\dfrac{1}{\sqrt{9}} = \dfrac{1}{3}$

28. The correct answer is (C).

$$5\left(\frac{2}{3}\right) = \frac{5}{1} \bullet \frac{2}{3} = \frac{10}{3} \qquad \left(\frac{5}{3}\right)2 = \frac{5}{3} \bullet \frac{2}{1} = \frac{10}{3}$$

29. The correct answer is (C). A triangle inscribed in a parallelogram is equal in area to one-half the parallelogram. Therefore, the area of $\triangle DEC$ equals the combined areas of $\triangle ADE$ and $\triangle EBC$.

30. The correct answer is (A).

$$x^3 + x^2 - x + 1 =$$
$$(-1)^3 + (-1)^2 - (-1) + 1$$
$$= -1 + 1 + 1 + 1$$
$$= 2$$
$$x^3 - x^2 + x - 1 =$$
$$(-1)^3 - (-1)^2 + (-1) - 1$$
$$= -1 - 1 - 1 - 1$$
$$= -4$$

$\therefore$ Column A > Column B

31. The correct answer is (C).

$$e^3 = 27 \qquad 6e^2 = 54$$
$$e = 3 \qquad\quad e^2 = 9$$
$$\qquad\qquad\quad e = 3$$

$\therefore$ Column A = Column B

32. The correct answer is (A).

$$\frac{\frac{1}{2}+\frac{1}{3}}{\frac{2}{3}} = \frac{\frac{3+2}{6}}{\frac{2}{3}} = \frac{\frac{5}{6}}{\frac{2}{3}}$$

(multiplying numerator and denominator by $\frac{3}{2}$)

$$= \frac{\frac{15}{12}}{1} = \frac{15}{12} = \frac{5}{4}$$

$$\frac{\frac{2}{3}}{\frac{1}{2}+\frac{1}{3}} = \frac{\frac{2}{3}}{\frac{3+2}{6}} = \frac{\frac{2}{3}}{\frac{5}{6}}$$

(multiplying numerator and denominator by $\frac{6}{5}$)

$$= \frac{\frac{12}{15}}{1} = \frac{12}{15} = \frac{4}{5}$$

$$\frac{5}{4} > \frac{4}{5} \therefore \text{ Column A > Column B}$$

33. The correct answer is (D). We cannot determine the areas of the circles unless the value of x is known.

34. The correct answer is (A).

$$\begin{pmatrix} \text{Area of} \\ \text{shaded} \\ \text{portion} \end{pmatrix} = \begin{pmatrix} \text{Area of} \\ \text{larger} \\ \text{circle} \end{pmatrix} - \begin{pmatrix} \text{Area of} \\ \text{smaller} \\ \text{circle} \end{pmatrix}$$

$$= \pi(10^2) - \pi(7^2)$$
$$= 100\pi - 49\pi$$
$$= 51\pi$$

$$\begin{pmatrix} \text{Area of} \\ \text{smaller} \\ \text{circle} \end{pmatrix} = \pi r^2$$

$$= \pi(7^2)$$
$$= 49\pi$$

$$51\pi > 49\pi$$

$\therefore$ Column A > Column B

35. The correct answer is (D). A number smaller than 0 is a negative number, so a is a negative number. A negative number squared becomes a positive number. Without knowing absolute values of a and b there is insufficient information to determine the answer to this question.

Section 3: Reading Comprehension

1. C	9. C	17. C	25. B	33. B
2. B	10. A	18. A	26. B	34. A
3. D	11. A	19. C	27. A	35. C
4. C	12. C	20. D	28. D	36. A
5. B	13. D	21. D	29. D	37. A
6. D	14. A	22. B	30. A	38. C
7. D	15. B	23. D	31. D	39. C
8. A	16. B	24. A	32. C	40. D

1. **The correct answer is (C).** The selection graphically details the movement of a snake. While much of the description is in terms of legs and feet, the point of the selection is to fully describe the means of locomotion.

2. **The correct answer is (B).** The second sentence of the second paragraph makes this statement. The remainder of the paragraph expands on the theme.

3. **The correct answer is (D).** This word appears in line 16. Read carefully and you can figure out the meaning from the context. *Terrain* means *earth*, with reference to its topographical features.

4. **The correct answer is (C).** The detail in this selection indicates that the author knows a good deal about snakes.

5. **The correct answer is (B).** The last sentence of the first paragraph tells us that rope is absolutely vital for docking.

6. **The correct answer is (D).** The second sentence serves by way of definition.

7. **The correct answer is (D).** In lines 15–16 we learn that the ship is secured by nine-inch or ten-inch mooring lines. Since rope is measured by circumference rather than by diameter (lines 31–32), choice (D) is the correct answer.

8. **The correct answer is (A).** Check back and eliminate. Sisal does not come from the Philippines.

9. **The correct answer is (C).** Since State Department clerks took charge of getting the Constitution and Declaration of Independence out of Washington before the British burned the city, these important documents must have been housed in the State Department offices.

10. **The correct answer is (A).** See the first sentence of the last paragraph.

11. **The correct answer is (A).** The last sentence enumerates the disasters protected against.

12. **The correct answer is (C).** The documents were removed in 1814 to protect them from the War of 1812; in 1941, they were removed for protection from possible damage in World War II.

13. **The correct answer is (D).** Great blank spaces on a population map indicate very small population.

14. **The correct answer is (A).** (See line 9.) You may eat the vegetables at a winter dinner, but the farm produces only the vegetables; it does not cook the dinner.

15. **The correct answer is (B).** In lines 15–16 we learn that broadcloth is made from silky cotton grown in Egypt.

16. **The correct answer is (B).** The third paragraph makes the statement that desert civilizations have made important cultural contributions. The last paragraph tells what these contributions are.

17. The correct answer is (C). See lines 32–35.

18. The correct answer is (A). The name of the town is *Ekalaka*, but they call it "Skeleton Flats."

19. The correct answer is (C). The answer to this main-idea question should be clear. The article is about the various fossil finds.

20. The correct answer is (D). Lines 10–12 give the definition: " . . . paleontologists, scientists who use fossils to study prehistoric life forms." Walter Peck's hobby was geology, and in the course of pursuing his hobby he made the first find, but he was not a paleontologist.

21. The correct answer is (D). The third paragraph discusses the people of Ekalaka in terms of their enthusiasm for digging and fossil discovery.

22. The correct answer is (B). See the last sentence.

23. The correct answer is (D). The selection describes the properties of zirconium in its various forms.

24. The correct answer is (A). Consider the use of the word *docile* as applied to solid zirconium, in contrast to the use of the word *violent* as applied to powdered zirconium.

25. The correct answer is (B). An emphasis of the selection is that increasing uses are being found for zirconium.

26. The correct answer is (B). The first paragraph makes this point.

27. The correct answer is (A). In both the second and third paragraphs, zirconium is described as a metal.

28. The correct answer is (D). If zirconium is too dangerous to be used in ammunition, it is most certainly too dangerous to be used in fireworks.

29. The correct answer is (D). The selection is about the beginning of Hudson ferryboat service.

30. The correct answer is (A). See lines 7–9.

31. The correct answer is (D). The next-to-last sentence discusses Fulton's invention of floating docks for the ferryboats.

32. The correct answer is (C). 1812 was in the nineteenth century.

33. The correct answer is (B). In the context of the paragraph, *shock* must refer to the *impact* of the boat running into the dock.

34. The correct answer is (A). The first paragraph describes the original trail as a path. The road is also described as an east-west route. It presented travelers with surprisingly few obstacles.

35. The correct answer is (C). The frontier outpost, Ithaca, was at the western end of the highway.

36. The correct answer is (A). See line 12.

37. The correct answer is (A). Guides are not mentioned in the selection.

38. The correct answer is (C). We are told that five positions for botanists have been created. The implication is that these are *new* positions.

39. The correct answer is (C). See lines 18–22. The Department says that listing and delisting are equally important.

40. The correct answer is (D). This is a difficult question. You can instantly eliminate choices (A) and (B), but choice (C) appears possible. If you reread the selection carefully a few more times, you will realize that past concepts of success are not really spelled out. Therefore, choice (D) would seem the most likely correct answer. The writer is anticipating a criticism and answering it in advance.

Section 4: Mathematics Achievement

1. D	10. A	19. A	28. C	37. D
2. A	11. A	20. C	29. D	38. B
3. C	12. D	21. C	30. A	39. C
4. A	13. A	22. A	31. B	40. D
5. D	14. A	23. B	32. C	41. D
6. B	15. C	24. D	33. A	42. B
7. C	16. A	25. C	34. D	43. C
8. A	17. D	26. C	35. B	44. D
9. B	18. C	27. D	36. A	45. D

1. **The correct answer is (D).**
   Area = length × width

   Area of square = 8 × 8 = 64 sq. in.

   Area of rectangle = (8 + 4) (8 − 2) = 12 × 6 = 72 sq. in.

   72 − 64 = 8 sq. in.

2. **The correct answer is (A).**

   $r = 35 − (9) (−n)$

   $r = 35 − (9) (−2)$

   $r = 35 − (−18)$

   $r = 35 + 18 = 53$

   To subtract signed numbers, change the sign of the subtrahend and proceed as in algebraic addition.

3. **The correct answer is (C).** First perform the operation within the parentheses. To cube a number, multiply it by itself, two times.

   $(3 + 4)^3 = (7)^3 = 7 × 7 × 7 = 343$

4. **The correct answer is (A).** Copper and aluminum in the ratio of 10:1 means 10 parts copper to 1 part aluminum.

   Let x = weight of aluminum

   Then $10x$ = weight of copper

   $10x + x = 77$

   $11x = 77$

   $x = 7$

5. **The correct answer is (D).**

   Volume = L × W × H

   Volume of carton = 2' × 3' × 4'

   = 24 cubic feet

   Volume of one box = 2" × 3" × 4"

   = 24 cubic inches

   1 cubic foot = 12" × 12" × 12"

   = 1,728 cubic inches

   $\dfrac{1,728 \times \overset{1}{\cancel{24}}}{\underset{1}{\cancel{24}}}$ = 1,728 boxes will fit in the carton

6. **The correct answer is (B).** $\dfrac{3}{5}$ of 200

   = 120 columns by machine @ 40 columns per hour = 3 hours

   200 − 120 = 80 columns without machine @ 20 columns per hour = 4 hours

   3 hours + 4 hours = 7 hours to complete the job.

7. **The correct answer is (C).** His total income is equal to 7% of his sales plus $150; 7% of his sales is $945 × .07 = $66.15.

   $66.15 + $150 = $216.15

8. **The correct answer is (A).**

   If $x^2 + 5 = 41$

   $$x^2 = 41 - 5$$

   $$x^2 = 36$$

   $$x = \pm 6$$

9. **The correct answer is (B).** Perimeter $= 2l + 2w$

   If the two long sides are together, the perimeter will be

   $$5 + 3 + 3 + 5 + 3 + 3 = 22$$

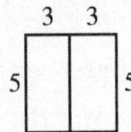

   If the two short sides are together, the perimeter will be

   $$3 + 5 + 5 + 3 + 5 + 5 = 26$$

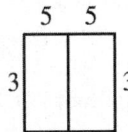

   $26 - 22 = 4$ feet shorter

10. **The correct answer is (A).** 5 hours

    30 minutes $= 5\dfrac{1}{2}$ hours

    1,000 miles $\div 5\dfrac{1}{2}$ hours $=$

    $$1,000 \div \frac{11}{2} = 1,000 \times \frac{2}{11} = 181\frac{9}{11} \text{ mph}$$

11. **The correct answer is (A).** 500 dozen @ \$.40 per dozen = purchase of two years ago

    75% of 500 dozen = 375 dozen pencils purchased this year

    20% of \$.40 = \$.08 increase in cost per dozen

    $375 \times \$.48 = \$180$ spent on pencils this year

12. **The correct answer is (D).** A child's ticket costs x dollars. Each adult ticket costs twice as much, or $2x$ dollars. $2(2x)$ = 2 adult tickets; $3x$ = 3 children's tickets. Write a simple equation, and solve for x.

    $$2(2x) + 3x = \$49$$

    $$4x + 3x = \$49$$

    $$7x = \$49$$

    $$x = \$7$$

    \$7 is the cost of a child's ticket; \$14 is the cost of an adult's ticket.

13. **The correct answer is (A).**

    $$\frac{x}{2} + 36 = 37.25$$

    $$\frac{x}{2} = 37.25 - 36$$

    $$\frac{x}{2} = 1.25$$

    $$x = 2.50$$

14. **The correct answer is (A).** One person raised 35% of \$690.

    $\$690 \times .35 = \$241.50$.

    The remainder raised by the others was $\$690 - 241.50 = \$448.50$

15. **The correct answer is (C).** For the length, 29 feet would be represented by 29 units of $\frac{1}{4}$", resulting in $\frac{29}{4}$, or $7\frac{1}{4}$ inches. For the width, 23 feet would be represented by 23 units of $\frac{1}{4}$", resulting in $\frac{23}{4}$, or $5\frac{3}{4}$ inches.

16. **The correct answer is (A).**
    Area = length × width

    = 176 ft. × 79 ft.

    = 13,904 sq. ft.

17. The correct answer is (D).

$$63 \div \frac{1}{9} = 63 \times \frac{9}{1} = 567$$

This is a good answer to estimate. By dividing a number by $\frac{1}{9}$, you are, in effect, multiplying it by 9. Only one of the suggested answers is close.

18. The correct answer is (C). The problem asks, "What number is $13.23 18% of?" $13.23 ÷ .18 = $73.50.

19. The correct answer is (A). Each fast worker is equivalent to two slow workers; therefore, the three men are the equivalent of five slow workers. The whole job, then, requires 5 × 56 = 280 minutes for one slow worker. It also requires half that time, or 140 minutes, for one fast worker, and half again as much, or 70 minutes, for two fast workers.

20. The correct answer is (C). Subtract from the total population of 18,000 the 756 children and the 2,244 married people. 18,000 − 756 − 2,244 = 15,000 single men and women.

Because there are $1\frac{1}{2}$ times as many men as women, we know that 60% of the 15,000 single people are men, and 40% are women. 60% of 15,000 = 9,000.

21. The correct answer is (C). No calculations are needed here. Note that a 20-mile trip at 60 mph (which is 1 mile per minute), would take 20 minutes. Since the vehicle is traveling half as fast (30 mph), the 20-mile trip should take twice as long, or 40 minutes.

22. The correct answer is (A).

$$2x^2 + 3 = 21$$
$$2x^2 = 21 - 3$$
$$2x^2 = 18$$
$$x^2 = 9$$
$$x = \pm 3$$

You should have been able to predict that x would be a small number, since, according to the equation, twice its square is no larger than 21.

23. The correct answer is (B). The area of a circle is A = πr^2, when the radius equals $\frac{1}{2}$ the diameter. $r = 3$, and $\pi = \frac{22}{7}$, or 3.14.

A = πr^2
A = $\pi(3)^2$
A = 9π
A = 9(3.14) = 28.26 sq. in.

24. The correct answer is (D). The scale is $\frac{1}{8}$" = 25 miles. In $3\frac{7}{8}$" there are 31 $\frac{1}{8}$" units. The distance is 31 • 25 = 775 miles.

25. The correct answer is (C). The amount the house was insured for is 80% of $83,000, or $66,400. The insurance is calculated at 45¢ per hundred, or $4.50 per thousand of value. Since there are 66.4 thousands of value, 66.4 × $4.50 per thousand equals the yearly premium of $298.80.

26. The correct answer is (C). The size of the job can be thought of this way: 18 clerks working for 26 days do 18 × 26 or 468 clerk-days of work. To do 468 clerk-days of work in only 12 days would require 468 ÷ 12 = 39 clerks.

27. **The correct answer is (D).** The digits are all alike, so you do not need to calculate. Move the decimal point of the divisor two places to the right; do the same for the dividend.

28. **The correct answer is (C).** Solve this problem as you would any mixture-value problem. The numbers of cars sold are all related to the number of those sold for $4,200. Call the number of $4,200 cars sold x. Then, the number of $5,400 cars sold is $3x$, and the number of $4,800 cars is $2x$.

   The value of $4,200 cars sold is $4,200 • x.

   The value of $4,800 cars sold is $4,800 • $2x$.

   The value of $5,400 cars sold is $5,400 • $3x$.

   The sum of these values equals the total sales.

   ($4,200 • x) + ($4,800 • $2x$) + (5,400 • $3x$) = $360,000

   $4,200x + $9,600x + $16,200x = $360,000

   $30,000x = $360,000

   $x = $360,000 ÷ $30,000

   $x = 12$

   Since $x = 12$, $4,200 cars, $3x$, or 36 of the $5,400 model, were sold.

29. **The correct answer is (D).** There is not enough information to answer this problem. We must know how many attended the game to determine how many paid full price.

30. **The correct answer is (A).** You must borrow one day's worth of hours and one hour's worth of minutes and rewrite the problem as:

   6 days 26 hr. 80 min.

   − 4 days   9 hr. 31 min.

   2 days 17 hr. 49 min.

31. **The correct answer is (B).** The formula for the area of a triangle is A = $\frac{1}{2}$ bh. Plug in the numbers:

   $A = \frac{1}{2} • 12 • 14$

   A = 84 sq. ft.

32. **The correct answer is (C).** This is a tricky question. It doesn't ask for 150% of 72, but rather to increase 72 by 150%. Since 150% of 72 = 108, we add 72 and 108 for the correct answer, 180.

33. **The correct answer is (A).** Choice (B) is read, "Four times the square of a certain number minus 6 equals 2." Choice (C) is read, "Four times the square of a number divided by 3 minus 6 equals 2." Choice (D) is read, "One-fourth a given number divided by 3 minus 6 equals 2."

34. **The correct answer is (D).** Write down both equations and add them together.

   $14x − 2y = 32$

   $+ x + 2y = 13$

   $15x = 45$

   $x = 3$

35. **The correct answer is (B).** An ordinary die has six sides, each having a different number of dots. The chance of any face coming up is the same: $\frac{1}{6}$.

36. **The correct answer is (A).** First, pick the two longest times, then compare them. 1,440 minutes and 25 hours are obviously the longest periods. 25 hours contains 1,500 minutes.

37. **The correct answer is (D).** The cars are traveling toward each other, so the distance between them is being reduced at 60 + 50 or 110 miles per hour. At a rate of 110 mph, 550 miles will be covered in 5 hours. If both cars left at 1 p.m., they should meet at 6 p.m.

38. **The correct answer is (B).** Choice (A) is 4,930; choice (C) is 483; choice (D) is 133.

39. **The correct answer is (C).** If 10 men earn \$5,400 in 12 days, each man earns \$540 in 12 days, or \$45 per day. Therefore, 6 men working for 15 days at \$45 per day will earn \$4,050.

40. **The correct answer is (D).** The map distance is $4\frac{1}{2}"$, or $\frac{9}{2}"$ or $\frac{36}{8}"$. Each $\frac{3}{8}" = 5$ miles, and we know there are $12\frac{3}{8}"$-units in $\frac{36}{8}"$. Therefore, the $12\frac{3}{8}"$-units correspond to 60 miles in actuality.

41. **The correct answer is (D).** The area of a circle is found by $A = \pi r^2$. The radius is half the diameter. To find the diameter when the area is known, divide the area by π to find the square of the radius.

$$78.5 \div 3.14 = 25$$

Since the square of the radius is 25, we know the radius is 5, and the diameter is twice the radius, or 10 inches.

42. **The correct answer is (B).** If $a = 6$, $ab + 4 = 52$ becomes $6b + 4 = 52$.

If $6b + 4 = 52$

$$6b = 52 - 4$$

$$6b = 48$$

$$b = 8$$

43. **The correct answer is (C).** If $\frac{2}{3}$ of the jar is filled in 1 minute, then $\frac{1}{3}$ of the jar is filled in $\frac{1}{2}$ minute. Since the jar is $\frac{2}{3}$ full, $\frac{1}{3}$ remains to be filled. The jar will be full in another $\frac{1}{2}$ minute.

44. **The correct answer is (D).** First convert to a 24-hour clock.

$$3{:}30 \text{ p.m.} = 15{:}30 \text{ o'clock}$$

$$15{:}30 = 14{:}90$$

$$\underline{- 8{:}50 = -8{:}50}$$

$$6{:}40 = 6 \text{ hours } 40 \text{ minutes}$$

To subtract a larger number of minutes from a smaller number of minutes, borrow 60 minutes from the hour to enlarge the smaller number.

45. **The correct answer is (D).**

Assign arbitrary values to solve this problem:

A square 10 ft. × 10 ft. = 100 sq. ft.

A rectangle 9 ft. × 11 ft. = 99 sq. ft.

$$100 - 99 = 1; \ \frac{1}{100} = 1\%$$

Section 5: Essay

Example of a well-written essay.

If I could spend an afternoon with any author, I would have a wonderful conversation with Jules Verne. I think of Jules Verne as the father of science fiction. We would talk about his books and why they make such good reading. I would tell him how much of his fiction has become fact. Then we would probably talk about recent science fiction and about the latest scientific and technological advances. Perhaps we would predict future developments.

The first book I would mention is my favorite, *Twenty Thousand Leagues under the Sea*. I would ask Mr. Verne how he thought up the book and would tell him how much I admire his works and how I respect his imagination. Then I would tell him about submarines and submarine warfare and would describe all the deep sea explorations that I know about. It is hard to predict a conversation in advance, but *Around the World in Eighty Days* would certainly be a good next topic, and we might well consume the remainder of the afternoon with discussion of modern travel and of all the countries and cultures that can be visited today.

No conversation with Jules Verne could conclude without mention of modern science fiction and of how predictive it might be. I wonder what Jules Verne would think of *Star Trek*. Finally I would tell him about space exploration, moon landings, satellites, and all the exciting space work that is unfolding.

The prospect of a conversation with Jules Verne is very appealing. Even though I know it cannot happen, I am thinking of more and more things I would like to discuss with him. What a stimulating afternoon it would be.

SCORE YOURSELF

Scores on the ISEE are determined by comparing each student's results against all other students in his or her grade level who took that particular test. A scaled score is then calculated. You can use the following calculations to determine how well you did on this practice test, but keep in mind that when you take the actual test, your score might vary.

Test	Raw Score ÷ No. questions	× 100 =	%
Synonyms	÷ 20	× 100 =	%
Sentence Completions	÷ 20	× 100 =	%
Total Verbal Ability	÷ 40	× 100 =	%
Multiple-Choice Quantitative	÷ 17	× 100 =	%
Quantitative Comparisons	÷ 18	× 100 =	%
Total Quantitative Ability	÷ 35	× 100 =	%
Reading Comprehension	÷ 40	× 100 =	%
Mathematics Achievement	÷ 45	× 100 =	%

High percentage scores should make you feel very good about yourself, but low percentages do not mean that you are a failure.

Remember:

- Scores are not reported as percentages. A low percentage may translate to a respectable scaled score.
- The same test is given to students in grades 8 through 12. Unless you have finished high school, you have not been taught everything on the test. You are not expected to know what you have not been taught.
- You will be compared only to students in your own grade.

Use your scores to plan further study if you have time.

ANSWER SHEET PRACTICE TEST 5: ISEE (Upper Level)

Section 1: Verbal Reasoning

1 Ⓐ Ⓑ Ⓒ Ⓓ	11 Ⓐ Ⓑ Ⓒ Ⓓ	21 Ⓐ Ⓑ Ⓒ Ⓓ	31 Ⓐ Ⓑ Ⓒ Ⓓ
2 Ⓐ Ⓑ Ⓒ Ⓓ	12 Ⓐ Ⓑ Ⓒ Ⓓ	22 Ⓐ Ⓑ Ⓒ Ⓓ	32 Ⓐ Ⓑ Ⓒ Ⓓ
3 Ⓐ Ⓑ Ⓒ Ⓓ	13 Ⓐ Ⓑ Ⓒ Ⓓ	23 Ⓐ Ⓑ Ⓒ Ⓓ	33 Ⓐ Ⓑ Ⓒ Ⓓ
4 Ⓐ Ⓑ Ⓒ Ⓓ	14 Ⓐ Ⓑ Ⓒ Ⓓ	24 Ⓐ Ⓑ Ⓒ Ⓓ	34 Ⓐ Ⓑ Ⓒ Ⓓ
5 Ⓐ Ⓑ Ⓒ Ⓓ	15 Ⓐ Ⓑ Ⓒ Ⓓ	25 Ⓐ Ⓑ Ⓒ Ⓓ	35 Ⓐ Ⓑ Ⓒ Ⓓ
6 Ⓐ Ⓑ Ⓒ Ⓓ	16 Ⓐ Ⓑ Ⓒ Ⓓ	26 Ⓐ Ⓑ Ⓒ Ⓓ	36 Ⓐ Ⓑ Ⓒ Ⓓ
7 Ⓐ Ⓑ Ⓒ Ⓓ	17 Ⓐ Ⓑ Ⓒ Ⓓ	27 Ⓐ Ⓑ Ⓒ Ⓓ	37 Ⓐ Ⓑ Ⓒ Ⓓ
8 Ⓐ Ⓑ Ⓒ Ⓓ	18 Ⓐ Ⓑ Ⓒ Ⓓ	28 Ⓐ Ⓑ Ⓒ Ⓓ	38 Ⓐ Ⓑ Ⓒ Ⓓ
9 Ⓐ Ⓑ Ⓒ Ⓓ	19 Ⓐ Ⓑ Ⓒ Ⓓ	29 Ⓐ Ⓑ Ⓒ Ⓓ	39 Ⓐ Ⓑ Ⓒ Ⓓ
10 Ⓐ Ⓑ Ⓒ Ⓓ	20 Ⓐ Ⓑ Ⓒ Ⓓ	30 Ⓐ Ⓑ Ⓒ Ⓓ	40 Ⓐ Ⓑ Ⓒ Ⓓ

Section 2: Quantitative Reasoning

1 Ⓐ Ⓑ Ⓒ Ⓓ	13 Ⓐ Ⓑ Ⓒ Ⓓ	25 Ⓐ Ⓑ Ⓒ Ⓓ	37 Ⓐ Ⓑ Ⓒ Ⓓ
2 Ⓐ Ⓑ Ⓒ Ⓓ	14 Ⓐ Ⓑ Ⓒ Ⓓ	26 Ⓐ Ⓑ Ⓒ Ⓓ	38 Ⓐ Ⓑ Ⓒ Ⓓ
3 Ⓐ Ⓑ Ⓒ Ⓓ	15 Ⓐ Ⓑ Ⓒ Ⓓ	27 Ⓐ Ⓑ Ⓒ Ⓓ	39 Ⓐ Ⓑ Ⓒ Ⓓ
4 Ⓐ Ⓑ Ⓒ Ⓓ	16 Ⓐ Ⓑ Ⓒ Ⓓ	28 Ⓐ Ⓑ Ⓒ Ⓓ	40 Ⓐ Ⓑ Ⓒ Ⓓ
5 Ⓐ Ⓑ Ⓒ Ⓓ	17 Ⓐ Ⓑ Ⓒ Ⓓ	29 Ⓐ Ⓑ Ⓒ Ⓓ	41 Ⓐ Ⓑ Ⓒ Ⓓ
6 Ⓐ Ⓑ Ⓒ Ⓓ	18 Ⓐ Ⓑ Ⓒ Ⓓ	30 Ⓐ Ⓑ Ⓒ Ⓓ	42 Ⓐ Ⓑ Ⓒ Ⓓ
7 Ⓐ Ⓑ Ⓒ Ⓓ	19 Ⓐ Ⓑ Ⓒ Ⓓ	31 Ⓐ Ⓑ Ⓒ Ⓓ	43 Ⓐ Ⓑ Ⓒ Ⓓ
8 Ⓐ Ⓑ Ⓒ Ⓓ	20 Ⓐ Ⓑ Ⓒ Ⓓ	32 Ⓐ Ⓑ Ⓒ Ⓓ	44 Ⓐ Ⓑ Ⓒ Ⓓ
9 Ⓐ Ⓑ Ⓒ Ⓓ	21 Ⓐ Ⓑ Ⓒ Ⓓ	33 Ⓐ Ⓑ Ⓒ Ⓓ	45 Ⓐ Ⓑ Ⓒ Ⓓ

answer sheet

Section 3: Reading Comprehension

1 Ⓐ Ⓑ Ⓒ Ⓓ	11 Ⓐ Ⓑ Ⓒ Ⓓ	21 Ⓐ Ⓑ Ⓒ Ⓓ	31 Ⓐ Ⓑ Ⓒ Ⓓ
2 Ⓐ Ⓑ Ⓒ Ⓓ	12 Ⓐ Ⓑ Ⓒ Ⓓ	22 Ⓐ Ⓑ Ⓒ Ⓓ	32 Ⓐ Ⓑ Ⓒ Ⓓ
3 Ⓐ Ⓑ Ⓒ Ⓓ	13 Ⓐ Ⓑ Ⓒ Ⓓ	23 Ⓐ Ⓑ Ⓒ Ⓓ	33 Ⓐ Ⓑ Ⓒ Ⓓ
4 Ⓐ Ⓑ Ⓒ Ⓓ	14 Ⓐ Ⓑ Ⓒ Ⓓ	24 Ⓐ Ⓑ Ⓒ Ⓓ	34 Ⓐ Ⓑ Ⓒ Ⓓ
5 Ⓐ Ⓑ Ⓒ Ⓓ	15 Ⓐ Ⓑ Ⓒ Ⓓ	25 Ⓐ Ⓑ Ⓒ Ⓓ	35 Ⓐ Ⓑ Ⓒ Ⓓ
6 Ⓐ Ⓑ Ⓒ Ⓓ	16 Ⓐ Ⓑ Ⓒ Ⓓ	26 Ⓐ Ⓑ Ⓒ Ⓓ	36 Ⓐ Ⓑ Ⓒ Ⓓ
7 Ⓐ Ⓑ Ⓒ Ⓓ	17 Ⓐ Ⓑ Ⓒ Ⓓ	27 Ⓐ Ⓑ Ⓒ Ⓓ	37 Ⓐ Ⓑ Ⓒ Ⓓ
8 Ⓐ Ⓑ Ⓒ Ⓓ	18 Ⓐ Ⓑ Ⓒ Ⓓ	28 Ⓐ Ⓑ Ⓒ Ⓓ	38 Ⓐ Ⓑ Ⓒ Ⓓ
9 Ⓐ Ⓑ Ⓒ Ⓓ	19 Ⓐ Ⓑ Ⓒ Ⓓ	29 Ⓐ Ⓑ Ⓒ Ⓓ	39 Ⓐ Ⓑ Ⓒ Ⓓ
10 Ⓐ Ⓑ Ⓒ Ⓓ	20 Ⓐ Ⓑ Ⓒ Ⓓ	30 Ⓐ Ⓑ Ⓒ Ⓓ	40 Ⓐ Ⓑ Ⓒ Ⓓ

Section 4: Quantitative (Math)

1 Ⓐ Ⓑ Ⓒ Ⓓ	13 Ⓐ Ⓑ Ⓒ Ⓓ	25 Ⓐ Ⓑ Ⓒ Ⓓ	37 Ⓐ Ⓑ Ⓒ Ⓓ
2 Ⓐ Ⓑ Ⓒ Ⓓ	14 Ⓐ Ⓑ Ⓒ Ⓓ	26 Ⓐ Ⓑ Ⓒ Ⓓ	38 Ⓐ Ⓑ Ⓒ Ⓓ
3 Ⓐ Ⓑ Ⓒ Ⓓ	15 Ⓐ Ⓑ Ⓒ Ⓓ	27 Ⓐ Ⓑ Ⓒ Ⓓ	39 Ⓐ Ⓑ Ⓒ Ⓓ
4 Ⓐ Ⓑ Ⓒ Ⓓ	16 Ⓐ Ⓑ Ⓒ Ⓓ	28 Ⓐ Ⓑ Ⓒ Ⓓ	40 Ⓐ Ⓑ Ⓒ Ⓓ
5 Ⓐ Ⓑ Ⓒ Ⓓ	17 Ⓐ Ⓑ Ⓒ Ⓓ	29 Ⓐ Ⓑ Ⓒ Ⓓ	41 Ⓐ Ⓑ Ⓒ Ⓓ
6 Ⓐ Ⓑ Ⓒ Ⓓ	18 Ⓐ Ⓑ Ⓒ Ⓓ	30 Ⓐ Ⓑ Ⓒ Ⓓ	42 Ⓐ Ⓑ Ⓒ Ⓓ
7 Ⓐ Ⓑ Ⓒ Ⓓ	19 Ⓐ Ⓑ Ⓒ Ⓓ	31 Ⓐ Ⓑ Ⓒ Ⓓ	43 Ⓐ Ⓑ Ⓒ Ⓓ
8 Ⓐ Ⓑ Ⓒ Ⓓ	20 Ⓐ Ⓑ Ⓒ Ⓓ	32 Ⓐ Ⓑ Ⓒ Ⓓ	44 Ⓐ Ⓑ Ⓒ Ⓓ
9 Ⓐ Ⓑ Ⓒ Ⓓ	21 Ⓐ Ⓑ Ⓒ Ⓓ	33 Ⓐ Ⓑ Ⓒ Ⓓ	45 Ⓐ Ⓑ Ⓒ Ⓓ
10 Ⓐ Ⓑ Ⓒ Ⓓ	22 Ⓐ Ⓑ Ⓒ Ⓓ	34 Ⓐ Ⓑ Ⓒ Ⓓ	
11 Ⓐ Ⓑ Ⓒ Ⓓ	23 Ⓐ Ⓑ Ⓒ Ⓓ	35 Ⓐ Ⓑ Ⓒ Ⓓ	
12 Ⓐ Ⓑ Ⓒ Ⓓ	24 Ⓐ Ⓑ Ⓒ Ⓓ	36 Ⓐ Ⓑ Ⓒ Ⓓ	

Practice Test 5: ISEE (Upper Level)

SECTION 1: VERBAL REASONING

40 Questions • 20 Minutes

Directions: Each question is made up of a word in CAPITAL letters followed by four choices. Choose the one word that is most nearly the same in meaning as the word in CAPITAL letters, and mark its letter on your answer sheet.

1. IMPLIED
   (A) acknowledged
   (B) stated
   (C) predicted
   (D) hinted

2. FISCAL
   (A) critical
   (B) basic
   (C) personal
   (D) financial

3. STRINGENT
   (A) demanding
   (B) loud
   (C) flexible
   (D) clear

4. PERMEABLE
   (A) penetrable
   (B) durable
   (C) unending
   (D) allowable

5. SCRUPULOUS
   (A) conscientious
   (B) unprincipled
   (C) intricate
   (D) neurotic

6. STALEMATE
   (A) pillar
   (B) deadlock
   (C) maneuver
   (D) work slowdown

7. REDUNDANT
   (A) concise
   (B) reappearing
   (C) superfluous
   (D) lying down

8. SUPPLANT
   (A) prune
   (B) conquer
   (C) uproot
   (D) replace

9. COMMENSURATE
   (A) identical
   (B) of the same age
   (C) proportionate
   (D) measurable

10. ZENITH
    (A) depths
    (B) astronomical system
    (C) peak
    (D) solar system

11. SUCCOR
    (A) assistance
    (B) nurse
    (C) vitality
    (D) distress

12. DISPATCH
    (A) omit mention of
    (B) send out on an errand
    (C) tear
    (D) do without

13. PORTABLE
    (A) drinkable
    (B) convenient
    (C) having wheels
    (D) able to be carried

14. VERBOSE
    (A) vague
    (B) brief
    (C) wordy
    (D) verbal

15. SUBVERSIVE
    (A) secret
    (B) foreign
    (C) evasive
    (D) destructive

16. MALLEABLE
    (A) changeable
    (B) equalizing
    (C) decisive
    (D) progressing

17. PETTY
    (A) lengthy
    (B) communal
    (C) small
    (D) miscellaneous

18. INTREPID
    (A) willing
    (B) fanciful
    (C) cowardly
    (D) fearless

19. NEGOTIATE
    (A) argue
    (B) think
    (C) speak
    (D) bargain

20. STERILE
    (A) antique
    (B) germ-free
    (C) unclean
    (D) perishable

Directions: Each of the following questions is made up of a sentence containing one or two blanks. The sentences with one blank indicate that one word is missing. Sentences with two blanks have two missing words. Each sentence is followed by four choices. Choose the one word or pair of words that will best complete the meaning of the sentence as a whole, and mark the letter of your choice on your answer sheet.

21. Undaunted by his many setbacks, Joshua _____.
    (A) crumpled
    (B) drew back
    (C) canceled
    (D) persevered

22. Nationwide, college arts and science departments are taking _____ measures to attract students.
    (A) no
    (B) puny
    (C) innovative
    (D) few

23. With less capital available and fewer deals being done, it has clearly become a(n) _____ market.
   (A) heinous
   (B) inflationary
   (C) sellers'
   (D) buyers'

24. The penalty for violating the law would _____ for multiple offenses.
   (A) accede
   (B) nullify
   (C) diminish
   (D) escalate

25. The hotel was a world-class _____ property and, thanks to recent refurbishing and clever marketing efforts, it is experiencing a _____.
   (A) luxury .. renaissance
   (B) communal .. withdrawal
   (C) opulent .. decline
   (D) decadent .. stalemate

26. Some colleges, rather than _____ students to take arts courses, simply force them.
   (A) requiring
   (B) enticing
   (C) demanding
   (D) allowing

27. Requiring _____ by the criminal to the victim would be a far better way of dealing with many lawbreakers than _____, she argued.
   (A) punishment .. freedom
   (B) imprisonment .. pardon
   (C) restitution .. imprisonment
   (D) mea culpa .. negligence

28. Knowledge gained from books without the benefit of practical experience is usually not so profitable in everyday work as the opposite, _____ without _____.
   (A) culture .. manners
   (B) experiments .. science
   (C) experience .. scholarship
   (D) learning .. knowing

29. To _____ some of its _____ over the huge increase in state insurance premiums for employees, the school district invited one insurance expert to speak at a recent board meeting.
   (A) quell .. anxiety
   (B) dispel .. myths
   (C) aggravate .. nervousness
   (D) foment .. trepidation

30. While many elderly indeed are _____, poverty is _____ among the millions of older Americans who rely solely on Social Security.
   (A) penurious .. rampant
   (B) invalid .. abolished
   (C) absolute .. widespread
   (D) comfortable .. pervasive

31. A police officer's _____ job is to prevent crime.
   (A) primary
   (B) only
   (C) ostentatious
   (D) ostensible

32. In view of the extenuating circumstances and the defendant's youth, the judge recommended _____.
   (A) conviction
   (B) a defense
   (C) a mistrial
   (D) leniency

33. Despite religious differences, the family _____ clashes by respecting each other's values.
   (A) denied
   (B) averted
   (C) condescended
   (D) declined

34. While marketing to health-conscious consumers will _____ a restaurant change, it will also have an effect in supermarkets.
   (A) denigrate
   (B) cancel
   (C) encourage
   (D) emit

35. Despite the politician's overwhelming loss, he _____ his popularity with a small core of followers.
   (A) revoked
   (B) maintained
   (C) restrained
   (D) encouraged

36. The decision to seek therapeutic treatment is often provoked by a(n) _____, such as an arrest or a domestic dispute.
   (A) dearth
   (B) crisis
   (C) enigma
   (D) casualty

37. Knowing that any particular new business can _____, Joshua avoided investing in one even if the potential _____ was high.
   (A) succeed .. down side
   (B) reduce .. profit
   (C) do well .. monies
   (D) fail .. payoff

38. Because of the _____ caused by the flood, living conditions in the area have _____; many people have lost all of their belongings.
   (A) trepidation .. augmented
   (B) morass .. careened
   (C) devastation .. deteriorated
   (D) vertigo .. ameliorated

39. The management is providing all needed building facilities to help the scientists _____ their research project.
   (A) magnify
   (B) retard
   (C) relinquish
   (D) implement

40. We can easily forgo a _____ we have never had, but once obtained it often is looked upon as being _____.
   (A) requirement .. unusual
   (B) gift .. useless
   (C) luxury .. essential
   (D) bonus .. unearned

STOP END OF SECTION 1. IF YOU HAVE ANY TIME LEFT, GO OVER YOUR WORK IN THIS SECTION ONLY. DO NOT WORK IN ANY OTHER SECTION OF THE TEST.

SECTION 2: QUANTITATIVE REASONING

35 Questions • 35 Minutes

Note: You may assume that all figures accompanying Quantitative Reasoning questions have been drawn as accurately as possible EXCEPT when it is specifically stated that a particular figure is not drawn to scale. Letters such as x, y, and n stand for real numbers. The Quantitative Reasoning Test includes two types of questions. There are separate directions for each type of question.

> **Directions:** For questions 1–17, work each problem in your head or in the margins of the test booklet. Mark the letter of your answer choice on the answer sheet.

1. If the decimal point in a number is moved one place to the right, the number has been
   (A) divided by 10.
   (B) multiplied by 10.
   (C) divided by 100.
   (D) multiplied by 100.

2. What is the total number of degrees found in angles A and C in the triangle below?

   (A) 180°
   (B) 100°
   (C) 90°
   (D) 75°

3. Using exponents, write 329 in expanded form.
   (A) $(3^2 \times 10) + (2 \times 10) + 9$
   (B) $(3 \times 10^2) + (2 \times 10) + 9$
   (C) $(3 \times 10^2) + (2 \times 10^2) + 9$
   (D) $(3 \times 10^3) + (2 \times 10) + 9$

4. Find the circumference of a circle whose radius is 21 feet.
   (A) 65.94 feet
   (B) 132 feet
   (C) 153 feet
   (D) 1,769.4 feet

5. If $x > -4$, and $y < 2$, then $x \cap y$ includes
   (A) $-4, 0, 1, 2$
   (B) $-2, -1, 1, 2$
   (C) $1, 2, 3, 4$
   (D) $-3, -2, 0, 1$

6. $(6 \times 2) + (7 \times 3) = ?$
   (A) $(6 \times 7) + (2 \times 3)$
   (B) $(7 - 6) + (3 - 2)$
   (C) $(7 \times 3) + (6 \times 2)$
   (D) $(7 \times 3) \times (6 \times 2)$

7. Which of the following will substitute for x and make the statement below true?

$56 - (7 - x) = 53$

(A) 4

(B) 3

(C) 2

(D) 1

8. An angle that is greater than 90° and less than 180° is a(n)

(A) acute angle.

(B) right angle.

(C) reflex angle.

(D) obtuse angle.

9. $\dfrac{17}{30}$ is greater than

(A) $\dfrac{7}{8}$

(B) $\dfrac{9}{20}$

(C) $\dfrac{8}{11}$

(D) $\dfrac{20}{25}$

10. 1 centimeter equals what part of a meter?

(A) $\dfrac{1}{10}$

(B) $\dfrac{1}{100}$

(C) $\dfrac{1}{1,000}$

(D) $\dfrac{1}{10,000}$

11. What is the lowest common denominator for the fractions $\dfrac{3}{4}, \dfrac{6}{9}, \dfrac{2}{6}$, and $\dfrac{5}{12}$?

(A) 24

(B) 32

(C) 36

(D) 48

12. The set of common factors of 36 and 64 is

(A) {1, 2, 4}

(B) {1, 2, 3, 4}

(C) {1, 2, 4, 6, 18}

(D) {1, 2, 3, 4, 6}

13. If one angle of a triangle measures 115°, then the sum of the other two angles is

(A) 245°

(B) 195°

(C) 75°

(D) 65°

14.

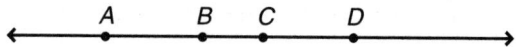

$\overline{AB} \cup \overline{BC}$

(A) $\overline{BD}$

(B) $\overline{BC}$

(C) $\overline{AD}$

(D) $\overline{AC}$

15. If a playing card is drawn from a standard deck, what are the chances it will be a 6?

(A) $\dfrac{1}{4}$

(B) $\dfrac{4}{13}$

(C) $\dfrac{4}{52}$

(D) $\dfrac{6}{52}$

16. The scale on a map is $\frac{1}{2}" = 8$ miles. If 2 towns are 28 miles apart, how many inches will separate them on a map?

(A) $1\frac{3}{4}$

(B) $1\frac{5}{8}$

(C) $1\frac{1}{2}$

(D) $1\frac{3}{8}$

17. A certain highway intersection has had A accidents over a 10-year period, resulting in B deaths. What is the yearly average death rate for the intersection?

(A) $A + B - 10$

(B) $\frac{B}{10}$

(C) $10 - \frac{A}{B}$

(D) $\frac{A}{10}$

Directions: For questions 18–35, two quantities are given—one in Column A and the other in Column B. In some questions, additional information concerning the quantities to be compared is centered above the entries in the two columns. Compare the quantities in the two columns, and mark your answer sheet as follows:

(A) if the quantity in Column A is greater

(B) if the quantity in Column B is greater

(C) if the quantities are equal

(D) if the relationship cannot be determined from the information given

Column A	Column B

18.

$$x = -2$$

| $3x^2 + 2x - 1$ | $x^3 + 2x^2 + 1$ |

19.

| AC | BC |

	Column A	Column B
20.	$(16 \div 4) + (8 \times 2) - 8$	$(3 \times 4) + (10 \div 5) - 3$

21.   A radio priced at \$47.25 includes a 5% profit (based on cost)

\$44.89	The original cost before profit

22.

$$a - b = -1$$

$$-b - a = -3$$

b	a

23.   25% of the 300 girls in the school have blonde hair

The ratio of girls with blonde hair to those without blonde hair	$\dfrac{1}{3}$

24.

$$e + c = 90°$$

$b + a + d + f$	270

25.

$ABCD$ is a parallelogram inscribed in circle O

$a° + c°$	$b° + d°$

Column A	Column B

26. Difference between $\dfrac{9}{8}$ and $\dfrac{3}{5}$ | .5

27.

A can do a job alone in 4 days

B can do a job alone in 3 days

The number of days it takes A and B working together to do the job | 2 days

28.

In a certain college, the ratio of the number of freshmen to the number of seniors is 3:1

$\dfrac{1}{3}$ | The ratio between the number of seniors and the total enrollment

29.

m | n

30.

$a + b = x$

$a - b = y$

x | y

31.

5 | AB

	Column A	Column B

32.

$$\sqrt[3]{125}$$

$$\sqrt{25}$$

33.

$$x > 0$$

$$y < 0$$

$x - y$	$x + y$

34. During a store sale, a $43.50 radio can be purchased at a 15% discount

The selling price of the radio with the discount	$36

35.

75% of $\dfrac{1}{2}$	50% of $\dfrac{3}{4}$

STOP END OF SECTION 2. IF YOU HAVE ANY TIME LEFT, GO OVER YOUR WORK IN THIS SECTION ONLY. DO NOT WORK IN ANY OTHER SECTION OF THE TEST.

SECTION 3: READING COMPREHENSION

40 Questions • 40 Minutes

Directions: Each reading passage is followed by questions based on its content. Answer the questions on the basis of what is stated or implied in the passage. On your answer sheet, mark the letter of the answer you choose.

Coming into the relay station with a rush, the Pony Express rider swung down from his exhausted mount and up onto a fresh horse with his precious
(5) mochilla, the saddle bag containing the mail. He was off again without a moment's delay. He was expected to reach the next station, and he did, or he died trying.

(10)   A rider might come into a station at dawn only to find that the station had been burned, the keepers killed, and the horses run off by attacking Indians. In that case he would con-
(15) tinue to the next station without food or rest.

"Buffalo Bill," a boy of 18, made the longest continuous run in the history of the Pony Express, 384 miles.
(20) By riding 280 miles in just 22 hours, Jim Moore earned the distinction of having made the fastest run.

Ninety riders covered the trail at all times of the day and night, often
(25) risking their lives to get the mail through within the ten-day limit. Most made it in eight days.

On the average, the riders could travel 11 miles an hour, a quick pace
(30) over terrain that might require the horse to swim rivers or cat-foot its way along narrow cliff trails.

The Pony Express riders carried the mail between Missouri and
(35) California for less than two years. They stopped riding in 1861 when a telegraph line offered a swifter means of communication.

1. The Pony Express rider stopped at a station to
   (A) get a few hours, sleep.
   (B) get a fresh mount.
   (C) sort the mail.
   (D) escape Native American attacks.

2. The *mochilla* refers to the
   (A) Pony Express rider's saddle bags.
   (B) Pony Express horses.
   (C) stations.
   (D) trails.

3. This passage implies that most of the Pony Express riders were
   (A) sure-footed.
   (B) faithful to their jobs.
   (C) mountain-bred.
   (D) killed.

4. Those sending mail by Pony Express could expect that it would reach its destination within
   (A) ten days.
   (B) five days.
   (C) a month.
   (D) before dawn.

5. The longest continuous run was
   (A) completed within 22 hours.
   (B) 280 miles.
   (C) made by traveling 11 miles per hour.
   (D) 384 miles.

Hatting was one of the first industries to develop in the colonies. As early as 1640, American hats were one of the domestic products used for barter (5) and exchange.

Wool was the principal raw material used by hatters, but large numbers of hats were also made of fur felt that came from native beaver pelts. (10) The average price of a wool hat was between 40 and 80 cents, and beaver hats ranged from $2.50 to $3.50.

By the beginning of the eighteenth century, hatting had become one of (15) New England's most important industries, and in the 1730s, hats were being exported from the colonies in sufficient numbers to arouse uneasiness among hatters in England. Pressure (20) was exerted, and Parliament passed a law prohibiting the export of hats from one colony to another, and from any colony to Great Britain.

6. The title that best expresses the main idea of this selection is
   (A) "Colonial Exports."
   (B) "Kinds of American Hats."
   (C) "An Early American Industry."
   (D) "How Colonial Hats Were Made."

7. A law restricting hat exports was enacted by Parliament in response to complaints by
   (A) colonists.
   (B) English hatmakers.
   (C) English noblemen.
   (D) citizens of foreign countries.

8. This law made it illegal for
   (A) Great Britain to export hats.
   (B) the colonies to import hats.
   (C) the hatters to use beaver fur.
   (D) the colonies to export hats.

9. American hats
   (A) were made principally of wool.
   (B) did not suit customers in Great Britain.
   (C) were an unimportant part of New England's industry.
   (D) were not made until 1730.

10. Beaver felt hats were
    (A) unpopular.
    (B) cheaper than wool hats.
    (C) more expensive than wool hats.
    (D) not exported.

The use of wood as a material from which to make paper was first suggested by René de Réaumer, a celebrated French naturalist, in 1719.
(5) Réaumer had observed wasps as they built their nests, and he concluded that the wood filaments used by these insects to construct their paper-like nests could also be used in the manu-
(10) facture of paper.

Wasps look for dry wood which they saw or rasp in their jaws. This material is then mixed with a gluey substance secreted by the wasp's body
(15) to make a paste that, when spread, becomes the paper substance of the nest.

Wasp nests are exceptionally lightweight, dark in color, and bound
(20) repeatedly by bands of paper to the place where they are suspended. The nests are nearly waterproof because of their rounded tops and the fact that the paper strips overlap like the
(25) shingles on the roof of a house.

11. The word *filaments* as used in line 7 of this passage probably means
(A) large chunks.
(B) threadlike pieces.
(C) files.
(D) dust.

12. The man who first suggested making paper from wood was a
(A) farmer.
(B) industrialist.
(C) lumberjack.
(D) naturalist.

13. According to the passage, a wasp nest is usually
(A) attached to a house.
(B) exceptionally lightweight.
(C) waterproofed with a gluey substance.
(D) constructed with chunks of wood.

14. The primary material used by wasps in nest building is
(A) dirt.
(B) water.
(C) paste.
(D) wood.

15. Wasp nests are waterproof because
(A) they are constructed of heavy materials.
(B) they hang from the boughs of trees.
(C) the strips of paper overlap.
(D) bands are placed around them.

About 86 percent of the total weight of a glass of milk is water. The remaining 14 percent is a combination of nutritious solids suspended in the water.
(5) The solids consist of milk sugar, fat, protein, minerals, and vitamins.

Milk is a unique food because it meets most of the body's requirements for growth and health. It is especially
(10) rich in Vitamins A and B and the minerals calcium and phosphorus, none of which can be easily obtained from other foods. These substances are essential for normal development
(15) and maintenance of healthy bones and teeth.

In spite of this, it is fortunate for us that we do not have to live on milk alone, as it does not supply us with
(20) the iron we need to prevent anemia. In its natural state, milk also lacks Vitamin D, whose production within the body can be stimulated by sunshine, and the commercial prepara-
(25) tion of milk eliminates its Vitamin C. It is therefore necessary to get these essential vitamins and minerals from other food sources.

16. The largest part of milk is

(A) water.

(B) sugar.

(C) vitamins.

(D) minerals.

17. Milk is an especially important food because

(A) it is cheap.

(B) it is easily available.

(C) it contains so much protein.

(D) a number of its nutrients are not easily obtained from other food sources.

18. Milk does not contain

(A) phosphorus.

(B) iron.

(C) fat.

(D) Vitamin A.

19. According to the article, sunshine is important in the production of

(A) Vitamin A.

(B) Vitamin C.

(C) Vitamin D.

(D) calcium.

For generations, historians and boat lovers have been trying to learn more about the brave ship that brought the Pilgrims to America. The task is a
(5) difficult one because *Mayflower* was such a common name for ships back in early seventeenth-century England that there were at least twenty of them when the Pilgrims left for the
(10) New World.

An exact duplicate of the *Mayflower* has been built in England and given to the people of the United States as a symbol of good will and
(15) common ancestry linking Britons and Americans. The Pilgrims' *Mayflower* apparently was built originally as a fishing vessel. It seems to have been 90 feet long by 22 feet wide, displacing
(20) 180 tons of water. The duplicate measures 90 feet by 26 feet, displaces 183 tons, and has a crew of 21, as did the original vessel. The new *Mayflower* has no motor but travels faster than
(25) the old boat.

What happened to the historic boat? So far as can be told, the *Mayflower* went back to less colorful jobs and, not too many years later,
(30) was scrapped. What happened to the beams, masts, and planking is questionable. In the English city of Abingdon, there is a Congregational church that contains two heavy
(35) wooden pillars. Some say these pillars are masts from the *Mayflower*. A barn in the English town of Jordans seemed to be built of old ship timbers. Marine experts said these timbers
(40) were impregnated with salt and, if put together, would form a vessel 90 feet by 22 feet. The man who owned the farm when the peculiar barn was built was a relative of the man who
(45) appraised the *Mayflower* when it was scrapped.

So the original *Mayflower* may still be doing service ashore while her duplicate sails the seas again.

20. A long search was made for the Pilgrims' boat because it
(A) contained valuable materials.
(B) might still do sea service.
(C) has historical importance.
(D) would link Great Britain and America.

21. It has been difficult to discover what happened to the original *Mayflower* because
(A) many ships bore the same name.
(B) it was such a small vessel.
(C) the search was begun too late.
(D) it has become impregnated with salt.

22. The British recently had a duplicate of the *Mayflower* built because
(A) the original could not be located.
(B) they wanted to make a gesture of friendship.
(C) parts of the original could be used.
(D) historians recommended such a step.

23. Compared with the original *Mayflower*, the modern duplicate
(A) is longer.
(B) is identical.
(C) carries a larger crew.
(D) is somewhat wider.

24. When the author says that the original boat may still be doing service ashore, he means that
(A) it may be whole and intact somewhere.
(B) present-day buildings may include parts of it.
(C) it may be in a boat lover's private collection.
(D) it may be in the service of pirates.

Few animals are as descriptively named as the varying hare (*Lepus americanus*), also commonly known as the snowshoe hare, white rabbit, or
(5) snowshoe rabbit. The species derives its various names from its interesting adaptations to the seasonal changes affecting its habitat.

The color changes are effected by
(10) means of a molt, and are timed (although the hares have no voluntary control over them) to coincide with the changing appearances of the background. The periods of transition—
(15) from white to brown in the spring, and from brown to white in the fall— require more than two months from start to completion, during which time the hares are a mottled brown and
(20) white. In addition to the changes in color, in the fall the soles of the feet develop a very heavy growth of hair that functions as snowshoes.

In New York State, hares are
(25) most abundant in and around the Adirondack and Catskill Mountains. Thriving populations, with less extensive ranges, are found in Allegany, Cattaraugus, Rensselaer, and
(30) Chenango counties. Smaller colonies of limited range are found in scattered islands.

25. The title that best expresses the main idea of this selection is

(A) "Seasonal Changes in Birds."

(B) "The Varying Hare."

(C) "An American Animal."

(D) "The Abundance of Hares."

26. Terms used to name these rabbits are related to their

(A) abundance in many parts of New York State.

(B) sensitivity to weather conditions throughout the state.

(C) ability to adapt to the change of seasons.

(D) thick white coats.

27. These rabbits have both brown and white markings in

(A) summer and winter.

(B) spring and fall.

(C) spring and summer.

(D) fall and winter.

28. The parts of New York State where rabbit populations are most plentiful are

(A) Allegany, Cattaraugus, Rensselaer, and Chenango counties.

(B) Adirondack and Catskill Mountain regions.

(C) islands within the state.

(D) snowy areas in the hills.

29. Which statement about these rabbits is *true* according to the selection?

(A) They are becoming fewer in number.

(B) They are capable of leaping great distances.

(C) They are more plentiful in winter.

(D) They have no control over their color changes.

Like the United States today, Athens had courts where a wrong might be righted. Since any citizen might accuse another of a crime, the Athenian
(5) courts of law were very busy. In fact, unless a citizen was unusually peaceful or very unimportant, he would be sure to find himself in the courts at least once every few years.

(10)   At a trial, both the accuser and the person accused were allowed a certain time to speak. The length of time was marked by a water clock. Free men testified under oath as they do today,
(15) but the oath of a slave was counted as worthless.

    To judge a trial, a jury was chosen from the members of the assembly who had reached 30 years of age. The
(20) Athenian juries were very large, often consisting of 201; 401; 501; 1,001; or more men, depending upon the importance of the case being tried. The juryman swore by the gods to listen
(25) carefully to both sides of the question and to give his honest opinion of the case. Each juryman gave his decision by depositing a white or black stone in a box. To keep citizens from being
(30) too careless in accusing each other, there was a rule that if the person accused did not receive a certain number of negative votes, the accuser was condemned instead.

30. The title that best expresses the main idea of this selection is

    (A) "Athens and the United States."

    (B) "Justice in Ancient Athens."

    (C) "Testifying Under Oath."

    (D) "The Duties of Juries."

31. People in Athens were frequently on trial in a law court because

    (A) they liked to serve on juries.

    (B) a juryman agreed to listen to both sides.

    (C) any person might accuse another of a crime.

    (D) the slaves were troublesome.

32. An Athenian was likely to avoid accusing another without a good reason because

    (A) the jury might condemn the accuser instead of the accused.

    (B) the jury might be very large.

    (C) cases were judged by men over 30 years old.

    (D) there was a limit on the time a trial could take.

33. Which statement is *true* according to the selection?

    (A) An accused person was denied the privilege of telling his side of the case.

    (B) The importance of the case determined the number of jurors.

    (C) A jury's decision was handed down in writing.

    (D) A citizen had to appear in court every few years.

The temperature of the earth's upper atmosphere is one of the most revealing properties of the earth's near environment. Not only does it vary
(5) widely with time and location but it also reacts strongly to changes in solar activity. The variation of temperature with altitude and with time reflects directly the different energy sources
(10) that in large measure govern the dynamic behavior of the upper atmosphere. The temperature also controls the rate of change of density with altitude through the requirement of
(15) hydrostatic balance. In hydrostatic balance the atmospheric pressure at any height equals the total weight of the overlying gas, a condition that requires that the pressure and density
(20) of the gas decrease exponentially at a rate inversely proportional to the temperature.

Thus, if the altitude profile of the temperature is known, one can
(25) calculate the altitude profiles of pressure and density provided the mean molecular weight of the gas is also known. This proviso is necessary because the rate of decrease of
(30) pressure and density is proportional to the mean molecular weight. Since heavy gases, such as argon and carbon dioxide, are more tightly bound by the earth's gravitational field, they tend
(35) to concentrate at low altitudes, while the density of light constituents, such as hydrogen and helium, decreases very slowly with height. At altitudes below about 110 kilometers, however,
(40) this tendency toward gravitational separation of the constituents is fully counteracted by turbulent mixing processes so the mean molecular weight of the atmosphere varies very little
(45) from its sea-level value of 29 atomic mass units (amu). At higher altitudes there is little mixing. The heavy constituents become progressively more rare, and the dominant atmospheric
(50) constituent changes, with increasing altitude, from molecular nitrogen (28 amu), to atomic oxygen (16 amu), to

helium (4 amu), and, at very high altitudes, to atomic hydrogen (1 amu).

34. All of the following affect the temperature of the earth's upper atmosphere EXCEPT
   (A) sun.
   (B) altitude.
   (C) time.
   (D) weather.

35. Which of the following most strongly affects the upper atmosphere?
   (A) Lack of oxygen
   (B) Seasonal changes
   (C) Air pressure
   (D) Heat of the sun

36. At the highest altitude one would find
   (A) helium.
   (B) oxygen.
   (C) hydrogen.
   (D) nitrogen.

37. Which statement best reflects the main idea of this article?
   (A) There is a great variability in the temperature of the earth from place to place and from time to time.
   (B) Control of the earth's upper atmosphere depends upon control of its temperature.
   (C) Our environment is controlled by the earth's temperature.
   (D) High altitude temperature tells much about the earth's atmosphere.

On May 8, 1939, folk song collector and scholar Herbert Halpert arrived in Mississippi to document folklore and folk music during a recording tour
(5) of the South sponsored by the Joint Committee on the Arts of the Works Progress Administration (WPA). He drove into the state in an old ambulance outfitted with cabinets, a small
(10) cot, food, and clothes. The ambulance also had specially built shelves for the latest in recording equipment— an acetate disc recorder lent by the Archive of American Folk Song at the
(15) Library of Congress.

To take full advantage of Halpert's short visit, local WPA workers acted as intermediaries, preceding the recording truck to make arrangements
(20) with the folk musicians he would visit and grouping artists in convenient places to minimize travel and maximize recording time. Following their schedule, with a few side trips
(25) to pursue a couple of leads of his own, Halpert cut 168 records between May 8 and June 11, 1939. Abbott Ferriss, a Mississippi native, assisted him.

In addition to helping with the ac-
(30) tual recording, Ferriss kept field notes on the trip and took photographs of the musicians, their families, homes, and surroundings. At the project's conclusion the recordings became
(35) part of the folk-music collections at the Library of Congress. The photographs and much of the manuscript material related to the project remained in Mississippi.

38. According to the passage, the purpose of Halpert's journey to Mississippi was to
   (A) make arrangements for the writing of folk songs.
   (B) consult with a local native.
   (C) record the folk music of Mississippi performers.
   (D) photograph the Mississippi landscape.

39. Which of the following is NOT stated in the passage?
   (A) The WPA sponsored a recording project in the South.
   (B) Local workers helped Halpert by searching for musicians.
   (C) The local workers sought to minimize Halpert's travel time.
   (D) The photographs were sent to the Library of Congress.

40. Which of the following can be reasonably inferred about the WPA?
   (A) It was only interested in folk music.
   (B) It took full advantage of short visits to the Library of Congress.
   (C) It was a national organization with local offices.
   (D) It was sponsored by the Joint Committee on the Arts.

STOP END OF SECTION 3. IF YOU HAVE ANY TIME LEFT, GO OVER YOUR WORK IN THIS SECTION ONLY. DO NOT WORK IN ANY OTHER SECTION OF THE TEST.

SECTION 4: MATHEMATICS ACHIEVEMENT

45 Questions • 40 Minutes

Directions: Each question is followed by four answer choices. Choose the correct answer to each question, and mark its letter on your answer sheet.

1. A recipe for 6 quarts of punch calls for $\frac{3}{4}$ cup of sugar. How much sugar is needed for 9 quarts of punch?
   (A) Five-eighths of a cup
   (B) Seven-eighths of a cup
   (C) $1\frac{1}{8}$ cups
   (D) $2\frac{1}{4}$ cups

2. How many yards of ribbon will it take to make 45 badges if each badge uses 4 inches of ribbon?
   (A) 5
   (B) 9
   (C) 11
   (D) 15

3. As an employee at a clothing store, you are entitled to a 10% discount on all purchases. When the store has a sale, employees are also entitled to an additional 20% discount offered to all customers. What would you have to pay for a $60 jacket bought on a sale day?
   (A) $6
   (B) $10.80
   (C) $36
   (D) $43.20

4. A section of pavement that is 10 feet long and 8 feet wide contains how many square feet?
   (A) 18 sq. ft.
   (B) 80 sq. ft.
   (C) 92 sq. ft.
   (D) 800 sq. ft.

5. In 1972, approximately 19,000 fatal accidents were sustained in industry. There were approximately 130 non-fatal injuries to each fatal injury. The number of nonfatal accidents during 1972 was approximately
   (A) 146,000
   (B) 190,000
   (C) 1,150,000
   (D) 2,500,000

6. What is the value of x when $5x = 5 \times 4 \times 2 \times 0$?
   (A) 6
   (B) 8
   (C) 1
   (D) 0

7. A particular store has a 100% mark-up from wholesale to retail prices. A dress that costs $130 retail will cost how much wholesale?
   (A) $260
   (B) $100
   (C) $90
   (D) $65

8. The scale used on a blueprint is $\frac{1}{8}$" = 1 foot. If a room is actually 17' × 22', how large will it be on the drawing?

   (A) $1\frac{1}{8}$" × $2\frac{1}{4}$

   (B) $2\frac{1}{8}$" × $2\frac{3}{4}$"

   (C) $2\frac{1}{2}$" × 3

   (D) $2\frac{3}{4}$" × $3\frac{1}{8}$"

9. A roll of carpeting contains 90 square feet of carpet. How many rolls will be required to carpet a room 28' × 20' ?

   (A) $6\frac{2}{9}$

   (B) 6

   (C) $5\frac{8}{9}$

   (D) $5\frac{3}{8}$

10. $100 - x = 5^2$. What is the value of x?

    (A) 75

    (B) 50

    (C) 25

    (D) 5

11. If $72x = 6y$, and $y = 2$, $x =$

    (A) $\frac{1}{2}$

    (B) $\frac{1}{6}$

    (C) 6

    (D) 12

12.   60 hr.   21 min.
    − 5 hr.   37 min.

    (A) 54 hr. 44 min.

    (B) 54 hr. 84 min.

    (C) 55 hr. 44 min.

    (D) 55 hr. 84 min.

13. Which of the following represents one half of a certain number squared, minus 6?

    (A) $6 = \frac{1}{2}x^2$

    (B) $\frac{1}{2}x - 6$

    (C) $\frac{\frac{x^2}{1} - 6}{2}$

    (D) $\frac{1}{2}x^2 - 6$

14. A mixture contains 20 gallons of water and 5 gallons of nitric acid. If 10 more gallons of water are added, the part that is water is

    (A) $\frac{1}{7}$

    (B) $\frac{2}{9}$

    (C) $\frac{1}{4}$

    (D) $\frac{6}{7}$

15. Which is the longest time?

    (A) $\frac{1}{24}$ of a day

    (B) $1\frac{1}{2}$ hours

    (C) 100 minutes

    (D) $\frac{1}{30}$ of a month

16. What percentage of a circle graph would be represented by a portion having a right angle?

    (A) 90%

    (B) 45%

    (C) 25%

    (D) 20%

17. Find the perimeter of a rectangle with the dimensions 115' × 63'.

    (A) 7,245'

    (B) 356'

    (C) 187'

    (D) 178'

18. 6.28 × 1.003 =

    (A) .629884

    (B) 6.29884

    (C) 62.9442

    (D) 629.884

19. Solve for x: $\dfrac{x^2}{2.5} = 10$

    (A) ± 5

    (B) ± 10

    (C) ± 20

    (D) ± 25

20. If $2,000 were borrowed at 12% simple interest for two years, what would the total interest charge be?

    (A) $240

    (B) $360

    (C) $420

    (D) $480

21. The pup tent shown is 3 feet wide and 2 feet high. Find its volume if it is 6 feet long.

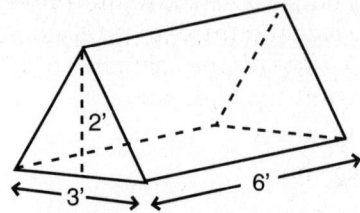

    (A) 36 sq. ft.

    (B) 18 cu. ft.

    (C) 24 cu. ft.

    (D) 36 cu. ft.

22. A board 30' long is cut into three unequal parts. The first is three times as long as the second. The third is twice as long as the first. How long is the longest piece?

    (A) 6'

    (B) 9'

    (C) 12'

    (D) 18'

23. A wine merchant has 32 gallons of wine worth $1.50 a gallon. If he wishes to reduce the price to $1.20 a gallon, how many gallons of water must he add?

    (A) 10

    (B) 9

    (C) 8

    (D) 7

24. Six is four more than $\frac{2}{3}$ of what number?

    (A) 1

    (B) 3

    (C) 4

    (D) 6

25. The winner of a race received $\frac{1}{3}$ of the total purse. The third-place finisher received one-third of the winner's share. If the winner's share was $2,700, what was the total purse?

   (A) $8,100
   (B) $2,700
   (C) $1,800
   (D) $900

26. Two cars start toward each other along a straight road between two cities that are 450 miles apart. The speed of the first car is 35 mph, and that of the second is 48 mph. How much time will elapse before they meet?

   (A) 6.01 hours
   (B) 5.42 hours
   (C) 5.25 hours
   (D) 4.98 hours

27. A stock clerk had 600 pads on hand. He then issued $\frac{3}{8}$ of his supply of pads to Division X, $\frac{1}{4}$ to Division Y, and $\frac{1}{6}$ to Division Z. The number of pads remaining in stock is

   (A) 48
   (B) 125
   (C) 240
   (D) 475

28. One man can load a truck in 25 minutes, a second can load it in 50 minutes, and a third can load it in 10 minutes. How long would it take the three together to load the truck?

   (A) $5\frac{3}{11}$ minutes
   (B) $6\frac{1}{4}$ minutes
   (C) $8\frac{1}{3}$ minutes
   (D) 10 minutes

29. If $4x - y = 20$, and $2x + y = 28$, then $x =$
   (A) 24
   (B) 16
   (C) 8
   (D) 6

30. If $6 + x + y = 20$, and $x + y = k$, then $20 - k =$
   (A) 0
   (B) 6
   (C) 14
   (D) 20

31.

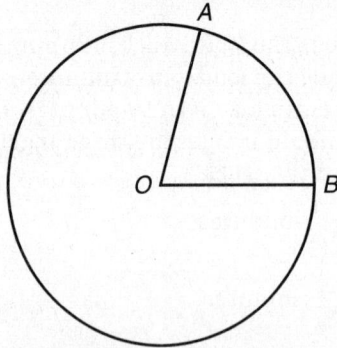

In the figure above, $m\angle AOB = 60°$. If O is the center of the circle, then minor arc AB is what part of the circumference of the circle?

(A) $\dfrac{1}{2}$

(B) $\dfrac{1}{3}$

(C) $\dfrac{1}{6}$

(D) $\dfrac{1}{8}$

32. If all P are S and no S are Q, it necessarily follows that

(A) all Q are S.

(B) all Q are P.

(C) no P are Q.

(D) no S are P.

33. A is older than B. With the passage of time the

(A) ratio of the ages of A and B remains unchanged.

(B) ratio of the ages of A and B increases.

(C) ratio of the ages of A and B decreases.

(D) difference in their ages varies.

34. From a temperature of 15°, a drop of 21° would result in a temperature of

(A) 36°

(B) −6°

(C) −30°

(D) −36°

35.

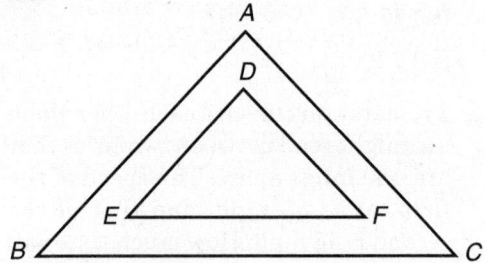

In the figure above, the sides of $\triangle ABC$ are respectively parallel to the sides of $\triangle DEF$. If the complement of A is 40°, then the complement of D is

(A) 20°

(B) 40°

(C) 50°

(D) 60°

36. A line of print in a magazine article contains an average of 6 words. There are 5 lines to the inch. If 8 inches are available for an article that contains 270 words, how must the article be changed?

(A) Add 30 words.

(B) Delete 30 words.

(C) Delete 40 words.

(D) Add 60 words.

37.

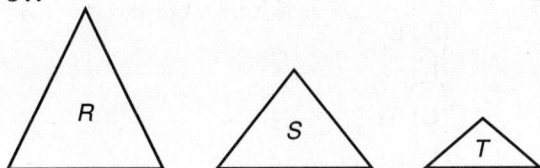

The area of triangle R is 3 times triangle S. The area of triangle S is 3 times triangle T. If the area of triangle $S = 1$, what is the sum of the areas of the three triangles?

(A) $2\frac{1}{3}$

(B) $3\frac{1}{3}$

(C) $4\frac{1}{3}$

(D) 6

38. If 5 pints of water are needed to water each square foot of lawn, the minimum gallons of water needed for a lawn 8' by 12' is

(A) 5

(B) 20

(C) 40

(D) 60

39. In the formula $l = p + prt$, what does l equal when $p = 500$, $r = 20\%$, $t = 2$?

(A) 700

(B) 8,000

(C) 10,000

(D) 12,000

40. A car owner finds he needs 12 gallons of gas for each 120 miles he drives. If he has his carburetor adjusted, he will need only 80% as much gas. How many miles will 12 gallons of gas then last him?

(A) 90

(B) 96

(C) 150

(D) 160

41. What is the maximum number of books each $\frac{1}{4}$ inch thick that can be placed standing on a shelf 4 feet long?

(A) 16

(B) 48

(C) 96

(D) 192

42. In a bag there are red, green, black, and white marbles. If there are 6 red, 8 green, 4 black, and 12 white, and one marble is to be selected at random, what is the probability it will be white?

(A) $\frac{1}{5}$

(B) $\frac{2}{5}$

(C) $\frac{2}{15}$

(D) $\frac{4}{15}$

43.

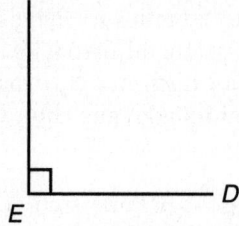

In the diagram above, $\overline{CE} \perp \overline{ED}$. If $CE = 7$ and $ED = 6$, what is the shortest distance from C to D?

(A) 6

(B) 7

(C) $\sqrt{85}$

(D) $4\sqrt{12}$

44. If $a = 3$, then $a^a \cdot a =$

(A) 9

(B) 18

(C) 51

(D) 81

45. $(3 + 2)(6 - 2)(7 + 1) = (4 + 4)(x)$. What is the value of x?

(A) $13 + 2$

(B) $14 + 4$

(C) $4 + 15$

(D) $8 + 12$

STOP   END OF SECTION 4. IF YOU HAVE ANY TIME LEFT, GO OVER YOUR WORK IN THIS SECTION ONLY. DO NOT WORK IN ANY OTHER SECTION OF THE TEST.

SECTION 5: ESSAY

30 Minutes

Directions: Write a legible, coherent, and correct essay on the following topic.

Topic: Tell about one extracurricular activity in which you hope to participate in high school. Give reasons why you have chosen this activity.

_____

_____

_____

_____

_____

_____

_____

_____

_____

_____

_____

_____

_____

_____

_____

_____

_____

_____

_____

_____

ANSWER KEY AND EXPLANATIONS

Section 1: Verbal Reasoning

1. D	9. C	17. C	25. A	33. B
2. D	10. C	18. D	26. B	34. C
3. A	11. A	19. D	27. C	35. B
4. A	12. B	20. B	28. C	36. B
5. A	13. D	21. D	29. A	37. D
6. B	14. C	22. C	30. D	38. C
7. C	15. D	23. D	31. A	39. D
8. D	16. A	24. D	32. D	40. C

1. **The correct answer is (D).** To IMPLY is to *indicate indirectly*, to *suggest*, or to *hint*. By her strange smile, the Mona Lisa implies that she knows a secret.

2. **The correct answer is (D).** That which is FISCAL has to *do with money*. A fiscal year is the twelve-month period between settlement of accounts.

3. **The correct answer is (A).** STRINGENT means *rigidly controlled*, *strict*, or *severe*. Prospective firefighters must pass a stringent physical exam to prove that they can meet the demands of the job.

4. **The correct answer is (A).** That which is PERMEABLE can be *penetrated*, especially by *fluids*. The word meaning "allowable" is "permissible"; that meaning "durable" or "unending" is "permanent." The rain barrel was covered with a permeable cloth that strained out solid particles.

5. **The correct answer is (A).** SCRUPULOUS means *careful to do the right, proper, or correct in every detail*. The legislator took scrupulous care to fill out the ethics form accurately.

6. **The correct answer is (B).** A STALEMATE is a *deadlock* or *impasse*. Neither the union nor management would concede a point, so the negotiations were at a stalemate.

7. **The correct answer is (C).** REDUNDANT means *more than necessary* or *superfluous*. The word "join" indicates that units are put together; therefore, in the expression "join together" the word "together" is redundant.

8. **The correct answer is (D).** To SUPPLANT is to *supersede* or to *replace*. The Constitution supplanted the Articles of Confederation.

9. **The correct answer is (C).** COMMENSURATE means *proportionate*. The 2-year-old's vocabulary was commensurate with her age.

10. **The correct answer is (C).** The ZENITH is the *point directly overhead* or the *highest point*. The sun reaches its zenith at noon.

11. **The correct answer is (A).** SUCCOR is *aid*, *help*, or *relief*. It is treason to give succor to the enemy by distributing false propaganda.

12. **The correct answer is (B).** To DISPATCH is to *send out quickly*. Do not rely on the mails; dispatch a messenger to deliver the package.

13. **The correct answer is (D).** PORTABLE means *easily moved or carried*. The word meaning "drinkable" is "potable." A television set with a three-inch screen is a portable set.

14. **The correct answer is (C).** VERBOSE means *containing too many words* or *long-winded*. The speaker was so verbose that we thought the evening would never end.

15. **The correct answer is (D).** SUBVERSIVE means *seeking to overthrow* or to *destroy something established*. Subversive elements in the government are extremely dangerous to stability.

16. **The correct answer is (A).** That which is MALLEABLE tends to be *changeable*. Before it cools, hot metal is quite malleable and can be twisted into different shapes.

17. **The correct answer is (C).** PETTY means *trivial*, *narrow*, or *small*. The crotchety old man was full of petty complaints.

18. **The correct answer is (D).** INTREPID means *bold*, *brave*, and *fearless*. The intrepid astronauts went on their mission as if there had never been an accident.

19. **The correct answer is (D).** To NEGOTIATE is to *make arrangements* or to *bargain*. The buyer and seller of a property must negotiate to reach a fair price.

20. **The correct answer is (B).** STERILE means *extremely clean*, *barren*, or *germ-free*. For the safety of the patient, the surgeon must work in a sterile environment.

21. **The correct answer is (D).** Since Joshua was undaunted (not discouraged) by his failures, a positive word is necessary. PERSEVERED is the only positive word.

22. **The correct answer is (C).** In order to attract students, INNOVATIVE (new, novel) methods are necessary.

23. **The correct answer is (D).** Since there is less money available and fewer business transactions are being conducted, BUYERS have the upper hand in how they spend their money.

24. **The correct answer is (D).** Multiple offenses would require an *increased* penalty; therefore, ESCALATE is the only correct choice.

25. **The correct answer is (A).** All the adjectives describing the hotel are positive; therefore, a positive description is necessary.

26. **The correct answer is (B).** The opposite of forcing students to take courses is ENTICING them to do so.

27. **The correct answer is (C).** An innovative method of dealing with criminals is being suggested in contrast to the usual method, which is IMPRISONMENT.

28. **The correct answer is (C).** The sentence mentions "knowledge gained without experience" and then asks for the opposite condition, which must be EXPERIENCE without SCHOLARSHIP.

29. **The correct answer is (A).** By having an insurance expert discuss the changes, the school system was attempting to reduce, or QUELL, ANXIETY over those increased fees.

30. **The correct answer is (D).** The first half of the sentence requires a word that contrasts with poverty (COMFORTABLE). The second word must show that poverty is widespread among older Americans.

answers practice test 5

31. **The correct answer is (A).** A little common sense should give you this answer immediately. Choice (C) makes no sense at all. A police officer's job is to prevent crime, but that is not the officer's only job, just the PRIMARY job.

32. **The correct answer is (D).** Extenuating circumstances mitigate the seriousness of a crime. A young defendant also tends to be offered a "second chance." It is therefore most plausible that the judge would have recommended LENIENCY.

33. **The correct answer is (B).** The fact that the family respected one another means that they AVERTED clashes.

34. **The correct answer is (C).** Health-conscious consumers will ENCOURAGE change.

35. **The correct answer is (B).** Although the politician lost the election, he MAINTAINED his popularity with some followers.

36. **The correct answer is (B).** An arrest or domestic dispute is considered a serious CRISIS.

37. **The correct answer is (D).** A negative word (FAIL) must be followed by a positive word (PAYOFF).

38. **The correct answer is (C).** A flood that destroys people's belongings causes devastation. Living conditions in the area can be said to have deteriorated (worsened).

39. **The correct answer is (D).** The word "help" indicates the need for a positive word to complete this sentence. Therefore, you need consider only choices (A) and (D). Of these two, IMPLEMENT (meaning put into action) is a better choice than magnify (meaning to make larger).

40. **The correct answer is (C).** The words required to complete the thought must be opposites. A LUXURY is something we can easily do without, but once we have had that luxury for awhile we can no longer do without it and it becomes a necessity (an ESSENTIAL).

Section 2: Quantitative Reasoning

1. B	8. D	15. C	22. A	29. C
2. C	9. B	16. A	23. C	30. D
3. B	10. B	17. B	24. C	31. B
4. B	11. C	18. A	25. C	32. C
5. D	12. A	19. D	26. A	33. A
6. C	13. D	20. A	27. B	34. A
7. A	14. D	21. B	28. A	35. C

1. **The correct answer is (B).** It is useful to know that you multiply and divide by 10, 100, 1,000, and so on, by moving the decimal point.

2. **The correct answer is (C).** The sum of the angles of a triangle is 180°. Angle B is 90°. Angles A and C, therefore, must total 180° − 90°, or 90°.

3. **The correct answer is (B).** (3×10^2) $+ (2 \times 10) + 9$

4. **The correct answer is (B).** Circumference = π • diameter; diameter = 2 • radius; $\pi = \dfrac{22}{7}$

   $C = \pi \cdot 21 \cdot 2$

   $C = 42 \cdot \pi = 42 \cdot \dfrac{22}{7} = 132'$

   You can also estimate this problem and choose the closest answer.

5. **The correct answer is (D).** The set $\{x, y\}$ includes all those numbers larger than −4 and smaller than 2. Considering only whole numbers, this set includes −3, −2, −1, 0, 1.

6. **The correct answer is (C).** The order in which numbers are added does not affect the sum.

7. **The correct answer is (A).** We want the amount in the parentheses to be equal to 3. The value of x that will make the amount in parentheses equal to 3 is 4.

8. **The correct answer is (D).** Refer to the Geometry Review section if necessary.

9. **The correct answer is (B).** Note that $\dfrac{17}{30}$ is slightly larger than $\dfrac{15}{30}$, or $\dfrac{1}{2}$. Choices (A), (C), and (D) are closer in value to 1 than to $\dfrac{1}{2}$.

10. **The correct answer is (B).** 100 centimeters = 1 meter. Each centimeter is $\dfrac{1}{100}$ of a meter.

11. **The correct answer is (C).** Find the LCM (least common multiple) of 4, 9, 6, and 12, and this becomes the least common denominator.

12. **The correct answer is (A).** The set of factors of 36 is: {1, 2, 3, 4, 6, 9, 12, 18, 36}.

    The set of factors of 64 is: {1, 2, 4, 8, 16, 32, 64}.

    The set of common factors is:

    {1, 2, 4}.

13. **The correct answer is (D).** The sum of the angles of a triangle is 180°.

    $180° − 115° = 65°$

14. **The correct answer is (D).** The union of the two adjacent line segments creates one continuous line segment.

15. **The correct answer is (C).** The 52 playing cards in a deck consist of 4 suits of 13 cards each. There is one 6 in each of the four suits, making the probability of drawing a 6 $\dfrac{4}{52}$ or $\dfrac{1}{13}$.

16. **The correct answer is (A).** Every 8 miles is represented on the map by $\dfrac{1}{2}$ inch. $28 \div 8 = 3\dfrac{1}{2}$, so $3\dfrac{1}{2}$-inch units are needed to represent 28 miles.

    $3\dfrac{1}{2} \times \dfrac{1}{2} = \dfrac{7}{2} \times \dfrac{1}{2} = \dfrac{7}{4} = 1\dfrac{3}{4}$. You may solve the problem another way: If $\dfrac{1}{2}''$ = 8 miles, 1″ = 16 miles. $28 \div 16 = 1\dfrac{3}{4}$, so $1\dfrac{3}{4}''$ are required to represent 28 miles.

17. The correct answer is (B). The number of accidents is irrelevant to the question, so A has no place in the equation.

B (total deaths) ÷ 10 years = $\dfrac{B}{10}$ average deaths per year.

18. The correct answer is (A).

$3x^2 + 2x - 1$	$x^3 + 2x^2 + 1$
$3(-2)^2 + 2(-2) - 1$	$(-2)^3 + 2(-2)^2 + 1$
$3(4) - 4 - 1$	$8 + 8 + 1$
$12 - 4 - 1$	$+1$
7	

Column A > Column B

19. The correct answer is (D). The relationship between column A and column B cannot be determined from the information given.

20. The correct answer is (A).

$(16 \div 4) + (8 \times 2) - 8$	$(3 \times 4) + (10 \div 5) - 3$
$4 + 16 - 8$	$12 + 2 - 3$
$20 - 8$	$14 - 3$
12	11

Column A > Column B

21. The correct answer is (B). Original Cost + Profit = Selling Price

Let x = original cost

then $x + .05(x) = \$47.25$

$1.05x = \$47.25$

$x = \$45$

$\$45 > \$44.89$

Column B > Column A

22. The correct answer is (A).

$a - b = -1$	$a - b = -1$
$\underline{a - b = -3}$	$a - (2) = -1$
$-2b = -4$	$a = 1$
$b = 2$	

Column A > Column B

23. The correct answer is (C).

$.25(300) = 75$ (girls with blonde hair)

$300 - 75 = 225$ (girls without blonde hair)

$$\frac{75}{225} = \frac{1}{3}$$

Column A = Column B

24. The correct answer is (C). The sum of the angles of a triangle equal 180°.

$a + b + c = 180$

and $d + e + f = 180$

$a + b + c + d + e + f = 360$

also $e + c = 90$

Therefore, $a + b + d + f = 270$ (subtraction)

Column A = Column B

25. The correct answer is (C). A parallelogram inscribed in a circle is a rectangle. Therefore, all angles equal 90°.

Hence, $a + c = b + d$

Column A = Column B

26. The correct answer is (A).

$$\frac{9}{8} = 1.125$$

$$\frac{3}{5} = .60$$

$$1.125 - .60 = .525$$

$$.525 > .5$$

Column A > Column B

27. **The correct answer is (B).** Let x = the number of days A and B take working together.

A can do the job in 4 days; thus, A's rate is $\frac{1}{4}$.

B can do the job in 3 days; thus, B's rate is $\frac{1}{3}$.

$$\frac{x}{4} + \frac{x}{3} = 1$$

$$\frac{7x}{12} = 1$$

$$x = 1\frac{5}{7} \text{ days}$$

$$2 \text{ days} > 1\frac{5}{7} \text{ days}$$

Column B > Column A

28. **The correct answer is (A).** The ratio between seniors and the total of seniors and freshmen is 1:4. The ratio between seniors and the total enrollment (including sophomores and juniors) would actually decrease.

Column A > Column B

29. **The correct answer is (C).** The sum of the three angles of a triangle equals 180°. Thus, $x + x + 60° = 180°$

$$2x = 120°$$

$$x = 60°$$

Therefore, the triangle is equilateral. Hence, side m = side n.

Column A = Column B

30. **The correct answer is (D).** The relationship cannot be determined from the information given.

31. **The correct answer is (B).** The sum of the angles of a triangle equals 180°. Thus,

$$x + 2x + 90° = 180°$$

$$3x = 90°$$

$$x = 30°$$

Therefore ΔABC is a 30°-60°-90° right triangle. In a 30°-60°-90° right triangle the hypotenuse is equal to twice the side opposite the 30° angle.

$$AB = 8$$

$$8 > 5$$

Column B > Column A

32. **The correct answer is (C).**

$$\sqrt[3]{125} = 5 \quad \text{and} \quad \sqrt{5} = 5$$

Column A = Column B

33. **The correct answer is (A).**

$x > 0$, x is positive

$y < 0$, y is negative

Substitute some arbitrary figures of your choosing, for example: $x = 10$; $y = -2$

$x - y =$ $x + y =$

$10 - (-2) = 12$ $10 + (-2) = 8$

Column A > Column B

34. **The correct answer is (A).**

$$15\% = .15$$

$$.15\,(43.50) = 6.525$$

$$\$43.50 - 6.53 = 36.97$$

$$\$36.97 > \$36$$

Column A > Column B

35. **The correct answer is (C).**

$75\% = \frac{3}{4}$ $50\% = \frac{1}{2}$

$\frac{3}{4}\left(\frac{1}{2}\right) = \frac{3}{8}$ $\frac{1}{2}\left(\frac{3}{4}\right) = \frac{3}{8}$

Column A = Column B

Section 3: Reading Comprehension

1. B	9. A	17. D	25. B	33. B
2. A	10. C	18. B	26. C	34. D
3. B	11. B	19. C	27. B	35. D
4. A	12. D	20. C	28. B	36. C
5. D	13. B	21. A	29. D	37. D
6. C	14. D	22. B	30. B	38. C
7. B	15. C	23. D	31. C	39. D
8. D	16. A	24. B	32. A	40. C

1. **The correct answer is (B).** See the first sentence.

2. **The correct answer is (A).** This definition is given in the explanatory statement at the end of the first sentence.

3. **The correct answer is (B).** The entire selection extols the dedication of the Pony Express riders in the face of the hazards they met.

4. **The correct answer is (A).** The fourth paragraph tells us that there was a ten-day limit in which the route must be covered.

5. **The correct answer is (D).** See paragraph 3. Buffalo Bill made the longest continuous run of 384 miles; Jim Moore made the fastest run, 280 miles in 22 hours.

6. **The correct answer is (C).** The selection discusses hatmaking as an early American industry, touching on materials, costs, and markets.

7. **The correct answer is (B).** See lines 19–21.

8. **The correct answer is (D).** Prohibition of export of hats from one colony to another and from any colony to Great Britain was an effective ban on export of hats altogether.

9. **The correct answer is (A).** See the second paragraph.

10. **The correct answer is (C).** Price comparisons are in the second paragraph.

11. **The correct answer is (B).** The dictionary definition of *filament* is "a very slender thread or fiber." You do not need to know the dictionary definition to answer this question. Wasps could not possibly be handling large chunks or files. The word *filaments* in the selection appears in the plural. If the meaning were "dust," the word would be in the singular.

12. **The correct answer is (D).** The first sentence describes René de Réaumer as a French naturalist.

13. **The correct answer is (B).** See the beginning of the third paragraph.

14. **The correct answer is (D).** The entire selection describes the manner in which wasps use wood to make the paper from which they construct nests.

15. **The correct answer is (C).** See the last sentence.

16. **The correct answer is (A).** See the first sentence.

17. **The correct answer is (D).** See lines 9–13.

18. **The correct answer is (B).** See lines 19–20.

19. **The correct answer is (C).** See lines 22–24.

20. **The correct answer is (C).** Clues may be found in the first sentence, which states that historians are trying to learn more about the *Mayflower*, and in the first sentence of the third paragraph, which describes the boat as historic.

21. **The correct answer is (A).** If you got this wrong, reread the second sentence of the first paragraph.

22. **The correct answer is (B).** See the first sentence of the second paragraph.

23. **The correct answer is (D).** The original *Mayflower* was 22 feet wide; the duplicate is 26 feet wide. The lengths are both 90 feet.

24. **The correct answer is (B).** You can infer this meaning from the fact that the author describes two buildings in England that may contain parts of the *Mayflower*.

25. **The correct answer is (B).** The selection describes the varying hare.

26. **The correct answer is (C).** As the names imply, the rabbits vary their appearance with the seasons.

27. **The correct answer is (B).** The rabbits are mottled brown and white while in the middle of the molting process during spring and fall.

28. **The correct answer is (B).** See the first sentence of the last paragraph.

29. **The correct answer is (D).** A parenthetical statement in the second paragraph states that the hares have no voluntary control over the changes in their appearance.

30. **The correct answer is (B).** The entire selection is about court practices in ancient Athens.

31. **The correct answer is (C).** The answer is in the second sentence.

32. **The correct answer is (A).** See the last sentence.

33. **The correct answer is (B).** See lines 20–23. The accused was allowed a certain time to speak; the jury voted by depositing black or white stones in a box.

34. **The correct answer is (D).** The second sentence tells us that the temperature of the earth's upper atmosphere varies with time, location (altitude), and solar activity (the sun). No mention is made of the weather.

35. **The correct answer is (D).** The first paragraph makes clear that the temperature (the heat of the sun) directly affects many other measures and dimensions in the upper atmosphere.

36. **The correct answer is (C).** See the last sentence.

37. **The correct answer is (D).** See the first sentence.

38. **The correct answer is (C).** See the first sentence.

39. **The correct answer is (D).** The last sentence tells us that the photographs remained in Mississippi. The recordings themselves were sent to the Library of Congress.

40. **The correct answer is (C).** The second paragraph tells of local WPA workers and the assistance they gave.

answers practice test 5

Section 4: Mathematics Achievement

1. C	10. A	19. A	28. B	37. C
2. A	11. B	20. D	29. C	38. D
3. D	12. A	21. B	30. B	39. A
4. B	13. D	22. D	31. C	40. C
5. D	14. D	23. C	32. C	41. D
6. D	15. D	24. B	33. C	42. B
7. D	16. C	25. A	34. B	43. C
8. B	17. B	26. B	35. B	44. D
9. A	18. B	27. B	36. B	45. D

1. **The correct answer is (C).** First find out how much sugar is needed for one quart of punch:

$$\frac{3}{4} \text{ cup} \div 6 = \frac{3}{4} \times \frac{1}{6} = \frac{\overset{1}{\cancel{3}}}{4} \times \frac{1}{\underset{2}{\cancel{6}}} = \frac{1}{8}$$

For 9 quarts of punch you need:

$$9 \times \frac{1}{8} = \frac{9}{8} = 1\frac{1}{8}$$

2. **The correct answer is (A).** 45 badges × 4 inches each = 180 inches needed. There are 36 inches in one yard: 180 inches ÷ 36 = 5 yards of ribbon needed.

3. **The correct answer is (D).** $60 × .10 = $6 (employee discount)

$60 − $6 = $54

$54 × .20 = $10.80 (sale discount)

$54 − $10.80 = $43.20

4. **The correct answer is (B).** Area equals Length times Width.

A = L × W

A = 10 ft. × 8 ft.

A = 80 sq. ft.

5. **The correct answer is (D).** For each of the 19,000 fatal accidents there were 130 nonfatal injuries. To find the total number of nonfatal accidents, we multiply 19,000 × 130 = 2,470,000. There were approximately 2,500,000 nonfatal accidents in 1972.

6. **The correct answer is (D).** Any number multiplied by 0 equals 0. Since one multiplier on one side of the = sign is 0, the product on that side of the sign must be 0. The value on the other side of the = sign must also be 0.

$5x = 5 \times 4 \times 2 \times 0$

$5x = 40 \times 0$

$5x = 0$

$x = 0$

7. **The correct answer is (D).** An item marked up 100% has a retail price twice the wholesale price. The coat now costs $130, which is twice $65.

8. **The correct answer is (B).** The width of the room will be $17 \times \frac{1}{8}$ ", or $2\frac{1}{8}$ ".

The length of the room will be $22 \times \frac{1}{8}$ ", or $2\frac{3}{4}$ ".

9. **The correct answer is (A).** The room has an area of 28' × 20' = 560 sq. ft. Each roll of carpet can cover 90 sq. ft. The number of rolls required is 560 ÷ 90 = $6\frac{2}{9}$ rolls.

10. **The correct answer is (A).** To square a number, multiply it by itself.

$$100 - x = 5^2$$
$$100 - x = 5 \times 5$$
$$100 - x = 25$$
$$100 - 25 = x$$
$$x = 75$$

11. **The correct answer is (B).** If $y = 2$, then

$$72x = 6(2)$$
$$72x = 12$$
$$x = \frac{1}{6}$$

12. **The correct answer is (A).** Borrow 60 minutes and rewrite as:

$$
\begin{array}{rr}
59 \text{ hr.} & 81 \text{ min.} \\
- \ 5 \text{ hr.} & 37 \text{ min.} \\
\hline
54 \text{ hr.} & 44 \text{ min.}
\end{array}
$$

13. **The correct answer is (D).** $\frac{1}{2}x^2 - 6$

14. **The correct answer is (D).** Ten more gallons of water would bring the volume of the mixture to 30 gallons of water + 5 gallons of acid = 35 gallons. The part that is water is $\frac{30}{35}$, or $\frac{6}{7}$.

15. **The correct answer is (D).** $\frac{1}{30}$ of a month is about one day.

16. **The correct answer is (C).** A circle graph contains 360°, while a right angle contains 90°. A right angle, therefore, contains $\frac{1}{4}$, or 25%, of the circle.

17. **The correct answer is (B).** The perimeter is the sum of the lengths of the four sides. A rectangle has two pairs of sides of equal length. The perimeter then is (2 × 115) + (2 × 63) = 356 feet.

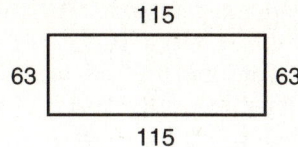

$$115 + 63 + 115 + 63 = 356$$

This is a good problem to solve by estimation. You can readily discard three of the possible answers without doing any calculation.

18. **The correct answer is (B).** Don't bother to calculate here! Notice that your answer will be very close to 6 × 1. There is only one answer anywhere near that estimate.

19. **The correct answer is (A).** The square of a number divided by 2.5 equals 10. The square of the number, then, equals 10 multiplied by 2.5.

$$x^2 = 10 \times 2.5$$
$$x^2 = 25$$
$$x = \pm 5$$

20. **The correct answer is (D).** Each year, 12% is charged as interest. On $2,000, 12% interest is $2,000 × .12 = $240. For two years, the amount is $240 × 2 = $480.

21. **The correct answer is (B).** Find the volume by finding the area of the triangular end and multiplying by the length. $A = \frac{1}{2}bh$. The area of the triangular end is $A = \frac{1}{2}(3)(2) = 3$ sq. ft. Multiply 3 sq. ft. by the length to find the volume: 3 sq. ft. × 6 ft. = 18 cu. ft.

22. **The correct answer is (D).** Note that the second piece is the shortest. We don't know its exact length, so call it x feet long. The first piece is three times as long as the second, or $3x$ feet long. The third is twice as long as the first, or $6x$ feet long. All the pieces total $x + 3x + 6x = 10x$ feet. The board is 30 feet long, and the pieces are $10x$ feet long. $10x = 30$, so $x = 3$, which is the length of the shortest piece. The largest piece is six times the shortest, or 18 feet long.

23. **The correct answer is (C).** We assume that the merchant wants to have the same total value of wine after reducing the price. He now has (32 • $1.50), or $48 worth of wine. At $1.20 per gallon, he would need 40 gallons to have $48 worth. Therefore, he must add 8 gallons of water.

24. **The correct answer is (B).** If six is four more than $\frac{2}{3}$ of a number, then $6 - 4$ equals $\frac{2}{3}$ of the number. Since $6 - 4 = 2$, we know that 2 is $\frac{2}{3}$ of the number, so the number is 3. Another way to solve this problem is to write an equation, and solve for x:

$$\frac{2}{3}x + 4 = 6$$
$$\frac{2}{3}x = 2$$
$$x = 3$$

25. **The correct answer is (A).** You have to read only the first and third sentences of the problem. The information in the second sentence contains information not relevant to the problem. The winner received $\frac{1}{3}$ of the total, or $2,700. Thus, the total purse was $2,700 × 3 = $8,100.

26. **The correct answer is (B).** The distance between the cars is being reduced at a rate equal to the sum of their speeds. They are coming closer together at $35 + 48 = 83$ miles per hour. Since the distance between them was 450 miles, the time required for traveling is $450 \div 83 = 5.42$ hours. Remember that distance is the product of rate and time, or $d = rt$.

27. **The correct answer is (B).** Of his total, he issued $\frac{3}{8} + \frac{1}{4} + \frac{1}{6} = \frac{19}{24}$, so he had $\frac{5}{24}$ pads remaining. His total in stock was 600. $600 \cdot \frac{5}{24} = 125$ pads remaining.

28. **The correct answer is (B).** The first man can load $\frac{1}{25}$ of the truck in 1 minute. The second man can load $\frac{1}{50}$ of the truck in 1 minute. The third man can load $\frac{1}{10}$ of the truck in 1 minute. Together they can load $\frac{1}{25} + \frac{1}{50} + \frac{1}{10}$ of the truck each minute.

$$\frac{1}{25} + \frac{1}{50} + \frac{1}{10} = \frac{2}{50} + \frac{1}{50} + \frac{5}{50}$$
$$= \frac{8}{50} = \frac{4}{25}$$

of the truck loaded per minute. The whole job then requires $\frac{25}{4}$ minutes, or $6\frac{1}{4}$ minutes.

29. **The correct answer is (C).** This is a difficult question unless you have had some algebra. The equations are "added." The y term is eliminated, leaving x only.

$$\begin{aligned} 4x - y &= 20 \\ + \; 2x + y &= 28 \\ \hline 6x &= 48 \\ x &= 8 \end{aligned}$$

30. **The correct answer is (B).**

$$6 + x + y = 20$$

$x + y = 14 = k$; now substitute

$$20 - 14 = 6$$

31. **The correct answer is (C).** A circle is 360°; 60° is $\dfrac{1}{6}$ of 360°.

32. **The correct answer is (C).** Diagram this problem:

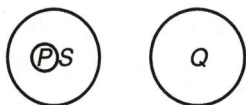

33. **The correct answer is (C).** Pick a pair of ages and try for yourself. A is 4; B is 2; the ratio of their ages is 4 to 2 or 2 to 1. In two years, A is 6 and B is 4. The ratio of their ages is 6 to 4 or 3 to 2.

34. **The correct answer is (B).** $15° - 21° = -6°$

35. **The correct answer is (B).** If the sides are parallel, the angles are congruent.

36. **The correct answer is (B).** 6 words per line × 5 lines per inch = 30 words per inch.

30 words per inch × 8 inches = 240 words.

If the article has 270 words and there is space for only 240 words, then 30 words must be deleted.

37. **The correct answer is (C).**

$$S = 1; R = 3 \times 1; T = \frac{1}{3}$$

$$1 + (3 \times 1) + \left(\frac{1}{3}\right) = 4\frac{1}{3}$$

38. **The correct answer is (D).** The lawn is 8' × 12' = 96 sq. ft.

96 × 5 = 480 pints of water needed

8 pts. in 1 gal.; 480 ÷ 8 = 60 gallons needed

39. **The correct answer is (A).**

$$l = 500 + (500 \times .20 \times 2)$$

$$l = 500 + 200$$

$$l = 700$$

40. **The correct answer is (C).** Right now, he gets 120 mi. ÷ 12 gal. = 10 mpg. With 80% more efficiency, he will need 80% of 12, or 9.6 gal. to go 120 miles. He will then get 120 mi. ÷ 9.6 gal. = 12.5 mpg.

12 gal. × 12.5 mpg = 150 miles on 12 gal.

41. **The correct answer is (D).** 4 feet = 48 inches; $48 \div \dfrac{1}{4} = 48 \times 4 = 192$ books

42. **The correct answer is (B).** There are 6 + 8 + 4 + 12 = 30 marbles.

$$12 \div 30 = .40 = \frac{2}{5}$$

43. **The correct answer is (C).** $\overline{CD}$ is a hypotenuse, so use the Pythagorean Theorem:

$$CD = \sqrt{CE^2 + ED^2}$$
$$CD = \sqrt{7^2 + 6^2} = \sqrt{49 + 36} = \sqrt{85}$$

answers practice test 5

44. The correct answer is (D). $3^3 \times 3 =$
$27 \times 3 = 81$

45. The correct answer is (D).
$(3 + 2)(6 - 2)(7 + 1) = (4 + 4)(x)$

$$(5)(4)(8) = 8x$$

$$8x = 160$$

$$x = 20 = 8 + 12$$

Section 5: Essay

Example of a well-written essay.

When I enter high school, I plan to become an active member of the drama club. The drama club offers a variety of activities within one organization. In the course of a single year, a member of the drama club can get involved in acting, set building, lighting design, publicity, ticket sales, and much more. And because of the variety of activities, I expect to make friends with classmates with varied interests and abilities.

People involved with theater appear to be having a lot of fun. While there may be some competition among stars, a production is generally a cooperative effort. Teamwork is key to making an amateur production appear to be professional. Even in kindergarten I got high marks from my teachers in "works and plays well with others," and I would like to carry this aspect of my personality into joining a cast and crew that creates theater.

Another reason for joining the drama club is that it will give me a chance to perform. I have always been a bit of a show-off. Being on stage will allow me to strut about without being criticized. I hope that my acting will contribute to successful productions along with my work as part of the behind-the-scenes crew.

Finally, any cooperative effort must be a social activity. There should be lots of give and take and conversation during preparations and rehearsals. And I do look forward to cast parties when the show closes. Drama club seems like the perfect extracurricular activity; I will have a good time while doing something worthwhile.

SCORE YOURSELF

Scores on the ISEE are determined by comparing each student's results against all other students in his or her grade level who took that particular test. A scaled score is then calculated. You can use the following calculations to determine how well you did on this practice test, but keep in mind that when you take the actual test, your score might vary.

Test	Raw Score ÷ No. Questions	× 100 =	%
Synonyms	÷ 20	× 100 =	%
Sentence Completions	÷ 20	× 100 =	%
Total Verbal Ability	÷ 40	× 100 =	%
Multiple-Choice Quantitative	÷ 17	× 100 =	%
Quantitative Comparisons	÷ 18	× 100 =	%
Total Quantitative Ability	÷ 35	× 100 =	%
Reading Comprehension	÷ 40	× 100 =	%
Mathematics Achievement	÷ 45	× 100 =	%

High percentage scores should make you feel very good about yourself, but low percentages do not mean that you are a failure.

Remember:

- Scores are not reported as percentages. A low percentage may translate to a respectable scaled score.
- The same test is given to students in grades 8 through 12. Unless you have finished high school, you have not been taught everything on the test. You are not expected to know what you have not been taught.
- You will be compared only to students in your own grade.

Use your scores to plan further study if you have time.

practice test

PARENT'S GUIDE TO PRIVATE SCHOOLS

Why Choose an Independent School?

Patrick F. Bassett
President of the National Association of Independent Schools (NAIS)

Why do families choose independent schools for their children? Many cite the intimate school size and setting, individualized attention, and high academic standards. The National Educational Longitudinal Study (NELS), conducted by the U.S. Department of Education, confirms what independent school families have known for years: Compared to students in public, parochial, and other private schools, larger percentages of students in independent schools are enrolled in advanced courses. Independent school students:

- Do twice as much homework as their counterparts

- Watch only two-thirds as much television

- Are significantly more likely to participate in varsity or intramural sports

- Are more likely to agree that students and teachers get along well, discipline is fair, and teaching is good

Other longitudinal research confirms the wisdom of choosing an independent school. Roughly speaking, students from independent schools are twice as likely to:

- Take Algebra I and foreign language in the eighth grade

- Enroll in an Advanced Placement course as a sophomore

- Have a teacher who has graduated from a selective college

- Complete precalculus or higher level of mathematics

- Participate in extracurricular sports, arts, academics, and community service

These patterns begin in our elementary schools, which place a strong emphasis on creating a positive learning climate for each child. The patterns are sustained through our middle and upper schools, where children are encouraged and expected to do well academically and urged to participate in extracurricular activities.

Why are these patterns important? Simply stated, they reflect two critical elements that make independent school students well prepared for college and for life: mastery of a serious academic program and being a "player."

WHAT VALUE WILL I SEE IN AN INDEPENDENT SCHOOL FOR MY CHILD?

Parents often consider independent schools as they would consider any other "investment," expecting a "return" and "value." Research shows that the choice of a child's peer group may be the single most important factor in determining educational success. Parents choose a peer group largely by the school they choose for their child. Data show that virtually all independent school graduates succeed by completing college (as opposed to about 40 percent of the general population). This "persistence factor" is largely attributable to attending a school with high expectations for all students and a culture that reinforces achievement. The ethos of independent schools contributes to this equation, since "everybody" is expected to work hard and succeed academically and since "everybody" is expected be a "player." Choosing an independent school, and the right independent school for your child, can be one of life's most important and rewarding investments.

WHICH ARE THE "HIGHEST RANKING" OR "BEST" INDEPENDENT SCHOOLS?

Independent schools are as individual as your child. Each has a unique mission, culture, and personality. Among independent schools, there are different shapes and sizes. There are day schools, boarding schools, and combination day-boarding. Some independent schools have a few dozen students; others have several thousand. Some are coed; others are single-sex. Some independent schools have a religious affiliation; some are nonsectarian. Most serve students of average to exceptional academic ability, but some serve exclusively those with learning differences, and others exclusively serve the gifted. Virtually all independent schools are "college-prep." Because independent schools have different missions and different student populations, NAIS discourages ranking, since no single set of objective criteria could apply.

WHAT ARE THE MYTHS AND MISCONCEPTIONS ABOUT INDEPENDENT SCHOOLS?

It is important to note that independent schools, contrary to popular belief and their portrayal in the media, are not "elitist" in any way except in terms of academic expectations. The typical independent school *chooses* to commit to diversity (racial, ethnic, and socioeconomic). Socioeconomic diversity, for example, is supported by a significant commitment to financial aid: Independent school students come from all family income levels, and approximately 20 percent of them are supported by financial aid. On average nationally, 17 percent of independent school students are students who are members of minority groups.

WHAT KIND OF RELATIONSHIP DOES AN INDEPENDENT SCHOOL HAVE WITH PARENTS?

Independent schools seek a solid partnership with parents. Independent schools seek to speak with a unified voice about a common set of goals and values. It is this coalescing of parental and school voices that points students, like a beacon, toward achievement, decent behaviors, and good citizenship. In the final analysis, children prosper when the key adults in their lives reinforce a common set of values and speak with a common voice. The great achievement of American education is that it offers parents many choices of schooling so that they can find a school with a voice and vision to match their own.

Another Option: Independent Day Schools

Lila Lohr

For those of us who are fortunate enough to be able to send our children to an independent day school, it seems to offer the best of both worlds. Our children are able to reap the enormous benefits of an independent school education and we, as parents, are able to continue to play a vital, daily role in the education of our children. Parents enjoy being seen as partners with day schools in educating their children.

As more and more independent day schools have sprung up in communities across the country, more and more parents are choosing to send their children to them, even when it might involve a lengthy daily commute. Contrary to some old stereotypes, parents of independent school students are not all cut from the same mold, living in the same neighborhood with identical dreams and aspirations for their children. Independent school parents represent a wide range of interests, attitudes, and parenting styles.

They also have several things in common. Most parents send their children to independent day schools because they think their children will get a better education in a safe, value-laden environment. Many parents are willing to pay substantial annual tuition because they believe their children will be held to certain standards, challenged academically, and thoroughly prepared for college.

This willingness to make what is for many substantial financial sacrifices reflects the recognition that much of one's character is formed in school. Concerned parents want their children to go to schools where values are discussed and reinforced. They seek schools that have clear expectations and limits. The nonpublic status allows independent schools to establish specific standards of behavior and performance and to suspend or expel students who don't conform to those expectations.

Understanding the power of adolescent peer pressure, parents are eager to have their children go to school with other teens who are academically ambitious and required to behave. They seek an environment where it is "cool" to be smart, to work hard, and to be involved in the school community. In independent day schools, students spend their evenings doing homework, expect to be called on in class, and participate in sports or clubs.

Successful independent schools, whether elementary or high school, large or small, single-sex or coed, recognize the importance of a school-parent partnership in educating each child. Experienced faculty members and administrators readily acknowledge that, while they are experts on education, parents are the experts on their own children. Gone are the days when parents simply dropped their children off in the morning, picked them up at the end of the day, and assumed the school would do the educating. Clearly, children benefit enormously when their parents and teachers work together, sharing their observations and concerns openly and frequently.

Independent schools encourage this two-way give-and-take and are committed to taking it well beyond the public school model. Annual back-to-school nights are attended by more than 90 percent of parents. Teacher-parent and student-teacher-parent conferences, extensive written comments as part of the report cards, and adviser systems that encourage close faculty-student relationships are all structures that facilitate this parent-school partnership. Although more and more independent school parents work full-time, they make time for these critical opportunities to sit down and discuss their children's progress.

Most independent schools welcome and encourage parental involvement and support. Although the individual structures vary from school to school, most include opportunities beyond making cookies and chaperoning dances. Many parents enjoy being involved in community service projects, working on school fund raisers, participating in admission activities, sharing their expertise in appropriate academic classes, and even offering student internships. Most schools have made a concerted effort to structure specific opportunities for working parents to participate in the life of the school.

Independent day schools recognize the benefits of parent volunteers and of extending themselves so that parents feel that they are an important part of the school family. Buddy systems that pair new parents with families who have been at the school for several years help ease the transition for families who are new to the independent school sector.

Independent schools have also responded to increased parental interest in programs focusing on parenting skills. Recognizing the inherent difficulties of raising children, independent day schools have provided forums for discussing and learning about drugs, depression, stress management, peer pressure, and the like. Book groups, panel discussions, and workshops provide important opportunities for parents to share their concerns and to get to know the parents of their children's classmates. Schools recognize that this parent-to-parent communication and networking strengthens the entire school community.

Many current day school parents would contend that when you choose an independent day school for your child you are really choosing a school for the entire family. The students become so involved in their academic and extracurricular activities, and the parents spend so much time at school supporting those activities that it does become the entire family's school.

_____

Lila Lohr is the former Head of School at Princeton Day School in Princeton, New Jersey. She has been a teacher and an administrator in independent day schools for more than thirty years and is the mother of 3 independent day school graduates.

Finding the Perfect Match

Helene Reynolds

One of the real benefits of independent education is that it allows you to deliberately seek out and choose a school community for your child. If you are like most parents, you want your child's school years to reflect an appropriate balance of academic challenge, social development, and exploration into athletics and the arts. You hope that through exposure to new ideas and sound mentoring your child will develop an awareness of individual social responsibility, as well as the study skills and work ethic to make a contribution to his or her world. It is every parent's fondest wish to have the school experience spark those areas of competence that can be pursued toward excellence and distinction.

An increasing number of parents realize that this ideal education is found outside their public school system, that shrinking budgets, divisive school boards, and overcrowded classrooms have resulted in schools where other agendas vie with education for attention and money. In this environment there is less time and energy for teachers to focus on individual needs.

The decision to choose a private school can be made for as many different reasons as there are families making the choice. Perhaps your child would benefit from smaller classes or accelerated instruction. Perhaps your child has needs or abilities that can be more appropriately addressed in a specialized environment. Perhaps you are concerned about the academic quality of your local public school and the impact it may have on your child's academic future. Or perhaps you feel that a private school education is a gift you can give your child to guide him or her toward a more successful future.

Every child is an individual, and this makes school choice a process unique to each family. The fact that your father attended a top-flight Eastern boarding school to prepare for the Ivy League does not necessarily make this educational course suitable for all of his grandchildren. In addition to determining the school's overall quality, you must explore the appropriateness of philosophy, curriculum, level of academic difficulty, and style before making your selection. The right school is the school where your child will thrive, and a famous name and a hallowed reputation are not necessarily the factors that define the right environment. The challenge is in discovering what the factors are that make the match between your child and his or her school the right one.

No matter how good its quality and reputation, a single school is unlikely to be able to meet the needs of all children. The question remains: How do families begin their search with confidence that they will find what they are looking for? How do they make the right connection?

As a parent, there are a number of steps you can follow to establish a reasoned and objective course of information gathering that will lead to a subjective discussion of this information and the way it applies to the student in question. This can only occur if the first step is done thoroughly and in an orderly manner. Ultimately, targeting a small group of schools, any of which could be an excellent choice, is only possible after information gathering and discussion have taken place. With work and a little luck, the result of this process is a school with an academically sound and challenging program based on an educational philosophy that is an extension of the family's views and which will provide an emotionally and socially supportive milieu for the child.

STEP 1: IDENTIFY STUDENT NEEDS

Often the decision to change schools seems to come out of the blue, but, in retrospect, it can be seen as a decision the family has been leading up to for some time. I would urge parents to decide on their own goals for the search first and to make sure, if possible, that they can work in concert toward meeting these goals before introducing the idea to their child. These goals are as different as the parents who hold them. For one parent, finding a school with a state-of-the-art computer program is a high priority. For another, finding a school with a full dance and music program is important. Others will be most concerned about finding a school that has the best record of college acceptances and highest SAT scores.

Once you have decided your own goals for the search, bring the child into the discussion. I often say to parents that the decision to explore is *not* the decision to change schools but only the decision to gather information and consider options. It is important to be aware that everyone has an individual style of decision making and that the decision to make a change is loaded with concerns, many of which will not be discovered until the process has begun.

If you have already made the decision to change your child's school, it is important to let your child know that this aspect of the decision is open to discussion but not to negotiation. It is equally important that you let your child know that he or she will have responsibility in choosing the specific school. Without that knowledge, your son or daughter may feel that he or she has no control over the course of his or her own life.

Some students are responsible enough to take the lead in the exploration; some are too young to do so. But in all cases, children need reassurance about their future and clarity about the reasons for considering other school settings. Sometimes the situation is fraught with disparate opinions that can turn school choice into a family battleground, one in which the child is the ultimate casualty. It is always important to keep in mind that the welfare of the child is the primary goal.

The knowledge that each individual has his or her own agenda and way of making decisions should be warning enough to pursue some preliminary discussion so that you, as parents, can avoid the pitfall of conflicting goals and maintain a united front and a reasonably directed course of action. The family discussion should be energetic, and differences of opinion should be encouraged as healthy and necessary and expressed in a climate of trust and respect.

There are many reasons why you may, at this point, decide to involve a professional educational consultant. Often this choice is made to provide a neutral ground where you and your child can both speak and be heard. Another reason is to make sure that you have established a sound course of exploration that takes both your own and your child's needs into consideration. Consultants who are up-to-date on school information, who have visited each campus, and who are familiar with the situations of their clients can add immeasurably to the process. They can provide a reality check, reinforcement of personal impressions, and experience-based information support for people who are doing a search of this type for the first time. All the research in the world cannot replace the experience and industry knowledge of a seasoned professional. In addition, if the specific circumstances of the placement are delicate, the educational consultant is in a position to advocate for your child during the placement process. There are also situations in which a family in crisis doesn't have the time or the ability to approach school choice in a deliberate and objective manner.

These are some of the many reasons to engage the services of a consultant, but it is the family guidance aspect that most families overlook at the start of the process and value most highly after they have completed it. A good consultant provides neutral ground and information backup that are invaluable.

STEP 2: EVALUATE YOUR CHILD'S ACADEMIC PROFILE

If your child's academic profile raises questions about his or her ability, learning style, or emotional profile, get a professional evaluation to make sure that your expectations for your child are congruent with the child's actual abilities and needs.

Start gathering information about your child from the current school. Ask guidance counselors and teachers for their observations, and request a formal meeting to review the standardized testing that virtually every school administers. Question their views of your child's behavior, attentiveness, and areas of strength and weakness. Make sure you fully understand the reasons behind their recommendations. Do not feel shy about calling back to ask questions at a later date, after you have had time to think and consider this important information. Your child's future may depend on the decisions you are making; don't hesitate to keep asking until you have the information you need.

If a picture of concern emerges, ask the guidance counselor, other parents, or your pediatrician for suggestions regarding learning specialists or psychologists in the community who work with children and can provide evaluation of their academic ability, academic achievement, and learning style. The evaluation should be reviewed in-depth with the specialist, who should be asked about specific recommendations for changes in the youngster's schooling.

Remember, as the parent, it is ultimately your responsibility to weigh the ideas of others and to decide if the difficulty lies with your child or the environment, either of which could indicate a need for a change of school.

STEP 3: REVIEW THE GOALS OF PLACEMENT

Discuss your differences of opinion about making a change. Identify a list of schools that creates a ballpark of educational possibilities. (An educational consultant can also be helpful at this stage.)

It is important that both you and your child take the time to consider what characteristics, large and small, you would like in the new school and which you would like to avoid. As you each make lists of priorities and discuss them, the process of school choice enters the subjective arena. The impersonal descriptions of school environments transform into very personal visualizations of the ways you and your child view the child in a new setting.

A chance to play ice hockey, a series of courses in Mandarin Chinese, the opportunity to take private flute lessons, or a desire to meet others from all over the world may sound like a bizarre mix of criteria, but the desire to explore and find all of these options in a single environment expresses the expansiveness of the student's mind and the areas he or she wants to perfect, try out, or explore. Don't expect perfectly logical thinking from your child as he or she considers options; don't take everything he or she says literally or too seriously. Open and respectful discussion will allow a child to embrace a new possibility one day and reject it the next—this is part of the process of decision making and affirmation and part of the fun of exploration.

STEP 4: SET AN ITINERARY

Set an itinerary for visits and interviews so that you and your child can compare campuses and test your preconceived ideas of the schools you have researched against the reality of the campus community; forward standardized testing scores and transcripts to the schools prior to visits so that the admission office has pertinent information in advance of your meeting.

In order to allow your child the freedom to form opinions about the schools you visit, you may want to keep these pointers in mind:
- Parents should allow their child to be front and center during the visits and interviews—allow your child to answer questions, even if they leave out details you think are important.
- Parents should stay in the background and have confidence that the admission officers know how to engage kids in conversation.
- This may be the first time your child has been treated by a school as an individual

and responsible person—enjoy watching him or her adjust to this as an observer, not as a protector or participant.

- Don't let your own anxiety ruin your child's experience.
- Discuss dress in advance so it doesn't become the issue and focus of the trip.

Keep your ideas and impressions to yourself and allow your child first shot at verbalizing opinions. Remember that immediate reactions are not final decisions; often the first response is only an attempt to process the experience.

STEP 5: USE THE APPLICATION PROCESS FOR PERSONAL GUIDANCE

Make sure your child uses the application process not only to satisfy the school's need for information but also to continue the personal guidance process of working through and truly understanding his or her goals and expectations.

Application questions demand your child's personal insight and exploration. Addressing questions about significant experiences, people who have influenced his or her life, or selecting four words that best describe him or her are ways of coming to grips with who your child is and what he or she wants to accomplish both at the new school and in life. Although parents want their children to complete seamless and perfect applications, it is important to remember that the application must be the work of the child and that the parent has an excellent opportunity to discuss the questions and answers to help guide the student in a positive and objective self-review.

It is more important that the application essays accurately reflect the personality and values of the student than that they be technically flawless. Since the school is basing part of its acceptance decision on the contents of the application, the school needs to meet the real student in the application. The child's own determination of what it is important for the school to know about them is crucial to this process. That being said, parents can play an important role in helping the child understand the difference between unnecessarily brutal honesty and putting his or her best foot forward.

STEP 6: TRUST YOUR OBSERVATIONS

Although the process of school exploration depends on objectivity, it is rare that a family will embrace a school solely because of its computer labs, endowment, library, SAT scores, or football team. These objective criteria frame the search, but it tends to be the intangibles that determine the decision. It is the subjective—instinctive responses to events on campus, people met, quality of interview, unfathomable vibes—that makes the match.

It is important to review what aspects of the school environment made you feel at home. These questions apply equally to parent and child. Did you like the people you met on campus? Was the tour informational but informal, with students stopping to greet you or the tour guide? Was the tone of the campus (austere or homey, modern or traditional) consistent with the kind of educational atmosphere you are looking for? Are the sports facilities beyond your wildest expectation? Does the college-sending record give you confidence that your child will find an intellectually comfortable peer group? How long do the teachers tend to stay with the school, and do they send their own children there? If it is a boarding school, do teachers live on campus? How homey is the dorm setup?

The most fundamental questions are: Do people in the school community like where they are, trust each other, have respect for each other, and feel comfortable there? Is it a family you would care to join? These subjective responses will help you recognize which schools will make your child feel he or she is part of the community, where he or she will fit in and be respected for who he or she is and wants to become.

_____

Helene Reynolds is a former educational consultant from Princeton, New Jersey.

Understanding the Admission Application Form

Gregg W. M. Maloberti
Dean of Admission
The Lawrenceville School
Lawrenceville, New Jersey

Although an attractive option for college applicants for many years, the Admission Application Form (formerly known as the Common Application) for independent boarding and day schools has only recently been made available and has just begun to grow in popularity among candidates. The Admission Application Form has been sanctioned by members of The Association of Boarding Schools (TABS). It represents the collaborative spirit of boarding schools and their commitment to helping students find the right school. Steve Ruzicka, former Executive Director of TABS, organized the nationwide effort that led to the publication of the Admission Application Form. "We opened an Internet-driven discussion that led to many suggestions, alterations, and refinements of what is now the Admission Application Form accepted by more than 200 schools. A version of the Admission Application Form is available for day schools as well. My goal is to have every school accept this application." The current version of the Admission Application Form is available in TABS *Boarding Schools Directory* and in electronic form from the TABS Web site: http://www.schools.com/forms/applicationform.pdf.

There are a few schools that accept only the recommendation forms from the Admission Application Form. It's best to check with each school to find out which forms are preferred. The list of schools accepting the Admission Application Form is available at this TABS Web site: http://www.schools.com/forms/school_list.pdf.

THE ADMISSION APPLICATION FORM EXPLAINED

Anxious parents' lingering doubts about the use of the Admission Application Form are hard to ignore: Will the substitution of the Admission Application Form for the individual school's application cause the admission committee to be offended and compromise my child's chances for admission? Parents should rest assured that schools agreeing to accept the Admission Application Form believe that a fair and effective admission decision can be made on the basis of the Admission Application Form and that its use in no way erodes the quality of their selection process.

All applications begin with a biographical sketch of the candidate: name, address, birth date, mailing address, parents' names, and schools attended. Information regarding sibling or legacy relationships, interest in financial aid, citizenship, language spoken, and even racial and ethnic diversity is collected as well. Except for the order in which these questions appear, there is little variation in these question types from one school's application to another. The Admission Application Form certainly relieves candidates of the burden of providing the very same biographical information over and over again.

The second section of an application generally reveals a candidate's accomplishments and ambitions. Often, the applicants are asked to catalog their interests and activities in list or narrative form. Schools want to know what the candidate has done, for how long, with whom, and to what distinction, if any. In a few cases, some schools ask for a series of short answers to a combination of questions or look for the applicant to complete a sentence. There are generally no "right" answers to these questions—but honest answers can help the school begin to characterize the applicant's curiosity, maturity, ambition, and self-esteem. Here again, great similarity exists in the manner and style with which this information is gathered. While the Admission Application Form asks these question types in a more direct manner, it is no less effective than the individual school's application, and its use affords a candidate a genuine measure of efficiency without compromising individuality.

Schools that advocate the use of their own applications over that of the Admission Application Form often bitterly defend the third and final portion of their applications since it generally includes essay questions. With few exceptions, these questions, while occasionally posed in a unique or original manner, seek to probe much the same territory covered by the three choices listed in the essay section of the Admission Application Form:

1. Describe a person you admire or who has influenced you a great deal.
2. What makes you the interesting person that you are?
3. Explain the impact of an event or activity that has created a change in your life or in your way of thinking.

While the candidate's ability to write well is certainly under review in the essay question, the exercise investigates a candidate's values and explores the individual experiences that have shaped his or her character. These questions give candidates a chance to reveal such qualities as independence, self-reliance, creativity, originality, humility, generosity, curiosity, and genius. Viewed in this light, answering these questions becomes a tall order. The best advice may be to just answer them. In addition, candidates should recognize that although the content of their essays is always of interest, grammar, spelling, punctuation, organization, and the inclusion of evidence or examples are of equal importance.

Candidates who come from disadvantaged backgrounds often find this section of the application the most challenging and occasionally exclusionary. Some schools assume that all applicants have access to such things as summer camps, music instruction, and periodicals and newspapers. Whatever the case, the Admission Application Form is more inclusive of a broader set of experiences. In fact, many outreach agencies who seek to identify and place disadvantaged students in independent schools have either used the Admission Application Form or developed their own applications in lieu of individual school application forms.

If a student fears that using the Admission Application Form will somehow fail to convey a unique aspect of his or her individuality or that the essay question answers will not speak to the unique qualities of why a particular school might be a good match, he or she may want to think about including an extra essay. Just because a candidate uses the Admission Application Form does not mean that he or she must use a common approach to completing it. Imagine how welcome a splash of creativity might be to an individual reader or committee of admission officers who may read hundreds or even thousands of applications each admission season. An application that parrots the list of school courses, sports, and activities offers little insight into the candidate. A well-written application will be as unique as the individual who wrote it.

Applicants and their parents are not the only winners when the Admission Application Form is used. The teachers who dutifully complete countless recommendation forms enjoy the convenience of having to complete only one form for each of their students applying to independent schools. Practically speaking, if there is ever a time that a student wants to be in good favor with his or her teacher, it is the moment at which a reference is being given. With only one form to complete, most teachers will provide longer and more informative answers that are far more helpful to admission officers. The Admission Application Form is a great remedy for the fatigue and frustration endured by teachers who have been overwhelmed by a barrage of recommendation forms. Currently, there are even more schools accepting the recommendation forms than there are schools accepting the entire Admission Application Form. Before discounting the benefits of the Admission Application Form, be sure to consider at least the use of the recommendation forms.

COUNSELORS AND CONSULTANTS SPEAK OUT

Lee Cary, Director of Admissions, Shore Country Day School in Beverly, Massachusetts, has been advising eighth graders for many years and finds the workload associated with the application process unreasonable for most of her students. "It is inconceivable to expect a 14-year-old student to write upwards of eight individual essays, all of top quality. From taking time for school visits, making up missed schoolwork, organizing forms, completing paperwork, and polishing writing, the act of applying to secondary school becomes a whole second job for eighth- and ninth-grade students." Considering that the average application includes up to ten documents, some of which must pass between the applicant, the sending school, and back to the applicant or the receiving school, an eighth grader and his or her parents are now looking at completing more than eighty documents! On top of the testing process and applying for financial aid, this amounts to an enormous administrative challenge.

Karl Koenigsbauer, Director of Secondary School Placement, Eaglebrook School in Deerfield, Massachusetts, agrees that the Admission Application Form makes the process more efficient, but he worries about how it might erode the process as well. "My goal is to help students find the school that will be the best match for their abilities and interests. The essay questions from some schools really help the candidate to understand more about what qualities of mind and spirit a school values. When a candidate comes to me and says a particular question is too difficult, too simplistic, or just plain confusing, it gives me an opportunity to help him or her see how that question represents the identity of that particular school and why it may or may not be a good match. I worry that the Admission Application Form will homogenize the application process to the point where I lose this opportunity to fine-tune the placement process."

Faith Howland, an independent educational consultant in Boston, Massachusetts, and a member of the Independent Educational Consultants Association (IECA), works with families to find the right school and is also often contacted for help when a student's first round of applications has not been successful. "The application process can be near overwhelming for 13- and 14-year-olds. To write as many as eight different applications, each with different essays, just when you are expected to get great grades and continue your sports commitments and other extracurriculars—not to mention working to prepare for entrance tests. This is high stress! Use of the Admission Application Form would be supportive to students and would be extremely helpful in streamlining the teacher recommendations. For those kids who need to submit a second round of applications, the Admission Application Form could be invaluable. These youngsters are coping with disappointment while needing to research new possibilities. If schools were willing to share the Admission Application Form, it's conceivable that many more students who might simply give up if not successful on their first applications could be placed."

MANY SCHOOLS, ONE APPLICATION

Increased acceptance of the Admission Application Form could lead to a marked increase in applications. The Admission Application Form is especially helpful to the candidate who fails to earn any acceptance letters at the end of the application process. Traditionally, if a candidate wants to apply to a new list of schools, he or she must start from scratch and complete a new set of forms. The Admission Application Form certainly speeds up this process.

More than half of the candidates who apply to independent schools come from public schools and do not enjoy the benefit of placement counselors at their schools nor do they seek the advice of independent counselors. Regardless, most candidates are well served in using the Admission Application Form when applying to multiple schools. One strategy may be to complete a few individual applications and then submit the Admission Application Form to a few other schools—identifying some additional options and increasing the likelihood of having meaningful choices after the decision letters are mailed. Many candidates find it much easier to figure out which school they want once they know which school wants them.

Few schools realize how difficult the application process can be for families who are applying to more than one school. The Admission Application Form makes the process of applying to multiple schools a much more manageable endeavor. The use of the Admission Application Form affords families much more time and energy to devote to other aspects of the application and interview process. By reducing the duplicated paperwork of recommendations and the need to complete so many essays, applicants and their parents are granted a greater opportunity to discuss the real issues surrounding school selection, such as the compatibility of curriculum, style of teaching, and program offerings. Rather than creating folders for each school and chasing down multiple letters of recommendation, applicants and their parents can focus on just a few essays and remove the stress associated with sorting and tracking multiple documents.

Candidates and their families can be assured of the professionalism of admission officers and feel free to use the Admission Application Form. The Admission Application Form represents the efforts of the very best admission officers who have put the interests of the applicant at the fore—shifting the focus away from the school and back to the candidate. Candidates can be confident that the Admission Application Form will more than adequately allow them to make a strong case for their own admission at any school accepting the form.

Paying for a Private Education

Mark J. Mitchell
Vice President, School Information Services
National Association of Independent Schools (NAIS)

Imagine asking a car dealer to sell you a $15,000 sedan for $5000 because that is all you can afford. When you buy a car, you know that you will be paying more than it cost to design, build, ship, and sell the car. The sales staff will not offer you a price based on your income. At best, you may receive discounts, rebates, or other incentives that allow you to pay the lowest price the dealer is willing to accept. As a buyer, you even accept the notion that the car's value will depreciate as soon as you drive it off the lot. No matter how you look at it, you pay more than the car cost to make and ultimately more than it's worth.

Tuition at many private schools can easily approach the cost of a new car; however, paying for a private school education is not the same as buying a car. One difference is the availability of financial aid at thousands of schools in the United States and abroad to help offset the tuition. Imagine asking a school to accept $5000 for a $15,000 tuition because that is all you can afford to pay. That is exactly what private schools that provide need-based financial aid programs accomplish. Learning about the financing options and procedures available at private schools nationwide can make this imagined scenario a reality for many families.

NEED-BASED FINANCIAL AID

Many private schools offer assistance to families who demonstrate financial need. They take the tuition of the school and re-evaluate how much of it a family will pay based on financial ability. As a result, the price a family pays varies according to the amount of financial assistance received. Through a school's financial aid program, the tuition price listed is not always the tuition price you can expect to pay.

In fact, for academic year 2005–06, 946 NAIS-member schools provided an average of $14,520 for boarding students and $9213 for day students. The schools themselves fund the vast majority of the $879.3 million in financial aid provided to students. These need-based grants do not require repayment and

673

are used to offset the school's tuition. Schools make this substantial commitment as one way of ensuring a socioeconomically diverse student body and to help ensure that every student qualified for admission has the best chance to enroll, regardless of his or her financial circumstances.

HOW FINANCIAL NEED IS DETERMINED

Many schools use a process of determining financial need that requires the completion of applications and the submission of tax forms and other documentation to help them decide how much help each family needs. Currently, more than 2,400 schools nationwide require families to complete The School and Student Service (SSS) Parents' Financial Statement (PFS) online at www.nais.org. The PFS gathers information about family size, income and expenses, parents' assets and indebtedness, and the child's assets. From this and other information, schools are provided with an estimate of the amount of discretionary income (after several allowances are made for basic necessities) available for education costs. Schools review each case individually and use this estimate, along with such supporting documentation as most recent income tax forms, to make a final decision on your need for a financial aid grant. You must pay for this service online by credit card unless you receive a fee waiver from the school. You can apply for aid at up to six schools for 12 children on a single PFS. Since most schools will only accept one PFS per family, be sure to list all children in your PFS. For more information, call the School and Student Service for Financial Aid (SSS) at 866-387-2601 or visit their Web site at https://sss.ets.org/.

The amount of a need-based award varies from person to person and school to school. Just as individuals have different financial resources and obligations that dictate their need for assistance, schools have different resources and policies that dictate their ability to meet your financial need. Tuition costs, endowment incomes, and awarding philosophies are a few of the things that can affect how much a school can offer. If your decision to send your child to a private school depends heavily on getting financial help, you would benefit from applying for aid at more than one school.

MERIT-BASED AWARDS

While the majority of aid offered is based on a family's financial situation, not everyone who receives financial assistance must demonstrate financial need. Private schools offer millions of dollars in merit-based scholarships to thousands of students. In the 2005–06 academic year, 310 NAIS-member schools awarded an average annual merit award worth $3545 to students, totaling more than $25.7 million. Even with this level of commitment, such awards are rare (fewer than 5 percent of all enrolled students receive this type of aid) and, therefore, highly competitive. They may serve to reward demonstrated talents or achievements in areas ranging from academics to athletics to the arts.

Some additional resources may be available from organizations and agencies in your community. Civic and religious groups, philanthropies, and even your employer may sponsor scholarships for students at private schools. Unfortunately, these options tend to be few and far between, limited in number and size of award. Be sure to ask a financial aid officer at the school(s) in which you are interested if he or she is aware of such organizations and opportunities.

Whether it is offered by the school or a local organization, be sure to understand the requirements or conditions on which a merit-based scholarship is based. Ask if the award is renewable and, if so, under what conditions. Often, certain criteria must be met (such as minimum GPA, community service, or participation in activities) to ensure renewal of the award in subsequent years. (Some merit awards are available for just one year.)

TUITION FINANCING OPTIONS

Whether or not you qualify for grants or scholarships, another way to get financial help involves finding ways to make tuition payments easier on your family's monthly budget. One common option is the tuition payment plan. These plans allow you to spread tuition payments (less any forms of financial aid you receive) over a period of eight to ten months. In most cases, payments start before the school year begins, but this method can be more feasible than coming up with one or two huge lump sums before the beginning of a semester. Payment plans may be administered by the schools themselves or by a private company approved by the school. They do not normally require credit checks or charge interest; however, they typically charge an application or service fee, which may include tuition insurance.

Since a high-quality education is one of the best investments they can make in their child's future, many parents finance the cost just as they would any other important investment. Many schools, banks, and other agencies offer tuition loan programs specifically for elementary and secondary school expenses. While such loans are subject to credit checks and must be repaid with interest, they tend to offer rates and terms that are more favorable than those of other consumer loans. These programs are growing in popularity, so it pays to compare the details of more than one type of loan program to find the best one for your needs. Although they should always be regarded as an option of last resort, tuition loan programs can be helpful. Of course, every family must consider both the short- and long-term costs of borrowing and make its decision part of a larger plan for education financing.

A FINAL WORD

Although the primary responsibility to pay for school costs rests with the family, there are options available if you need help. As you can see, financing a private school education can result in a partnership between the family, the school, and sometimes outside agencies or companies, with each making an effort to provide ways to meet the costs. The financial aid officer at the school is the best source of information about your options and is willing to help you in every way he or she can. Always go to the financial aid officer at a school in which you are interested whenever you have any questions or concerns about these programs and the application process. Understanding your responsibilities, meeting deadlines, and learning about the full range of options is your best strategy for obtaining assistance. Though there are no guarantees, with proper planning and the right questions, your family just might get that $15,000 education for $5000.

APPENDIX

Private Schools At-a-Glance

Private Schools
At-a-Glance

In the following pages you will find valuable data on private secondary schools from *Peterson's Guide to Private Secondary Schools 2008*. This chart will guide your search, whether it's focused on a specific geographic region of the U.S. or around the world. We've provided quick answers to key questions about each school, such as:

- Are its students boarding, day, or both?
- Is it coeducational?
- What grades are offered at the school?
- How many students are enrolled?
- What is the student/faculty ratio?

The chart also provides information about Advanced Placement subject areas and sports.

Once you've used the following chart to help you identify prospective schools, be sure to check out *Peterson's Guide to Private Secondary Schools 2008*, the only comprehensive private school guide available. You'll find detailed profiles on approximately 1,500 accredited private schools worldwide, as well as valuable advice on planning your search and financing a private school education.

appendix

PRIVATE SCHOOLS AT-A-GLANCE	STUDENTS ACCEPTED				GRADES			STUDENT/FACULTY			STUDENT OFFERINGS (number)	
	Boarding		Day									
	Boys	Girls	Boys	Girls	Lower	Middle	Upper	Total	Upper	Student/ Faculty Ratio	Advanced Placement Subject Areas	Sports
UNITED STATES												
Alabama												
The Altamont School, Birmingham			X	X	5–8		9–12	376	228	5:1	18	18
American Christian Academy, Tuscaloosa			X	X	K–6	7–9	10–12	858	154	12:1	4	35
Briarwood Christian High School, Birmingham			X	X	K–6	7–8	9–12	1,920	551	23:1	5	17
Indian Springs School, Indian Springs	X	X	X	X			8–12	300	300	8:1	14	19
Lyman Ward Military Academy, Camp Hill	X				6–8		9–12	75	55	12:1	3	35
Madison Academy, Madison			X	X	PS–6		7–12	800	400	15:1		7
Marion Academy, Marion			X	X	K4–3	4–6	7–12	88	34	9:1		7
Mars Hill Bible School, Florence			X	X	K–4	5–8	9–12	635	196	14:1	5	10
Pickens Academy, Carrollton			X	X	K4–6		7–12	309	147	20:1		12
Randolph School, Huntsville			X	X	K–6	7–8	9–12	876	268	13:1	15	16
Saint James School, Montgomery			X	X	PK–5	6–8	9–12	1,115	325	20:1	13	20
St. Paul's Episcopal School, Mobile			X	X	PK–4	5–8	9–12	1,491	558	12:1	7	16
Shades Mountain Christian School, Hoover			X	X	K4–6	7–8	9–12	465	148	22:1	2	15
Sumiton Christian School, Sumiton			X	X	K–5	6–8	9–12	637	231	12:1		36
Tuscaloosa Academy, Tuscaloosa			X	X	PK–4	5–8	9–12	408	125	16:1	12	12
Westminster Christian Academy, Huntsville			X	X	K4–5	6–8	9–12	659	234	12:1	5	18
Alaska												
Grace Christian School, Anchorage			X	X	K–6	7–8	9–12	669	242	15:1	6	8
Heritage Christian High School, Anchorage			X	X	PK–5	6–8	9–12	121	67	11:1	1	9
Arizona												
Blueprint Education, Phoenix												
Brophy College Preparatory, Phoenix			X				9–12	1,270	1,270	15:1	16	44
Faith Christian School, Mesa			X	X	K–6	7–8	9–12	68	22	10:1		3
Immaculate Heart High School, Tucson			X	X			9–12	72	72	7:1		8
Lourdes Catholic High School, Nogales			X	X	PK–5	6–8	9–12	410	94	8.5:1		3
New Way Learning Academy, Scottsdale			X	X	K–5	6–8	9–12	139	43	4:1		
Oak Creek Ranch School, West Sedona	X	X				6–8	9–12	79	68	8:1		60
Phoenix Christian Unified Schools, Phoenix			X	X	PS–6	7–8	9–12	732	315	20:1	8	17
Phoenix Country Day School, Paradise Valley			X	X	PK–4	5–8	9–12	741	262	9:1	15	16
St. Gregory College Preparatory School, Tucson			X	X		6–8	9–PG	344	196	10:1	17	23
Saint Mary's High School, Phoenix			X	X			9–12	837	837	18:1	8	18
St. Paul's Preparatory Academy, Phoenix	X		X				8–12	75	75	8:1		20
Salpointe Catholic High School, Tucson			X	X			9–12	1,196	1,196	14:1	11	22
Seton Catholic High School, Chandler			X	X			9–12	529	529	14:1	10	15
Southwestern Academy, Rimrock	X	X	X	X			9–PG	32	32	3:1	2	37
Valley Lutheran High School, Phoenix			X	X			9–12	150	150	8:1		16
Verde Valley School, Sedona	X	X	X	X			9–PG	108	108	5:1		57
Xavier College Preparatory, Phoenix				X			9–12	1,152	1,152	22:1	17	29
Arkansas												
Episcopal Collegiate School, Little Rock			X	X		6–8	9–12	376	206	10:1	13	15
Harding Academy, Searcy	X	X	X	X	K–6		7–12	589	288	11:1	6	10
Pulaski Academy, Little Rock			X	X	PK–4	5–8	9–12	1,310	373	13:1	20	21
Subiaco Academy, Subiaco	X		X				8–12	170	170	9:1	10	46
California												
Academy of Our Lady of Peace, San Diego				X			9–12	740	740	15:1	10	11
Anacapa School, Santa Barbara			X	X	7–8		9–12	69	45	12:1	1	23
Archbishop Riordan High School, San Francisco			X				9–12	650	650	14:1	13	26
Army and Navy Academy, Carlsbad	X		X			7–8	9–12	320	273	12:1	10	43
Arrowhead Christian Academy, Redlands			X	X		7–8	9–12	545	400	12:1	7	13
The Athenian School, Danville	X	X	X	X		6–8	9–12	450	296	10:1	11	15

	STUDENTS ACCEPTED				GRADES			STUDENT/FACULTY			STUDENT OFFERINGS (number)	
	Boarding		Day									
	Boys	Girls	Boys	Girls	Lower	Middle	Upper	Total	Upper	Student/ Faculty Ratio	Advanced Placement Subject Areas	Sports
Bakersfield Christian High School, Bakersfield			X	X			9–12	506	506	17:1	5	12
Bellarmine College Preparatory, San Jose			X				9–12	1,570	1,570	14:1	7	20
Bentley School, Oakland			X	X	K–5	6–8	9–12	679	327	8:1	15	15
Berean Christian High School, Walnut Creek			X	X			9–12	420	420	13:1		11
Besant Hill School, Ojai	X	X	X	X			9–12	100	100	4:1	3	36
Bishop Alemany High School, Mission Hills			X	X			9–12	1,460	1,460	18:1	11	16
Bishop Conaty-Our Lady of Loretto High School, Los Angeles				X			9–12	356	356	13:1	1	6
Bishop Garcia Diego High School, Santa Barbara			X	X			9–12	307	307	12:1	8	25
Bishop Quinn High School/St. Francis Middle School, Palo Cedro			X	X			9–12	100	100	15:1		23
The Branson School, Ross			X	X			9–12	320	320	9:1	14	15
Brentwood School, Los Angeles			X	X	K–6	7–8	9–12	991	469	8:1	18	40
Brethren Christian Junior and Senior High Schools, Huntington Beach			X	X		7–8	9–12	406	302	12:1	6	13
Bridgemont High School, San Francisco			X	X		6–8	9–12	69	54	4:1	3	13
Bridges Academy, Studio City			X	X		6–8	9–12	92	59	9:1		2
Calvin Christian High School, Escondido			X	X	PK–5	6–8	9–12	550	186	10:1	5	13
Campbell Hall (Episcopal), North Hollywood			X	X	K–6	7–8	9–12	1,090	530	8:1	19	19
Cardinal Newman High School, Santa Rosa			X				9–12	436	436	15:1	8	17
Carondelet High School, Concord				X			9–12	800	800	25:1	6	22
Castilleja School, Palo Alto				X		6–8	9–12	415	235	7:1	18	12
Cate School, Carpinteria	X	X	X	X			9–12	265	265	5:1	19	34
Central Catholic High School, Modesto			X	X			9–12	437	437	17:1	8	14
Chadwick School, Palos Verdes Peninsula			X	X	K–6	7–8	9–12	826	356	6:1	11	19
Chaminade College Preparatory, West Hills			X	X			9–12	1,176	1,176	15:1	15	26
Chinese Christian Schools, San Leandro			X	X	K–5	6–8	9–12	915	225	12:1	12	11
Christian Junior–Senior High School, El Cajon			X	X		7–8	9–12	634	451	14:1	8	13
The College Preparatory School, Oakland			X	X			9–12	342	342	8:1	11	12
Cornelia Connelly School, Anaheim				X			9–12	312	312	9:1	10	14
Crespi Carmelite High School, Encino			X				9–12	605	605	23:1	13	14
Crossroads School for Arts & Sciences, Santa Monica			X	X	K–5	6–8	9–12	1,134	498	17:1		21
Crystal Springs Uplands School, Hillsborough			X	X		6–8	9–12	354	247	9:1	15	10
Damien High School, La Verne			X				9–12	1,100	1,100	22:1	19	24
De La Salle High School, Concord			X				9–12	1,039	1,039	28:1	9	18
Drew School, San Francisco			X	X			9–12	245	245	8:1	8	24
Dunn School, Los Olivos	X	X	X	X		6–8	9–12	250	180	6:1	12	37
Eastside College Preparatory School, East Palo Alto	X	X	X	X		6–8	9–12	222	164	8:1	5	4
Emerson Honors High Schools, Orange	X	X	X	X	K–6		7–12	180	85	15:1	4	10
Escondido Adventist Academy, Escondido			X	X	K–5	6–8	9–12	215	105	10:1	8	4
Faith Christian High School, Yuba City			X	X			9–12	119	119	10:1	3	7
Flintridge Preparatory School, La Canada Flintridge			X	X		7–8	9–12	519	408	8:1	12	17
Flintridge Sacred Heart Academy, La Canada Flintridge		X		X			9–12	406	406	10:1	14	21
Fresno Christian Schools, Fresno			X	X	K–6	7–8	9–12	733	276	23:1	4	23
The Frostig School, Pasadena			X	X	1–5	6–8		120	48	6:1		4
Garces Memorial High School, Bakersfield			X	X			9–12	709	709	28:1	5	15
Grace Brethren School, Simi Valley			X	X	K–6	7–8	9–12	896	261	7:1	7	7
The Grauer School, Encinitas			X	X		6–8	9–12	123	63	7:1	2	25
Halstrom High School, Vista			X	X		7–8	9–12	20	16	1:1		
The Harker School, San Jose			X	X	K–5	6–8	9–12	1,702	665	10:1	18	23
Harvard-Westlake School, North Hollywood			X	X		7–9	10–12	1,609	870	8:1	19	21
Head-Royce School, Oakland			X	X	K–5	6–8	9–12	797	344	9:1	20	20
Highland Hall, A Waldorf School, Northridge			X	X	N–6	7–8	9–12	390	103	6:1		6
Hillcrest Christian School, Thousand Oaks			X	X	K–6	7–8	9–12	313	48	12:1	4	7
Holy Names High School, Oakland				X			9–12	270	270	11:1	6	10

PRIVATE SCHOOLS AT-A-GLANCE	STUDENTS ACCEPTED				GRADES			STUDENT/FACULTY			STUDENT OFFERINGS (number)	
	Boarding		Day									
	Boys	Girls	Boys	Girls	Lower	Middle	Upper	Total	Upper	Student/Faculty Ratio	Advanced Placement Subject Areas	Sports
Idyllwild Arts Academy, Idyllwild	X	X	X	X			9–PG	268	268	12:1	1	31
International High School, San Francisco			X	X	PK–5	6–8	9–12	944	327	10:1	14	24
Jesuit High School, Carmichael			X				9–12	1,080	1,080	18:1	12	15
Junipero Serra High School, Gardena			X	X			9–12	582	582	25:1	9	10
Kings Christian School, Lemoore			X	X	PK–6	7–8	9–12	326	116	15:1	2	18
La Cheim School, Antioch			X	X	4–5	6–8	9–12	16	8	4:1		2
Laguna Blanca School, Santa Barbara			X	X	K–4	5–8	9–12	423	202	7:1		18
La Salle High School, Pasadena			X	X			9–12	735	735	12:1	12	18
Laurel Springs School, Ojai					1–4	5–8	9–12	3,608	2,170	1:1		
Le Lycee Francais de Los Angeles, Los Angeles			X	X	PS–5	6–8	9–12	802	147	15:1	10	8
Lick-Wilmerding High School, San Francisco			X	X			9–12	428	428	9:1	15	17
Linfield Christian School, Temecula			X	X	K–5	6–8	9–12	898	412	19:1	7	11
Lodi Academy, Lodi			X	X			9–12	104	104	10:1		6
Los Angeles Baptist Junior/Senior High School, North Hills			X	X		7–8	9–12	848	612	22:1	11	11
Los Angeles Lutheran High School, Sylmar			X	X		6–8	9–12	224	146	16:1	1	11
Louisville High School, Woodland Hills				X			9–12	484	484	25:1	15	12
Loyola High School, Jesuit College Preparatory, Los Angeles			X				9–12	1,214	1,214	15:1	20	14
Lutheran High School, La Verne			X	X			9–12	184	184	10:1	6	15
Lycee International de Los Angeles, Los Angeles			X	X	PK–5	6–8	9–12	460	92	10:1	3	10
Marin Academy, San Rafael			X	X			9–12	404	404	9:1	12	35
Marlborough School, Los Angeles				X		7–9	10–12	537	277	5:1	21	13
Marymount High School, Los Angeles				X			9–12	413	413	8:1	17	20
Mary Star of the Sea High School, San Pedro			X	X			9–12	503	503	16:1		10
Mayfield Senior School, Pasadena				X			9–12	300	300	8:1	12	21
Menlo School, Atherton			X	X		6–8	9–12	750	530	10:1	19	16
Mercy High School, Red Bluff			X	X							5	13
Mercy High School College Preparatory, San Francisco				X			9–12	498	498	14:1	11	8
Mesa Grande Seventh-Day Academy, Calimesa			X	X	K–6	7–8	9–12	305	148	10:1		8
Midland School, Los Olivos	X	X	X	X			9–12	92	92	5:1	2	19
Mid-Peninsula High School, Menlo Park			X	X			9–12	122	122	8:1		7
Milken Community High School of Stephen S. Wise Temple, Los Angeles			X	X		7–8	9–12	768	561	7:1	20	17
Montclair College Preparatory School, Van Nuys	X	X	X	X	6–8		9–12	439	282	15:1	14	21
Moreau Catholic High School, Hayward			X	X			9–12	930	930	18:1	13	20
Mountain View Academy, Mountain View			X	X			9–12	157	157	10:1	2	6
Nawa Academy, French Gulch	X	X				7–8	9–12	50	45	8:1		84
Newbury Park Adventist Academy, Newbury Park			X	X								13
New Heights Preparatory School, Northridge	X	X	X			6–8	9–12	75	42	10:1		5
Notre Dame Academy, Los Angeles				X			9–12	470	470	12:1	8	9
Notre Dame High School, Belmont				X			9–12	652	652	16:1	12	13
Oak Grove School, Ojai	X	X	X	X	PK–6	7–8	9–12	200	42	7:1	1	22
Oakwood School, North Hollywood			X	X	K–6		7–12	764	476	7:1	12	48
Ojai Valley School, Ojai	X	X	X	X	PK–5	6–8	9–12	328	125	6:1	10	37
Orangewood Adventist Academy, Garden Grove			X	X	PK–6	7–8		268	96	10:1	3	7
Orinda Academy, Orinda			X	X		7–8	9–12	124	117	9:1	2	4
Oxford School, Rowland Heights			X	X		7–8	9–12	90	85	15:1	1	4
Pacific Academy, Encinitas			X	X		7–8		30	24	5:1		
Pacific Hills School, West Hollywood			X	X		6–8	9–12	289	216	15:1	6	12
Palma High School, Salinas			X			7–8	9–12	630	472	16:1	14	13
Paraclete High School, Lancaster			X	X			9–12	827	827	18:1	6	12
Pilgrim School, Los Angeles			X	X	PK–5	6–8	9–12	335	112	10:1	15	15
Polytechnic School, Pasadena			X	X	K–5	6–8	9–12	856	372	17:1		16
Providence High School, Burbank			X	X			9–12	555	555	20:1	11	14

	Boarding Boys	Boarding Girls	Day Boys	Day Girls	Lower	Middle	Upper	Total	Upper	Student/Faculty Ratio	Advanced Placement Subject Areas	Sports
Redwood Adventist Academy, Santa Rosa			X	X	K–4	5–8	9–12	127	53	5:1		5
Redwood Christian Schools, Castro Valley			X	X	K–6	7–8	9–12	726	250	24:1	1	8
Riblfet Academy, Los Angeles			X	X	PK–5	6–8	9–12	408	184	10:1	13	32
Rio Lindo Adventist Academy, Healdsburg	X	X	X	X			9–12	162	162	9:1	2	19
Ripon Christian Schools, Ripon			X	X	K–5	6–8	9–12	703	257	18:1	3	13
Rolling Hills Preparatory School, San Pedro			X	X		6–8	9–12	240	140	9:1	8	18
Rosary High School, Fullerton				X			9–12	687	687	15:1	9	12
Sacramento Adventist Academy, Carmichael			X	X	K–6	7–8	9–12	283	115	12:1		5
Sacramento Country Day School, Sacramento			X	X	PK–5	6–8	9–12	515	152	10:1	12	12
Sacred Heart High School, Los Angeles				X			9–12	369	369	15:1		6
Saddleback Valley Christian School, San Juan Capistrano			X	X	K–6	7–8	9–12	633	230	12:1		7
Sage Hill School, Newport Coast			X	X			9–12	454	454	14:1	16	25
St. Augustine High School, San Diego			X				9–12	700	700	28:1	14	16
St. Catherine's Military Academy, Anaheim	X		X		K–6	7–8		160	70	7:1		23
Saint Elizabeth High School, Oakland			X	X			9–12	247	247	15:1	2	8
Saint Francis High School, La Canada Flintridge			X				9–12	685	685	15:1	13	9
Saint Francis High School, Mountain View			X	X			9–12	1,618	1,618	28:1	19	31
Saint John Bosco High School, Bellflower			X				9–12	1,041	1,041	16:1	12	15
St. Joseph High School, Santa Maria			X	X			9–12	642	642			15
Saint Mary's College High School, Berkeley			X	X			9–12	630	630	16:1	9	15
St. Michael's Preparatory School of the Norbertine Fathers, Silverado	X						9–12	64	64	3:1	6	11
Salesian High School, Richmond			X	X			9–12	580	580	25:1	7	8
San Diego Jewish Academy, San Diego			X	X	K–5	6–8	9–12	622	181	18:1	15	25
San Domenico School, San Anselmo		X	X	X	PK–5	6–8	9–12	566	152	8:1	10	14
San Francisco University High School, San Francisco			X	X			9–12	385	385	8:1	18	22
San Francisco Waldorf High School, San Francisco			X	X			9–12	129	129	15:1		17
Santa Catalina School, Monterey		X	X	X	PK–5	6–8	9–12	561	283	7:1	19	39
Servite High School, Anaheim			X				9–12	877	873	19:1	13	13
Southwestern Academy, San Marino	X	X	X	X		6–8	9–PG	123	107	6:1	3	22
Squaw Valley Academy, Olympic Valley	X	X	X	X		6–8	9–12	84	76	7:1	4	68
Stanbridge Academy, San Mateo			X	X	K–6	7–8	9–12	93	48	8:1		12
Stevenson School, Pebble Beach	X	X	X	X	PK–5	6–8	9–12	756	548	10:1	18	34
Summerfield Waldorf School, Santa Rosa			X	X	K–6	7–8	9–12	379	96	4:1	3	5
The Thacher School, Ojai	X	X	X	X			9–12	249	249	5:1	17	43
Tri-City Christian Schools, Vista			X	X	PK–6	7–8	9–12	1,132	298	12:1	5	17
Upland Christian Schools, Upland			X	X	K–5	6–8	9–12	606	224	11:1	4	10
The Urban School of San Francisco, San Francisco			X	X			9–12	344	344	9:1	8	34
Ursuline High School, Santa Rosa				X			9–12	316	316	14:1	7	11
Vacaville Christian Schools, Vacaville			X	X	K–5	6–8	9–12	1,358	378	20:1		10
Valley Christian School, San Jose			X	X	K–5	6–8	9–12	2,233	1,216	17:1	14	20
Victor Valley Christian School, Victorville			X	X	K–6	7–8	9–12	440	155	15:1	5	10
Viewpoint School, Calabasas			X	X	K–5	6–8	9–12	1,205	480	10:1	22	24
Village Christian Schools, La Tuna Canyon			X	X	JK–5	6–8	9–12	1,616	630	25:1	11	16
Villanova Preparatory School, Ojai	X	X	X	X			9–12	330	330	10:1	5	17
The Waverly School, Pasadena			X	X	PK–6	7–8	9–12	312	93	8:1	10	12
The Webb Schools, Claremont	X	X	X	X			9–12	385	385	7:1	20	34
Westridge School, Pasadena				X	4–6	7–8	9–12	510	273	9:1	14	15
Whittier Christian High School, La Habra			X	X			9–12	712	712	10:1	5	14
Windward School, Los Angeles			X	X		7–8	9–12	477	328	7:1	10	6
Woodside International School, San Francisco			X	X		6–8	9–12	85	80	5:1	4	4
Woodside Priory School, Portola Valley	X	X	X	X		6–8	9–12	352	257	10:1	18	18
York School, Monterey			X	X			8–12	222	222	9:1	14	6

PRIVATE SCHOOLS AT-A-GLANCE	STUDENTS ACCEPTED				GRADES			STUDENT/FACULTY			STUDENT OFFERINGS (number)	
	Boarding		Day									
	Boys	Girls	Boys	Girls	Lower	Middle	Upper	Total	Upper	Student/Faculty Ratio	Advanced Placement Subject Areas	Sports
Colorado												
Accelerated Schools, Denver	X	X	X	X	K–5	6–8	9–12	52	39	7:1	4	22
Bridge School, Boulder			X	X		6–8	9–12	73	44	6:1		4
Colorado Academy, Denver			X	X	PK–5	6–8	9–12	885	328	8:1	16	21
The Colorado Rocky Mountain School, Carbondale	X	X	X	X			9–12	156	156	5:1	8	30
The Colorado Springs School, Colorado Springs			X	X	PK–5	6–8	9–12	456	147	6:1	8	12
Colorado Timberline Academy, Durango	X	X	X	X			9–12	50	50	5:1		30
Denver Academy, Denver			X	X	1–6	7–8	9–12	435	262	6:1		32
Denver Christian High School, Denver			X	X			9–12	230	230	18:1		7
Denver Lutheran High School, Denver			X	X			9–12	223	223	17:1	2	14
Eagle Rock School, Estes Park	X	X	X	X					80	4:1		38
Forest Heights Lodge, Evergreen	X				K–5	6–8	9–12	24	3	5:1		36
Fountain Valley School of Colorado, Colorado Springs	X	X	X	X			9–12	250	250	6:1	18	35
Front Range Christian High School, Littleton			X	X	K–6	7–8	9–12	487	193	16:1	5	9
Kent Denver School, Englewood			X	X		6–8	9–12	655	436	7:1	16	27
The Lowell Whiteman School, Steamboat Springs	X	X	X	X			9–12	108	108	7:1	5	65
Regis Jesuit High School, Aurora			X	X			9–12	910	910	16:1	8	24
St. Mary's Academy, Englewood			X	X	K–5	6–8	9–12	720	263	10:1	11	14
St. Mary's High School, Colorado Springs			X	X			9–12	389	389	11:1	6	14
Telluride Mountain School, Telluride			X	X	PK–4	5–8	9–12	85	10	5:1		28
Vail Mountain School, Vail			X	X	K–5	6–8	9–12	362	116	10:1	6	41
Connecticut												
Academy of Our Lady of Mercy, Milford				X			9–12	432	432	12:1		17
Avon Old Farms School, Avon	X		X				9–PG	412	412	7:1	15	50
Brunswick School, Greenwich			X		PK–4	5–8	9–12	893	330	6:1	19	17
Canterbury School, New Milford	X	X	X	X			9–PG	347	347	6:1	19	28
Chase Collegiate School, Waterbury			X	X	PK–5	6–8	9–12	518	185	9:1	19	23
Cheshire Academy, Cheshire	X	X	X	X		6–8	9–PG	381	333	7:1	14	28
Choate Rosemary Hall, Wallingford	X	X	X	X			9–12	848	848	6:1	22	43
Christian Heritage School, Trumbull			X	X	K–6	7–8	9–12	528	166	9:1	10	11
Convent of the Sacred Heart, Greenwich				X	PS–4	5–8	9–12	748	268	5:1	12	18
Eagle Hill School, Greenwich	X	X			1–6		7–9	230	115	4:1		33
Eagle Hill-Southport, Southport			X	X				110	34	4:1		9
East Catholic High School, Manchester			X	X			9–12	759	759	13:1	5	20
The Ethel Walker School, Simsbury		X		X		6–8	9–12	267	199	4:1	17	45
Fairfield College Preparatory School, Fairfield			X				9–12	900	900	15:1	11	28
The Forman School, Litchfield	X	X	X	X			9–12	187	187	3:1	2	32
Franklin Academy, East Haddam	X	X	X	X			9–PG	81	81	2:1		30
The Glenholme School, Washington	X	X	X	X				105	90	12:1		38
Greens Farms Academy, Greens Farms			X	X	K–5	6–8	9–12	624	266	6:1	15	38
Greenwich Academy, Greenwich				X	PK–4	5–8	9–12	793	319	7:1	19	29
Grove School, Madison	X	X	X	X		7–8	9–13	99	94	3:1		65
The Gunnery, Washington	X	X	X	X			9–PG	298	298	7:1	9	21
Hamden Hall Country Day School, Hamden			X	X	PK–6	7–8	9–12	574	249	8:1	13	18
Hopkins School, New Haven			X	X		7–8	9–12	679	524	6:1	15	38
The Hotchkiss School, Lakeville	X	X	X	X			9–PG	584	584	6:1	19	46
Hyde School, Woodstock	X	X	X	X			9–12	159	159	6:1	6	18
Indian Mountain School, Lakeville	X	X	X	X	PK–4	5–6	7–9	261	160	4:1		17
Kent School, Kent	X	X	X	X			9–PG	574	574	7:1	22	37
King & Low-Heywood Thomas School, Stamford			X	X	PK–5	6–8	9–12	648	265	7:1	15	25
Kingswood-Oxford School, West Hartford			X	X		6–8	9–12	595	401	8:1	16	19
The Loomis Chaffee School, Windsor	X	X	X	X			9–PG	723	723	5:1	14	50
Marianapolis Preparatory School, Thompson	X	X	X	X			9–PG	315	315	10:1	9	35
The Marvelwood School, Kent	X	X	X	X			9–12	143	143	4:1		32

	STUDENTS ACCEPTED										STUDENT OFFERINGS (number)	
	Boarding		Day		GRADES			STUDENT/FACULTY				
	Boys	Girls	Boys	Girls	Lower	Middle	Upper	Total	Upper	Student/ Faculty Ratio	Advanced Placement Subject Areas	Sports
The Master's School, West Simsbury			X	X	K–6	7–8	9–12	275	126	7:1	6	20
Mercy High School, Middletown				X			9–12	697	697	14:1	10	15
Miss Porter's School, Farmington		X		X			9–12	327	327	8:1	18	40
Northwest Catholic High School, West Hartford			X	X			9–12	640	640	12:1	14	35
The Norwich Free Academy, Norwich			X	X						22:1	15	27
The Oxford Academy, Westbrook	X						9–PG	38	38	1:1	8	16
Pomfret School, Pomfret	X	X	X	X			9–PG	345	345	6:1	19	29
The Rectory School, Pomfret	X	X	X	X	K–4	5–9		230	153	4:1		48
Rumsey Hall School, Washington Depot	X	X	X	X	K–5	6–9		305	192	8:1		50
Sacred Heart Academy, Hamden				X			9–12	508	508		9	4
St. Joseph High School, Trumbull			X	X			9–12	837	837	14:1	7	11
Saint Thomas More School, Oakdale	X					8	9–PG	210	194	7:1		40
Salisbury School, Salisbury	X		X				9–PG	295	295	11:1	11	21
South Kent School, South Kent	X		X				9–PG	145	145	4:1	5	25
Suffield Academy, Suffield	X	X	X	X			9–PG	406	406		14	27
The Taft School, Watertown	X	X	X	X			9–PG	576	576	6:1	19	46
Watkinson School, Hartford			X	X		6–8	9–PG	276	193	7:1		25
Westminster School, Simsbury	X	X	X	X			9–PG	385	385	5:1	19	26
Westover School, Middlebury		X		X			9–12	194	194	8:1	15	46
The Williams School, New London			X	X		7–8	9–12	312	245	6:1	10	14
The Woodhall School, Bethlehem	X		X				9–PG	42	42	4:1	2	34
Wooster School, Danbury			X	X	K–5	6–8	9–12	346	151	10:1	11	15
Delaware												
Archmere Academy, Claymont			X	X			9–12	513	513	10:1	18	20
The Cedars Academy, Bridgeville	X	X				6–8	9–12	40	25	6:1		25
St. Mark's High School, Wilmington			X	X			9–12	1,606	1,606	15:1	18	19
Salesianum School, Wilmington			X				9–12	1,040	1,040	12:1	17	21
Sanford School, Hockessin			X	X	PK–4	5–8	9–12	677	241	8:1	13	13
The Tatnall School, Wilmington			X	X	N–4	5–8	9–12	706	268	8:1	15	18
Tower Hill School, Wilmington			X	X	PK–4	5–8	9–12	743	216	7:1	17	21
Ursuline Academy, Wilmington			X	X	PK–6	7–8	9–12	638	224	5:1	16	16
District of Columbia												
The Field School, Washington			X	X		7–8	9–12	315	252	6:1	1	19
Georgetown Day School, Washington			X	X	PK–5	6–8	9–12	1,031	458	7:1	19	8
Georgetown Visitation Preparatory School, Washington				X			9–12	479	479	10:1	10	18
Gonzaga College High School, Washington			X				9–12	935	935	10:1	17	27
Maret School, Washington			X	X	K–4	5–8	9–12	600	292	6:1	15	19
St. Albans School, Washington	X		X		4–8		9–12	579	314	7:1	17	38
St. Anselm's Abbey School, Washington			X			6–8	9–12	242	138	5:1	16	14
St. John's College High School, Washington			X	X			9–12	1,062	1,062	13:1	12	39
Universal Ballet Academy, Washington	X		X	X		6–8	9–12	66	58	8:1		1
Washington International School, Washington			X	X	PK–5	6–8	9–12	894	254	7:1		10
Florida												
Academy of the Holy Names, Tampa			X	X	PK–4	5–8	9–12	868	328	15:1	14	21
Admiral Farragut Academy, St. Petersburg	X	X	X	X	P4–5	6–8	9–12	406	249	15:1	9	32
Allison Academy, North Miami Beach			X	X		6–8	9–12	113	89	15:1	3	18
American Academy, Plantation			X	X	1–6	7–8	9–12	429	208	12:1		21
American Heritage School, Plantation			X	X	PK–6		7–12	2,157	1,300	13:1	17	16
Argo Academy, Sarasota	X	X					12	38	38	4:1		12
The Benjamin School, North Palm Beach			X	X	PK–5	6–8	9–12	1,300	415	9:1	18	20
Berkeley Preparatory School, Tampa			X	X	PK–5	6–8	9–12	1,200	500	8:1	16	27
Bishop Verot High School, Fort Myers			X	X			9–12	740	740	18:1	8	18
The Bolles School, Jacksonville	X	X	X	X	PK–5	6–8	9–12	1,730	788	10:1	13	18

PRIVATE SCHOOLS AT-A-GLANCE	Boarding Boys	Boarding Girls	Day Boys	Day Girls	Lower	Middle	Upper	Total	Upper	Student/ Faculty Ratio	Advanced Placement Subject Areas	Sports
Bradenton Christian School, Bradenton			X	X	PK–6	7–8	9–12	592	190	14:1		14
Canterbury School, Fort Myers			X	X	PK–5	6–8	9–12	697	214	10:1	14	13
The Canterbury School of Florida, St. Petersburg			X	X	PK–4	5–8	9–12	430	105	4:1	13	27
Cardinal Newman High School, West Palm Beach			X	X			9–12	879	879	25:1	7	18
Carrollton School of the Sacred Heart, Miami				X	PK–3	4–6	7–12	710	380	9:1	7	14
Chaminade-Madonna College Preparatory, Hollywood			X	X			9–12	872	872	19:1	10	15
Christian Home and Bible School, Mount Dara			X	X	K–5	6–8	9–12	670	224	13:1	2	12
Clearwater Central Catholic High School, Clearwater			X	X			9–12	620	620	16:1	7	20
The Community School of Naples, Naples			X	X	PK–5	6–8	9–12	799	281	12:1	18	21
Donna Klein Jewish Academy, Boca Raton			X	X	K–4	5–8	9–12	704	84	5:1	10	14
Eckerd Youth Alternatives, Clearwater	X	X			5–5	6–8	9–12	91	67	10:1		6
Episcopal High School of Jacksonville, Jacksonville			X	X		6–8	9–12	908	603	10:1	16	22
Father Lopez High School, Daytona Beach			X	X			9–12	266	266	20:1	6	16
Florida Air Academy, Melbourne	X	X	X	X		6–8	9–12	385	295	11:1	6	56
Forest Lake Academy, Apopka	X	X	X	X			9–12	516	516	19:1	1	12
Fort Lauderdale Preparatory School, Fort Lauderdale			X	X	PK–6		7–12	220	120	9:1	7	
The Geneva School, Winter Park			X	X	K4–6	7–8	9–12	452	87	9.8:1	6	9
Glades Day School, Belle Glade			X	X	PK–6	7–8	9–12	617	281	15:1	2	14
Gulliver Preparatory School, Miami			X	X	PK–4	5–8	9–12	2,062	886	8:1	20	36
Jesuit High School of Tampa, Tampa			X				9–12	644	644	12:1	9	16
La Salle High School, Miami			X	X			9–12	743	743	15:1	10	22
Miami Country Day School, Miami			X	X	JK–5	6–8	9–12	1,000	402	9:1	18	24
Montverde Academy, Montverde	X	X	X	X	PK–5	6–8	9–PG	628	285	12:1	10	36
The North Broward Preparatory Upper School, Coconut Creek	X	X	X	X	PK–5	6–8	9–12	1,775	735	12:1	16	31
Northside Christian School, St. Petersburg			X	X	PS–5	6–8	9–12	877	221	11:1	5	15
Orangewood Christian School, Maitland			X	X	K4–5	6–8	9–12	701	210	11:1	8	21
Out-Of-Door-Academy, Sarasota			X	X	PK–6	7–8	9–12	601	196	9:1	13	18
Pensacola Catholic High School, Pensacola			X	X			9–12	599	599	18:1	4	
Pine Crest School, Fort Lauderdale			X	X	PK–5	6–8	9–12	1,692	775	9:1	18	23
Pope John Paul II High School, Boca Raton			X	X			9–12	582	582	28:1	6	19
Rabbi Alexander S. Gross Hebrew Academy, Miami Beach			X	X	N–5	6–8	9–12	590	197	4:1	8	4
Ransom Everglades School, Miami			X	X		6–8	9–12	1,035	591	14:1	22	22
Right Way Academy, Tallahassee	X	X	X	X								27
Saddlebrook Preparatory School, Wesley Chapel	X	X	X	X	3–5	6–8	9–12	99	76	11:1		2
Saint Andrew's School, Boca Raton	X	X	X	X	K–5	6–8	9–12	1,154	604	9:1	17	18
Saint Edward's School, Vero Beach			X	X	PK–5	6–8	9–12	877	307	17:1	15	16
St. Joseph Academy, St. Augustine			X	X			9–12	348	348	13:1	4	16
Saint Stephen's Episcopal School, Bradenton			X	X	PK–6	7–8	9–12	730	265	11:1	13	28
St. Thomas Aquinas High School, Fort Lauderdale			X	X			9–12	2,151	2,151	18:1	18	22
Shorecrest Preparatory School, Saint Petersburg			X	X	PK–4	5–8	9–12	993	273	12:1	22	14
Trinity Preparatory School, Winter Park			X	X		6–8	9–12	831	492	12:1	17	20
University School of Nova Southeastern University, Fort Lauderdale			X	X	PK–5	6–8	9–12	1,805	627	10:1	22	18
The Vanguard School, Lake Wales	X	X	X	X		5–8	9–PG	133	112	10:1		23
Westminster Christian School, Miami			X	X	PK–5	6–8	9–12	1,149	437	11:1	13	13
Windermere Preparatory School, Windermere			X	X	PK–4	5–8	9–12	732	81	17:1		20
Georgia												
Athens Academy, Athens			X	X	N–4	5–8	9–12	875	300	8:1	8	11
Atlanta International School, Atlanta			X	X	PK–5	6–8	9–12	937	279	5:1		12
Augusta Preparatory Day School, Martinez			X	X	PS–4	5–8	9–12	551	203	9:1	13	3
Benedictine Military School, Savannah			X				9–12	339	339	11:1	5	21
Ben Franklin Academy, Atlanta			X	X			9–12	130	130	3:1		4
Blessed Trinity High School, Roswell			X	X			9–12			12:1		17

	STUDENTS ACCEPTED				GRADES			STUDENT/FACULTY			STUDENT OFFERINGS (number)	
	Boarding		Day									
	Boys	Girls	Boys	Girls	Lower	Middle	Upper	Total	Upper	Student/ Faculty Ratio	Advanced Placement Subject Areas	Sports
Brandon Hall School, Atlanta	X		X	X		4–8	9–PG	101	75	3:1	5	5
Brenau Academy, Gainesville		X		X			9–PG	70	70	8:1		13
Brentwood School, Sandersville			X	X	PK–6	7–8	9–12	407	104	11:1	4	10
Brookstone School, Columbus			X	X	PK–4	5–8	9–12	836	287	10:1	13	12
Bulloch Academy, Statesboro			X	X	PK–5	6–8	9–12	482	122	16:1	6	17
Chatham Academy, Savannah			X	X	1–5	6–8	9–12	107	39	10:1		18
The Cottage School, Roswell			X	X		6–8	9–12	182	125	9:1		26
Darlington School, Rome	X	X	X	X	PK–5	6–8	9–PG	914	473	10:1	16	30
Deerfield-Windsor School, Albany			X	X	PK–5	6–8		767	263	18:1	5	12
Dominion Christian High School, Marietta			X	X			9–12	246	246	11:1	6	9
Eckerd Academy of the Blue Ridge, Suches	X	X	X	X		5–8	9–12			10:1		20
Excel Christian Academy, Cartersville			X	X	K–5	6–8	9–12	428	100	20:1	2	9
First Presbyterian Day School, Macon			X	X	PK–5	6–8	9–12	982	362	12:1	8	16
Flint River Academy, Woodbury			X	X		6–8	9–12	363	102	14:1	2	14
The Galloway School, Atlanta			X	X	PK–4	5–8	9–12	715	222	8:1	11	14
George Walton Academy, Monroe			X	X	K–5	6–8	9–12	998	355	10:1	10	20
Greater Atlanta Christian Schools, Norcross			X	X	P4–5	6–8	9–12	1,945	645	13:1	19	21
The Heritage School, Newnan			X	X	PK–4	5–8	9–12	404	130	5:1	13	26
Hidden Lake Academy, Dahlonega	X	X					7–PG	130	60	10:1		53
Holy Innocents' Episcopal School, Atlanta			X	X	PS–5	6–8	9–12	1,390	409	10:1	11	17
Horizons School, Atlanta	X	X	X	X	K–5	6–7	8–PG	100	60	10:1	2	1
John Hancock Academy, Sparta			X	X	K–5	6–8	9–12	106	46	8:1		11
King's Ridge Christian School, Alpharetta			X	X	K–5	6–8	9–12	555		8:1		16
La Grange Academy, La Grange			X	X	K–5	6–8	9–12	258	86	17:1	5	12
Landmark Christian School, Fairburn			X	X	K4–5	6–8	9–12	782	240	9:1	7	16
The Lovett School, Atlanta			X	X	K–5	6–8	9–12	1,560	605	8:1	21	50
Marist School, Atlanta			X	X			7–12	1,067	1,067	11:1	16	19
Memorial Day School, Savannah			X	X	PK–5	6–8	9–12	220	103	16:1	5	8
Monroe Academy, Forsyth			X	X	PK–5	6–8	9–12	185	79	15:1	3	12
North Cobb Christian School, Kennesaw			X	X	PK–5	6–8	9–12	970	294	6:1		20
Oak Mountain Academy, Carrollton			X	X	K4–5	6–8	9–12	272	78	6:1	5	10
Pace Academy, Atlanta			X	X	K–5	6–8	9–12	949	376	7:1	17	20
The Paideia School, Atlanta			X	X	PK–6	7–8	9–12	929	396	9:1	7	15
Piedmont Academy, Monticello			X	X	PK–5	6–8	9–12	391	117	12:1	5	16
Rabun Gap-Nacoochee School, Rabun Gap	X	X	X	X		6–8	9–12	354	267	8:1	14	37
Riverside Military Academy, Gainesville	X		X			7–8	9–12	358	300	10:1	8	48
St. Andrew's on the Marsh School, Savannah			X	X	PK–3	4–8	9–12	494	169	9:1	7	16
St. Francis School, Alpharetta			X	X	P3–5	6–8	9–12	852	297	14:1		16
St. Pius X Catholic High School, Atlanta			X	X			9–12	1,000	1,000	15:1	19	20
Saint Vincent's Academy, Savannah				X					364	13:1	5	13
Savannah Christian Preparatory School, Savannah			X	X	PK–5	6–8	9–12	1,519	478	14:1	8	13
The Savannah Country Day School, Savannah			X	X	PK–5	6–8	9–12	1,007	308	10:1	16	27
Stratford Academy, Macon			X	X	PK–5	6–8	9–12	899	300	13:1	16	10
Tallulah Falls School, Tallulah Falls	X	X	X	X		6–8	9–12	145	84	10:1	6	36
Trinity Christian School, Dublin			X	X	K4–5	6–8	9–12	500	163	12:1		14
Valwood School, Valdosta			X	X	PK–5	6–8	9–12	421	111	6:1	3	11
The Walker School, Marietta			X	X	PK–5	6–8	9–12	1,089	392	14:1		19
The Weber School, Sandy Springs			X	X			9–12	220	220	8:1	8	9
Wesleyan School, Norcross			X	X	K–4	5–8	9–12	1,069	416	7:1	9	18
The Westfield Schools, Perry			X	X	PK–4	5–8	9–12	610	201	14:1	6	16
The Westminster Schools, Atlanta			X	X	K–5	6–8	9–12	1,821	792	15:1	14	36
Westminster Schools of Augusta, Augusta			X	X	PK–5	6–8	9–12	502	139	9:1	11	9
Whitefield Academy, Mableton			X	X	PK–5	6–8	9–12	683	242	8:1	10	16
Woodward Academy, College Park			X	X	PK–6	7–8	9–12	2,919	1,071		22	20

PRIVATE SCHOOLS AT-A-GLANCE	STUDENTS ACCEPTED				GRADES			STUDENT/FACULTY			STUDENT OFFERINGS (number)	
	Boarding		Day									
	Boys	Girls	Boys	Girls	Lower	Middle	Upper	Total	Upper	Student/ Faculty Ratio	Advanced Placement Subject Areas	Sports
Hawaii												
Academy of the Pacific, Honolulu			X	X		6–8	9–12	111	99	8:1	2	18
Hanalani Schools, Mililani			X	X	PK–6		7–12	758	299	12:1	4	20
Hawaiian Mission Academy, Honolulu	X	X	X	X			9–12	128	128	12:1		2
Hawaii Baptist Academy, Honolulu			X	X	K–6	7–8	9–12	1,073	436	12:1	8	21
Hawai`i Preparatory Academy, Kamuela	X	X	X	X	K–5	6–8	9–12	590	349	8:1	14	25
Iolani School, Honolulu			X	X	K–6		7–12	1,842	1,299	12:1	17	27
La Pietra–Hawaii School for Girls, Honolulu				X		6–8	9–12	247	143	10:1	5	24
Lutheran High School of Hawaii, Honolulu			X	X			9–12	133	133	10:1	2	8
Mid-Pacific Institute, Honolulu			X	X	K–5	6–8	9–12	1,515	836	19:1	7	31
The Parker School, Kamuela			X	X	K–5	6–8	9–12	296	120	8:1	5	11
Punahou School, Honolulu			X	X	K–5	6–8	9–12	3,761	1,732	18:1	14	21
St. Andrew's Priory School, Honolulu				X	K–4	5–8	9–12	515	200	7:1	8	34
St. Anthony's Junior-Senior High School, Wailuku			X	X		7–8	9–12	304	218	10:1	4	25
Saint Francis School, Honolulu			X	X	K–6	7–8	9–12	389	281	20:1	7	22
Saint Joseph Junior-Senior High School, Hilo			X	X		7–8	9–12	193	143	12:1	5	11
Seabury Hall, Makawao			X	X		6–8	9–12	420	288	10:1	12	15
Idaho												
Bishop Kelly High School, Boise			X	X			9–12	665	665	17:1	9	19
Elk Mountain Academy, Clark Fork	X						9–12	21	21	8:1	3	
Gem State Adventist Academy, Caldwell	X	X	X	X			9–12	101	101	8:1	1	7
Greenleaf Academy, Greenleaf			X	X	K–6	7–8	9–12	239	90	16:1		12
Riverstone International School, Boise			X	X	K–5	6–8	9–12	310	105	5:1		22
Illinois												
Aurora Central High School, Aurora			X	X			9–12	483	483	16:1	10	29
Bishop McNamara High School, Kankakee			X	X			9–12	442	442	23:1	8	23
Boylan Central Catholic High School, Rockford			X	X			9–12	1,251	1,251	14:1	10	28
Brehm Preparatory School, Carbondale	X	X	X	X		6–8	9–PG	83	77	8:1		10
Carmel High School, Mundelein			X	X			9–12	1,440	1,440	16:1		17
The Chicago Academy for the Arts, Chicago			X	X			9–12	164	164	16:1	7	
Elgin Academy, Elgin			X	X	PS–4	5–8	9–12	614	118	7:1	14	13
Fox River Country Day School, Elgin	X	X	X	X	PK–5	6–8		193		12:1		25
Fox Valley Lutheran Academy, Elgin			X	X			9–12	21	21	3:1		3
Francis W. Parker School, Chicago			X	X	PK–5	6–8	9–12	913	316	5:1		26
Gordon Technical High School, Chicago			X	X			9–12	585	585	15:1	8	10
The Governor French Academy, Belleville	X	X	X	X	1–8		9–12	216	66	6:1	5	24
Guerin College Preparatory High School, River Grove			X	X			9–12	660	660	16:1	6	16
Hales Franciscan High School, Chicago			X				9–12	185	185	18:1		14
Holy Trinity High School, Chicago			X	X			9–12	420	420	15:1		10
Illiana Christian High School, Lansing			X	X			9–12	675	675	18:1	6	13
Immaculate Conception School, Elmhurst			X	X			9–12	243	243	11:1	4	15
Josephinum High School, Chicago				X		6–8	9–12	134	103	10:1	2	3
Keith Country Day School, Rockford			X	X	PK–5	6–8	9–12	358	113	13:1	8	7
Lake Forest Academy, Lake Forest	X	X	X	X			9–12	390	390	6:1	17	26
Loyola Academy, Wilmette			X	X			9–12	2,000	2,000	17:1	22	55
Luther High School North, Chicago			X	X			9–12	255	255	16:1	3	13
Luther High School South, Chicago			X	X		6–8	9–12		214	11:1	4	12
Marian Central Catholic High School, Woodstock			X	X			9–12	782	782	15:1	5	16
Marist High School, Chicago			X	X			9–12	1,810	1,810	19:1	16	25
Marmion Academy, Aurora			X				9–12	520	520	11:1	8	21
Marquette High School, Ottawa			X	X			9–12	239	239	20:1		19
Mooseheart High School, Mooseheart	X	X	X	X	K–5	6–8	9–12	215	110	6:1		6
Morgan Park Academy, Chicago			X	X	PK–5	6–8	9–12	520	181	5:1	11	18
Mother McAuley High School, Chicago				X			9–12	1,469	1,469	15:1	10	15

	STUDENTS ACCEPTED				GRADES			STUDENT/FACULTY			STUDENT OFFERINGS (number)	
	Boarding		Day									
	Boys	Girls	Boys	Girls	Lower	Middle	Upper	Total	Upper	Student/ Faculty Ratio	Advanced Placement Subject Areas	Sports
Mount Carmel High School, Chicago			X				9–12	895	895	18:1	11	17
Nazareth Academy, LaGrange Park			X	X			9–12	770	770	17:1	15	15
North Shore Country Day School, Winnetka			X	X	PK–5	6–8	9–12	487	190	8:1	10	14
Notre Dame High School for Boys, Niles			X							14:1	6	28
Queen of Peace High School, Burbank				X						16:1		
Resurrection High School, Chicago				X			9–12	754	754	14:1	8	14
Roycemore School, Evanston			X	X	PK–4	5–8	9–12	254	83	9:1	12	5
Sacred Heart/Griffin High School, Springfield			X	X			9–12	858	858	17:1		
Saint Anthony High School, Effingham			X	X			9–12	226	226	10:1	3	11
Saint Edward Central Catholic High School, Elgin			X	X			9–12	468	468	12:1	7	15
Saint Joseph High School, Westchester			X	X			9–12	815	815	17:1	6	15
Saint Patrick High School, Chicago			X				9–12	964	964	25:1	4	14
St. Scholastica Academy, Chicago				X			9–12	250	250	9:1	5	11
Saint Viator High School, Arlington Heights			X	X			9–12	1,089	1,089	12:1		19
Schlarman High School, Danville			X	X			9–12	193	193	17:1	3	19
Timothy Christian High School, Elmhurst			X	X	K–6	7–8	9–12	1,036	398	13:1	7	12
Trinity High School, River Forest				X			9–12	470	470	12:1		11
University of Chicago Laboratory Schools, Chicago			X	X	N–4	5–8	9–12	1,746	498	10:1	15	14
Wheaton Academy, West Chicago			X	X			9–12	630	630	14:1	6	33
The Willows Academy, Des Plaines				X		6–8	9–12	229	154	10:1	5	7
Woodlands Academy of the Sacred Heart, Lake Forest		X	X				9–12	166	166	9:1	6	4
Indiana												
Bishop Luers High School, Fort Wayne			X	X			9–12	548	548	15:1	4	21
Canterbury High School, Fort Wayne			X	X	K–4	5–8	9–12	754	277	7:1	15	15
Cathedral High School, Indianapolis			X	X			9–12	1,286	1,286	13:1	18	31
The Culver Academies, Culver	X	X	X	X			9–PG	792	792	9:1	21	73
Evansville Day School, Evansville			X	X	PK–4	5–8	9–12	314	66	10:1	9	11
Howe Military School, Howe	X	X	X	X	5–8		9–12	141	97	9:1	4	15
Lakeland Christian Academy, Winona Lake			X	X		7–8	9–12	159	105	15:1		8
La Lumiere School, La Porte	X	X	X	X			9–PG	165	165	7:1	6	49
Lutheran High School, Indianapolis			X	X			9–12	309	309	16:1	5	14
Marian High School, Mishawaka			X	X			9–12	764	764	20:1	6	30
Marquette High School, Michigan City			X	X					211	10:1	5	13
New Horizon Youth Ministries, Marion	X	X	X	X		7–8	9–12	26	26	4:1		39
Oldenburg Academy, Oldenburg			X	X			9–12	208	208	12:1	9	4
Park Tudor School, Indianapolis			X	X	PK–5	6–8	9–12	985	423	9:1	16	17
Iowa												
Columbus High School, Waterloo			X	X			9–12	304	304	15:1	5	9
Dowling Catholic High School, West Des Moines			X	X			9–12	1,226	1,226	14:1	9	21
Maharishi School of the Age, Fairfield	X	X	X	X	PS–6	7–9	10–12	231	84	8:1		32
Rivermont Collegiate, Bettendorf			X	X	PS–5	6–8	9–12	174	32	4:1	8	12
Scattergood Friends School, West Branch	X	X	X	X			9–PG	54	54	2:1		29
Kansas												
Bishop Ward High School, Kansas City			X	X			9–12	345	345	18:1	4	15
Hayden High School, Topeka			X	X			9–12	517	517	15:1	6	20
Hyman Brand Hebrew Academy of Greater Kansas City, Overland Park			X	X	K–5	6–8	9–12	242	72	5:1	5	6
Independent School, Wichita			X	X	PK–5	6–8	9–12	772	251	10:1	9	16
Kapaun Mt. Carmel Catholic High School, Wichita			X	X			9–12	884	884	15:1	7	18
Maur Hill-Mount Academy, Atchison	X	X	X	X			9–12	238	238	8:1		35
St. John's Military School, Salina	X					7–8	9–12	122	108	10:1		30
Saint Thomas Aquinas High School, Overland Park			X	X			9–12	1,184	1,184	15:1		18

PRIVATE SCHOOLS AT-A-GLANCE

| | STUDENTS ACCEPTED | | | | GRADES | | | STUDENT/FACULTY | | | STUDENT OFFERINGS (number) | |
| | Boarding | | Day | | | | | | | | | |
PRIVATE SCHOOLS AT-A-GLANCE	Boys	Girls	Boys	Girls	Lower	Middle	Upper	Total	Upper	Student/Faculty Ratio	Advanced Placement Subject Areas	Sports
Trinity Academy, Wichita			X	X			9–12	279	279	12:1		15
Wichita Collegiate School, Wichita			X	X	PS–4	5–8	9–12	996	243	10:1	17	13
Kentucky												
Assumption High School, Louisville				X			9–12	1,004	1,004	10:1	19	21
Beth Haven Christian School, Louisville			X	X	K4–5	6–8	9–12	361	104	13:1	4	7
Calvary Christian Academy, Covington			X	X	K4–6	7–8	9–12	636	197	14:1	7	15
Community Christian Academy, Independence			X	X	PS–6	7–8	9–12	203	47	20:1		4
Kentucky Country Day School, Louisville			X	X	JK–4	5–8	9–12	902	269	7:1	13	19
Landmark Christian Academy, Louisville			X	X	K4–6	7–8	9–12	164	33	10:1	3	4
Lexington Catholic High School, Lexington			X	X			9–12	880	880	14:1	13	23
Louisville Collegiate School, Louisville			X	X	K–5	6–8	9–12	630	195	8:1	18	16
Oneida Baptist Institute, Oneida	X	X	X	X		6–8	9–12	350	250	11:1	5	10
Sacred Heart Academy, Louisville				X						15:1	13	11
Saint Xavier High School, Louisville			X				9–12	1,402	1,402	12:1	18	38
Sayre School, Lexington			X	X	PK–5	6–8	9–12	644	239	10:1	12	13
Shedd Academy, Mayfield	X	X	X	X	1–5	6–8	9–12	16	3	3:1		22
Trinity High School, Louisville			X				9–12	1,355	1,355	13:1	17	40
Louisiana												
Academy of the Sacred Heart, Grand Coteau		X		X	PK–4	5–8	9–12	415	121	8:1	5	15
Academy of the Sacred Heart, New Orleans				X	PK–4	5–8	9–12	783	246	16:1	9	21
Archbishop Rummel High School, Metairie			X			8	9–12	1,200	1,020	10:1	5	11
Archbishop Shaw High School, Marrero			X			8–9	10–12	655	415	24:1	5	14
Episcopal High School, Baton Rouge			X	X	K–5	6–8	9–12	1,035	390	14:1	13	18
The Episcopal School of Acadiana, Cade			X	X	P3–5	6–8	9–12	497	226	6:1	14	15
Hanson Memorial High School, Franklin			X	X						13:1		11
Holy Savior Menard Catholic High School, Alexandria			X	X		7–8	9–12	537	355	25:1	3	13
Isidore Newman School, New Orleans			X	X	PK–5	6–8	9–12	967	362	18:1	15	15
Jesuit High School of New Orleans, New Orleans			X			8	9–12	1,364	1,113	12:1	12	22
Metairie Park Country Day School, Metairie			X	X	K–5	6–8	9–12	615	203	7:1	12	12
Notre Dame High School, Crowley			X	X			9–12	500	500	25:1		14
Ridgewood Preparatory School, Metairie			X	X	PK–4	5–8	9–12	281	156	25:1		7
St. Joseph's Academy, Baton Rouge				X			9–12	834	834	13:1	7	15
St. Martin's Episcopal School, Metairie			X	X	PK–5	6–8	9–12	634	235	9:1	10	13
St. Michael High School, Baton Rouge			X	X			9–12	778	778	12:1		23
Saint Thomas More Catholic High School, Lafayette			X	X			9–12	1,085	1,085	21:1	8	15
Teurlings Catholic High School, Lafayette			X	X			9–12	674	674	22:1	2	23
University Christian Preparatory School, Shreveport			X	X	K–5	6–8	9–12	150	86	16:1		24
Vandebilt Catholic High School, Houma			X	X			8–12	898	894	25:1		8
Xavier University Preparatory School, New Orleans				X		7–8	9–12	337	261	11:1		9
Maine												
Bangor Christian School, Bangor			X	X	K4–5	6–8	9–12	315	112	10:1	1	11
Berwick Academy, South Berwick			X	X	K–4	5–8	9–12	602	261	12:1	10	10
Bridgton Academy, North Bridgton	X		X				PG	180	180	10:1		34
Carrabassett Valley Academy, Carrabassett Valley	X	X	X	X	8–9		10–13	126	97	6:1		37
Catherine McAuley High School, Portland				X			9–12	252	252	9:1	5	22
Cheverus High School, Portland			X	X			9–12	541	541	12:1	9	24
Community School, Camden	X	X	X	X					8	1:1		
Deck House School, Edgecomb	X						9–12	12	12	2:1		
Elan School, Poland	X	X				7–8	9–12	82	82	7:1		46
Foxcroft Academy, Dover-Foxcroft	X	X	X	X			9–12	439	439	16:1	7	20
Fryeburg Academy, Fryeburg	X	X	X	X			9–PG	691	691	10:1	13	63
George Stevens Academy, Blue Hill	X	X	X	X			9–12	317	317	10:1	7	41
Gould Academy, Bethel	X	X	X	X			9–PG	244	244	6:1	5	12

	STUDENTS ACCEPTED				GRADES			STUDENT/FACULTY			STUDENT OFFERINGS (number)	
	Boarding		Day									
	Boys	Girls	Boys	Girls	Lower	Middle	Upper	Total	Upper	Student/ Faculty Ratio	Advanced Placement Subject Areas	Sports
Hebron Academy, Hebron	X	X	X	X		6–8	9–PG	260	219	7:1	9	24
Hyde School, Bath	X	X	X	X			9–12	200	200	7:1		27
John Bapst Memorial High School, Bangor			X	X			9–12	473	473	13:1	13	20
Kents Hill School, Kents Hill	X	X	X	X			9–PG	226	226	5:1	11	35
Lee Academy, Lee	X	X	X	X			9–PG	263	263	10:1	5	63
Maine Central Institute, Pittsfield	X	X	X	X			9–PG	485	485	15:1	4	38
North Yarmouth Academy, Yarmouth			X	X		6–8	9–12	330	197	8:1	14	17
Saint Dominic Regional High School, Auburn			X	X			9–12	276	276	12:1	13	13
Washington Academy, East Machias	X	X	X	X			9–12	380	380	14:1	7	22
Waynflete School, Portland			X	X	PK–5	6–8	9–12	566	248	5:1		27
Maryland												
Academy of the Holy Cross, Kensington				X			9–12	626	626	14:1	12	19
Archbishop Curley High School, Baltimore			X				9–12	609	609	14:1	6	20
Archbishop Spalding High School, Severn			X	X			9–12	1,153	1,153	15:1	14	40
The Baltimore Actors' Theatre Conservatory, Baltimore			X	X				12		3:1	5	
The Barrie School, Silver Spring			X	X	N–5	6–8	9–12	395	111	7:1	8	38
The Bryn Mawr School for Girls, Baltimore			X	X	K–5	6–8	9–12	795	315	7:1	18	41
Calvert Hall College High School, Baltimore			X				9–12	1,230	1,230	12:1	17	26
The Calverton School, Huntingtown			X	X	PK–5	6–8	9–12	408	124	11:1	10	7
The Catholic High School of Baltimore, Baltimore				X			9–12	287	287	12:1	5	16
Chelsea School, Silver Spring			X	X		5–8	9–12	80	67	8:1		5
Connelly School of the Holy Child, Potomac				X		6–8	9–12	371	272	16:1	9	51
DeMatha Catholic High School, Hyattsville			X				9–12	1,015	1,015	12:1	16	20
Elizabeth Seton High School, Bladensburg				X			9–12	600	600	13:1	12	40
Friends School of Baltimore, Baltimore			X	X	PK–5	6–8	9–12	999	382	11:1	14	16
Garrison Forest School, Owings Mills		X	X	X	N–5	6–8	9–12	696	263	8:1	13	22
Georgetown Preparatory School, North Bethesda	X		X				9–12	457	457	8:1	16	53
Gilman School, Baltimore			X		P1–5	6–8	9–12	988	442	8:1	16	29
Glenelg Country School, Ellicott City			X	X	PK–5	6–8	9–12	807	265	6:1	19	26
Griggs University and International Academy, Silver Spring			X	X	PK–6	7–8	9–12	1,310	837			
Gunston Day School, Centreville			X	X			9–12	141	141	6:1	11	20
The Heights School, Potomac			X		3–5	6–8	9–12	460	193	7:1	13	18
The Holton-Arms School, Bethesda				X	3–6	7–8	9–12	655	333	6:1	13	19
The Key School, Annapolis			X	X	PK–4	5–8	9–12	716	205	8:1	14	30
Landon School, Bethesda			X		3–5	6–8	9–12	678	338	6:1	15	29
Loyola-Blakefield, Baltimore			X			6–8	9–12	1,003	765	10:1	13	27
Maryvale Preparatory School, Brooklandville				X		6–8	9–12	389	294	9:1	9	13
McDonogh School, Owings Mills	X	X	X	X	K–4	5–8	9–12	1,283	558	9:1	16	25
Mount De Sales Academy, Catonsville				X			9–12	464	464	12:1		11
New Dominion School, Oldtown	X							47		6:1		29
The Newport School, Silver Spring			X	X	N–4	5–8	9–12	124	19	4:1		6
The Nora School, Silver Spring			X	X			9–12	60	60	5:1		24
Notre Dame Preparatory School, Towson				X		6–8	9–12	762	586	9:1	19	23
Oldfields School, Glencoe		X		X			8–12	164	164	6:1	12	46
Our Lady of Good Counsel High School, Olney			X	X			9–12	1,200	1,200	14:1	11	21
Queen Anne School, Upper Marlboro			X	X		6–8	9–12	206	124	7:1	7	18
Roland Park Country School, Baltimore				X	K–5	6–8	9–12	701	287	7:1	19	21
St. Andrew's Episcopal School, Potomac			X	X		6–8	9–12	455	324	7:1	9	16
Saint James School, St. James	X	X	X	X		8	9–12	235	211	7:1	13	23
St. John's Catholic Prep, Frederick			X	X			9–12	275	275	10:1		22
Saint Maria Goretti High School, Hagerstown			X	X			9–12	225	225	15:1	6	6
Saint Mary's High School, Annapolis			X	X			9–12	555	555	17:1	4	16
St. Mary's Ryken High School, Leonardtown			X	X			9–12	712	712	13:1	17	16

PRIVATE SCHOOLS AT-A-GLANCE

| | STUDENTS ACCEPTED | | | | GRADES | | | STUDENT/FACULTY | | | STUDENT OFFERINGS (number) | |
| | Boarding | | Day | | | | | | | | | |
	Boys	Girls	Boys	Girls	Lower	Middle	Upper	Total	Upper	Student/ Faculty Ratio	Advanced Placement Subject Areas	Sports
St. Paul's School, Brooklandville			X	X	P1–4	5–8	9–12	853	331	9:1	14	27
St. Paul's School for Girls, Brooklandville				X		5–8	9–12	461	271	7:1	14	23
Saints Peter and Paul High School, Easton			X	X			9–12	214	214	8:1	7	11
St. Timothy's School, Stevenson		X		X			9–12	151	151	5:1		23
St. Vincent Pallotti High School, Laurel			X	X			9–12	512	512	18:1		19
Sandy Spring Friends School, Sandy Spring	X	X	X	X	PK–5	6–8	9–12	561	240	8:1	10	20
Severn School, Severna Park			X	X		6–8	9–12	586	387	13:1	11	23
Stone Ridge School of the Sacred Heart, Bethesda			X	X	JK–4	5–8	9–12	675	305	9:1	16	25
Washington Waldorf School, Bethesda			X	X	PS–4	5–8	9–12	291	68	7:1	1	5
West Nottingham Academy, Colora	X	X	X	X			9–PG	123	123	6:1	5	19
Worcester Preparatory School, Berlin			X	X	PK–5	6–8	9–12	615	206	10:1	9	11
Massachusetts												
The Academy at Charlemont, Charlemont	X	X	X	X		7–8	9–PG	108	77	7:1		15
Academy at Swift River, Cummington	X	X					9–12	100	100	8:1		62
Academy of Notre Dame, Tyngsboro			X	X	K–5	6–8	9–12	694	195	7:1		17
The Arlington School, Belmont			X	X		8–8	9–12					
Bancroft School, Worcester			X	X	K–5	6–8	9–12	557	226	8:1	14	14
Beaver Country Day School, Chestnut Hill			X	X		6–8	9–12	419	299	8:1		27
Belmont Hill School, Belmont	X		X			7–9	10–12	419	223	8:1	10	22
The Bement School, Deerfield	X	X	X	X	K–5		6–9	246	111	7:1		35
Berkshire School, Sheffield	X	X	X	X			9–PG	371	371	6:1	13	31
Bishop Feehan High School, Attleboro			X	X			9–12	986	986	13:1	10	20
Bishop Stang High School, North Dartmouth			X	X			9–12	824	824	14:1	7	37
Boston College High School, Boston			X			7–8	9–12	1,543	1,305	13:1	19	20
Boston University Academy, Boston			X	X			9–12	148	148	8:1		9
Brooks School, North Andover	X	X	X	X			9–12	366	366	5:1	18	18
Buckingham Browne & Nichols School, Cambridge			X	X	PK–6	7–8	9–12	968	473	7:1	19	26
Buxton School, Williamstown	X	X	X	X			9–12	93	93	5:1		25
The Cambridge School of Weston, Weston	X	X	X	X			9–PG	333	333	7:1	10	49
Chapel Hill–Chauncy Hall School, Waltham	X	X	X	X			9–12	174	174	6:1	2	23
Commonwealth School, Boston			X	X			9–12	150	150	5:1	13	16
Concord Academy, Concord	X	X	X	X			9–12	364	364	6:1		34
Cotting School, Lexington			X	X				119	62	3:1		8
Cushing Academy, Ashburnham	X	X	X	X			9–PG	441	441	8:1	15	37
Dana Hall School, Wellesley		X		X		6–8	9–12	485	349	12:1	14	34
Deerfield Academy, Deerfield	X	X	X	X			9–PG	599	599	5:1	19	40
Doctor Franklin Perkins School, Lancaster	X	X	X	X						4:1		27
Eaglebrook School, Deerfield	X		X			6–9		282	258	4:1		67
Eagle Hill School, Hardwick	X	X	X	X		8	9–12	140	130	4:1		36
Falmouth Academy, Falmouth			X	X		7–8	9–12	225	145	4:1	4	3
Fay School, Southborough	X	X	X	X	1–5	6–9		380	217	6:1		36
The Fessenden School, West Newton	X		X		K–4	5–6	7–9	482	206	7:1		24
Gann Academy (The New Jewish High School of Greater Boston), Waltham			X	X			9–12	309	309	6:1		13
The Governor's Academy (formerly Governor Dummer Academy), Byfield	X	X	X	X			9–12	376	376	5:1	14	21
Groton School, Groton	X	X	X	X		8	9–12	352	317	7:1	13	34
Hillside School, Marlborough	X		X		5–6	7–9		139	106	6:1		46
Holyoke Catholic High School, Granby			X	X			9–12	305	305	10:1	4	16
The John Dewey Academy, Great Barrington	X	X					10–PG	30	30	3:1		
The Judge Rotenberg Educational Center, Canton	X	X						130	130			1
Landmark School, Prides Crossing	X	X	X	X	1–5	6–7	8–12	454	310	3:1		13
Lawrence Academy, Groton	X	X	X	X			9–12	396	396	8:1	11	26
Lexington Christian Academy, Lexington			X	X		6–8	9–12	345	236	11:1	6	26

| | STUDENTS ACCEPTED | | | | GRADES | | | STUDENT/FACULTY | | | STUDENT OFFERINGS (number) | |
| | Boarding | | Day | | | | | | | | | |
	Boys	Girls	Boys	Girls	Lower	Middle	Upper	Total	Upper	Student/ Faculty Ratio	Advanced Placement Subject Areas	Sports
Linden Hill School, Northfield	X		X					24	7	3:1		36
The MacDuffie School, Springfield	X	X	X	X		6–8	9–12	232	186	7:1	10	27
Matignon High School, Cambridge			X	X			9–12	302	302	15:1	6	21
Middlesex School, Concord	X	X	X	X			9–12	346	346	5:1	17	22
Miss Hall's School, Pittsfield		X		X			9–12	195	195	5:1	11	30
Montrose School, Medfield				X		6–8	9–12	140	75	10:1	2	5
The Newman School, Boston			X	X			9–PG	230	230	14:1	6	17
Newton Country Day School of the Sacred Heart, Newton				X		5–8	9–12	394	230	7:1	19	29
Noble and Greenough School, Dedham	X	X	X	X		7–8	9–12	571	458	7:1	16	18
Northfield Mount Hermon School, Mount Hermon	X	X	X	X			9–PG	635	635	7:1	15	27
Notre Dame Academy, Hingham				X			9–12	578	578	10:1	13	24
Notre Dame Academy, Worcester				X			9–12	302	302	11:1	12	23
The Penikese Island School, Woods Hole	X						8–12	9	9	2:1		26
Phillips Academy (Andover), Andover	X	X	X	X			9–PG	1,090	1,090	5:1	14	48
The Pingree School, South Hamilton			X	X			9–12	332	332	7:1	10	32
Pioneer Valley Christian School, Springfield			X	X	PS–5	6–8	9–12	319	130	7:1	2	12
Presentation of Mary Academy, Methuen				X			9–12	300	300	15:1		14
The Rivers School, Weston			X	X		6–8	9–12	433	327	8:1	15	18
Riverview School, East Sandwich	X	X	X	X		6–8	9–12	95	85	8:1		18
The Roxbury Latin School, West Roxbury			X				7–12	288	288	8:1	11	10
St. John's Preparatory School, Danvers			X				9–12	1,200	1,200	12:1	16	47
Saint Mark's School, Southborough	X	X	X	X			9–12	356	356	5:1	14	24
St. Sebastian's School, Needham			X			7–8	9–12	354	257	7:1	17	18
Sparhawk School, Salisbury			X	X	K–5	6–8	9–12	159	57	4:1		6
The Sudbury Valley School, Framingham			X	X				180		16:1		
Tabor Academy, Marion	X	X	X	X			9–12	500	500	6:1	14	21
Trinity Catholic High School, Newton			X	X					253	13:1	5	19
Ursuline Academy, Dedham				X		7–8	9–12	400	181	11:1	6	14
Valley View School, North Brookfield	X					5–8	9–12	56	30	6:1		42
The Waldorf High School of Massachusetts Bay, Belmont			X	X			9–12	59	59	7:1		3
Walnut Hill School, Natick	X	X	X	X			9–12	300	300	6:1	6	6
Waring School, Beverly			X	X		6–8	9–12	150	99	8:1	5	11
Wilbraham & Monson Academy, Wilbraham	X	X	X	X		6–8	9–PG	360	301	7:1	18	44
The Williston Northampton School, Easthampton	X	X	X	X		7–8	9–PG	542	455	7:1	14	36
Willow Hill School, Sudbury			X	X		6–8	9–12	60	35	4:1		24
The Winchendon School, Winchendon	X	X	X	X			8–PG	240	240	8:1	5	46
The Winsor School, Boston				X		5–8	9–12	433	244	7:1	7	13
The Woodward School, Quincy				X		6–8	9–12	146	93	8:1	5	5
Worcester Academy, Worcester	X	X	X	X		6–8	9–PG	655	503	7:1	14	22
Xaverian Brothers High School, Westwood			X				9–12	974	974	22:1	12	28
Michigan												
Academy of the Sacred Heart, Bloomfield Hills			X	X	N–4	5–8	9–12	601	156	7:1	4	11
Brother Rice High School, Bloomfield Hills			X				9–12	715	715	13:1	18	25
Cardinal Mooney Catholic College Preparatory High School, Marine City			X	X			9–12	195	195	10:1	5	11
Cranbrook Schools, Bloomfield Hills	X	X	X	X	PK–5	6–8	9–12	1,620	774	8:1	16	50
Detroit Country Day School, Beverly Hills	X	X	X	X	PK–5	6–8	9–12	1,623	677	8:1	17	29
Divine Child High School, Dearborn			X	X			9–12	903	903	14:1	6	11
Gabriel Richard High School, Riverview			X	X			9–12	463	463	15:1	9	16
Greenhills School, Ann Arbor			X	X		6–8	9–12	528	323	7:1	10	15
Heritage Christian Academy, North Branch			X	X	PK–6	7–8	9–12	92	6	6:1		6
Interlochen Arts Academy, Interlochen	X	X	X	X			9–PG	455	455	6:1	3	44
Ladywood High School, Livonia				X			9–12	447	447	14:1	10	23
Lutheran High School Northwest, Rochester Hills			X	X			9–12	302	302	16:1	4	18

PRIVATE SCHOOLS AT-A-GLANCE	Boarding Boys	Boarding Girls	Day Boys	Day Girls	Lower	Middle	Upper	Total	Upper	Student/ Faculty Ratio	Advanced Placement Subject Areas	Sports
Marian High School, Bloomfield Hills				X			9–12	559	559	14:1	12	15
Mercy High School, Farmington Hills				X						14:1	5	12
Montcalm School, Albion	X	X				6–8	9–12	58	58	10:1		58
Powers Catholic High School, Flint			X	X			9–12	691	691	16:1	8	29
The Roeper School, Bloomfield Hills			X	X	PK–5	6–8	9–12	616	200	10:1	14	11
St. Mary's Preparatory School, Orchard Lake	X		X				9–12	540	540	10:1	8	39
Southfield Christian High School, Southfield			X	X	K–5	6–8	9–12	572	239	20:1	6	18
University Liggett School, Grosse Pointe Woods			X	X	PK–5	6–8	9–12	509	209	8:1	14	16
University of Detroit Jesuit High School and Academy, Detroit			X			7–8	9–12	809	704	15:1	14	18
Valley Lutheran High School, Saginaw			X	X			9–12	365	365	17:1	2	6
The Valley School, Flint			X	X	PK–4	5–8	9–12			12:1	2	4
West Catholic High School, Grand Rapids			X	X			9–12	638	638	16:1	7	25
Minnesota												
Ambassador Preparatory (formerly International School of Minnesota), St. Paul	X	X	X	X		6–9		40	40	5:1		11
Benilde–St. Margaret's School, St. Louis Park			X	X		7–8	9–12	1,154	873	12:1	12	25
The Blake School, Hopkins			X	X	PK–5	6–8	9–12	1,390	512	8:1	14	15
Breck School, Minneapolis			X	X	PK–4	5–8	9–12	1,213	421	7:1	9	19
Convent of the Visitation School, Mendota Heights			X	X	PK–5	6–8	9–12	596	324	10:1	11	18
Cotter Schools, Winona	X	X	X	X		7–8	9–12	454	349	16:1	17	18
Cretin-Derham Hall, Saint Paul			X	X			9–12	1,319	1,319	15:1	7	25
The International School of Minnesota, Eden Prairie			X	X	PS–5	6–8	9–12	550	95	20:1	13	9
Lutheran High School, Bloomington			X	X		7–8	9–12	123	106	15:1	5	7
Lutheran High School in Mayer, Mayer			X	X			9–12	247	247	14:1	2	15
Marshall School, Duluth			X	X		5–8	9–12	453	288	11:1	10	18
Mounds Park Academy, St. Paul			X	X	PK–4	5–8	9–12	653	255	9:1	4	16
St. Croix Lutheran High School, West St. Paul	X	X	X	X			9–12	377	377	15:1	7	16
Saint John's Preparatory School, Collegeville	X	X	X	X		7–8	9–PG	341	263	11:1	6	50
St. Paul Academy and Summit School, St. Paul			X	X	K–5	6–8	9–12	866	358	7:1		19
Saint Thomas Academy, Mendota Heights			X			7–8	9–12	690	526	10:1	10	28
Shattuck-St. Mary's School, Faribault	X	X	X	X		6–8	9–12	417	360	7:1	11	24
Mississippi												
Bass Memorial Academy, Lumberton	X	X	X	X					99	12:1		8
Brookhaven Academy, Brookhaven			X	X			7–12	481	227	20:1		11
Chamberlain-Hunt Academy, Port Gibson	X		X	X		7–8	9–12	133	92	5:1	3	45
The Education Center, Jackson			X	X	1–6	7–8	9–12	166	124	10:1	1	
Jackson Academy, Jackson			X	X	PK–6	7–9	10–12	1,324	289	15:1	10	13
Jackson Preparatory School, Jackson			X	X		6–9	10–12	800	360	11:1	9	15
Madison-Ridgeland Academy, Madison			X	X	K–5	6–8	9–12	953	244	13:1	13	13
New Summit School, Jackson			X	X	K–5	6–8	9–12	94	36	10:1		11
Parklane Academy, McComb			X	X	PK–3	4–6	7–12	957	422	16:1	4	11
St. Andrew's Episcopal School, Ridgeland			X	X	PK–4	5–8	9–12	1,206	337	9:1	19	20
St. Stanislaus College, Bay St. Louis	X		X			6–8	9–12	444	310	12:1	6	10
Vicksburg Catholic School, Vicksburg			X	X	PK–6	7–8	9–12	582	170	10:1	3	15
Washington County Day School, Greenville			X	X	PK–5	6–8	9–12	753	256	20:1		11
Missouri												
Chaminade College Preparatory School, St. Louis	X		X			6–8	9–12	890	570	11:1	18	17
Crossroads College Preparatory School, St. Louis			X	X		7–8	9–12	219	139	8:1	6	22
De Smet Jesuit High School, Creve Coeur			X				9–12			14:1	7	30
Greenwood Laboratory School, Springfield			X	X	K–6	7–8	9–12	343	98	28:1		8
John Burroughs School, St. Louis			X	X					602	8:1	7	29
Kansas City Academy of Learning, Kansas City			X	X		6–8	9–12	66	44	6:1		

| | STUDENTS ACCEPTED | | | | GRADES | | | STUDENT/FACULTY | | | STUDENT OFFERINGS (number) | |
| | Boarding | | Day | | | | | | | | | |
	Boys	Girls	Boys	Girls	Lower	Middle	Upper	Total	Upper	Student/ Faculty Ratio	Advanced Placement Subject Areas	Sports
Logos School, St. Louis			X	X		7–8	9–12	156	135	6:1		4
Lutheran High School North, St. Louis			X	X			9–12	378	378	13:1	5	12
Lutheran High School South, St. Louis			X	X			9–12	544	544	13:1	6	18
Mary Institute and St. Louis Country Day School (MICDS), St. Louis			X	X	JK–4	5–8	9–12	1,225	583	8:1	18	29
Nerinx Hall, Webster Groves				X			9–12	618	618	11:1		13
New Covenant Academy, Springfield			X	X	PK–6	7–8	9–12	432	132	10:1		3
Notre Dame High School, St. Louis				X			9–12	400	400	10:1	6	11
The Pembroke Hill School, Kansas City			X	X	PS–5	6–8	9–12	1,188	436	11:1	15	18
Saint Elizabeth Academy, St. Louis				X					208	10:1		20
Saint Louis Priory School, St. Louis			X			7–8	9–12	394	250	9:1	14	17
Saint Paul Lutheran High School, Concordia	X	X	X	X			9–12	179	179	12:1		19
Saint Pius X High School, Kansas City	X	X						422	422	18:1	3	14
Saint Teresa's Academy, Kansas City				X			9–12	529	529	12:1		24
Springfield Catholic High School, Springfield			X	X			9–12	356	356	16:1	10	11
Thomas Jefferson School, St. Louis	X	X	X	X		7–8	9–PG	82	63	7:1	12	11
Valle Catholic High School, Ste. Genevieve			X	X			9–12	132	132	8:1		13
Vianney High School, St. Louis			X				9–12	586	586	13:1	2	29
Villa Duchesne/Oak Hill School, St. Louis			X	X	JK–6		7–12	772	444	9:1	9	13
Visitation Academy of St. Louis County, St. Louis			X	X	PK–6		7–12	614	410	9:1	12	12
Wentworth Military Academy and Junior College, Lexington	X	X	X	X			9–12	140	140	10:1		52
Whitfield School, St. Louis			X	X			6–12	470	470	8:1	7	14
Montana												
Loyola-Sacred Heart High School, Missoula			X	X			9–12	195	195	17:1	5	12
Lustre Christian High School, Lustre	X	X	X	X			9–12	36	36	6:1		4
Montana Academy, Marion	X	X						70	70	2:1	4	47
Summit Preparatory School, Kalispell	X	X					9–12	65	65	6:1		47
Valley Christian School, Missoula			X	X	K–5	6–8	9–12	303	105	8:1	3	7
Nebraska												
Brownell-Talbot School, Omaha			X	X	PK–4	5–8	9–12	464	126	9:1	13	16
Central Catholic Mid-High School, Grand Island			X	X		6–8	9–12	294	174	15:1	2	13
Duchesne Academy of the Sacred Heart, Omaha				X			9–12	289	289	9:1	6	15
Mount Michael Benedictine School, Elkhorn	X		X				9–12	172	172	7:1	5	19
Nebraska Christian Schools, Central City	X	X	X	X	K–6	7–8	9–12	186	97	10:1		6
Pius X High School, Lincoln			X	X			9–12	1,005	1,005	14:1	8	16
Saint Cecilia High School, Hastings			X	X		6–8	9–12	335	202	10:1	2	20
Scotus Central Catholic High School, Columbus			X	X		7–8	9–12	345	206	11:1	1	6
Nevada												
Bishop Gorman High School, Las Vegas			X	X			9–12	1,050	1,050	25:1	14	21
Bishop Manogue High School, Reno			X	X			9–12	676	676	17:1	11	17
Faith Lutheran High School, Las Vegas			X	X		6–8	9–12	1,279	716	17:1	7	18
The Meadows School, Las Vegas			X	X	PK–5	6–8	9–12	910	266	11:1	17	15
Sage Ridge School, Reno			X	X		5–8	9–12	228	82	8:1	12	14
New Hampshire												
Bishop Brady High School, Concord			X	X			9–12	446	446	15:1	7	27
Bishop Guertin High School, Nashua			X	X			9–12	884	884	23:1	12	34
Brewster Academy, Wolfeboro	X	X	X	X			9–PG	363	363	5:1	8	31
Cardigan Mountain School, Canaan	X		X			6–9		199	186	4:1		39
Coe-Brown Northwood Academy, Northwood			X	X			9–12	709	709	12:1	4	12
Community School, South Tamworth			X	X		7–8	9–12	30	27	6:1		21
The Derryfield School, Manchester			X	X		6–8	9–12	383	246	8:1	8	22

PRIVATE SCHOOLS AT-A-GLANCE	STUDENTS ACCEPTED				GRADES			STUDENT/FACULTY			STUDENT OFFERINGS (number)	
	Boarding		Day									
	Boys	Girls	Boys	Girls	Lower	Middle	Upper	Total	Upper	Student/Faculty Ratio	Advanced Placement Subject Areas	Sports
Dublin Christian Academy, Dublin	X	X	X	X	K–6	7–8	9–12	136	81	8:1	2	11
Dublin School, Dublin	X	X	X	X			9–12	123	123	5:1	4	32
Hampshire Country School, Rindge	X				3–6		7–12	20	15	4:1		27
High Mowing School, Wilton	X	X	X	X			9–12	117	117	4:1		41
Holderness School, Plymouth	X	X	X	X			9–PG	281	281	6:1	12	48
Kimball Union Academy, Meriden	X	X	X	X			9–PG	344	344	6:1	16	34
New Hampton School, New Hampton	X	X	X	X			9–PG	321	321	5:1	5	42
Phillips Exeter Academy, Exeter	X	X	X	X			9–PG	1,045	1,045	5:1	19	43
Portsmouth Christian Academy, Dover			X	X	PK–5	6–8	9–12	797	244	11:1	4	12
Proctor Academy, Andover	X	X	X	X			9–12	347	347	5:1	11	58
St. Paul's School, Concord	X	X					9–12	527	527	5:1	19	32
St. Thomas Aquinas High School, Dover			X	X			9–12	721	721	15:1	9	18
Tilton School, Tilton	X	X	X	X			9–PG	243	243	5:1	11	26
Trinity High School, Manchester			X	X			9–12	462	462	16:1	3	21
Wediko School and Treatment Program, Windsor	X		X					40		2:1		40
The White Mountain School, Bethlehem	X	X	X	X			9–PG	95	95	5:1	3	41
New Jersey												
Academy of the Holy Angels, Demarest				X			9–12	586	586	11:1	12	16
The American Boychoir School, Princeton	X		X		4–5	6–8		44	25	3:1		22
Barnstable Academy, Oakland			X	X		5–8	9–12	139	104	8:1	5	15
Bishop Eustace Preparatory School, Pennsauken			X	X			9–12	759	759	13:1	15	20
Bishop George Ahr High School, Edison			X	X			9–12	950	950		7	16
Blair Academy, Blairstown	X	X	X	X			9–PG	441	441	7:1	17	42
Christian Brothers Academy, Lincroft			X				9–12	935	935	14:1	16	15
Community High School, Teaneck			X	X				180	180			7
The Craig School, Mountain Lakes			X	X	3–8		9–12	153	46	6:1		4
Delbarton School, Morristown			X			7–8	9–12	545	484	10:1	19	28
DePaul Catholic High School, Wayne			X	X						19:1	10	20
Dwight-Englewood School, Englewood			X	X	PK–5	6–8	9–12	954	453	9:1	15	16
Eastern Christian High School, North Haledon			X	X	PK–4	5–8	9–12	827	351	9:1	6	30
Gill St. Bernard's School, Gladstone			X	X	PK–4	5–8	9–12	676	238	8:1	8	16
The Hudson School, Hoboken			X	X		5–8	9–12	203	95	10:1	12	15
The Hun School of Princeton, Princeton	X	X	X	X		6–8	9–PG	586	489	8:1	14	37
Immaculata High School, Somerville			X	X			9–12	813	813	15:1	7	12
Immaculate Conception High School, Lodi				X			9–12	182	182	11:1	3	14
Immaculate Conception High School, Montclair			X	X			9–12	317	317	12:1		14
Kent Place School, Summit			X	X	N–5	6–8	9–12	647	263	7:1	18	17
The King's Christian High School, Cherry Hill			X	X	PK–5	6–8	9–12	446	164	18:1	5	9
The Lawrenceville School, Lawrenceville	X	X	X	X			9–PG	797	797	8:1	11	10
Marist High School, Bayonne			X	X				510	510	25:1		12
Mary Help of Christians Academy, North Haledon				X			9–12	230	230	8:1	4	7
Marylawn of the Oranges, South Orange				X			9–12	197	197	15:1	1	11
Monsignor Donavan High School, Toms River			X	X			9–12	990	990	14:1	10	21
Montclair Kimberley Academy, Montclair			X	X	PK–3	4–8	9–12	1,046	433	7:1	15	21
Moorestown Friends School, Moorestown			X	X	PS–4	5–8	9–12	727	285	9:1	14	17
Morristown-Beard School, Morristown			X	X		6–8	9–12	529	390	7:1	10	23
Mt. Saint Dominic Academy, Caldwell				X			9–12	334	334	10:1	8	21
Newark Academy, Livingston			X	X		6–8	9–12	555	410	12:1	19	32
The Newgrange School, Hamilton			X	X	2–5	6–8	9–12	107	46	3:1		6
Notre Dame High School, Lawrenceville			X	X			9–12	1,289	1,289	15:1	12	31
Oak Knoll School of the Holy Child, Summit			X	X	K–6		7–12	553	311	8:1	14	16
Our Lady of Mercy Academy, Newfield				X			9–12	222	222	11:1		19
Peddie School, Hightstown	X	X	X	X			9–PG	518	518	6:1	11	23
The Pennington School, Pennington	X	X	X	X		6–8	9–12	474	374	8:1	14	21

	STUDENTS ACCEPTED				GRADES			STUDENT/FACULTY			STUDENT OFFERINGS (number)	
	Boarding		Day									
	Boys	Girls	Boys	Girls	Lower	Middle	Upper	Total	Upper	Student/ Faculty Ratio	Advanced Placement Subject Areas	Sports
The Pingry School, Martinsville			X	X	K–5	6–8	9–12	1,048	51	9:1	17	22
Pope John XXIII Regional High School, Sparta			X	X			9–12	935	935	13:1		14
Princeton Day School, Princeton			X	X	JK–4	5–8	9–12	900	375	8:1	13	24
Purnell School, Pottersville		X		X			9–12	125	125	8:1		23
Queen of Peace High School, North Arlington			X	X			9–12	625	625	15:1	3	21
Ranney School, Tinton Falls			X	X	N–5	6–8	9–12	815	241		19	16
Rutgers Preparatory School, Somerset			X	X	PK–4	5–8	9–12	722	335	6:1	19	12
Saddle River Day School, Saddle River			X	X	K–5	6–8	9–12	318	162	7:1	13	17
Saint Augustine Preparatory School, Richland			X				9–12	647	647	13:1	11	23
St. Benedict's Preparatory School, Newark			X		7–8		9–12	556	486	11:1		19
Saint Dominic Academy, Jersey City				X			9–12	483	483	12:1	8	12
Saint Joseph High School, Hammonton			X	X			9–12	525	525	17:1	4	24
Saint Joseph Regional High School, Montvale			X				9–12	501	501	12:1		18
Saint Joseph's High School, Metuchen			X				9–12	843	843	17:1	11	22
Saint Mary High School, Rutherford			X	X			9–12	342	342	10:1	5	11
St. Mary's Hall–Doane Academy, Burlington			X	X	PK–6		7–12	197	110	6:1	11	14
St. Peter's Preparatory School, Jersey City			X				9–12	915	915	13:1	9	29
SciCore Academy, Princeton Junction			X	X	5–5	6–8	9–12	89	38	7:1		2
Seton Hall Preparatory School, West Orange			X				9–12	969	969	8:1	14	19
Stuart Country Day School of the Sacred Heart, Princeton			X	X	PS–5	6–8	9–12	506	148	12:1	12	12
Villa Victoria Academy, Ewing				X	PK–6	7–8	9–12	213	81	6:1	8	10
Villa Walsh Academy, Morristown				X		7–8	9–12	248	220	8:1	13	10
The Wardlaw-Hartridge School, Edison			X	X	PK–5	6–8	9–12	429	148	4:1	19	18
Wildwood Catholic High School, North Wildwood			X	X			9–12	266	266	20:1	4	13
Woodcliff Academy, Wall			X	X	3–6	7–8	9–12	55	35	3:1		10
New Mexico												
Albuquerque Academy, Albuquerque			X	X		6–8	9–12	1,089	653	8:1	18	27
Bosque School, Albuquerque			X	X		6–8	9–12	523	264	9:1		10
Chamisa Mesa High School, Taos			X	X			9–12	26	26			
Desert Academy, Santa Fe			X	X		7–8	9–12	159	108	7:1		8
McCurdy School, Espanola			X	X	PK–6	7–8	9–12	327	126	14:1	3	13
Navajo Preparatory School, Inc., Farmington	X	X	X	X					198	15:1		7
New Mexico Academy for Sciences and Mathematics, Sante Fe			X	X						8:1		22
St. Michael's High School, Santa Fe			X	X		7–8	9–12	840	464	25:1	3	15
Sandia Preparatory School, Albuquerque			X	X		6–8	9–12	667	388	9:1		27
The United World College--USA, Montezuma	X	X					11–12	200	200	7:1		55
New York												
Academy of Mount Saint Ursula, Bronx				X			9–12	420	420	17:1	5	9
Academy of Our Lady of Good Counsel High School, White Plains				X			9–12	331	331	11:1		8
Allendale Columbia School, Rochester			X	X	N–5	6–8	9–12	447	137	8:1	16	12
Bay Ridge Preparatory School, Brooklyn			X	X	K–5	6–8	9–12			5:1		12
The Beekman School, New York			X	X			9–PG	80	80	8:1	19	
Berkeley Carroll School, Brooklyn			X	X	N–4	5–8	9–12	785	215	8:1	9	15
The Birch Wathen Lenox School, New York			X	X	K–5	6–8	9–12	500	175	12:1	10	23
Bishop Grimes High School, East Syracuse			X	X		7–8	9–12	555	357	14:1	8	20
Bishop Loughlin Memorial High School, Brooklyn	X		X	X			9–12	850	850		2	23
Blessed Sacrament-St. Gabriel High School, New Rochelle			X	X			9–12	343	343			10
The Brearley School, New York				X	K–4	5–8	9–12	687	207	6:1	10	26
The Browning School, New York			X		K–4	5–8	9–12	389	113	19:1	14	9
The Buffalo Seminary, Buffalo				X			9–12	173	173	10:1	15	21
The Calhoun School, New York			X	X	N–4	5–8	9–12	740	181	5:1	6	16
Cascadilla School, Ithaca	X	X	X	X			9–PG	60	60	6:1	13	46

PRIVATE SCHOOLS AT-A-GLANCE

	STUDENTS ACCEPTED				GRADES			STUDENT/FACULTY			STUDENT OFFERINGS (number)	
	Boarding		Day									
	Boys	Girls	Boys	Girls	Lower	Middle	Upper	Total	Upper	Student/ Faculty Ratio	Advanced Placement Subject Areas	Sports
The Chapin School, New York				X	K–3	4–7	8–12	665	237	4:1	11	63
Christian Brothers Academy, Albany			X			6–8	9–12	449	324	12:1	6	25
Christian Brothers Academy, Syracuse			X	X			7–12	740	740		13	17
Christian Central Academy, Williamsville			X	X	K–6	7–8	9–12	411		6:1	4	8
Columbia Grammar and Preparatory School, New York			X	X	PK–6		7–12	1,128	554	7:1	18	26
Convent of the Sacred Heart, New York				X	PK–4	5–7	8–12	673	241	16:1	18	23
The Dalton School, New York			X	X	K–3	4–8	9–12	1,280	441	7:1	11	16
Darrow School, New Lebanon	X	X	X	X			9–PG	121	121	5:1		22
Doane Stuart School, Albany			X	X	N–4	5–8	9–12	279	107	5:1		5
The Dominican Academy of the City of New York, New York				X			9–12	237	237	10:1	11	9
The Dwight School, New York			X	X	PK–4	5–8	9–12	435	254	6:1	6	25
Emma Willard School, Troy		X		X			9–PG	318	318	5:1	16	35
The Ethical Culture Fieldston School, Bronx			X	X	PK–5	7–8	9–12	1,669	566	10:1		47
The Family Foundation School, Hancock	X	X				6–8	9–12	250	242	8:1		22
Fontbonne Hall Academy, Brooklyn				X			9–12	538	538	12:1		17
Fordham Preparatory School, Bronx			X				9–12	919	919	11:1	18	23
French-American School of New York, Mamaroneck			X	X	N–5	6–8	9–11	798	109	7:1	2	8
Friends Academy, Locust Valley			X	X	N–5	6–8	9–12	749	357	6:1	19	17
Friends Seminary, New York			X	X	K–4	5–8	9–12	670	270	7:1	13	10
Garden School, Jackson Heights			X	X	N–6		7–12	350		11:1	6	7
The Gow School, South Wales	X					7–9	10–PG	144	97	4:1		57
Green Meadow Waldorf School, Chestnut Ridge			X	X	N–8		9–12	379	84	9:1		8
Hackley School, Tarrytown	X	X	X	X	K–4	5–8	9–12	833	380	6:1	19	27
The Harley School, Rochester			X	X	N–4	5–8	9–12	516	165	8:1	14	13
The Harvey School, Katonah	X	X	X	X		6–8	9–12	344	229	7:1	10	22
Hebrew Academy-the Five Towns, Cedarhurst			X	X			9–12	488	488		13	7
Holy Trinity Diocesan High School, Hicksville			X	X			9–12	1,580	1,580		8	19
Hoosac School, Hoosick	X	X	X	X			8–PG	125	125	5:1	5	26
The Horace Mann School, Riverdale			X	X	N–5	6–8	9–12	1,757	714	9:1	19	39
Houghton Academy, Houghton	X	X	X	X		7–8	9–PG	170	147	15:1		18
Immaculata Academy, Hamburg				X			9–12	223	223	13:1		12
Iona Preparatory School, New Rochelle			X				9–12	769	769	13:1	12	36
Kildonan School, Amenia	X	X	X	X	2–6	7–9	10–PG	137	56	6:1		18
The Knox School, St. James	X	X	X	X		6–8	9–12	126	109	5:1	7	30
La Salle Academy, New York			X				9–12	423	423	15:1	3	7
Little Red School House and Elisabeth Irwin High School, New York			X	X	N–4	5–8	9–12	566	181	7:1		15
Long Island Lutheran Middle and High School, Brookville			X	X		6–8	9–12	615	412	9:1	11	21
Loyola School, New York			X	X			9–12	199	199	8:1	9	14
Lycee Franlfcais de New York, New York			X	X	PK–5	6–9	10–12	1,338	278	9:1	6	34
Manlius Pebble Hill School, DeWitt			X	X	PK–5	6–8	9–12	593	274	6:1	20	25
Maplebrook School, Amenia	X	X	X	X				77	62	8:1		41
Martin Luther High School, Maspeth			X	X			9–12	362	362	15:1	7	19
The Mary Louis Academy, Jamaica Estates				X			9–12	1,008	1,008	13:1	7	18
Marymount School, New York			X	X	N–3	4–7	8–12	567	234	6:1	18	22
The Masters School, Dobbs Ferry	X	X	X	X		5–8	9–12	564	410	6:1	17	28
McQuaid Jesuit, Rochester			X			7–8	9–12	877	668	14:1	16	50
Millbrook School, Millbrook	X	X	X	X			9–12	254	254	5:1	11	22
Mother Cabrini High School, New York				X			9–12	415	415	13:1		6
Mount St. Michael Academy, Bronx			X			6–8	9–12	1,144	978	18:1	5	17
Nardin Academy, Buffalo			X	X	PK–8		9–12	954	474	10:1	10	30
National Sports Academy at Lake Placid, Lake Placid	X	X	X	X		8	9–PG	84	82	7:1	4	24
New York Military Academy, Cornwall-on-Hudson	X	X	X	X		7–8	9–12	146	123	10:1	4	17
The Nichols School, Buffalo			X	X		5–8	9–12	561	388	8:1	20	18

| | STUDENTS ACCEPTED | | | | GRADES | | | STUDENT/FACULTY | | | STUDENT OFFERINGS (number) | |
| | Boarding | | Day | | | | | | | | | |
	Boys	Girls	Boys	Girls	Lower	Middle	Upper	Total	Upper	Student/ Faculty Ratio	Advanced Placement Subject Areas	Sports
The Nightingale-Bamford School, New York				X	K–4	5–8	9–12	550	169	7:1	12	16
North Country School, Lake Placid	X	X	X	X		4–9		88	68	3:1		39
Northwood School, Lake Placid	X	X	X	X			9–12	172	172	6:1	3	49
Notre Dame- Bishop Gibbons School, Schenectady			X	X		6–8	9–12	337	208	11:1		15
Oakwood Friends School, Poughkeepsie	X	X	X	X		6–8	9–12	174	148	5:1	7	22
Our Lady of Mercy High School, Rochester				X		7–8	9–12	665	485	14:1	11	16
Our Saviour Lutheran School, Bronx			X	X	PK–3	4–6	7–12	340	200	14:1	3	6
The Packer Collegiate Institute, Brooklyn			X	X	PK–4	5–8	9–12	941	306	7:1	16	4
The Park School of Buffalo, Snyder			X	X	N–4	5–8	9–12	232	101	9:1	6	9
Poly Prep Country Day School, Brooklyn			X	X	N–4	5–8	9–12	1,014	469	7:1	13	24
Portledge School, Locust Valley			X	X	N–5	6–8	9–12	408	157	8:1	11	11
Poughkeepsie Day School, Poughkeepsie			X	X	PK–4	5–8	9–12	353	112	7:1	4	25
Professional Children's School, New York			X	X		6–8	9–12	200	170	8:1		
Rambam Mesivta, Lawrence			X				9–12	155	155	4:1	9	8
Redemption Christian Academy, Troy	X	X	X	X	K–6	7–8	9–PG			10:1		3
Regis High School, New York			X				9–12	546	546	15:1		9
Rice High School, New York			X				9–12	275	275	15:1		9
Riverdale Country School, Riverdale			X	X	PK–5	6–8	9–12	1,084	456	8:1	17	21
Robert Louis Stevenson School, New York			X	X			7–PG	79	79	5:1		27
The Rockland Country Day School, Congers			X	X	PK–5		6–12	159	99	6:1	14	23
Ross School, East Hampton	X	X	X	X	1–4	5–8	9–12	560	220			11
Rudolf Steiner School, New York			X	X	PK–6	7–8	9–12	320	80	4:1		18
Rye Country Day School, Rye			X	X	PK–4	5–8	9–12	870	386	6:1	17	24
Saint Edmund High School, Brooklyn			X	X						15:1	10	12
St. Thomas Choir School, New York	X				3–6		7–8	36	21	5:1		21
Salesian High School, New Rochelle			X				9–12	550	550	11:1	6	20
School for Young Performers, New York			X	X	K–5	6–8	9–12	51	18	2:1	20	
School of the Holy Child, Rye				X		5–8	9–12	334	229	9:1	14	20
Seton Catholic Central High School, Binghamton			X	X			9–12	350	350	23:1	12	19
Smith School, New York			X	X		7–8	9–12	55	47	4:1		10
Soundview Preparatory School, Yorktown Heights			X	X		6–8	9–PG	74	58	6:1	5	9
The Spence School, New York				X	K–4	5–8	9–12	657	208	6:1	2	10
Staten Island Academy, Staten Island			X	X	PK–4	5–8	9–12	400	126	10:1	12	11
Stella Maris High School and the Maura Clarke Junior High Program, Rockaway Park			X	X	8–8		9–12	376	363	10:1	2	11
The Stony Brook School, Stony Brook	X	X	X	X		7–8	9–12	346	266	8:1	17	15
Storm King School, Cornwall-on-Hudson	X	X	X	X		7–8	9–12	124	111	6:1	5	55
Trevor Day School, New York			X	X	N–5	6–8	9–12	768	227	6:1	7	13
Trinity-Pawling School, Pawling	X		X			7–8	9–PG	315	287	8:1	17	34
Trinity School, New York			X	X	K–4	5–8	9–12	970	440	7:1	11	15
United Nations International School, New York			X	X	K–4	5–8	9–12	1,564	484	10:1		63
The Waldorf School of Saratoga Springs, Saratoga Springs			X	X	PK–8		9–12	233	51	4:1		1
The Windsor School, Flushing			X	X		6–8	9–13	147	141	14:1	5	11
Winston Preparatory School, New York			X	X		6–8	9–12	240	142	3:1		10
Xavier High School, New York			X						941	14:1	8	18
York Preparatory School, New York			X	X		6–8	9–12	336	238	5:1	3	26
North Carolina												
Asheville School, Asheville	X	X	X	X			9–12	251	251	7:1	12	48
Auldern Academy, Siler City		X					9–12	40	40	6:1		25
Camelot Academy, Durham			X	X	K–6		7–12	93	45	10:1	6	6
Cannon School, Concord			X	X	PK–4	5–8	9–12	915	340	9:1	14	26
Cape Fear Academy, Wilmington			X	X	PK–5	6–8	9–12	653	225	8:1	11	12
Cardinal Gibbons High School, Raleigh			X	X			9–12	1,132	1,132	25:1	18	19
Carolina Day School, Asheville			X	X	PK–5	6–8	9–12	654	169	10:1	14	11

PRIVATE SCHOOLS AT-A-GLANCE	STUDENTS ACCEPTED				GRADES			STUDENT/FACULTY			STUDENT OFFERINGS (number)	
	Boarding		Day									
	Boys	Girls	Boys	Girls	Lower	Middle	Upper	Total	Upper	Student/ Faculty Ratio	Advanced Placement Subject Areas	Sports
Cary Academy, Cary			X	X		6–8	9–12	710	408	14:1		49
Charlotte Country Day School, Charlotte			X	X	PK–4	5–8	9–12	1,637	476	12:1	20	20
Charlotte Latin School, Charlotte			X	X	K–5	6–8	9–12	1,368	474	8:1	14	29
Christ School, Arden	X		X			8–8	9–12	215	200	6:1	8	48
Durham Academy, Durham			X	X	PK–4	5–8	9–12	1,129	384	12:1	18	22
Fayetteville Academy, Fayetteville			X	X	PK–5	6–8	9–12	422	135	13:1	9	14
Forsyth Country Day School, Lewisville			X	X	PK–4	5–8	9–12	1,017	424	12:1	13	15
Greenfield School, Wilson			X	X	PS–4	5–8	9–12	324	80	3:1	4	7
Guilford Day School, Greensboro			X	X	1–5	6–8	9–12	144	61	8:1		8
Harrells Christian Academy, Harrells			X	X	K–5	6–8	9–12	492	136	11:1	6	8
The Hill Center, Durham Academy, Durham			X	X	K–5	6–8	9–12	180	80	4:1		
Oak Ridge Military Academy, Oak Ridge	X	X	X	X		6–8	9–12	160	130	11:1		24
The O'Neal School, Southern Pines			X	X	PK–4	5–8	9–12	446	174	10:1	10	11
The Patterson School, Patterson	X	X	X	X		7–8	9–12	58	58	5:1		15
Providence Day School, Charlotte			X	X	PK–5	6–8	9–12	1,513	506	7:1	18	23
Ravenscroft School, Raleigh			X	X	PK–5	6–8	9–12	1,229	446	7:1	16	22
Ridgecroft School, Ahoskie			X	X	PK–5	6–8	9–12	352	94	11:1	3	12
Rocky Mount Academy, Rocky Mount			X	X	PK–5	6–8	9–12	450	147	8:1	8	14
St. David's School, Raleigh			X	X	K–4	5–8	9–12	545	214	10:1	15	16
Saint Mary's School, Raleigh		X		X			9–12	294	294	7:1	13	16
Salem Academy, Winston-Salem		X		X			9–12	182	182	7:1	10	21
Salem Baptist Christian School, Winston Salem			X	X	P3–4	5–8	9–12	330	125	10:1	4	6
Stone Mountain School, Black Mountain	X					6–8	9–12	58	39	4:1		42
Wayne Country Day School, Goldsboro			X	X	PK–6		7–12	260	125	15:1	6	11
Westchester Country Day School, High Point			X	X	K–5	6–8	9–12	435	135	6:1	15	12
North Dakota												
Bismark St. Mary's Central, Bismark			X	X			9–12	345	345	12:1	3	21
Oak Grove Lutheran School, Fargo			X	X		6–8	9–12	308	184	12:1		15
Northern Mariana Islands												
Mount Carmel School, Saipan			X	X	1–5	6–8	9–12	416	152	15:1	3	11
Ohio												
Andrews Osborne Academy, Willoughby	X	X	X	X	PK–4	5–8	9–12	304	106	5:1	7	14
Archbishop Alter High School, Kettering			X	X			9–12	648	648	16:1		19
Archbishop Hoban High School, Akron			X	X			9–12	909	909	13:1		23
Benedictine High School, Cleveland			X				9–12	398	398	11:1	6	22
Bishop Fenwick High School, Franklin			X	X					565	18:1	6	17
Central Christian High School, Kidron			X	X	K–4	5–8	9–12	290	145	13:1	1	12
Chaminade-Julienne High School, Dayton			X	X			9–12	985	985	16:1	14	24
Cincinnati Country Day School, Cincinnati			X	X	PK–5	6–8	9–12	800	253	9:1	11	14
Cleveland Central Catholic High School, Cleveland			X	X			9–12		509	14:1		6
The Columbus Academy, Gahanna			X	X	PK–4	5–8	9–12	1,055	366	8:1	17	13
Columbus School for Girls, Columbus				X	PK–5	6–8	9–12	661	231	12:1	13	38
Delphos Saint John's High School, Delphos			X	X			9–12	282	282	14:1		13
Elyria Catholic High School, Elyria			X	X			9–12	567	567	14:1	5	15
Excel Academy, Inc., Newark			X	X	K–5	6–8	9–12	136	48	3:1		
Gilmour Academy, Gates Mills	X	X	X	X	PK–6	7–8	9–12	735	415	10:1	15	38
The Grand River Academy, Austinburg	X						9–12	111	111	6:1	3	62
Hathaway Brown School, Shaker Heights			X	X	PS–4	5–8	9–12	860	339	8:1	13	12
Hawken School, Gates Mills			X	X	PS–5	6–8	9–12	972	437	10:1	15	16
Laurel School, Shaker Heights			X	X	PS–4	5–8	9–12	606	229	8:1	16	12
Lawrence School, Sagamore Hills			X	X	1–6	7–8	9–12	315	134	11:1	2	31
Lehman High School, Sidney			X	X			9–12	261	261	12:1	4	17
Lutheran East High School, Cleveland Heights			X	X			9–12	134	134	13:1	4	7
Magnificat High School, Rocky River				X			9–12	873	873	12:1		13

| | STUDENTS ACCEPTED | | | | GRADES | | | STUDENT/FACULTY | | | STUDENT OFFERINGS (number) | |
| | Boarding | | Day | | | | | | | | | |
	Boys	Girls	Boys	Girls	Lower	Middle	Upper	Total	Upper	Student/ Faculty Ratio	Advanced Placement Subject Areas	Sports
Maumee Valley Country Day School, Toledo			X	X	N–6	7–8	9–12	485	184	10:1	9	14
McAuley High School, Cincinnati				X			9–12	860	860			
McNicholas High School, Cincinnati			X	X			9–12	776	776	19:1	14	18
The Miami Valley School, Dayton			X	X	PK–5	6–8	9–12	461	173	9:1	12	16
Notre Dame-Cathedral Latin School, Chardon			X	X			9–12	744	744	15:1	5	17
Olney Friends School, Barnesville	X	X	X	X			9–12	62	62	5:1	4	26
Padua Franciscan High School, Parma			X	X			9–12	958	958	18:1	8	39
Regina High School, South Euclid				X			9–12	230	230	12:1	5	12
St. Francis de Sales High School, Toledo			X				9–12	596	596	14:1	18	17
Saint Peter Chanel High School, Bedford			X	X			9–12	343	343	13:1	6	14
Saint Vincent-Saint Mary High School, Akron			X	X			9–12	655	655	15:1	7	18
Saint Xavier High School, Cincinnati			X				9–12	1,574	1,574	14:1	19	17
The Seven Hills School, Cincinnati			X	X	PK–5	6–8	9–12	1,050	310	9:1	14	13
The Summit Country Day School, Cincinnati			X	X	PK–4	5–8	9–12	1,060	341	9:1	19	18
Trinity High School, Garfield Heights			X	X			9–12	410	410	13:1	5	17
The Wellington School, Columbus			X	X	PK–4	5–8	9–12	616	210	12:1	13	13
Western Reserve Academy, Hudson	X	X	X	X			9–12	385	385	6:1	19	44
Oklahoma												
Bishop McGuinness Catholic High School, Oklahoma City			X	X	9–10		11–12	679	326	20:1	7	17
Cascia Hall Preparatory School, Tulsa			X	X		6–8	9–12	578	375	12:1	12	18
Heritage Hall, Oklahoma City			X	X	PS–4	5–8	9–12	860	343	16:1	13	19
Holland Hall, Tulsa			X	X	PK–3	4–8	9–12	993	340	9:1	8	16
Oregon												
The Academy at Sisters, Bend		X				7–8	9–12			12:1		33
Academy for Global Exploration, Ashland	X	X					9–12	8	8	3:1		53
Blanchet School, Salem			X	X		7–8	9–12	309	201	18:1	3	8
Canyonville Christian Academy, Canyonville	X	X	X	X			9–12	124	124	15:1	4	11
Central Catholic High School, Portland			X	X								
The Delphian School, Sheridan	X	X	X	X	K–4	5–7	8–12	266				9
East Linn Christian Academy, Lebanon			X	X	PK–6	7–8	9–12	311	119	12:1		7
Hosanna Christian School, Kamath Falls			X	X	PK–5	6–8	9–12	297	76	15:1		7
Lifegate School, Eugene			X	X	P4–5	6–8	9–12	101	36	8:1	2	4
Milo Adventist Academy, Days Creek	X	X	X	X			9–12	140	140	11:1	5	21
Mount Bachelor Academy, Prineville	X	X						101		4:1		20
The Northwest Academy, Portland			X	X		6–8	9–12	114	68	15:1		
Oregon Episcopal School, Portland	X	X	X	X	PK–5	6–8	9–12	839	305	7:1	11	14
Pacific Crest Community School, Portland			X	X		7–8	9–12	85	70	9:1		11
Portland Christian Schools, Portland			X	X	PS–6	7–8	9–12	810	234	10:1	6	8
Portland Lutheran School, Portland	X	X	X	X	PK–5	6–8	9–12	251	91	15:1	1	12
St. Mary's School, Medford			X	X		6–8	9–12	434	283	11:1	20	20
Santiam Christian School, Corvallis			X	X	PS–6	7–8	9–12	825	323	17:1		12
Valley Catholic High School, Beaverton			X	X	K–6	7–8	9–12	480	364	11:1	8	16
Wellsprings Friends School, Eugene			X	X			9–12	58	58	6:1		9
Pennsylvania												
Academy of Notre Dame de Namur, Villanova				X		6–8	9–12	504	361	8:1		16
Academy of the New Church Boys' School, Bryn Athyn	X		X							8:1	6	5
The Agnes Irwin School, Rosemont				X	PK–4	5–8	9–12	693	248	7:1	14	27
The Baldwin School, Bryn Mawr				X	PK–5	6–8	9–12	613	211	7:1	9	17
Bishop Carroll High School, Ebensburg			X	X			9–12	238	238	12:1		11
Bishop McDevitt High School, Wyncote			X	X			9–12	718	718	20:1	5	20
Blue Mountain Academy, Hamburg	X	X	X	X			9–12	247	247	10:1	3	8
Cardinal Dougherty High School, Philadelphia			X	X					885	20:1	8	14
Carson Long Military Institute, New Bloomfield	X					6–8	9–12	179	150	11:1		21

PRIVATE SCHOOLS AT-A-GLANCE	STUDENTS ACCEPTED				GRADES			STUDENT/FACULTY			STUDENT OFFERINGS (number)	
	Boarding		Day									
	Boys	Girls	Boys	Girls	Lower	Middle	Upper	Total	Upper	Student/ Faculty Ratio	Advanced Placement Subject Areas	Sports
Cathedral Preparatory School, Erie			X				9–12	609	609	14:1	19	23
Central Catholic High School, Pittsburgh			X				9–12	833	833	15:1	9	22
CFS, The School at Church Farm, Paoli	X		X			7–8	9–12	175	141	7:1	5	17
Chestnut Hill Academy, Philadelphia			X		PK–5	6–8	9–12	570	222	7:1	11	18
Christopher Dock Mennonite High School, Lansdale			X	X			9–12	417	417	13:1	3	11
The Concept School, Westtown			X	X		4–8	9–12	46	33	8:1		16
Country Day School of the Sacred Heart, Bryn Mawr				X	PK–4	5–8	9–12	354	185	10:1	5	9
Delaware County Christian School, Newtown Square			X	X	PK–5	6–8	9–12	907	348	12:1	9	14
Delaware Valley Friends School, Paoli			X	X		7–8	9–12	207	181	5:1		14
Devon Preparatory School, Devon			X			6–8	9–12	295	228	10:1	16	11
The Ellis School, Pittsburgh				X	PK–4	5–8	9–12	469	159	7:1	12	10
Father Judge High School, Philadelphia			X				9–12	1,258	1,258	28:1		23
Friends' Central School, Wynnewood			X	X	PK–4	5–8	9–12	982	379	9:1		11
Friends Select School, Philadelphia			X	X	PK–5	6–8	9–12	536	184	10:1	3	10
George School, Newtown	X	X	X	X			9–12	513	513	7:1	13	34
Germantown Academy, Fort Washington			X	X	PK–5	6–8	9–12	1,122	485	8:1	14	20
Germantown Friends School, Philadelphia			X	X	K–5	6–8	9–12	894	362	9:1		16
Girard College, Philadelphia	X	X			1–5	6–8	9–12	749	233	16:1	2	21
The Grier School, Tyrone		X				7–8	9–PG	200	173	6:1	5	31
Gwynedd Mercy Academy, Gwynedd Valley				X			9–12	411	411	10:1	8	14
The Haverford School, Haverford			X		PK–5	6–8	9–12	963	363	7:1		24
The Hill School, Pottstown	X	X	X	X			9–PG	464	464	7:1	14	25
The Hill Top Preparatory School, Rosemont			X	X		6–8	9–12	79	61	4:1		37
Holy Ghost Preparatory School, Bensalem			X				9–12	512	512	11:1	16	18
Holy Name High School, Reading			X	X			9–12	459	459	12:1	5	16
Jack M. Barrack Hebrew Academy (formerly Akiba Hebrew Academy), Bryn Mawr			X	X		6–8	9–12	317	235	9:1	9	12
The Janus School, Mount Joy			X	X	1–7		8–12	61	37	4:1		
Kennedy Christian High School, Hermitage			X	X			9–12	306	306	18:1	4	22
Keystone National High School, Bloomsburg							9–12	7,700	7,700			
The Kiski School, Saltsburg	X		X				9–PG	205	205	6:1	14	34
Lancaster Country Day School, Lancaster			X	X	PS–5	6–8	9–12	513	157	5:1	11	13
Lansdale Catholic High School, Lansdale			X	X			9–12	820	820		13	24
Lebanon Catholic Junior / Senior High School, Lebanon			X	X	K4–5	6–8	9–12	397	150	20:1	5	8
Lehigh Valley Christian High School, Allentown			X	X			9–12	166	166	12:1	3	8
Linden Hall, Lititz		X		X		6–8	9–PG	125	83	6:1	11	20
Marian Catholic High School, Tamaqua			X	X			9–12	354	354	11:1	2	8
Mercersburg Academy, Mercersburg	X	X	X	X			9–PG	438	438	5:1	20	41
Mercyhurst Preparatory School, Erie			X	X			9–12	611	611	16:1		22
Mercy Vocational High School, Philadelphia			X	X								
MMI Preparatory School, Freeland			X	X		6–8	9–12	253	153	9:1	9	14
Moravian Academy, Bethlehem			X	X	PK–5	6–8	9–12	803	287	7:1	9	9
Mount Alvernia High School, Pittsburgh				X				93	93	8:1	2	6
Mount Saint Joseph Academy, Flourtown				X			9–12	562	562	10:1	14	15
Nazareth Academy High School for Girls, Philadelphia				X			9–12	484	484	9:1	11	14
Notre Dame Junior/Senior High School, East Stroudsburg			X	X			9–12	264	264	15:1	4	15
The Oakland School, Pittsburgh			X	X			8–12	55	55	6:1	3	32
Our Lady of the Sacred Heart, Coraopolis			X	X			9–12	345	345	13:1	2	18
The Pathway School, Norristown	X	X	X	X				170		6:1		5
Perkiomen School, Pennsburg	X	X	X	X		5–8	9–PG	281	233	7:1	13	18
The Phelps School, Malvern	X		X				7–PG	127	127	5:1	1	21
Pine Forge Academy, Pine Forge	X	X	X	X			9–12	173	173	15:1	4	6
Quigley Catholic High School, Baden			X	X			9–12	183	183	12:1	3	17
Saint Basil Academy, Jenkintown				X			9–12	418	418	13:1	9	11
St. Joseph's Preparatory School, Philadelphia			X				9–12	976	976	16:1	14	25

	STUDENTS ACCEPTED				GRADES			STUDENT/FACULTY			STUDENT OFFERINGS (number)	
	Boarding		Day									
	Boys	Girls	Boys	Girls	Lower	Middle	Upper	Total	Upper	Student/Faculty Ratio	Advanced Placement Subject Areas	Sports
Serra Catholic High School, McKeesport			X	X			9–12	350	350	18:1	4	17
Sewickley Academy, Sewickley			X	X	PK–5	6–8	9–12	782	299	9:1	16	14
Shady Side Academy, Pittsburgh	X	X	X	X	PK–5	6–8	9–12	938	494	8:1	6	23
The Shipley School, Bryn Mawr			X	X	PK–5	6–8	9–12	875	342	7:1	17	25
Solebury School, New Hope	X	X	X	X		7–8	9–PG	219	196	5:1	8	25
Springside School, Philadelphia				X	PK–4	5–8	9–12	655	196	7:1	18	27
Valley Forge Military Academy and College, Wayne	X		X			7–8	9–PG	302	275	13:1	6	27
Villa Joseph Marie High School, Holland				X			9–12	385	385	14:1	13	12
Villa Maria Academy, Erie			X	X			9–12	335	335	9:1	6	13
Villa Maria Academy, Malvern				X			9–12	449	449	9:1		16
Westtown School, Westtown	X	X	X	X	PK–5	6–8	9–12	795	401	8:1	10	41
William Penn Charter School, Philadelphia			X	X	K–5	6–8	9–12	906	429	9:1	14	17
Winchester Thurston School, Pittsburgh			X	X	PK–5	6–8	9–12	615	198	7:1	16	23
The Woodlynde School, Strafford			X	X	1–5	6–8	9–12	302		6:1	2	10
Wyoming Seminary, Kingston	X	X	X	X	PK–8		9–PG	812	461	7:1	17	34
York Country Day School, York			X	X	PS–5	6–8	9–12	213	61	4:1	8	8
Puerto Rico												
American School, Bayamon			X	X	PK–4	5–8	9–12	1,000		18:1		6
Baldwin School of Puerto Rico, Inc., Bayamlfon			X	X	PK–6	7–8	9–12	832	203	10:1	7	11
Colegio de San Antonio Abad, Humacao			X	X		7–9	10–12	442	213	26:1	3	14
Colegio Puertorriqueno de Ninas, Guaynabo				X	PK–6	7–8	9–12	594	169	11:1	7	14
Colegio San Jose, San Juan			X			7–9	10–12	521	259		5	13
Commonwealth Parkville School, San Juan			X	X	PK–6	7–8	9–12	729	163	8:1	6	25
Guamani Private School, Guayama			X	X	1–6	7–8	9–12	606	164	13:1	4	6
Saint John's School, San Juan			X	X	PK–5	6–8	9–12	703	175	8:1	13	8
Wesleyan Academy, Guaynabo			X	X	PK–6		7–12	922	332	23:1	2	11
Rhode Island												
La Salle Academy, Providence			X	X		7–8	9–12	1,460	1,375	12:1	10	24
Lincoln School, Providence			X	X	N–5	6–8	9–12	380	157	4:1	15	25
Moses Brown School, Providence			X	X	N–5	6–8	9–12	789	399	8:1	10	22
Mount Saint Charles Academy, Woonsocket			X	X			7–12	988	988	14:1	12	23
Portsmouth Abbey School, Portsmouth	X	X	X	X			9–12	359	359	7:1	14	19
The Prout School, Wakefield			X	X			9–12	657	657	12:1		28
Providence Country Day School, East Providence			X	X		5–8	9–12	290	210	6:1	11	18
Rocky Hill School, East Greenwich			X	X	PS–5	6–8	9–12	349	159	7:1	11	18
St. Andrew's School, Barrington	X	X	X	X		6–8	9–12	216	182	5:1	2	32
St. George's School, Middletown	X	X	X	X			9–12	350	350	5:1	19	20
The Wheeler School, Providence			X	X	N–5	6–8	9–12	816	339	13:1	11	20
South Carolina												
Aiken Preparatory School, Aiken			X	X	PK–5	6–8	9–12	170	55	5:1	5	9
Ben Lippen Schools, Columbia	X	X	X	X	K–5	6–8	9–12	776	351	15:1	8	17
The Byrnes Schools, Florence			X	X	PK–6	7–8	9–12	270	83	9:1	8	13
Camden Military Academy, Camden	X					7–8	9–12	305	236	12:1	5	7
Cardinal Newman School, Columbia			X	X		7–8	9–12	443	285	10:1	1	15
Cherokee Creek Boys School, Westminster	X					5–9		36	32	6:1		40
Christ Church Episcopal School, Greenville			X	X	K–4	5–8	9–12	1,016	303	10:1	15	9
Glenforest School, West Columbia			X	X	1–5	6–8	9–12	93	51	4:1		21
Hammond School, Columbia			X	X	PK–4	5–8	9–12	994	265	9:1	14	39
Heathwood Hall Episcopal School, Columbia			X	X	N–4	5–8	9–12	886	266	11:1	14	44
Hilton Head Preparatory School, Hilton Head Island			X	X	K–5	6–8	9–12	461	174	12:1	15	15
International Junior Golf Academy, Hilton Head Island	X	X	X	X			6–PG	140	140	10:1	6	1
Porter-Gaud School, Charleston			X	X	K–5	6–8	9–12	919	325	15:1	13	18
St. Joseph's Catholic School, Greenville			X	X		6–8	9–12	507	269	13:1	12	14

PRIVATE SCHOOLS AT-A-GLANCE	Boarding Boys	Boarding Girls	Day Boys	Day Girls	Lower	Middle	Upper	Total	Upper	Student/ Faculty Ratio	Advanced Placement Subject Areas	Sports
Shannon Forest Christian School, Greenville			X	X	PK–5		6–12	568	312	17:1	9	10
Trident Academy, Mt. Pleasant	X	X	X	X	K–5	6–8	9–12	101	33	4:1		12
Trinity Collegiate School, Darlington			X	X								11
Westminster Catawba Christian, Rock Hill			X	X	PK–6	7–8	9–12	633	152		5	10
Wilson Hall, Sumter			X	X	PS–5	6–8	9–12	845	231	12:1	14	29
South Dakota												
Freeman Academy, Freeman	X	X	X	X	5–8		9–12	94	64	8:1		6
Sioux Falls Christian High School, Sioux Falls			X	X	K–5	6–8	9–12	722	213	17:1	4	8
Tennessee												
Battle Ground Academy, Franklin			X	X	K–4	5–8	9–12	953	378	11:1	12	33
Baylor School, Chattanooga	X	X	X	X		6–8	9–12	1,065	720	8:1	17	50
Boyd-Buchanan School, Chattanooga			X	X	K4–5	6–8	9–12	934	319	15:1	7	11
Brentwood Academy, Brentwood			X	X		6–8	9–12	780	444	10:1	8	27
Chattanooga Christian School, Chattanooga			X	X	K–5	6–8	9–12	1,102	430	18:1	10	49
Columbia Academy, Columbia			X	X	K–6		7–12	607	266	13:1	3	14
Currey Ingram Academy, Brentwood			X	X	K–4	5–8	9–12	290	58	6:1		8
David Lipscomb High School, Nashville			X	X	PK–4	5–8	9–12	1,369	519	14:1	4	13
Donelson Christian Academy, Nashville			X	X	K–5	6–8	9–12	832	292	16:1	6	17
The Ensworth School, Nashville			X	X	K–5	6–8	9–12	1,007	405	7:1		
Evangelical Christian School, Cordova			X	X	K4–5	6–8	9–12	1,515	519	11:1	5	15
Ezell-Harding Christian School, Antioch			X	X	K–4	5–8	9–12	875	273	12:1	3	15
Father Ryan High School, Nashville			X	X			9–12	873	873	12:1	17	27
Franklin Road Academy, Nashville			X	X	PK–4	5–8	9–12	945	266	9:1	10	24
Friendship Christian School, Lebanon			X	X	PK–4	5–8	9–12	720	219	15:1	2	8
Girls Preparatory School, Chattanooga				X		6–8	9–12	703	401	8:1	19	48
Grace Baptist Academy, Chattanooga			X	X	K4–5	6–8	9–12	800	209	20:1		13
The Harpeth Hall School, Nashville				X		5–8	9–12	625	373	8:1	13	37
Hutchison School, Memphis				X	PK–4	5–8	9–12	894	223	16:1	13	12
Jackson Christian School, Jackson			X	X	K–5	6–8	9–12	886	302	19:1		10
The King's Academy, Seymour	X	X	X	X	K4–5	6–8	9–12	400	154	20:1	3	22
Knoxville Catholic High School, Knoxville			X	X			9–12	649	649	14:1	9	21
Lausanne Collegiate School, Memphis			X	X	PK–4	5–8	9–12	768	239	10:1	14	47
The McCallie School, Chattanooga	X		X			6–8	9–12	911	651	9:1	13	59
Memphis University School, Memphis			X		7–8		9–12	653	433	10:1	12	13
Montgomery Bell Academy, Nashville			X			7–8	9–12	680	449	9:1	16	20
Nashville Christian School, Nashville			X	X	K4–5	6–8	9–12	499	181	18:1	5	17
Notre Dame High School, Chattanooga			X	X			9–12	577	577	10:1		41
St. Andrew's–Sewanee School, Sewanee	X	X	X	X		6–8	9–12	255	180	7:1	6	31
St. Benedict at Auburndale, Cordova			X	X			9–12	960	960	13:1	6	23
St. Cecilia Academy, Nashville				X			9–12	229	229	9:1	13	20
St. George's Independent School, Collierville			X	X	PK–5	6–8	9–12		400	9:1		
St. Mary's Episcopal School, Memphis				X	PK–4	5–8	9–12	860	231	13:1	11	12
University School of Jackson, Jackson			X	X	PK–5	6–8	9–12	1,262	362	12:1	11	16
University School of Nashville, Nashville			X	X	K–4	5–8	9–12	1,008	358	12:1	19	19
The Webb School, Bell Buckle	X	X	X	X		6–8	9–PG	300	211	7:1	7	43
Webb School of Knoxville, Knoxville			X	X	K–5	6–8	9–12	1,047	477	11:1	18	19
Texas												
The Alexander School, Dallas			X	X		8–8	9–12	49	44	5:1	7	11
Alexander Smith Academy, Houston			X	X						7:1	4	16
Allen Academy, Bryan			X	X	PK–5	6–8	9–12	286	80	10:1	8	14
All Saints' Episcopal School of Fort Worth, Fort Worth			X	X	K–6	7–8	9–12	805	270	9:1	9	25
Bishop Lynch Catholic High School, Dallas			X	X			9–12	1,034	1,034	12:1	13	27
The Brook Hill School, Bullard	X	X	X	X	PK–5	6–8	9–12	507	169	9:1	3	16

| | STUDENTS ACCEPTED | | | | | | | | | | | STUDENT OFFERINGS (number) | |
| | Boarding | | Day | | GRADES | | | STUDENT/FACULTY | | | | | |
	Boys	Girls	Boys	Girls	Lower	Middle	Upper	Total	Upper	Student/ Faculty Ratio		Advanced Placement Subject Areas	Sports
Central Catholic High School, San Antonio			X				9–12	510	510	21:1		7	19
Cistercian Preparatory School, Irving			X			5–8	9–12	344	173	8:1		19	12
Dallas Academy, Dallas			X	X	3–6	7–8	9–12	156	93	6:1			11
Dallas Christian School, Mesquite			X	X	PK–5	6–8	9–12	721	249	15:1			13
Duchesne Academy of the Sacred Heart, Houston				X	PK–4	5–8	9–12	665	241	7:1		11	14
The Emery Weiner School, Houston			X	X		6–8	9–12	412	213	8:1			17
Episcopal High School, Bellaire			X	X			9–12	629	629	9:1		9	18
The Episcopal School of Dallas, Dallas			X	X	PK–4	5–8	9–12	1,139	395	8:1		18	18
Excel Academy, Conroe	X	X					9–12	75	75	15:1			4
Fairhill School, Dallas			X	X	1–5	6–8	9–12	240	89	12:1			8
First Baptist Academy, Dallas			X	X	K–4	5–8	9–12	677	272	11:1		3	14
Fort Worth Country Day School, Fort Worth			X	X	K–4	5–8	9–12	1,125	387	10:1		21	21
Gateway School, Arlington			X	X		5–8	9–12	30	19	10:1			8
Greenhill School, Addison			X	X	PK–4	5–8	9–12	1,242	437	18:1		11	32
The Hockaday School, Dallas		X		X	PK–4	5–8	9–12	1,028	443	14:1		19	55
Houston Learning Academy-Central Campus, Houston			X	X			9–12	54	54	15:1			
Huntington-Surrey School, Austin			X	X			9–12	61	61	4:1			
Hyde Park Baptist School, Austin			X	X	K–6	7–8	9–12	749	227	7:1		11	14
Incarnate Word Academy, Houston				X			9–12	248	248	11:1		9	13
Jesuit College Preparatory School, Dallas			X				9–12	1,030	1,030	11:1		16	22
The John Cooper School, The Woodlands			X	X	PK–5	6–8	9–12	952	323	12:1		14	10
Keystone School, San Antonio			X	X	K–4	5–8	9–12	428	125	10:1		7	10
Lakehill Preparatory School, Dallas			X	X	K–4	5–8	9–12	400	106	9:1		12	13
Loretto Academy, El Paso			X	X	PK–5	6–8	9–12	707	396	20:1		6	13
Lydia Patterson Institute, El Paso			X	X		8	9–12	452	280	20:1		1	9
Marine Military Academy, Harlingen	X						8–12	402	402	12:1		6	27
Mount Carmel High School, Houston			X	X						10:1			12
The Oakridge School, Arlington			X	X	PS–4	5–8	9–12	870	287	10:1		18	14
Prestonwood Christian Academy, Plano			X	X	PK–4	5–8	9–12	1,463	432	9:1		8	13
St. Agnes Academy, Houston				X			9–12	838	838	15:1		12	17
St. Anthony Catholic High School, San Antonio	X	X	X	X			9–12	443	443	22:1			16
St. John's School, Houston			X	X	K–5	6–8	9–12	1,210	537	7:1		19	16
St. Mark's School of Texas, Dallas			X		1–4	5–8	9–12	838	353	8:1		14	34
Saint Mary's Hall, San Antonio			X	X	PK–5	6–8	9–PG	968	333	6:1		22	19
St. Pius X High School, Houston			X	X			9–12	630	630	13:1		6	15
St. Stephen's Episcopal School, Austin	X	X	X	X		6–8	9–12	646	452	7:1		16	34
St. Thomas High School, Houston			X				9–12	675	675	13:1		10	10
San Marcos Baptist Academy, San Marcos	X	X	X	X		7–8	9–12	260	203	7:1		3	23
Second Baptist School, Houston			X	X	PK–4	5–8	9–12					17	9
Shelton School and Evaluation Center, Dallas			X	X	PS–4	5–8	9–12	846	233	8:1			10
Southwest Christian School, Inc., Fort Worth			X	X	PK–6	7–8	9–12	855	300	10:1		7	19
Strake Jesuit College Preparatory, Houston			X				9–12	893	893	12:1		10	10
The Tenney School, Houston			X	X		6–8	9–12	58	46	1:1		2	
Texas NeuroRehab Center, Austin	X	X						53		4:1			
TMI--The Episcopal School of Texas, San Antonio	X	X	X	X		6–8	9–12	365	248	8:1		14	20
Trinity Christian Academy, Addison			X	X	K–4	5–8	9–12	1,515	482	10:1		14	19
Trinity School of Texas, Longview			X	X	K–5	6–8	9–12	249	78	6:1		10	10
Trinity Valley School, Fort Worth			X	X	K–4	5–8	9–12	963	337	10:1		15	11
Tyler Street Christian Academy, Dallas			X	X	P3–6	7–8	9–12	198	47	6:1		1	7
The Ursuline Academy of Dallas, Dallas				X			9–12	808	808	10:1		13	13
Vanguard College Preparatory School, Waco			X	X		7–8	9–12	154	119	8:1		7	10
Westbury Christian School, Houston			X	X	PK–6	7–8	9–12	538	254	11:1		13	15
The Winston School, Dallas			X	X	1–6	7–8	9–12	223	118	6:1			17
The Winston School San Antonio, San Antonio			X	X	K–6	7–8	9–12	216	80	10:1			15

PRIVATE SCHOOLS AT-A-GLANCE	STUDENTS ACCEPTED				GRADES			STUDENT/FACULTY			STUDENT OFFERINGS (number)	
	Boarding		Day									
	Boys	Girls	Boys	Girls	Lower	Middle	Upper	Total	Upper	Student/ Faculty Ratio	Advanced Placement Subject Areas	Sports
Utah												
Alpine Academy, Erda		X				7–8	9–12	44	40	4:1		30
Bridgerland Applied Technology Center, Logan										16:1		
Cedar Ridge Academy, Roosevelt	X	X					9–12	50	50	9:1		7
Cross Creek Programs, LaVerkin	X	X				7–8	9–12	308	276	15:1		27
Intermountain Christian School, Salt Lake City			X	X	PK–5	6–8	9–12	339	103	20:1	7	7
New Haven, Provo		X				8–9	10–12	64	54	5:1		25
Oakley School, Oakley	X	X					9–PG	101	101	10:1		34
Pine Ridge Academy, Draper	X	X	X	X		7–9	10–12	42	24	4:1		
Rowland Hall-St. Mark's School, Salt Lake City			X	X	PK–5	6–8	9–12	981	287	8:1	17	36
St. Joseph's High School, Ogden			X	X			9–12	170	170	10:1	9	5
Salt Lake Lutheran High School, Salt Lake City			X	X			9–12	82	82	7:1		13
Sorenson's Ranch School, Koosharem	X	X					7–12	75	75	7:1		50
SunHawk Academy, St. George	X	X					8–12	70	70	12:1		14
Wasatch Academy, Mt. Pleasant	X	X	X	X				200	200	10:1	9	70
The Waterford School, Sandy			X	X	PK–5	6–8	9–12	1,022	285	5:1	14	27
Vermont												
Bromley Brook School, Manchester Center		X					9–12	80	80	6:1		21
Burke Mountain Academy, East Burke	X	X	X	X			7–PG	70	70	7:1	2	8
Burr and Burton Academy, Manchester	X	X	X	X			9–12	686	686		6	21
The Greenwood School, Putney	X							44		2:1		10
King George School, Sutton	X	X						45		3:1	8	44
Lyndon Institute, Lyndon Center	X	X	X	X		8–8	9–12	626	626	10:1	4	27
Pine Ridge School, Williston	X	X	X	X				98	98	2:1		38
The Putney School, Putney	X	X	X	X			9–12	226	226	7:1	2	60
Rock Point School, Burlington	X	X	X	X			9–12	37	37	5:1		32
St. Johnsbury Academy, St. Johnsbury	X	X	X	X			9–PG	958	958	5:1	17	41
Stratton Mountain School, Stratton Mountain	X	X	X	X		7–8	9–PG	116	90	6:1		12
Vermont Academy, Saxtons River	X	X	X	X			9–PG	266	266	7:1	16	80
Virgin Islands												
St. Croix Country Day School, Kingshill			X	X	N–6	7–8	9–12	502	171	12:1	8	12
Virginia												
Benedictine High School, Richmond			X				9–12	274	274	9:1	8	22
Bishop Denis J. O'Connell High School, Arlington			X	X				1,433	1,433	14:1	18	19
Bishop Ireton High School, Alexandria			X	X			9–12	804	804	14:1	11	24
The Blue Ridge School, St. George	X						9–12	197	197	6:1		45
Cape Henry Collegiate School, Virginia Beach			X	X	PK–5	6–8	9–12	1,020	329	10:1	12	45
Carlisle School, Axton	X	X	X	X	PK–5	6–8	9–12	469	131	10:1		17
Christchurch School, Christchurch	X		X	X			8–PG	218	218	7:1	11	20
The Collegiate School, Richmond			X	X	K–4	5–8	9–12	1,563	498	15:1	11	25
Eastern Mennonite High School, Harrisonburg			X	X	K–5	6–8	9–12	388	226	10:1	3	11
Episcopal High School, Alexandria	X	X					9–12	435	435	6:1	18	44
Fishburne Military School, Waynesboro	X		X			8	9–12	180	165	9:1	3	34
Flint Hill School, Oakton			X	X	JK–4	5–8	9–12	1,090	484	9:1	15	31
Fork Union Military Academy, Fork Union	X		X			6–8	9–PG	509	446	15:1	5	38
Foxcroft School, Middleburg		X		X			9–12	180	180	7:1	17	24
Fredericksburg Academy, Fredericksburg			X	X	PK–5	6–8	9–12	552	135	6:1		11
Fuqua School, Farmville			X	X	PK–5	6–8	9–12	521	152	16:1	4	12
Hampton Roads Academy, Newport News			X	X		6–8	9–12	499	302	10:1	18	18
Hargrave Military Academy, Chatham	X		X			7–8	9–PG	373	350	11:1	2	47
Highland School, Warrenton			X	X	PK–4	5–8	9–12	552	228	6:1	19	33
Isle of Wight Academy, Isle of Wight			X	X	PK–7		8–12	521	176	13:1	6	8
Little Keswick School, Keswick	X							31		4:1		16

| | STUDENTS ACCEPTED | | | | GRADES | | | STUDENT/FACULTY | | | STUDENT OFFERINGS (number) | |
| | Boarding | | Day | | | | | | | | | |
	Boys	Girls	Boys	Girls	Lower	Middle	Upper	Total	Upper	Student/ Faculty Ratio	Advanced Placement Subject Areas	Sports
The Madeira School, McLean		X		X			9–12	316	316	6:1	13	18
Massanutten Military Academy, Woodstock	X	X	X	X		7–8	9–PG	194	169	8:1	4	66
Miller School, Charlottesville	X	X	X	X		8–8	9–12	148	133	6:1	13	41
New Dominion School, Dillwyn	X	X					6–12	88	88	6:1		10
Norfolk Academy, Norfolk			X	X	1–6	7–9	10–12	1,229	344	10:1	15	26
Norfolk Christian School, Norfolk			X	X	PK–5	6–8	9–12	763	234	10:1	10	
Norfolk Collegiate School, Norfolk			X	X	K–5	6–8	9–12	918	357	10:1	16	15
North Cross School, Roanoke			X	X	JK–5	6–8	9–12	500	137	6:1	11	13
Notre Dame Academy, Middleburg			X	X			9–12	261	261	9:1	11	19
Oak Hill Academy, Mouth of Wilson	X	X	X	X			8–12	137	137	10:1		34
Oakland School, Keswick	X	X	X	X						5:1		32
The Potomac School, McLean			X	X	K–3	4–8	9–12	930	349	6:1	14	25
Randolph-Macon Academy, Front Royal	X	X	X	X		6–8	9–PG	398	313	9:1	10	29
St. Anne's–Belfield School, Charlottesville	X	X	X	X	PK–4	5–8	9–12	838	322	7:1	11	14
St. Catherine's School, Richmond				X	PK–4	5–8	9–12	862	231	6:1	22	36
St. Christopher's School, Richmond			X		JK–5	6–8	9–12	961	317	7:1	18	23
Saint Gertrude High School, Richmond				X			9–12	277	277	9:1	6	13
St. Margaret's School, Tappahannock		X		X			8–12	158	158	6:1	5	25
St. Stephen's & St. Agnes School, Alexandria			X	X	JK–5	6–8	9–12	1,144	450	9:1	17	26
Shenandoah Valley Academy, New Market	X	X	X	X			9–12	173	173	11:1		14
Stuart Hall, Staunton		X	X	X	K–5	6–8	9–12	319	122	15:1	10	12
Tandem Friends School, Charlottesville			X	X		5–8	9–12	243	132	8:1	10	10
Timber Ridge School, Cross Junction	X					6–8	9–12	85	64	10:1		4
Trinity Episcopal School, Richmond			X	X			8–12	445	445	10:1	14	33
Virginia Beach Friends School, Virginia Beach			X	X	1–5	6–8	9–12	210	55	5:1	5	10
Virginia Episcopal School, Lynchburg	X	X	X	X			9–12	262	262	8:1	19	32
Wakefield School, The Plains			X	X	PK–5	6–8	9–12	500	120	14:1	19	15
Woodberry Forest School, Woodberry Forest	X						9–12	395	395	8:1	19	59
Washington												
Annie Wright School, Tacoma		X	X	X	PS–5	6–8	9–12	477	139	7:1	8	5
Auburn Adventist Academy, Auburn	X	X	X	X			9–12	300	300	12:1		24
Bellevue Christian School, Clyde Hill			X	X	PK–6	7–8	9–12	1,300	360	21:1		21
Bishop Blanchet High School, Seattle			X	X			9–12	1,045	1,045	14:1	8	20
The Bush School, Seattle			X	X	K–5	6–8	9–12	578	238	6:1	8	28
Charles Wright Academy, Tacoma			X	X	PK–5	6–8	9–12	733	315	8:1	11	23
Chrysalis School, Woodinville					K–6	7–8	9–12	257	198	1:1		
DeSales Catholic Middle/High School, Walla Walla			X	X			9–12	131	131	15:1	5	8
Eastside Catholic High School, Bellevue			X	X			9–12	560	560	13:1	6	20
Explorations Academy, Bellingham			X	X				12		5:1	2	
John F. Kennedy Memorial High School, Burien	X	X	X	X			9–12	972	972	17:1	13	26
King's High School, Seattle			X	X	PK–6	7–8	9–12	1,144	424	17:1	8	13
King's West School, Bremerton			X	X	K–6		7–12	380	211	9:1		7
Lakeside School, Seattle			X	X		5–8	9–12	775	518	10:1		15
The Northwest School, Seattle	X	X	X	X		6–8	9–12	458	329	9:1		13
Northwest Yeshiva High School, Mercer Island			X	X			9–12	95	95	4:1		6
O'Dea High School, Seattle			X				9–12	481	481	13:1	3	17
The Overlake School, Redmond			X	X		5–8	9–12	499	290	9:1	14	23
Saint George's School, Spokane			X	X	K–5	6–8	9–12	399	153	7:1	11	9
Seattle Academy of Arts and Sciences, Seattle			X	X		6–8	9–12	581	354	8:1		25
Seattle Christian Schools, Seattle			X	X	K–6	7–8	9–12	712	273	22:1	6	21
Seattle Lutheran High School, Seattle			X	X			9–12	172	172	16:1	6	18
Shoreline Christian, Shoreline			X	X	PS–6	7–8	9–12	254	96	7:1		8
University Prep, Seattle			X	X		6–8	9–12	477	277	8:1	12	13
Upper Columbia Academy, Spangle	X	X	X	X			9–12	246	246	6:1	4	9

PRIVATE SCHOOLS AT-A-GLANCE	STUDENTS ACCEPTED				GRADES			STUDENT/FACULTY			STUDENT OFFERINGS (number)	
	Boarding		Day									
	Boys	Girls	Boys	Girls	Lower	Middle	Upper	Total	Upper	Student/Faculty Ratio	Advanced Placement Subject Areas	Sports
West Virginia												
The Linsly School, Wheeling	X	X	X	X	5–8		9–12	444	283	10:1	11	52
Wisconsin												
Columbus High School, Marshfield			X	X	1–5	6–8	9–12	585	152	10:1	4	17
Conserve School, Land O' Lakes	X	X					9–12	125	125	8:1	10	72
Fox Valley Lutheran High School, Appleton			X	X			9–12	633	633	14:1	4	12
Marquette University High School, Milwaukee			X				9–12	1,050	1,050	15:1	18	21
Milwaukee Lutheran High School, Milwaukee			X	X			9–12	731	731	16:1	7	36
The Prairie School, Racine			X	X	PK–4	5–8	9–12	722	255	17:1	11	9
Saint Joan Antida High School, Milwaukee				X			9–12	391	391	18:1	4	
St. John's Northwestern Military Academy, Delafield	X		X			7–8	9–12	360	280	12:1		11
Saint Joseph High School, Kenosha			X	X		7–8	9–12	447	289	20:1	4	8
St. Lawrence Seminary, Mount Calvary	X						9–12	215	215	10:1		25
University Lake School, Hartland			X	X	PK–5	6–8	9–12	324	84	9:1	9	11
University School of Milwaukee, Milwaukee			X	X	PK–4	5–8	9–12	1,062	364	9:1	13	18
Wayland Academy, Beaver Dam	X	X	X	X			9–12	238	238	8:1	12	42
Wisconsin Academy, Columbus	X	X	X	X			9–12	108	108	6:1		7
CANADA												
Academie Sainte Cecile International School, Windsor, ON	X	X	X	X	1–8		9–12	247	140	12:1		25
The Academy for Gifted Children (PACE), Richmond Hill, ON			X	X	1–3	4–7	8–12	283	120	15:1	5	37
Airdrie Koinonia Christian School, Airdrie, AB			X	X	K–6		7–12	283	114	14:1		15
Albert College, Belleville, ON	X	X	X	X	JK–6	7–8	9–PG	337	178	8:1	5	66
Appleby College, Oakville, ON	X	X	X	X		7–8	9–12	736	592	7:1	10	31
Arrowsmith School, Toronto, ON			X	X				60	20	8:1		
Ashbury College, Ottawa, ON	X	X	X	X	4–8		9–12	646	486	17:1		31
Balmoral Hall School, Winnipeg, MB		X	X	X	N–5	6–8	9–12	469	199	7:1	9	67
Banbury Crossroads School, Calgary, AB			X	X	1–3	4–6	7–12	46	35	10:1		19
Bearspaw Christian School, Calgary, AB			X	X	1–6	7–9	10–12	433	82	20:1		11
Bishop's College School, Sherbrooke, QC	X	X	X	X		7–9	10–12	246	154	8:1	13	44
The Bishop Strachan School, Toronto, ON		X		X	PK–6		7–12	895	645	10:1	16	52
Bodwell High School, North Vancouver, BC	X	X	X	X		8–9	10–12	360	260	15:1	4	43
Brampton Christian School, Caledon, ON			X	X	JK–5	6–8	9–12	489	179	11:1		18
Brentwood College School, Mill Bay, BC	X	X	X	X			8–12	434	434	9:1		74
British Columbia Christian Academy, Port Coquitlam, BC			X	X	PK–3	4–7	8–12	229	85	5:1		8
Calgary Academy, Calgary, AB			X	X	2–6		7–12	630	450	8:1		46
Cariboo Adventist Academy, Williams Lake, BC			X	X						7:1		
Centennial Academy, Montreal, QC			X	X			7–11	302	302	10:1		23
Century High School, Vancouver, BC			X	X			8–12	250	250	20:1		
Community Hebrew Academy, Downsview, ON			X	X			9–12	1,500	1,500	8:1		
Concordia High School, Edmonton, AB	X	X	X	X				133		10:1		14
The Country Day School, King City, ON			X	X	JK–6	7–8	9–12	720	320	10:1	2	25
Covenant Canadian Reformed School, Neerlandia, AB			X	X	K–6	7–9	10–12	170	31	10:1		16
Crescent School, Willowdale, ON			X		3–6	7–8	9–12	666	351	10:1	12	24
Crestwood Preparatory College, Toronto, ON										16:1	17	15
Crofton House School, Vancouver, BC				X	1–6		7–12	708	440	10:1	9	16
Edison School, Okotoks, AB			X	X	K–4	5–8	9–12	198	48	12:1	7	7
Elmwood School, Rockcliffe Park, Ottawa, ON			X	X	JK–5	6–8	9–12	375	125	8:1		11
Foothills Academy, Calgary, AB			X	X	1–6	7–8	9–12	201	93	12:1		40
Gateway Christian School, Prince George, BC			X	X	K–3	4–6	7–12	87	36			32
Glen Eden School, Vancouver, BC			X	X								

	STUDENTS ACCEPTED				GRADES			STUDENT/FACULTY			STUDENT OFFERINGS (number)	
	Boarding		Day									
	Boys	Girls	Boys	Girls	Lower	Middle	Upper	Total	Upper	Student/Faculty Ratio	Advanced Placement Subject Areas	Sports
The Glenfir School, Summerland, BC			X	X	JK–6	7–9	10–12			5:1		41
Glenlyon Norfolk School, Victoria, BC			X	X	JK–5	6–8	9–12	680	284	8:1		28
Great Lakes Christian College, Beamsville, ON	X	X	X	X			9–12	101	101	9:1		15
GreenHill Village Academy, Thornhill, ON			X	X	JK–4	5–8	9–12	248	53	7:1		26
Hamilton District Christian High, Ancaster, ON	X	X	X				9–12	515	515	19:1		23
Havergal College, Toronto, ON		X		X	JK–6	7–8	9–12	910	473	9:1	4	79
Heritage Christian Academy, Calgary, AB			X	X	K–5	6–9	10–12	494	92	10:1		50
Heritage Christian School, Kelowna, BC			X	X	1–6		7–12	342	162	17:1	4	22
Heritage Christian School, Jordan, ON			X	X	K–8		9–12	568	168	15:1		5
Hillfield Strathallan College, Hamilton, ON			X	X	PK–4	5–8	9–12	1,112	400	9:1	8	32
Hope Christian School, Champion, AB			X	X						5:1		
Imperial College of Toronto, Etobicoke, ON	X	X					11–12	201	201	22:1		
King David High School, Vancouver, BC			X	X			8–12	205	205	8:1	1	9
King's College School, Caledon, ON			X	X	3–6	7–8	9–12	28	20	4:1		35
King's-Edgehill School, Windsor, NS	X	X	X	X		6–9	10–12	365	255	10:1	2	33
The King's School, Langley, BC			X	X	K–7		8–12	120	40	10:1		3
Kingsway College, Oshawa, ON	X	X	X	X			9–12	191	191	11:1		18
Koinonia Christian School, Red Deer, AB			X	X	K–5	6–8	9–12	173	60	12:1		3
Lakefield College School, Lakefield, ON	X	X	X	X			7–12	365	365	7:1	7	31
Landmark East School, Wolfville, NS	X	X	X	X		6–9	10–12	65	41	2:1		34
The Laureate Academy, Winnipeg, MB			X	X	1–5	6–8	9–12	95	45	5:1		30
Laurel View Academy, Barrie, ON			X	X						10:1		
Lester B. Pearson United World College of the Pacific, Victoria, BC	X	X	X	X								
Lighthouse Christian School, Sylvan Lake, AB			X	X	PK–5	6–9	10–12	89	14	15:1		
Linden Christian School, Winnipeg, MB			X		K–4	5–8	9–12	832	238	13:1		13
The Linden School, Toronto, ON				X	1–6	7–8	9–12	140	45	3:1	2	42
Luther College High School, Regina, SK	X	X	X	X			9–12	463	463	16:1		18
Lycee Claudel, Ottawa, ON			X	X	1–5	6–9	10–12	932	156	10:1		
MacLachlan College, Oakville, ON			X	X	JK–8		9–12	344	133	10:1	7	36
Maxwell International Baha'i School, Shawnigan Lake, BC	X	X	X	X		7–9	10–12	127	91	9:1	4	40
Meadowridge School, Maple Ridge, BC			X	X	JK–5		6–12	500	199	9:1		17
Mennonite Collegiate Institute, Gretna, MB	X	X	X	X			9–12	147	147	11:1	1	9
Mentor College, Mississauga, ON			X	X	JK–4	5–8	9–12	1,580	640	14:1	1	32
Metropolitan Preparatory Academy, Toronto, ON			X	X		6–8	9–12	435	335	18:1		15
Miss Edgar's and Miss Cramp's School, Montreal, QC				X	K–5	6–8	9–11	346	120	9:1	2	16
Nancy Campbell Collegiate Institute, London, ON	X	X	X	X	JK–6	7–8	9–12	219	162	10:1		29
New Tribes Mission Academy, Durham, ON			X	X	K–4	5–8	9–12	34	7	3:1		13
Niagara Christian Community of Schools, Fort Erie, ON	X	X	X	X	JK–6	7–8	9–12	381	256	17:1	3	18
Notre Dame Regional Secondary, Vancouver, BC			X	X			8–12	575	575	16:1	1	18
Okanagan Adventist Academy, Kelowna, BC			X	X	K–7		8–12	100	44			6
Pickering College, Newmarket, ON	X	X	X	X	JK–8		9–13	422	243	9:1		36
Pinehurst School, St. Catharines, ON	X	X			7–8	9–10	11–12	23	12	10:1		71
Queen Margaret's School, Duncan, BC		X	X	X	JK–7		8–12	315	160	7:1		37
Queensway Christian College, Etobicoke, ON			X	X	JK–5	6–8	9–12	115	45	7:1		22
Quinte Christian High School, Belleville, ON			X	X			9–12	146	146	15:1		8
Richmond Christian School, Richmond, BC			X	X	K–7		8–12	286	286	16:1	2	6
Ridley College, St. Catharines, ON	X	X	X	X	1–4	5–8	9–PG	634	492	9:1	12	69
Rocklyn Academy, Meaford, ON		X					9–12	27	27	3:1		25
Rockway Mennonite Collegiate, Kitchener, ON	X	X	X	X		6–8	9–12	385	293	10:1		30
Ron Pettigrew Christian School, Dawson Creek, BC			X	X	K–6	7–8	9–12	99	26	5:1		
Rosseau Lake College, Rosseau, ON	X	X	X	X		7–8	9–12	141	113	7:1		87
Rothesay Netherwood School, Rothesay, NB	X	X	X	X		6–8	9–12	255	200	8:1	11	50
Royal Canadian College, Vancouver, BC			X	X		8–10	11–12	57	40	15:1		5

PRIVATE SCHOOLS AT-A-GLANCE	STUDENTS ACCEPTED				GRADES			STUDENT/FACULTY			STUDENT OFFERINGS (number)	
	Boarding		Day									
	Boys	Girls	Boys	Girls	Lower	Middle	Upper	Total	Upper	Student/ Faculty Ratio	Advanced Placement Subject Areas	Sports
Rundle College, Calgary, AB			X	X	PK–6	7–9	10–12	771	250	14:1		20
Sacred Heart School of Halifax, Halifax, NS			X	X	K–6		7–12	388	188	15:1	7	15
St. Andrew's College, Aurora, ON	X		X			6–8	9–12	550	412	10:1	9	62
St. Andrew's Regional High School, Victoria, BC			X	X						14:1		
St. Clement School, Ottawa, ON			X	X		7–8	9–12	33	20	13:1		10
St. Clement's School, Toronto, ON				X	1–6	7–9	10–13	448	177	9:1	16	36
St. George's School, Vancouver, BC	X		X		1–7		8–12	1,157	761	10:1	13	33
St. George's School of Montreal, Montreal, QC			X	X	PK–6		7–11	503	316	17:1	6	24
St. John's-Kilmarnock School, Breslau, ON			X	X	JK–5	6–8	9–12	454	199	12:1	8	35
St. John's-Ravenscourt School, Winnipeg, MB	X	X	X	X	1–5	6–8	9–12	799	345	9:1	7	31
Saint John's School of Alberta, Stony Plain, AB	X	X	X	X		7–9	10–12	86	61	10:1		21
St. Margaret's School, Victoria, BC		X		X	JK–6		7–12	373	226	8:1	5	66
St. Michael's College School, Toronto, ON			X			7–8	9–12	1,083	881	16:1	3	23
St. Patrick High School, Yellowknife, NT			X	X			9–12	525	525			
St. Patrick's Regional Secondary, Vancouver, BC			X	X				500				
St. Paul's High School, Winnipeg, MB			X				9–12	582	582	14:1	3	20
St. Thomas More Collegiate, Burnaby, BC			X	X			8–12	669	669	26:1		26
Scarborough Christian School, North York, ON			X	X	JK–8			133	48	12:1		6
Sedbergh School, Montebello, QC	X	X	X	X		7–8	9–12	80	67	5:1		58
Selwyn House School, Westmount, QC			X		K–6	7–8	9–11	570	175	9:1		19
Shawnigan Lake School, Shawnigan Lake Postal Bag 2000, BC	X	X	X	X			8–12	438	438	9:1	8	49
Sheila Morrison School, Utopia, ON	X	X	X	X	4–6	7–8	9–12	39	21	3:1		58
Shoore Centre for Learning, Toronto, ON			X	X		8–8	9–12	27	22	6:1		
SICES International Academy, Edmonton, AB	X	X						50	32	20:1		7
Smithville District Christian High School, Smithville, ON			X	X			9–12	217	217	11:1		10
Solomon Learning Institute, Ltd., Edmonton, AB			X	X						20:1		
Southridge School, Surrey, BC			X	X	K–3	4–7	8–12	666	326	10:1	9	35
Stanstead College, Stanstead, QC	X	X	X	X		7–9	10–12	187	128	8:1	10	43
Strathcona-Tweedsmuir School, Okotoks, AB			X	X	1–6	7–9	10–12	711	264	20:1		15
The Study School, Westmount, QC				X	K–3	4–6	7–11	387	175	8:1		34
Tapply Binet College, Ancaster, ON			X	X				17	11	3:1		1
Toronto District Christian High School, Woodbridge, ON			X	X			9–12	452	452	14:1		2
Town Centre Private High School, Markham, ON			X	X	1–6	7–8	9–12	1,400	200	15:1	4	19
Trafalgar Castle School, Whitby, ON		X		X				228	208	9:1	2	12
Trinity College School, Port Hope, ON	X	X	X	X		5–8	9–12	608	510	8:1	11	39
United Mennonite Educational Institute, Leamington, ON			X	X			9–12	80	80	15:1		13
University of Toronto Schools, Toronto, ON			X	X		7–8	9–12	540		12:1	5	49
Westgate Mennonite Collegiate, Winnipeg, MB			X	X		7–9	10–12	302	155	15:1	5	31
West Island College, Calgary, AB			X	X		7–9	10–12	465	229	17:1	10	39
Windsor Christian Fellowship Academy, Windsor, ON			X	X	K–5	6–8	9–12	76	21	12:1		7
The Yorkland School, Willowdale, ON			X	X		7–8	9–12	358	240	15:1		27
The York School, Toronto, ON			X	X	1–6		7–12	520	300	12:1		26
INTERNATIONAL												
Aruba												
International School of Aruba, Oranjenstad			X	X	PK–5	6–8	9–12	173	45	8:1	5	8
Australia												
Mercedes College, Springfield			X	X	1–5	6–9	10–12	1,189	444	12:1		25
Austria												
The American International School, Vienna			X	X	PK–5	6–8	9–PG	796	255	6:1		18

	Boarding Boys	Boarding Girls	Day Boys	Day Girls	Lower	Middle	Upper	Total	Upper	Student/Faculty Ratio	Advanced Placement Subject Areas	Sports
Belgium												
International School of Brussels, Brussels			X	X	N–6	7–9	10–13	1,387	344	10:1	7	16
Bermuda												
Saltus Grammar School, Hamilton HMJX			X	X	K–5	6–8	9–12	1,083	258	13:1	14	16
Brazil												
Chapel School, Sao Paulo			X	X	PK–6		7–12	631	237	7:1		6
Escola Americana de Campinas, Campinas-SP			X	X	PK–5	6–8	9–12	485	85	7:1	5	27
Escola Americana do Rio de Janeiro, Rio de Janeiro			X	X	N–5	6–8	9–12	705	215	7:1		27
China												
Hong Kong International School, Tai Tam, Hong Kong			X	X	PK–5	6–8	9–12	2,631	737	11:1	22	37
Colombia												
Colegio Bolivar, Cali			X	X	PK–5	6–8	9–12	1,268	327	10:1	5	13
Colegio Nueva Granada, Bogota			X	X	PK–5	6–8	9–12	1,744	451	20:1	11	8
Cyprus												
American International School in Cyprus, Nicosia			X	X	K–5	6–8	9–12	255	94	15:1		15
Denmark												
Copenhagen International School, 2900 Hellerup			X	X	PK–5		6–12	584	300	7:1		4
Ecuador												
Academia Cotopaxi, Quito			X	X	PK–8		9–12	462	129	7:1		5
Alliance Academy, Quito	X	X	X	X	PK–6		7–12	424	222	7:1	8	22
El Salvador												
Academia Britanica Cuscatleca, Santa Tecla			X	X	PK–5		6–12	1,389	532	9:1		23
France												
American School of Paris, Saint Cloud			X	X	PK–5	6–8	9–13	778	348	7:1	8	11
The Lycee International, American Section, Saint-Germain-en-Laye Cedex			X	X	PK–5	6–9	10–12	674	179	18:1	2	17
Germany												
Black Forest Academy, Kandern	X	X	X	X	1–5	6–8	9–12	361	242	8:1	10	9
International School Hamburg, Hamburg			X	X	PK–5	6–8	9–12	670	188	7:1		3
Munich International School, Starnberg			X	X	PK–4	5–8	9–12	1,312	414	9:1		24
Greece												
American Community Schools of Athens, Athens			X	X	JK–5	6–8	9–12	702	302	18:1	1	11
International School of Athens, Kifissia--Athens			X	X	PK–6	7–9	10–12	323	86	9:1		9
Pinewood--The International School of Thessaloniki, Greece, Thessaloniki	X	X	X	X	PK–5	6–9	10–12	167	39	5:1	9	12
Honduras												
Mazapan School, La Ceiba			X	X					92	12:1		10
India												
Kodaikanal International School, Kodaikanal	X	X	X	X	PS–5	6–10	11–12	535	213	5:1		37
Woodstock School, Uttarakhand	X	X	X	X	N–5	6–8	9–12	468	260	15:1	12	18
Indonesia												
Jakarta International School, Jakarta			X	X	PK–5	6–8	9–12	2,460	990	19:1	14	27
Italy												
American School of Milan, Noverasco di Opera, Milan			X	X	N–5	6–8	9–12	525	163	7:1		16
International School of Milan, 20146 Milan			X	X	K–5	6–9	10–13	1,250	250	7:1		16

PRIVATE SCHOOLS AT-A-GLANCE	STUDENTS ACCEPTED				GRADES			STUDENT/FACULTY			STUDENT OFFERINGS (number)	
	Boarding		Day									
	Boys	Girls	Boys	Girls	Lower	Middle	Upper	Total	Upper	Student/ Faculty Ratio	Advanced Placement Subject Areas	Sports
Marymount International School, Rome			X	X	PK–5	6–8	9–12	729	206	15:1	1	7
St. Stephen's School, Rome, Rome	X	X	X	X			9–PG	218	218	7:1	9	8
Jamaica												
Belair School, Mandeville			X	X	K–4	5–6	7–12	692	300	15:1		11
Japan												
Canadian Academy, Kobe	X	X	X	X	PK–5	6–8	9–13	793	248	11:1	1	9
Columbia International School, Tokorozawa, Saitama	X	X	X	X	1–6	7–8	9–12	271	133	12:1		38
Hokkaido International School, Sapporo	X	X	X	X	PK–6	7–9	10–12	195	51	10:1	5	11
Marist Brothers International School, Kobe			X	X	PK–6		7–12	295	118	8:1	6	6
Saint Maur International School, Yokohama			X	X	PK–5	6–8	9–12	452	128	4:1	10	8
Seisen International School, Tokyo			X	X	K–6	7–8	9–12	728	173	4:1		26
Yokohama International School, Yokohama			X	X	N–5	6–8	9–12	709	227	5.5:1		17
Jordan												
Ahliyyah School for Girls, Amman				X	1–6	7–10	11–12	1,001	149	4:1		42
Kuwait												
New English School, Hawalli			X	X	K–2	4–6	7–13	2,244	1,114	7:1		20
Malaysia												
Alice Smith School, Kuala Lumpur			X	X	7–9	10–11	12–13	632	81	9:1		28
Mont'Kiara International School, Kuala Lumpur			X	X	1–5	6–8	9–12	868	189	9:1		14
Malta												
Verdala International School, Pembroke	X	X	X	X	PK–5	6–8	9–12	265	104	7:1		4
Mexico												
The American School Foundation, Mexico City, D.F.			X	X	PK–5	6–8	9–12	2,420	624	10:1	13	9
The American School of Puerto Vallarta, Puerto Vallarta, Jalisco			X	X	N–6	7–9	10–12	368	79	7:1	7	5
Monaco												
The International School of Monaco, Monte Carlo			X	X	K–6	7–9	10–13	385	72	8:1		7
Netherlands												
American International School Rotterdam, Rotterdam			X	X	PK–5	6–8	9–12	240	53	6:1		7
The American School of The Hague, Wassenaar			X	X	PK–4	5–8	9–12	1,060	380	6:1	14	11
International School Eerde, Ommen	X	X	X	X								18
International School of Amsterdam, Amstelveen			X	X	PS–5	6–8	9–12	883	200	6:1		15
Pakistan												
Karachi American School, Karachi			X	X	PS–5	6–8	9–12	380	150	6:1	14	39
Peru												
Colegio Franklin D. Roosevelt, Lima 12			X	X	N–5	6–8	9–12	1,329	360	11:1		22
Philippines												
Brent School-Baguio, Baguio City	X	X	X	X	PK–5	6–8	9–12	270	97	6:1		14
International School Manila, 1634 Taguig City			X	X	PK–5	6–8	9–12	1,760	665	9:1	6	18
Portugal												
Carlucci American International School of Lisbon, Linho, Sintra			X	X	N–5	6–8	9–12	557	154	9:1		4
St. Dominic's International School, Portugal, Sao Domingos de Rana			X	X	1–6	7–11	12–13	645	91	7:1		15

6. **Rate each of the following aspects of this book on a scale of 4 to 1 (4 = Excellent and 1 = Poor).**

	4	3	2	1
Comprehensiveness of the information	❏	❏	❏	❏
Accuracy of the information	❏	❏	❏	❏
Usability	❏	❏	❏	❏
Cover design	❏	❏	❏	❏
Book layout	❏	❏	❏	❏
Special features (e.g., CD, flashcards, charts, etc.)	❏	❏	❏	❏
Value for the money	❏	❏	❏	❏

7. **This book was recommended by:**
   - ❏ Guidance counselor
   - ❏ Parent/guardian
   - ❏ Family member/relative
   - ❏ Friend
   - ❏ Teacher
   - ❏ Not recommended by anyone—I found the book on my own
   - ❏ Other (please specify) _____

8. **Would you recommend this book to others?**

Yes	Not Sure	No
❏	❏	❏

9. **Please provide any additional comments.**

_____

_____

_____

_____

_____

Remember, you can tear out this page and mail it to us at:

Publishing Department
Peterson's, a Nelnet company
2000 Lenox Drive
Lawrenceville, NJ 08648

or you can complete the survey online at **www.petersons.com/booksurvey.**

Your feedback is important to us at Peterson's, and we thank you for your time!

If you would like us to keep in touch with you about new products and services, please include your e-mail address here: _____

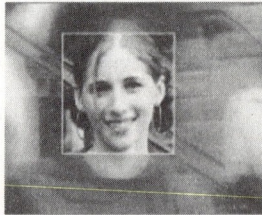

Peterson's
Book Satisfaction Survey

Give Us Your Feedback

Thank you for choosing Peterson's as your source for personalized solutions for your education and career achievement. Please take a few minutes to answer the following questions. Your answers will go a long way in helping us to produce the most user-friendly and comprehensive resources to meet your individual needs.

When completed, please tear out this page and mail it to us at:

Publishing Department
Peterson's, a Nelnet company
2000 Lenox Drive
Lawrenceville, NJ 08648

You can also complete this survey online at **www.petersons.com/booksurvey.**

1. **What is the ISBN of the book you have purchased? (The ISBN can be found on the book's back cover in the lower right-hand corner.)** _____

2. **Where did you purchase this book?**
   ❑ Retailer, such as Barnes & Noble
   ❑ Online reseller, such as Amazon.com
   ❑ Petersons.com
   ❑ Other (please specify) _____

3. **If you purchased this book on Petersons.com, please rate the following aspects of your online purchasing experience on a scale of 4 to 1 (4 = Excellent and 1 = Poor).**

	4	3	2	1
Comprehensiveness of Peterson's Online Bookstore page	❑	❑	❑	❑
Overall online customer experience	❑	❑	❑	❑

4. **Which category best describes you?**

   ❑ High school student
   ❑ Parent of high school student
   ❑ College student
   ❑ Graduate/professional student
   ❑ Returning adult student

   ❑ Teacher
   ❑ Counselor
   ❑ Working professional/military
   ❑ Other (please specify) _____

5. **Rate your overall satisfaction with this book.**

Extremely Satisfied	Satisfied	Not Satisfied
❑	❑	❑

NOTES

NOTES

NOTES

NOTES

NOTES

	STUDENTS ACCEPTED				GRADES			STUDENT/FACULTY			STUDENT OFFERINGS (number)	
	Boarding		Day									
	Boys	Girls	Boys	Girls	Lower	Middle	Upper	Total	Upper	Student/Faculty Ratio	Advanced Placement Subject Areas	Sports
Republic of Korea												
Seoul Foreign School, Seoul			X	X	PK–5	6–8	9–12	1,476	415	9:1	1	11
Seoul International School, Seoul			X	X	PK–5	6–8	9–12	1,032	313	10:1	12	12
Singapore												
International School Singapore, Singapore			X	X	PK–4	5–8	9–12	673	225	10:1	1	29
Overseas Family School, Singapore 238515			X	X	PK–5	6–8	9–12	2,600	550	9:1		8
Spain												
The American School of Madrid, Madrid			X	X	PK–5	6–8	9–12	865	257	9:1		8
International College Spain, Madrid			X	X	PK–5	6–8	9–12	678	216	10:1		25
Switzerland												
Ecole d'Humanitlfe, CH 6085 Hasliberg Goldern	X	X	X	X	3–6	7–9	10–12	144	88	5:1	7	20
Gstaad International School, Gstaad	X	X	X	X		8–9	10–12	23	10	5:1	5	25
International School of Berne, Guemligen 3073			X	X	PK–5		6–12	293	156	5:1		16
The International School of Geneva, Geneva			X	X	PK–6		7–13	4,030	2,340	11:1		16
International School of Lausanne, Le Mont-sur-Lausanne			X	X	PK–5	6–8	9–12	597	193	7:1		29
Neuchatel Junior College, 2002 Neuchlf]tel	X	X					12	105	105	10:1	11	18
Riverside School, Zug			X	X				185	65	7:1	14	31
St. George's School in Switzerland, 1815 Clarens/Montreux		X	X	X	K–5	6–8	9–12	399	111	7:1		25
TASIS, The American School in Switzerland, Montagnola-Lugano	X	X	X	X	1–6	7–8	9–PG	516	347	5:1	17	35
Zurich International School, Wlfpdenswil			X	X	PS–5	6–8	9–13	1,211	391	7:1	13	15
Taiwan												
Taipei American School, Taipei			X	X	PK–5	6–8	9–12	2,189	840	18:1		15
Thailand												
International School Bangkok, Pakkret			X	X	PK–5	6–8	9–12	1,837	704	10:1	11	15
Trinidad and Tobago												
International School of Port-of-Spain, Westmoorings			X	X	K–5	6–8	9–12	164	164	7:1	12	11
United Arab Emirates												
Dubai American Academy, Dubai			X	X	PK–5	6–8	9–12	1,996	504	12:1		6
United Kingdom												
ACS Cobham International School, Cobham, Surrey	X	X	X	X	N–4	5–8	9–12	1,315	436	9:1	10	15
ACS Egham International School, Surrey			X	X	N–5	6–8	9–12	553	143	9:1		14
ACS Hillingdon International School, Hillingdon, Middlesex			X	X	PK–4	5–8	9–12	584	242	9:1	12	10
The American School in London, London			X	X	PK–4	5–8	9–12	1,338	477	10:1	19	18
Brockwood Park School, Bramdean, Hampshire	X	X						65	65	7:1		
The International School of London, London W3 8LG			X	X	K–6	7–10	11–13	350	60			7
Marymount International School, Surrey		X		X		6–8	9–12	240	185	7:1		16
Merchiston Castle School, Edinburgh	X		X						196	9:1		26
St Leonards School and Sixth Form College, Fife, Scotland	X	X	X	X	N–7	8–11	12–13	464	122	7:1		56
TASIS The American School in England, Thorpe, Surrey	X	X	X	X	N–5	6–8	9–13	745	340	8:1	19	45
Zimbabwe												
Harare International School, Harare			X	X	K–5	6–8	9–12	442	128	10:1		25